W9-AKX-876

Microsoft®
Office 2003
All-in-One

by Joe Habraken

800 East 96th Street, Indianapolis, Indiana 46240 USA

Microsoft® Office 2003 All-in-One

Copyright © 2004 by Que Publishing

International Standard Book Number: 0-7897-2936-9

Library of Congress Catalog Card Number: 2003103664

Printed in the United States of America

First Printing: November 2003

08   07   06   6   7   8

Trademarks

All terms mentioned in this book that are known to be trademarks or service marks have been appropriately capitalized. Que Publishing cannot attest to the accuracy of this information. Use of a term in this book should not be regarded as affecting the validity of any trademark or service mark.

Microsoft is a registered trademark of Microsoft Corporation.

Warning and Disclaimer

Every effort has been made to make this book as complete and as accurate as possible, but no warranty or fitness is implied. The information provided is on an "as is" basis. The author and the publisher shall have neither liability nor responsibility to any person or entity with respect to any loss or damages arising from the information contained in this book.

Bulk Sales

Que Publishing offers excellent discounts on this book when ordered in quantity for bulk purchases or special sales. For more information, please contact

> U.S. Corporate and Government Sales
> 1-800-382-3419
> corpsales@pearsontechgroup.com

For sales outside the U.S., please contact

> International Sales
> international@pearsoned.com

Associate Publisher
Greg Wiegand

Acquisitions Editor
Stephanie J. McComb

Development Editor
Todd Brakke

Managing Editor
Charlotte Clapp

Project Editor
Tonya R. Simpson

Copy Editor
Margaret Berson

Indexer
Heather McNeill

Proofreader
Leslie Joseph

Technical Editor
Mark Hall

Team Coordinator
Sharry Lee Gregory

Interior Designer
Gary Adair

Cover Designer
Anne Jones

Page Layout
Julie Parks

Indexer
Heather McNeill

Contents

Part II: Migrating to Office 2003   67

Part III: Outlook 97

Part V: Excel   453

Part VII: PowerPoint   703

Part VIII: Publisher   797

About the Author

Joe Habraken is a best-selling author, information technology professional, and educator. He is currently an assistant professor at the University of New England, where he teaches a variety of information technology classes introducing undergraduate students to computer basics, software applications, Web design, and the use of personal computers in business settings. His books include the *Absolute Beginner's Guide to Networking* (4th Edition), *Practical Cisco Routers*, and *Sams Teach Yourself Microsoft Server 2003 in 24 Hours*. With more than 15 years as a trainer and consultant, Joe, who is a Microsoft Certified Professional and a Cisco Certified Network Associate, enjoys taking difficult computer concepts and making them accessible to readers and students.

Dedication

To Kim, my wonderful spouse, thanks for all your love, understanding, and support; I love you!

Acknowledgments

Creating books like this takes a real team effort. I would like to thank Stephanie McComb, our acquisitions editor, who worked very hard to assemble the team that made this book a reality and kept us all on track as the book evolved toward completion. I would also like to thank Todd Brakke, who served as the development editor for this book and who came up with many great ideas for improving its content. Also a tip of the hat and a thanks to Mark Hall, who, as the technical editor for the project, did a fantastic job making sure that everything was correct and suggested a number of additions that made the book even more technically sound. Finally, a great big thanks to our project editor, Tonya Simpson, who ran the last leg of the race and made sure the book made it to press on time—what a great team of professionals.

We Want to Hear from You!

As the reader of this book, *you* are our most important critic and commentator. We value your opinion and want to know what we're doing right, what we could do better, what areas you'd like to see us publish in, and any other words of wisdom you're willing to pass our way.

As an associate publisher for Que Publishing, I welcome your comments. You can email or write me directly to let me know what you did or didn't like about this book—as well as what we can do to make our books better.

Please note that I cannot help you with technical problems related to the topic of this book. We do have a User Services group, however, where I will forward specific technical questions related to the book.

When you write, please be sure to include this book's title and author as well as your name, email address, and phone number. I will carefully review your comments and share them with the author and editors who worked on the book.

Email: feedback@quepublishing.com

Mail: Greg Wiegand
           Associate Publisher
           Que Publishing
           800 East 96th Street
           Indianapolis, IN 46240 USA

For more information about this book or another Que Publishing title, visit our Web site at www.quepublishing.com. Type the ISBN (excluding hyphens) or the title of a book in the Search field to find the page you're looking for.

Introduction

Congratulations! You are about to harness the incredible features and tools of the latest version of Microsoft Office. Office 2003 provides you with all the applications that you need to do everything from creating letters to balancing your sales books, to managing your contacts, to creating great presentations and Web pages. It's all here: word processing, spreadsheets, databases, personal information management, publication design, and much, much more. This book is designed to get you up and running quickly on all the Office applications, such as Word, Excel, Access, PowerPoint, Publisher, and Outlook, and to make it easy for you to use their basic features and a number of their advanced features.

Microsoft Office 2003 provides you with all the familiar Office applications and many new enhancements that make it easier for you to create your various Office documents. Microsoft Office 2003 includes the following applications:

- **Word**—A versatile word-processing application that enables you to create every possible type of document from simple letters to newsletters to reports that include charts and tables.
- **Excel**—A powerful spreadsheet program that enables you to create simple worksheets or specialty worksheets such as invoices and financial statements. Excel provides all the tools and formulas for doing simple math or special statistical and financial calculations.
- **Access**—A relational database application that is extremely powerful, yet very straightforward to use. Access provides several database wizards that help you create your own databases quickly and efficiently.
- **PowerPoint**—An easy-to-use presentation application that enables you to create eye-catching and impressive slide shows that can be shown from your computer monitor or other video output device. PowerPoint also enables you to print presentation outlines and speakers' notes for your presentations.
- **Outlook**—A personal information manager that will help you keep organized. Outlook not only helps you manage your contacts, appointments, and tasks, it also serves as your e-mail and fax client. Outlook has been redesigned and greatly improved in the 2003 edition and now includes the Business Contact Manager, which makes it easy to manage business contacts and accounts.
- **Publisher**—A desktop publishing application that makes it easy to create special publications such as brochures, flyers, and business cards.

Using This Book

Microsoft Office 2003 All-in-One is designed to help you learn the applications in the Office 2003 suite. All the most important and useful tasks are covered in this book, and the short, concise lessons make it easy for you to learn a particular feature quickly.

This book is organized into eight parts. Part I covers new features found in the Microsoft Office 2003 applications and also provides you with information on common Office features such as the Help system and the Speech feature. Part I of the book also contains lessons that teach you the basics of navigating the menus and toolbars provided by the Office applications.

Part II provides information on upgrading to the new versions of the Office applications found in Office 2003. A lesson is provided for each application: Outlook, Word, Excel, Access, PowerPoint, and Publisher. Information on new features found in the applications is discussed and tips related to upgrading from previous versions of these applications are also included.

Parts III through VIII each cover a specific Office application: Outlook, Word, Excel, Access, PowerPoint, and Publisher. Working through the lessons in a particular section will provide you with a solid knowledge of how to be productive with a particular application.

Conventions Used in This Book

Each lesson in this book includes step-by-step instructions for performing specific tasks. To help you as you work through these steps and to help you move through the lessons easily, additional information is included and identified by the following icons:

Term   New or unfamiliar terms are defined to help you as you work through the various steps in the lesson.

Tip   Read these tips for ideas that cut corners and confusion. Tips also provide additional information related to the topic you are currently reading. Use them to expand your knowledge of a particular software feature or concept.

CAUTION

Caution This icon identifies areas where new users often run into trouble; these hints offer practical solutions to those problems.

In addition to the icons discussed, the following conventions are also used:

Text you should type	Information you need to type appears in **bold monospace type**.
Items you select	Commands, options, and icons you are to select and keys you are to press appear in **bold type**.

Office Introduction and Shared Features

What's New in Office 2003?

In this lesson, you learn about the new features that the Office 2003 application suite provides.

Introducing Microsoft Office 2003

Microsoft Office 2003 is the latest version of the popular Office application suite. Microsoft Office 2003 comes in different editions that include a different set of Office applications. For example, the Microsoft Office Professional Edition, which we cover in this book, includes Word 2003, Excel 2003, PowerPoint 2003, Outlook 2003 with the Business Contact Manager, Publisher, and Access 2003. Table 1.1 provides a look at each of the Microsoft Office 2003 editions.

Table 1.1 The Different Editions of Microsoft Office 2003

Edition:	Microsoft Office Professional Edition 2003	Microsoft Office Small Business Edition 2003	Microsoft Office Standard Edition 2003	Microsoft Office Student and Teacher Edition 2003
Applications Included				
	Word 2003	Word 2003	Word 2003	Word 2003
	Excel 2003	Excel 2003	Excel 2003	Excel 2003
	PowerPoint 2003	PowerPoint 2003	PowerPoint 2003	PowerPoint 2003
	Outlook 2003 with Business Contact Manager	Outlook 2003 with Business Contact Manager	Outlook 2003	Outlook 2003
	Publisher 2003	Publisher 2003		
	Access 2003			

No matter which edition of Office you use, you are provided with different software applications that you can use to tackle a large variety of business and personal tasks on the computer. For example, Word allows you to create reports, letters, and other documents, and Excel allows you to tackle spreadsheets, invoices, and do a wide variety of number-crunching tasks. Each application provides a specialized set of tools and environments for addressing your productivity needs.

Microsoft Office 2003 offers a number of new enhancements to the Office suite. This lesson serves as a quick overview of some of these new features. Other new features are highlighted in Part II of the book ("Migrating to Office 2003"). You will also use some new features as you explore each of the Office applications discussed in this book.

Office 2003 and the Document Workspace

An exciting new feature, the Document Workspace, allows users who don't have the option of sharing documents on a corporate network to collaborate on the Web. The Document Workspace is actually an extension of Microsoft Windows SharePoint Services, which allows you to store documents for collaboration on a SharePoint server. Multiple users can access the document in the shared workspace, and tasks can be assigned associated with the collaborative effort.

The Document Workspace is a fairly advanced feature offered by Office 2003, so the full details related to the use of this powerful feature are beyond the scope of this introduction. However, creating a new workspace is surprisingly easy. It does, however, require that you are connected to the Internet and have access to a SharePoint server maintained by your company or you have subscribed to a SharePoint hosting service such as those offered by Microsoft. Let's take a look at creating a Document Workspace in Microsoft Word.

To create a Document Workspace, follow these steps (these steps assume Microsoft Word is already open):

1. Open the document that will be available in the shared workspace.
2. Select **Tools** and then **Shared Workspace**. The Shared Workspace task pane opens as shown in Figure 1.1.
3. Type the URL (Uniform Resource Locator or Web address) for the workspace that will serve as the holding area for the shared document in the Location for New Workspace box.
4. Click the **Create** button in the task pane.
5. A connection box will appear that requires you to enter your user name and password for the shared workspace. After entering the information, click OK.
6. The shared workspace will be created (on the Web site you designated) and a copy of the current document is placed in the workspace.

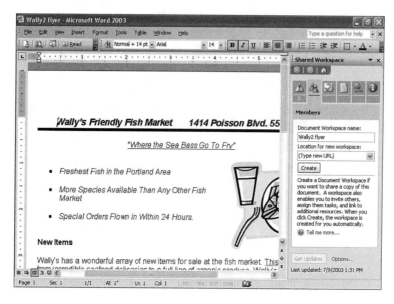

Figure 1.1   A shared workspace can be created for your Office documents.

As the creator of the site, you are designated as the site owner. This allows you to add new members to the site, add additional documents, and manage the workspace. You can also view who is currently online and working on the document. Figure 1.2 shows a document that is shared in a workspace. Note that the Shared Workspace task pane lists the current users of the workspace and whether or not they are currently online. Tools provided in the task pane allow you to quickly e-mail workspace users and to update the workspace status.

TIP   **Tasks Can be Created Using the Shared Workspace Task Pane**   A useful feature related to the Shared Workspace feature is the ability to create tasks and assign them to users of the workspace. Click the **Tasks** icon at the top of the Shared Workspace task pane and then click the **Add New Task** link. To name the task, use the Task dialog box that appears, and set the other task parameters, such as who the task is assigned to and when the task is due.

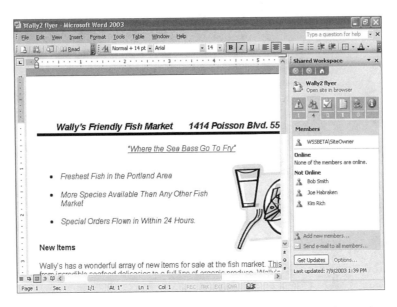

Figure 1.2 The Shared Workspace task pane allows you to manage the workspace and its users.

Getting Help in Office 2003

Microsoft Office 2003 uses a streamlined Help system that is primarily accessed using the new Help task pane. Options available in previous versions of Office such as the Office Assistant and the Ask a Question box are also available in Office 2003 for accessing help.

You can open the Help task pane by selecting the **Help** menu and then accessing the Help command for the current application. For example, to access the Help task pane in Word, select **Help** and then **Microsoft Word Help**. The Help task pane appears as shown in Figure 1.3.

The Help task pane enables you to search using keywords. You also have access to up-to-date help via Office online. For more about the new Office Help system, see Lesson 5, "Getting Help in Microsoft Office."

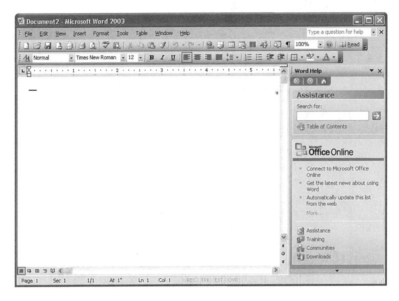

Figure 1.3   The Help task pane allows you to search for help and access online Office resources.

Using the New Research Feature

Another new feature that Office 2003 provides is the Research task pane. The Research task pane allows you to access basic tools such as the Thesaurus, but it also provides you with the ability to access online resources that range from business Web sites, to stock information, to online encyclopedias such as Microsoft's Expedia.

For example, I might want to search for information on a key term as shown in Figure 1.4. The Research task pane is discussed in more detail in Lesson 3, "Using Office Task Panes," and in the Word section of the book (Part IV) in Lesson 4, "Using Proofreading Tools."

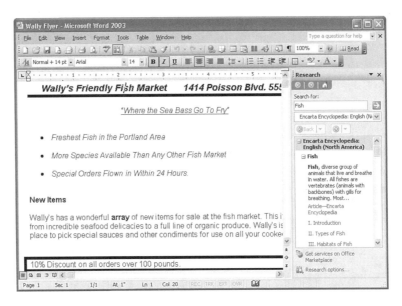

Figure 1.4   The Research task pane allows you to search for business data and other information from inside your Office application.

Faxing over the Internet

Another addition to Office 2003 is the ability to send faxes from your Office applications over the Internet. This feature requires that you sign up for an Internet fax service. These services provide you with the ability to send and receive faxes over the Internet. This means that you do not require a fax modem on your computer to work with faxes.

Sending the current document from any Office application as an Internet fax is quite easy: You click the **File** menu, point at **Send To**, and then select **Recipient Using Internet Fax Service**. The first time you use this command, you will have the option of being taken to a Web page that allows you to sign up for a fax service. Pricing for this service varies by provider as do the steps required to prepare a fax cover page and send your Office document. Faxing is discussed in more detail in Lesson 8, "Faxing and E-Mailing in Office 2003."

Office 2003 and XML Data

XML (Extensible Markup Language) is fast becoming the standard for data exchange on the World Wide Web. In Office 2003, instead of saving documents in their default formats, you can save Office documents as XML documents.

 TERM   **XML**   or Extensible Markup Language is a markup language (HTML being an example of another markup language) that can be used to tag data so that it can be transferred between applications and also interpreted and validated. XML is rapidly becoming an important format for moving data between servers on the Web.

Saving in XML format is particularly useful in situations where you want to convert Excel or Access data to an XML format for use on the Web. Although using XML data on the Web is beyond the scope of this book, you will find that if required, you can quickly save data in an Office application such as Excel in the XML format.

Follow these steps:

1. Select **File**, then **Save As**. The Save As dialog box will open.

2. In the Save As dialog box, select the **Save as Type** drop-down box and select **XML Data** (see Figure 1.5). You can also change the filename if you want.

3. When you have made the necessary changes in the Save As dialog box, click **Save**.

Figure 1.5   Office data can be saved in the XML format.

Office Instant Messaging

Microsoft Office XP introduced smart tags to the Office applications. A *smart tag* is a special shortcut menu that provides you with additional options related to a particular feature. There are paste smart tags, AutoCorrect smart tags, and smart tags for dates, times, and addresses that you place in your Office documents. Office 2003 has added a new Person Name smart tag that flags contact names that you have added to your Outlook Contacts list and provides the Windows Messenger address for the contact.

 TIP **Make Sure the Person Name Smart Tag Is Active** The Person Name smart tag must be applied to names in your documents if you want to send instant messages. Select **Tools**, then **AutoCorrect Options**. In the AutoCorrect dialog box, click the **Smart Tags** tab and make sure that the **Person Name (English)** smart tag has a check mark next to it.

For example, if you create a document that includes the person's name, the name will be flagged with the Person Name tag (the name will be underlined with a dashed red line). Point at the name and click the smart tag icon that appears (the icon looks like the Windows Messenger icon, see Figure 1.6). On the menu that appears, select **Send Instant Message**.

Smart tag icon

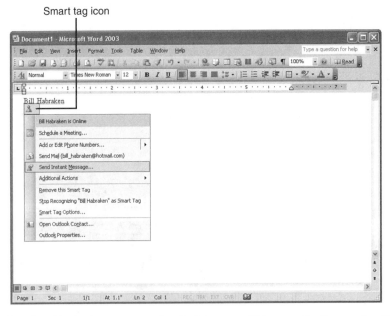

Figure 1.6 Send instant messages directly from your Office applications using the Person Name smart tag.

A Windows Messenger window will open. You can now send your instant message as needed.

CAUTION

Your Message Recipient Must Be Online   To send an instant message to a person using the new Person Name smart tag, that person must currently be online using Windows Messenger. If they are not online, the Send Instant Message menu choice is not available.

Using Common Office Features

In this lesson, you learn how to use common Office features such as menus, toolbars, and dialog boxes.

Starting Office Applications

The Microsoft Office applications can be quickly started from the Windows Start menu. Desktop icons can also be quickly created for an Office application to provide quick access to that application.

To start an Office application from the Start menu, follow these steps:

1. From the Windows XP desktop, click **Start**, point at **All Programs**, and then point at the **Microsoft Office** folder. The Office programs installed on your computer will appear as shown in Figure 2.1 (for Windows 2000, point at **Programs,** then **Microsoft Office**).

2. To open a particular Office application, click that application's icon on the menu. The program window for that application appears.

Starting an Application by Choosing a Document Template

You can also start a particular Office application by choosing the type of Office document that you are going to create. This is done using the Start menu.

1. From the Windows desktop, click **Start**, **All Programs**, then **New Office Document**. The New Office Document dialog box appears (see Figure 2.2).

2. All the Office application templates are available on the different tabs of the New Office Document dialog box. You can create blank documents or special documents from the templates that are provided (specific templates are discussed in more detail in the various parts of this book as they relate to a particular Office application). Select a particular template in the dialog box.

Figure 2.1   Use the Start menu to start your Office applications.

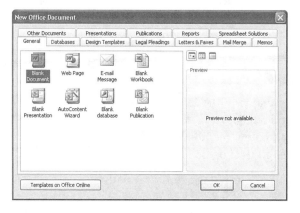

Figure 2.2   The New Office Document dialog box can be used to quickly start a new document in any Office application.

3. Click **OK**. The application that uses that particular template opens (such as Word if you select the Blank Document icon), and the new document appears in the application window.

Creating Desktop Icons

You can also create shortcut icons for your Office applications on the Windows desktop. To create desktop icons for Office applications, follow these steps:

1. From the Windows desktop, click **Start** and then point at **All Programs**, **Microsoft Office**.

2. Right-click the Office application icon that you want to use to create the desktop icon.

3. Select **Copy** from the shortcut menu that appears.

4. Click anywhere on the desktop to close the Start menu.

5. Right-click the Windows desktop and select **Paste Shortcut** from the shortcut menu that appears.

A desktop icon for the selected application appears on the Windows desktop. You can double-click the icon to start the specific application. You can also use the steps discussed in this section to create shortcut icons for your other programs (including non-Office applications), as needed.

TIP **More Shortcuts** You can also pin an application to the Start menu in Windows XP. This provides quick access to the application. Right-click on a Start menu icon and select Pin to Start menu.

Using the Menu System

The menu bar that you find in the Office applications gives you access to all the commands and features a particular application provides. These specific menu systems are found below the title bar and are activated by selecting a particular menu choice. The menu then opens, providing you with a set of command choices.

The Office 2003 applications use a personalized menu system that was first introduced in Microsoft Office 2000. It enables you to quickly access the commands you use most often. When you first choose a particular menu, you find a short list of menu commands. As you use commands, the Office application adds them to the menu list.

To access a particular menu, follow these steps:

1. Select the menu by clicking its title. The most recently used commands appear; hover the mouse pointer for just a moment and all the commands on a particular menu appear; if you don't like to hover, click the Expand icon (the double down-pointing arrow on the bottom of the menu) to view all the menu choices.

2. Select the command on the menu that invokes a particular feature.

You will find that several of the commands found on the menu are followed by an ellipsis (…). These commands, when selected, open a dialog box or a task pane. Dialog boxes require you to provide the application with additional information before the particular feature or command can be used (more information on working with dialog boxes appears later in this lesson).

Some of the menus also contain a submenu or a cascading menu that you can use to make your choices. The menu commands that produce a submenu are indicated by an arrow to the right of the menu choice. If a submenu is present, you point at the command (marked with the arrow) on the main menu to open the submenu.

 TIP   **Activating Menus with the Keyboard**   You can also activate a particular menu by holding down the **Alt** key and then pressing the keyboard key that matches the underscored letter, also called a hotkey, in the menu's name. For example, to activate the File menu in Office applications, press **Alt**+**F**.

If you would rather have access to all the menu commands (rather than just those you've used recently), you can turn off the personalized menu system. To do this, follow these steps in any Office application:

1. Click the **Tools** menu, and then click **Customize**.

2. In the Customize dialog box, click the **Options** tab.

3. To show all the commands on the menus (without delay), click the **Always Show Full Menus** check box.

4. Click **OK** to close the dialog box.

Using Shortcut Menus

A fast way to access commands that are related to a particular item on an Office document, such as selected text or a picture, is to right-click that item. This opens a shortcut menu that contains commands related to the particular item with which you are working.

For example, if you select a chart on an Excel worksheet, right-clicking the chart (see Figure 2.3) opens a shortcut menu with commands such as Cut, Copy, and Paste.

You will learn about shortcut menus as you work with the Office applications in the various parts of this book.

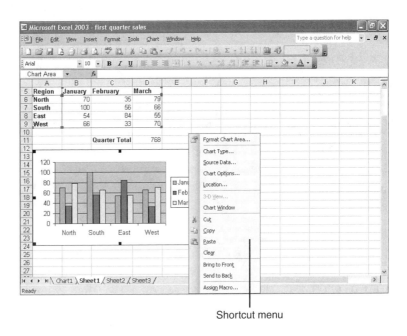

Shortcut menu

Figure 2.3 Shortcut menus provide quick access to application commands.

As you learned in Lesson 1, some items in your Office application documents are also marked with smart tags. Pointing at an item underscored with a dotted red line allows you to access the smart tag menu and access options related to that document item, such as a pasted item.

Working with Toolbars

Toolbars provide you with a very quick and straightforward way of accessing commands and features in the Office applications. When you first start one of the Office applications, you typically see the Standard and Formatting toolbars sharing one row, as shown in Figure 2.4.

To access a particular command using a toolbar button, click the button. Depending on the command, you see an immediate result in your document (such as the removal of selected text when you click the **Cut** button), or a dialog box might appear, requesting additional information from you.

 TIP **Finding a Toolbar Button's Purpose** You can place the mouse pointer on any toolbar button to view a ScreenTip that describes that tool's function.

Menu bar   Toolbar

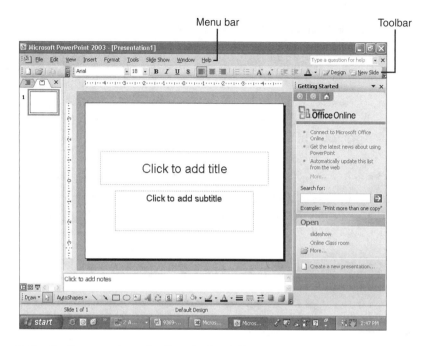

Figure 2.4   Toolbars, such as the Standard and Formatting toolbars in this PowerPoint window, provide quick access to an application's features and commands.

Other toolbars, such as the Drawing toolbar and toolbars that are specific to a particular Office application, open when you access a particular application. You can also open them manually by right-clicking any visible toolbar and then selecting the toolbar you want to use from the list that is provided. You can also use this method to close a toolbar you no longer need.

CAUTION

Missing Toolbar Buttons?   The Standard and Formatting toolbars have been configured to share one row by default, so you might not be able to see every button on the toolbars. To find a hidden button, click the **More Buttons** button on the end of either toolbar. Another alternative is to click the **Toolbar Options** button on the Standard or Formatting toolbar and select **Show Buttons on Two Rows**. This gives each toolbar its own row.

In Lesson 6, "Customizing Your Office Applications," you learn how to customize common Office features. We will work with toolbar settings and other options related to the various application settings.

Understanding Dialog Boxes

When you are working with the various commands and features found in Office applications, you will invariably come across dialog boxes. Dialog boxes are used when an Office application needs more information from you before it can complete a particular command or take advantage of a special feature. Dialog boxes always appear when you select a menu command that is followed by an ellipsis. Dialog boxes also appear when you invoke this same command using the appropriate toolbar button.

Figure 2.5 shows Word's Font dialog box. This dialog box enables you to make selections using check boxes and drop-down lists. Other dialog boxes use option buttons, spinner boxes, and other methods of enabling you to quickly make selections in a particular box.

Figure 2.5   Dialog boxes enable you to make your choices related to a particular feature.

In most cases, when you complete your selections in a dialog box, you click the **OK** button to close the box and complete the command. You also have the option of clicking the **Cancel** button if you want to close the dialog box without saving any changes you made.

Using Office Task Panes

In this lesson, you learn how to use Office 2003's task panes.

Understanding the Task Pane

A major change to the previous version of Office, Office XP, was the introduction of task panes. Office 2003 also uses task panes, which have replaced many of the dialog boxes that were a common feature in Office 97 and Office 2000. Office 2003 has also added new task panes such as the Research task pane (which we discuss later in this lesson).

A task pane is a multipurpose window pane that appears on the right side of the window of an Office application. The list that follows describes the global task panes that you will find in all the Office applications:

- **New File Task Pane**—Enables you to start a new file in a particular application (for example, in Word it is called the New Document task pane; in Excel it is called the New Workbook task pane). It also provides access to various document templates and the capability to open recently used files.

- **Office Clipboard Task Pane**—Enables you to view items that you copy and cut to the Office Clipboard. You can manage up to 24 items on the Clipboard and paste them within an application or between applications.

- **Clip Art Task Pane**—Enables you to search the Office Clip Gallery and insert clip art into your Office application documents.

- **Search Task Pane**—Enables you to search for files from any of the Office applications.

- **Research Task Pane**—This new task pane allows you to take advantage of a number of research and reference services. A number of these references are accessed via online services such as Microsoft Encarta.

You look at the Research, Search, Clip Art, and Clipboard task panes in more detail later in the lesson.

Task panes also house features that handle specific purposes in each of the Office applications. For example, in PowerPoint, the Slide Layout task pane (shown in Figure 3.1) is used to select a design format for a new or existing PowerPoint presentation slide. You learn about the different task panes in the Office applications as you use them in the different parts of this book.

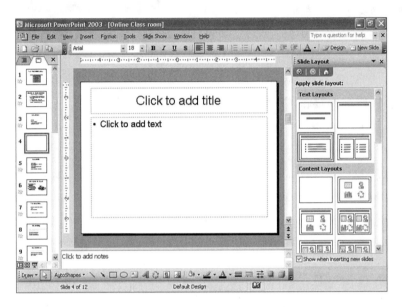

Figure 3.1 The task pane provides specific features in the different Office applications.

When you are working in an Office application, such as Word or Excel, you can open a task pane and switch between the different task pane features offered in that particular application. To open a task pane, follow these steps:

1. In the Office application window, select the **View** menu and select **Task Pane**. The New File task pane appears on the right side of the application window (the New File task pane is the default task pane for the Office applications).

2. To switch to a particular task pane that is available in the current Office application, click the task pane's drop-down arrow (see Figure 3.2).

3. Click the item on the task pane menu that you want to use.

You will find that the task pane also pops up when you select specific features in an application. For example, in Word, when you select **Format** and then **Styles and Formatting**, the Styles and Formatting task pane appears in the Word window.

Figure 3.2   Use the task pane's menu to switch to a particular task pane in an application.

TIP   **Help Is Now a Task Pane**   Office Help is now accessed through a task pane. Getting help in Office is discussed in Lesson 5, "Getting Help in Microsoft Office."

The Research Task Pane

The newest Office task pane is the Research task pane. The Research task pane provides a tool that can be used to access all sorts of information related to a selection in a Word document, Excel worksheet, or PowerPoint Presentation. These tools can be standard tools such as the Thesaurus and can also consist of specialized data sources created to find specific kinds of information. For example, Figure 3.3 shows the results of a Research task pane search for the term "Microsoft." The results provide company information including employee numbers and yearly revenue.

To use the Research task pane, follow these steps:

1. From an Office application window, select the term or phrase that will be used in the Research task pane search.

2. Select the **View** menu and then select **Task Pane** to open the task pane.

3. Select the task pane drop-down arrow and select Research. The Research task pane will open.

4. Your selected term or phrase will appear in the Search For box.

Figure 3.3 The Research task pane can be used to find a variety of information from any Office application.

5. Click the **Services** drop-down list and select the research services you want to use for the search. You can select **All Research Sites**, **Factiva News Search**, **All Business and Financial Sites**, and a number of other resource services.

6. After selecting the service or services, the search will be performed. A list of found information will appear in the task pane.

7. To switch from the initial source to the next source (found in the search), click **Next**.

8. To expand any of the found information, click the plus symbol next to a source heading.

If you want to conduct another search, type the keyword or phrase in the Search For box and then click the **green Search arrow**. Results are returned in the task pane. When you have finished working with the Research task pane, click the **Close** button to close it.

The Basic File Search Task Pane

The Basic File Search task pane enables you to locate files stored on your computer or company network without leaving the Office application that is currently open. To use the Search task pane, follow these steps:

1. From an Office application window, select the **File** menu and then select **Search** to open the Search task pane (see Figure 3.4).

Figure 3.4 Use the Search task pane to locate files on your computer or network.

2. Type the keyword or keywords that you want to use for the search into the Search text box.

3. To specify the locations that should be searched, click the **Selected Locations** drop-down box. You can expand any of the locations listed, such as My Computer, by clicking the plus (**+**) symbol to the left of the location. This enables you to view folders and subfolders at that location. Use the check boxes to the left of each location to specify whether that location should be searched.

4. To specify the types of files that are located during the search, click the **Selected File Types** drop-down list. Select or deselect the check boxes for particular Office applications (such as Word or Excel) to specify the types of files that should be included in the search.

5. When you are ready to run the search, click the **Go** button.

The files that meet your search criteria appear in the Search task pane. To open one of the files (in the application that it was created in), click the filename.

TIP **Run an Advanced Search** You can also click the Advanced Search link in the Search task pane to run an advanced search. The Advanced Search task pane enables you to create a search that uses conditional statements and allows you to search by file type, the date that the file was last modified, and a number of other parameters.

Other Standard Task Panes

Two other standard task panes that you will probably use a lot are the Clip Art and Office Clipboard task panes. Although using these task panes is covered within the context of specific Office applications in the parts of this book, you can take a brief look at both of them in the following sections.

The Clip Art Task Pane

How you find and insert clip art in the Office applications has been made much easier by the introduction of the Clip Art task pane. This task pane enables you to quickly search for clip art using a keyword search. Clip art that matches your search parameters is then immediately shown in the Clip Art task pane as thumbnails.

To use the Clip Art task pane, follow these steps:

1. In an Office application such as Word or Excel, select **Insert**, point at **Picture**, and then select **Clip Art**. The Clip Art task pane appears (see Figure 3.5).

Figure 3.5 Search for clip art by keywords using the Clip Art task pane.

2. In the task pane's Search For box, type keywords that Office can use to find your clip art images.

3. Use the **Search In** drop-down box to specify the collections you want to include in the clip art search. Selected collections are marked with a check mark in their check box that you can toggle on and off with a simple click of the mouse.

4. Use the Results Should Be drop-down box to specify the type of files that should be included in the search. You can select or deselect file types such as Clip Art, Movies, and Sounds.

5. When you have finished setting your search parameters, click the **Search** button. When the search is complete, the clip art that meets your search criteria appears in the task pane.

6. In the Image list, locate the image that you want to place into your Office document. Then, click the image. The application inserts clip art document.

Using the Office Clipboard

Microsoft Office 2003 provides a new version of the Office Clipboard that enables you to accumulate a list of 24 copied or cut items. This makes it very easy to paste items within an Office document, between Office documents in an Office application, or to copy, cut, and paste items among your different Office applications.

To use the Office Clipboard, follow these steps:

1. In an Office application, select **Edit** and then select **Office Clipboard**. The Office Clipboard task pane opens.

2. As you cut or copy items from your various Office applications, the items are placed on the Office Clipboard, as shown in Figure 3.6.

3. To paste an item from the Clipboard, place the insertion point in your Office document at the place where you want to insert the item, and then click the item on the Office Clipboard task pane.

You can remove items from the Office Clipboard at any time by placing the mouse on the item. A drop-down arrow appears; click the drop-down arrow and select **Delete** from the shortcut menu that appears. You can clear the entire Clipboard by clicking the **Clear All** button at the top of the task pane.

Figure 3.6   Use the Office Clipboard to copy, cut, and paste multiple items in your Office applications.

Using the Office Speech Feature

4

In this lesson, you learn how to train and use the Office Speech feature.

Training the Speech Feature

Microsoft Office 2003 provides you with the ability to enter information into the Office applications using a microphone. You can also enable access to an application's menu system using voice commands. The Speech feature was first made available with Office XP.

Before you can really take advantage of the Speech feature, you must provide it with some training so that it can more easily recognize your speech patterns and intonation. After the Speech feature is trained, you can effectively use it to dictate text entries or access various application commands without a keyboard or mouse.

The Speech feature is actually installed and then trained in Microsoft Word. So, you must run it for the first time from within Word. After you train the Speech feature in Word, you can then use it in your other applications, such as Excel and PowerPoint. Follow these steps to get the Speech feature up and running:

1. In Microsoft Word, select the **Tools** menu and select **Speech**. You will be asked if you want to install the Speech feature; click Yes to continue. After the installation, the Welcome to Office Speech Recognition dialog box appears. To begin the process of setting up your microphone and training the Speech feature, click the **Next** button.

2. The first screen of the Microphone Wizard that appears asks you to make sure that your microphone and speakers are connected to your computer. If you have a headset microphone, this screen shows you how to adjust the microphone for use. Click **Next** to continue.

3. The next wizard screen asks you to read a short text passage so that your microphone volume level can be adjusted (see Figure 4.1). When you have finished reading the text, click **Next** to continue.

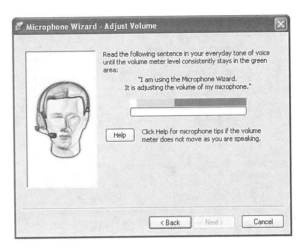

Figure 4.1 The Microphone Wizard adjusts the volume of your microphone.

4. On the next screen, you are asked to read another passage. The text is then played back to you. This is to determine whether the microphone is placed at an appropriate distance from your mouth; when you get satisfactory playback, click **Finish**.

When you finish working with the Microphone Wizard, the Voice Training Wizard appears. This wizard collects samples of your speech and, in essence, educates the Speech feature as to how you speak.

To complete the voice training process, follow these steps:

1. The opening Wizard screen provides you with a Sample button that allows you to hear how you should read the text that is supplied during the training session. After reading the directions provided on the opening screen, click **Next** to begin the voice training process.

2. On the next screen, you are asked to begin reading a sample passage (see Figure 4.2). If you need to pause during the process (the initial training takes about 15 minutes), click the **Pause** button.

3. You are asked to read text on several subsequent screens. Words are selected as the wizard recognizes them.

 TIP **Some Words Might Not Be Recognized** If the wizard becomes stuck on a word that it cannot recognize during the training session, click the **Skip Word** button. This skips the current word and allows you to continue the training session.

Figure 4.2 You read text passages to train the Speech feature.

4. When you complete the training screens, your profile is updated. Click **Finish** on the wizard's final screen.

You are now ready to use the Speech feature. The next two sections discuss using the Voice Dictation and Voice Command features.

CAUTION

The Speech Feature Works Better Over Time Be advised that the voice feature's performance improves as you use it. If you pronounce your words carefully and consistently, the Speech feature tunes itself to your speech patterns. You might need to do additional training sessions to fine-tune the Speech feature.

Using Voice Dictation

When you are ready to start dictating text into an Office application such as Word, put on your headset microphone or place your standalone microphone in the proper position that you determined when you used the Microphone Wizard. When you're ready to go, select the **Tools** menu and then select **Speech**. The Language bar appears, as shown in Figure 4.3. If necessary, click the **Dictation** button on the toolbar (if the Dictation button is not already activated or depressed).

After you enable the Dictation button, you can begin dictating your text into the Office document. Figure 4.3 shows text being dictated into a Word document. When you want to put a line break into the text, say "new line." Punctuation is placed in the document by saying the name of a particular punctuation mark, such as "period" or "comma."

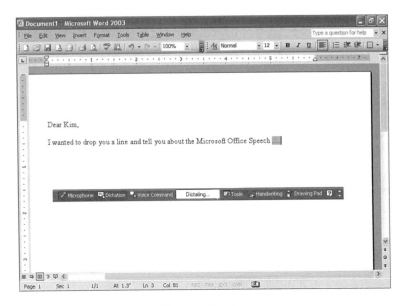

Figure 4.3 Dictating text into the Office application.

CAUTION

How Do I Insert the Word "Comma" Rather Than the Punctuation Mark? Because certain keywords, such as "period" or "comma," are used to insert punctuation during dictation, you must spell these words out if you want to include them in the text. To do this, say "spelling mode," and then spell out the word, such as c-o-m-m-a. As soon as you dictate an entire word, the spelling mode ends.

When you have finished dictating into the document, click the **Microphone** button on the Language bar. When you click the **Microphone** button, the Language bar collapses, hiding the **Dictation** and the **Voice Command** buttons. You can also stop Dictation mode by saying "microphone."

You can minimize the Language bar by clicking the **Minimize** button on the right end of the bar. This sends the Language bar to the Windows system tray.

With the Language bar minimized in the system tray, you can quickly open it when you need it. Click the **Restore** icon in the system tray.

Using the Dictation feature correctly requires that you know how to get the Speech feature to place the correct text or characters into an Office document. For more help with the dictation feature, consult the Microsoft Office Help system from any Office application.

Using Voice Commands

Another tool the Speech feature provides is voice commands. You can open and select menus in an application and even navigate dialog boxes using voice commands.

To use voice commands, open the Language bar (click **Tools**, **Speech** or restore the Language Bar from the system tray). Click the **Microphone** icon, if necessary, to expand the Language bar. Then, click the **Voice Command** icon on the bar (or say "voice command").

To open a particular menu such as the Format menu, say "format." Then, to open a particular submenu such as Font, say "font." In the case of these voice commands, the Font dialog box opens.

You can then navigate a particular dialog box using voice commands. In the Font dialog box, for example, to change the size of the font, say "size"; this activates the Size box that controls font size. Then, say the size of the font, such as "14." You can also activate other font attributes in the dialog box in this manner. Say the name of the area of the dialog box you want to use, and then say the name of the feature you want to turn on or select.

When you have finished working with a particular dialog box, say "OK" (or "Cancel" or "Apply," as needed) and the dialog box closes and provides you with the features you selected in the dialog box. When you have finished using voice commands, say "microphone," or click the **Microphone** icon on the Language bar.

Believe it or not, you can also activate buttons on the various toolbars using voice commands. For example, you could turn on bold by saying "bold." The Bold button on the Formatting toolbar becomes active. To turn bold off, say "bold" again.

A Final Word About the Speech Feature

The Speech feature actually provides a number of possibilities for using voice dictation and voice commands. You will probably want to practice on some documents that aren't important to your work as you become familiar with the different features provided.

If you find that you aren't getting very good results with either voice dictation or voice commands, you can do some additional training for the Speech feature. On the Language bar, click the **Tools** icon and then select **Training** from the shortcut menu that appears. The Voice Training Wizard appears (see Figure 4.4). Do the additional training exercises that the wizard supplies.

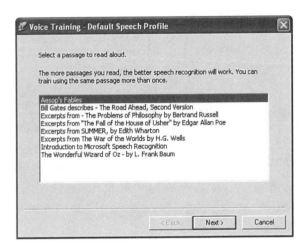

Figure 4.4   Use the Language bar's Tools button to select the Training feature.

Getting Help in Microsoft Office

In this lesson, you learn how to access and use the Help system in Microsoft Office.

Help: What's Available?

Microsoft Office supplies a Help system that makes it easy for you to look up information on application commands and features as you work in a particular Office application. Because people have different preferences, the Office Help system can be accessed in several ways. You can

- Ask a question in the Ask a Question box.
- Ask the Office Assistant for help.
- Use the Help task pane.
- Access the Office on Microsoft.com Web site to view Web pages containing help information (if you are connected to the Internet).

Using the Ask a Question Box

The Ask a Question box is the easiest way to quickly get help. An Ask a Question box resides at the top right of every Office application.

For example, if you are working in Excel and would like to get some help with Excel functions (functions are discussed in Lesson 5, "Performing Calculations with Functions," of the Excel part of this book), type **functions** into the Ask a Question box. Then press the **Enter** key. A search will be performed on the Help system and the results of the search (based on your keywords) will appear in the Search Results task pane (see Figure 5.1).

To access one of the Help topics supplied, select the appropriate link in the Search Results task pane. The Help window will appear. In the Help window, you can use the links provided to navigate the Help system. Click on a particular link to read more about that topic. The topic will be expanded in the Help window. When you have finished working with the Help window, click its Close button.

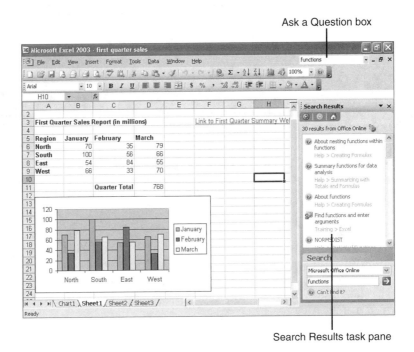

Ask a Question box

Search Results task pane

Figure 5.1 The Ask a Question box provides a list of Help topics in the Search Results task pane.

Using the Office Assistant

Another way to get help in an Office Application is to use the Office Assistant. The Office Assistant supplies the same type of access to the Help system as the Ask a Question box. You ask the Office Assistant a question, and it supplies you with a list of possible answers that provide links to various Help topics. The next two sections discuss how to use the Office Assistant.

Turning the Office Assistant On and Off

By default, the Office Assistant is off. To show the Office Assistant in your application window, select the **Help** menu and then select **Show the Office Assistant**.

You can also quickly hide the Office Assistant if you no longer want it in your application window. Right-click the Office Assistant and select **Hide**. If you want to get rid of the Office Assistant completely so that it isn't activated when you select the Help feature, right-click the Office Assistant and select **Options**. Clear the **Use the Office Assistant** check box, and then click **OK**. You can always get the Office Assistant back by selecting **Help**, **Show Office Assistant**.

Asking the Office Assistant a Question

When you click the Office Assistant, a balloon appears above it, as shown in Figure 5.2. Type a question into the text box. Then click the **Search** button.

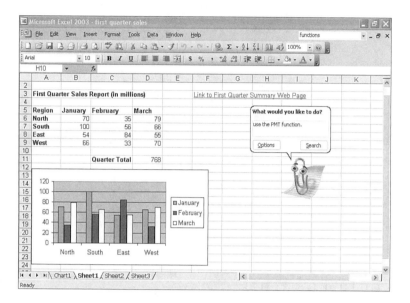

Figure 5.2   Ask the Office Assistant a question to get help.

When you click Search, the Search Results task pane appears, containing a list of results. Click a particular topic to open the Help window. Using the Office Assistant actually provides you with the same type of results you receive when you use the Ask a Question box.

Although not everyone likes the Office Assistant because having it enabled means that it is always sitting in your application window, it can be useful at times. For example, when you access particular features in an application, the Office Assistant can automatically provide you with context-sensitive help on that particular feature. If you are brand new to Microsoft Office, you might want to use the Office Assistant to help you learn the various features that the Office applications provide.

TIP   **Select Your Own Office Assistant**   Several different Office Assistants are available in Microsoft Office. To select your favorite, click the Office Assistant and select the **Options** button. On the Office Assistant dialog box that appears, select the **Gallery** tab. Click the **Next** button repeatedly to see the different Office Assistants that are available. When you locate the assistant you want to use, click **OK**.

Using the Help Task Pane

You can also forgo either the Type a Question box or the Office Assistant and get your help from the Help task pane; select **Help** and then the help command for the application you are using, such as **Microsoft Word Help.** You can also press the **F1** key to make the Help task pane appear (see Figure 5.3).

Figure 5.3   Open the Help task pane to search for help by topic.

The Help task pane provides you with the ability to do a search using a keyword or keywords. You can also open the Help table of contents for the application that you are currently working in.

To do a search using the Help task pane, click in the Search box and type a keyword, phrase, or question. Then click the **Start Searching** arrow. The results of the search will appear in the Search Results task pane. Click a particular result and the Help window will open as shown in Figure 5.4.

To expand any of the help topics provided in the Help window, click a particular link. If you want to expand all the topics provided, click **Show All**.

TIP   **View the Help Window Tabs**   If you don't see the different tabs in the Help window, click the **Show** button on the Help window toolbar.

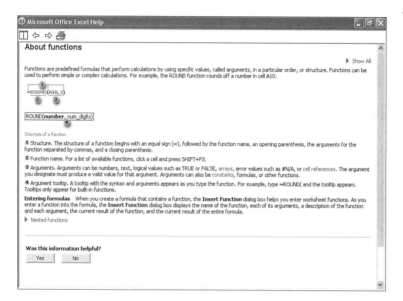

Figure 5.4   The Help window provides access to all the help information provided for a particular application.

Searching For Help Online

If you don't find the help you need using the different ways we discussed in this lesson to access the Help window, you can connect to the Microsoft Office Web site. The site provides a search engine and other information on the different Microsoft Office applications. To connect to the Office Web site, follow these steps:

1. Open the Help task pane (select **Help** and then your application's help command, or press **F1**).

2. In the Help task pane, click the **Connect to Office on Microsoft.com** link.

3. The Microsoft Office Web site will open in your Web browser window. Use the links to the various articles and the Search engine provided to find the help that you need.

TIP   **Take Advantage of ScreenTips**   Another Help feature provided by the Office applications is the ScreenTip. All the buttons on the different toolbars provided by your Office applications have a ScreenTip. Other buttons or tools in an Office application window can also provide ScreenTips. Place the mouse on a particular button or icon, and the name of the item (which often helps you determine its function) appears in a ScreenTip.

Customizing Your Office Applications

In this lesson, you learn how to customize your Office applications.

Navigating Options Settings

Office applications provide you with a great deal of control over the desktop environment that you work in. You can control options such as how the application window looks for a particular Office application and where the application should store files, by default, when you save them.

Every one of the Office applications has an Options dialog box that provides access to different settings that you can customize. First, you take a look at how you open and navigate the Options dialog box in an Office application. Then, you look at several of the applications and some of the key options they offer that you might want to customize.

CAUTION

Customizing Office Applications   You might want to work with the Office applications described in this book before you change a lot of options for the applications. A good way for you to do this is to explore the other parts of this book and then return to this lesson when you are ready to customize some of the options in the Office applications you use most.

To open and navigate the Options dialog box in an Office application, follow these steps:

1. In an Office application (such as Word), select **Tools, Options**. The Options dialog box for that application appears (see Figure 6.1).
2. To switch between the different options, click the appropriate tab on the Options dialog box. Each tab controls a subset of the options available in that application.
3. To change settings on the various tabs, use the check boxes, drop-down lists, or spinner boxes to make your selections for various features.
4. When you have finished customizing the various options in the Options dialog box, click **OK**. You are returned to the application window.

Figure 6.1 The Options dialog box in an application enables you to customize various settings.

You will find that you can set a large number of options in the Options dialog box for each Office application. This doesn't mean that you have to change them all (if you're not sure what you're doing, in many cases you shouldn't change them). Next, take a look at some of the common settings that you might want to change in your Office applications; you'll look at Word, Excel, PowerPoint, and Access individually in the sections that follow.

 TIP **Customizing Outlook** Because Outlook is customized differently than the other Office applications, see Lesson 20, "Customizing Outlook," in the Outlook section of this book (Part III).

Setting Options in Word

When you work in Word, you are probably going to create letters and envelopes for mailings. One of the options related to Word that you will want to set up is your user information. This way, the return address on any letters and envelopes you create with Word are inserted automatically into certain documents.

Another set of options that you might want to customize in Word are the options related to the Spelling and Grammar Checker. For example, you might want to customize the types of things that are automatically flagged by the Spelling and Grammar Checker when you run these features in Word.

To customize some of the Word options, follow these steps:

1. In Word, select **Tools** and then select **Options** to open the Options dialog box.

2. Click the **User Information** tab on the Options dialog box (see Figure 6.2).

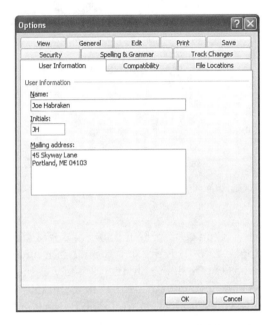

Figure 6.2   Provide your name and address on the User Information tab.

3. If necessary, type your name into the Name box on the User Information tab. Type your address into the Mailing Address box. That takes care of the User Information tab.

4. To set options related to the Spelling and Grammar features, click the **Spelling & Grammar** tab (see Figure 6.3).

5. Check boxes are provided that allow you to check spelling as you type or to hide any typing errors in the document (by default, typing errors are flagged as you type with a red underscore). You can also determine whether you want the Spelling feature to ignore uppercase words, words with numbers, and Internet and file addresses. Select or deselect check boxes as needed.

6. Use the Grammar box on the Spelling & Grammar tab to set options such as Check Grammar As You Type. You can also set whether the grammar in the document is checked whenever you run the Spelling and Grammar Checker (select **Check Grammar with Spelling**).

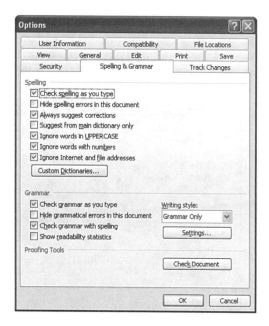

Figure 6.3 Set Spelling and Grammar options on the Spelling & Grammar tab.

7. When you have finished setting options on the two Options dialog box tabs discussed in these steps, click **OK** to close the Options dialog box. If you don't want any of your changes to take effect, click **Cancel**.

Setting Options in Excel

When you work with Excel, you work with numbers and calculations. As you learn in the Excel section of this book (Part V), Excel is a number cruncher. It is built to do math and provide you with correct results when it does calculations.

Two of the options that you might want to adjust related to Excel specify when it recalculates all the formulas in an Excel workbook and the rules that it uses to check for errors in an Excel worksheet.

Follow these steps:

1. In Excel, select **Tools** and then select **Options**. The Options dialog box opens.

2. Click the **Calculation** tab on the Options dialog box (see Figure 6.4).

3. When you work with very large worksheets and worksheets that are linked to other Excel workbook files, your worksheet is recalculated every time you change or add data on the worksheet. If you have a computer with marginal processing power and memory, this process can take a while. You can turn off the automatic recalculation feature on the Calculations tab by clicking the **Manual** option button. If you do this, you must press **F9** to make Excel recalculate the sheet.

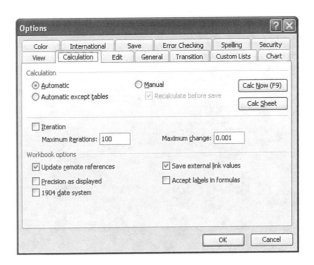

Figure 6.4   Set options related to calculations on the Calculation tab.

4. You might want to look at another set of options on the **Error Checking** tab (click it). This tab contains a list of errors that Excel can automatically check for as you work on your worksheet (see Figure 6.5).

5. To set a default color for errors found in a worksheet, click the **Error Indicator Color** drop-down box and select a color from the color palette (because the Spelling Checker and smart tags use red, don't pick red).

6. You should probably leave the error rules listed all in force. However, notice in Figure 6.5 that the Formulas Referring to Empty Cells check box is not selected. This is because you typically enter formulas into worksheets even before data is entered. After creating a worksheet, you might want to select this option, especially if you are working on a large, complex worksheet. This ensures that you get all the data into the appropriate cells, or Excel will start sending error messages your way.

7. When you have finished setting these options, click **OK** to close the Options dialog box (or **Cancel** to discard changes).

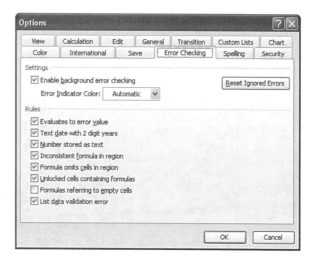

Figure 6.5   Error checking helps make sure that your worksheet data is entered correctly.

Setting Options in PowerPoint

After you work in PowerPoint for a while, you might find that you want to specify a view to be the default view when you open presentations that you have created. Another option you might want to set is the default location where presentations that you save are placed.

Follow these steps to change these PowerPoint options:

1. In PowerPoint, select **Tools** and then select **Options** to open the Options dialog box.

2. Click the **View** tab on the Options dialog box (see Figure 6.6).

3. Click the **Open All Documents Using This View** drop-down list and select a view that you want to use whenever you open a saved presentation. The views range from **Normal-Outline, Notes,** and **Slide** to **Slide Sorter**.

4. Another option you might want to set is the default folder that is used when you first save a presentation. Click the **Save** tab on the Options dialog box.

5. In the Default File Location box, type the path that you want to use.

6. When you have finished changing your settings, click **OK** (or **Cancel** to reject any changes made).

Figure 6.6   Set the default view that will be used when you open a saved presentation.

Setting Special Options in Access

When you work in Access, you spend a lot of time in the Datasheet view, adding and manipulating records in a database table. Although forms can be used to handle some of the data entry and editing chores (as discussed in the Access section of this book [Part VI]), you still will work a great deal with table datasheets. Therefore, you might want to customize the Datasheet view to make it easier to work with and provide an environment that is a little easier on your eyes.

Follow these steps to customize Access options:

1. In Access, select **Tools** and then select **Options**. The Options dialog box opens.

2. Click the **Datasheet** tab on the Options dialog box (see Figure 6.7).

3. Use the Font drop-down box to select a color for the font used in the Datasheet view.

4. The Background and Gridlines drop-down boxes can be used to adjust the colors of these items to complement the Font color you select.

5. If you want to change the Default Cell Effect, select either the **Raised** or **Sunken** option buttons.

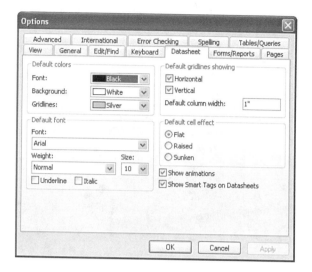

Figure 6.7 You can edit the datasheet colors and other settings on the Datasheet tab.

6. You can also specify a wider default column width for your datasheets in the Default Column Width box.

7. When you have finished making your changes, click **OK** (or **Cancel** to discard any changes made).

Customizing Toolbars

You might find as you use your Office applications that you would like to customize your toolbars. This enables you to add or remove buttons from the toolbars so that they provide you with quick access to the commands and features you use the most often.

For example, suppose you would like to add or remove buttons from a particular toolbar, such as the Formatting toolbar (which is common to a number of Office applications). Follow these steps:

1. In any application (such as Word), place the mouse on a toolbar's drop-down arrow (on the far right of the toolbar). Click the drop-down arrow to open a shortcut menu.

2. On the toolbar shortcut menu, point at **Add or Remove Buttons**, and then point at the toolbar's name on the pop-up menu that appears. A list of all the buttons available for that toolbar appears (see Figure 6.8). The buttons that are being used on the toolbar have a check mark to the left of them.

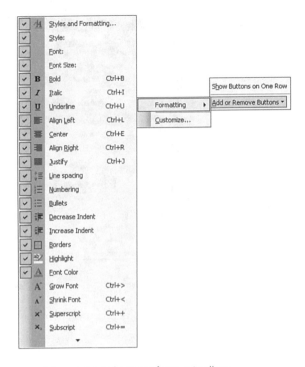

Figure 6.8   You can add or remove buttons from a toolbar.

3. Click a button to deselect it (remove it), or click one of the unselected buttons listed to add it.

4. Repeat step 4 until you have customized the buttons shown on the toolbar. Then, click anywhere in the application window to close the Button drop-down list.

TIP   **Resetting a Toolbar**   If you want to reset a toolbar and start from scratch with the default buttons, open the Button drop-down list for a particular toolbar and then click **Reset Toolbar** at the very bottom of the Button drop-down list.

Another setting related to toolbars that you might want to adjust is for the Standard and Formatting toolbars in your Office applications, which are set up, by default, to share one line. This limits the number of buttons that can be shown on either of the toolbars at any one time. To place each of these toolbars on its own line, follow these steps:

1. In any application (such as Word or Excel), select the **Tools** menu and then select **Customize**.

2. The Customize dialog box opens. Click the **Options** tab, if necessary.

3. On the Options tab, click the **Show Standard and Formatting Toolbars on Two Rows** check box.

4. Click **Close**.

 TIP   **Get Toolbars in Two Rows Quickly**   You can also quickly place the Standard and Formatting toolbars on two rows by clicking the **Toolbar Options** button on the Standard toolbar (when the toolbars are in a single row) and selecting **Show Buttons on Two Rows**.

Using Office Web Integration Features

In this lesson, you learn how to use various Web features in your Office applications.

Adding Hyperlinks to Office Documents

Microsoft Office provides several features that allow you to integrate features that you typically associate with the World Wide Web into the Office documents that you create. Office documents can be saved in the HTML format and then incorporated into Web pages. Hyperlinks can be placed into Office documents, including Excel workbooks and even Access tables. A *hyperlink* is a text entry or a graphic that, when clicked, opens a Web page on the World Wide Web, a file on your hard disk, or a file on a local network.

Hyperlinks are basically pointers that enable you to quickly access Web content or another file when the hyperlink is clicked. Hyperlinks can also take the form of an e-mail address and can be used to quickly fire off an e-mail message when the link is selected.

Adding a hyperlink to an Office document follows pretty much the same procedure in all the Office applications. In fact, the Insert Hyperlink dialog box is identical in Excel, Word, PowerPoint, Publisher, and Access (you can also add hyperlinks to Outlook e-mails in a Insert Hyperlink dialog box that requires you to type the hyperlink address).

Next, take a look at adding a hyperlink to an Excel worksheet. To add a hyperlink, follow these steps:

1. Select the text or graphic you want to use for the hyperlink (in Excel, select a cell; in Access, click in a Table field).
2. Select the **Insert** menu and then select **Hyperlink**. The Insert Hyperlink dialog box appears, as shown in Figure 7.1.
3. Type the address of the Web page to be used by the hyperlink into the Address box at the bottom of the dialog box.

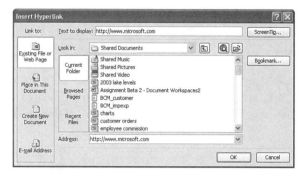

Figure 7.1 Insert a hyperlink into an Office document, such as an Excel worksheet.

4. If you would like to select the address of the Web page from a list of Web sites that you have recently browsed with Internet Explorer, click the **Browsed Pages** button in the dialog box. Click a link in the list that appears. It will be placed into the Address box.

5. If the link is to an e-mail address rather than to a Web page or file on your computer, click the **E-Mail Address** icon on the left of the dialog box.

6. A list of recently used e-mail addresses that you can select from appears in the dialog box, or you can type the e-mail address into the **E-Mail Address** box, as shown in Figure 7.2.

Figure 7.2 Hyperlinks to e-mail addresses can also be inserted the Insert Hyperlink dialog box.

7. To display a ScreenTip when the mouse pointer rests on the hyperlink, click the **ScreenTip** button; in the dialog box that appears, enter the description you want to display. Click **OK**.

8. Click **OK** to close the Insert Hyperlink dialog box. The text or graphic that was selected becomes a hyperlink. Text hyperlinks appear in a blue font and are underlined.

Figure 7.3 shows a text hyperlink that has been added to an Excel worksheet on the words "Link to First Quarter Summary Web page." The link could be used to quickly access a Web page that has information related to the worksheet shown in the figure.

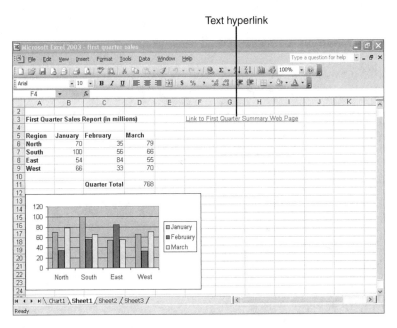

Figure 7.3 Hyperlinks provide quick access to Web pages and files.

When you move the mouse pointer over this link, it changes to a hand. Next to the hand, you can see the address of the link. Click the link and you jump to the appropriate worksheet, Web page, file, or e-mail program. The text color of the link changes to purple to indicate that you have used the link.

TIP **Creating Hyperlinks to Documents on Your Computer** To insert a hyperlink for a document on your computer, use the Look In box in the Insert Hyperlink dialog box to find the drive that the file resides on, and then open the appropriate folder to locate the file. Select the file in the dialog box to create the link.

Saving Office Documents As Web Pages

You can save any of your Office documents, such as Word documents, Excel worksheets, and PowerPoint presentations as HTML documents (you can also convert Publisher publications to the HTML format using the **Publish to the Web** command on the **File** menu). After you save an Office document in the HTML format, you can view the document in the Internet Explorer Web browser.

 HTML   Short for Hypertext Markup Language, HTML is the language in which data is presented on the World Wide Web. Office uses the term "Web Page" to define the format type in which you save an Office document for the Web. You are actually converting the document to HTML format.

Saving Office documents as Web pages is similar regardless of whether you are using Word, Excel, or PowerPoint. The Save As Web Page command on the File menu is used to save an Office document in the HTML format. Access is the exception, however: Access objects, such as tables, can be made into Web pages using the Export command on the Access File menu.

Before you save a Word document, Excel worksheet, or a PowerPoint presentation as a Web page, you might want to preview the document as it would appear in a Web browser. For example, suppose you have a PowerPoint presentation and you would like to see how it would look on the Web.

Select the **File** menu and then select **Web Page Preview**. It might take a moment as your file is prepared; when it's ready, Internet Explorer opens and your Office document appears in the browser window. Figure 7.4 shows a PowerPoint presentation in the Internet Explorer window. Notice that links to all the slides in the presentation have been automatically created for the Web version of the presentation.

After you preview your Office document as a Web page, if things look good, you can quickly save it as a Web page in the HTML format. Next, take a look at saving a PowerPoint presentation as a Web page to get the overall feel for converting any Office document to the HTML format (the procedure is similar in Word and Excel). Follow these steps:

1. Choose the **File** menu and then choose **Save As Web Page**. The Save As dialog box appears (see Figure 7.5).

2. In the **File Name** text box, enter a filename for the Web page document or go with the default name provided (it will be the current name of the file). Notice that in the Save As Type box, the file type is Web Page.

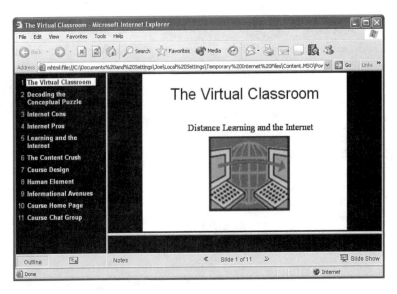

Figure 7.4 You can preview an Office document as a Web page.

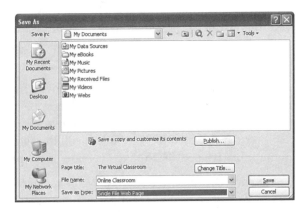

Figure 7.5 Office documents can be saved as Web pages.

3. If you want to change the page title for the presentation, click the **Change Title** button. Type a new title and then click **OK**.

4. Click **Save**. Your Office document (in this case, a presentation) is saved.

TIP   **PowerPoint Enables You to Select the Slides for the Web Page**   In the case of PowerPoint, you can select the slides in the presentation that you actually want to include in the Web page document that you are creating. Click the **Publish** button and select the slides you want to include in the HTML document. You can also specify in the Publish dialog box which Web browsers (such as Internet Explorer or Netscape Navigator) the PowerPoint Web page should support.

When you save an Office document, such as a Word document or PowerPoint presentation, as a Web page, you have the choice of saving the file as a single file Web page (where all the pictures and other items are made part of that file), or you can save the file as a "typical" Web page that actually creates several files. Any graphics, objects, or other special elements in the document are saved as separate files in the appropriate format for the Web.

For example, in the case of PowerPoint, if the presentation file named Broadway.ppt is saved as a Web page (not as a single file Webpage), the home page would be named Broadway.htm. Then, PowerPoint creates a folder named *Presentation Name* Files (for example, Broadway Files) that contains all the other HTML, graphics, and other files needed to display the complete presentation. If you are transferring the HTML presentation to another PC (which is very likely, if you are going to make it available on the World Wide Web), you must transfer not only the lone HTML home page, but also the entire associated folder.

Adding an FTP Site to Your Save In Box

After you save an Office document as a Web page or create a Web page using Microsoft Word or Publisher, you may need to load that file onto a Web server. You can save the Web pages that you create in the Office applications directly to a Web server that also functions as an FTP site.

FTP FTP (File Transfer Protocol) is a protocol that allows you to download and upload files to an FTP server. An FTP server is a computer connected to the Internet that hosts an FTP site and provides space for file transfers (this includes file uploads and downloads).

You can save your Web files to an FTP site on the Internet (or a company intranet), provided you have the permission to do so. The first step is to add the FTP site to the Save As dialog box:

1. Open the **Save In** list and select **Add/Modify FTP Locations**. The Add/Modify FTP Locations dialog box appears, as shown in Figure 7.6.

2. In the **Name of FTP Site** text box, enter the site's address, such as **ftp.microsoft.com**.

3. Select **Log On As**, either **Anonymous** or **User**, and enter a password, if necessary.

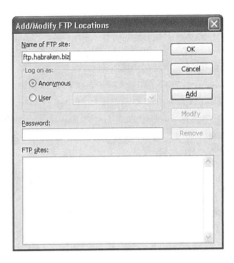

Figure 7.6   Saving to an FTP site can get files onto the Web or a company's intranet.

4. Click **OK**.

5. After the site has been added to the Save As dialog box, you can select it from the FTP Locations folder in the Save In list.

Faxing and E-Mailing in Office 2003

In this lesson, you learn how to fax and e-mail documents from Office applications.

Understanding E-Mails and Faxes in Office

The capability to send e-mail and faxes directly from your Office applications enables you to quickly take the information on your screen and either fax it or e-mail it to a recipient. When you send an e-mail message directly from an Office application client, such as Word, Excel, Access, or PowerPoint, you are actually using your default e-mail client, such as Outlook, to send the message.

All the Office applications allow you to send the current document as an attachment. Word and Excel also provide the option of sending the document as part of the e-mail message.

There are two options for faxing documents from within an Office application. You can either send the fax using an Internet Fax Service, which allows you to actually fax the document over the Internet, or you can outfit your computer with a fax modem. Fax modems actually supply faxing capabilities as an extension of your computer's printing services.

TIP **Sign Up for an Internet Fax Service** If you want to fax documents over the Internet, you need to sign up for an Internet Fax Service. Several Internet Fax Services exist, which not only allow you to fax information over the Internet but may also enable you to receive faxes over the Internet and have them sent to you as e-mail messages. The first time you attempt to use the Internet Fax Service to send a fax from a Microsoft Application, you are provided with the option of navigating to a Web page that lists Internet Fax Providers. The cost related to these services will vary.

Word makes the process of sending a fax easy and provides a Fax Wizard to walk you through the steps. The other Office applications send faxes in two different ways: either by "printing" to a fax modem or by using the Send To command on the File menu to send an Internet fax (Word also provides this option). Sending a fax from the Office applications via a fax modem is discussed later in the lesson.

To send a fax from any Office application using an Internet Fax Service, you click **File**, and then point at **Send To**. On the menu that appears, select **Recipient Using Internet Fax Service**. You can then complete the process by providing the recipient's fax number and other information required for a fax cover page.

Internet Fax Services provide their own cover page and set of instructions for sending a fax. The actual number of steps that you have to complete to send an Office document as a fax over the Internet depends on the actual service that you use.

Using the Word Fax Wizard

The Word Fax Wizard walks you through the steps of preparing your Word document. You can send your fax using a fax modem (attached to your computer) or using an Internet Fax Service.

 TIP **Setting Up a Fax Modem and the Fax Service**   Most "new" fax modems embrace plug-and-play technology as do Microsoft Windows XP and Microsoft Windows 2000. In most cases all you will have to do to get a fax modem up and running is to attach the modem to the computer (or install it internally) and then restart the PC. Windows XP requires that you add the Microsoft Fax Service to your computer to send and receive faxes. You add this service in the Printers and Faxes window of the Control Panel. When you open this window, click the Install Faxing link on the left side of the window and follow the prompts. Make sure you have your Windows XP CD available because files need to be copied to your system to enable the fax service.

To use the Word Fax Wizard and send a fax using a fax modem (in the Windows XP environment), follow these steps:

1. Select **File**, point to **Send To**, and then select **Recipient Using a Fax Modem** from the cascading menu. The Word Fax Wizard starts (see Figure 8.1).

2. The Fax Wizard starts to walk you through the process of sending the current document as a fax. Click **Next** to continue the process.

3. On the next wizard screen, a drop-down list enables you to select whether to send the current document or select another open document (see Figure 8.2). After making your selection, click **Next** to continue.

4. On the next screen, you select your fax service. Microsoft Fax is the default. If you use a different fax program on your computer, select the option button labeled **A Different Fax Program Which Is Installed on This System**, and then select your fax program from the **Fax Service** drop-down list. Then click **Next** to continue.

Figure 8.1   The Fax Wizard walks you through the process of sending the current document as a fax.

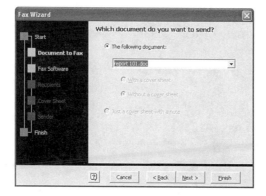

Figure 8.2   You can select whether to send the current document or select another open document.

5. At this point the Fax Wizard has completed the initial process of selecting the document and fax service. When you click **Finish**, the Send Fax Wizard appears. Click **Next** to bypass the initial Wizard screen.

6. On the next screen (see Figure 8.3), enter the recipient and the fax number into the appropriate boxes. If you have the recipient listed in your e-mail program's address book (such as the Outlook Contacts folder), click the **Address Book** button and select the person from the Address Book list. If a fax number is listed in the address book (as it is in Microsoft Outlook), all you have to do is select the recipients from the address book for your Word fax, and the fax numbers are entered for you automatically. When you have finished entering the recipient information for the fax, click **Next** to continue.

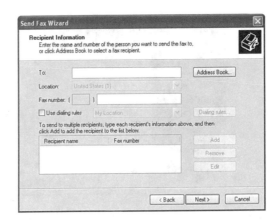

Figure 8.3　Enter the recipient (or recipients) information for the fax.

7. On this screen, select the cover page template you want to use for your fax cover page. Also provide a subject line and note (optional); click **Next** to continue.

8. On the next screen, you choose the schedule for when the fax should be sent. The default is Now, but you can also select a specific time. This screen also allows you to specify the priority for the fax: High, Normal (the default), or Low.

9. On the final screen of the Fax Wizard, you are can choose to preview the fax. Click the **Preview Fax** button to see the fax cover page and accompanying document. When you are ready to send the fax, click **Finish**.

Your fax modem will connect to your phone line and send the fax (if you chose to send the fax "Now"). If you want to view sent faxes or view a list of faxes waiting to be sent by the Microsoft Fax Service, you can open the Fax Console. Select **Start**, **All Programs**, **Accessories**, **Fax**, and then click on the **Fax Console**. The Fax Console operates much like an e-mail client. It provides an Inbox, Outbox, and Sent Items folders that store your received, pending, and sent faxes respectively.

Sending Faxes from Other Office Applications

You can also send faxes directly from other Office applications. You "print" the document to the fax service installed on your computer.

Follow these steps to send a fax from an Office application such as Excel or Access:

1. Select **File** and then select **Print** to open the Print dialog box.

2. In the Name box in the Print dialog box, select the fax service that you have installed on your computer (see Figure 8.4).

Figure 8.4   Select your fax service as the printer in the Print dialog box.

3. Click **OK**. Depending on the fax service you are using on your computer, a dialog box or wizard specific to the fax service opens. For example, if you have the Windows fax service installed on your computer, the Send Fax Wizard opens. You would then click **Next** to advance past the opening screen provided by the wizard.

4. Follow steps 5 through 8 in the preceding section if you are using the Windows Fax Service. At the completion of the process, click **Finish** to send your fax.

Sending E-Mails from Office Applications

If you have an e-mail client (software for sending and receiving e-mail) on your computer, such as Microsoft Outlook, you can send Office documents in e-mails. You can send a Word document, an Excel worksheet, or even an entire PowerPoint presentation with an e-mail message.

E-Mail Client   The e-mail program installed on your computer that you use to send and receive e-mail.

The process for sending e-mail from the different Office applications is the same for Word, Excel, PowerPoint, and Access. You use the Send To command on the File menu.

You can send Word or Excel files embedded in the e-mail message or you can send them as attachments. In the case of PowerPoint and Access, the file you currently have open can only be sent with the e-mail message as an attachment.

In most cases, sending the file as an attachment makes it easier for the recipient to manipulate the file after they receive it. To send an Excel worksheet as an attachment, follow these steps:

1. Select **File** and then point at **Send To**. Select **Mail Recipient (as Attachment)** from the cascading menu that appears. A new e-mail message opens (in your default e-mail client, such as Outlook) with the Excel file attached (see Figure 8.5).

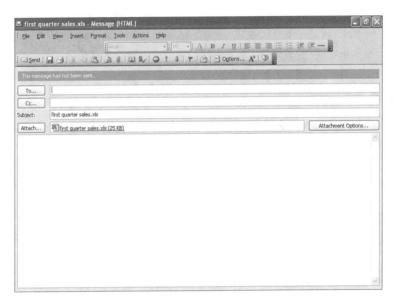

Figure 8.5   The new e-mail message contains the Excel file as an attachment.

2. Type the e-mail address of the recipient into the To box, or click the **To** icon and select an e-mail address from an address book, such as your Outlook Contacts list.

3. When you are ready to send the e-mail, click **Send**.

Your e-mail is sent. You can view the sent e-mail by opening your e-mail client and then opening the Sent Items folder.

TIP   **Sending Word and Excel Files Using the Mail Recipient Command**
As already mentioned, Word and Excel can send documents as the body of an
e-mail. When you select **File**, **Send To** and then **Mail Recipient,** a mail window
actually opens at the top of the Word or Excel document. You enter the recipient
and other information required and then click the **Send This Sheet** button (in
Excel) or **Send a Copy** button (in Word) that is provided on the Mail toolbar. For
recipients to view this e-mail correctly they will need to be using Outlook. If they use
another type of e-mail client, you are better off sending the file as an attachment.

One thing to remember when you are e-mailing documents directly from Office
applications is that you must be connected to the Internet or your company's network to actually send the mail. If you use a dial-up connection to access the Internet
(and Internet e-mail), connect to the Internet before sending the e-mail from the
Office application.

Migrating to Office 2003

Upgrading to Outlook 2003

In this lesson you learn what's new in Outlook 2003.

What's New in Outlook 2003?

Outlook 2003 is the latest version of Microsoft's popular personal information manager (PIM). Outlook 2003 has a new look and a number of new features. Outlook 2003 is further enhanced by the addition of the Business Contact Manager, which is an add-on to Outlook that provides you with the ability to organize and track business activities.

 TIP **Business Contact Manager Lessons** The Business Contact Manager is covered in Lessons 21 and 22 of the Outlook section (Part III) of this book.

A number of enhancements have been made to Outlook 2003. Some of these changes are as follows:

- **New Navigation Pane**—The new Navigation pane provides icons that allow you to navigate the major areas of Outlook such as the Mail, Calendar, and Contacts. Subpanes are also provided that make it easier to access data in a particular Outlook tool; for example, the All Mail Folders pane appears when you select Mail on the Navigation pane. (These subpanes are also referred to as panes).

- **New Reading Pane**—The preview pane found in previous versions has been upgraded to the new Reading pane, which provides a vertical orientation for reading e-mail messages.

- **Junk E-mail Filter**—A junk e-mail filter has been added to Outlook and helps to rid your Inbox of useless junk e-mail. For more protection against unwanted e-mail, you can design your own e-mail rules as in previous versions of Outlook.

- **Research Task Pane**—The new Research task pane is available in Outlook (and the other Office applications) and can be used to look up stock, financial, and other information from a variety of online resources.

- **Business Contact Manager**—The biggest change to Outlook is the addition of the Business Contact Manager. It provides a repository for entering and tracking business contacts, accounts, and opportunities.

- **Search Folders**—Search Folders allow you to set up search criteria for e-mail messages. The messages that match the search criteria are then listed in the specific Search Folder. This provides a great way to see lists of messages that are grouped by different criteria. Search Folders are discussed in this lesson. Lesson 18, "Saving and Finding Outlook Items," in the Outlook section of this book (Part III) also discusses Search Folders and their relationship to the Find and Advanced Search features.

- **Favorite Folders Pane**—This pane is available when you select **Mail** on the Navigation pane (it is only available in the Mail view). It allows you quick access to any mail folders in Outlook. By default, the Inbox and Sent Items folders are included in the Favorite Folders pane. To add other mail folders to the pane, such as those you create, right-click a folder containing mail and select **Add to Favorite Folders** on the shortcut menu that appears.

We take a quick look at some of these listed new features and other new features in the remainder of this lesson. For more details related to working in Outlook, see Part III of this book.

Using the New Navigation Pane

The new Outlook Navigation pane makes it easier to access the different tools in Outlook such as the Mail, Contacts, Calendar, and Tasks features. Each Outlook tool has its own button on the Navigation pane. To access a particular tool, such as Mail, click the appropriate icon on the Navigation pane.

The Navigation pane provides additional navigational features that make it an improvement over the Outlook bar that was used for navigation in previous versions of Outlook. For example, when you click the Mail icon on the Navigation pane, the Favorite Folders and All Mail Folders subpanes appear on the Navigation pane as shown in Figure 1.1.

The Favorite Folders pane makes it easy for you to access unread mail and messages that you have sent. The All Mail Folders pane provides access to other e-mail accounts that you have configured in Outlook (such as a Hotmail account) and also provides access to Outlook archived files.

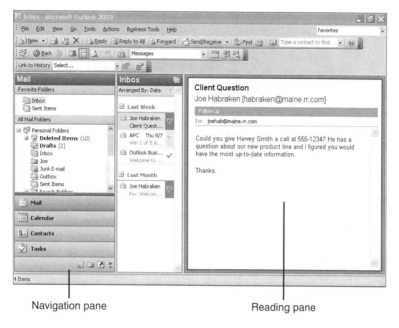

Navigation pane   Reading pane

Figure 1.1 The Navigation pane provides easy access to e-mail messages and accounts.

Not only does the Navigation pane make it easier to access your e-mails, but it also makes it easier to access information in any of the Outlook tools such as the Calendar and Contacts. Figure 1.2 shows the Navigation pane after Contacts has been selected. It provides you with access to the different types of contacts stored in Outlook and also provides different views for viewing your contacts.

TIP **Outlook Section Provides Overview of Using Outlook** For more about working in Outlook and sending e-mail, creating contacts, and working with the calendar, see Part III of this book.

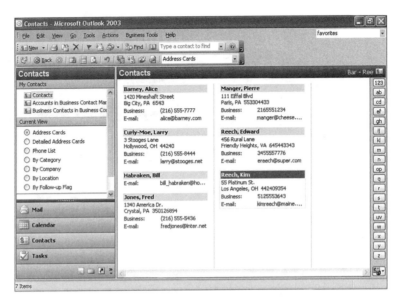

Figure 1.2 The Navigation pane provides easy access to different views of your contacts.

Creating Search Folders

Another new feature provided by Outlook is the Search Folder. A Search Folder is a way to logically group information such as mail or contacts and then view the information. A Search Folder that you create is really a virtual folder; it doesn't actually exist as the mail or contacts folders exist, but it groups information such as mail, contacts, or appointments according to your search criteria. Because Search Folders can be saved (you are actually saving the search criteria that make the Search Folder), they can be used to quickly view data in Outlook whenever needed.

To create a search folder for e-mail messages, follow these steps:

1. Select the **File** menu, point at **New**, and then select **Search Folder**. The New Search Folder dialog box opens (see Figure 1.3).

2. Select the type of Search Folder that you will create from the New Search Folder dialog box such as Mail from Specific People or Mail with Attachments.

3. After selecting the type of search folder, you have to supply additional information. For example, in the case of a Mail from Specific People search folder, you have to specify the e-mail senders that will be used to logically group the mail in the search folder. To see a list of people in your Contacts or other list, click the **Choose** button at the bottom of the New Search Folder dialog box.

Figure 1.3   Logically group Outlook information in search folders.

4. The Select Names dialog box will open. You can use the drop-down list on the right of the dialog box to view your Contacts folder or other list (such as the Business Contacts folder). Select the name or names to use for the search folder. Then click the **From** button.

5. When you have completed adding the names the search folder will use, click **OK**. You will be returned to the New Search Folder dialog box. Click **OK** to create the new folder.

The new search folder appears in the Outlook window and lists the items such as mail that meet the criteria that you specified for the folder. Search folders that you create can be accessed by opening your personal folders in the All Mail Folders pane and then opening the Search Folders icon. This will list all search folders available in Outlook.

TIP   **Search Folders Exist by Default**   Some search folders are available in Outlook by default. For example, the Mail search folders provided are the Unread Mail and For Follow Up folders found in the All Mail Folders pane.

Introducing the Business Contact Manager

An important change to Outlook is the addition of the Business Contact Manager (BCM). The BCM allows you to manage business contacts, business accounts, and business opportunities in the familiar Outlook environment. The BCM is an add-on program and adds a Business Tools menu to the Outlook menu bar (see Figure 1.4).

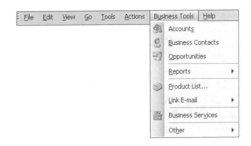

Figure 1.4   The Business Tools menu provides access to the BCM features.

The BCM data such as Business Contacts and Accounts are accessed via the Contacts button on the Navigation pane. Your business opportunities are accessed via the Tasks button on the Navigation pane. For more about the Business Contact Manager, see Lessons 21 and 22 in the Outlook section (Part III) of this book.

Importing E-Mail Accounts and Other Data

For those of you who have used other e-mail clients in the past and are just now upgrading to Outlook as your e-mail software, you may want to import your e-mail settings and even your mail messages from another e-mail software package that is installed on your computer. Outlook can import e-mail accounts, messages, and other data such as contacts. Outlook can import e-mail accounts and messages from Outlook Express and Eudora.

TIP   **Settings from Previous Versions of Outlook Used by Outlook 2003**
When you upgrade a previous version of Outlook to Outlook 2003, settings, accounts, and preferences that you made in the previous version of Outlook are used in Outlook 2003.

Data can also be imported from other programs used to manage calendars and contacts such as Act! and Lotus Organizer. Let's take a look at the steps used to import e-mail settings into Outlook 2003.

1. Select the **File** menu, point at **Import and Export**, and then select **Standard**. The Import and Export Wizard will appear.

2. On the Import and Export Wizard screen, select **Import Internet E-mail Account Settings** and then select **Next**.

3. The next wizard screen (which starts the Internet Connection Wizard) provides a list of e-mail clients that you have installed on your computer (see Figure 1.5). Select the e-mail client that contains the settings. Click **Next** to continue.

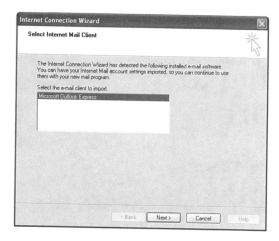

Figure 1.5 You can import settings from other e-mail clients.

4. The next screen asks you to provide the name that you want to appear in the From box when you send e-mail. Type the name (or go with the default, which is imported from the other e-mail client) and then click **Next** to continue.

5. Your e-mail account will appear on the next screen (as it was set up for the e-mail client). Click **Next** to continue.

6. On the next screen the e-mail servers for the account will appear (the POP and SMTP servers). Click **Next** to continue.

7. On the next screen, the account name you used for e-mail will appear. You also have to enter your e-mail password. Click **Next**.

8. The next screen shows the connection type that you use to connect to the Internet such as a phone line or a LAN connection. Check to make sure these settings are correct and then click **Next**.

9. The final screen will appear, letting you know that all the information needed has been collected. Click **Finish**.

The imported e-mail account settings will be added to Outlook. If you also want to import mail messages or contacts from the other e-mail client, run the Import and Export Wizard again and make the appropriate choices.

Upgrading to Word 2003

In this lesson, you learn what's new in Word 2003.

What's New in Word 2003?

Microsoft Word 2003 offers a number of new features that make it an even more efficient and easy-to-use word processor and desktop publishing environment than its predecessors. These new features range from the new shared Document Workspace to the new Reading Layout view to the new Research task pane. Some of the new Word features that you will explore in this book are as follows:

- **Document Workspace**—Using a SharePoint server, you can create an online workspace that allows users at different sites to view and edit the same Word document. The Document Workspace is discussed in Lesson 1 in Part I of this book.

- **Research Task Pane**—The Research task pane allows you to access online resources that range from business Websites, to stock information, to online encyclopedias such as Microsoft's Expedia. Figure 2.1 shows the Research task pane in the Word workspace. The Research task pane is discussed in more detail in Lesson 4, "Using Proofreading and Research Tools," in the Word section of the book (Part IV).

- **Reading Layout View**—The Reading Layout view allows you to view a document as it will print and also edit the document as you read it. The Reading Layout view is discussed briefly in Lesson 8, "Examining Your Documents in Different Views," of the Word section of this book.

- **Compare Side by Side With**—This new command found on the Window menu allows you to compare documents side by side on the Windows desktop.

Word 2003 also offers other enhancements. These include the ability to create XML documents (discussed later in the lesson), Tablet PC support, and better integration with the Office Online Web site.

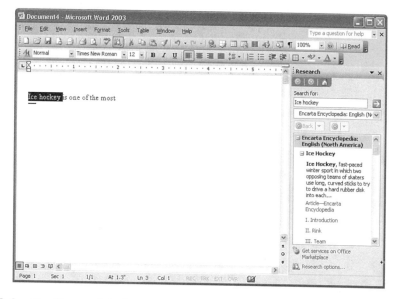

Figure 2.1 The Research task pane makes it easy for you to quickly look up information in a variety of online reference tools.

Understanding File Format Issues

Word 2003 saves Word documents by default in the Word file format that is also embraced by Word 2000 and Word 2002. If you plan to use an earlier version of Word (such as Word 6.0) on another computer or will share Word documents with users who still use an earlier version of Word, you will need to save your documents in the appropriate file format.

The easiest way to manage file formats in Word is to save all documents in the Word file format and then use the Save As command to save documents in a format that will be used by collaborators who use an earlier version of the Word software.

To save a document in a file format compatible with earlier versions of Word, follow these steps:

1. Open the document that you want to save in a different file format (**File**, **Open**).

2. Select **File**, then **Save As** to open the Save As dialog box as shown in Figure 2.2.

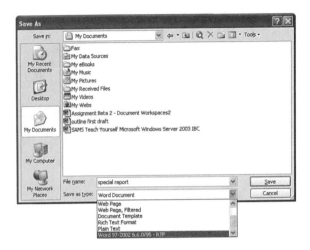

Figure 2.2 Select a different file format in the Save As dialog box.

3. Click the **Save as Type** drop-down box in the Save As dialog box and select the Word 97-2002&6.0/95-RTF file format. This file format is compatible with any version of Word from Word 95 to Word 2003.

4. Type a new filename for the document (if necessary).

5. Click **Save** to save the document in the new file format.

Word and XML Documents

XML or eXtensible Markup Language is a markup language that allows you to tag the contents of a document; the tags not only define the tagged contents of the document (as HTML codes do) but also allow for the validation and transmission of data in the document. Although XML is beyond the scope of this book, the ability for a user to create XML documents directly in Word is an important advance to the Word environment (as was the addition of Web site creation tools to earlier versions of Word).

Not only does Word provide a platform for the creation of XML documents, but it also provides for user-defined schemas for the XML codes. A schema defines what the actual XML codes do in the document when the XML code is read (by an application that is versed in XML such as a Web browser like Internet Explorer).

Task Panes and Smart Tags

For those of you upgrading from a version of Word prior to Word 2002 (such as Word 2000), the biggest changes in the Word workspace will be the various task panes and smart tags. Task panes have replaced a number of dialog boxes that were used to configure or use certain features. For example, Word styles are now created and modified using the Styles and Formatting task pane as shown in Figure 2.3.

Figure 2.3   Task panes have replaced many Word dialog boxes.

A number of new task panes have been added to Word 2003 including the following: Getting Started task pane, Help task pane, Search Results task pane, Shared Workspace task pane, and Research task pane. Many of these task panes are discussed in the Word section of this book.

A smart tag is a special shortcut menu that provides you with additional options related to a particular feature. Word 2003 has a number of smart tags including paste smart tags and AutoCorrect smart tags.

For example, when you cut or copy information from a Word document and then paste it to a new location, you will find that a paste smart tag appears at the bottom of the pasted item. This enables you to access options related to your paste job, such as whether the information pasted should maintain its original formatting or be formatted the same as text or numbers that are in the same part of the document where you pasted the new information.

Figure 2.4 shows the Person Name smart tag. This smart tag flags proper names and provides you with the option of pulling information about the person (such as their address) from your Outlook Contacts.

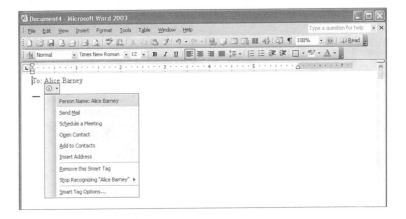

Figure 2.4   Smart tags flag certain text elements in a document.

Upgrading to Excel 2003

In this lesson, you learn what's new in Excel 2003.

Introducing Excel 2002

Excel 2003 is a powerful spreadsheet program that can help you create worksheets and invoices and do both simple and sophisticated number crunching; it is designed to help you calculate the results of formulas and analyze numerical data. Excel 2003 provides a number of enhancements over previous versions of Excel. Some of these enhancements are as follows:

- **Designate a Range as a List**—Excel allows you to designate a range of cells as a list. You can then manipulate the list using list menus provided at the heading row of the list. You can quickly sort or filter data in the list.

- **Statistical Functions Improved**—Although you won't necessarily "see" the enhancements that have been made to the statistical functions in Excel such as standard deviation and the forecast function, a number of Excel's statistical functions have been made to compute and round more accurately.

- **Document Workspaces**—Document workspaces can be created on a SharePoint server that is accessible from the Web. This allows different users to collaborate on Excel workbooks that are stored in the workspace.

- **Compare Side by Side With**—A new command on the Windows menu allows you to compare two worksheets side by side in the Excel window. This makes it easy to view changes that have been made to a worksheet where other users have made changes to the original worksheet.

- **Research Task Pane**—As with the other applications in Office 2003, Excel has access to the Research task pane, which can be used to find financial and other information stored on the Web.

Excel 2003 has had the latest makeover from the previous version of Excel when compared to the other members of the newest version of Office (such as Outlook and Access). We take a broad look at a number of Excel features in Part V of this book. In the balance of this lesson we will look at two new features found in Excel 2003, creating a list from a worksheet range and comparing worksheets side by side.

Creating Worksheet Lists

For users upgrading from versions of Excel prior to Excel 2002, the biggest changes to the Excel environment will be the introduction of task panes. Users upgrading from Excel 2002 to Excel 2003 will find that many changes made to Excel are quite subtle such as the list feature. Most Excel users are familiar with worksheet ranges, a grouping of contiguous cells. You can now specify data in a row or a column as a list and then manipulate the data. This means that even data already in a range can be manipulated as a list.

Creating a list is very straightforward; just follow these steps:

1. Select the range of cells that you want to include in the list. This can be data or other information in several rows or columns.

2. To create the list, select **Data**, point at **List**, and then select Create List.

3. The Create List dialog box opens showing the range of selected cells that will be included in the list. Click **OK** to create the list.

The list will be marked in the worksheet by a yellow frame as shown in Figure 3.1. Notice that drop-down arrows also appear at the top of each column in the list, which can be used to quickly manipulate the data in the list. For example, you can quickly filter the data in the list by selecting a salesperson's name from the drop-down list that appears.

When you create a list in a worksheet, the List and XML toolbar will appear in the Excel workspace. You can use the toolbar to add a Total row to your data list and then choose from several different formulas by clicking in the Total row.

CAUTION

Remove a Worksheet List   Lists provide a fast way to manipulate a selected range of data that may be part of a larger data set. When you have finished working with a list, you can remove it by right-clicking on the list and pointing at List on the menu that appears. Select **Convert to Range** and then select **Yes** to complete the conversion.

Drop-down arrow

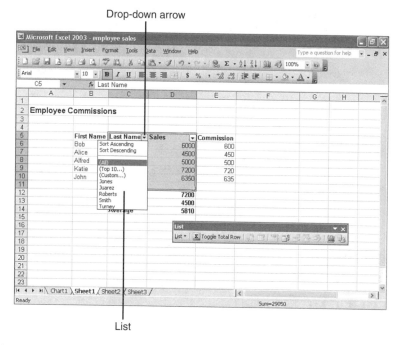

List

Figure 3.1   Lists can be created using ranges in a worksheet.

Comparing Worksheets Side by Side

Excel 2003 makes it easy for users to collaborate on Excel workbooks. For example, the Document Workspace feature allows users to access an Excel workbook on the Web. You may find that you need to compare an original worksheet with an updated or edited version of the worksheet. This can be done in the Excel window by comparing the two sheets side by side.

Follow these steps:

1. Open the workbooks that contain the sheets that you want to compare.

2. From one of the worksheets that you want to compare, select **Window**, then **Compare Side By Side** (followed by the workbook's name). The second workbook will appear in the Excel window (see Figure 3.2).

3. By default, scrolling is synchronized between the two windows. Scroll in either worksheet to scroll in both.

4. When you have finished comparing the worksheets, click the **Close Side By Side** button on the Compare Side by Side toolbar.

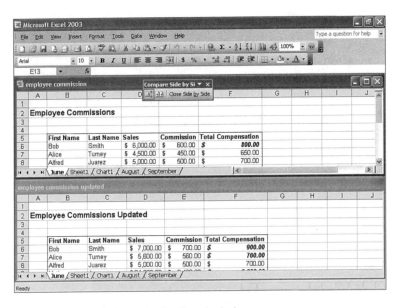

Figure 3.2 Compare worksheets in the Excel window.

You will also work with other Excel enhancements as you work through the lessons in Part V of this book.

Upgrading to Access 2003

In this lesson, you learn what's new in Access 2003.

What's New in Access 2003?

Access 2003 is similar in look and feel to its recent predecessors, Access 2002 and 2000; for those of you upgrading from Access 2000, task panes will be new. Data is held in tables and can be directly entered into a table or by using a form. Data tables can then be related, which allows for the filtering and sorting of data using queries and reports.

Although Access 2003 does not sport a major makeover as some of the other Office 2003 applications do (such as Outlook 2003), improvements and enhancements have been added to this latest version of Access. Some of the enhancements to Access 2003 are as follows:

- **Error Checking in Forms and Reports**—You can check controls in reports and forms using the new Error Checking feature. This feature is used in the form or report Design view and is discussed in more detail later in this lesson.

- **Back Up and Restore Databases**—Access 2003 makes it easy for you to back up a database file. This allows you to protect your valuable data. You can then restore the database if necessary. Backing up and restoring a database is discussed in more detail later in this lesson.

- **AutoCorrect Options**—Because database text entries are often peculiar unto themselves, you may not always want the AutoCorrect feature to correct certain text entries. An AutoCorrect Option button now appears next to text that is corrected by AutoCorrect, allowing you to quickly undo the correction.

- **SharePoint Server Compatibility**—Other Office 2003 applications such as Word and Excel provide the Document Workspace feature, which allows you to store and share files on the Web using a Microsoft SharePoint server. Access also provides the ability to store tables on a SharePoint server and link to data lists on the Web.

Other new features related to using Access are covered in Part VI of this book. For an overview of new features in Office, see Chapter 1, "What's New in Office 2003?" in Part I of this book.

Access File Format Issues

The file format that you select as the default file format will determine whether your Access databases can be opened in previous versions of the Access software. This is important if you are going to share Access files with users who use previous versions of Access (such as Access 2000) or if you are going to also use a computer that is running an earlier version of Access.

To set the default file format for Access databases, follow these steps:

1. In the Access window, select **Tools**, then **Options**. The Options dialog box will open.

2. Select the **Advanced** tab on the Options dialog box (see Figure 4.1).

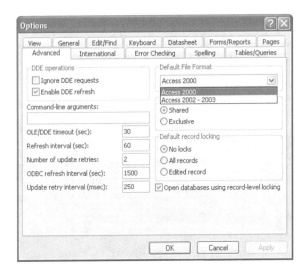

Figure 4.1   Set the default file format for your Access databases.

3. On the Advanced tab, click the **Default File Format** drop-down list. The default file format is Access 2000, which provides a file format that is compatible with Access 2000, 2002, and 2003. If you will not be using Access 2000 to work on the database, you may change the file format to Access 2002-2003 (which is compatible with both Access 2002 and 2003).

4. After making your selection, click OK. You will be returned to the Access window.

Access Error Checking

Another new feature provided by Access 2003 is the form and report control error-checking feature. This feature allows controls on forms and reports to automatically be checked for errors. Creating and modifying forms in Access is discussed in the Access portion of this book (Part VI) in Lessons 10, 11, and 12; creating and modifying reports is discussed in Lessons 17 and 18.

The form and report error-checking feature is controlled via the Error Checking tab on the Options dialog box. To view the Error Checking properties, follow these steps:

1. In the Access window, select **Tools**, then **Options**. The Options dialog box will open.

2. Select the Error Checking tab on the Options dialog box (see Figure 4.2).

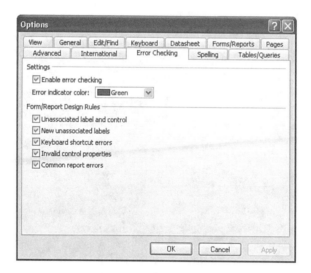

Figure 4.2 The form and report error-checking feature.

3. You can turn error checking off (it is on by default), by clearing the Enable Error Checking check box. You can also determine the rules that error checking uses on forms and reports. Clear the appropriate rule check box to disable a rule.

4. When you have finished viewing the Error Checking properties, click OK to close the Options dialog box.

When you create a form or report in the Design view, labels and controls are created and associated with fields in the tables that make up the database or with formulas that provide summary information. One of the error-checking rules provided by the Error Checking feature is to find labels that are not associated with controls (which are typically associated with a field in a table).

Figure 4.3 shows a label that is not associated with a control. Notice that an error icon has been placed on the label by the Error Checking feature. You can correct the error by clicking on the error icon and selecting a remedy from the list. For example, you can associate the new label with an existing control (a control already on the form) by clicking the **Associate Label with a Control** menu choice. This opens a list of controls on the form so that you can select the associated control. Other possibilities include **Help on this Error**, which opens the Help system and provides you with help on the problem, and **Ignore Error**, which removes the error icon.

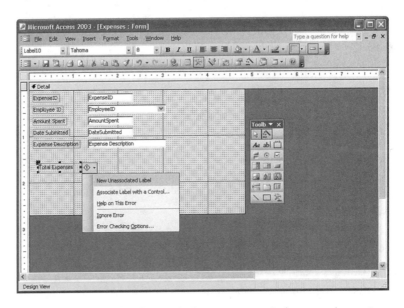

Figure 4.3   The Error Checking feature helps spot errors in forms and reports.

The new Error Checking feature provides you with help in minimizing label and control errors in forms and reports. See the Access section (Part VI) of this book for more about forms and reports.

Backing Up an Access Database

Another new feature that Access 2003 provides is the ability to back up and restore database files. This provides added protection for your valuable data. When you back up the database, it is actually saved in the default database file format (not a compressed or special) backup format. This makes it very easy for you to open a backup database at a later date because it really is just a copy of the original database file.

When you create a database backup, the database file created is timestamped. This allows you to easily differentiate the backups that you create for a database because they will all be date-specific.

To create a database backup, follow these steps:

1. With the database that you want to back up open in the Access window, click **File**, then **Back Up Database**. The Save Backup As dialog box will open (see Figure 4.4).

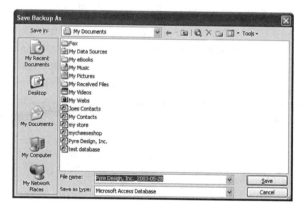

Figure 4.4   Back up an Access database file.

2. Supply the location to save the backup in using the **Save In** drop-down list. The new filename for the backup will be the original filename including the current date (see Figure 4.4).

3. Click **Save** to save the backup database file.

Backup databases can be opened as any database file can be opened. For more about saving and opening database files, see Lesson 2, "Creating a New Database," in Part VI of this book.

Upgrading to PowerPoint 2003

In this lesson, you learn what's new in PowerPoint 2003.

What's New in PowerPoint 2003?

PowerPoint 2003 provides the powerful slide creation and organization tools that are available in its predecessors, PowerPoint 2002 and 2000. PowerPoint 2003 also provides a number of enhancements that makes it even easier to create eye-catching and informative presentations.

Some of the new features provided by PowerPoint 2003 are as follows:

- **Package to CD**—This new feature is used to write a PowerPoint presentation directly to a CD. When the CD is created, a copy of the new PowerPoint Viewer is also placed on the CD to allow you to easily play the presentation on any computer. Packaging a presentation on a CD is discussed later in this lesson.

- **New Slide Show Toolbar**—The Slide Show toolbar provides easy access to slide show tools such as the pen and highlighter options. The Slide Show toolbar is discussed in Lesson 12, "Presenting an Onscreen Slide Show," which is in the PowerPoint section of this book (Part VII).

- **Document Workspaces**—PowerPoint embraces the Document Workspace feature (as do Word and Excel), which allows you to make presentation files available on the Web through the use of a Microsoft SharePoint server. Document Workspace is discussed in Lesson 1, "What's New in Office 2003," in Part I of this book.

PowerPoint File Format Issues

By default PowerPoint presentations saved in PowerPoint 2003 are saved using the presentation file format that is compatible with PowerPoint 2002 and 2000. If you are upgrading from a version of PowerPoint that precedes PowerPoint 2000, you should be aware of some file compatibility issues.

For example, when you open a PowerPoint presentation saved in PowerPoint 97 or 95, the presentation will be upgraded as it is loaded by PowerPoint 2003. You can then save the presentation in the newer presentation file format (the standard for PowerPoint 2000, 2002, and 2003). If you are planning on editing or playing a presentation on a computer that is running a pre-2000 version of PowerPoint, you can save the presentation in a legacy file format ("legacy" simply means an older file format).

To save presentations in a pre-2000 file format, follow these steps:

1. With the presentation open in the PowerPoint window, select **File**, then **Save As**. The Save As dialog box opens (see Figure 5.1).

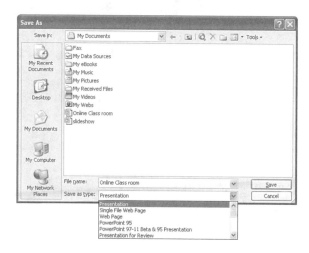

Figure 5.1   Use the Save As dialog box to save a presentation in a legacy file format.

2. Click the **Save as Type** drop-down box and select the PowerPoint 95 or PowerPoint 97 file format (see Figure 5.1).

3. Change the filename if you want. Click **Save** to save the file.

Packaging a Presentation to a CD

For those of you who used the Pack and Go feature provided by previous versions of PowerPoint, PowerPoint 2003 has upgraded the feature to the Package to CD tool. It allows you to quickly place a presentation on a CD. The process also includes the copying of the PowerPoint Viewer to the CD. You can then play the presentation on any Windows computer.

To package a presentation to a CD, follow these steps:

1. Place a writable CD (a CD-R or CD-RW disc) in your CD-RW drive. With the presentation you want to package open in PowerPoint, select **File**, then **Package for CD**. The Package for CD dialog box opens (see Figure 5.2).

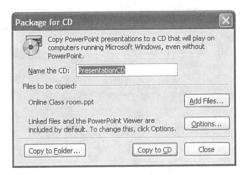

Figure 5.2 Package a presentation to a CD.

2. Type the name for the CD in the Name the CD box (if you want).

3. If you want to add additional files or other presentations to the CD, click the **Add Files** button. The Add Files dialog box will open.

4. Select additional files using the Add Files dialog box and then click Add. The files will be added to the file list in the Files to Be Copied area of the Package for CD dialog box.

 TIP **PowerPoint Viewer Added to CD by Default** The PowerPoint Viewer is added to the CD by default. If you do not want to include the viewer on the CD, select the **Options** button in the Package for CD Dialog box. Clear the **PowerPoint Viewer** check box in the Options dialog box and then click **OK**.

5. When you are ready to copy the presentation (and any additional files), click the **Copy to CD** button.

The presentation and any other files are copied to the CD. A message box will appear asking if you want to copy the files to another CD; click **No** to complete the process. When you open the CD files in Windows Explorer, you will find that the presentation has been copied to the CD (and any other files that you specified) along with the pptview file, which is the PowerPoint Viewer file (other files, such as some bearing the .DLL extension, which are required for the Viewer, are also copied to the CD). The CD is also written to autorun. This means when you place the CD in the computer, the PowerPoint Viewer automatically opens your presentation as a screen presentation.

Upgrading to Publisher 2003

6

In this lesson, you learn what's new in Publisher 2003.

What's New in Publisher 2003?

Publisher 2003 provides an easy-to-use environment for creating personal and business publications. Publisher 2003 provides an environment similar to that in previous editions of Publisher, but it also provides enhancements that make creating publications even easier.

Some of the enhancements to Publisher 2003 are as follows:

- **New Master Design Sets**—Master design sets allow you to create a family of publications such as envelopes, business cards, and stationery that share the same color and design elements. Master design sets are discussed in Lesson 3, "Using Design Sets," in the Publisher section of this book (Part VIII).

- **New Publication Types**—PowerPoint 2003 also provides support for several new publication types. New greeting card and invitation templates are provided, and PowerPoint now allows you to quickly create CD/DVD labels and e-mail publications such as an e-mail newsletter. E-mail publications are discussed later in this lesson.

- **New Publication Task Pane**—The redesigned New Publication task pane allows you to quickly select a new publication from several different categories such as Publications for Print, Design Sets, and Blank Publications.

- **Commercial Printing Features**—Features used to prepare a publication for commercial printing have also been enhanced in PowerPoint 2003. Some of these features are discussed in Lesson 11, "Printing Publisher Publications," in Part VIII of this book.

Publisher also embraces a number of enhancements that are common to the Office 2003 applications such as the Research task pane and Office 2003 Help system. New features found in Office 2003 are discussed in Lesson 1, "What's New in Office 2003?" and the help system is discussed in Lesson 5, "Getting Help in Microsoft Office." Both of these lessons are found in Part I of this book.

TIP **Upgrading From Publisher 2000 or Earlier?** If you are upgrading to Publisher 2003 from Publisher 2000 or earlier, you will need to become familiar with task panes and other features that have been recently added to the Office suite. Check out the lessons in Part I of this book before working through the lessons in the Publisher section (Part VIII) of this book.

Creating E-Mail Publications

One of the enhancements to Publisher 2003 is the availability of a number of new publication types. One of the new categories of publications is the e-mail publication. You have probably noticed that you get newsletters, flyers, and a variety of other publication types as e-mail. Publisher now makes it easy for you to create these special electronic publications. Let's look at how you create an e-mail publication. The basics of creating other publication types are covered in Part VIII of this book.

Follow these steps:

1. In the Publisher window (select **Start**, **All Programs**, **Microsoft Office**, then **Publisher** to open Publisher), select **Web Sites and E-Mail** in the New Publication task pane.

2. Select **E-Mail**. The e-mail publication templates will appear in the Publisher window (see Figure 6.1).

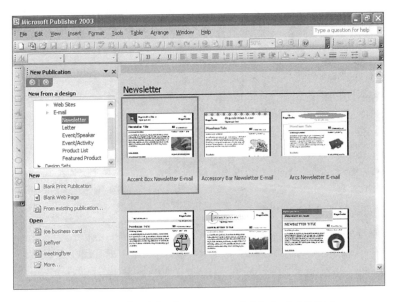

Figure 6.1 A number of e-mail publications are available in Publisher.

3. Select the e-mail publication template you want to use to create your new publication.

The new publication will appear in the PowerPoint workspace. You can now edit the template (replacing placeholder text with your own text) and add images to the publication. Completing a Publisher publication is discussed in Lesson 5, "Working with Existing Publications," which is found in Part VIII of this book.

Publisher File Format Issues

You can become familiar with the Publisher 2003 interface and the tools that have been added to this most recent version of this popular desktop publishing tool by working through the lessons in Part VIII of this book. If you are planning on sharing Publisher files with users who still use previous versions of Publisher, or you plan on using a previous version of Publisher on another computer, there are some compatibility issues that you should be aware of.

Publisher 2003 uses a default file format that is also compatible with the 2002 version. If you plan on creating publications and then sharing them with users who use previous versions of Publisher, such as Publisher 2000 and 98, you will have to save the completed publication in a different file format.

To save a Publisher 2003 publication in a different file format, follow these steps:

1. In the Publisher window (with the publication open), select **File**, then **Save As**. The Save As dialog box will open (see Figure 6.2).

Figure 6.2   Use the Save As dialog box to save Publisher files in different file formats.

2. Select the **Save as Type** drop-down box and select the file format that you want to save the file in (such as Publisher 98 or Publisher 2000).

3. You can change the filename or use the **Save In** drop-down box to specify a new location to save the file.

4. Click **Save** to save the file (in the new file format).

After the file is saved in the legacy format (meaning older file format), you can provide the file to users of previous versions of Publisher.

Outlook

Getting Started in Outlook

1

In this lesson, you learn how to start and exit Outlook, identify parts of the Outlook window, and use the mouse to get around the program.

Starting Outlook

You start Outlook from the Windows desktop. After starting the program, you can leave it open, or you can minimize it to free up the desktop for other applications. Either way, you can access it at any time.

To start Microsoft Outlook, follow these steps:

1. From the Windows XP desktop, click the **Start** button, choose **All Programs**, point at **Microsoft Office**, and then select **Microsoft Office Outlook 2003**. (For Windows 2000, select **Start**, **Programs**, point at **Microsoft Office**, and then click **Microsoft Office Outlook 2003**.)

 TIP **Shortcut to Launching Outlook** In Windows XP, you can click the **Outlook** icon, which is pinned to the Start menu or click the **Outlook** icon on the Quick Launch toolbar on the Windows taskbar (next to the Start button).

2. If your PC is set up for multiple users, the Choose Profile dialog box appears; click **OK** to accept the default profile or choose your profile and open Microsoft Outlook. Figure 1.1 shows the Outlook screen that appears.

TERM **Profile** The profile includes information about you and your e-mail accounts and is created automatically when you install Outlook (the e-mail accounts are added to the profile when Outlook is set up for the first time, as discussed in Lesson 2, "Understanding the Outlook E-Mail Configurations"). Multiple profiles become an issue only if you share your computer with other users.

If you connect to the Internet using a modem dial-up connection, the Connection Wizard attempts to make a dial-in connection as Outlook opens. This enables Outlook to check your e-mail server.

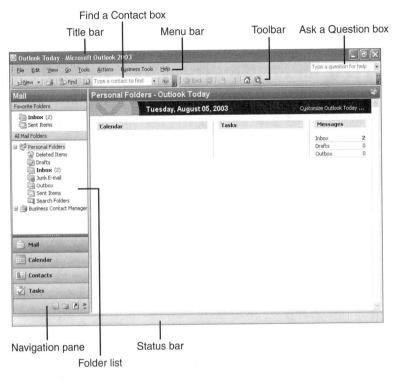

Find a Contact box

Title bar   Menu bar   Toolbar   Ask a Question box

Navigation pane   Status bar

Folder list

Figure 1.1   The Outlook window includes all the icons and items you need to access its various features.

Understanding the Outlook Window

The Outlook window includes items you can use to navigate in and operate the program. If you do not see some of the items listed in Figure 1.1 on your screen, open the **View** menu and select the command for the appropriate element (such as **Toolbars**, **Status Bar**, or **Outlook Bar**). A check mark in front of an item means the item is currently showing.

Table 1.1 describes the elements you see in the opening screen.

Table 1.1   Elements of the Outlook Window

Element	Description
Title bar	Includes the name of the application and current folder, plus the Minimize, Maximize, and Close buttons.
Toolbar	Includes icons that serve as shortcuts for common commands, such as creating a new message or printing a message.

Table 1.1   Continued

Element	Description
Navigation pane	Displays icons representing folders: Inbox, Calendar, Contacts, and so on. Click an icon to change to the folder it names. The Outlook Shortcuts, My Shortcuts, and Other Shortcuts buttons on the bar list specific groups of folders (for example, the My Shortcuts button lists icons related to your e-mail, such as the Drafts, Outbox, and Sent items).
Show Folder List	Displays the current folder. Click this to display a list of personal folders you can open. In this latest version of Outlook, the Folder List is now part of the Outlook bar.
Status bar	Displays information about the items currently shown in the Information Viewer.
Find a Contact box	This box allows you to search for a contact that you have entered in your Contacts folder.
Ask a Question box	This box allows you to quickly ask the Outlook Help system a question. It also allows you to forgo using the Office Assistant to access the Help system.

TIP   **Finding a Toolbar Button's Purpose**   You can place the mouse pointer on any toolbar button to view a description of that tool's function.

Using the Mouse in Outlook

As in most Windows-based programs, you can use the mouse in Outlook to select items, open e-mail and folders, move items, and so on. In general, clicking selects an item, and double-clicking selects it and performs some action on it (for example, displaying its contents). In addition to clicking and double-clicking, there are some special mouse actions you can use in Outlook:

- **Drag**—To move an object to another position on the screen (to transfer a mail message to another folder, for example), you can drag the object with the mouse. To drag an object to a new location onscreen, point to the object and press and hold down the left mouse button. Move the mouse pointer to the new location and then release the mouse button.

- **Right-click**—You can display a shortcut menu by clicking the right mouse button when pointing to an item. For example, you can right-click a folder in the Outlook bar or a piece of e-mail. A shortcut menu appears, which usually contains common commands relating to that particular item.

- **Multiselect**—You can act on multiple items at once by selecting them before issuing a command. To select multiple contiguous items, hold down the **Shift** key and click the first and last items you want to select. To select noncontiguous items (those that are not adjacent to each other), hold down the **Ctrl** key and click each item.

If you have a mouse, such as the Microsoft IntelliMouse, that includes a scroll wheel, you can use it in Outlook. Turn the wheel toward you to move down through any list in Outlook, such as your Contacts list, or move the wheel up to scroll up in a list.

 TIP **Keyboard Shortcuts** Many shortcuts are provided that allow you to access Outlook features using the keyboard. For example, you can go to your mail by pressing Ctrl+1 or to the Calendar by pressing Ctrl+2. Check out the Outlook Go menu (on the Menu bar) for more keyboard shortcuts. You can also access Outlook menus by pressing the **Alt** key and then pressing the underlined letter in the menu name (press **Alt+F** to open the File menu, for instance). The Alt menu shortcuts are common to all the Office applications.

Working Offline

If you use a modem connection to access your e-mail server, you can close the connection while still working in Outlook. This allows you to free up your phone line or, if you pay for your connection based on the time you are connected, save on connection time. Working offline in Outlook does not affect any Outlook features or capabilities. E-mail that you create while working offline is held in the Outbox until you reconnect to your Internet connection.

To work offline, select the **File** menu and then select **Work Offline**. If you are prompted to confirm the closing of your dial-in connection, click **Yes**. To go back online, click **File** then **Work Online**.

Exiting Outlook

When you are finished working in Outlook, you can exit the application in several ways. You can use the File menu: select **File**, **Exit**. Or you can close Outlook by clicking the Outlook window's **Close (X)** button. If you are connected to the Internet using a dial-up connection, you are prompted as to whether you want to log off your connection. If you want to close the dial-up connection, select **Log Off** in the message box.

 TIP **Exiting Outlook Before Mail Is Sent or Received** Outlook will complete any send or receive operations via your modem before it will actually allow you to exit the application.

Understanding the Outlook E-Mail Configurations

In this lesson, you learn how to set up Outlook for different types of electronic mail.

Types of Outlook E-Mail Configurations

The type or flavor of e-mail that you use in Outlook depends on who provides your e-mail account. Outlook contains support for the three most common providers of e-mail service:

- **ISP**—When you sign up for an Internet service provider (ISP), the company usually provides you with at least one e-mail account.
- **Exchange**—In networked environments (most offices, for example), an e-mail server such as Microsoft Exchange may control delivery of e-mail.
- **Web**—Outlook also provides you with the capability to connect to Microsoft's Hotmail Web-based e-mail service.

Because Outlook serves not only as your e-mail client, but also as your personal information manager (allowing you to build a contacts list and keep track of your appointments and tasks), it is designed to operate either in a standalone environment or in a corporate service environment. When you use Outlook as a standalone application, your contacts, appointments, and tasks are stored locally on your computer and you access your e-mail through the Internet. However, in a corporate environment, your calendar and tasks folders are kept on a corporate communication server (typically Microsoft Exchange Server) where your information can be shared with other users.

E-Mail Client   Software that is configured on a user's computer to connect to e-mail services on a company's network or on the Internet.

Making Your E-Mail Choice

For Outlook to function as your e-mail client, you must communicate to Outlook the type of e-mail account that you use on your computer. Outlook assists you in this task with the E-mail Accounts Wizard.

TIP **Add a New Directory with the Wizard** You can also add address books to your Outlook installation using the E-Mail Accounts Wizard. This includes Web-based directories that verify e-mail addresses and information (this would be a service provided by your Internet service provider or corporate network) and other personal address books supported by Outlook such as the Outlook Address Book.

To start the Wizard, select **Tools**, then **E-mail Accounts**. The E-Mail Accounts screen appears as shown in Figure 2.1.

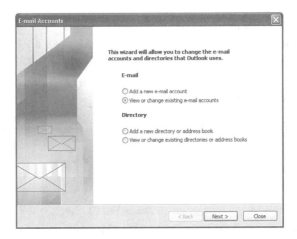

Figure 2.1 The E-Mail Accounts Wizard helps you set up your e-mail accounts.

TIP **Working with a New Installation of Outlook** If you have just completed a new installation of Outlook on a computer that is not running another e-mail client or previous version of Outlook, the Accounts Wizard will open the first time you start the Outlook software.

To configure an e-mail account for use in Outlook, make sure that the **Add a New E-mail Account** option button is selected, and then click **Next** to continue. The next screen presents a selection of different e-mail servers, as shown in Figure 2.2.

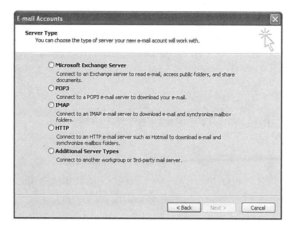

Figure 2.2 Outlook can function as an e-mail client for several e-mail server types.

How your e-mail functions depends on which option you select to configure Outlook as a specific e-mail client. The possibilities are

- **Microsoft Exchange Server**—This type of account makes Outlook an Exchange Server client; mail boxes and other resources, such as shared public folders, are managed on the Exchange Server computer. If this is what your Outlook installation requires, your network system administrator should provide these settings for you.

- **POP3**—POP3 is a protocol that most ISPs use, which allows a POP3 e-mail server to function as a mail drop.

    This means that your Internet e-mail is forwarded to the POP3 server and sits there until you connect with your e-mail client (Outlook) and download the mail to your computer.

 POP3 (Post Office Protocol Version 3) A set of software protocols or rules used to download mail to your computer. Your e-mail resides on the POP3 server until you connect and download it to your computer.

- **IMAP**—IMAP is a protocol that allows Outlook to download e-mail from an IMAP mail server. IMAP differs from POP3 in that your e-mail is not removed from the mail server when you connect to the server with your e-mail client (Outlook). Instead, you receive a list of saved and new messages, which you can then open and read. IMAP is particularly useful when one e-mail account can be accessed by more than one computer, allowing the messages to be available from more than one computer.

You might think that IMAP is a good idea because it leaves the e-mail on the mail server. However, you can use IMAP only if your ISP or company provides an IMAP mail server. In most cases, ISPs don't want your mail taking up too much space on their server, so they use POP3, which sends the mail to your computer when you connect.

IMAP (Internet Message Access Protocol) A set of software rules used by an e-mail client to access e-mail messages on a shared mail server as if the messages were stored locally.

- **HTTP**—The Hypertext Transfer Protocol is the protocol and set of rules that enable you to browse Web sites using a Web browser. HTTP e-mail is accessed through a Web site, and your inbox actually resides on a server that is hosted by the provider of the e-mail Web site. The HTTP selection is designed to allow you to set up Outlook to read your Microsoft MSN/Hotmail.

- **Additional Server Types**—This selection allows you to configure Outlook as a mail client for other e-mail server types, such as Microsoft Mail or third-party e-mail server software. It also provides you with the capability to create a special e-mail account that allows you to receive faxes in the Outlook Inbox.

The two most common uses for Outlook are as a Microsoft Exchange Server e-mail client or as an Internet e-mail client using POP3, IMAP, or HTTP. The option you chose in the Server Type dialog box shown earlier, in Figure 2.2, determines where you go from here. In the following sections, you take a closer look at the configuration steps for setting up your first POP3 or HTTP account. You can run the wizard again, at any time to add additional e-mail accounts to Outlook's configuration.

Importing E-Mail Settings If you are already using an e-mail client, such as Outlook Express, you can import all the e-mail messages and the settings for your e-mail accounts into Outlook. Outlook actually prompts you to perform this import when you start it for the first time. If you import mail settings, you won't be required to add an e-mail account as outlined in this section. You can use the information in this lesson, however, to add any additional e-mail accounts that you might need.

Internet POP3 E-Mail

If you connect to the Internet using a modem, a DSL router, a broadband satellite connection, or a broadband cable modem, your Internet connection is of the type that an Internet service provider (ISP) provides. Most ISPs provide e-mail to their users in the form of a POP3 account. This means that the ISP's e-mail server holds your e-mail until you connect and download your messages to Outlook.

ISP (Internet service provider) A commercial, educational, or government institution that provides individuals and companies access to the Internet.

ISPs that provide e-mail service also must have some mechanism for you to send e-mail to other users on the Internet. A computer called an SMTP server handles the sending of e-mail from your computer, over the Internet, to a final destination. That destination is typically the POP3 server that serves as the mail drop for the person to whom you are sending the Internet e-mail.

 SMTP (Simple Mail Transfer Protocol) A set of rules used to transfer Internet mail; your ISP goes through an SMTP host, or relay, server to get your mail to you.

If you do not use an e-mail account (such as a POP3 account) that your ISP supplies to you, you can still use Outlook for Internet e-mail. In this case, sign up for an HTTP e-mail account on the Web and configure Outlook to use it. Configuring HTTP e-mail is discussed in a moment, but first take a look at the steps required to configure a POP3 e-mail account as Outlook's initial e-mail account.

The first thing Outlook needs you to provide is information related to the POP3 account, such as your username, password, and SMTP and POP3 servers, all of which your ISP must provide. To complete the configuration of your POP3 account, follow these steps:

1. Select the **POP3** button on the E-Mail Accounts screen (refer to Figure 2.2), and then click **Next** to continue.

2. On the next screen, shown in Figure 2.3, enter your name, your e-mail address, your username, and your password. You also must provide the name of your ISP's POP3 (incoming server) and SMTP server (outgoing server) in the appropriate box. If your ISP uses Secure Password Authentication, which provides a second layer of authentication for their mail servers, click the Log on Using Secure Password Authentication (SPA) box. (If SPA is used, you are provided a second username and password, other than your e-mail username, to log on to the servers; most ISPs do not use SPA.)

3. You can test your new account settings to make sure that they work; be sure you are connected to the Internet, and then click the **Test Account Settings** button. Outlook tests the user account and the servers listed. A Test Account Settings dialog box appears, as shown in Figure 2.4. To close the dialog box, click **Close**.

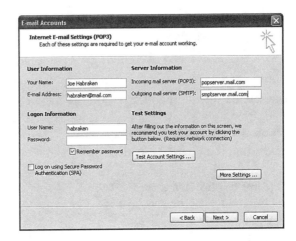

Figure 2.3 You must supply all the information listed on the Internet E-mail Settings (POP3) screen.

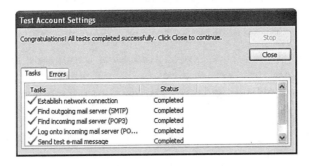

Figure 2.4 You can check your Internet e-mail settings after entering the appropriate information.

4. When you have completed your POP3 configuration settings (and tested them), click the **Next** button.

CAUTION

If the Account Test Fails Check your account name, password and the name of the POP3 and SMTP servers that you have provided. This information must be entered correctly for the text to work. If you are still having trouble, check with your Internet service provider or network administrator to verify the account and other information.

5. A final screen appears, letting you know that you have provided all the necessary information. Click **Finish** to end the process and open the Outlook Inbox.

TIP **Configuring for IMAP** The steps to configure an IMAP account are the same as those listed to configure the POP3 Internet e-mail account. The only differences are that you select IMAP on the initial setup screen and then make sure that the IMAP server name is provided on the configuration screen rather than the POP3 server name.

HTTP E-Mail Accounts

Although most people use either an Exchange Server (configured by a system administrator) or a POP3 account as their primary e-mail account, Web-based HTTP accounts, such as Microsoft Hotmail, are convenient for checking personal e-mail from any computer. Typically, you must log on to the appropriate Web site and provide a username and password to access your HTTP e-mail account. Although this offers a degree of flexibility that is appealing to many users, others are often put off because, in the past, this has prevented them from checking their e-mail using Outlook.

Fortunately, Outlook now has the capability to access HTTP e-mail accounts for users who have MSN/Hotmail accounts from Microsoft. Before you can add an MSN or Hotmail account to the Outlook configuration, you must sign up for an account. See www.msn.com or www.hotmail.com for more information. Then, follow these steps to configure the HTTP e-mail account:

1. Rather than selecting POP3, as you did in the previous section, select the **HTTP** option button on the E-Mail Accounts dialog box (shown previously in Figure 2.2). Click **Next** to continue.

2. On the next screen, shown in Figure 2.5, enter your name, your e-mail address, your username, and your password (supplied by Microsoft for your MSN or Hotmail account).

3. Click **Next** after entering all the necessary information. On the final screen that appears, click **Finish**.

You are then returned to the Outlook window. When you add an HTTP account, such as a Hotmail account, to Outlook, a second set of folders appears in the Outlook folder listings, including Deleted Items, Inbox, Outbox, and Sent Items. Figure 2.6 shows this new set of folders.

A second set of folders will be created in the All Mail Folder list that you can use to access the HTTP account, such as Hotmail. You will also find that a folder for Hotmail (or MSN) is added to the All Folders list in Outlook. The main Inbox for Outlook will still be reserved for your POP3 or Microsoft Exchange e-mail.

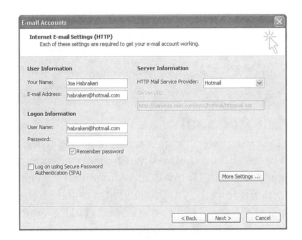

Figure 2.5   You must supply all the information listed on the HTTP E-mail Settings screen.

Folders specific to an
HTTP-based e-mail account

Figure 2.6   The HTTP mail folders, such as Hotmail, appear on the Outlook Folders list.

Adding Other Types of E-Mail Accounts

As previously mentioned, Outlook is typically used as an e-mail client for either
Exchange Server environments or for Internet e-mail where an ISP supplies either a
POP3, an IMAP, or an HTTP e-mail account. However, many users find that they
have more than one type of account at their disposal. Very often, users get one or

more accounts through their ISP, but also sign up for an HTTP account that they can have easy access to from multiple locations (these HTTP accounts are usually free).

 TIP   **Configuring Exchange Server E-Mail Accounts**   If you are using Outlook on a corporate network that uses an Exchange Server as the e-mail server, your account will typically be set up on your computer by the network administrator. The name of the Exchange Server and your network user name are required to complete the configuration. If you use Outlook on a corporate network, consult your network administrator for help in configuring Outlook. Using Outlook for e-mail on an Exchange Server network enables several e-mail features that are not available when you use Outlook for Internet e-mail, such as a POP3 account. On a network, you can redirect replies, set message expirations, and even grant privileges to other users who can then monitor your e-mail, calendar, contacts, and tasks.

You can use the following steps to add e-mail accounts to the Outlook settings after you have already made your initial configuration, as discussed in the previous sections of this lesson. Remember, you can add any type of e-mail account to Outlook after the fact.

In the Outlook window:

1. Select **Tools, E-Mail Accounts**. The E-Mail Accounts dialog box opens.

2. Select the **Add a New E-mail Account** option button, and click **Next** to continue.

3. The Server Type screen opens with a list of the different types of e-mail accounts (this is the same screen provided during the initial e-mail configuration for Outlook, shown in Figure 2.2).

4. Select the type of e-mail account you want to add to the Outlook configuration, and then click the **Next** button.

The information needed to configure a particular e-mail type is requested on the next screen, as previously discussed in this lesson.

Deleting or Changing E-Mail Accounts

As you've seen in this lesson, configuring Outlook with different types of e-mail accounts is a pretty straightforward process. You might also find, on occasion, that you want to delete an e-mail account from the Outlook configuration. To do so, follow these steps:

1. Select **Tools, E-Mail Accounts**. In the E-Mail Accounts dialog box, select the **View or Change Existing E-Mail Accounts** option button, and then click **Next** (refer to Figure 2.1).

2. The E-mail Accounts dialog box appears as shown in Figure 2.7. To delete an account, select the account, and then click the **Remove** button.

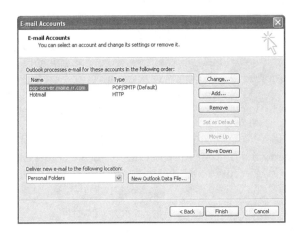

Figure 2.7   E-mail accounts are managed in the E-Mail Accounts dialog box.

3. You are asked to confirm the deletion of the account. Click **Yes** to continue.

You can also use the E-Mail Accounts dialog box to edit the settings for any of the e-mail accounts that you have created. Select the appropriate account, and then select the **Change** button. A dialog box for that specific account opens (refer back to Figure 2.3) and you can change settings as required.

In some cases, you might need to configure special settings for an e-mail account, such as how your computer connects to the Internet when you are using a particular e-mail account. Select the **More Settings** button on the E-mail Accounts Settings dialog box. The Internet E-Mail Settings dialog box appears for the e-mail account.

The Internet E-Mail Settings dialog box has a series of tabs that differ depending on the type of e-mail account you are editing. Two tabs that you many want to adjust are the General tab and the Connection tab. When you open the dialog box, it defaults to the General tab. On the General tab you can supply a "friendly" name that will be used to refer to the account. It is this name that appears in the E-mail Accounts dialog box that lists your Outlook e-mail accounts. You can also specify a Reply E-Mail that sends any replies to e-mail sent by your account to a secondary e-mail address (this is useful when you are handling customer support and you want e-mail replies to go to a different e-mail account).

On the Connection tab (shown in Figure 2.8), you can specify how Outlook connects to the Internet when you are checking this particular account for e-mail. This is useful in cases where you use a modem to connect to the Internet. You can work offline and then have Outlook connect via your modem when you send or receive mail from the account.

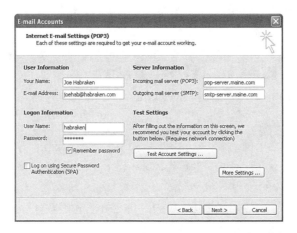

Figure 2.8   Special settings related to an e-mail account can be reached by clicking the More Settings button.

After completing the addition of any special settings to the Internet E-Mail Settings dialog box, click **OK** to close it. You are returned to the dialog box for the e-mail account. Click **Next** to return to the E-Mail Accounts dialog box, and then click **Finish** to return to Outlook.

Using Outlook's Tools

In this lesson, you learn how to change views in Outlook, how to use the Navigation pane, and how to use the Folder list.

Using the Navigation Pane

Microsoft Outlook 2003 has greatly enhanced the user environment in the Outlook workspace. The new Navigation pane replaces the Outlook bar and serves as the main navigational tool when you are working in Outlook. You will find that the Navigation pane has a button for each of the Outlook folders. Each Outlook organizational tool has its own folder. You have a folder for e-mail (Inbox), a folder for the calendar (Calendar), and so on.

To use the Navigation pane to switch to a different folder, select the appropriate button. Figure 3.1 shows the Navigation pane and some of the other areas of the Outlook window.

As already mentioned, the different Outlook folder buttons on the Navigation pane enable you to access your work in Outlook. This includes your e-mail messages, appointments, contact list, and so on. Table 3.1 describes each of the folders provided on the Navigation pane.

Table 3.1 Outlook Folders

Folder	Description
Mail	Includes messages you've sent and received by e-mail and fax.
Calendar	Contains your appointments, events, scheduled meetings, and so on.
Contacts	Lists names and addresses of the people with whom you communicate.
Tasks	Includes any tasks you have on your to-do list.
Notes	Lists notes you write to yourself or others.

The Outlook 2003 Navigation pane also provides shortcuts that help you access the information in a particular folder. For example, when you access a Mail folder, you are also provided with two areas on the pane: Favorite Folders and All Mail Folders. These lists can be used to quickly access different mail-related folders found in Outlook.

All Mail Folders

Favorite Folders

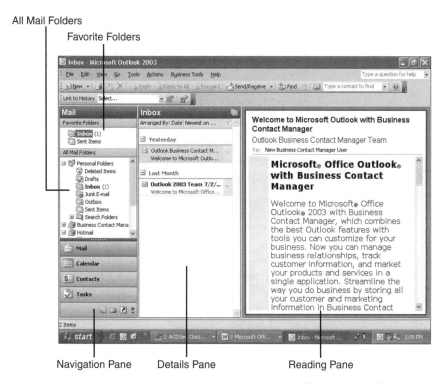

Navigation Pane   Details Pane   Reading Pane

Figure 3.1   Use the Navigation pane to view your e-mail, appointments, and so on.

The Navigation pane also allows you to control how the information is actually viewed in the Details pane of a particular folder. For example, you can choose from a number of current views to browse the records in your Contacts folder as shown in Figure 3.2.

The Navigation pane also makes it easy for you to quickly access the Folder list, custom shortcuts, and tools that allow you to configure the overall "feel" of the Navigation pane. Four buttons are provided along the bottom of the Navigation pane (see Figure 3.2) that allow you to access these features:

- **Notes**—This button opens the Notes pane and allows you to create reminder notes. See Lesson 16, "Using Outlook Notes," for more information.

- **Folder list**—This button opens the Folder list in the Navigation pane (it is open by default when you start Outlook). The Folder list is used to view all your Outlook Personal folders.

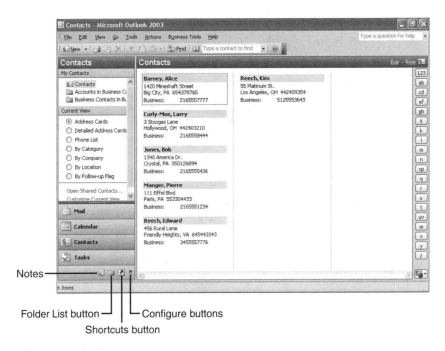

Figure 3.2 Different views can be quickly accessed from the Navigation pane.

- **Shortcuts**—This button allows you to access special shortcut icons such as those for Outlook Today (which provides an overview of current Calendar, mail, and tasks) and Outlook Update (which connects you to Microsoft and allows you to quickly update the Outlook software). You can also add custom shortcuts to the Shortcuts list by adding groups using the Add New Group link.
- **Configure Buttons**—This button opens a shortcut menu that allows you to change the size of the buttons on the Navigation pane, and change the order of the buttons that appear on the bar. You can also even add or remove buttons if you want to customize your Navigation pane further.

Using the Folder List

Although the Navigation pane provides quick access to your Outlook folders (such as Mail or the Calendar), you can view all your personal folders using the Folder List. To use the Folder List, click the **Folder List** button at the bottom of the Navigation pane (see Figure 3.3).

Complete list of folders ——

Figure 3.3 The Folder List shows all your personal folders.

Choose any folder from the list, and the Outlook Details pane changes to reflect your selection. If you want to display another folder in the Details pane, click the folder to display its contents.

Using the Advanced Toolbar

As already mentioned in relation to the Contacts folder, you are provided with different views when you work with the information in your various folders. Although these different views can be accessed for some folders (such as Contacts and the Calendar) via the Navigation pane, another way to select the different views provided for each of your Outlook folders is to use the Current View drop-down box that is provided on the Advanced toolbar. To open the Advanced toolbar (it doesn't matter which Outlook folder you currently have selected), follow these steps:

1. Point to the Standard toolbar for an Outlook folder (such as the Inbox) and click the right mouse button.

2. A shortcut menu appears; click **Advanced**. The Advanced toolbar appears.

3. To access one of the views available for the current folder (such as the Mail folder as shown in Figure 3.4), click the Current View drop-down list on the Advanced toolbar and make your selection.

Current View drop-down list   Advanced toolbar

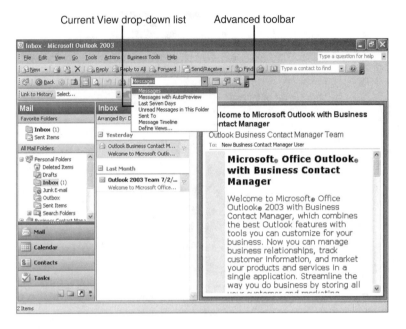

Figure 3.4   Select a view from the Current View list.

As you can see in Figure 3.4, you can change your view of the Inbox so that you can see the following:

- **Messages**—All messages
- **Messages with AutoPreview**—Messages and their first three lines of text
- **Last Seven Days**—Messages from the last seven days
- **Unread Messages in this folder**—Unread messages only
- **Sent To**—Messages by recipient
- **Message Timeline**—Messages arranged in a timeline

Similarly, the Calendar folder, which is arranged in the Day/Week/Month view type by default, enables you to view your appointments and events by Active Appointments, Day/Week/Month with AutoPreview, Events, Recurring Appointments, and several other view types.

You can also change the view type for any of your folders by selecting the **View** menu pointing at **Arrange By**, and then pointing at **Current View**. The View list appears at the top of the Current View submenu.

As you work your way through the Outlook part of this book, you'll see examples of some of the different view types as they are used when you are working in Outlook. When you change folders in Outlook, take a quick look at the available views in the Current View drop-down list.

 TIP **Open the Advanced Toolbar Once** After you've opened the Advanced toolbar for a folder, such as the Calendar or Mail, it will be available for all the other Outlook folders.

You will also find that each folder, such as Mail, Calendar, Contacts, and so on, has a different set of buttons on the Standard and Advanced toolbars. This is because the commands and features that you access on a toolbar are particular to the folder that you currently have selected.

Creating Custom Views

In addition to Outlook's many precompiled views (for each folder type), you can also create custom views of the information in your Outlook folders. To create a custom view for one of your Outlook folders, follow these steps:

1. Click the **View** menu, point at **Arrange By**, and then point at **Current View**. Select **Define Views**. The Custom View Organizer dialog box for the currently selected folder opens.

2. Click the **New** button in the Custom View Organizer dialog box. The Create a New View dialog box appears, as shown in Figure 3.5.

3. Enter a name for your new view and select a view type from the list in the Type of View box.

   You can select different view types for a custom view:

   - **Table**—Presents items in a grid of sorts in rows and columns. Use this view type to view mail messages, tasks, and details about any item.

   - **Timeline**—Displays items as icons arranged in chronological order from left to right on a time scale. Use this to view journal entries and other items in this type of view.

   - **Card**—Presents items such as cards in a card file. Use this to view contacts.

   - **Day/Week/Month**—Displays items in a calendar view in blocks of time. Use this type for meetings and scheduled tasks.

   - **Icon**—Provides graphical icons to represent tasks, notes, calendars, and so on.

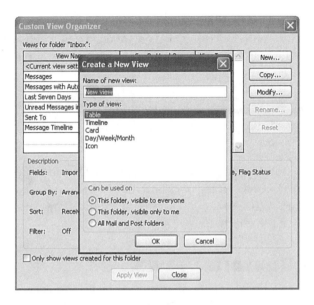

Figure 3.5 You can create custom views for your Outlook folders.

TIP **Using the Create a New View Option Buttons** If you work on a network where Outlook folders are shared on an Exchange Server, you can create your new view so that you see only the information in the view. Alternatively, you can share the view with other users who access the information. The default option in the Create a New View dialog box is **This Folder, Visible to Everyone**. To reserve the custom view for yourself, click the **This Folder, Visible Only to Me** option button.

4. After you've selected the type of view you want to create, click the **OK** button. A View Settings dialog box appears based on your selection. In this box, you determine which fields you want to have in the view and the fonts and other view settings you want to use.

5. After you've selected the fields and view settings, click **Apply View**. The items in the current folder appear in the new view.

Fields A specific type of information that you want to appear in your custom view. For a custom Inbox view using the Timeline view type, the fields include Received (when the message was received), Created (when the message was created), and Sent (when the message was sent).

Your newly created view appears on the Current View list on the Advanced toolbar. You can select it by clicking the list's drop-down arrow and then clicking the custom view's name.

Should I Design My Own Views?   Designing your own views can be
complicated. Outlook provides several views for each folder on the Navigation pane.
You might want to explore all these possibilities before you begin to create your own
CAUTION   views.

Using Outlook Today

Outlook Today is a great way to get a snapshot view of your day. This feature provides a window that lists all your messages, appointments, and tasks associated
with the current day.

To open the Outlook Today window, click **Personal Folders** in the folder list (or you
can click the **Shortcuts** button at the bottom of the Navigation pane and then select
the **Outlook Today** shortcut folder). Icons for your Calendar, Messages, and Tasks
appear in the Outlook Today window, as shown in Figure 3.6. Items for the current
day are listed below the icons.

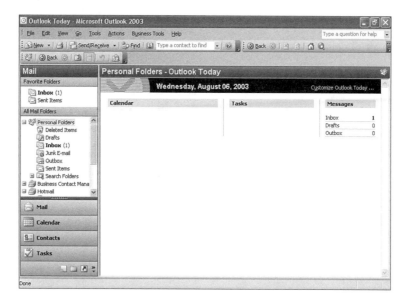

Figure 3.6   Outlook Today provides a list of all the items associated with the current day.

You can click any of the listed items (a particular appointment or task) to open the
appropriate folder and view the details associated with the items. You can even
update the items.

The Outlook Today Standard toolbar also provides the Type a Contact to Find box that you can use to quickly find people in your Contacts folder. Type a name into the Type a Contact to Find box (on the left of the Standard toolbar), and then press **Enter**. A Contact window appears for the person. You can edit the person's information or close the Contact box by clicking the **Close** button.

After you have viewed the items in the Outlook Today window, you can return to any of your folders by clicking their icons on the Navigation pane. Outlook Today is an excellent way to get a handle on what your day has in store for you.

Creating Mail

In this lesson, you learn how to compose a message, format text, check your spelling, and send e-mail. You also learn how to use different e-mail formats such as plain text and HTML.

Composing a Message

You can send an e-mail message to anyone for whom you have an e-mail address, whether that address is in your list of contacts or scribbled on a scrap of paper. In addition to sending a message to one or more recipients, in Outlook you can forward or copy messages to individuals in your Contacts list. You can even e-mail groups of people who are listed in your various distribution lists.

To open a new e-mail message while in the Outlook Inbox, select **File**, point at **New**, and then select **Mail Message** in the Outlook Inbox window (you can also click the **New** button on the Standard toolbar). A new message window appears (see Figure 4.1).

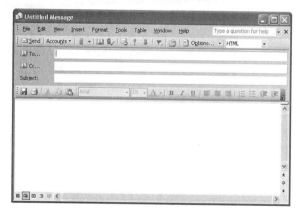

Figure 4.1   Compose a new message in the Untitled Message window.

E-mail addresses can be placed in the To box of a message that you want to send (a message you create from scratch or an existing message that you are forwarding) in several ways. You can

- Use your Outlook Contacts list
- Use your Outlook Address Book
- Type in an e-mail address that you don't currently have in any of your lists

In the case of e-mail messages that you reply to, the e-mail address of the person who sent you the message is automatically placed in the To box, making it ready to be sent.

Choosing from e-mail addresses listed in either your Contacts list or the Outlook Address Book is the easiest way to add an e-mail address to a message. It also helps you keep organized, and that is probably one of the reasons why you're using Outlook in the first place. You will also find that having e-mail addresses readily available in an Outlook list makes it easier to send carbon copies (duplicate e-mails) or blind carbon copies of messages when you are composing a particular message.

 Blind Carbon Copy   A blind carbon copy (Bcc) of a message is a copy sent to someone in secret; the other recipients have no way of knowing that you are sending the message to someone as a blind carbon copy.

You can find more information on using Outlook's Personal Address Book in Lesson 10, "Using the Outlook Address Books." Lesson 11, "Creating a Contacts List," shows you how to use contacts.

To address a new e-mail message, follow these steps:

1. In the message window, click the **To** button to display the Select Names dialog box. Names that have been entered in your Contacts list appear on the left side of the dialog box. If you want to switch to a different list, such as the Outlook Address Book, click the drop-down list on the upper-right corner of the dialog box and make a new selection.

   If the e-mail address you want isn't in your Contacts list, instead of clicking the **To** button, type the e-mail address directly into the To text box (if you do this, you can then skip steps 3 through 7).

2. From the list of addresses that appears on the left of the dialog box, choose the name of the intended recipient and select the **To** button (or you can double-click the name). Outlook copies the name to the Message Recipients list. You can also add any distribution lists to the To box that appear in your address list. To send a carbon copy or blind carbon copy to a recipient, use the **Cc** or **Bcc** buttons.

Figure 4.2 shows a message that is addressed to an individual whose address was contained in the Contacts list and also to a group of people who are listed in a distribution list (you can enter as many addresses as you want).

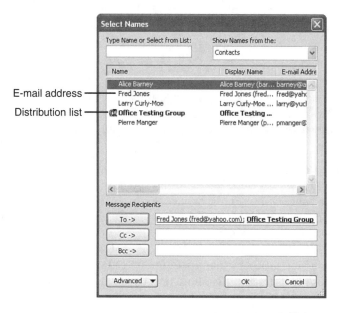

E-mail address ——

Distribution list ——

Figure 4.2 Add e-mail addresses or distribution list names quickly with the Select Names dialog box.

3. Click **OK** to return to the message window. Click in the Subject box and type the subject of your message.

4. Click in the text area, and then enter the text of the message. You do not have to press the Enter key at the end of a line; Outlook automatically wraps the text at the end of a line for you. You can use the Delete and Backspace keys to edit the text you enter.

5. When you finish typing the message, you can send the message, or you can format the message or check the spelling as detailed later in this lesson. To send the message, click the **Send** button on the message's Standard toolbar.

CAUTION

No Address If you try to send a message without entering at least one address in the To, CC, or BCC address boxes, Outlook displays a message that you must include at least one e-mail address in one of those boxes. Make sure you provide an address; either type in an address or select an address from your Contacts list or Address Book.

Formatting Text

You can enhance the format of the text in your message to make it more attractive, to make it easier to read, or to add emphasis. Any formatting you do transfers to the recipient with the message if the recipient has Outlook or another e-mail client that can work with HTML or Rich Text Format messages. However, if the recipient doesn't have an e-mail client that can handle these special message formats, formatting might not transfer and the message will be received in plain text.

HTML   Hypertext Markup Language is used to design Web pages for the World Wide Web. Outlook can send messages in this format, providing you with several text formatting options. Graphics can even be pasted into an HTML message.

Rich Text Format   A special e-mail format developed by Microsoft for use with Microsoft mail systems. Outlook can send and receive messages in Rich Text Format. This enables you to send and receive messages with special formatting, such as bold, italic, various fonts, and other special characters and graphics.

You format text in two ways. You can format the text after you type it by selecting it and then choosing a font, size, or other attribute; or you can select the font, size, or other attribute to toggle it on, and then enter the text, which will be formatted as you type.

To format the text in your message, you use various formatting buttons that appear on the message's toolbar. If you are using Word as your e-mail editor, the formatting buttons will appear on the E-mail toolbar. If you are not using Word as your e-mail editor, the formatting buttons are provided on the Formatting toolbar. You can open either of these toolbars (as needed) by selecting the **View** menu on the message's menu bar and then pointing at **Toolbars**. Select the required toolbar from the list provided.

Figure 4.3 shows a message with the E-mail toolbar displayed (Word is being used as the e-mail editor, which is the default when you install Microsoft Office). Formatting options have also been applied to the text in the message. Table 4.1 explains the buttons found on the E-mail toolbar (these same buttons would be available on the Formatting toolbar).

The Formatting Buttons Don't Work   Only messages sent in HTML or Rich Text Format can be formatted using the formatting buttons. Plain-text messages don't supply you with any formatting options. Selecting the message type (such as HTML or plain text) is discussed in the section "Selecting the E-mail Message Format," found later in this lesson.

CAUTION

Italics   Bold text   E-mail toolbar

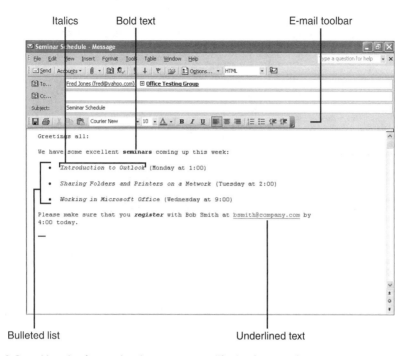

Bulleted list   Underlined text

Figure 4.3   Use the formatting buttons to modify the format of your message text.

Table 4.1   Formatting Buttons

Button	Name
A	Font Color
B	Bold
I	Italic
U	Underline
≡	Align Left
≡	Center
≡	Align Right
≡	Numbering

Table 4.1 Continued

Button	Name
![Bullets button]	Bullets
![Decrease Indent button]	Decrease Indent
![Increase Indent button]	Increase Indent

To change font attributes in a mail message, follow these steps:

1. To apply a new font to selected text, click the down arrow in the **Font** box. Scroll through the font list, if necessary, to view all fonts on the system, and then click the font you want to apply to the text. Make sure that you select an easy-to-read font such as Arial or Times New Roman. Using a highly stylized font such as Bauhaus 93 or Chiller can make the message difficult to read.

2. Assign a size by clicking the down arrow beside the **Font Size** drop-down list and choosing the size; alternatively, you can type a size into the Font Size text box (typically you should use a font size of 10 to 12 points).

3. To choose a color, click the **Color** button and select a color from the palette box that appears.

4. Choose a type style to apply to text by clicking the **Bold**, **Italic**, and/or **Underline** buttons.

5. Choose an alignment by selecting the **Align Left**, **Center**, or **Align Right** button from the toolbar.

6. Add bullets to a list by clicking the **Bullets** button on the toolbar. If you prefer a numbered list, click the **Numbering** button.

7. Create text indents or remove indents in half-inch increments by clicking the **Increase Indent** or **Decrease Indent** buttons (each time you click the Indent button, the indent changes by one-half inch).

TIP   **Yuck, No Thanks!**   If you assign formatting to your text and don't particularly like it, click **Edit** and select **Undo** (or press Ctrl+Z) to remove the last formatting that you assigned the text.

Selecting the E-Mail Message Format

The default message format in Outlook is HTML. If you send most of your messages to individuals who don't have mail clients that can read the HTML format, you might want to change the default to plain text. On corporate networks, you might find an advantage to using the Rich Text Format as the default text format for your messages. This file format was developed for the Exchange Server mail environment used on many business networks.

The default format is set in the Outlook Options dialog box on the Mail Format tab. Fortunately, Outlook makes it very easy for you to switch the format of a mail message while you are composing the message. First, let's take a look at how to set the default mail type, and then look at how to change the message format while composing the message.

To set the default message format:

1. Click **Tools**, **Options**. The Options dialog box appears.

2. Click the **Mail Format** tab (see Figure 4.4).

 TIP   **Include Hyperlinks**   If you use the HTML or Rich Text Format message formats, you can include hyperlinks in your e-mails. Hyperlinks are Web addresses and e-mail addresses that can be accessed by clicking them in the message. Just type the Web address or e-mail address, and the hyperlink is created automatically in the message.

Figure 4.4   You can send your messages in HTML, Rich Text Format, or plain-text format.

3. To select the message format, click the **Compose in This Message Format** drop-down box. Select **HTML**, **Rich Text**, or **Plain Text**. If you want to use Microsoft Word as your e-mail editor, click the **Use Microsoft Word to Edit E-mail Messages** check box (if it is not already selected).

TIP   **Using HTML Stationery**   If you use the HTML format for your messages, you can also select to use a particular stationery on the Mail Format tab. Stationery types can be previewed using the **Stationery Picker** button. Be advised that HTML stationery will slow down the loading of e-mail messages on the recipient's computer, and not everyone will have a mail client that can view the stationery. You probably should use the stationery only for personal messages to friends and family members who also use Outlook as their e-mail client.

Checking Spelling

If you send business-related e-mails, you will certainly want to check the spelling in your mail messages before you send them. Outlook includes a spelling checker you can use for that purpose. If you are using Word as your e-mail editor, you will use the Word Spelling and Grammar features. (Using Word as your e-mail editor also allows you to check for grammar errors.) These features are discussed in Lesson 4 of the Word section (Part IV) of this book, "Using Proofreading and Research Tools."

To check the spelling in a message, follow these steps:

1. In a message window, choose **Tools**, and then select **Spelling** or press **F7**. If the spelling checker finds a word whose spelling it questions, it displays the Spelling dialog box (shown in Figure 4.5). (If no words are misspelled, a dialog box appears saying that the spelling check is complete; choose **OK** to close the dialog box.)

Figure 4.5   Check your spelling before sending a message.

2. Your response to the questions in the Spelling dialog box will vary. If you recognize that Outlook has correctly flagged a misspelled word, choose one of the following:

   • **Suggestions**—Select the correct spelling in this text box, and it automatically appears in the Change To text box.

   • **Change**—Click this button to change this particular occurrence of the word in question to the spelling in the Change To text box.

   • **Change All**—Click this button to change the word in question to the spelling listed in the Change To text box every time the spelling checker finds the word in this message.

   If Outlook checks a word that you know is already spelled correctly (such as a proper name), choose one of the following:

   • **Not in Dictionary**—Enter the correct spelling into this text box.

   • **Ignore**—Click this button to continue the spelling check without changing this occurrence of the selected word.

   • **Ignore All**—Click this button to continue the spelling check without changing any occurrence of the word in question throughout this message.

   • **Add**   Click this button to add the current spelling of the word in question to the dictionary so that Outlook will not question future occurrences of this spelling.

   • **Undo Last**—Click this button to undo your last spelling change and return to that word.

3. Continue until the spelling check is complete (or click **Cancel** to quit the spelling check).

4. Outlook displays a message box telling you that the spell check is complete. Click **OK** to close the dialog box.

 TIP   **Set Your Spelling Options**   Click the **Options** button in the Spelling dialog box to set options that tell Outlook to do such things as ignore words with numbers, ignore original message text in forwarded messages or replies, always check spelling before sending, and so on.

Adding a Signature

You can further personalize your e-mails by adding a signature to the message. A signature can be as simple as just your name, or the signature can include your phone number or extension or other information. Some people even add a favorite quote to their signature. If you use HTML as your message format, you can even include signature files that contain graphics. Plain-text signatures (for use with plain-text messages) will consist only of text characters.

First, take a look at how you can create a signature. Then you can take a look at how you apply it to a message.

Creating a Signature

1. Choose **Tools, Options** to open the Options dialog box, and then select the **Mail Format** tab.

2. Click the **Signatures** button at the bottom of the dialog box. The Create Signature dialog box opens.

3. Click the **New** button; the Create New Signature dialog box opens as shown in Figure 4.6.

Figure 4.6   Outlook walks you through the steps of creating a signature.

4. Type a name for your new signature, and then click **Next**.

5. The Edit Signature dialog box appears. Enter the text you want included in the signature. You can use the Paragraph or Font buttons to add formatting to the text in the signature.

6. When you have finished creating your signature, click the **Finish** button. Click **Close** to close the Create New Signature dialog box, and then click **OK** to close the Options dialog box.

 TIP   **You Can Edit Signatures**   To edit a signature, select the signature in the Create New Signature dialog box and then click **Edit**.

Inserting the Signature

After you've created a signature or signatures, you can quickly add it to any message by placing the insertion point where you want to place the signature, choosing **Insert**, and then choosing **Signature**; all the signatures that you have created appear on the menu. Select the signature from the list you want to use in the message you are currently composing.

You can also preview the signatures before inserting them; choose **Insert**, **Signature**, and then select **More** from the cascading menu. The Select a Signature dialog box opens. Select any of your signatures to view a preview of the signature. When you find the signature you want to use, click **OK**.

Sending Mail

You probably know that after you add recipient addresses, compose your message, format the text, spell check the message, and insert a signature in the e-mail, you are ready to send the message. But you can use a couple of ways to actually send the message on its way.

The fastest way to send the message using the mouse is to click the **Send** button on the Message toolbar. If you prefer, press **Ctrl+Enter**. In either case, your message is heading out to its destination. If you are working offline, the message is placed in the Outbox until you connect to the Internet and send and receive your messages.

Recalling a Message

If you use Outlook as an e-mail client in a Microsoft Exchange Server environment, you can actually recall or replace e-mail messages that you have sent. But you can only recall or replace messages that have not been opened by the recipient or moved to another folder by a recipient.

If the Folder List is not visible, click the **View** menu, and then click **Folder List**.

1. Click the **My Shortcuts** button on the Navigation pane, and then select the **Sent Items** folder.

2. Double-click to open the message that you want to recall.

3. In the message window, click the **Actions** menu, and then click **Recall This Message**. The Recall This Message dialog box opens as shown in Figure 4.7.

Figure 4.7   Messages that have not been read can be recalled or replaced.

4. To recall the message, click the **Delete Unread Copies of This Message** option button, and then click **OK**. A notice appears in the message window informing you that you attempted to recall this message on a particular date and at a particular time.

5. If you want to replace the message with a new message, click the **Delete Unread Copies and Replace with New Message** option button. When you click **OK**, a new message window opens with a copy of the message you want to recall in it. Just change the message text or address and then send the message.

6. You eventually receive a notification in your Inbox (as new mail) notifying you whether the recall was successful.

Although you can't recall messages that are sent as Internet e-mail, you can use this feature to notify the recipients of a particular e-mail message that you want them to ignore the message. Use the message recall feature as detailed in the steps in this section. When you "recall" the message, a new message is sent to the original recipient (or recipients) that states you would like to recall the previous message. This doesn't remove the original message from their inbox but it at least provides them with a follow-up message that lets them know that the original message is essentially invalid.

Working with Received Mail

In this lesson, you learn how to read your mail, save an attachment, answer mail, and close a message.

Reading Mail

When you open Outlook, the Outlook Today window appears by default (unless you have specified that your Inbox should open; see the Tip that follows for how to open the Inbox by default). To switch to your Inbox, select the **Mail** button on the Navigation pane.

TIP **Change the Startup View to Your Inbox** To have the inbox open by default in Outlook, select **Tools** and then **Options**. In the Options dialog box, select the **Other** tab and then select the **Advanced Options** button. In the Advanced Options dialog box, set the **Startup in This Folder** option to the **Inbox**.

New e-mail is downloaded when you open Outlook and connect to your mail server; this is either accomplished automatically if you have a persistent connection to the Internet (such as through network, DSL, or cable modem connections) or when you connect to your Internet service provider via your modem. You can check if any new mail is available on your mail server as you are working in Outlook by clicking the Send/Receive button on the Outlook toolbar.

No matter what the connection situation, after you download any new e-mail to your computer, the new mail appears in the Outlook Inbox (see Figure 5.1). The Inbox list and the Reading pane (formerly the Preview pane) have been enhanced in Outlook 2003.

As you can see in Figure 5.1, the Inbox provides a list of messages that you have received. Outlook 2003 lists your e-mails in logical groupings. By default, messages are listed in subsets according to when they were received, such as Today, Yesterday, Last Week, and so on. Notice that at the top of the Inbox, it says: "Arranged By: Date." You can change how the e-mails are grouped by clicking on **Arrange By: Date** and selecting another grouping from the menu that appears. You can group the messages in the Inbox by sender (From), subject (Subject), and even by e-mails from different senders that were part of an overall conversation (Conversation).

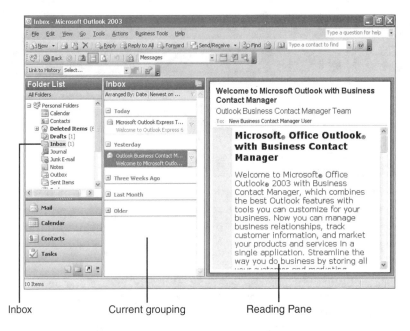

Inbox   Current grouping   Reading Pane

Figure 5.1   The Inbox provides a list of received messages.

To expand one of the groups that appear in the Inbox, click the **Expand** button (the plus sign) to the left of the group name. If you want to expand all the groups shown in the Inbox, select **View**, then point at **Expand/Collapse Groups**, and then select **Expand All Groups**.

TIP   **Use the Expand/Collapse Groups Menu to Expand or Collapse a Specific Group**   If you have a message selected in the Inbox that is in a particular group (such as Today), you can expand or collapse the group using the Expand/Collapse menu or the Expand/Collapse icon on the group itself.

Additional information about a particular message, such as the actual date sent, the message subject, and the message size can be viewed by placing the mouse pointer on the message. The message statistics will appear. To read a message, you can select it, and its contents appear in the Reading pane (see Figure 5.1). The Reading pane is a vertical window (by default) that replaces the Outlook Preview pane found in earlier versions of Outlook.

You can also open a message in its own window; double-click a mail message to open it. Figure 5.2 shows an open message.

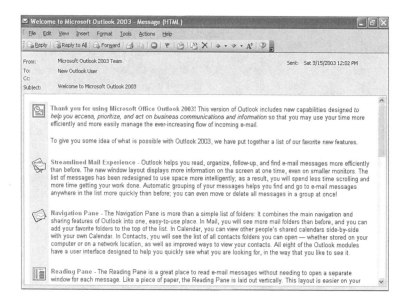

Figure 5.2   The message window displays the message and tools for responding to the message or moving to the previous or next message in the Inbox.

 To read the next or previous mail message in the Inbox when you have opened a mail message, click either the **Previous Item** or the **Next Item** button on the message window toolbar.

To access more view choices, click the drop-down arrow next to either the Previous Item or Next Item button; submenu choices are provided for each of these buttons that allow you to jump to another item, an unread item, or to an item found under a particular conversation topic.

Item   Outlook uses the word *item* to describe a mail message, an attached file, an appointment or meeting, a task, and so on. Item is a generic term in Outlook that describes the currently selected element.

Saving an Attachment

You often receive messages that have files or other items attached to them, such as documents or pictures. In the Inbox list of messages, a paper clip icon beside the message subject represents the presence of an attachment. You can save any attachments sent to you so that you can open, modify, print, or otherwise use the attached document or image. Messages can contain multiple attachments.

CAUTION

What About Viruses? Unfortunately, there is a chance that an attachment to a message can be a virus or other malicious software. Computer viruses can really wreak havoc on your computer system. When you receive an e-mail message from someone you don't know and that message has an attachment, the best thing to do is delete the message without opening it or the attachment. Detecting questionable mail is difficult; mail with no body text or a vague subject can be good indicators that a mail message contains a malicious attachment. You can also check questionable attachments with an antivirus program before you open the file.

To save an attachment, follow these steps:

1. Open the message containing an attachment by double-clicking the message. The attachment appears as an icon below the subject area of the message (see Figure 5.3).

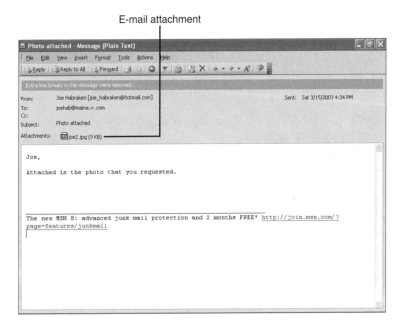

Figure 5.3 An icon represents the attached file.

2. (Optional) You can open the attachment from within the message by double-clicking the attachment icon. A message appears, as shown in Figure 5.4, warning you that you should only open attachments received from reliable sources.

To open the file, click the **Open** button. The attachment will be opened in the application in which it was created (such as Word or Excel) or the default application assigned to that particular file type (such as an image editor that you have installed on our computer). When you have finished looking at the attachment, you can return to the e-mail message by closing the open application.

3. If you choose **Save** in the Opening Mail Attachment dialog box, a Save As dialog box appears (as shown in Figure 5.5).

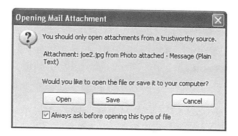

Figure 5.4   You can open or save an attachment by double-clicking its icon.

4. (Optional) There is also an additional option for saving an attachment (other than the option provided in step 2). This method makes it easier to save multiple attachments. In the message window, select **File, Save Attachments**. The Save Attachment dialog box appears (see Figure 5.5).

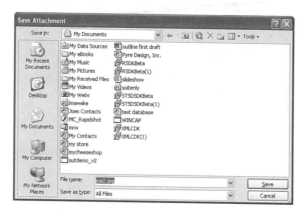

Figure 5.5   Save the attachment to a convenient folder.

5. Choose the folder in which you want to save the attachment or attachments and click **Save**. The dialog box closes and returns to the message window. You can change the name of the file in the File Name box, if you want. After you save the attachment, you can open the attachment, which is now like any other saved file on your computer, at any time from the application in which it was created.

 TIP **Use the Right Mouse Button** You can also quickly save an attachment by right-clicking the attachment icon. On the shortcut menu that appears, click **Save As**, and then save the attachment to an appropriate folder.

Answering Mail

You might want to reply to a message after you read it. The message window enables you to answer a message immediately as you read it. To reply to any given message, follow these steps:

1. Select the message in the Inbox window, and then click the **Reply** button on the Inbox toolbar.

   If you have the message open, click the **Reply** button in the message window. The Reply message window appears, with the original message in the message text area and the sender of the message already filled in for you (see Figure 5.6).

E-mail address is automatically filled in

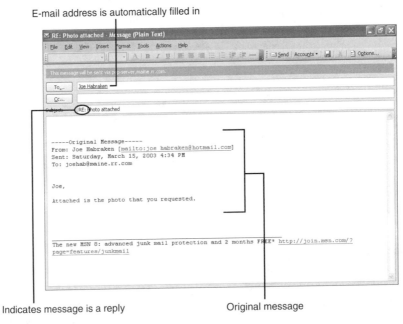

Indicates message is a reply   Original message

Figure 5.6   You can reply to a message quickly and easily.

TIP   **Reply to All**   If you receive a message that has also been sent to others—as either a message or a carbon copy (Cc)—you can click the **Reply to All** button to send your reply to each person who received the original message.

2. The insertion point is automatically placed above the message text that you are replying to. Enter your reply text.

3. When you finish your reply, click the **Send** button. Outlook sends the message.

The next time you open a message to which you've replied, there is a reminder at the top of the message window telling you the date and time you sent your reply. Don't forget that the purple arrow next to a message in the Inbox window shows that the message has been replied to.

Printing Mail

You can print mail messages, either directly from the Inbox when they have been selected or from a message window when you have opened a particular message. To print an unopened message, select the message in the message list of the Inbox or other folder and choose **File**, **Print**. The Print dialog box opens; click **OK** to send the message to the printer. If the message is already open, you can follow these steps:

1. Open the message in Outlook.

2. Choose **File** and then select **Print**, to open the Print dialog box.

3. In the Print dialog box, click **OK** to print one copy of the entire message using the printer's default settings. See Lesson 17, "Printing in Outlook," in this section of the book for detailed information about configuring pages and changing printer options.

TIP   **Print a Message from the Inbox**   You can also print a message or messages from the Inbox. Select the message or messages in the Inbox list and then click the **Print** button on the Outlook toolbar.

When you finish reading or printing a message, click the **Close** button on the message window.

Managing Mail

In this lesson, you learn how to delete and undelete messages, forward messages, and create folders. You also learn how to move messages to these folders.

Deleting Mail

You will want to delete a number of the messages that you receive, read, and respond to (or ignore). You can easily delete messages in Outlook. Messages that you want to save can actually be organized into folders that you create so that they don't clutter your Inbox. This is discussed in Lesson 8, "Saving Drafts and Organizing Messages."

The easiest way to delete a selected message, such as a message selected in the Inbox, is to click the **Delete** button on the Outlook toolbar. If the message is open, just click the **Delete** button on the message window toolbar instead.

If you want to delete several messages in the Inbox, just select the messages using the mouse. To select several contiguous messages, click the first message, and then hold down the **Shift** key when you click the last message in the series. To select non-contiguous messages, hold down the **Ctrl** key and click each message. When you have all the messages selected that you want to delete, click the **Delete** button (or you can select the **Edit** menu and then select **Delete**).

Undeleting Items

If you change your mind and want to get back items you've deleted, you can usually retrieve them from the Deleted Items folder. By default, when you delete an item, it doesn't disappear from your computer; it is moved to the Deleted Items folder. Items stay in the Deleted Items folder until you delete them from that folder—at which point they are unrecoverable. Typically, when you exit Outlook, the Deleted Items folder is emptied automatically.

TIP Determining When the Deleted Items Folder Should Be Emptied You can choose whether or not the Deleted Items folder should be emptied when you close Outlook. Select Tools, Options. In the Options dialog box select the Other tab and then select Empty the Deleted Items Folder Upon Exiting. Then click OK. If you are using Outlook on an Exchange Server network, see your system manager for information related to discarding deleted items.

To retrieve a deleted item from the Deleted Items folder, follow these steps:

1. With the Inbox selected in the Navigation pane, click the **Deleted Items** folder in the All Mail Folders group.

2. Select the items you want to retrieve; you can then drag them back to the Inbox by dragging them and dropping them onto the Inbox icon in the Navigation pane. Or if you don't like dragging messages, select the files you want to move from the Deleted Items folder, and then select **Edit, Move to Folder**. The Move Items dialog box appears as shown in Figure 6.1.

Figure 6.1   Deleted messages can be moved out of the Deleted Items folder back into the Inbox.

3. Select the folder you want to move the items into (such as the Inbox) and then click the **OK** button.

 TIP   **Use Undo Immediately**   If you want to undelete a message or messages that you just deleted, select the **Edit** menu, and then select **Undo Delete** (or type Ctrl+Z).

Emptying the Deleted Items Folder

If you're sure you no longer need them, you can completely discard the item or items in\ the Deleted Items folder. To "completely delete" items in the Deleted Items folder, follow these steps:

1. On the Navigation pane, choose the **Mail** icon. In the All Mail Folders group, expand the Personal Folders icon. The Deleted Items folder will appear in the All Mail Folders group. Select the Deleted Items folder; deleted items in that folder appear in the message list, as shown in Figure 6.2.

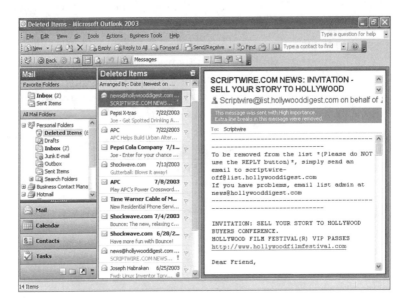

Figure 6.2 Deleted messages remain in the Deleted Items folder until you permanently delete them or empty the folder.

2. To permanently delete an item or items, select it (or them) in the Deleted Items folder.

3. Click the **Delete** button. Outlook displays a confirmation dialog box asking whether you're sure you want to permanently delete the message. Choose **Yes** to delete the selected item.

If you typically are pretty confident about the status of messages that you delete (you know you won't want to undelete them), you can empty all the messages out of the Deleted Items folder (rather than emptying it piecemeal, message by message). Right-click on the **Deleted Items** folder icon in the All Mail Folders group on the Navigation bar.

On the shortcut menu that appears, select **Empty "Deleted Items" Folder**. You will be asked to confirm the emptying of the folder; click **Yes**. The Deleted Items folder will be emptied. All messages or other items in the folder can no longer be retrieved.

TIP **Automatic Permanent Delete** You can set Outlook to empty the contents of the Deleted Items folder every time you exit the program. To do so, in the Outlook window choose **Tools**, and then click **Options**. Select the **Other** tab of the Options dialog box and click the **Empty the Deleted Items Folder Upon Exiting** check box. Then click **OK**.

Forwarding Mail

You can forward mail that you receive to a co-worker or anyone else with an e-mail address. When you forward a message, you can also add your own comments (or even attachments) to the message if you want.

 TERM **Forward Mail** When you forward mail, you send a copy of a message you have received to another person; you can add your own comments to the forwarded mail, if you want.

You can forward an open message or a message selected in the message list in the Inbox in the same way. To forward mail, follow these steps:

1. Select or open the message you want to forward. Then click the **Forward** button. The FW Message window appears (see Figure 6.3).

2. In the To text box, enter the addresses of the people to whom you want to forward the mail. If you want to choose an address or addresses from a list, click the **To** button to display the Select Names dialog box, and then select the address or addresses from your Contacts list.

3. (Optional) In the Cc text box, enter the addresses of anyone to whom you want to forward copies of the message.

4. In the message area of the window, enter any message you want to send with the forwarded text.

 TIP **Attachments Are Forwarded, Too** If the message that you forward contains attached files, the attachments are also forwarded.

5. When you are ready to send the message, click the **Send** button.

"FW:" indicates a forwarded message

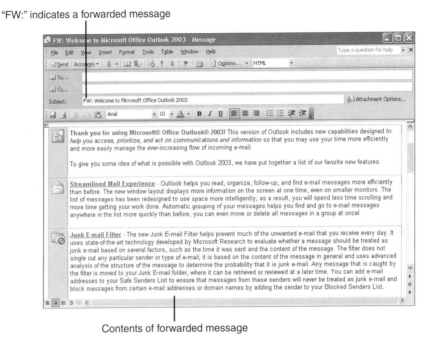

Contents of forwarded message

Figure 6.3   When you forward a message, the original message appears at the bottom of the message window.

Creating Folders

Although Outlook provides you with an Inbox, an Outbox, a Sent Items folder, an Unread Mail folder, and a Deleted Items folder, you might find it advantageous to create your own folders. This provides you with alternative places to store items and can make finding them in the future easier (rather than just having all your messages languish in the Inbox). Folders can also be used to store items other than messages, so you could even create subfolders for your Contacts folder or Calendar.

TIP   **Folders Aren't the Only Way to Get Organized**   Although the creation of folders can help you organize messages and other items that you want to store in Outlook, another tool called the Organizer has been designed to help you move, delete, and even color-code received e-mail messages. You will take a look at the Organizer in Lesson 8, "Saving Drafts and Organizing Messages."

To create a folder, follow these steps:

1. Click the **Folder List** button at the bottom of the Navigation pane. The Folder List appears in the Navigation pane.

2. To create a folder in the Folder List, right-click the Personal Folders icon.

3. On the shortcut menu that appears (see Figure 6.4), select **New Folder**. The Create New Folder dialog box appears.

Figure 6.4 Folders can be created anywhere in the Folder List.

TIP **Create Folders from the File Menu** You can also open the Create New Folder dialog box from the File menu. Just select **File**, point at **New**, and then select **Folder**.

4. In the Create New Folder dialog box, type a name for the folder into the Name box.

5. Use the Folder Contains drop-down list in the New Folder dialog box to select the type of folder that you want to create. For example, if you want to hold mail messages in the folder, select **Mail and Post Items** from the list (see Figure 6.5).

6. Use the folder locations provided in the Select Where to Place Your Folder list to select the location for the new folder. If you want to nest the new folder in an existing folder, such as the Inbox, select that folder on the list. If you want to create the new folder as a first-level folder, select **Personal Folders**.

Figure 6.5 Folders can be created to hold mail messages, contacts, and even calendar appointments.

7. When you have finished making your entries and selections in the New Folder dialog box, click **OK** to create the folder.

The new folder appears on the Navigation pane in the Folder List.

CAUTION

I Want to Delete a Folder If you add a folder and then decide you don't want it, right-click the folder in the Folder List and select **Delete** from the shortcut menu. You then must verify the deletion; click **Yes**.

Moving and Copying Items to Another Folder

You can move items from one folder in Outlook to another; for example, you can create a folder to store all messages pertaining to a specific account or just make a folder that holds personal messages instead of business-related messages. You can easily move any messages to a new folder and then open them later to read them or to reply to them.

To move an item to another folder, follow these steps:

1. From the Inbox or any Outlook folder, select the message or messages you want to move.

2. Select **Edit, Move to Folder**. The Move Items dialog box appears (see Figure 6.6).

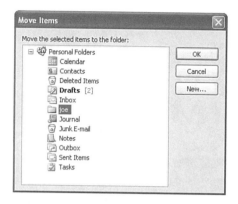

Figure 6.6   Choose the folder in which you want to store the message or messages.

3. In the Move Items dialog box, select the folder to which you want to move the message or messages.

4. Click **OK**. The message or messages are moved to the destination folder.

TIP   **Quickly Move Items**   You can quickly move any message or other Outlook item by dragging it from the open folder in which it resides to any folder icon in the Outlook bar.

You can also copy items from one folder to another (rather than moving them). Select the items you want to copy. Then select **Edit, Copy to Folder**. Specify the location that you want to copy the items to in the Copy Items dialog box (which is similar to the Move Items dialog box shown in Figure 6.6) and then click **OK**.

Attaching Files and Items to a Message

In this lesson, you learn how to attach a file and Outlook items to an e-mail message.

Attaching a File

You can attach any type of file to an Outlook message, which makes for a convenient way of sending your files to your co-workers or sending pictures to anyone (anywhere in the world) who has access to Internet e-mail. You can send Word documents, Excel spreadsheets, a family photo (taken from a digital camera or scanned from a photograph), or any other file you have on your hard drive.

When you attach a file, it appears as an icon in an attachment box that resides in the message window right below the Subject box, as shown in Figure 7.1. A button to the left of the attached file can be used to quickly access the Insert File dialog box if you want to change the attached file or add additional attachments before sending the message.

You can also open or view any files that you attach to your e-mail messages (before or after you send them) by double-clicking the file. Next, you take a look at attaching and viewing attachments, such as files created in other applications and picture files. Then, you can take a look at attaching an Outlook item such as a contact or appointment to an e-mail message.

 TIP   **E-mail Attachments and E-mail Clients**   Depending on the e-mail client they are using, the way recipients of your file attachments retrieve them will vary. For example, some e-mail packages do not show the attachment as an icon, but save the attachment directly to a specific folder on the recipient's computer after the e-mail message is received.

To attach a file to a message, follow these steps:

 1. In the new message window, choose **Insert** and then select **File,** or click the **Insert File** button on the toolbar. The Insert File dialog box appears (see Figure 7.2).

Attached file

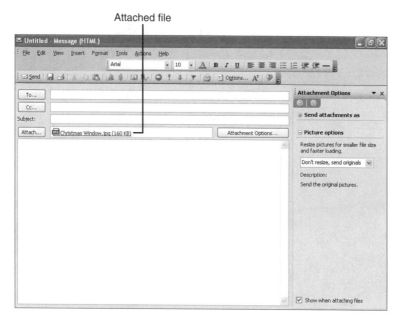

Figure 7.1   Attached files appear as an icon in the Attach box.

Figure 7.2   Select the file you want to attach to a message.

2. From the **Look In** drop-down list, choose the drive and folder that contain the file you want to attach.

3. Select the file you want to attach.

4. Click **Insert** to insert the file into the message.

An Attach box appears below the Subject box on the message, and an icon and the filename are inserted. If you attached a photo file to your Outlook message, the Attachment Options Task Pane also appears (see Figure 7.3).

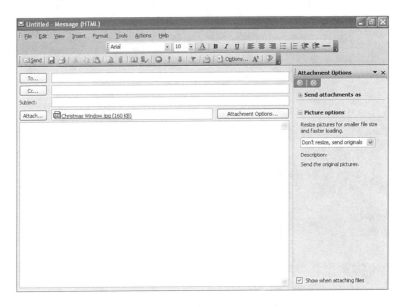

Figure 7.3 Select the file you want to attach to a message.

 TIP **Where Is the Attachment Options Task Pane?** If you don't see the Attachment Options Task Pane, click the **Attachment Options** button to the right of the Attachment box on the e-mail message.

The Attachment Options Task Pane allows you to control how the attachments are sent and also allows you to change the size of an image attachment.

To control how the attachments are sent, click the **Send Attachments As** heading. You are provided with two possibilities:

- **Regular Attachments**: The default setting for attachments sends a set of attachments to each recipient of the e-mail.
- **Shared Attachments**: This option allows you to provide each recipient with a copy of the attachments and also to place the attachments on a Document Workspace located on the Web (you must have access to a Web server for this feature to work). You must supply a Web address (URL) that is the address of the Web server that will hold the file attachments.

Select the option that is appropriate to your needs. All file attachments including documents, databases, and images can be configured so that they are shared attachments available on a particular Website.

The Attachments Options Task Pane also allows you the option of changing the size of image file attachments (this option is not available for documents, databases, and other file types). For example, if you have attached a large digital camera photo to an e-mail, you can have Outlook resize the attachment so that it is sent as a smaller file size. This allows recipients with slow Internet connections to download the e-mail message and its attachments faster.

Be advised, however, that this feature can't be used to make a small file larger. You can shrink picture attachments but you can't enlarge them.

To select the size options for the image attachment, click the Picture options dropdown list and select one of the following:

- **Don't Resize, Send Originals**—The default setting, the images are sent as attached (the original file size).
- **Small (448×336)**—This option lowers the resolution of the image making the file smaller.
- **Medium (640×480)**—This option lowers the resolution less drastically than the Small option but also gives you a slightly small file size.
- **Large (1024×768)**—This option provides a higher resolution file that may actually increase the file size of the image you are sending.

After making your selections in the Attachments Options Task Pane, you can complete your e-mail message (address it, add a message text). When you send the message, the options you selected in the Task Pane will be used in relation to the attached file.

 TIP   **Large Files Take Time**   Sending an extremely large file can take a great deal of time, depending on your connection speed. Some ISPs and Web-based e-mail providers, such as America Online and Yahoo! Mail, set a limit for attachment file size for sent or received attachments.

Attaching Outlook Items

In addition to attaching files from other programs, you can also attach an Outlook item to a message. An Outlook item can be any item saved in one of your personal folders, including an appointment, a contact, a note, and so on. You can attach an Outlook item in the same manner you attach a file.

Follow these steps to attach an Outlook item:

1. In the message window, choose **Insert, Item** (or click the drop-down arrow next to the Insert File icon and select **Item**). The Insert Item dialog box appears (see Figure 7.4).

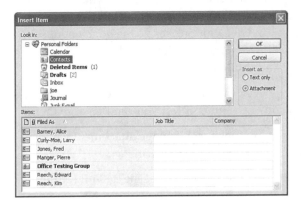

Figure 7.4   Select items from any folder in Outlook, such as a contact's information from the Contacts folder.

2. From the **Look In** list, choose the folder containing the item you want to include in the message.

3. Select from the items that appear in the **Items** list when you have the appropriate folder selected. To select multiple adjacent items, hold down the **Shift** key and click the first and last desired items; to select multiple nonadjacent items, hold down the **Ctrl** key and click the items.

4. In the Insert As area, choose from the following option buttons:

   - **Text Only**—Inserts the file as text into the message, such as the contact's information or the text in an e-mail message.

   - **Attachment**—Attaches the e-mail message or Contact record as an attachment to the current e-mail message.

5. Click **OK**, and Outlook inserts the selected items into your message (either as an attachment or as inserted text).

Figure 7.5 shows an attached contact record in an Outlook e-mail message. When the e-mail recipient receives the message, he or she can access the contact information by double-clicking the attachment icon. The recipient can then save the contact information to their Contacts folder.

An attached contact item

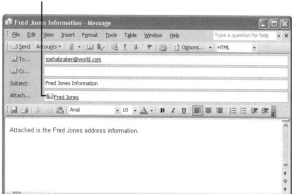

Figure 7.5 Select an item from any folder in Outlook, such as a contact's information, and attach it to your e-mail message.

  TIP **It Doesn't Work Without Outlook** If recipients don't have Outlook on their computers, they will not be able to view the attached item, such as an Outlook contact record. If you know that a recipient doesn't have Outlook, insert the contact information into the message as text using the Text Only option in the Insert Item dialog box.

Saving Drafts and Organizing Messages

In this lesson, you learn how to save a draft, view messages that you've sent, and manage messages using the Outlook Organizer. You also learn how to create rules to manage messages.

Saving a Draft

Suppose you start a message but you are called away or need to do something else before you can finish it. You don't have to lose the message by canceling, forcing you to start over again later; you can save the message in the Drafts folder and then open it later to complete it. The easiest way to save a draft is to click the Save button on the message toolbar.

However, if you inadvertently close a message before you either send it or save it as a draft, follow these steps to save it:

1. When you click the **Close** button, a dialog box appears, asking whether you want to save changes, as shown in Figure 8.1.

Figure 8.1 Click **Yes** to save the message in the Drafts folder for later completion.

2. Click **Yes**. Outlook places the current message into the Drafts Folder.

To open the message and continue working on it at another time, follow these steps:

1. Click the **Drafts** folder icon in the All Mail Folders group on the Navigation pane (when Mail is the selected group), or choose **Drafts** from the Folder List.

2. The message will be listed in the Drafts pane. Double-click the message to open it. At the top of the Message tab, you'll see a reminder that reads: This Message Has Not Been Sent.

3. Continue your work on the message. If you need to store it again before you're finished, click the **Close** button and answer **Yes** to the message box that asks you to save the file. Alternatively, you can choose to save changes that you have made to the message by clicking the **Save** button on the message toolbar and then closing the message. The message remains in the Drafts folder until you move or send it.

4. When you've actually completed the entire message and are ready to send it, click the **Send** button to send the message.

Viewing Sent Items and Changing Defaults

By default, Outlook saves a copy of all e-mail messages that you send. It keeps these copies in the Sent Items folder, which can be opened using the Sent Items icon found in the All Mail Folders group (or the Folders List) on the Navigation pane. You can view a list of sent items at any time, and you can open any message in that list to review its contents.

Viewing Sent Items

To view sent items, follow these steps:

1. In the Navigation pane, select the **Mail** icon.

 TIP **Save Time Using the Folder List** You can select the Sent Items folder from the Folder List instead of using the icon in the My Shortcuts group.

2. In the All Mail Folders group on the Navigation pane, click the **Sent Items** folder; Outlook displays a list of the contents of that folder. Figure 8.2 shows the Sent Items list. All messages you send remain in the Sent Items folder until you delete or move them.

3. (Optional) To view a sent item, select it to view its contents in the Reading pane, or double-click it to open it. When you have finished viewing its contents, click the **Close** (**X**) button (if you have opened it in a separate window).

 TIP **Open the Reading Pane** If you don't see the Reading pane when you are working in the Sent Items folder, select the **View** menu, point at **Reading Pane**, and then select **Right** or **Bottom** to place the pane.

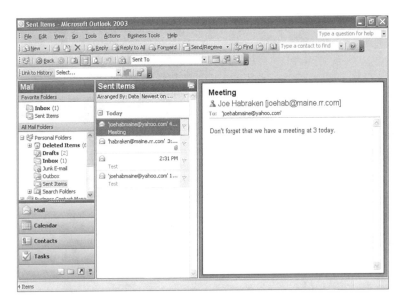

Figure 8.2   You can open any sent message by double-clicking it.

Changing Sent E-Mail Defaults

You can control whether Outlook saves copies of your sent messages (this is also true for unsent messages that are, by default, saved to the Drafts folder). Follow these steps:

1. Select **Tools**, **Options**, and the Options dialog box appears.

2. Select the **Preferences** tab on the Options dialog box.

3. Click the **E-mail Options** button. The E-mail Options dialog box appears (see Figure 8.3). This dialog box provides a series of check boxes that you can use to toggle several e-mail–related features on and off; to make sure that saved copies of messages are placed in the Sent Items folder, click the **Save Copies of Messages in Sent Items Folder** check box. To have e-mail that is not sent automatically saved in the Outbox, click the **Automatically Save Unsent Messages** check box.

The E-mail Options tab also gives you control over several other features related to the management of your e-mail. More mail option settings are discussed in the next lesson.

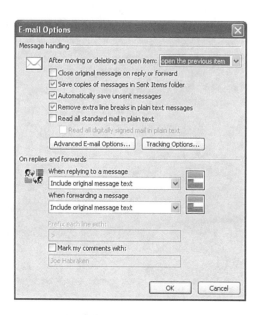

Figure 8.3   The E-mail Options dialog box gives you control over various features related to sending and saving unsent e-mail messages.

Using the Organize Tool

You have already learned how to create folders and move e-mail messages to folders to help keep your Outlook information organized (look back at Lesson 7, "Attaching Files and Items to a Message," for more info). Outlook also provides an easy-to-use tool, called the Organize tool, that can help you move, delete, or color-code received and sent mail.

Suppose that you decide to move a message or messages to a new location in Outlook. You can use the Move Message command and place the items into a different folder.

To use the Organize tool to manage messages, follow these steps:

1. In your Inbox, select a message or messages that you want to work with.

2. Click the **Tools** menu and then click **Organize**. The Organize window appears (see Figure 8.4).

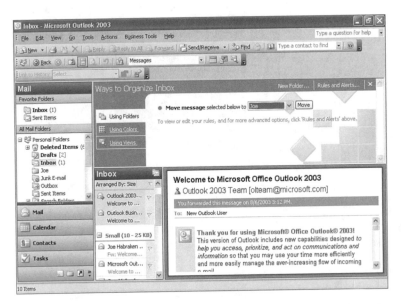

Figure 8.4 The Organize tool helps you manage messages using folders, colors, and views.

The Organize tool helps you manage and organize your messages using these methods:

- **Using Folders**—This method is used to move or delete selected messages; they can be moved to a folder that you create or moved to the Deleted Items folder.

- **Using Colors**—This option enables you to color-code messages according to the sender or receiver of the message.

- **Using Views**—This option allows you to categorize messages by their view (Last Seven Days, Unread Messages, and so on).

To manually move the currently selected message or messages to another folder, follow these steps:

1. Click **Using Folders**.

2. In the Move Message Selected Below To box, click the drop-down arrow and select the Outlook folder to which you would like to move the message.

3. Click the **Move** button and the message (or messages) is moved to the new location.

4. If you want to move other messages, select the message (or several messages) in the Message list and repeat steps 2 and 3.

As already mentioned you can also color-code messages. This Organizer feature allows you to color-code messages from specific senders, making it easy to locate these messages in the message list. When you specify that messages from a particular sender should be color-coded in your Inbox, you are actually creating a rule that color-codes the messages based on the sender's name. We talk more about creating rules in the next section.

Follow these steps to color-code messages:

1. In your Inbox, select a message from the sender. All messages in the Inbox from this sender will be color-coded.

2. Click the Tools menu and then click Organize.

3. Select the Using Colors tab in the Organize pane (see Figure 8.5).

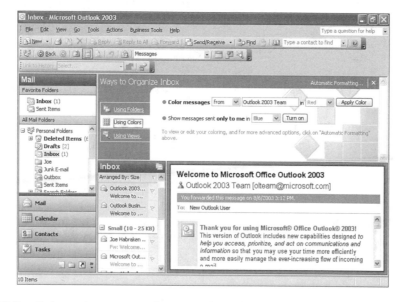

Figure 8.5   Color-code messages from specific senders.

4. The sender's name will appear on the Color messages from line. Click the color drop-down box (the default is red) and select the color that will be assigned to messages from this sender.

5. When you are ready to apply the color, click Apply Color.

The color will be assigned to all messages from the sender. You can also use color-coding in your Sent Items folder to color code messages that you have sent to a particular recipient.

TIP   **Turning Colors Off**   To turn off the color-coding on a particular group of messages (from a particular sender for example) click the Automatic Formatting link at
the top of the Organizer pane. In the Automatic Formatting dialog box, clear the
check box next to the rule that color-coded the messages; it will appear as "Mail
received from" and then the name of the sender. After clearing the checkbox, click
OK to close the dialog box.

Creating Rules

If you want to automate some of the management of your e-mail messages (rather
than relying on the Organize tool and moving the messages manually), you can create rules. Rules can be used to automatically move messages from a particular
sender or automatically send certain messages to the Deleted Items folder. Rules
can use different criteria to act upon a message such as the sender, subject, and
message text.

TERM   **Rules**   Rules are a set of conditions (such as a particular e-mail address or message content) that you identify to move, delete, or otherwise manage incoming e-
mail messages (including color-coding).

TIP   **Rules and Attachments**   The rules you create to organize your messages can
look at such things as sender, receiver, message subject, and message text.
Attachments to a message are not governed by the rules that you create, so the
content of file attachments to a message does not govern how they are handled by
the Organize tool or rules.

You can create a rule by using the Organize pane or by clicking on the Rules and
Alerts icon on the Outlook Advanced toolbar. Rules are created using the Rules
Wizard. The Rules Wizard enables you to create pretty sophisticated rules using sim-
ple sentences.

To open the Rules Wizard, follow these steps:

1. Select the Rules and Alerts icon on the Outlook Advanced toolbar (or from the
Organizer pane, when Using Folders is selected, click **Rules and Alerts**). The
Rules and Alerts dialog box appears (see Figure 8.6).

2. To create a new rule, click the **New Rule** button. The Rules Wizard walks you
through the rule-creation process. The first screen asks you to choose either to
create the rule from an existing template or create a new, blank rule. Templates
provide you with the easiest way to quickly create a new rule. Step 3 describes
creating a rule using a template (although the process of creating a blank rule
follows a similar set of options provided by the wizard).

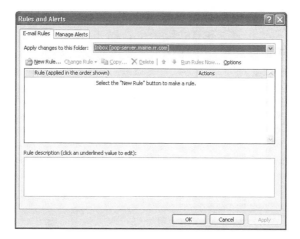

Figure 8.6 The Rules and Alerts dialog box helps you create and manage rules for managing mail messages.

3. Select one of the templates provided by the Rule wizard. For example, you might select the **Move Messages with Specific Words in the Subject to a Folder Template** (see Figure 8.7). After selecting a particular template, click **Next**.

Figure 8.7 In the Rules Wizard, you select the type of rule you want to create and the template used to create the rule.

4. The next screen asks you to select all the conditions that the new rule is to use (see Figure 8.8). These conditions range from words found in the subject line to who the message is from to the importance level for the message. Any conditions that you select in the conditions list will require fine-tuning in the Edit the Rule Description box of the Rules Wizard. Select conditions using the check boxes provided in the Step 1 Select Conditions Box.

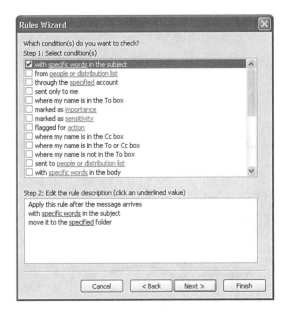

Figure 8.8   You select the conditions that are to be used by the rule.

 TIP   **Conditions That Require Input from You**   Some conditions such as From People or Distribution List or Specific Words require that you provide a list of people for the condition to use or certain words. Conditions requiring additional information have an underlined selection for you to click in the Step 2 box.

5. In the Step 2: Edit the Rule Description box, select any underlined items associated with the conditions you select in the Step 1 box. You will have to provide the information required by each condition. For example, the Specific Words in the Subject condition (shown in Figure 8.8) requires that you click the Specific Words link and provide a list of words for the rule to use. This condition also requires that you specify the folder to which the e-mail messages meeting the condition are moved. After providing the required information, click **Next**.

6. The next wizard screen provides you with a second chance to specify what should be done with a message that meets the condition of the rule. If you used a template that set specific actions when a message met the conditions of the rule, actions for the rule and the overall rule description should be completed at this point. Click **Next** to continue.

7. The next wizard screen provides you with the ability to configure any exceptions that you may want to have for this rule. For example, if you create a rule that moves messages with certain words in the subject line directly to the Deleted Items folder, you could create an exception for messages that are received from certain senders. After setting any exceptions to the rule, click the **Next** button to continue.

8. On the next wizard screen, provide a name for the new rule (see Figure 8.9). The rule is turned on by default. You can also check the Run This Rule Now on Messages Already in "Inbox" if you want to apply the rule to previously received messages. After setting these options, click **Finish**.

Figure 8.9 Provide a name for the rule and determine if you want to apply the rule to previously received messages.

The new rule will appear in the Rules and Alerts dialog box. You can create additional rules at this point, or you can close the Rules and Alerts dialog box by clicking **OK**. After using a particular rule, you may find that you want to fine-tune and edit the rule. All you have to do is open the Rules and Alerts dialog box (click the **Rules and Alerts** icon on the Advanced toolbar) and then double-click on the rule. You can then edit the various settings as you did when you first created the rule.

TIP **Delete "Bad" Rules** If you find that a rule or rules that you have created are actually doing things to messages that you hadn't planned, you can delete the rules. Rules created with the Organize tool can also be deleted in this manner. Open the Rules and Alerts dialog box (click **Tools**, then **Rules and Alerts**). In the dialog box, select rules that you want to delete and then select **Delete**. They will be removed from the rule list.

When you use the Rules Wizard for the first time, you may want to create a simple rule or two that handle messages that you do not consider extremely important. A poorly designed rule could delete important messages that you receive. A good general rule is to use the Organize tool first and let it create simple rules, and if you need more advanced message-management help, use the Rules Wizard.

Using the Junk E-Mail Filter

Junk e-mail has become a real scourge for e-mail users worldwide. No matter how careful you are about sharing your e-mail address, it doesn't take very long, even with a new e-mail account, before you begin receiving junk e-mail. Outlook 2003 has improved your ability to control received junk e-mail by providing a new Junk E-Mail Filter.

The Junk E-Mail Filter can provide different levels of protection from junk e-mail. By default the filter is set to low, which only moves messages received in the Inbox to the Junk E-Mail folder if they are obvious junk e-mail messages. You can change the level of protection using the Junk E-Mail Options dialog box (which we discuss in a moment).

TIP **How Does the Junk E-Mail Filter Work?** the Junk E-Mail filter analyzes the overall content and structure of a message to determine if it is junk e-mail. Depending on the level of protection that you set for the filter, you may have legitimate messages placed in the Junk E-Mail folder.

The Junk E-Mail Filter provides you with the ability to immediately deal with the status of Junk E-Mail and specify received messages in your Inbox as junk (and the sender of the message as a junk sender). You can also create lists of senders that are considered trusted, so that their messages are never flagged as junk. Let's look at the Junk E-Mail commands available on the Actions menu and then we will look at how you set the various Junk E-Mail Options.

Using the Junk E-Mail Commands

As you receive e-mail, the Junk E-Mail Filter will move any e-mail to the Junk E-Mail folder that it considers junk. You can view mail that has been placed in the Junk E-Mail folder by selecting Junk E-Mail in the All Mail Folders group.

By default the Junk E-Mail filter is set to low, so you may still receive messages in your inbox that you would like to be considered junk. You can quickly change the status of a message to junk using the Junk E-Mail command.

Select a message (or messages) in your Inbox that you would like to flag as junk e-mail. Then select the **Actions** menu, and point at **Junk E-Mail**. As shown in Figure 8.10, options are provided for how you handle the selected message (or messages).

Figure 8.10   Junk e-mail commands allow you to specify how a message should be handled.

- **Add Sender to Junk Senders List**—Selecting this menu command adds the sender address to the junk senders list. All future e-mail from this sender will be treated as junk e-mail.

- **Add Sender to Trusted Senders List**—Selecting this menu command adds the sender address to the trusted senders list. All e-mail from this sender, no matter the content, will be treated as regular mail and not sent to the Junk E-Mail folder.

- **Add to Trusted Recipients List**—This menu command allows you to add mailing lists and other domain subscription lists that you subscribe to so that messages from them are not considered junk e-mail no matter the content.

You can repeat the process described in the preceding steps until you have added any number of message senders to the Junk Senders list or the trusted recipients list. After you have built these various lists to contain a number of senders, you can consider raising the Junk E-Mail Filter's protection level. Setting filter options is discussed in the next section.

Setting the Junk E-Mail Options

You can set the level of protection that the Junk E-Mail Filter provides. Select Actions, then point at Junk E-mail, and select Junk E-mail Options. The Junk E-Mail Options dialog box appears as shown in Figure 8.11.

Figure 8.11   You can set the level of protection provided by the Junk E-mail Filter.

As already mentioned, the protection level is set to Low by default. You can raise the Junk E-Mail Filter protection level to high by selecting the **High** option button. Be advised that selecting the High option may mean that some non-junk mail may end up in the Junk E-Mail folder.

If you have built an extensive list of trusted senders, you may even want to raise the level of protection so that only e-mails from trusted senders are treated as non-junk. Select the **Trusted Lists Only** option.

If you want to add trusted senders, trusted recipients, or junk senders to a particular list, select the appropriate tab on the Junk E-mail Options dialog box. You can add e-mail names to any of these lists using the **Add** button on the appropriate tab.

Setting Mail Options

In this lesson, you learn how to set options for messages related to message priority and the delivery of messages. You also learn how to work with message flags.

Working with Message Options

Outlook provides options that enable you to mark any message with certain options that emphasize a certain aspect of the message's importance. You can use Priority status so that the recipient knows you need a quick response. Using a sensitivity rating makes it so that not just anyone can change your message after it is sent. With other options you can enable the recipients of your message to vote on an issue by including voting buttons in your message and having the replies sent to a specific location.

You also can set delivery options. For example, you can schedule the delivery of a message for a specified delivery time or date if you don't want to send it right now.

CAUTION

Recognizing Priority Levels   Not all e-mail packages recognize the priority levels that you assign to messages you send (as discussed in the next section). These priority levels work ideally in a network situation, where Outlook is the e-mail client for all users. Microsoft's Outlook Express e-mail client also has the capability to recognize priority levels that you use on sent messages.

To set message options, open a new e-mail and click the **Options** button on the toolbar (or select **View, Options**). As you can see in Figure 9.1, the Message Options dialog box is separated into four areas. The next four sections discuss each group of options in detail.

CAUTION

I Don't See Options on the View Menu   If you are using Word 2003 as your e-mail editor (the default setting for Outlook if Word is also installed on the computer), the Options command does not appear on the View menu. You must select **Options** on the message toolbar to open the Options dialog box.

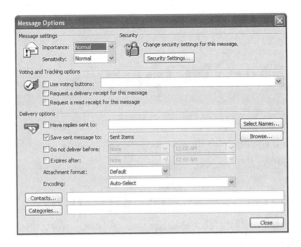

Figure 9.1   Use the Message Options dialog box to govern how your message is sent.

Message Settings

In the Message Settings area, set any of the following options for your message:

- Click the **Importance** drop-down arrow and choose a priority level of **Low**, **Normal**, or **High** from the list. Low priority is denoted on a message by a down-pointing arrow, whereas a high priority is denoted by a red exclamation point. When importance isn't specified, the message is given Normal importance.

- Click the **Sensitivity** drop-down arrow and choose one of the following options:

  - **Normal**—Use this option to indicate that the message contents are standard or customary.

  - **Personal**—Use this option to suggest that the message contents are of a personal nature. A banner is placed at the top of the message that reads "Please treat this as Personal."

  - **Private**—Use this option to prevent the message from being edited (text changes, copy, paste, and so on) after you send it. A banner is placed at the top of the message that reads "Please treat this as Private."

  - **Confidential**—Use this option to indicate that the message contents are restricted or private. Confidential messages can be edited by the recipient. Marking the message Confidential is only to suggest how the recipient should handle the contents of the message. A banner is placed at the top of the message that reads "Please treat this as Confidential."

TIP **Mark All Messages As Private** You can mark all your new messages as private automatically. Choose **Tools**, **Options**. On the **Preferences** tab, click the **E-mail Options** button. In the E-mail Options dialog box, click the **Advanced E-mail Options** button. Use the **Sensitivity** drop-down box at the bottom of the Advanced E-mail Options dialog box to set the default sensitivity for all your new e-mail messages.

Only message recipients who use Outlook as their e-mail client will be able to view the sensitivity banners placed on sent e-mails when you assign them a sensitivity level. Outlook Express users cannot view the banners such as "Please treat this as Confidential" that are placed on the messages.

Security Settings

Outlook also supplies you with options related to the security settings for a message. You can choose to encrypt the contents of your message or add a digital signature to the message. You can access the security options by clicking the Security Settings button in the Message Options dialog box (which you can open by clicking the Options button on the message toolbar).

 Digital Signature A digital ID that is electronically stamped on messages that you send. This allows recipients of the message to verify that the message is truly sent by you.

To set the security option for the message, click the **Security Settings** button. This opens the Security Properties dialog box, as shown in Figure 9.2.

If you want to encrypt the message, click the **Encrypt Message Contents and Attachments** check box. If you want, you can also add a digital signature to the message that verifies you are the sender; click the **Add Digital Signature to This Message** check box.

 Encryption Messages are coded so that they remain secure until the recipient opens them.

Before you can use either the encryption or the digital-signature features, you must obtain a digital ID, which is also often called a certificate. Digital IDs are issued by an independent certifying authority. Microsoft's certifying authority of choice is VeriSign Digital ID. For a fee, you can obtain, download, and install your digital ID from VeriSign by following the steps on their Web page at `http://digitalid.verisign.com/`.

Figure 9.2   You can set security options for a message, such as encryption and the use of a digital signature.

Most e-mail traffic doesn't really require encryption or the use of digital signatures. You will have to determine for yourself whether your e-mails require extra security precautions such as encryption and digital signatures.

Voting and Tracking Options

The Voting and Tracking Options enable you to control special features such as voting buttons (these allow recipients of the message to reply with a click of the mouse), which supply you with the means to track the receipt of your message. The delivery and read notification options allow you to receive notification that the recipient of the message has received the message or opened and read it, respectively.

- In the Message Options dialog box, select the **Use Voting Buttons** check box to add the default choices (Approve and Reject) to your message. You can also add Yes and No choices (meeting requests, for example) or Yes, No, and Maybe choices using the drop-down list to the right of the Use Voting Buttons check box. If you want to provide other choices, enter your own text into the text box (using semicolons to break up your choices). When you send a message with voting buttons to several people, you can view a summary of all the voting results by clicking the voting summary message on any of the e-mail responses.

- Select **Request a Delivery Receipt for This Message** to receive an e-mail notification that the intended recipient has received the message.

- Select **Request a Read Receipt for This Message** to receive e-mail confirmation that the recipient has opened the message.

Delivery Options

In addition to voting and tracking options, you can set certain delivery options, such as having replies sent to individuals you select. You can also choose a folder where a copy of the message is saved, or schedule the time of the delivery. In the Delivery Options area of the Message Options dialog box, choose any of the following check boxes:

- Normally, a reply to an e-mail message returns to the e-mail address of the sender. Sometimes, especially if you have multiple e-mail accounts, you might want replies to your message to go to a different e-mail address than the one you're sending from. Choose the **Have Replies Sent To** check box and specify in the text box the e-mail address to which you want the replies sent (see Figure 9.3). You can use the **Select Names** button to view your Contacts or Outlook Address Book and choose an e-mail address or addresses from the selected list.

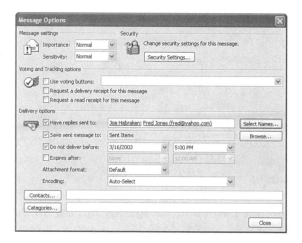

Figure 9.3   You can specify that responses to a message be sent to specific e-mail addresses (including or excluding your own).

- Select the **Save Sent Message To** check box to save your message to a folder other than the Sent Items folder. The Sent Items folder is specified by default, but you can choose to save the sent message to any folder in Outlook. Use the **Browse** button and the resulting Select Folder dialog box to specify a particular folder.

- Select the **Do Not Deliver Before** option to specify a delivery date. Click the down arrow in the text box beside the option to display a calendar on which you can select the day. This option enables you to send out e-mail even when you are not at your computer (or in the office). The message will be held in your Outbox folder until the specified time. If you are using Internet e-mail, your computer and Outlook must be up and running for the e-mail to be sent. In a corporate environment where Exchange Server is used, the e-mail is stored on the mail server and is sent automatically on the delivery date.

- Select the **Expires After** check box to include a day, date, and time of expiration. You can click the down arrow in the text box to display a calendar from which you can choose a date, or you can enter the date and time yourself. Messages marked to expire are made unavailable after the expiration date. This means the message is basically recalled from any computer where the message has not been read (this feature works only in networked environments using Microsoft Exchange Server).

The delivery options are really great in cases where someone other than you needs to keep track of the responses related to an e-mail message that you sent or in cases where you don't want to immediately deliver a message using the Do Not Deliver Before option. Using the Expire option means that people who have been on vacation won't have to read old messages that you have sent; they will no longer be available because of the expiration date.

Assigning Contacts to a Message

The Message Options dialog box also enables you to link a contact or contacts to a message. Linking a contact (or contacts) to a message allows you to view the message on that contact's Activities tab (when you are viewing the contact's actual record in the Contacts folder). The use of the Activities tab on a contact's record is discussed in Lesson 11, "Creating a Contacts List."

CAUTION

Do Contact Links and Categories Appear on Sent Messages? When you link contacts and categories to messages, you are actually just applying organizational tags to the e-mails. You can then view all the e-mail sent to a particular contact in the Contacts folder or sort sent e-mail by a particular category. The recipient of e-mail that you have tagged in this manner does not know that you created the link.

To assign a contact link to the message, click the **Contacts** button in the Message Options dialog box. The Select Contacts dialog box opens, showing all your contacts. Double-click a contact to add it to the Contacts box on the Message Options dialog box. Now the sent message is linked to a particular contact or contacts and can be accessed for later consideration when you are working with that contact or contacts in the Contacts folder.

Assigning Categories to a Message

Another option that Outlook provides for organizing sent messages is the use of categories. You can assign your messages to different categories, such as Business, Goals, Hot Contacts, Phone Calls, and so on. You set the category for a message in the Categories dialog box.

Categories   Categories offer a way of organizing messages to make them easier to find, sort, print, and manage. To find all the items in one category, choose **Tools**, **Find Items**. Click the **More Choices** tab, choose **Categories**, and check the category for which you're searching.

To assign a category, follow these steps:

1. In the Message Options dialog box, click the **Categories** button. The Categories dialog box appears (see Figure 9.4).

Figure 9.4   Organize your messages with categories.

2. To assign an existing category, select the category or categories that best suit your message from the Available Categories list. To assign a new category, enter a new category into the **Item(s) Belong to These Categories** text box, and then click the **Add to List** button.

3. Click **OK** to close the Categories dialog box and return to the Message Options dialog box.

TIP **Create Your Own Categories** If you want to create a new category to assign to your e-mail messages, click the **Master Category List** button on the Categories dialog box. The Master Category List dialog box appears. Type the name of the new category in the New category box, and then click **Add** (repeat as necessary). To return to the Categories dialog box, click **OK**. Your new categories appear in the Categories dialog box.

When you have set all the options for the current message, click the **Close** button to close the Message Options box and return to the message window.

The whole point of tagging sent messages with categories is so that you can view messages by category when you open the Sent Items folder. For example, you might want to quickly check the messages that have been tagged with the Competition category.

1. Use the Mail Favorite Folders group or the All Mail Folders group on the Navigation pane to open the Sent Items folder.

2. To view the messages by category (in the mail list), select View, point at Arrange By, and then select Categories. The messages will be arranged by category.

3. Click any of the categories to expand the list to view the messages in a particular category. If you want to expand all the categories, click the **View** menu, point at **Collapse/Expand Groups**, and then select **Expand All Groups**.

TIP **Categories Can Be Used to Find Messages** You can search for messages or other Outlook items that have been assigned a particular category using Outlook's Advanced Search feature. Finding Outlook items is discussed in Lesson 18, "Saving and Finding Outlook Items."

Using Message Flags

Another tool for tagging messages is a message flag. A message flag enables you to mark a message as important, either as a reminder for yourself or as a signal to the message's recipient. When you send a message flag, a red flag icon appears in the recipient's message list, and Outlook adds text at the top of the message telling which type of flag you are sending. In addition, you can add a due date to the flag, and that date appears at the top of the message.

The following list outlines the types of flags you can send in Outlook:

Call   No Response Necessary

Do Not Forward   Read

Follow Up	Reply
For Your Information	Reply to All
Forward	Review

Using these various flags is like sticking a brief note on the message that provides you with a clue as to what type of follow-up might be required by a particular message. Flagged messages show a colored flag (the color depending on the type of the flag) to the right of the message sender and subject when you view the message in your Inbox list or other mail list. To use a message flag, follow these steps:

1. Open a new message or existing message that you want to flag. In the message window, click **Actions**, point at **Follow Up**, and then select **Add Reminder**. The Flag for Follow Up dialog box appears (see Figure 9.5).

Figure 9.5   Flag a message to show its importance or as a reminder for your follow-up.

2. Click the **Flag To** drop-down arrow and choose the flag type you want to add to the message.

3. Click the **Due By** drop-down arrow and use the calendar that appears to enter a date into the text box. Use the **Time** drop-down box to set a specific time. Assigning a due date and time makes you act on the message as dictated by the flag by a particular date.

4. Click **OK** to return to the message window.

Marking messages with the Follow Up flag is a great way to remind yourself that you need to attend to a particular issue. All received messages that you flag can easily be viewed because they are listed in the For Follow Up Folder, which is accessed via the Mail Favorite Folders group. Flagging messages for your e-mail recipients helps them prioritize responses, so you receive the needed reply within a particular time frame.

TIP   **Flag Existing Messages with Colored Flags**   Existing messages can be flagged with different colored flags. This allows you to flag an e-mail without actually adding a particular reminder to it. Right-click on any message in any of your mail folders (such as the Inbox or Sent Mail) and point at Follow Up on the shortcut menu that appears. You can quickly add a red, blue, yellow, green, orange, or purple flag. If you want to remove an existing flag from a message, select **Clear Flag**.

When you double-click a flagged message (the flag appears to the right of the message as an icon when the message appears in the Inbox list) and open it in a message window (see Figure 9.6), the flag type (not the flag itself) appears at the top of the message as a gray banner, just above the From box.

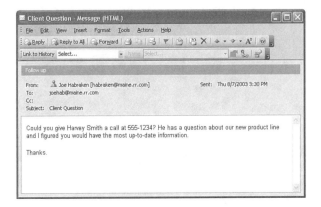

Figure 9.6   To view the type of flag attached, open the message.

Viewing the flag type on the message provides you with a quick reminder as to what your next action should be regarding the particular message.

Using the Outlook Address Books

In this lesson, you learn about different Outlook address books and how to import lists to Outlook from other applications.

Understanding the Outlook Address Books

Outlook has the capability to access different stores or lists of information that can provide you with people's e-mail addresses and other contact information, such as phone numbers and addresses. The address books that you can access include the Personal Address Book, your Contacts list, and other directory lists that are provided by other e-mail systems and communication servers. For example, in a corporate network, a Microsoft Exchange Server can provide you with a Global Address list that is shared by all users on the Exchange network. The e-mail addresses of any users on the network are then easily found in one resource.

 The Contacts List You might notice contacts in the list of address books; this list contains entries you create in your Contacts list. For more information about the Contacts list, see Lesson 11, "Creating a Contacts List."

Where your e-mail addresses and other contact information are stored depends on whether you are using Outlook on a corporate network that uses Active Directory (a network that deploys Microsoft Windows network servers), a network that uses Exchange Server, or as a standalone product where you use an Internet e-mail account. However, no matter where your contact information is kept, Outlook makes it easy for you to access your different address books using the Address Book feature.

 Using Address Books On a home computer Outlook provides the Contacts List as the primary location for contact information and e-mail addresses (although you may also have access to the Outlook Address Book, depending on your Outlook configuration). If you imported settings from another e-mail client such as Outlook Express, you may also have Personal Address Book or other directory. On a network using Exchange Server, corporate contact information is supplied by the Windows Active Directory, which is a database of all users on the network. In most cases it is a best practice to place your new contacts in the Contacts List instead of the Address Book.

Using the Address Book

The Address Book is basically a launch pad that allows you to access information lists (they are all considered address books) that contain e-mail addresses and other contact information. Because you create your own Contacts list, you always have this resource available, even if you aren't connected to a special network server and you access your e-mail by connecting to the Internet. You can find more information about building your Contacts list in Lesson 11, "Creating a Contacts List."

As already mentioned, Outlook also has the capability to access a number of different address lists. If Outlook is used as a mail client for the Microsoft Exchange Server mail system, Outlook will be able to access distribution lists as well as the entire Exchange Server e-mail catalog.

You can open the Address Book feature by clicking the **To** button or **Cc** button on a new message or by clicking the **Address Book** icon on the Outlook toolbar. After the Address Book dialog box is open (see Figure 10.1), you can use the **Show Names from the** drop-down list to select the specific address book (such as your Outlook Address Book or Contacts list) that you want to view.

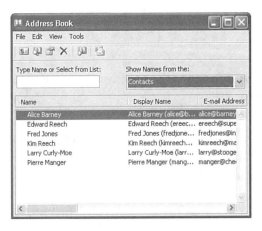

Figure 10.1 The Address Book provides access to your various e-mail address and contacts lists.

Finding Records in an Address Book

The Address Book dialog box also makes it easy for you to search through a particular address book for a particular person. In the Type Name box, begin to type the name of a contact you want to find in the list; as soon as you type enough of the contact's name for Outlook to find that particular contact, it will be highlighted in the list provided.

For cases where you want to search for a record or records by a particular character string (such as all records in the address book that have the last name of Smith), the Address Book provides you with a Find dialog box.

 Click the **Find Items** button on the Address Book toolbar. The Find dialog box appears as shown in Figure 10.2.

Figure 10.2   You can search a particular address book by keywords or text strings using the Find dialog box.

Type your search string into the Find Names Containing box. Then, click **OK** to run the search. The search results appear in the Address Book dialog box. Only the records that match your search parameters appear in the list.

Adding Records to an Address Book

You can also add records to any of the address books that you have access to. For example, you can add records to your Personal Address book or to your Contacts list directly in the Address Book window. Keep in mind that in a corporate environment, your network administrator probably controls some address books, such as the Global Address Book. This means that you won't be able to add information to these address books; you can use them only as resources to find information such as e-mail addresses.

To add a record to an address book that you do control:

1. In the Address Book dialog box, make sure that you have the address book selected that you want to add the new record to.

 2. Click the **New Entry** button on the Address Book toolbar. The New Entry dialog box appears (see Figure 10.3).

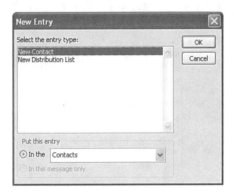

Figure 10.3   You can add new records to address books using the New Entry dialog box.

3. Use the **Put This Entry In the** drop-down box at the bottom of the New Entry dialog box to make sure that your new record ends up in the correct address book. To add a new record (a new contact, for example), click **New Contact** and then click **OK**.

 Distribution List   A distribution list allows you to create a record that includes the e-mail addresses for several people. This makes it easy to send e-mails to a group of people. You can create distribution lists in the New Entry dialog box. You will learn how to create distribution lists in the next lesson.

4. A blank record appears for your new entry. Enter the appropriate information for the new record, such as the person's name, e-mail address, and so on into the appropriate text boxes. When you have finished entering the information, click **OK** to save the new entry. In the case of new contacts added to the Contacts list, click the **Save and Close** button.

The blank records that open for your new entries look slightly different, depending on the address book in which you are creating the new record. In the case of new contacts (which is discussed in the next chapter), you can enter information for the new entry that includes the person's address, phone number, fax number, and even a Web page address. Some address books may allow you to enter only the name and e-mail address of the person.

TIP 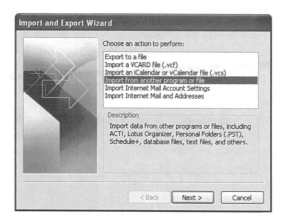 **Create a New Message from the Address Book Dialog Box**   If you opened the Address Book using the **Address Book** icon on the Outlook toolbar (or selected **Tools, Address Book**), you can open a new message for any of the contacts listed in one of the address books. Select the particular person, and then click the **New Message** icon on the Address Book icon. A new message opens addressed to that particular person.

Importing Address Books and Contact Lists

If you are migrating from another personal information manager or e-mail client and want to import your address book or Contacts list, Outlook contains different conversion filters for this purpose. Outlook even provides you with an Import/Export Wizard that walks you through the steps of importing address lists and address books from these other software packages.

To start the Outlook Import/Export Wizard, follow these steps:

1. Click **File**, and then select **Import and Export**. The Outlook Import and Export Wizard opens (see Figure 10.4).

Figure 10.4   The Import and Export Wizard walks you through the process of importing your old address books or information from other applications.

2. On the first wizard screen, you can choose to import e-mail and contacts information from another e-mail client, such as Outlook Express or Netscape, by selecting **Import Internet Mail and Addresses**. Then, click **Next**.

3. On the next screen, select the e-mail client, such as Outlook Express, that holds the information that you will import to Outlook (remember that this feature

imports e-mail messages and address information from the e-mail client to Outlook). Then, click **Next**.

4. The next wizard screen asks you to select the Outlook address book that will hold the imported information. Select the **Personal Address Book** option button or the **Outlook Contacts Folder** option button to specify the destination for the imported records. Additional option buttons on this screen allow you to specify how duplicate records are handled; select one of the following:

- **Replace Duplicates with Items Imported**: This option replaces any records currently in the address book with duplicates from the imported file.

- **Allow Duplicates to be Created**: Any duplicates currently in the address book are not overwritten during the import and duplicate records are placed in the address book.

- **Do Not Import Duplicate Items**: Any duplicate items found in the address book that is being imported are not imported into Outlook.

5. After making your selections, click **Finish**.

The e-mail messages and the e-mail address records are imported into the Outlook address book that you chose. A message appears letting you know how many records were imported. The address records are placed in the address book that you chose. Imported e-mail is placed in the appropriate Outlook folder, such as your Inbox and Sent Items folders.

 TIP **Importing Information from Database Programs** If you want to import address records or other information from programs such as Microsoft Access or Lotus Notes, select the Import from Another Program or File option on the initial Import and Export Wizard screen. The wizard then walks you through the steps of selecting the program and file that holds the data that you want to import. You will have the option of selecting the Outlook Contacts list or another address book, such as the Personal Address Book, to hold the information after it is imported.

Exporting Outlook Address Records

There might be occasions where you would like to take the records in one of your Outlook address books such as the Contacts list and export this information to another software package. For example, you may want to place all the records in your Contacts list in an Access database file (this is particularly useful in cases where you might be using Outlook to hold information about your customers or clients). Outlook records can be exported using the Import and Export Wizard.

Follow these steps:

1. Click **File**, and then select **Import and Export**. The Outlook Import and Export Wizard opens.

2. Select **Export to a File**, and then click **Next**.

3. On the next screen, you are provided with a list of file types that you can use for your export file (see Figure 10.5). If you want to export to another Microsoft Office application such as Microsoft Excel or Access, make the appropriate selection. If you want to export the information so that you can then import it into another e-mail client or contact management software package, your best bet is the Comma Separated Values (Windows) option. After selecting a file type, click **Next**.

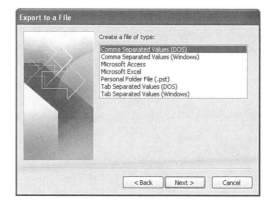

Figure 10.5   Select the file format for your export.

4. On the next screen, you are asked to select the Outlook folder that contains the information that you will export. Select the appropriate folder such as **Contacts**. Then, click **Next**.

5. On the next screen, type a name for the file in the Save Exported File As box. If you want to specify a specific location on your computer for the file to be saved, use the **Browse** button to open the Browse dialog box. When you have returned to the wizard (click **OK** to close the Browse dialog box), click **Next**.

6. The next screen lists the folder that will be exported. Click **Finish**. The export file is created.

After the information has been exported to the new file (it is actually copied to the new file; your Contacts list remains intact in Outlook), you can open the file using the destination application. For example, if you created an Access database using the export feature, you can open the file created using Microsoft Access.

Creating a Contacts List

In this lesson, you learn how to create and view a Contacts list and how to send mail to someone on your Contacts list. You also learn how to create a distribution list.

Creating a New Contact

You use the Contacts folder to create, store, and access your Contacts list. You can enter any or all of the following information about each contact:

- Name
- Job title
- Company name
- Address (street, city, state, ZIP code, and country)
- Phone (business, home, business fax, mobile)
- E-mail address
- Web page address
- Comments, notes, or descriptions
- Categories

 Contact In Outlook, a contact is any person or company for which you've entered a name, address, phone number, or other information. You can communicate with a contact in Outlook by sending an e-mail message, scheduling a meeting, sending a letter, and so on.

You also can edit the information at any time, add new contacts, or delete contacts from the list. To open the Contacts folder and create a new contact, follow these steps:

1. To open the Contacts folder, click the **Contacts** button on the Navigation pane. The Contacts folder opens.

2. To create a new contact, select **Actions** and then choose **New Contact**, or click the **New Contact** button on the Standard toolbar. The Contact dialog box appears, with the General tab displayed (see Figure 11.1).

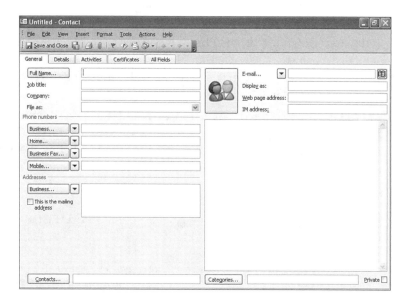

Figure 11.1   You can enter as much or as little information about each contact as you need.

3. Enter the contact's name into the Full Name text box. If you want to add more detailed information for the name, click the **Full Name** button to display the Check Full Name dialog box, and then enter the contact's title and full name (including first, middle, and last names) and any suffix you want to include. Click **OK** to close the Check Full Name dialog box and return to the Contact dialog box.

4. Press the **Tab** key to navigate from one field in this dialog box to the next. After the name field, the insertion point moves down to the contact's job title and then the company name. This information is optional.

5. In the **File As** drop-down box, enter or select the method by which you want to file your contact's names. You can choose **Last Name First** or **First Name First**, or you can enter your own filing system, such as by company or state.

> **TIP   Keep It Simple**   The default filing method for contacts is last name first, which makes it easy to quickly find the contact when you need it.

6. Enter the address into the Address box and choose whether the address is **Business**, **Home**, or **Other**. Alternatively, you can click the **Address** button to enter the street, city, state, ZIP code, and country in specified areas instead of all within the text block. You can add a second address (the Home address, for example) if you want. Address information is optional.

7. In the drop-down lists in the **Phone Numbers** area, choose the type of phone number—Business, Callback, Car, Home Fax, ISDN, Pager, and so on—and then enter the number. You can enter up to 19 numbers into each of the four drop-down boxes in the Phone area of the dialog box.

8. You can enter up to three e-mail addresses into the **E-Mail** text box. Click the drop-down arrow next to E-Mail to specify the e-mail address (E-Mail, E-Mail 2 or E-Mail 3) that you are currently entering. The box below the e-mail address allows you to enter how the e-mail address appears when you send a message to a person (for example, `smith@mail.com` could appear as Bob Smith); in the **Web Page Address** text box, enter the address for the company or contact's URL on the World Wide Web. You can also enter an **IM** (Instant Messenger) address for the contact.

> **TIP**   **Add a Picture of the Contact**   If you have a scanned or digital camera picture of the contact, you can add it by clicking the **Add Contact Picture** icon to the left of the E-mail and Web Page Address boxes.

As already mentioned, you can enter multiple e-mail addresses for the individual (using the drop-down arrow next to E-Mail). The first e-mail address that you enter for the individual serves as the default when you send e-mail to this individual.

> **TIP**   **Sending an E-mail to a Contact Using An E-mail Address Other than the Default**   When you address an e-mail to a particular contact using the Address Book, the default e-mail address is used. If you want to use a different e-mail address for the contact, double-click the contact's name in the Message To box and select one of the other e-mail addresses in the contact's Properties box.

> **TERM**   **URL (Uniform Resource Locator)**   The address for a Web page on the World Wide Web. A typical URL is written `http://www.companyname.com`, such as `http://www.quepublishing.com`.

9. In the comment text box (the large text box on the right of the Contact dialog box), enter any descriptions, comments, or other pertinent information. Then, select or enter a category to classify the contact.

10. After you have finished entering the new contact information, click the **Save and Close** button to return to the Contacts folder. You can also save the new contact by opening the **File** menu and choosing one of the following commands:

- **Save and Close**—Saves the record and closes the Contact dialog box.
- **Save and New**—Saves the record and clears the Contact dialog box so that you can enter a new contact.

TIP   **Other Tabs in the Contacts Window**   Most of the information that you need to enter for a contact is contained on the General tab. You can also add additional information, such as the person's nickname or spouse's name, on the Details tab. The Certificates tab allows you to specify a certificate to use to send encrypted e-mail to this particular contact (certificates are discussed in Lesson 9, "Setting Mail Options").

You can edit the information for a contact at any time by double-clicking the contact's name in the Contacts list; this displays the contact's information window. Alternatively, you can work on the fields in a record directly in the Contacts list window. Click within the information listed below a contact's name (such as the phone number or address) to position the insertion point in the text and then delete or enter text. Press **Enter** to complete the modifications you've made and move to the next contact in the list.

Viewing the Contacts List

By default, you see the contacts in an Address Cards view. You can quickly change the view by using the Current View options on the Navigation pane or by selecting from the current View list on the Outlook Advanced toolbar. The information you see displays the contact's name and other data, such as addresses and phone numbers. The contact's company name, job title, and comments, however, are not displayed by default. Figure 11.2 shows the Contacts list in the default Address Cards view.

You can use the horizontal scrollbar to view more contacts, or you can click a letter in the index (on the right side of the screen) to display contacts beginning with that letter in the first column of the list.

You can change how you view the contacts in the list by choosing one of the options from the Current View list on the Navigation pane:

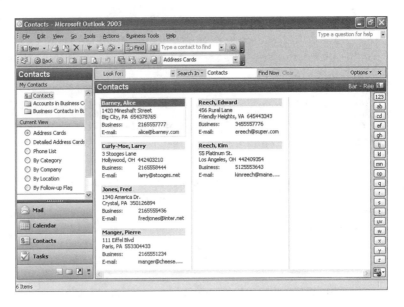

Figure 11.2   View your contacts in Address Cards view.

- **Address Cards**—Displays full name, addresses, and phone numbers of the contacts, depending on the amount of information you've entered, in a card format.

- **Detailed Address Cards**—Displays full name, job title, company, addresses, phone numbers, e-mail addresses, categories, and comments in a card format.

- **Phone List**—Displays full name, job title, company, File As name, department, phone numbers, and categories in a table, organizing each entry horizontally in rows and columns.

- **By Category**—Displays contacts in rows by categories. The information displayed is the same as what's displayed in a phone list.

- **By Company**—Displays contacts in rows, grouped by their company. The information displayed is the same as what's displayed in a phone list.

- **By Location**—Displays contacts grouped by country. The information displayed is the same as what's displayed in a phone list.

- **By Follow-Up Flag**—Displays contacts grouped by follow-up flags. The view also displays the due date for the follow-up that you specified when you marked the contact with a flag (flags are discussed in Lesson 8, "Saving Drafts and Organizing Messages," and can be assigned to Contacts in the same way they are assigned to e-mail messages).

TIP   **Accessing Shared Contacts**   If you are using a system that allows you to share Contacts with other users, you can access these shared contacts by clicking the **Open Shared Contacts** link at the bottom of the Current View list on the Navigation pane.

Viewing a Contacts Activities Tab

Although the Contacts folder provides different views for perusing the actual contacts in the Contacts list, these views really don't give you any indication of the messages that you have sent to a particular contact or the tasks that you might have assigned to a particular contact (assigning a task to a contact is covered later in this lesson).

You can view all the activities related to a particular contact on the contact's Activities tab. With the Contacts folder open, follow these steps:

1. Double-click a contact in the Contacts folder to open the contact.
2. Click the **Activities** tab on the contact's window. All the activities, such as sent and received e-mails and any assigned tasks, appear on the Activities tab (see Figure 11.3).

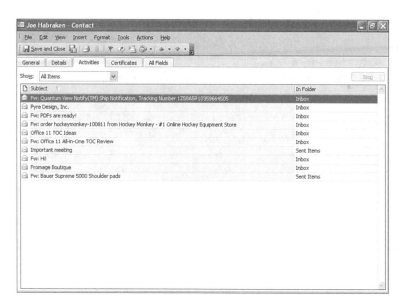

Figure 11.3   You can view all the activities related to a particular contact.

3. To see a subset of the Activities list, click the **Show** drop-down box. You can choose to view only E-Mail, Notes, or Upcoming Tasks/Appointments related to that particular contact (any items that you delete in the Activities list are removed from the list and the folder that contained them).

4. You open any of the items on the Activities list by double-clicking that item. Close an opened item by clicking its **Close (x)** button.

5. When you have finished viewing the activities related to a particular contact, you can close the contact's window.

Using Distribution Lists

If you find that you are sending e-mail messages or assigning tasks to multiple recipients, you might want to create a distribution list. A distribution list enables you to group several contacts. Then, to send an e-mail to all the contacts in the distribution list, you address the e-mail with the name of the distribution list.

The distribution lists that you create are listed in your Contacts folder. You can open an existing distribution list by double-clicking it. You can then add or delete members of the list.

To create a distribution list, follow these steps:

1. Select the **Actions** menu, and then select **New Distribution List**, or you can right-click an empty space of the Contacts folder and select **New Distribution List** from the shortcut menu that appears. The Distribution List dialog box appears (see Figure 11.4).

2. To enter a name for the distribution list, type the name into the Name box.

3. To add contacts to the distribution list, click the **Select Members** button, which opens the Select Members dialog box. Use the **Show Names From The** drop-down list to select the address book, such as the Contacts list, that you want to use to add names to the distribution list.

4. Select a contact to add to the distribution list, and then click the **Members** button to add the contact to the list (see Figure 11.5).

5. To select multiple contacts at once, hold down the **Ctrl** key, click the mouse on each contact, and then click the **Members** button.

6. When you have finished adding the contacts to the distribution list, click the **OK** button on the Select Members dialog box. You are returned to the Distribution List dialog box.

7. To save the distribution list, click the **Save and Close** button on the list's toolbar.

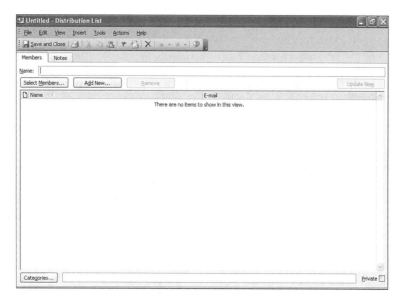

Figure 11.4   You can add contacts to a distribution list for mass e-mail mailings.

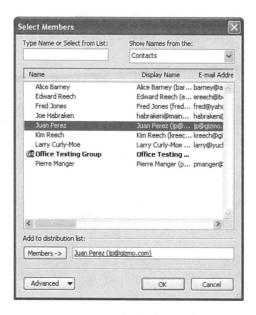

Figure 11.5   Add your contacts to the list from any of your address books.

After you have saved the distribution list, it appears as a contact listing in your Contacts folder. You can use the distribution list's name in the To box of an e-mail message to send the message to all the contacts listed in the distribution list.

If you find that you want to remove names from a distribution list, open the distribution list from the Contacts folder. In the Distribution List window, select the name or names you want to remove from the list. Then, click the **Remove** button. Make sure that you save the changes that you have made to the distribution list.

 TIP   **Add People to the Distribution List Who Are Not Current Contacts**   If you want to add names and associated e-mail addresses for people who are not in an address book to a distribution list, click the **Add New** button in the Distribution List window. The Add New dialog box allows you to enter a name and e-mail address for a new member of the distribution list.

Communicating with a Contact

You can send messages to any of your contacts, arrange meetings, assign tasks, or even send a letter to a contact from within Outlook (this also includes any distribution lists that you have created in the Contacts folder). To communicate with a contact, make sure you're in the Contacts folder. You do not need to open the specific contact's information window to perform any of the following procedures.

Sending Messages

To send a message to a contact, you must make sure you've entered an e-mail address in the General tab of the Contact dialog box for that particular contact. If Outlook cannot locate the e-mail address, it displays a message dialog box letting you know.

To send a message from the Contacts folder, select the contact, select **Actions**, and then select **New Message to Contact** (or you can right-click the contact or the distribution list and select **New Message to Contact** from the shortcut menu that appears).

In the Untitled - Message dialog box, enter the subject and message and set any options you want. When you're ready to send the message, click the **Send** button.

Scheduling a Meeting with a Contact

To schedule a meeting with a contact (or with contacts contained in a distribution list), you must first select the contact or distribution list (as with sending mail messages, the contacts involved must have an e-mail address). After you've selected the contact or list, select **Actions**, and then select **New Meeting Request to Contact** to open the Untitled - Meeting dialog box.

Enter the subject, location, time, date, and other information you need to schedule the meeting, and then notify the contact by sending an invitation (invitations are sent automatically during the process of creating the meeting). For more information about scheduling meetings, see Lesson 13, "Planning a Meeting."

Assigning a Task to a Contact

As with mail messages and meetings, for you to assign a task to an individual, that person's contact information must include an e-mail address. To assign a task to a contact, select the contact (tasks cannot be assigned to distribution lists), select **Actions**, and then select **New Task for Contact**. The Task dialog box appears. Enter the subject, due date, status, and other information, and then send the task to the contact; just click the Send Task button on the task's toolbar. For detailed information about assigning tasks, see Lesson 14, "Creating a Task List."

Sending a Letter to a Contact

If you want to create a hard copy letter and send it using "snail mail" (that is, sending it using the postal system), Outlook can help you create the letter based on the information in a particular Contact's record. Outlook uses the Microsoft Word Letter Wizard to help you create a letter to send to a contact. Within the Word Letter Wizard, you follow directions as they appear onscreen to complete the text of the letter.

CAUTION

Word Must Be Installed to Use the Word Letter Wizard   You must have Microsoft Word installed on your computer to take advantage of the feature discussed in this section. If you are running Outlook as a standalone version and have not installed other Office applications such as Word, you will not be able to take advantage of the integration features that Office offers to each component application such as Outlook.

To send a letter to the contact, select the contact in the Contacts folder and choose **Actions**, and then select **New Letter to Contact**. Word opens the Letter Wizard onscreen. The Letter Wizard helps you format and complete the letter (see Figure 11.6). Just follow the onscreen directions to create the letter.

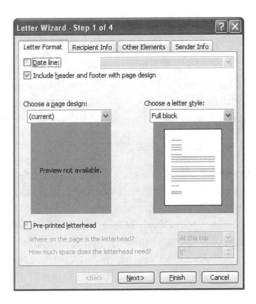

Figure 11.6 Use Word's Letter Wizard to create a letter to a contact.

Calling a Contact

Another obvious way to communicate with a contact is over the telephone. For Outlook to dial the phone number for you, your computer must be configured with a modem that can dial out for you. With the right equipment, Outlook makes it easy for you to make a phone call to a contact by dialing the phone number for you.

For Outlook to manage your calls, you must have a modem hooked to your computer that can dial out for you. If you're in a networked environment that has access to a network modem pool, you can also dial out using your computer. The line you dial out on, however, must also be accessible by your telephone.

To initiate a phone call to a contact, select the contact in the Contact list and follow these steps:

1. Select **Actions**, point at **Call Contact**, and then select the appropriate phone number from the cascading menu that appears (all the phone numbers for the selected contact appear, including business, home, and fax). You can also click the **Dial** button on the Standard toolbar and select the appropriate phone number from the drop-down list. In both cases, the New Call dialog box appears (see Figure 11.7).

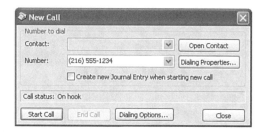

Figure 11.7   You can initiate phone calls from Outlook without having to dial the number.

2. Click the **Start Call** button to allow Outlook to dial the contact's phone number using your modem.

3. The Call Status dialog box appears. Pick up your phone and click the **Talk** button in the Call Status dialog box. This engages the phone and you can speak to your contact when they answer your call.

Using the Calendar

In this lesson, you learn how to navigate the Calendar, create appointments, and save appointments. You also learn how to insert an Office object, such as an Excel workbook, in an appointment.

Navigating the Calendar

You can use Outlook's Calendar to schedule appointments and create a task list. If necessary, Outlook can also remind you of appointments and daily or weekly tasks. You can schedule appointments months in advance, move appointments, cancel appointments, and so on. The Calendar makes it very easy to identify the days on which you have appointments.

To open the Outlook Calendar, click the **Calendar** button on the Navigation pane, or select the **Calendar** folder from the Folder List. Figure 12.1 shows the Calendar in Outlook.

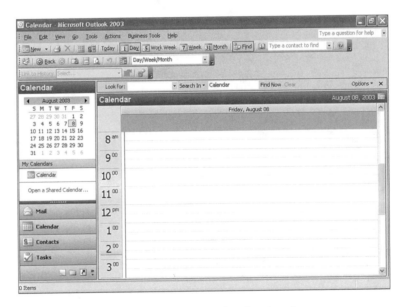

Figure 12.1   You can view all appointments and tasks at a glance.

By default the Calendar shows the current day and will list all the appointments that you have scheduled for that day. You can scroll through the hours of the day to view scheduled appointments.

On the Navigation pane, the current month is shown. To see the appointments for a day in the current month, click that day on the Calendar. If you want to see multiple days in the Appointment pane, select the first date on the Calendar and then hold down the Control key as you select other days. A column will appear for each day in the Appointment pane. If you want to move to a different month, use the navigation arrows on either side of the current month shown.

 TIP **Changing Calendar Views** You can change to different views of the Calendar by clicking the **Current View** drop-down arrow on the Advanced toolbar. Views including Active Appointments, Recurring Appointments, and By Category are available.

Another aspect of tracking activities in the Calendar is to be able to view tasks that you assigned to yourself or tasks that have been assigned to you by other users (creating tasks is discussed in Lesson 14, "Creating a Task List"). By default, tasks are not shown in the Calendar. To view the Task pane along with the Calendar, select the **View** menu, then select **Taskpad**. The Taskpad will be added to the Calendar. You can now track your appointments and tasks for a particular day (or days) simultaneously.

 TIP **Change the Date Quickly** To quickly go to today's date or to a specific date without searching through the Monthly Calendar pane, right-click in the Schedule pane and choose either **Today** or **Go to Date**.

Creating an Appointment

You can create an appointment on any day in the Outlook Calendar. When you create an appointment, you can add the subject, location, starting time, category, and even an alarm to remind you ahead of time.

Follow these steps to create an appointment:

1. On the Calendar in the Navigation pane, select the month and the date for which you want to create an appointment.
2. In the Schedule pane, double-click next to the time at which the appointment is scheduled to begin. The Untitled - Appointment dialog box appears, with the Appointment tab displayed (see Figure 12.2).

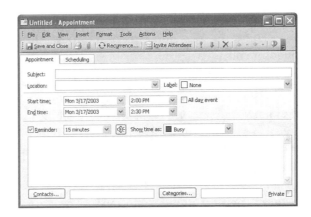

Figure 12.2   Enter all the details you need when scheduling an appointment.

3. Enter the subject of the appointment in the **Subject** text box (you can use a person's name, a topic, or other information).

4. In the **Location** text box, enter the meeting place or other text that will help you identify the meeting when you see it in your calendar.

5. Enter dates and times in the **Start Time** and **End Time** boxes (or click the drop-down arrows and select the dates and times).

TIP   **Autodate It!**   You can use Outlook's Autodate feature: Enter a text phrase such as **next Friday** into the Start time or End time box, and then press **Enter**; Outlook figures out the date for you and places it into the appropriate box.

6. If you want your PC to let you know when you're due for the appointment, select the **Reminder** check box and enter the amount of time before the appointment occurs that you want to be notified. If you want to set an audio alarm, click the **Alarm Bell** button and browse your hard drive to select a specific sound file for Outlook to play as your reminder.

7. From the **Show Time As** drop-down list, you can select how the appointment time block should be marked on the calendar. The default is Busy. But you can also block out the specified time as Free, Tentative, or Out of Office. The drop-down list uses different colors and patterns to specify each of the different appointment types.

8. In the large text box near the bottom of the Appointment tab, enter any text that you want to include, such as text to identify the appointment, reminders for materials to take, and so on.

9. Click the **Categories** button and assign a category (or categories) to the appointment.

10. Click the **Save and Close** button to return to the Calendar.

The Scheduling tab of the Appointment dialog box enables you to schedule a meeting with co-workers and enter the meeting on your calendar. See Lesson 13, "Planning a Meeting," for more information.

Scheduling a Recurring Appointment

Suppose you have an appointment that comes around every week or month or that otherwise occurs on a regular basis. Instead of scheduling every individual occurrence of the appointment, you can schedule that appointment in your calendar as a recurring appointment.

To schedule a recurring appointment, follow these steps:

1. With the Calendar selected on the Navigation pane, choose the **Actions** menu, and then **New Recurring Appointment**. The Appointment dialog box appears, and then the Appointment Recurrence dialog box appears on top of the Appointment dialog box (as shown in Figure 12.3).

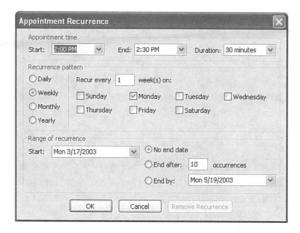

Figure 12.3   Schedule a recurring appointment once, and Outlook fills in the appointment for you throughout the Calendar.

2. In the Appointment Time area, enter the **Start** and **End** times for the appointment. Outlook calculates the duration of the appointment for you.

3. In the Recurrence Pattern area, indicate the frequency of the appointment: **Daily**, **Weekly**, **Monthly**, or **Yearly**. After you select one of these options, the rest of the Recurrence Pattern area changes to provide you with appropriate options, such as days of the week for a weekly recurring appointment or day-of-the-month options for a monthly recurring appointment.

4. Enter the day and month, as well as any other options in the Recurrence Pattern area that are specific to your selection in step 3.

5. In the Range of Recurrence area, enter appropriate time limits according to the following guidelines:

   - **Start**—Choose the date on which the recurring appointments begin.

   - **No End Date**—Choose this option if the recurring appointments are not on a limited schedule.

   - **End After**—Choose this option and enter the number of appointments if there is a specific limit to the recurring appointments.

   - **End By**—Choose this option and enter an ending date to limit the number of recurring appointments.

6. Click **OK** to close the Appointment Recurrence dialog box. The Appointment dialog box appears.

7. Fill in the Appointment dialog box using the steps in the "Creating an Appointment" section in this lesson. When you finish providing all the details for the recurring appointment, click the **Save and Close** button to return to the Calendar.

The recurring appointment appears in your calendar on the specified date and time. A recurring appointment contains a circular double-arrow icon to indicate that it is recurring.

 TIP **Make Any Appointment Recurring** If you have already started creating an appointment and then would like to make it recurring, click the **Recurrence** button on the appointment's toolbar. The Appointment Recurrence dialog box opens.

Planning Events

In the Outlook Calendar, an *event* is any activity that lasts at least 24 hours, such as a trade show or a conference. You can plan an event in the Calendar program to block off larger time slots than you would for normal appointments. In addition, you can schedule recurring events (such as a monthly seminar you attend that lasts all day).

To schedule an event, choose **Actions**, and then select **New All Day Event**. The Event dialog box appears (see Figure 12.4; it looks similar to the New Appointment dialog box).

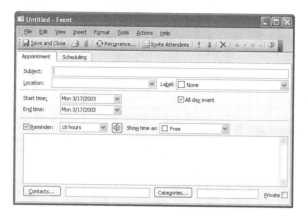

Figure 12.4   You can block out an entire day on the Calendar by scheduling an All Day Event.

Fill in the **Subject**, **Location**, **Start Time**, and **End Time** text boxes. Make sure the **All Day Event** check box is checked (that's the only difference between an event and an appointment). Click the **Save and Close** button to return to the Outlook Calendar. The appointment appears in gray at the beginning of the day for which you scheduled the event.

To schedule a recurring event, open a New All Day Event window and fill in the information as described earlier. To make the event recurring, click the **Recurrence** button in the Event window. The Event Recurrence dialog box opens; fill in the appropriate information and click **OK** (this dialog box is similar to the one for recurring appointments). Complete the information in the Event window, and then click the **Save and Close** button.

To edit an event or a recurring event, double-click the event in your calendar. As with a mail message or appointment, Outlook opens the event window so that you can change times, dates, or other details of the event.

Planning a Meeting

*In this lesson, you learn how to schedule a meeting, enter atten-
dees for a planned meeting, set the meeting date and time, and
invite others to the meeting.*

Scheduling a Meeting

Outlook enables you to plan the time and date of a meeting, identify the subject and
location of the meeting, invite others to attend the meeting, and identify resources
that will be needed for the meeting. You use the Calendar folder to plan and schedule meetings.

Meeting   In Outlook, a meeting is an appointment to which you invite people and
plan for the inclusion of certain resources.

Resources   Any equipment you use in your meeting, such as a computer, a slide
projector, or even the room itself.

To plan a meeting, follow these steps:

1. Click the icon for the Calendar on the Navigation pane. Then, in the Month
   pane, select the date on which you want to hold the meeting. To open a new
   meeting, select **Actions** and select **Plan a Meeting**. The Plan a Meeting dialog
   box appears (see Figure 13.1).

2. To enter the names of the attendees, click in the **All Attendees** list where it
   reads Click Here to Add a Name. You can type a name into the box and then
   press **Enter**. Continue adding new names as necessary. Names that you type
   into the list do not have to coincide with records in your Contacts list, but if
   you include new names, Outlook will not have an e-mail address for those particular attendees when invitations are sent for the meeting.

3. Another way (and perhaps a better way) to invite attendees to your meeting is
   to click the **Add Others** button, and then **Add from Address Book**. This allows
   you to choose the attendees from your Contacts list or other address book. This
   opens the Select Attendees and Resources dialog box, as shown in Figure 13.2.

You can add attendees and any resources needed for the meeting in this dialog box (select an attendee and then click the **Required** button). When you have finished adding attendees and resources, click **OK**.

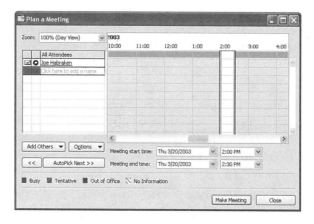

Figure 13.1   Choose the date and time of your meeting as well as the attendees.

Figure 13.2   Attendees of the meeting and resources that will be needed can be added using the Attendees and Resources dialog box.

TIP **A Word About Adding Resources** The Select Attendees and Resources dialog box enables you to add attendees and resources to a meeting. Because you probably don't list resources, such as overhead projectors, in your Contacts folder, you will have to type the resource names for the meeting as detailed in step 1 of this section (placing them in the Attendees list). In the case of resources, click the e-mail icon that appears to the left of the resource and select **Don't Send Meeting to This Attendee**. This keeps Outlook from trying to e-mail the resource. You can also use this option if you have listed attendees for the meeting who are not contained in your Contacts list.

4. To set a date for the meeting, open the **Meeting Start Time** drop-down list and select the date from the calendar, or just type the date into the text box. The ending date (in the **Meeting End Time** drop-down list) automatically shows the same date you set in the Meeting Start Time date box; you can change the End Time date if you want.

5. To set a start time for the meeting, do one of the following:
   - Open the **Meeting Start Time** drop-down list and select the time.
   - Type a time into the text box.
   - Drag the green bar in the Time Block pane to set the start time.

6. To set an end time for the meeting, do one of the following:
   - Open the **Meeting End Time** drop-down list and select the end time.
   - Type a time into the text box.
   - Drag the red bar in the Time Block pane of the dialog box to change the ending time of the meeting.

After you select the date and time for the meeting, notice that the time grid to the right of each attendee's name shows the currently scheduled appointments that they have on the day of the meeting. The times blocked out in each attendee's grid are based on appointments and meetings in their Outlook Calendar. Outlook is able to check your corporate network and check attendee availability by using their calendars. If you have a conflict between your meeting time and an attendee's appointment, you can adjust the time of your meeting and avoid availability conflicts.

TIP **Check the Availability of Internet Colleagues** On a corporate network that uses Exchange Server, it's easy for Outlook to check other people's calendars to see whether they have a conflict with a meeting that you are planning. If you aren't using Outlook in an Exchange Server environment, you can also avoid scheduling conflicts by having people you invite use Internet e-mail to subscribe to

Microsoft's Office Free/Busy Service. Outlook then periodically publishes a person's schedule to the service. All users who have subscribed can check the availability of participants using the service. The first time you schedule a meeting where other attendees' calendars cannot be accessed, a dialog box will open so that you can join the Free/Busy service. For more information about this service, go to `http://www.microsoft.com/office/` on the Web.

7. When you finish planning the meeting, click the **Make Meeting** button. The Meeting dialog box appears, allowing you to refine the meeting details. Details on using this dialog box are described in the next section.

Working Out Meeting Details

After you plan a meeting, Outlook enables you to send invitations, identify the subject of the meeting, and specify the meeting's location. You enter these details in the Meeting dialog box.

When you schedule a meeting, as described in the previous section, you finish by clicking the **Make Meeting** button in the Plan a Meeting dialog box. When you do that, Outlook displays the Meeting dialog box with the Appointment tab in front (see Figure 13.3).

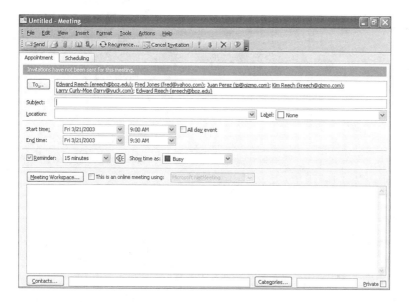

Figure 13.3   Specify the details related to the meeting in the Appointment tab of the Meeting dialog box.

Follow these steps to specify meeting details for a meeting you've already scheduled:

1. If you did not list the attendees in the Plan a Meeting dialog box, either click in the **To** text box and enter the names of the people that you want to attend the meeting, or click the **To** button to select the attendees from an address book or Contact list.

2. In the **Subject** text box, enter a subject for the meeting.

3. In the **Location** text box, enter a location for the meeting.

4. (Optional) You can change the starting and ending dates and/or times in the Appointment tab. You also can choose the Scheduling tab to view the meeting in a format similar to that of the Plan a Meeting dialog box; make any changes to attendees, time, dates, and so on in the Scheduling tab.

5. (Optional) Select the **Reminder** check box and enter a time for Outlook to sound an alarm to remind you of the meeting. See Lesson 12, "Using the Calendar," for more information on using the Reminder feature.

6. (Optional) Enter any special text you want to send the attendees in the text box provided beneath the Reminder fields.

TIP **Meetings Can Also Be Held On a Meeting Workspace Web Site** You can also schedule meetings on a SharePoint Portal server that supports Meeting Workspaces. Your company can deploy their own SharePoint server or you can subscribe to services provided by Microsoft. Click the Meeting Workspace button in the Meeting dialog box. The Meeting Workspace task pane will open on the right side of the Outlook Window. Click the Create button and then specify the Workspace Website that you are using for the meeting (this information will typically be supplied to you by your network administrator or by Microsoft when you subscribe to their SharePoint Services) and then configure other workspace parameters as needed. Click **OK** when the Workspace is configured for the meeting. Meeting Workspaces are similar to Document Workspaces, which are discussed in the first section of this book (Part I) in Lesson 1, "What's New in Office 2003."

7. After you have entered all the required information for the new meeting, you can send invitations. However, before you send the invitations, you might want to make sure that the recipients reply to your meeting invitation. Select the **Actions** menu and make sure that a selection check mark is next to **Request Responses**. If there isn't, click this selection to place a check mark next to it.

8. Now you can send the invitations; click the **Send** button. The meeting is saved and the Meeting dialog box closes.

Editing Meeting Details and Adding Attendees

You can edit the details of a meeting and change the date and time of the meeting at any time by opening the Meeting dialog box. Opening the Meeting dialog box also allows you to add attendees to the meeting.

Follow these steps:

1. In the Calendar folder, select the meeting date in the Monthly Calendar pane (any date that has scheduled appointments or meetings will be in bold on the Monthly Calendar pane). After you've opened the appropriate day, locate your appointment and double-click it to open it.

2. You can edit any information on the Appointment or Scheduling tabs. To see which contacts have responded to your meeting invitation, click the Tracking tab (see Figure 13.4).

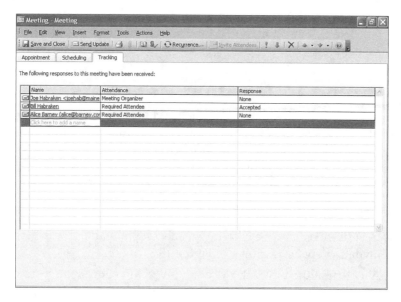

Figure 13.4 When you open an existing meeting, you can edit the settings for the meeting and view who has responded to your invitation.

3. You can also add additional attendees to your meeting. On either the Appointment tab or the Scheduling tab of the Meeting dialog box, use the **To** or **Add Others** buttons, respectively, to open the Select Attendees and Resources dialog box.

4. Open the **Show Names From The** drop-down list and choose either **Contacts** or another address book (you can also add a new record to the selected address book by clicking the **New** button; see Lesson 10, "Using the Outlook Address Books," for more information).

5. Select any name in the list on the left side of the dialog box and click the **Required** or **Optional** button to specify attendance requirements.

6. Click the **New** button to add resources to the list; then remember to notify the person who is in charge of those resources of your meeting.

7. Click **OK** to close the dialog box and add the new attendees to your list.

When you have finished editing the meeting and/or adding new attendees, click the **Save and Close** button on the meeting's toolbar. A message box appears asking you whether you want to send the new meeting details to your original and added attendees.

Because changing meeting details means that you also need to inform the attendees of any changes, click **Yes** to send the updated invitations. Attendees will be required to respond to the new invitation if the Request Responses option is selected on the Actions menu.

Responding to Meeting Requests

When a meeting is scheduled in Outlook and you are listed as one of the invitees, you will receive an invitation in the form of an e-mail message in your Inbox. This e-mail message provides the details of the meeting and also provides you with the ability to accept or decline the meeting invitation. If you accept the meeting invitation, the meeting is automatically added to your Outlook Calendar.

To accept a meeting invitation, follow these steps:

1. In your Inbox, double-click on the meeting invitation message. The Meeting invitation opens as shown in Figure 13.5.

2. A toolbar at the top of the Meeting invitation allows you to accept, tentatively accept (Tentative), or decline the meeting invitation. To accept the meeting, click the **Accept** button. A message box will appear detailing that you are accepting the meeting invitation and that it will be added to your Calendar. You are also provided with three options related to the sending of your acceptance response to the originator of the meeting; you must select one of the following:

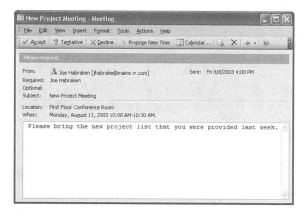

Figure 13.5   A new meeting invitation will be sent to you when you are included as a participant in a scheduled meeting.

- **Edit the Response Before Sending:** This allows you to include comments with the acceptance message that is sent to the meeting planner. Selecting this response opens a Meeting acceptance message box; you add your comments and then click **Send**.

- **Send Response Now:** An acceptance response will be sent immediately with no additional comments.

- **Don't Send a Response:** No acceptance response is sent to the meeting planner, but the meeting is still added to your calendar.

3. After selecting one of the three preceding options, click OK. Your response will be sent to the meeting planner (in the case of including comments with the acceptance, you will have to add the comments and then click **Send**).

TIP   **View the Proposed Meeting Date and Time on Your Calendar**   If you want to see how the proposed meeting fits into your overall schedule, click the **Calendar** icon on the Meeting invitation's toolbar. Your calendar will open showing the proposed meeting and other meetings and appointments you have scheduled on that day. When you have finished viewing your Calendar, switch back to your Inbox, by clicking the Mail icon on the Navigation pane.

In cases where you tentatively accept the meeting date (by selecting Tentative on the Meeting invitation's toolbar), the meeting is also added to your Calendar. You also have the same options related to the sending of the tentative response as were detailed in step 2. Declining the meeting means that the meeting is not placed on your Calendar; you will also have the same options as for an acceptance (as detailed in Step 2) for the sending of a rejection response.

In cases where you do not want to accept the meeting invitation but would like to propose a new time for the meeting, you can click the Propose New Time button on the Meeting invitation's toolbar. This opens the Propose New Time dialog box. It is very similar to the Plan a Meeting Dialog box shown in Figure 13.1. Edit the meeting start and ending times as needed and then click **Propose Time**. A New Proposed Time message box will open that allows you to comment on your proposed meeting time (see Figure 13.6). When you have finished adding comments to the message, click Send. The message will be sent to the original meeting planner.

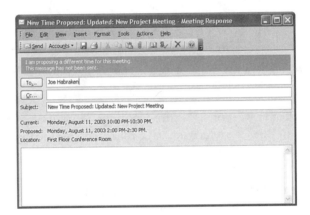

Figure 13.6   You can propose a new meeting time to the meeting planner.

Creating a Task List

In this lesson, you learn how to enter a task and record statistics about the task. You also learn how to assign tasks to other users.

Entering a Task

You can use the Tasks folder to create and manage tasks that you need to accomplish and don't want to forget about. You can list due dates, the status of a task, task priorities, and even set reminder alarms so your PC can keep you from forgetting a task entered in the list. To open the Tasks folder, click the **Tasks** button on the Navigation pane.

 TERM   **Tasks List**   A tasks list is a list of things you must do to complete your work, such as plan for a meeting, arrange an event, and so on. Various tasks might include making a phone call, writing a letter, printing a spreadsheet, or making airline reservations.

To enter a task, follow these steps:

1. In the Tasks folder, click the **New Task** button on the toolbar or double-click any empty space on the Tasks list. The Untitled - Task dialog box appears (see Figure 14.1).

> **TIP**   **Use the Menu to Start a New Task**   To start a new task from the Task folder menu, select **Actions**, **New Task**.

2. On the Task tab, enter the subject of the task into the **Subject** box.

3. Enter a date on which the task should be complete, or click the down arrow to open the **Due Date** drop-down calendar, and then choose a due date.

4. Enter a start date, or click the down arrow to open the **Start Date** drop-down calendar, and then choose a start date.

5. From the Status drop-down list, choose the current status of the project: **Not Started**, **In Progress**, **Completed**, **Waiting on Someone Else**, or **Deferred**.

6. In the Priority drop-down list, choose **Normal**, **Low**, or **High** priority.

7. In the % **Complete** text box, type a percentage or use the spinner arrows to enter one.

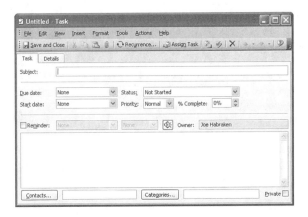

Figure 14.1 Enter data such as the subject of the task, due dates, and the task's priority.

8. (Optional) To set an alarm to remind you to start the task or complete the task, select the **Reminder** check box and enter a date and a time in the associated text boxes.

9. Enter any comments, descriptions, or other information related to the task in the comments text box located beneath the Reminder fields.

10. Click the **Categories** button and choose a category if you want to assign the task to a particular category, or enter your own category in the text box.

 TIP **Keeping a Task Private** If you are using Outlook on a corporate network that uses Exchange Server, your folders are kept on the Exchange Server and, to a certain extent, their contents can be viewed by other users. Select the **Private** check box if you don't want others to see information about a task that you are creating.

11. Click the **Save and Close** button when you're finished.

 TIP **Create Tasks in the Calendar Folder** You can also create tasks on the Task Pad of the Calendar folder. Double-click the Task Pad to start a new task.

Creating a Recurring Task

You can also create recurring tasks. For example, you might always have to hand in a weekly report every Friday; so why not schedule a recurring task that always reminds you to get that Friday report completed?

1. Double-click the Tasks Pad to open a new task window.

2. Enter the subject and other details of the task into the appropriate boxes.

3. 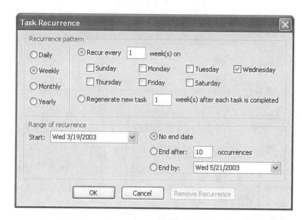 To make the task a recurring task, click the **Recurrence** button on the Task toolbar. The Task Recurrence dialog box opens.

4. You can set the recurrence of the task for Daily, Weekly, Monthly, or Yearly. After selecting an appropriate recurrence, such as Weekly, select how often the recurrence of the task occurs (see Figure 14.2).

Figure 14.2 Set the recurrence pattern for a recurring appointment.

5. When you have finished setting the recurrence options, click **OK** to return to the task window.

6. Click **Save and Close** to save the new task. Recurring tasks are labeled in the task folder by a small circular arrow icon (letting you know that the task recurs).

Assigning Tasks to Others

You can also assign tasks to others, such as co-workers or subordinates. Assigned tasks appear in your Task folder; however, the person you assign the task to has control over the task or the changing of the task parameters. To assign a task, follow these steps:

1. Double-click the Tasks pane to open a new task window.

2. Enter the subject and other details of the task into the appropriate boxes.

3. 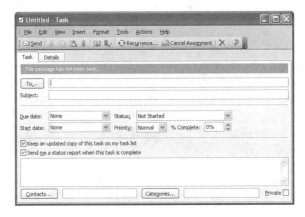 Click the **Assign Task** button on the Task toolbar. A To line is added at the top of the Task dialog box (see Figure 14.3).

Figure 14.3 Use the To button to assign the task to people in your Contacts list.

4. Click the **To** button on the task and the Select Task Recipient dialog box opens.

5. Select the appropriate address book, such as your Contacts list, and then assign the task to a person or persons. Click **OK** to close the Recipient dialog box after you have finished assigning the task.

6. Click **Send** on the Task toolbar to send the task to the recipient or recipients. A message appears saying that, because you no longer own this task (because you have assigned it), no reminder will be assigned to the task (meaning you are not reminded if the task becomes past due). Click **OK** to close the message box.

Outlook sends the new task to the recipient or recipients. The task is actually sent as an e-mail message. When the recipient opens the e-mail message in their Outlook Inbox, two buttons appear at the top of the message, Accept and Decline (see Figure 14.4).

When the **Accept** button is selected, a message box appears (see Figure 14.4). This message box lets the recipient know that a response will be sent to the originator of the task and that the task will be moved to the Task folder. To clear the message box, click **OK**. Now, when the recipient looks in the Outlook Task folder, they will find the task in the list.

If the task is declined (by clicking the **Decline** button), a message box appears saying that the task will be moved to the Deleted Items folder and that a message declining the task will be sent to the originator of the task (which in this case was you) and will appear in the originator's Inbox. Because a copy of the task is kept in your Task folder, you can open the task and assign it to another user.

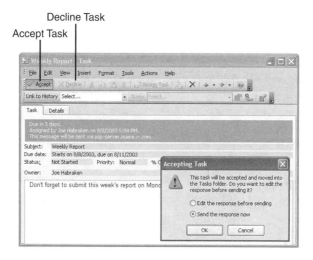

Figure 14.4   When a task recipient accepts the task, it is moved to their Task list.

Viewing Tasks

As in any Outlook folder, you can change how you view tasks in the list. When you have Tasks selected in the Navigation pane, a Current View pane is provided that gives you easy access to the different views for your tasks. You can also select the different views using the Current View drop-down list in the Standard toolbar. By default, the Tasks folder displays tasks in a Simple List view. Following is a description of the views you can use to display the Tasks folder:

- **Simple List**—Lists the tasks, completed check box, subject, and due date.
- **Detailed List**—Displays the tasks, priority, subject, status, percent complete, and categories.
- **Active Tasks**—Displays the same information as the detailed list but doesn't show any completed tasks.
- **Next Seven Days**—Displays only those tasks you've scheduled for the next seven days, including completed tasks.
- **Overdue Tasks**—Shows a list of tasks that are past due.
- **By Category**—Displays tasks by category; click the button representing the category you want to view.

- **Assignment**—Lists tasks assigned to you by others.
- **By Person Responsible**—Lists tasks grouped by the person who assigned the tasks.
- **Completed Tasks**—Lists only those tasks completed, along with their due dates and completion dates.
- **Task Timeline**—Uses the Timeline view to display tasks by day, week, or month. Figure 14.5 shows the tasks assigned within one week.

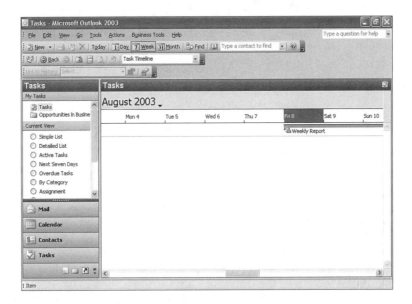

Figure 14.5 You can view your tasks in different views, such as the Task Timeline view.

Save What Settings? Depending on the changes you make to a view, Outlook might display the Save View Settings dialog box asking whether you want to save the view settings before you switch to a different view. Generally, you'll want to discard the current view settings and leave everything the way you found it.

CAUTION

Managing Tasks

When working with a task list, you can add and delete tasks, mark tasks as completed, and arrange the tasks within the list. You also can perform any of these procedures in most of the task views described in the previous sections. For information about printing a task list, see Lesson 17, "Printing in Outlook."

- To edit a task, double-click the task in the list. The Task dialog box appears.

- To mark a task as completed, click the check box in the second column from the left, or right-click the task and choose **Mark Complete** from the shortcut menu. Outlook places a line through the task.

- To delete a task, right-click the task and choose **Delete** from the shortcut menu.

- To assign an existing task to someone else, right-click the task and choose **Assign Task** from the shortcut menu. Fill in the name of the person to whom you want to assign the task (or use the To button to bring up the Select Task Recipient dialog box); after assigning the task, click the **Send** button to send the task to the recipient or recipients.

Recording Statistics About a Task

You can record statistics about a task, such as time spent completing the task, billable time, as well as other information, for your own records or for reference when sharing tasks with your co-workers. This feature is particularly helpful when you assign tasks to others; you can keep track of assigned tasks and find out when they're completed.

To enter statistics about a task, open any task in the task list and click the **Details** tab. Figure 14.6 shows a completed Details tab for a sample task.

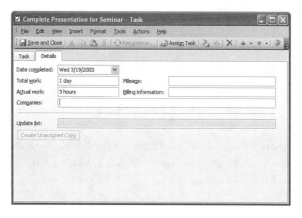

Figure 14.6   Fill in the statistics related to the completion of the task for later reference.

The following list describes the text boxes in the Details tab and the types of information you can enter:

- **Date Completed**—Enter the date the task was completed, or click the arrow to display the calendar and choose the date.
- **Total Work**—Enter the amount of time you expect the task to take.
- **Actual Work**—Enter the amount of time it actually took to complete the job. You can then compare the estimated time that you placed in the Total Work box with the actual time that it took (entered in the Actual Work box).
- **Mileage**—Enter the number of miles you traveled to complete the task.
- **Billing Information**—Enter any specific billing information, such as hours billed, resources used, charges for equipment, and so on.
- **Companies**—Enter the names of any companies associated with the contacts or with the project in general. Use semicolons to separate multiple names.
- **Update List**—Automatically lists the people whose task lists are updated when you make a change to your task. This is available only in situations where you are working in a Microsoft Exchange Server environment.
- **Create Unassigned Copy**—Copies the task so that it can be reassigned; use the button to send a task to someone other than an original recipient. This button is available only on tasks that you have assigned to other people.

Tracking Tasks

Outlook also enables you to track tasks that you assigned to others. You can even receive status reports related to a task that you have assigned to another person or persons. To track tasks, follow these steps:

1. On the **Tools** menu, click **Options**; the Options dialog box appears. Click the **Preferences** tab.
2. On the Preferences tab, click the **Task Options** button. The Task Options dialog box opens (see Figure 14.7).
3. To automatically track the progress of new tasks you assign to others, make sure a check mark appears in the **Keep Updated Copies of Assigned Tasks on My Task List** check box.
4. To automatically receive notification when an assigned task is complete, select the **Send Status Reports When Assigned Tasks Are Completed** check box.
5. After you've made your selections, click **OK** to close the Task Options dialog box, and then click **OK** to close the Options dialog box.

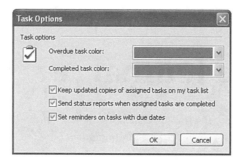

Figure 14.7   Make sure that you set task options so that you receive updated tasks and status reports for assigned tasks.

TIP   **Color Your Task List**   You can also set color options for overdue and completed tasks on the Task Options dialog box. Click the **Tools** menu, select **Options**, and from the Preferences tab, click the **Task Options** button.

Using the Journal

In this lesson, you learn how to create Journal entries manually and automatically and how to change views in the Journal.

Creating a Journal Entry

You can create a record of various actions so that you can track your work, communications, reports, and so on. In the Journal, you can manually record any activities, items, or tasks you want. For example, you might want to record the results of a telephone conversation.

You also can automatically record e-mail messages, meeting requests, meeting responses, task requests, and task responses. Additionally, you can automatically record activity related to documents created in the other Office applications: Access, Excel, PowerPoint, and Word.

The Journal is especially useful for recording information related to phone calls to and from people in your Contacts list. You can record information about the call and you can also time the conversation and enter its duration (which is very useful information if you need to record billable-hours information for a particular client).

 Journal   A folder within Outlook that you can use to record interactions, phone calls, message responses, and other activities important to your work.

Configuring the Journal

As already mentioned, you can automatically or manually record items in your Journal. Before you can take advantage of the Journal, however, you must configure it as to the type of events that you want the journal to record automatically. These settings are selected in the Journal Options dialog box (see Figure 15.1).

To open the Journal Options dialog box and configure the Journal, follow these steps:

1. Select **Tools** and then **Options**. On the Preferences tab of the Options dialog box, click the **Journal Options** button (it is in the lower half of the Preferences tab).

2. In the **Automatically Record These Items** list, check those items you want Outlook to automatically record in your Journal. (The items recorded correspond with the people selected in the list of contacts in step 3.)

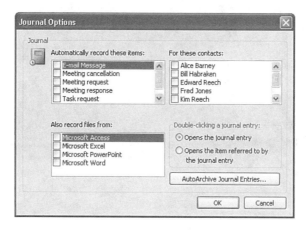

Figure 15.1   Click the check boxes in the Journal Options dialog box to have actions and events recorded automatically.

3. In the **For These Contacts** list, check any contacts you want automatically recorded in the Journal. Outlook records any items selected in step 1 that apply to the selected contacts.

4. In the **Also Record Files From** list, check the applications for which you want to record Journal entries. Outlook records the date and time you create or modify files in the selected programs.

5. When you have completed your selections, click the **OK** button. You will be returned to the Options dialog box, click **OK** to close it.

Now you can start the Journal. Click the Folder list button at the bottom of the Navigation pane. In the Folder list, click the **Journal** icon. The Journal opens and it is now ready to automatically record the items that you chose in the Journal Options dialog box.

Suppose that you wanted Excel sessions to be automatically recorded in the Task list. You would make sure that Excel was selected in step 3. Then, whenever you work in Excel, that event is recorded. Figure 15.2 shows a Journal entry for an Excel event.

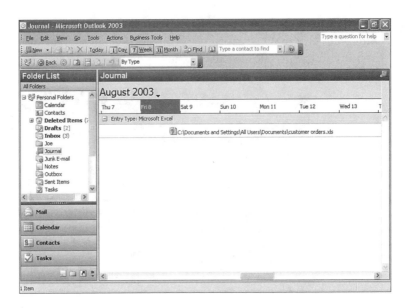

Figure 15.2 Journal entries for applications, such as Excel, are recorded automatically when you work in that application.

Recording an Entry Manually

You can also record items in the Journal manually using existing items such as e-mail messages. For example, you might add an e-mail message to the Journal that is not normally recorded (because you didn't select messages from that particular contact as something you want automatically recorded in the Journal).

To create a Journal entry manually, follow these steps:

1. In the Inbox folder (or any other folder in Outlook), select the item you want to record in the Journal and drag it onto the Journal folder icon in the Folder List. The Journal Entry dialog box appears (see Figure 15.3).

2. The information in the Subject, Entry Type, Contacts, and Company boxes and some other information is entered for you from the selected task, contact, or other selected item. However, you can change any of the statistics you want by entering new information into the following text boxes, drop-down lists, and buttons:

   - **Subject**—Displays the title or name of the Journal item.
   - **Entry Type**—Describes the item based on its point of origin, such as a Word document, a meeting or appointment, and so on.
   - **Company**—Lists the company or companies associated with the contacts.

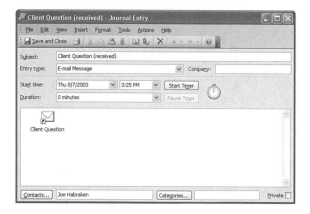

Figure 15.3 Drag an item onto the Journal icon, and the Journal Entry dialog box opens.

- **Start Time**—Displays the date and time of the meeting, appointment, or other item.

- **Start Timer**—Like a stopwatch, the timer records the time that passes until you click the Pause Timer button.

- **Pause Timer**—Stops the timer.

- **Duration**—Enter the amount of time for completing the item.

- **Shortcut icon**—This is a shortcut icon to the item you originally dragged onto the Journal icon to create a new entry (such as a Calendar appointment, a contact, or a message). You can actually open the item by double-clicking the shortcut icon. The icon appears in the large box below the Duration text box.

- **Contacts**—Lists the name(s) of any attendees, contacts, or other people involved with the selected item.

- **Categories**—Enter or select a category that you want to assign to the Journal entry.

3. Click **Save and Close** to complete the Journal entry.

If you want to create a new Journal entry, but you don't have a contact, a task, an e-mail, or other item that you want to use to create the entry, you can create a Journal entry from scratch (meaning it is not associated with any existing Outlook item such as an e-mail message). For example, you might want to create a Journal entry that holds information related to a phone call that you have made. Follow these steps:

1. Change to the Journal folder.

2. Choose **Actions**, and then select **New Journal Entry** or double-click any empty portion of the Journal pane. The Journal Entry dialog box appears.

3. Enter the subject for your new journal entry.

4. Select the type of entry you want to make; in this case, the default is already set to Phone Call. Leave the Journal Entry dialog box open on your desktop.

5. Make your phone call; you can actually have Outlook dial the phone call for you using the **AutoDialer** icon, which can be accessed on the toolbar in the Contacts folder (click the **Dial** icon's drop-down arrow, and then select **New Call**; use the **Contacts** drop-down list in the New Call dialog box to specify the contact that you want to call, and then click **Start Call**).

6. When your call is answered, click the **Start Timer** button in the Journal Entry dialog box. Type any notes that you want to record during the phone conversation in the entry's text box.

7. When you finish the call, click the **Pause Timer** button. Notice that the duration of the call is entered in the Duration box. To save the Journal entry, click the **Save and Close** button.

Changing Journal Settings

You might find that when you started the Journal for the first time, you didn't configure that many events to be automatically recorded by the Journal. No problem; you can return to the Journal settings and change the options related to the automatic recording items in the Journal.

In the Journal folder, choose **Tools**, **Options**. The Options dialog box appears. Click the **Preferences** tab if necessary, and then click the **Journal Options** button. The Journal Options dialog box appears.

You can also choose to have your Journal entries AutoArchived. Click the **AutoArchive Journal Entries** button, and then choose a folder on your computer where you want to have the Journal Archive file stored (selecting the default folder is your best bet). Then, click **OK** to complete the process (for more information about the AutoArchive feature, see Lesson 19, "Archiving Items").

When you have finished making changes to the Journal options, click **OK** to close the Journal Options dialog box. Then, click **OK** to close the Options dialog box.

Viewing Journal Entries

By default, the Journal folder displays information in the Timeline view and By Type, as shown in Figure 15.4. However, you can display the entries in various views, as described in the following list. To select a particular view, click the **Current View** drop-down button on the Advanced toolbar.

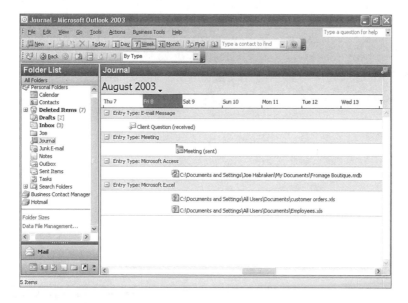

Figure 15.4   The default Journal view is the Timeline view.

TIP   **Save Settings?**   As in other views, Outlook might display the Save View Settings dialog box to ask whether you want to save the view settings before you switch to a different view. You're probably getting used to this dialog box by now.

- **By Type**—In Timeline view, this option groups Journal entries by type, such as e-mail messages, meetings, Word documents, and so on. Double-click a type to display its contents, and then position the mouse pointer over an entry to view its contents or name. When you switch to the Journal in the Type view, a Journal Options dialog box appears. This dialog box allows you to specify which e-mail messages will be recorded in the Journal, based on the contact they are received from. This dialog box also allows you to select which application use will also be recorded in the Journal, such as Excel, Word, or Access.

- **By Contact**—In Timeline view, this displays the name of each contact that you selected in the Options dialog box. Double-click any contact's name to view recorded entries.
- **By Category**—If you've assigned categories to your Journal entries and other items, you can display your Journal entries by category in the Timeline view.
- **Entry List**—Displays entries in a table with columns labeled Entry Type, Subject, Start, Duration, Contact, and Categories.
- **Last Seven Days**—Displays entries in an entry list but includes only those entries dated within the last seven days.
- **Phone Calls**—Lists all entries that are phone calls.

Using Outlook Notes

In this lesson, you learn how to create, sort, and view notes.

Creating Notes

If you've ever used a Post-it note to remind yourself of tasks, ideas, or other brief annotations, Outlook's Notes are for you. Notes are similar to paper sticky notes. You can use Notes to write down reminders, names, phone numbers, directions, or anything else you need to remember. In Outlook, all notes are kept in the Notes folder. You'll have to remember to look at the folder so you can view your notes.

 TIP **The Long and Short of It** You can enter pages and pages of text if you want. As you type, the page scrolls for you; use the arrow keys and the Page Up and Page Down keys to move through the note's text. Keep in mind, however, that the purpose of the note is a quick reminder, or information that you will eventually transfer to one of the other Outlook items, such as an appointment or task.

To create a note, click the **Notes** button on the Navigation pane and then follow these steps:

1. In the Notes folder, click the **New Note** button on the Outlook Standard toolbar or double-click an empty spot in the Notes pane. A new note appears, ready for you to type your text.
2. Enter the text for your note (see Figure 16.1).
3. When you finish, click the **Close** (**x**) button to close the note. You can reopen a note and edit the text as you need to.

If you press Enter after entering text in the note, you create a line break and you create a title, of sorts, at the same time. Only the text before the hard return displays when the note is closed. If you do not add a hard return but enter the note text so that it automatically wraps from line to line, the entire note text appears below the note in Icons view.

Notes already entered

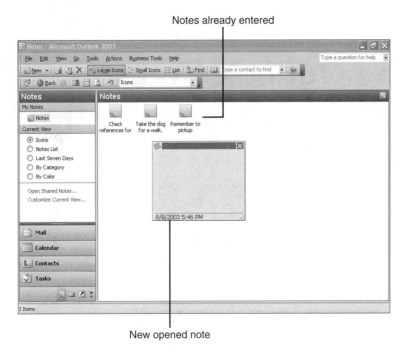

New opened note

Figure 16.1   A note automatically includes the date and time it was created.

Setting Note Options

You can change the default color and size of your notes. You also can change the default font used for your notes. To set note options, follow these steps:

1. In the Notes folder (or in any of the Outlook folders), choose **Tools**, **Options**. The Options dialog box appears. On the Preferences tab, click **Notes Options**; the Notes Options dialog box appears (see Figure 16.2).

Figure 16.2   You can customize your notes.

2. The Notes Options dialog box enables you to change the color, size, and font for your notes. Using the Color drop-down box, you can change the color to yellow, blue, green, pink, or white. The default is yellow.

3. Open the **Size** drop-down list and choose **Small**, **Medium**, or **Large** for the size of the notes. The default is Medium.

4. To change the font, click the **Font** button. The Font dialog box appears. Change the font, font style, size, color, and other options, and then click **OK**.

Managing Individual Notes

To open an existing note, double-click it in the Notes folder. You can edit the text in an open note the same as you would edit any text. To move a note, drag its title bar. You can delete, forward, or print notes; you can change the color of individual notes; and you can specify categories for your notes. You can also drag the notes to the Windows desktop and arrange them there.

Click an open note's Control Menu button (click the very upper left of the note) to display a menu with the following commands:

- **New Note**—Creates a new note but leaves the first note open.
- **Save As**—Enables you to save the note and its contents.
- **Delete**—Deletes a note and its contents. (You also can delete a note by selecting it in the Notes list and pressing the **Delete** key.)
- **Forward**—Enables you to send the note as an attachment in an e-mail message.
- **Cut, Copy, Paste**—Enables you to select text from the note and cut or copy it to the Clipboard. The Paste command enables you to paste items on the Clipboard at the insertion point in the note.
- **Color**—Choose another color for the individual note.
- **Categories**—Enter or choose a category.
- **Print**—Print the contents of the note.
- **Close**—Closes the note. (You can also click the **Close** (<u>X</u>) button in the note's title bar.)

Viewing Notes

The Notes folder provides various views for organizing and viewing your notes. The default view is Icons, but you can change the view using the Current View pane on the Navigation pane or the Current View drop-down list on the Advanced toolbar. Figure 16.3 shows the Notes folder in the default view.

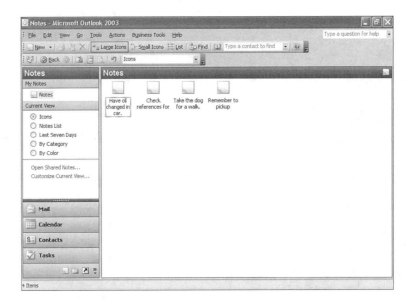

Figure 16.3   This view displays the notes in Icons view.

You can choose to display your Notes folder in any of the following views:

- **Icons**—Displays the notes as note icons with the message (or a portion of the message) displayed below the icon.

- **Notes List**—Displays the notes in a list, showing the title and note contents in the Subject column, the creation date and time, and the categories.

- **Last Seven Days**—Displays all notes written in the last seven days, by subject, creation date, and categories.

- **By Category**—Displays the categories; double-click a category to show its contents.

- **By Color**—Displays notes by their color. Double-click a color to display the notes.

Printing in Outlook

In this lesson, you learn how to print items in Outlook, change the page setup, preview an item before printing it, and change printer properties.

Choosing Page Setup

In Outlook, before you print, you choose the print style you want to use. Each folder—the Inbox, Calendar, Contacts, and so on—offers different print styles, and each style displays the data on the page in a different way.

 Page   In Outlook, this is the area of the paper that will actually be printed on. You might, for example, print two or four pages on a single sheet of paper.

 Print Style   The combination of paper and page settings that control printed output.

You can choose from Outlook's built-in print styles, modify the default print styles, or create your own print styles. These lists show the default print styles available for each folder. To access the print styles for a particular item, select **File**, **Print**. The Inbox, Contacts, and Tasks use the Table style and the Memo style; the Journal and Notes use only the Memo style.

 • **Table Style**—Displays data in columns and rows on an 8 1/2×11 sheet, portrait orientation, 1/2-inch margins.

 • **Memo Style**—Displays data with a header of information about the message and then straight text on an 8 1/2×11 sheet, portrait orientation, 1/2-inch margins.

The Calendar folder provides the Memo style as well as the following styles:

 • **Daily Style**—Displays one day's appointments on one page on an 8 1/2×11 sheet, portrait orientation, 1/2-inch margins.

 • **Weekly Style**—Displays one week's appointments per page on an 8 1/2×11 sheet, portrait orientation, 1/2-inch margins.

• **Monthly Style**—Displays one month's appointments per page on an 8 1/2×11 sheet, landscape orientation, 1/2-inch margins.

 • **Tri-fold Style**—Displays the daily calendar, task list, and weekly calendar on an 8 1/2×11 sheet, landscape orientation, 1/2-inch margins.

 • **Calendar Details Style**—Shows the currently displayed Calendar items and the body text of each item (such as an appointment) in a list format.

The Contacts folder provides the Memo style as well as the following styles:

 • **Card Style**—Two columns and headings on an 8 1/2×11 sheet, portrait orientation, 1/2-inch margins.

 • **Small Booklet Style**—One-column pages that print the contacts in a format similar to mailing labels by placing multiple contacts on a page. This style can be printed in Portrait or Landscape mode.

 • **Medium Booklet Style**—One column that equals 1/4 of a sheet of paper. Four pages are on one 8 1/2×11 sheet of paper, portrait orientation, with 1/2-inch margins.

 • **Phone Directory Style**—One column, 8 1/2×11 sheet of paper, portrait orientation, with 1/2-inch margins.

CAUTION

Will Page Setup Change My View? No matter how you set up your pages, it will not affect your view of tasks, calendars, or other Outlook items onscreen. Page setup applies only to a print job.

You can view, modify, and create new page setups in Outlook. To view or edit a page setup, follow these steps:

1. Change to the folder for which you're setting the page.

2. Choose **File** and then point at **Page Setup**. A secondary menu appears that lists the available print types.

3. Select the print type you want to view or edit, and the Page Setup dialog box appears (see Figure 17.1).

4. Click the **Format** tab to view and/or edit the page type, to choose options (in some cases), and to change fonts.

5. Click the **Paper** tab to view and/or edit paper size, page size, margins, and orientation.

6. Click the **Header/Footer** tab to view and/or edit headers for your pages.

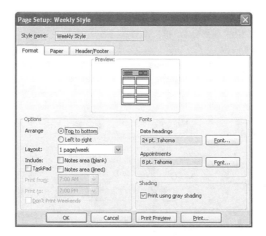

Figure 17.1 Customize the print style to suit yourself.

Previewing Before Printing

To make sure an item looks the way you want it to look, you can choose to preview it before printing it. If you do not like the way an item looks in preview, you can change the page setup.

Open the folder that contains the item that you want to preview. You can then open the item in the Print Preview view in any of the following ways:

- Click the **Print Preview** button in the Page Setup dialog box.
- Choose **File** and then select **Print Preview**.
- Click the **Print Preview** button on the Advanced toolbar.
- Click the **Preview** button in the Print dialog box.

Figure 17.2 shows a calendar in Print Preview. You can change the page setup by clicking the **Page Setup** button; the Page Setup dialog box appears. Click the **Print** button to send the job to the printer. Click the **Close** button to exit Print Preview and return to the Outlook folder.

 TIP **Enlarge the View** When the mouse pointer looks like a magnifying glass with a plus sign in it, you can click to enlarge the page. When the mouse pointer looks like a magnifying glass with a minus sign in it, you can click to reduce the view again.

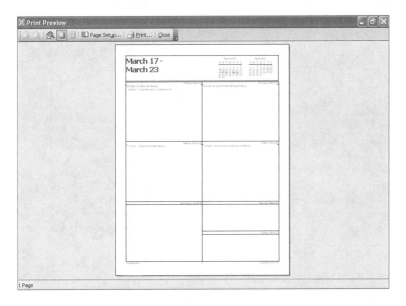

Figure 17.2 Preview the item before printing it.

Printing Items

After you choose the print style and preview an item to make sure it's what you want, you can print the item. You can indicate the number of copies you want to print, select a printer, change the print style or page setup, and set a print range.

When you're ready to print an item, follow these steps:

1. Choose **File**, and then select **Print** or click the **Print** button on the Standard toolbar. The Print dialog box appears, as shown in Figure 17.3.

2. Your default printer appears in the Printer area of the dialog box. If you have a different printer connected to your system that you would like to use, choose a different printer from the **Name** drop-down list.

3. In the Print Style area, choose a print style from the list. You also can edit the page setup (with the **Page Setup** button) or edit or create a new style (with the **Define Styles** button).

4. In the Copies area of the dialog box, choose **All**, **Even**, or **Odd** in **Number of Pages**, and enter the number of copies you want to print. This function is useful if you are going to print on both sides of the paper (this is called manual duplexing). You print the even pages, and then flip the sheets over in your printer and print the odd pages. Click the **Collate Copies** check box if you want Outlook to automatically assemble multiple copies.

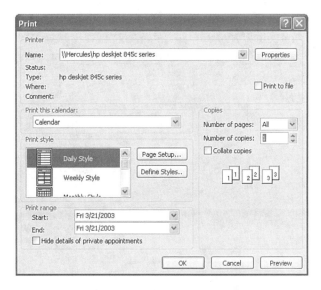

Figure 17.3 Set the printing options before printing the item.

5. Set the print range with the options in that area. (The Print Range options vary depending on the type of item you're printing.)

6. Click **OK** to print the item.

Printing Labels and Envelopes

A handy Outlook feature is the capability to print mailing labels and envelopes from your Contacts list. To take advantage of this feature, you also need to have Microsoft Word installed on your computer. Creating form letters, mailing labels or envelopes is called a *mail merge*. Basically, in Word, you create a main document (such as mailing labels, envelopes, and so on) that holds field codes that relate to the information you keep on each contact, such as name or address.

To actually start the merge process, open your Contacts folder and select **Tools**, **Mail Merge**. The Mail Merge Contacts dialog box opens (see Figure 17.4) and allows you to specify both the contacts for the merge and the Word document into which the contact information is merged. Using the option buttons at the top of the dialog box, you can specify that all the contacts or selected contacts are included in the mail merge. If you want to have only certain fields included in the mail merge, you can create a custom view of your Contacts folder (discussed in Lesson 3, "Using Outlook's Tools") before starting the Mail Merge.

After you specify the various options in the Mail Merge Contacts dialog box (see tip that follows) and click **OK**, you are taken to Word, where the mail merge is completed. Lesson 19 in the Word section of this book, "Creating Personalized Mass Mailings," covers mail merges using Word in greater detail.

Figure 17.4 Contact data can be merged with a document in Word for mass mailings.

 TIP **Setting Up a Mail Merge from Outlook**   The Mail Merge Contacts dialog box (refer to Figure 17.4) provides several options for customizing your mail merge using your Outlook Contacts. If you select the **Permanent File** check box, you can specify a filename and have your Contacts list saved as a data document for use in future Word mail merges (you won't have to start the merge from Outlook in the future if you select this option). You can also specify the type of document that Word creates during the mail merge using the Document Type drop-down list. You can create form letters, mailing envelopes, and mailing labels.

Setting Printer Properties

Whether you're printing to a printer connected directly to your computer or to a printer on the network, you can set printer properties. The properties you set apply to all print jobs you send to the printer until you change the properties again.

 TERM **Printer Properties**   Configurations specific to a printer connected to your computer or to the network. Printer properties include paper orientation, paper source, graphics settings, fonts, and print quality.

CAUTION

Access Denied? If you cannot change the printer properties to a network printer, it's probably because the network administrator has set the printer's configuration and you're not allowed access to the settings. If you need to change printer properties and cannot access the printer's Properties dialog box, talk to your network administrator.

To set printer properties, open the Print dialog box (by choosing **File, Print**). In the Printer area, select a printer from the Name drop-down list, and then click the **Properties** button. The printers' Properties dialog boxes differ depending on the make and model.

Most likely, you'll be able to set paper size, page orientation, and paper source using options on a Paper tab in the dialog box. In addition, you might see a Graphics tab, in which you can set the resolution, intensity, and graphics mode of your printer. A Fonts tab enables you to set options for TrueType fonts, font cartridges, and so on. You might also find a Device Options tab, in which you can set print quality and other options. For more information about your printer, read the documentation that came with it.

Saving and Finding Outlook Items

In this lesson, you learn how to use the Outlook Save As feature and find items in Outlook.

Using the Outlook Save As Feature

Generally, when you finish adding a new task, appointment, meeting, contact, or other item, Outlook automatically saves that item for you, or you're prompted to save the item yourself (and it is placed in the appropriate item folder). You can also save most items in Outlook in other file formats, such as text or some other format using the Save As command. Saving an item in a different format allows you to open that information in another application.

In fact, any application that supports the file format in which you save your Outlook item could be used to open that new file. For example, you might save an item—a journal entry or an appointment page—as a text file so that you can open the file in Word and include the journal information in a report (virtually every application that manipulates some form of a document is capable of opening text files).

 TIP **Using Save As** When you save an item using the File, Save As command, you can designate a drive, folder, and new filename for that item, as well as a file type.

 TERM **File Type** A file type is the same thing as a file format. When you save a file, you specify a file type that identifies the file as one that can be opened in specific applications. For example, the file extension `.doc` identifies a file type that you can open in Word, and the extension `.txt` represents a text-only format that you can open in nearly any word processor or other application.

The following are some of the available file formats:

- **Text Only**—Saves an item in ASCII format (ASCII is a basic coding system that is readable by most applications), which you can use in other applications, such as Word, Notepad, and so on. Save Outlook items in text-format only when you want to send them to someone who does not have Outlook and text-only format will suffice. Any special formatting in the item is lost when you save in this format. Files saved in other applications in text-only format can also be opened in Outlook.

- **Rich Text Format**—This file format was originally created for the Microsoft Exchange environment so that mail messages could include text formatting. You can use this format in Word, Outlook, or Lotus Notes. This format enables you to save items for use in other applications and maintains the text formatting, such as bold, underline, and other font attributes.

- **HTML**—Hypertext Markup Language is a file format designed for use as World Wide Web pages. It maintains all the font attributes, such as bold or italic, that you have placed in an Outlook item such as a message. All the Office applications can open HTML documents; they also can save files to this format.

- **Outlook Template**—This format enables you to take an Outlook item in the current view (such as a custom view that you have created) and save the item as a template. The template can be used to create custom forms for use in Outlook (this is an advanced feature and is typically used by a network administrator to create custom forms for use on a Microsoft Exchange network).

- **Message Format**—The Message format is embraced by Microsoft e-mail clients such as Outlook and Outlook Express. It can be used to save an e-mail message as a separate file in case you want to have a readily available backup of that particular e-mail message on your computer.

Figure 18.1 shows an e-mail message from Outlook saved as an HTML file and opened in Word. After opening a file such as the e-mail message shown, you can format it, cut or copy items to it, insert objects, print, edit, and otherwise manipulate the file. Because you used Save As to save the message as a new file, the original message is still available in your Outlook Inbox or Sent Items folder (depending on whether the message was received by you or sent by you).

 TIP **Getting Data from Other Applications** Although you can use Save As to quickly save an Outlook item in a format that can be used in another application, the best way to get external data into Outlook is to use the Import/Export Wizard. This wizard is discussed in Lesson 10, "Using the Outlook Address Books."

To save an item using Save As, follow these steps:

1. In the folder containing the item you want to save, choose **File**, **Save As**. The Save As dialog box appears (see Figure 18.2).

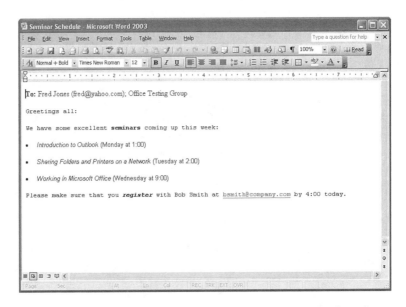

Figure 18.1 Exchanging data between applications makes your work easier.

Figure 18.2 Save Outlook files in different file formats for easy use in other applications.

Why Is Save As Dimmed? When the Save As command is dimmed, you must first select an item in the current folder—a message, an appointment, a meeting, a task, or a note—before you can save it using Save As.

CAUTION

2. From the **Save In** drop-down list, choose the drive to which you want to save the file. From the folders in that drive, select the one you want to save to. The Folder icons on the left of the dialog box give you quick access to your My Recent Documents, Desktop, My Documents, My Computer, and My Network Places.

3. In the **Save As Type** drop-down list, choose a file type. You can save the file in any of the file types discussed earlier in this section (Text, Rich Text, HTML, Outlook Template, or Message Format).

4. After you choose the type, enter a name for the item in the **File Name** text box or accept the default.

5. Click the **Save** button. The file is saved.

Finding Items

Outlook provides a Find feature that you can use to locate items in your various Outlook folders. You can search for messages, files, journal entries, notes, tasks, contacts, appointments, and so on, depending on which folder you are currently in. When you use the Find feature, it opens in its own pane at the top of the current folder window. You type in a key word or phrase, and the Find feature searches all the items in the current folder for your search word or words. When it finds items that match the search phrase, it lists them in the current folder window. Items not matching the search criteria are hidden.

To find an item in an Outlook folder, follow these steps:

1. Select the folder in which you want to conduct a search for an item. Choose **Tools**, point at **Find**, and then select **Find** or click the **Find** button on the Standard toolbar. The Find bar appears at the top of the current folder, as shown in Figure 18.3.

2. Type your search criteria in the **Look For** box. To include any subfolders that you have created under the current folder (such as additional e-mail folders under the Inbox), click the **Search In** drop-down list to include these folders.

3. When you are ready to run the search, click **Find Now**.

4. The items that match your search word or phrase appear in the Folder List (if no matches were found, the Folder List appears empty).

5. You can perform a new search by clicking the **Clear** button and repeating steps 2–4. When you have completed your search, you can close the Find bar by clicking its **Close (x)** button.

The Find bar

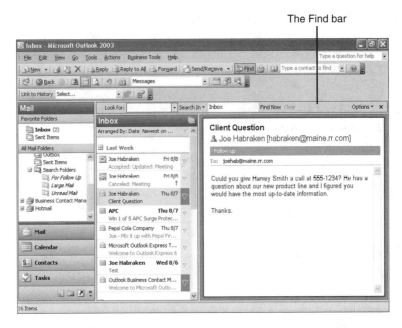

Figure 18.3 Use the Find feature to search for items in the current folder.

 TIP **Save Your Search as a Search Folder** You can save your searches using the Find bar as Search Folders. Search Folders are lists of messages that meet certain search criteria. To save your search as a Search Folder, run the search and then click **Options** on the Find bar. On the Options menu, click **Save Search as Search Folder**. The Save Search as Search Folder dialog box will appear. Provide a name for your Search Folder and then click **OK**. We discuss Search Folders in more detail later in the chapter.

Using the Advanced Find Feature

If the Find feature doesn't provide you with enough search muscle, you can use Advanced Find to perform more detailed searches. Using the Advanced Find feature, you can set multiple search criteria such as a category, from, sent to, and subject (when searching for mail messages, additional search criteria exist for each of the other items found in Outlook).

To use the Advanced Find feature, follow these steps:

1. Select **Tools**, point at **Find**, and then select **Advanced Find**. The Advanced Find dialog box appears (see Figure 18.4).

Figure 18.4 The Advanced Find dialog box provides you with more search parameters than the Find feature does.

2. In the Advanced Find dialog box, set the criteria for your search using the criteria boxes found on the various tabs that appear. For example, the Advanced Find dialog box includes tabs for Messages, More Choices, and Advanced. Each tab provides more advanced methods for conducting the search.

3. Set your search conditions on the various tabs. The More Choices tab is the same for each Outlook item and lets you search for items that have not been read or items that have an attachment.

4. When you've finished setting your criteria, click the **Find Now** button. A box opens at the bottom of the Advanced Find dialog box that lists the items that have met the search criteria. To open an item, double-click it.

 TIP **Save Your Advanced Search as a Search Folder** Run your search in the Advanced Find dialog box. Click **File** and then **Save Search as Search Folder**. The Save Search as Search Folder dialog box will appear. Provide a name for your Search Folder and then click **OK**. Search Folders are discussed in the next section.

Using Search Folders

A new feature provided by Outlook 2003 is the Search Folder. A *Search Folder* is actually a virtual folder that lists e-mail messages that match a particular search criterion. While the messages are listed in the Search Folder, they are not actually stored in the Search Folder; the messages actually reside in your Inbox, Sent Items folder, and other mail folders that you create. When you delete a Search Folder containing messages, the messages that were listed in that Search Folder are not deleted from the actual folder (such as the Inbox or Sent Items folder) that they reside in. However, if you open an e-mail in a Search Folder and delete that message, the message will be deleted from the actual folder that it is stored in.

CAUTION

Messages Deleted from a Search Folder Are Deleted from Outlook
Messages that are selected in or opened from a Search Folder and then deleted will delete the message from the folder that you have stored them in (such as the Inbox).

You access Search Folders by expanding the **Search Folders** icon in the Outlook All Mail Folders list (the Search Folders icon can also be accessed from the Folder List). By default, three Search Folders are available:

- **For Follow Up**—Any e-mail flagged for follow-up is listed in the For Follow Up Search Folder.

- **Large E-mail**—Any e-mail items that exceed 100KB are listed in the Large Mail Search Folder.

- **Unread Mail**—All your unread mail messages are listed in the Unread Mail Search Folder.

To access one of the default folders, click the appropriate folder in the All Mail Folders list (or the Folder list). Figure 18.5 shows the For Follow Up Search Folder and its listed messages (any messages flagged for follow-up).

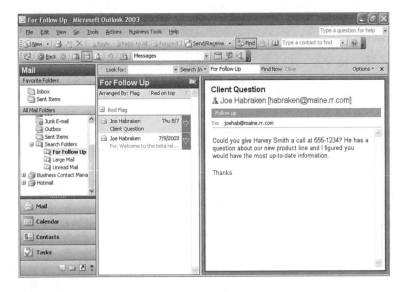

Figure 18.5 Search Folders, such as the For Follow Up Search Folder, list messages that meet particular search criteria.

You can also create your own Search Folders. Creating a Search Folder is not unlike doing an advanced search (as discussed in the preceding section of this lesson). However, because the Search Folder you create resides in the All Mail Folders list, you can quickly access the folder and view the messages that meet the folder's search criteria. Even new unread messages that you have received in your Inbox are listed in the Search Folder if they match the criteria. This means that you can view a constantly updated list of messages each time you click the Search Folder.

To create a Search Folder, follow these steps:

1. Select **Mail** on the Outlook Navigation pane.

2. Select **File**, point at **New**, and then select **Search Folder**. The New Search Folder dialog box opens (see Figure 18.6).

Figure 18.6 You can create your own Search Folders.

3. A number of predefined Search Folders are listed in the New Search Folder dialog box in three categories: Reading Mail, Mail from People and Lists, and Organizing Mail. To create a predefined Search Folder, click one of the predefined Search Folder types, such as **Mail from Specific People** or **Mail with Attachments**.

4. A Search Mail In drop-down box appears at the bottom of the New Search Folder dialog box. To specify where the Search Folder should look for mail that matches the search criteria, click the **Search Mail In** drop-down box and select a location such as Personal Folders or Business Contact Manager (other special mail folders that you have created such as Hotmail will also be listed in the

drop-down list). (Personal Folders is the default location for a new Search Folder.)

5. In cases where you are creating a Search Folder using one of the predefined folder types in the Mail from People and Lists category, you will also have to specify the people that will be used as the criteria for the folder. For example, if you create a Mail from Specific People Search Folder, you need to specify the people from your Contacts list or other address book. Click the **Choose** button at the bottom of the dialog box.

6. The Select Names dialog box will appear. Use the Show Name From drop-down list to specify the list (such as the Contacts list) that contains the names of the people that will be used as search criteria. Select names from the list as needed and click the From button to add them to the criteria. Click **OK** when finished.

7. You will be returned to the New Search Folder dialog box. Click **OK** to create the Search Folder.

The new Search Folder will appear in the Folder list. Click the folder to view the messages that it lists based on the criteria that you set. If you need to fine-tune a Search Folder, right-click on the folder and select **Customize** from the shortcut menu that appears. The Customize dialog for a Search Folder can be used to customize the criteria for the Search Folder or change the folders that it looks in when it creates its list based on your criteria.

If you want to delete a particular Search Folder, right-click on the Search Folder and select **Delete**. A message box will appear. Click **Yes** to delete the Search Folder.

 TIP   **Create Custom Search Folders**   You can also create custom Search Folders by clicking **Create a Custom Search Folder** in the New Search Folder dialog box (it is the last choice in the dialog box). Click **Choose**; the Custom Search Folder dialog box appears. Provide a name for the custom Search Folder and click **Criteria**. The Search Folder Criteria dialog box appears. It is extremely similar to the Advanced Find dialog box. Set up the criteria for the Search Folder in the Search Folder Criteria dialog box. Use the information in the "Using the Advanced Find Feature" section of this lesson to setup your criteria.

Archiving Items

In this lesson, you learn how to use AutoArchive and how to archive files, retrieve archived files, and delete archived files manually.

Using AutoArchive

You can configure Outlook so that mail messages and other items are periodically and automatically archived to a file. This feature, AutoArchive, cleans your Inbox for you but saves the specified messages in an archive file. AutoArchiving is similar to the backup procedure many people use to compress and save files on their computers in case they crash.

CAUTION

Be Wary of AutoArchive   The AutoArchive feature is set up by default to run every 14 days. This means that an AutoArchive dialog box will appear, asking you whether you want to archive Outlook items. Until you have had a chance to configure AutoArchive and use the feature as outlined in this lesson, you might want to click **Cancel** and not run the AutoArchive feature at that time.

The point of archiving is to save Outlook items, such as messages, for later reference, but also to remove some of the older items that are floating around your Outlook folders. Items autoarchived by Outlook are compressed and saved in a file. This file can then be transferred to a storage device such as a floppy disk, a rewritable CD, or other removable storage medium (such as an Iomega Zip drive or Imation Superdisk) for safekeeping.

TERM

Archive   To save items to a file that you can open at any time and print, view, or otherwise use. You might, for example, want to archive some of your mail messages to keep for your records instead of leaving those messages in your Inbox. Archived items are removed from the folder and copied to an archive file.

To use AutoArchive, follow these steps:

1. Choose **Tools, Options**. The Options dialog box appears.
2. Click the **Other** tab.
3. Click the **AutoArchive** button to display the AutoArchive options (see Figure 19.1).

Figure 19.1   Specify your options for automatically archiving items into an archive file.

4. Choose from the following check box options:

- **Run AutoArchive Every X Days**—Enter a number for how often (in days) you want Outlook to automatically archive items. If you enter **14**, for example, every 14th day it automatically archives the contents of your folders into an archive file.

- **Prompt Before AutoArchive Runs**—If you check this, Outlook displays a dialog box each time it is about to perform the AutoArchive; you can click **OK** to continue or **Cancel** to stop the operation.

- **Delete Expired Items (E-Mail Folders Only)**—Check this box to have Outlook delete messages from the Inbox after archiving them.

- **Archive or Delete Old Items**—This option allows you to customize how items are archived. It even allows you to permanently delete old items.

- **Show Archive Folder in Folder List**—This option, which is only available if Archive or Delete Old Items is enabled, makes the archive folder available from the Folder List, making it easier to access archived files. Each folder archived, such as the Inbox or Contacts folder, will appear as subfolders under the Archive folder. This allows you to view the contents in each of the archived folders as you would any other Outlook folder.

5. In the Default Folder Settings for Archiving area, use the click arrows to select the number of months, weeks, or days for the age of an item that should be archived. Use the drop-down box to select the unit, such as **Months**, **Weeks**, or **Days**.

6. In the Move Old Items To box, enter a path to where you want to save the file, and name it (if you don't want to use the default).

7. If you want to permanently delete old items rather than archive them, select the **Permanently Delete Old Items** option button.

8. To apply these settings to all folders, click the **Apply These Settings to All Folders Now** button.

9. Click **OK** to close the AutoArchive dialog box. Click **OK** to close the AutoArchive dialog box.

If you do not want to apply the AutoArchive options that you set in the AutoArchive dialog box to every Outlook folder, you can set AutoArchive options individually for each folder, such as Tasks, Calendar, and so on. To set an individual folder's AutoArchive options, follow these steps:

1. Right-click the folder icon in the Folder List to display a shortcut menu.

2. Choose **Properties**. The item's Properties dialog box appears.

3. Choose the **AutoArchive** tab. Figure 19.2 shows the Inbox's AutoArchive tab.

Figure 19.2 Set AutoArchive options for individual folders.

4. To set custom archiving options for this folder, select the **Archive This Folder Using These Settings** option button. You can set the age for items to be archived in Months, Weeks, or Days. You can also specify the path to be used for the archiving, or you can choose to have old items deleted rather than archived.

5. If you do not want to archive the items in the current folder, select the **Do Not Archive Items in This Folder** option button.

6. When you have finished setting the archiving options for the folder, click **OK** to close the dialog box.

Archiving Manually

If you are still feeling a little squeamish about using AutoArchive, you can choose to archive folder items manually. This feature allows you to archive only one folder at a time (and any subfolders it might hold), but the process does provide you with complete control over how and when the archives are created. The manual archive can be created using the current AutoArchive settings for a folder (such as the age of items that should be archived), or you can select new age-related parameters while doing the manual archive.

To manually create an archive, follow these steps:

1. Choose **File** and then select **Archive**. The Archive dialog box appears (see Figure 19.3).

Figure 19.3   Enter settings for manual archiving.

2. Choose one of the following options:

   • **Archive All Folders According to Their AutoArchive Settings**—Use this option to manually archive all the Outlook folders using their individual AutoArchive settings. Using this option is no different from running an AutoArchive, except that you are prompting Outlook to archive the folders immediately.

   • **Archive This Folder and All Subfolders**—Select this option to archive the selected folder. Using this option requires that you provide an age date for items to be archived, and you can also specify the path for the archive to be created.

3. Enter a date into the **Archive Items Older Than** text box, or select a date from the drop-down calendar (click the drop-down arrow on the right of the date box).

4. In the **Archive File** text box, enter a path and filename with which to save the file.

5. If you want to archive items in a folder that have been marked as Do Not AutoArchive in its Properties dialog box, select the **Include Items with "Do Not AutoArchive" Checked** check box.

6. Click **OK** to archive the selected folder.

Retrieving Archived Files

After you create an archive either by using the AutoArchive feature or by manually archiving a folder or folders, an Archive Folders icon is added to the Outlook Folder List as shown in Figure 19.4. To open the Folder List, click the Folder List arrow next to the name of the currently open folder; use the pushpin on the right of the Folder List to place the Folder List in the Outlook window. You can retrieve archived items from the subfolders in this Archive folder and copy or move them back to any of your Outlook folders.

To retrieve an archived file, follow these steps:

1. Open the Folder List. An Archive Folders icon will have been added to the list immediately after an archive file has been created (see Figure 19.4).

2. Click the **plus symbol** (+) to the left of the Archive Folders icon to expand the folder. Folders that you have automatically or manually archived are present as subfolders. For example, if you archived your Inbox, an Inbox folder is available under the Archive Folders.

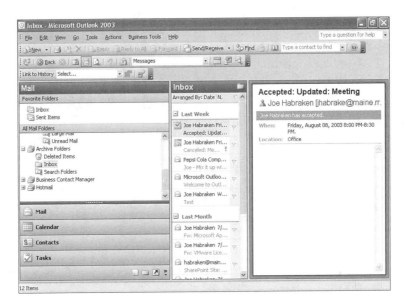

Figure 19.4   Archived items can be copied or moved from Archive Folders to other Outlook folders.

3. To view the archived items in a particular folder, select that folder (such as the Inbox or Calendar). The archived items, such as messages, appear in the Contents pane.

4. To move an item or items, select the items in the Contents pane and then drag them to an Outlook folder. For example, you could drag messages from the Archive Inbox folder to your Inbox.

Any or all items can be moved or copied from an archive folder to your Outlook folders such as the Calendar or the Inbox. The ability to quickly view the contents of an archived folder makes it easier for you to see how the archive options that you set for AutoArchive or a manual archive have actually archived items in a particular folder.

Customizing Outlook

20

In this lesson, you learn how to set e-mail, calendar, and other options in Outlook.

Setting Outlook Options

You can set all of Outlook's options by using the Options dialog box (see Figure 20.1). To open the Options dialog box, select **Tools** and then choose **Options**. The number of tabs on this dialog box depends on the situation in which you are using Outlook:

- On a company network that uses Microsoft Exchange Server for communications services such as e-mail

- At home or on a small network that uses an Internet service provider (ISP) for Internet e-mail

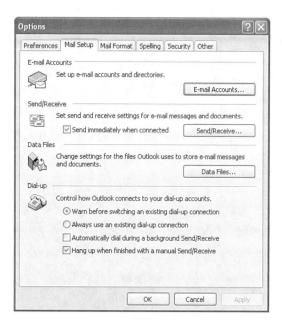

Figure 20.1   The Options dialog box gives you control over the various features of Outlook.

Figure 20.1 shows the Options dialog box provided for an Outlook user who uses a service provider for Internet e-mail. The only additional tab provided to users of Outlook on a Microsoft Exchange Server network is a Delegates tab. The Delegates tab allows users to "delegate" access of their Outlook folders to other users on the Exchange Server network. This is because all the personal folders of Outlook users connected to an Exchange Server are actually kept on the server (this makes it very easy to share information between users). You should rely on your network's system administrator to manage the settings for this tab.

Each tab on the Options dialog box controls a logical grouping of settings that you control with option buttons, text boxes, or check boxes. Each tab also contains buttons that are used to access additional groupings of more specific settings.

Setting E-Mail Options

E-Mail, Calendar, Tasks, Contacts, Journal, and Notes options are set on the Preferences tab of the Options dialog box. To open a more specific dialog box related to the features of each of the Outlook item types, click the appropriate button on the Preferences tab (see Figure 20.2).

Figure 20.2 Customize E-Mail, Calendar, Tasks, Journal, and Notes options on the Preferences tab.

To set e-mail options, click the **E-Mail Options** button. The E-Mail Options dialog box appears. This dialog box allows you to set items using check boxes and drop-down menus; buttons also exist for Advanced E-Mail Options and Tracking Options.

In the Message Handling box of the E-Mail Options dialog box, check the boxes of the options you want to activate, such as **Close Original Message on Reply**, **Forward**, and **Save Copies of Messages in Sent Items Folder**.

Two drop-down boxes in the On Replies and Forwards section provide you with options for replying to and forwarding messages. You can choose whether you want to include the original message text with replies and forwards or attach the original message as an attached file.

You can also set Advanced E-Mail options and Tracking options in this dialog box. When you click the **Advanced E-Mail Options** button, the Advanced E-Mail Options dialog box appears (see Figure 20.3). This dialog box allows you to control how unsent messages are handled, what happens when new mail arrives, and the default importance level of new messages that you send. When you've finished setting options in this dialog box, click **OK**.

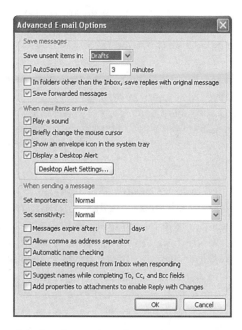

Figure 20.3 Options related to the saving of unsent messages and received messages are set in the Advanced E-Mail Options dialog box.

The **Tracking Options** button in the E-Mail Options dialog box opens the Tracking Options dialog box. In this box, you can set options that notify you when e-mail you send is received and when that e-mail is read. After setting options in this dialog box, click **OK**. Click **OK** again to close the E-Mail Options dialog box.

TIP   **Set Junk E-mail Options**   Outlook also gives you control over the level of protection that you set against junk e-mail messages. Click the **Junk E-Mail** button on the Preferences tab to select the level of junk e-mail protection. For more about the Junk E-Mail filter, see Lesson 8, "Saving Drafts and Organizing Messages."

There are other tabs on the Options dialog box that allow you to configure settings related to e-mail such as your e-mail accounts and the format of your e-mail messages. We look at these tabs in the next two sections.

Setting Mail Setup Options

The Mail Setup tab of the Options dialog box allows you to access existing e-mail accounts or create new accounts (look back at Figure 20.1). This tab also controls other options, such as which e-mail accounts are accessed when you use the Send and Receive command on the Outlook toolbar. An additional set of options related to your Outlook data files, such as your archive files and files that hold your personal folders, can also be accessed on this tab.

CAUTION

Outlook Data File Placement Is Crucial   Outlook places your personal folders and archive files based on whether you are working on an Exchange Server network or a PC connected to an Internet service provider. Therefore, you might want to forgo manipulating the names and placement of these files using the Data Files option on the Mail Setup tab. You could potentially cripple Outlook by changing these filenames or locations.

To set up a new e-mail account or edit a current e-mail account, click the **E-Mail Accounts** button. The E-Mail Accounts dialog box opens, providing you with options for creating a new e-mail account, editing an existing account, adding a new address book, or editing an existing address book. This dialog box can also be reached from Outlook by selecting **Tools, E-Mail Accounts**. Creating e-mail accounts is covered in detail in Lesson 2, "Understanding the Outlook E-Mail Configurations." When you have finished creating a new account or editing an existing account, you are returned to the Mail Setup tab.

To set options related to the Outlook Send/Review command, click the **Send/Receive** button on the Mail Setup tab. The Send/Receive Groups dialog box opens. By default, all accounts are included in an All Accounts group and checked for new messages, and any messages created using the account are also sent when you use the Send/Receive command (either on the Outlook toolbar or by selecting **Tools**, **Send/Receive**, **Send All**). New groups of e-mail accounts can be created using this dialog box (click **New** to create the group). After a new group has been created, you can double-click the group name to see a list of all e-mail accounts. Select the accounts you want to place in the new group.

Setting Mail Format Options

The Mail Format tab on the Options dialog box (see Figure 20.4) allows you to choose your message format, such as HTML, rich text, or plain text. You can also select whether to use Microsoft Word as your e-mail editor. The mail format that you use dictates any special fonts or stationery templates that are available to you (only HTML supports different stationery for your e-mail messages).

Figure 20.4   The Mail Format tab allows you to choose your message format and select Word as your e-mail editor.

To set the format for your messages, use the Compose in This Message Format drop-down list. If you want to use Word as your e-mail editor, click the **Use Microsoft Word to Edit E-Mail Messages** check box.

If you use HTML as the format for your messages, you can select a stationery type. Select stationery using the Use This Stationery by Default drop-down list. If you want to view the stationery, select the Stationery Picker button. In the Stationery Picker dialog box, select a stationery in the Stationery list to view it. When you have finished selecting your stationery, click **OK** to close the Stationery Picker dialog box.

TIP   **Applying Your Changes**   When you make changes on the tabs of the Options dialog box, you can apply these new options to Outlook by clicking the **Apply** button. The Options dialog box remains open so that you can configure other options.

Setting Calendar Options

Options related to the Outlook Calendar are also accessed from the Preferences tab of the Options dialog box. For example, if you don't work a typical Monday through Friday work week, you can change your default Calendar settings in the Calendar Options dialog box to reflect this. Suppose your work week runs from Tuesday through Saturday and your workday is from 4 a.m. to 12 noon. You can make changes to the Calendar so that it reflects your actual work week. You can also set your time zone and add holidays to your calendar.

To make changes to the Calendar Options, open the Calendar Options dialog box:

1. Click the **Calendar Options** button on the Preferences tab of the Options dialog box (see Figure 20.5). In the Calendar Work Week area, set your starting and ending time (the default is 8 a.m. to 5 p.m.).

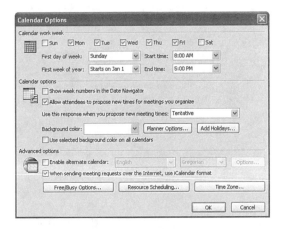

Figure 20.5   Calendar options are set in the Calendar Options dialog box.

2. To set the time zone for your area, click the **Time Zone** button, and then choose the zone that describes your location.

3. To add holidays to your calendar, click the **Add Holidays** button. Then, check the box representing your country (U.S. is the default) and click **OK**. Outlook imports the holidays from your selected region to the calendar.

4. When you finish setting the options in this dialog box, return to the Preferences tab by clicking **OK**.

The Preferences tab also allows you to set options for your other Outlook items, such as Tasks, the Journal, and Notes. For information on setting preferences for Tasks, the Journal, or Notes, see Lessons 14, 15, or 16, respectively.

Other Options Dialog Box Tabs

The Options dialog box also contains additional tabs that control other features associated with Outlook. Each tab is listed here with a description of the settings available:

- The Spelling tab enables you to change settings associated with Outlook's spell checker. You can choose (using check boxes) to have the spell checker always suggest replacements for misspelled words, always check spelling before sending, and ignore words in uppercase. A drop-down box also enables you to pick the language of the dictionary you want to use to spell check your Outlook items.

- The Security tab enables you to set options regarding whether outgoing messages should be encrypted or have digital signatures attached to them. An option also allows you to get a digital ID to use for your outgoing messages. Digital IDs and information on encrypting messages are covered in Lesson 9, "Setting Mail Options."

- The Other tab enables you to set options such as whether the Deleted Items folder is emptied when you exit Outlook. Other options included on this tab include Advanced Options (accessed by clicking the Advanced Options button), which allow you to specify the folder (such as the Inbox) that is selected when Outlook is opened. The Other tab also provides access to settings related to the AutoArchive feature, which is discussed in Lesson 19, "Archiving Items."

When you have finished all the changes you want to make to the various Outlook options, click **OK** to close the Options dialog box. This returns you to the currently selected Outlook folder (such as the Inbox or Contacts folder).

Introducing the Business Contact Manager

In this lesson, you learn about the Business Contact Manager. You learn how to create business contacts and create accounts.

Understanding the Business Contact Manager

Microsoft Office 2003 provides an extension to Microsoft Outlook called the Business Contact Manager. The Business Contact Manager makes it easy for you to organize business contacts and business opportunities. Because it is integrated with Microsoft Outlook, the Business Contact Manager provides a familiar interface and tools such as e-mail and faxing that make it a simple and effective small business tool.

When Business Contact Manager (BCM) is installed with Microsoft Outlook, it is integrated into the Outlook environment. You will find that a BCM mail folder is added to the available Outlook mail folders. BCM Account and Business Contacts are added to the Contact folders. An Opportunities list is also added to the Tasks folder.

You will also find that a Business Tools menu is added to the Outlook menu bar. The Business Tools menu provides you with access to the various BCM features including the ability to create reports based on your business contacts, accounts, and opportunities. Let's take a look at creating business accounts using the BCM.

Creating Business Contacts

Business contacts are created in the Business Contacts folder. To view your business contacts, select Contacts on the **Navigation pane**, then select **Business Contacts in the Business Contact Manager**. The first time you open the business contacts you will want to add new contacts.

Follow these steps:

1. Double-click in the Business Contacts pane. A new business contact will appear (see Figure 21.1).

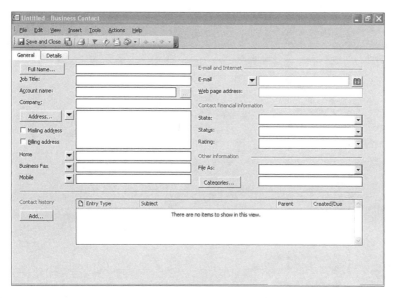

Figure 21.1 Create a new business contact.

2. Fill in the business contact's information in the appropriate text boxes, such as the contact name, address, financial information, and so on. You can also assign categories to the contact (creating a Business contact is very similar to creating an Outlook contact, which is discussed in Lesson 11, "Creating a Contacts List").

TIP **Keep the Contact Financial Information Up-to-Date** The contact financial information allows you to flag the overall financial "health" of a business contact. Select whether your financial association with the contact is Active or Inactive. You can also enter the status of the contact related to financial issues (such as payments) as Current or Overdue. A drop-down box also allows you to rate the contact's financials (such as Great, Good, Average, and so on).

3. When you have completed entering the general information for the business contact, you can also enter additional information related to the contact such as the contact's department, manager, and assistant and the contact's preferred method of communication (phone versus e-mail for example). Click the **Details** tab of the Business Contact dialog box (see Figure 21.2). Enter the data in the appropriate boxes as needed.

4. When you have completed entering all the information related to a business contact, click the **Save and Close** button to save the new contact.

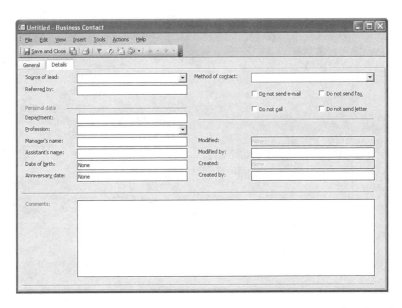

Figure 21.2 Enter additional information related to the contact on the Details tab.

To open a business contact record (for viewing or editing), double-click the record in the Business Contact list. You can also create and maintain a history of contact events that you have with a particular contact (such as an e-mail, meeting, and so on). For example, if you plan on sending an e-mail to the contact, you can send it via the business contact's record. This not only sends the e-mail but logs it in the contact history. To add an entry to the contact history, click the **Add** button. A menu appears as shown in Figure 21.3.

To send an item such as a new e-mail (and add the contact event to the Contact history list), click the appropriate icon. For example, if you select the **Mail Message** icon, a new blank e-mail opens in Outlook addressed to the contact. Complete the message and then send it. The new contact event appears in the Contact history list as shown in Figure 21.4.

TIP **Quickly Save Changes You Make to Business Contacts** As you edit a business contact record, you can save the changes that you make by pressing **Ctrl+S**. This saves the changes but does not close the contact window.

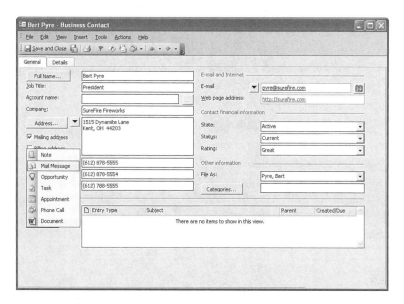

Figure 21.3   Log contact events such as e-mails with the contact from the business contact's record.

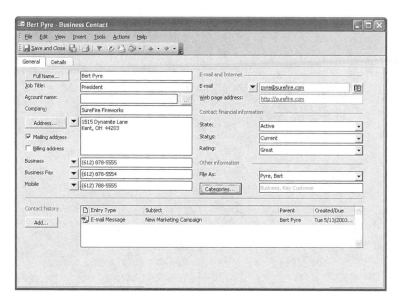

Figure 21.4   The contact event is logged and saved with the business contact record.

Creating Accounts

Creating business accounts allows you to track individuals that you do business with. Creating accounts in the BCM allows you to take a big-picture approach to managing business information. An *account* is a company, organization, or other institution that you do business with.

After different company accounts have been entered into the BCM, you can then associate individual business contacts with a particular account. For example, you may have several different employees from a business listed in your business contacts. Associating them with a particular account allows you to better document the interactions that you have with that company and their employees (we discuss associating contacts with an account later in the lesson).

 Account   A BCM entry for a particular business, organization, or institution that you do business with.

To create an account in the BCM, follow these steps:

1. Select Contacts on the **Navigation pane**, and then select **Accounts in the Business Contact Manager**.

2. Place the mouse on an empty spot in the Accounts pane, and double-click. A new Account dialog box will open (see Figure 21.5).

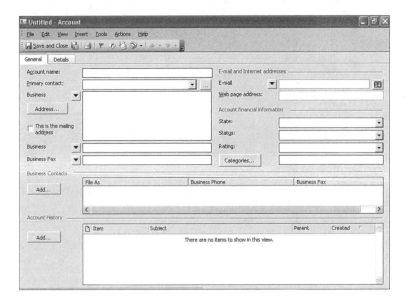

Figure 21.5   You can create accounts in Business Contact Manager.

3. Provide the account name for the account (such as a company name).

4. You can type the name of the primary contact, or you can select from your business contact list. To the right of the Primary contact text box, click the ellipse (...) button. A Contacts dialog box will appear showing the business contacts that you have entered in the BCM. Select a contact from the list and then click **OK**.

5. Enter the address and other information for the account including the Account financial information. You can also add categories to the account.

6. Click the **Details** tab of the Account dialog box. Enter the type of business, territory, and other information as needed. You can also add notes related to the business on the Details tab.

7. When you have completed entering the account information, click **Save and Close**.

You can open any of the accounts in the Account pane by double-clicking on the account. As with business contacts, you can also add Account History events such as e-mails and phone calls. Other items such as Word documents, Excel workbooks, and Access databases can also be associated with an account. We discuss linking items such as other Office documents to an account later in the lesson.

Adding Contacts to Accounts

After you have entered business contacts and accounts into the BCM, you can add the appropriate contacts to each of the accounts. This enables you to associate each business contact with the company or organization for whom they work.

Follow these steps:

1. Select Contacts on the **Navigation pane**, and then select **Accounts in the Business Contact Manager**.

2. In the Accounts pane, double-click on any account to open it.

3. In the Contact area of the Account dialog box, click the **Add** button. A list of the contacts in the BCM will appear (see Figure 21.6).

4. Select a contact in the left pane of the Contacts dialog box. Click the **Add** button (>) to add the contact to the Selected Items list. Add other contacts as needed.

5. When you have added the appropriate contacts to the account, click **OK**. You will be returned to the Account dialog box.

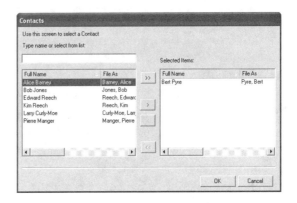

Figure 21.6   Add contacts to an account.

The contacts that you add to the account will appear in the Contact list in the account's dialog box. If you want to remove a contact from the list, select the contact and then press the **Delete** key. Make sure you save the changes that you make to the account before closing it.

TIP   **Contacts Specified as Primary Contact Are Automatically Added to the Contact List**   When you add the primary contact to an account by pulling a contact name from the business contact's list (as discussed in the previous section), that contact is automatically added to the contact list for the account.

Linking Items to Accounts

You can also link Office documents related to an account directly to the account record in the BCM. This allows you to link Word documents (such as letters), Excel workbooks, PowerPoint presentations, and Access databases to an account. This makes it very easy to find these documents when you need them because you can open them from the account.

To link an item to an account, follow these steps.

1. Open an account in the BCM (double-click on the account).

2. In the account's dialog box, click the **Add** button in the Account history area.

3. Select **Document** from the list that appears. An Open dialog box will appear.

4. Use the **Look In** drop-down box to locate the folder that holds your file. Select the file, such as an Excel workbook, that you want to link to the account.

5. Click **Open**. The file will be listed in the Account history box.

You can add additional documents to the account as needed. When you want to open a file linked to the account, double-click the file in the Account history box. The file will open in the appropriate Office application.

 TIP   **Link Office Documents to Business Contacts**   You can also link Word documents and other Office items such as Excel workbooks to business contacts. Open a business contact and then follow the steps provided for linking a document to an account.

Creating Business Contact Manager Opportunities and Reports

In this lesson, you learn how to use the Business Contact Manager to create opportunities and reports.

Creating Opportunities in Business Contact Manager

As you saw from the preceding lesson (Lesson 21, "Introducing the Business Contact Manager"), you can add business contacts and accounts to the Business Contact Manager (BCM). The BCM also enables you to create opportunities and track their progress. Entering the opportunity into the BCM and linking it to a contact or account allows you to more easily keep track of the progress of opportunities.

TERM　**Opportunity**　Best defined as a chance to sell your company's products or services to a client.

TIP　**Opportunities Are Accessed Using the Tasks Folder**　You access opportunities by using the Tasks button on the Navigation pane. Think of opportunities as another task that you must complete. You must "close the deal" in relation to the opportunity to sell your products or services.

To create an opportunity in the BCM, follow these steps:

1. Select the **Tasks** button on the Navigation pane.
2. In the My Tasks pane, select the **Opportunities in Business Contact Manager** link. The Opportunities pane will appear in the Reading pane.
3. To create the new opportunity, double-click in the Opportunities pane. The Opportunity dialog box will appear (see Figure 22.1).

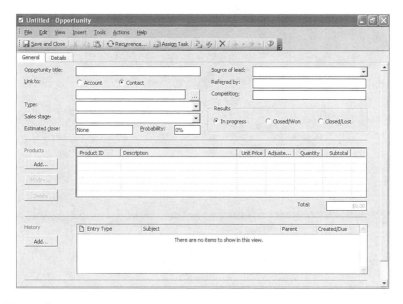

Figure 22.1   Create a new business opportunity.

4. Enter a title for the opportunity.

5. Use the **Type** drop-down box to specify the type of opportunity (Standard, Bulk Order, Delivery, Special Order).

6. Use the **Sales Stage** drop-down list to specify the stage for the opportunity.

7. Use the **Source of Lead** drop-down list to select a source type for the opportunity (such as advertisement or direct mail).

Complete the other information as needed. The next two sections discuss adding products and linking accounts and contacts to an opportunity.

 TIP   **Link Items to an Opportunity History**   You can link phone calls, e-mails, and documents related to an opportunity to the History area of the opportunity. For more about linking items in the BCM, see Lesson 21, "Introducing the Business Contact Manager."

Adding Products to an Opportunity

You can also add products to the opportunity. This allows you to keep track of the products, their unit price, and their quantity as related to the opportunity.

To add a product to an opportunity, follow these steps:

1. Select the **Add** button in the Products area of the Opportunity dialog box. The Add Product dialog box opens (see Figure 22.2).

Figure 22.2   Add products to the opportunity.

2. Provide the product ID, product name, and other information needed in the Add Product dialog box.

3. When you have completed adding the information, click **OK** to add the product or click **Add Next** to add the current product and then add another product.

Products that you add to the opportunity can also be edited. Click on the product in the Products list on the opportunity and then select **Modify**. After modifying the information click OK. If you want to delete any of the products listed on the opportunity, select the product and then click the **Delete** button.

As with other items that you create in the BCM, you will want to save your new opportunity. You cannot save the opportunity, however, until you link it to a BCM contact or account. This process is discussed in the next section.

Linking Contacts and Accounts to the Opportunity

Another aspect of creating opportunities is linking an opportunity to contacts or accounts that you have saved in the BCM. You must link the opportunity to a contact or account before you can save or close the opportunity. To link a contact or account to an opportunity, follow these steps:

1. Before attempting to save a new opportunity, select either the **Link to Account** or **Contact** option button in the Opportunity dialog box.

2. To link the account or contact, depending on the option button you selected, click the button marked with the ellipse (...) it is directly below the Link to Account and Contact option buttons). A menu will appear.

3. If you chose **Link to Account** in step 1, the menu will provide two choices, **Add Existing Account** and **Create New Account**. Select **Add Existing Account** to open The Accounts dialog box. Choose an account from the list and click **OK**. The account name is placed in the Opportunity dialog box. If you select

Create New Account, the Create an Account dialog box will open. Supply a name for the new account and click **OK**. The new account name is placed in the Opportunity dialog box.

If you chose **Contact** in Step 1, the menu provides two choices: **Add Existing Contact** and **Create New Contact**. To add an existing business contact, click Add Existing Contact to open the Business Contacts dialog box (see Figure 22.3). Select the business contact and click **OK**. The contact name is placed on the Opportunity dialog box. If you select **Create New Contact**, the Create A Business Contact dialog box opens. Supply a name for the new contact and click **OK**. The contact name is placed on the Opportunity dialog box.

Figure 22.3 Link contacts to the opportunity.

4. After providing the link information (and other data for the opportunity as needed), you can save and close the opportunity; click the **Save and Close** button.

TIP **You Must Fill In the Data for the New Account or Contact** If you chose to link a new account or BCM contact to the opportunity, you will have to open that new account or contact in the BCM and provide the appropriate data for the item. Only a blank account or contact is created in step 3 of the instructions provided.

TIP **View the Modification Date for the Opportunity** To view the last time an opportunity has been modified, click the Details tab on the Opportunity dialog box. The Modified date will be provided as well as the Created date for the opportunity.

Creating Reports

You can also create reports using the BCM. These reports allow you to print a hard copy of all your contacts (such as a phone list), create a quick account list, or print a report that details opportunities by product.

To create a BCM report, follow these steps:

1. Select the **Business Tools** menu and then point at **Report**. A submenu appears with choices for **Contacts**, **Accounts**, **Opportunities**, and **Other** (see Figure 22.4).

Figure 22.4   Select the type of report you want to create.

2. To create a specific report for Contacts, Accounts, or Opportunities, point at the category, and then select a report type. For example, for a contact phone list point at **Contact** and then select **Contacts Phone List**.

3. The report will appear in a business report window (see Figure 22.5).

4. You can zoom in and out on the report data and save or print the report. When you have completed working with the report, close it.

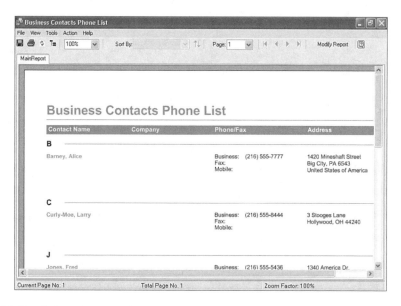

Figure 22.5   Select the type of report you want to create.

Word

Working in Word

In this lesson, you learn how to start Microsoft Word and navigate the Word window. You also learn how to use common tools such as menus, toolbars, and dialog boxes.

Starting Word

Microsoft Word is an efficient and full-featured word processor that provides you with all the tools you need to produce a wide variety of document types—everything from simple documents, such as memos and outlines, to complex documents, such as newsletters and Internet-ready HTML pages. You create your Word documents in the Word window, which provides easy access to all the tools you need to create all your documents.

Before you can take advantage of Word's proficient document processing features, you must open the Word application window. To start the Word program, follow these steps:

1. From the Windows XP desktop, click **Start**, **All Programs** (on Windows 2000, click **Start**, then **Programs**). The Programs menu appears (see Figure 1.1).

2. To start Word, point at the Microsoft Office icon and then click the **Word** icon. The Word application window appears.

 TIP **Pin a Program to the Windows XP Start Menu** For quick access to an application such as Word, right-click on the program icon when accessing the Programs menu. On the shortcut menu that appears, select **Pin to Start menu**. The application icon will now be available on the main Start menu, when you click **Start**.

Figure 1.1   Open the Programs menu and click the Word icon to start Word.

Understanding the Word Environment

When you start Word, the Word application window opens (see Figure 1.2). You create your documents in the Word window. The Word window also provides items that help you navigate and operate the application itself.

TIP   **Control the View**   If your view differs from the view shown in Figure 1.2 (the Normal view), or if you don't see all the Word window elements shown in the figure (particularly the ruler), you can easily change your view. Select **View**, and then choose the menu selection (such as **Normal** or **Ruler**) that matches your view to the figure.

Notice that the largest area of the window is blank; this is where you create your new document. All the other areas—the menu bar, the toolbar, and the status bar—either provide a fast way to access the various commands and features that you use in Word, or they supply you with information concerning your document, such as what page you are on and where the insertion point is currently located in your document.

Table 1.1 describes the elements you see called out in the Word application window.

Maximize/Restore button

Control Menu button | Title bar | Menu bar | Minimize button | Close button

Toolbar

Getting Started Task Pane

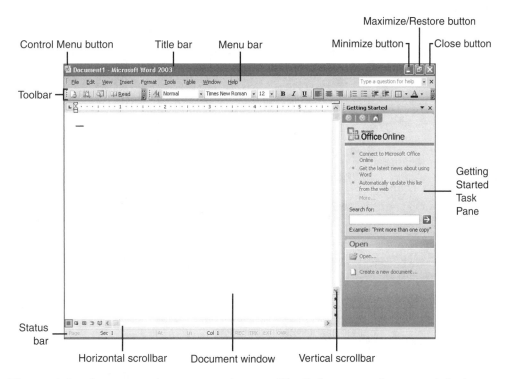

Status bar

Horizontal scrollbar | Document window | Vertical scrollbar

Figure 1.2 Create your documents and access Word's features and commands in the Word window.

Table 1.1 Elements of the Word Window

Element	Description
Title bar	Includes the name of the application and the current document, as well as the Minimize, Maximize, and Close buttons.
Control Menu button	Opens the Control menu, which provides such commands as Restore, Minimize, and Close.
Minimize button	Reduces the Word window to a button on the taskbar; to restore the window to its original size, click the button on the taskbar.
Maximize/Restore button	Enlarges the Word window to cover the Windows desktop. When the window is maximized, the Maximize button changes to a Restore button that you can click to return the window to its previous size.
Close (x) button	Closes the Word program. "x" is the icon for closing any window.
Menu bar	Contains menus of commands you can use to perform tasks in the program, such as Edit, Format, and Tools.

Table 1.1 Continued

Element	Description
Toolbar	Includes icons that serve as shortcuts for common commands, such as Save, Print, and Spelling.
Status bar	Displays information about the current document, including page number, the section in which you are located, and the current location of the insertion point (inches, line, and column). The status bar also shows you other information, such as whether you have turned on the Typeover (OVR) mode or turned on Word's track changes (TRK) feature.
Document window	This window is where you type and format your documents.
Scrollbars	The horizontal scrollbar is used to scroll your view of the current document in a left-to-right motion. The vertical scrollbar is used to scroll up and down through the current document.
Task pane	The column of information on the right side of the document is the task pane. This is where you can access features such as the Clipboard, styles, and formatting; you can also open another document or mail merge.

Using Menus and Toolbars

Word provides several ways to access the commands and features you use as you create your documents. You can access these commands by using the menus on the menu bar and the buttons on the various toolbars.

You can also access many Word commands using shortcut menus. Right-clicking a particular document element (a word or a paragraph, for example) opens these menus, which contain a list of commands related to the item on which you are currently working.

The Word Menu Bar

The Word menu bar gives you access to all the commands and features that Word provides. As in all Windows applications, Word's menus reside below the title bar and are activated by clicking a particular menu name. The menu then drops open, providing you with a set of command options.

Word (and the other Office applications) uses a menu system called personalized menus that enables you to quickly access the commands you use most often (while hiding those that you use less frequently). When you first choose a particular menu, you find only a short list of Word's most commonly used menu commands. When you've spent some time using Word, this list of commands will actually be the ones that you have used most recently on that particular menu.

If a menu has a small double arrow at the bottom of its command list, you can click that to gain access to other, less commonly needed, commands. As you use hidden commands, Word adds them to the normal menu list. This means that you are basically building the list of commands available on the menu as you use Word.

This personalized strategy is also employed by the toolbar system. As you use commands, they are added to the toolbar (this personalized toolbar feature is available only when you have the Standard toolbar and the Formatting toolbar on the same line in an application window). This provides you with customized menus and toolbars that are, in effect, personalized for you.

To access a particular menu, follow these steps:

1. Select the menu by clicking its title (such as **View**), as shown in Figure 1.3. The most recently used commands appear; wait just a moment for all the commands on a particular menu to appear (if the commands do not appear, click the down arrow at the bottom of the menu).

2. Select the command on the menu that invokes a particular feature (such as **Header and Footer**).

Denotes submenu

Opens separate dialog box when clicked

Figure 1.3   Select a particular menu to view, and then point to a Word command.

You will find that many of the commands found on Word's menus are followed by an ellipsis (...). These commands, when selected, open a dialog box that requires you to provide Word with additional information before the particular feature or command can be used. More information about understanding dialog boxes is included later in this lesson.

Some of the menus also contain a submenu or cascading menu from which you make choices. The menu commands that produce a submenu are indicated by an arrow to the right of the menu choice. When a submenu is present, you point at the command (marked with the arrow) on the main menu to open the submenu.

The menu system itself provides a logical grouping of the Word commands and features. For example, commands related to files, such as Open, Save, and Print, are all found on the File menu.

TIP **Activating Menus with the Keyboard** You can activate a particular menu by holding down the **Alt** key and then pressing the keyboard key that matches the underscored letter in the menu's name. This underscored letter is called the hotkey. For example, to activate the File menu in Word, press **Alt+F**.

If you find that you would rather have access to all the menu commands (rather than accessing only those you've used recently), you can turn off the personalized menu system. To do this, follow these steps:

1. Click the **Tools** menu, and then click **Customize**.
2. In the Customize dialog box, click the **Options** tab.
3. To show all the commands on the menus, click the **Always Show Full Menus** check box.
4. Click **OK** to close the dialog box.

Shortcut Menus

A fast way to access commands related to a particular document element is to select that document object and then right-click. This opens a shortcut menu that contains commands related to the particular object with which you are working.

Object Any element found in a document, such as text, a graphic, a hyperlink, or other inserted item.

For example, if you select a line of text in a document, right-clicking the selected text (see Figure 1.4) opens a shortcut menu with commands such as Cut, Copy, and

Paste, or it provides you with quick access to formatting commands, such as Font and Paragraph.

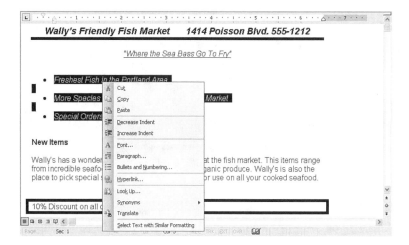

Figure 1.4 By right-clicking areas in Word, you can use shortcut menus to quickly access Word commands related to the item that was clicked.

Word Toolbars

The Word toolbars provide a very quick and straightforward way to access often-used commands and features. When you first start Word, the Standard and Formatting toolbars reside as one continuous toolbar found directly below the menu bar (as shown in Figure 1.2). You can quickly place the Standard and Formatting toolbars in their own row by selecting the Toolbar Options button on either toolbar, and then selecting Show Buttons on Two Rows (as shown in Figure 1.3 and 1.4).

To access a particular command using a toolbar button, click the button. Depending on the command, you see either an immediate result in your document (such as the removal of selected text when you click the **Cut** button) or the appearance of a dialog box requesting additional information from you.

TIP   **Finding a Toolbar Button's Purpose**   You can place (hover but do not click) the mouse pointer on any toolbar button to view a description of that tool's function. If you also want to see the shortcut keys associated with a toolbar button, select **Show Shortcut Keys in ScreenTips** on the Options tab of the Customize dialog box.

Word offers several toolbars; many of them contain buttons for a specific group of tasks. For example, the Drawing toolbar provides buttons that give you access to tools that enable you to draw graphical elements in your documents (such as text boxes, lines, and rectangles).

To place additional toolbars in the Word window, right-click any toolbar currently shown and select from the list that appears. Specific toolbars exist for working with tables, pictures, other Word features, and the World Wide Web.

You can also easily add or remove buttons from any of the toolbars present in the Word window. Each toolbar is equipped with a Toolbar Options button that you can use to modify the buttons shown on that particular toolbar.

To add or remove buttons from a specific toolbar, follow these steps:

1. Click the **Toolbar Options** button on any toolbar; a drop-down area appears.

2. Click **Add or Remove Buttons** and then select the name of the toolbar that appears on the pop-up menu. A list of all the buttons for the current toolbar appears, as shown in Figure 1.5.

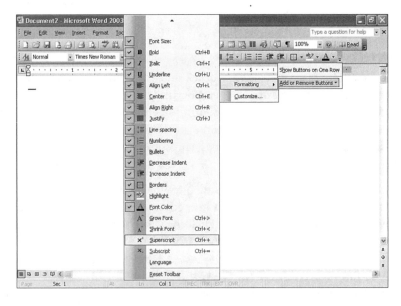

Figure 1.5   You can easily add or remove buttons from a toolbar using the button list.

3. For a button to appear on the toolbar, a check mark must appear to the left of the button in this list. For buttons without a check mark next to them, clicking this space puts the button on the toolbar. These buttons work as toggle switches; one click adds the check mark, another click removes it.

4. When you have completed your changes to the current toolbar, click outside the button list to close it.

The Word toolbars provide fast access to the commands you need most often. Buttons exist for all the commands that are available on the Word menu system.

 TIP **Moving Toolbars in the Word Window** You can rearrange toolbars in the Word window. Place the mouse on the dotted vertical handle on the left side of a toolbar and drag it to a new position. You can change the relative position of toolbars below the menu bar and you can also drag toolbars and nest them on the left side of the Word window. Toolbars dragged onto the document window will float and can be positioned as needed.

Exiting Word

When you have completed your initial survey of the Word application window or whenever you have completed your work in the program, you will want to exit the software. More than one way exists to close the Word window, which is the same as exiting the program.

You can exit Word by selecting the **File** menu and then **Exit**. Or you can close Word with one click of the mouse by clicking the Word **Close** (**x**) button in the upper-right corner of the application window.

When you close Word, you might be prompted to save any work that you have done in the application window. If you were just experimenting as you read through this lesson, you can click **No**. The current document will not be saved, and the Word application window closes. All the ins and outs of saving your documents are covered in Lesson 2, "Working with Documents."

Working with Documents

In this lesson, you learn how to start a new document and enter text. You also learn how to take advantage of Word document templates and Word document wizards.

Starting a New Document

When you choose to start a new document in Word, you can take three routes. You can

- Create a blank new document using Word's default *template.*
- Create a document using one of Word's many other templates or a custom one you created yourself.
- Create a document using one of the Word *wizards*, such as the Fax or Envelope Wizard.
- Create a document based on an existing document; using this method you are essentially opening a copy of an existing document, and you can then save it using a new filename.

Templates and wizards allow you to create more complex documents such as newsletters or Web sites. When you want to create a simple document, your best bet is to open a new blank document.

 Template A blueprint for a document that may already contain certain formatting options and text.

 Wizard A feature that guides you step by step through a particular process in Word, such as creating a new document.

When you create a new document from scratch, you are actually using a template—the Blank Document template. Documents based on the Blank Document template do not contain any premade text (as some of the other templates do), and the formatting contained in the document reflects Word's default settings for margins, fonts, and other document attributes (including any you customized specifically to your needs or preferences). To find more information on default Word settings involving font and document attributes, see Lesson 5, "Changing How Text Looks," and Lesson 9, "Working with Margins, Pages, and Line Spacing," respectively).

As covered in Lesson 1, Word automatically opens a new blank document for you when you open the Word application window. You can also open a new document when you are already working in Word.

To open a new document, follow these steps:

1. Select **File**, **New**. The New Document task pane opens on the right side of your screen. The task pane makes it easy for you to quickly create a new blank document, XML document (a document in the eXtensible Markup Language), Web page, or Email. For our purposes, let's look at available templates: under **Other templates**, select **On My Computer**. Word opens the Templates dialog box with a range of templates from which to choose (see Figure 2.1).

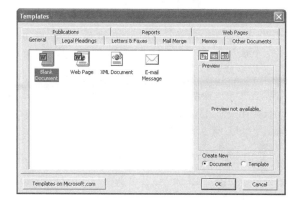

Figure 2.1 When you choose New on the File menu, the task pane opens and you can choose to open templates on your computer.

2. Make sure that the General tab is selected in the Templates dialog box, and then double-click the Word **Blank Document** icon. A new document appears in the Word application window.

Although the steps shown here are designed for you to create a new blank document, you could have chosen any of the templates available in the Templates dialog box to create a new document. The fastest way to create a new blank document is to click the **New Blank Document** icon on the Word Standard toolbar.

What Happened to My Previous Document?   If you were already working on a document, the new document will, in effect, open on top of the document you were previously working on. You can get back to the previous document by clicking the appropriately named document icon on the Windows taskbar (if you haven't yet named the first document, it might appear as Document1 on the taskbar). You can also select the **Windows** menu to see a list of currently opened documents. Click any document in the list to switch to it.

TIP   **Multiple Document Icons Are Grouped**   When you open a number of Word documents that exceed the number of single buttons that can be shown on the Windows Taskbar (which depends on your screen resolution), the document buttons are grouped under one Microsoft Word icon on the Taskbar. Click the single Word icon and a list of the currently open documents appears. As you close documents, the open documents remain grouped under the one icon until you close all but one of the documents (or all the documents by right-clicking on the Word icon and then selecting **Close Group**).

Using Document Templates

You don't have to base your new documents on a blank template. Instead, you can take advantage of one of the special document templates that Word provides. These templates make it easy for you to create everything from memos to newsletters.

Templates contain special text and document attributes; therefore, the look and layout of the document you create using a template are predetermined by the options contained in the template. This can include margins, fonts, graphics, and other document layout attributes.

To base a new document on a Word template, follow these steps:

1. Select the **File** menu, and then click **New**. The task pane opens in your current document window.

2. Several templates such as the Blank Document, Web Page, and XML Document templates, appear at the top of the New Document task pane. You can select any of these templates. Or you can use the Search box under Templates on Microsoft.com to search for online templates that Microsoft stores on the Office Web site. You can also select templates on your computer or templates held on other Web sites. To create a new memo from a template stored on your computer, click the **On My Computer** link under the Other Templates heading.

3. In the Templates dialog box that appears, choose the **Memos** tab (see Figure 2.2). Select your favorite style of memo and click **OK** (or double-click the icon of choice).

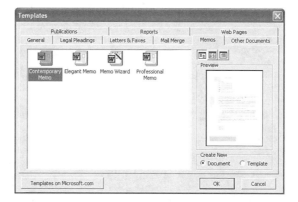

Figure 2.2   The document category tabs in the Templates dialog box contain templates for different document types.

4. The new document based on the template appears as shown in Figure 2.3.

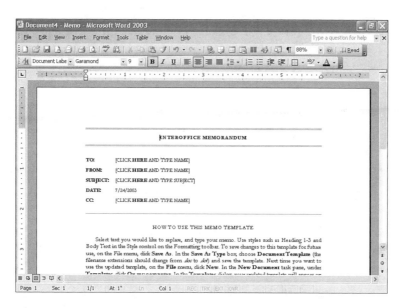

Figure 2.3   The new document contains predetermined text and formatting attributes derived from the template.

Most new documents based on templates already contain text, such as headings, and a variety of document layouts and text attributes, such as a particular font. For example, the document based on the Contemporary Memo template already contains the layout for a memo, and it automatically enters the current date in the memo for you.

You can easily enter text into the document using the Click Here and Type boxes that are placed in the document. Just click anywhere on the bracketed boxes provided and type the text you want to enter.

Many templates (the Contemporary Memo template, for example) contain text that gives you advice on how to use the template. Any of this explanatory text can be selected and removed or replaced with your own text (for more about selecting and editing text, see Lesson 3, "Editing Documents").

Using Word Wizards

If you find that you would like even more help as you create a new document, you can use any of a number of Word document wizards. These wizards actually walk you through the document creation process, and in many cases, they make sure that you enter the appropriate text in the proper place in the new document.

The wizards are found on the same tabs that housed the templates located in the Templates dialog box (reached through the task pane). The wizards can be differentiated from standard templates by a small wizard's wand that appears over the top right-hand corner of a template's icon.

To create a new document using one of the wizards, follow these steps:

1. Select the **File** menu, and then click **New** to open the New Document task pane.

2. Under the **Other Templates** heading, select the **On My Computer** link. In the Templates dialog box that appears, choose the new document tab of your choice (only the Legal Pleadings, Letterhead & Faxes, Memos, and other Documents tabs provide wizards).

3. To start the document creation process using the wizard, double-click the appropriate wizard icon (for example, the Memo Wizard on the Memos tab).

When you double-click the wizard icon, the wizard dialog box opens with an introductory screen and outlines the document creation process for the type of document you want to create. For example, the Memo Wizard shown in Figure 2.4 details the memo creation process on the left side of the wizard dialog box.

Figure 2.4   The various document wizards, such as the Memo Wizard, outline the new creation process and then walk you through the steps of creating the document.

If you find that you need help as you work with a wizard, you can click the **Office Assistant** button on the wizard dialog box. The Office Assistant, which appears as an animated paper clip by default, appears with context-sensitive help related to the wizard screen on which you are currently working. If the button is not available, cancel the wizard, select the **Help** menu, and then **Show the Office Assistant**; then repeat the steps necessary to open the particular document wizard.

To move to the next step in the document creation process, click the **Next** button at the bottom of the wizard screen.

The various document wizards walk you through the entire document creation process. After completing the steps for document creation, click the **Finish** button to close the wizard. A new document appears in the Word window based on the choices you made as you worked with the wizard. Figure 2.5 shows a new document created using the Memo Wizard.

The wizards you use vary in look and feel, depending on the type of document you are trying to create. For example, the Resume Wizard produces a decidedly different product than the Envelope Wizard does. A good rule to follow is to read each wizard screen carefully. Remember that you can always back up a step by clicking the **Back** button if you find that you've made an inappropriate choice (or you can close the unwanted document and start over).

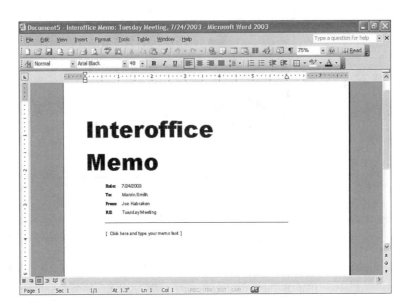

Figure 2.5 The Memo Wizard prompts you to input the appropriate information for a memo and provides the formatting for the new document.

Creating a New Document From an Existing Document

A new option that Word provides is the ability to quickly create a copy of an existing document. This allows you to open the existing document but have Word treat it as a new document without a filename. You can then edit the text and other items in the document as needed.

To create a new document from an existing document, click **File**, then **New**. The New Document task pane opens. Select the **From Existing Document** link under the New heading. The New from Existing Document dialog box opens (see Figure 2.6).

Use the **Look In** drop-down box to specify the drive where the file is located. Then double-click to open the appropriate folder. Select the file and then click **Create New** in the bottom right of the dialog box. A new document will open, which is a copy of the document you specified in the New from Existing Document dialog box. After making changes to the new document, you will want to save it under a new document name. The next section discusses saving a new document.

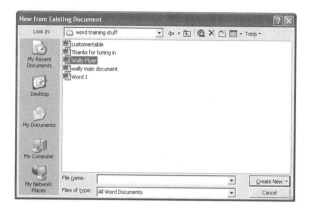

Figure 2.6 The New from Existing Document dialog box allows you to create a new document from an existing one.

Entering Text

After you have opened a new document, you are ready to start entering text. Notice that a blinking vertical element called the *insertion point* appears in the upper-left corner of your new document. This is where new text will be entered.

Begin typing text from the keyboard. The insertion point moves to the right as you type. As soon as you reach the end of the line, the text automatically wraps to the next line for you using word wrap.

When you reach the end of a paragraph in Word, you must press the **Enter** key to manually insert a paragraph break. If you want to view the manually placed paragraph breaks (called paragraph marks) in your document, click the **Show/Hide** button on the Word Standard toolbar.

If the Show/Hide button is not visible on the Word Standard toolbar, click the **Toolbar Options** button located at the end of the Standard toolbar. From the shortcut menu that appears, select **Add or Remove Buttons** and then **Standard**. A drop-down box of other buttons, including the Show/Hide button, appears. Clicking this button adds it to the Standard toolbar. When you are finished, click outside the drop-down box to return to your document. Now you can turn the Show/Hide option on and off as previously described.

TIP **How Word Views Paragraphs** Word considers any line or series of lines followed by a paragraph break (created when you press the Enter key) a separate paragraph. This concept becomes very important when you deal with paragraph formatting issues, such as line spacing, indents, and paragraph borders.

Saving a Document

Whether you create your new document using the Blank Document template, a Word template, a document wizard, or from an existing document, at some point you will want to save the new document. Saving your work is one of the most important aspects of working with any software application. If you don't save your Word documents, you could lose them.

CAUTION

Save and Save Often   You don't want to lose your valuable documents as you create them in Word. Power failures, an accidentally kicked-out power cord, or your computer locking up as you work can all lead to lost work. If you are really absent-minded about periodically saving your work, use the AutoSave feature. Select the **Tools** menu, then **Options**. Click the **Save** tab on the dialog box. Make sure the **Save AutoRecover Info Every** check box is selected. Use the minutes box to set the time interval between autosaves. This feature doesn't replace periodically saving your document using the Save command, but it will help you recover more of your document if there is a problem such as a power failure. I suggest setting AutoRecover to 10 or 15 minutes.

To save a document, follow these steps:

1. Click the **Save** button on the Word toolbar, or select the **File** menu and then **Save**. The first time you save your new document, the Save As dialog box appears.

2. Type a filename into the File Name box. If you want to save the file in a format other than a Word document (.doc), such as a text file (.txt), click the **Save As Type** drop-down arrow and select a different file type.

3. To save the file to a different location (the default location is My Documents), click the **Save In** drop-down arrow. After you select a particular drive, all the folders on that drive appear.

4. Double-click the desired folder in the Save In box to open that folder.

5. After you have specified a name and a location for your new document, select the **Save** button to save the file. Word then returns you to the document window.

As you edit and enhance your new document, you should make a habit of frequently saving any changes that you make. To save changes to a document that has already been saved under a filename, just click the **Save** button.

If you would like to keep a backup of a document (the version as it appeared the last time you saved it) each time you save changes to it, you need to set the backup option.

1. Click the **Tools** command on the toolbar, and then select **Options**.

2. In the Options dialog box, click the **Save** tab and then the **Always Create Backup Copy** check box. Click **OK** to return to the document.

3. Name your file and save it for the first time to an appropriate location such as My Documents or another folder on your computer or your network.

Now, when you use the Save command to save changes you've made to the document, a backup copy of the file (with the extension .wbk) is also saved. This backup copy is the previous version of the document before you made the changes. Each subsequent saving of the document replaces the backup file with the previous version of the document.

Occasionally, rather than using the backup option, you might want to save the current document under a new filename or drive location. You can do this using the Save As command. To save your document with a new filename, follow these steps:

1. Select **File**, **Save As**.

2. In the Save As dialog box, type the new filename into the File Name box (make sure that you are saving the document in the desired path).

3. Click **Save**. The file is saved under the new name.

Closing a Document

When you have finished working with a document, you need to save your changes and then close the document. To close a document, select the **File** menu and then select **Close**. You can also close a document by clicking the **Close (x)** button on the right side of the document window. If you are working with multiple documents, closing one of the documents does not close the Word application. If you want to completely end your Word session, select the **File** menu, and then select **Exit**. Before closing a document, Word checks to see whether it has changed since it was last saved. If it has, Word asks whether you want to save these changes before closing. If you don't want to lose any recent changes, click **Yes** to save the document.

Opening a Document

Opening an existing document is a straightforward process. You will find that the Open dialog box shares many of the attributes that you saw in the Save As dialog box.

To open an existing Word file, follow these steps:

1. Select the **File** menu, and then **Open** (or click the Open button on the Standard toolbar). The Open dialog box appears.

2. By default, Word begins showing the files and folders in your My Documents folder. If the document you need is located elsewhere on your computer, click the **Look In** drop-down arrow to select the drive on which the file is located, and navigate to the folder containing the document you need.

3. To open the file, click the file, and then click the **Open** button (you can also double-click the file). The file appears in a Word document window.

If you are working with text files or documents that have been saved in a format other than the Word document format (.doc), you must select the file type in the **Files of Type** drop-down box to see them.

Editing Documents

In this lesson, you learn how to do basic text editing in Word, including moving and copying text; you work with the mouse and keyboard to move your document, and you learn how to save existing documents under a new filename.

Adding or Replacing Text and Moving in the Document

After you have completed a draft of your document, you will find yourself in a situation where you want to add and delete text in the document as you edit your work. Word makes it very easy for you to add new text and delete text that you don't want. You also will find that, whether you use the mouse or the keyboard to move around in your document as you edit, Word offers a number of special keystrokes and other tricks that make moving within the document a breeze.

The primary tool for placing the insertion point into a document that already contains text using the mouse is the *I-beam*. It looks like an uppercase "I." Place it anywhere in the document and click the left mouse button. This places the insertion point in the document at the I-beam's current position.

 I-beam This is the shape that the mouse pointer takes when you place it over any text in a Word document. Use it to place the insertion point at a particular position in a document.

Adding New Text

You actually have two possibilities for adding text to the document: *insert* and *typeover*. To insert text into the document and adjust the position of the existing text, place the I-beam where you want to insert the new text. Click the mouse to place the insertion point at the chosen position. Make sure that the OVR indicator on the Status bar near the bottom of the screen is not active (it will be gray rather than bolded). This means that you are in the insert mode.

 Insert Mode The default text mode in Word. New text is added at the insertion point and existing text is pushed forward in the document so that it remains as part of the document.

Type your new text. It is added at the insertion point, and existing text (the text to the right of the inserted text) is pushed forward in the document.

Replacing Text with Typeover

If you want to add new text to a document and simultaneously delete text to the right of the insertion point, use the mouse to place the insertion point where you want to start typing over the existing text. Press the **Insert** key on the keyboard and add your new text. The added text types over the existing text, deleting it (see Figure 3.1). When you switch to Typeover mode using the **Insert** key, the Word status bar displays the message OVR. This means that you are currently in Typeover mode.

Appears in black text when in Typeover mode

Figure 3.1   When you are in Typeover mode, existing text is overwritten by the new text.

 TERM **Typeover Mode**   Press the **Insert** key to enter this mode; new text is added at the insertion point and types over the existing text, deleting it.

If you want to return to Insert mode, press the **Insert** key again (it toggles Word between the Insert and Typeover modes) and the OVR message on the status bar is dimmed (you can also double-click **OVR** on the status bar to toggle this feature on and off).

CAUTION   **Undo That Typeover**   If you inadvertently type over text in a document because you are in the Typeover mode, click the **Undo** button (it might take several clicks in cases where you have added several words to the document) on the toolbar to return the deleted text to the document (or press **Ctrl+Z**).

Moving Around the Document

Whether you are a mouse aficionado or prefer to stick close to your keyboard, Word provides several shortcuts and tools for moving around a document that you are trying to edit.

When you use the mouse, you can move to a different position on the current page by using the I-beam. You also can use the mouse to move through your document using the vertical and horizontal scrollbars. For example, clicking the up scroll arrow on the vertical scrollbar moves you up through the document. Clicking the down scroll arrow moves you down through the document. If you want to quickly move to a particular page in the document, you can drag the scroll box to a particular place on the vertical scrollbar. As soon as you click on the scroll box, a page indicator box appears that you can use to keep track of what page you are on as you drag the scroll box up or down on the vertical scrollbar.

The vertical scrollbar also provides Previous Page and Next Page buttons (the double-up arrow and double-down arrow buttons on the bottom of the scrollbar) that can be used to move to the previous page and next page, respectively. Use the mouse to click the appropriate button to move in the direction that you want to go in your document.

The horizontal scrollbar operates much the same as the vertical scrollbar; however, it offers the capability to scroll only to the left and the right of a document page. This is particularly useful when you have zoomed in on a document and want to scrutinize an area of the page in great detail.

You should be aware that clicking the mouse on the vertical scrollbar to change your position in a document allows you to view a different portion of a page or a different part of the document; however, it does not move the insertion point to that position on the page. To actually place the insertion point, you must move to a specific place or position in the document, and then click the mouse I-beam where you want to place the insertion point.

When you're typing or editing text, you might find that the fastest way to move through the document is with the help of the keyboard shortcuts shown in Table 3.1. Keeping your hands on the keyboard, rather than reaching out for the mouse, can be a more efficient way to move in a document while you compose or edit.

 TIP **Scroll Quickly with a Wheel Mouse**   You might want to purchase a wheel mouse, such as Microsoft's IntelliMouse, which provides a rolling device on the top of the mouse (between the click buttons). With your finger on the wheel device, you can literally "roll" the vertical scrollbar through the document at the pace of your choice—rapidly or slowly.

Table 3.1   Using the Keyboard to Move Through the

Key Combination	Movement
Home	Move to the beginning of a line
End	Move to the end of a line
Ctrl+Right arrow	Move one word to the right
Ctrl+Left arrow	Move one word to the left

Table 3.1   Continued

Key Combination	Movement
Ctrl+Up arrow	Move to the previous paragraph
Ctrl+Down arrow	Move to the next paragraph
PgUp	Move up one window
PgDn	Move down one window
Ctrl+PgUp	Move up one page
Ctrl+PgDn	Move down one page
Ctrl+Home	Move to the top of a document
Ctrl+End	document

Selecting Text

Having a good handle on the different methods for selecting text in a document makes it easy for you to take advantage of many features, including deleting, moving, and formatting text. You can select text with either the mouse or the keyboard. Both methods have their own advantages and disadvantages as you work on your documents.

Selecting Text with the Mouse

The mouse is an excellent tool for selecting text in your document during the editing process. You can double-click a word to select it and also use different numbers of mouse clicks (quickly pressing the left mouse button) or the mouse in combination with the Shift key to select sentences, paragraphs, or other blocks of text. You also can hold the left mouse button down and drag it across a block of text that you want to select.

How you use the mouse to select the text depends on whether the mouse pointer is in the document itself or along the left side of the document in the *selection bar*. The selection bar is the white space on the left edge of your document window, just in front of your text paragraphs. When you place the mouse in the selection bar, the mouse pointer becomes an arrow (in contrast to placing the mouse in the document where the pointer appears as an I-beam).

Selecting text lines and paragraphs from the selection bar makes it easy for you to quickly select either a single line or the entire document. Table 3.2 shows you how to select different text items using the mouse. Figure 3.2 shows the mouse pointer in the selection bar with a selected sentence.

Table 3.2 Using the Mouse to Quickly Select Text in the Document

Text Selection	Mouse Action
Selects the word	Double-click a word
Selects text block	Click and drag
	or
	Click at beginning of text, and then hold down the Shift key and click at the end of text block
Selects line	Click in selection bar next to line
Selects multiple lines	Click in selection bar and drag down through multiple lines
Selects the sentence	Hold Ctrl and click a sentence
Selects paragraph	Double-click in selection bar next to paragraph
	or
	Triple-click in the paragraph
Selects entire document	Hold down Ctrl and click in selection bar

You will find these mouse manipulations are particularly useful when you are editing the document. Selected text can be quickly deleted, moved, or copied.

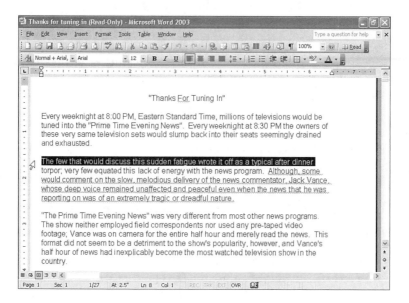

Figure 3.2 Place the mouse pointer in the selection bar to quickly select a line, a paragraph, or other text block.

Selecting Text with the Keyboard

You can also select text using only the keyboard. Press the F8 function key to turn on the extend (or select) feature; the EXT indicator becomes active on the Word status bar as soon as you press one of the arrow keys on the keyboard (meaning it is no longer "grayed" out).

To select text using the extend feature, use the arrow keys to move over and highlight characters, words, or sentences you want to select. You can quickly select entire words by placing the insertion point at the beginning of a word, pressing **F8** and then pressing the spacebar. To select an entire sentence, turn on the extend feature, and then press the period (.) key. You can select entire paragraphs using this method by pressing the **Enter** key. To turn off the extend feature, press the **Esc** key.

Finally, you can select text by pressing only the F8 function key. Press **F8** once to turn on the select feature where you want it, press it twice to select a word, three times to highlight an entire sentence, four times to select a paragraph, and five times to select your entire document.

Deleting, Copying, and Moving Text

Another important aspect of editing is being able to delete, move, or copy text in your document. Each of these tasks can be easily accomplished in Word and uses the mouse or the keyboard to select the text that you want to delete, move, or copy. Then, it's just a matter of invoking the correct command to delete, move, or copy the selected text.

Deleting Text

Deleting text can be accomplished in more than one way. The simplest way to remove characters as you type is with the Backspace key or the Delete key. If no text is selected, these keys work like this:

- **Delete**—Deletes the character to the right of the insertion point.
- **Backspace**—Deletes the character to the left of the insertion point.

You will probably find, however, that when you delete text you want to remove more than just one character, so use the keyboard or the mouse to select the text you want to delete. After the text is selected, press the **Delete** key. The text is then removed from the document.

You can also delete text and replace it with new text in one step. After the text is selected, type the new text. It replaces the entire existing, selected text.

CAUTION

Delete and Cut Are Different   When you want to erase a text block forever, use the **Delete** key. When you want to remove text from a particular place in the document but want to have access to it again to place it somewhere else, use the **Cut** command on the **Edit** menu. When you cut an item, it is automatically placed on the Office Clipboard. These steps are covered later in this lesson.

Copying, Cutting, and Pasting Text

Copying or cutting text and then pasting the copied or cut item to a new location is very straightforward. All you have to do is select the text as we discussed earlier in this lesson and then invoke the appropriate commands. Use the following steps to copy and paste text in your document:

1. Using the mouse or the keyboard, select the text that you want to copy.

2. Select the **Edit** menu, and then select **Copy**, or press **Ctrl+C** to copy the text.

3. Place the insertion point in the document where you want to place a copy of the copied text.

4. Select the **Edit** menu and then select **Paste**, or press **Ctrl+V**. A copy of the text is inserted at the insertion point.

TIP   **Use the Copy, Cut, and Paste Icons**   To quickly access the copy, cut, and paste features, use the Copy, Cut, and Paste icons on the Word toolbar, respectively.

After you paste your selected text, the Paste Smart Tag icon appears just below the text that you have pasted. When you click this icon, it provides a shortcut menu that allows you to keep the formatting that was applied to the source text that you copied, match the formatting supplied by the destination for the text (the paragraph you are placing the text in), or just paste the text into the new location with no formatting at all (which means it will assume the formatting that is provided at the current location). Figure 3.3 shows the Paste Smart Tag provided for pasted text.

TIP   **What Are Smart Tags?**   Smart Tags are shortcuts that are assigned to particular types of information in a Word document. For example, you will see that people's names are labeled with a smart tag (a purple dotted line below the text) that makes it easy to add a person to your Outlook Contact folder. Text that has been pasted to a new location is also flagged with a smart tag that makes it easy to format the pasted text.

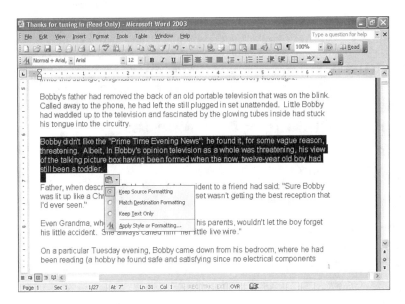

Figure 3.3   The Paste Smart Tag allows you to choose how the text is pasted into the new location.

Cutting text from the document and then pasting it to a new location is every bit as straightforward as using copy and paste. Select the text, and then press Ctrl+X or click the **Cut** button on the Standard toolbar. Click the I-beam to place the insertion point on the document, and then you can use Ctrl+V or the **Paste** button on the Standard toolbar to place the text in a new location. A Paste Smart Tag will appear below the pasted text as shown in Figure 3.3.

Using the Office Clipboard to Copy and Move Multiple Items

The Office Clipboard feature now resides in the task pane of your Office application windows as discussed in Lesson 3, "Using the Office Task Pane," which is found in Part I of this book. If you want to copy or cut more than one item and then be able to paste them into different places in the document, you must use the Office Clipboard. Follow these steps:

1. To open the Clipboard task pane, select the **Edit** menu and select **Office Clipboard**. The Clipboard appears in the task pane.

2. As shown in Figure 3.4, select and copy each item to the Clipboard.

Figure 3.4   The Clipboard can hold up to 24 separate items.

3. After you have copied your items onto the Clipboard, place the insertion point where you want the first item to be pasted. Then, return to the Clipboard and with the mouse, point to your first item and click; Word automatically inserts the item into the document.

4. Repeat step 3 as needed to paste other items from the Clipboard into your document.

If you want to cut and paste (or move) multiple items, you must use the Office Clipboard. Follow these steps:

1. To open the Clipboard, select the **Edit** menu and select **Clipboard**. The Clipboard appears in the task pane.

2. Select and cut each item to the Clipboard.

3. After you have your cut items on the Clipboard, place the insertion point where you want the first item to be pasted. Then, return to the Clipboard and with the mouse, point to your first item and click; it will automatically be inserted into the document.

4. Repeat step 3 as needed to paste other items from the Clipboard into your document.

Using Drag and Drop

One other way to move text is by selecting it and dragging it to a new location. This is called *drag and drop*. After the text is selected, place the mouse on the text block and hold down the left mouse button. A Move pointer appears, as shown in Figure 3.5.

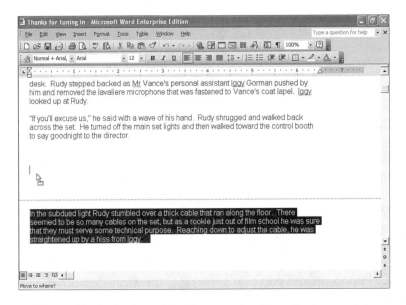

Figure 3.5 Drag a block of selected text to a new location with drag and drop.

Drag the Move pointer to the new location for the text. A dotted insertion point appears in the text. Place this insertion point in the appropriate position and release the mouse button. The text is moved to the new location.

Copying and Moving Text Between Documents

You can copy text easily between documents. All you have to do is open the appropriate documents and then use the methods already discussed for copying or moving text. You can even use drag and drop to move information from one document to another.

To copy information from one document to another, follow these steps:

1. Open the document you want to copy information from and the one you want to copy that information to (see Lesson 2, "Working with Documents," for more information on opening documents).

2. Switch to the document that contains the text you want to copy by clicking the document's button on the **Taskbar** or selecting the **Windows** menu and then the name of the document.

3. Select the text you want to copy, select the **Edit** menu, and then select the **Copy** command.

4. Using the instructions in step 2, switch to the document into which you want to paste the text.

5. Select the **Edit** menu, and then select **Paste**. The text is pasted into your document.

You can also use the preceding steps to move text from one document to another by substituting the Cut command for the Copy command. You can also use drag and drop to move text from one document to another. Working with multiple document windows can be tricky. You probably won't want to have more than two documents open if you want to use drag and drop, because you won't have enough space in the Word workspace to scroll through the documents and find the text you want to move or the final resting place for the text in the other document.

To view multiple document windows (all the documents you currently have open), select the **Window** menu and then select **Arrange All**. Each document is placed in a separate window in the Word workspace. The windows might be small if you have several documents open. Locate the text you want to move and select it. Drag it from the current document window to the document window and position where you want to place it.

Using Proofreading and Research Tools

In this lesson, you learn to check your documents for errors such as misspellings and improper grammar. You work with the spell checker and grammar checker and learn how to find synonyms with the thesaurus, how to proof your document as you type, and how to use the AutoCorrect feature. You learn how to add a service to the Research task pane.

Proofing As You Type

Word offers several excellent features for helping you to create error-free documents. Each of these features—the spell checker, the grammar checker, and the thesaurus—are explored in this lesson. Word also gives you the option of checking your spelling and grammar automatically as you type. You can also use the AutoCorrect feature to automatically make some proofing changes for you (for more about AutoCorrect, see "Working with AutoCorrect" in this lesson).

Proofing as you type simply means that errors in spelling and grammar can be automatically flagged as you enter text into your document. This enables you to quickly and immediately correct errors as you build your document.

When you proof as you type, spelling errors—words not found in the Word dictionary file or in your custom dictionary file—are flagged with a wavy red underline. Errors in grammar are underlined with a wavy green line. Spelling and grammar errors marked in this way can be corrected immediately, or you can correct them collectively by running the spelling and grammar checking features after you have finished entering all the text. For information on using the Spelling and Grammar Checker on a completed document, see the section "Using the Spelling and Grammar Checker," later in this lesson.

The check-as-you-type features are turned on in Word by default. To change the defaults associated with the automatic spelling and grammar checking features (or to turn them off completely), follow these steps:

1. Select the **Tools** menu, and then choose **Options**. The Options dialog box opens.
2. Make sure the **Spelling and Grammar** tab is selected, as shown in Figure 4.1.

Figure 4.1   You can turn the automatic spelling and grammar checking options on or off in the Options dialog box.

3. To toggle the automatic spelling checker on or off, click the **Check Spelling As You Type** check box in the Spelling area of the dialog box.

4. To toggle the automatic grammar checker on or off, click the **Check Grammar As You Type** check box in the Grammar area of the dialog box (near the bottom).

Several other options are also available in this dialog box that relate to how the Spelling and Grammar features operate when you use them in Word.

- **Hide Spelling Errors in This Document**—This option hides the wavy red lines that flag misspellings in the document.

- **Always Suggest Corrections**—This option provides a list of suggested corrections for each misspelled word when the spell checker is used.

- **Suggest from Main Dictionary Only**—This option uses only the main dictionary for spell checking the document. Any customized dictionaries that have been created are ignored.

- **Ignore Words in UPPERCASE**—This option ignores uppercase words in the document.

- **Ignore Words with Numbers**—This option ignores combinations of text and numbers in the document.

- **Ignore Internet and File Addresses**—This option ignores Web addresses and file-names (such as `C:\my documents\joe.doc`).

- **Hide Grammatical Errors in the Document**—This option hides the wavy green line that marks potential grammar errors in the document.

- **Check Grammar with Spelling**—This option is used to have Word also check the grammar in the document when you run the spell checker.

- **Show Readability Statistics**—This option is used to display different readability statistics that show you the readability level and grade level of your text.

After you have finished making your selections in the Options dialog box, click **OK**.

 TIP   **Understanding Readability Statistics**   Readability statistics provide you with a way to assess the reading level of a document. Two scales that are based on the average syllables per word and the number of words per sentence are provided: Flesch Reading Ease score and Flesch-Kincaid Grade Level score. Flesch Reading Ease uses a 100-point scale; the higher the number the easier the document is to read (you should aim for documents with a score of 60 to 70). Flesch-Kincaid Grade Level uses U.S. school grade levels. For example, a rating of 8.0 would be equivalent to an eighth grade reading level (aim for scores between 7.0 to 8.0).

With the check–as-you-type options enabled, suspected misspellings and grammatical errors are flagged with the appropriate colored wavy line.

Correcting Individual Spelling Errors

As mentioned, Word marks all words not found in its dictionary with a wavy red line. Because Word's dictionary isn't entirely complete, you might find that it marks correct words as misspelled. To correct words flagged as misspelled (whether they are or not), follow these steps:

1. Place the mouse pointer on the flagged word and click the right mouse button. A shortcut menu appears, as shown in Figure 4.2.

2. Word provides a list of possible correct spellings when it encounters a word not in its dictionary. If the correct spelling for the word you want appears in the list, simply click it, and Word replaces the incorrect spelling with the correct one.

    If the flagged word is correctly spelled (and just not in Word's dictionary) or the correct spelling is not in the suggestions list, you have two other options:

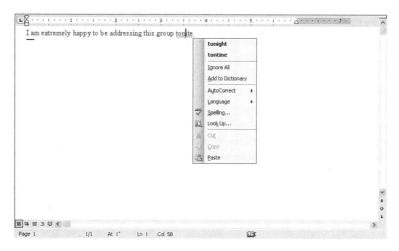

Figure 4.2   Right-click any flagged word to get a list of suggested spellings.

- If the word is correct and you don't want it flagged at all in the current document, you can click **Ignore All** and the wavy red line will be removed from all occurrences of the word.

- If the word is correct and you don't want it flagged in this or any other document, you can add the word to the dictionary file; click **Add to Dictionary**.

TIP   **Take Advantage of AutoCorrect**   If you find that you constantly misspell the word as it currently appears in your document, you can add the word to the AutoCorrect list (discussed later in this chapter). Right-click on the misspelled word and then point to AutoCorrect on the shortcut menu. Suggested spellings will be listed. Select a spelling from the list; the incorrect spelling and the correct spelling are entered into the AutoCorrect list. The word in your document is corrected, and the next time you type the word incorrectly, it is automatically corrected.

Correcting Individual Grammatical Errors

Correcting grammatical errors as you type is similar to correcting spelling errors that are flagged in the document. Suspected grammatical errors are marked with a green wavy line.

To correct a suspected grammatical error, follow these steps:

1. Right-click text blocks marked with the green wavy line.

2. The shortcut menu that appears might offer you a list of grammatically correct phrases. Select the phrase that corrects your text entry. In most cases, however, rather than providing a correct solution, the Grammar Checker provides the nature of the error such as passive voice or fragment. You will have to correct the error yourself, but Word at least provides information on why it was flagged.

3. If your text is not incorrect grammatically or requires that you manually make any necessary changes, click **Ignore Once**.

4. If you select Grammar on the shortcut menu, the Grammar dialog box will open. It offers suggestions related to the error and also gives you the option of ignoring the grammar rule that flagged the error in the document.

As soon as you make a selection from the shortcut menu or click **Ignore Once**, the shortcut menu closes. You can then either use the Grammar dialog box to fix the error or continue working on your document (the Spelling and Grammar features are discussed in the next section).

 TIP **How Good is the Grammar Checker?**   Although the Grammar Checker is useful, you will find that it will miss grammar errors and even flag correct sentences. The Grammar Checker does not have the ability to interpret the context of the words you use in a sentence. So, use it as an aid to writing, not necessarily the final word, however.

Using the Spelling and Grammar Checker

You might prefer not to correct spelling and grammatical errors as you type. If you're a touch typist, you might not even notice Word has flagged a word or sentence as incorrect. Waiting to correct the document until you have finished composing enables you to concentrate on getting your thoughts down without interruption. Then, you can check the entire document upon completion.

To use the Word Spelling and Grammar feature, follow these steps:

 1. Select **Tools**, **Spelling and Grammar**, or click the **Spelling and Grammar** button on the toolbar. The Spelling and Grammar dialog box appears as shown in Figure 4.3.

2. Words not found in the dictionary are flagged, and the text in which the word is contained is displayed in the Not in Dictionary box. You can manually correct the highlighted word in the box and then click **Change** to correct the word in the document. The following are other options available for the flagged word:

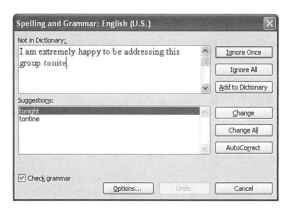

Figure 4.3 The Spelling and Grammar dialog box displays the suspected spelling and grammar errors in your document and offers you options for correcting them.

- Select the appropriate selection for the flagged word from the Suggestion box and click **Change**. If you want to correct all occurrences of the misspelled word (assuming you have consistently and knowingly misspelled it), click **Change All**.

- Ignore the flagged word if it is correctly spelled. Click **Ignore Once** to ignore this occurrence of the word, or click **Ignore All** to ignore all occurrences of the word in the document.

- You can also add the word to the dictionary; just click **Add**.

- If you would rather add the misspelled word and an appropriate correct spelling to the AutoCorrect feature, click **AutoCorrect**; the word is corrected, and future insertions of the word (even in other documents when they're opened) with the incorrect spelling are automatically corrected.

Regardless of which selection you make, the word is dealt with appropriately and the spelling checker moves on to the next flagged word. Make your selection either to correct or to ignore the word, as previously outlined.

If the Check Grammar check box in the Spelling and Grammar dialog box is selected, Word also checks the grammar in your document.

When the Spelling and Grammar dialog box flags a grammatical error in the document, the suspected error appears in the text box at the top of the Spelling and Grammar dialog box with a heading that describes the type of error. Figure 4.4 shows an error in subject-verb agreement that has been caught by the grammar checker.

Text specifies the nature of the problem

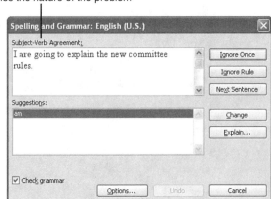

Figure 4.4   The grammar checker flags suspected grammar errors and offers suggestions and possible fixes for the problem.

Suggested corrections, if available, appear in the Suggestions box. In the case of the
fragment, the suggestion is to consider revising the fragment. In other cases, more
suggestions with actual sentence revisions might appear in this box. If the appropriate revision is present, select it and click **Change**.

You are also presented with different ignore options for flagged grammatical errors:

- You can choose to ignore the suspected grammatical error by clicking **Ignore**.
  This ignores only the currently flagged error.

- In some cases, **Ignore All** is also an option. If you click **Ignore All**, the grammar
  checker ignores all occurrences of this same grammatical error in the rest of the
  document.

- Word also provides you with the option of ignoring the actual grammar rule
  that was used to flag the current grammatical error; click **Ignore Rule** to do this
  throughout the document. This means that any error (not just the current error)
  that is flagged because of that particular rule (fragment or long sentence, for
  example) is not flagged as a grammatical error.

Use the Grammar feature to check the entire document using the options discussed
in this section. When you reach the end of the document and the Grammar check is
complete, a dialog box will appear letting you know that the spelling and grammar
check has been completed.

Finding Synonyms Using the Thesaurus

The Word thesaurus provides you with a tool that can be used to find synonyms for the words in your document. Synonyms are words that mean the same thing. Because the thesaurus can generate a list of synonyms for nearly any word in your document, you can avoid the constant use of a particular descriptive adjective (such as "excellent") and actually add some depth to the vocabulary that appears in your document.

 The thesaurus is now part of a new Research tool that has been added to Microsoft Office. Research tools like the Word thesaurus are accessed in the Research task pane, which you can open by clicking the Research button. The Research task pane can be used to search local resources such as the thesaurus and custom data sources specifically created by a company or institution. For example, a data source could be created that would allow a user to find information about a particular product they are writing about by accessing the custom data resource through the Research task pane.

The Research task pane also allows you to access remote data sources such as resources on the Internet. Although it is beyond the scope of this book to discuss the creation of custom data sources, we will look at how you can add additional resources to the Research task pane later in the lesson. We will get our feet wet using the new Research task pane by using the Word thesaurus.

> **TIP**   **The Thesaurus Also Lists Antonyms**   Depending on the word you select to find synonyms, you might find that a list of antonyms—words that mean the opposite—are also provided. Antonyms are marked with (antonym) to the right of the suggested word.

To use the thesaurus, follow these steps:

1. To select the word for which you want to find a synonym, double-click it.

2. Select the **Tools** menu, point at **Language**, and then select **Thesaurus**. (You can also click the **Research** button on the Standard toolbar.) The Research task pane appears as shown in Figure 4.5. By default the English (U.S.) thesaurus is used to find a list of synonyms for the selected word.

3. To replace the word with a synonym, place the mouse on the synonym in the synonym list, and then click on the drop-down arrow that appears to the right of the synonym. Click Insert from the menu that appears.

Figure 4.5   The Research task pane provides a list of synonyms for the selected word.

4. You can also choose to see a list of synonyms for any of the words listed in the synonym list. Double-click on the synonym. This can provide a greater number of possible words to use when you replace the particular word in your document. Synonyms provided for a word in the synonym list might be less close in meaning, however, to the word in your document. If you want to return to the original lists of synonyms (for the word you originally selected), click the **Back** button.

After you have selected a synonym and clicked **Replace**, the word is replaced in the document. If you want to close the Research task pane, click the Close button in the upper-right corner of the task pane.

TIP   **Right-Click for Synonyms**   A quick way to check for a list of synonyms for a word is to right-click that word in your document and then select **Synonyms** from the shortcut menu. A list of synonyms (if available for that word) appears. Select the appropriate word on the list to replace the currently selected word. Words flagged as misspelled or in a sentence marked as a grammar error will not provide a list of synonyms when you right-click them.

Adding Research Services

As we already discussed briefly, the new Research task pane provides a tool that can be used to access all sorts of information related to a selection in a document. These tools can be standard tools such as the thesaurus and can also consist of specialized data sources created to find specific kinds of information.

In the case of the Word thesaurus, you can actually access different thesaurus files. For example, by default you use the English (U.S.) thesaurus (if you installed the U.S. version of Office). But you can also access other thesaurus files such as the English (U.K.) or French (Canada or France). To access these additional reference books click the **Show Results From** drop-down list in the Research task pane.

You can also add new reference services to the Research task pane. These can be custom resources or resources provided by Microsoft. To add a new reference service, follow these steps:

1. Select **Tools**, and then select **Research** to open the Research task pane.

2. Select the Research options link at the bottom of the Research task pane. The Research Options dialog box will open as shown in Figure 4.6.

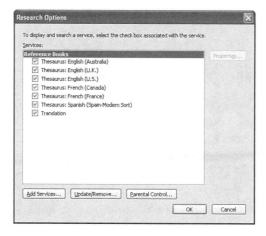

Figure 4.6 The Research Options dialog box allows you to view installed Research services and add new services.

3. Click **Add Services**. The Add Services dialog box appears. It will contain a list of services that are available for addition (this will typically consist of only Microsoft services).

4. To add a service, either click a service in the Available services list or provide the URL (the Web address) of the new service.

5. When you select a Microsoft service that is listed, an additional dialog box will open with service options. For example, you may be able to add Encarta dictionaries or other services such as MSN search to your Research services.

6. Select the specific services you want to add from the list and then click Install. The services will be added.

Now when you use the Research task pane the additional services will be available in the **Show Results From** drop-down list. You can use these new services for a variety of purposes. For example, if I have referenced a company name in a document, I can use the Research task pane to automatically search the Web for information on that company using an added service such as the MSN search tool from Microsoft. Follow these steps:

1. Click at the end of the company name or other information in the document.

2. Select **Tools**, and then select **Research** to open the Research task pane.

3. Select the **Show Results From** drop-down list and select the service you want to use (such as **MNS Search**).

4. A list of links or other information will appear in the results area of the Research Task pane. In the case of Web links you can click any of the links to open the referenced Web page. Internet Explorer will open to the referenced page.

Working with AutoCorrect

You will find that as you type some of your misspelled words are corrected automatically. AutoCorrect, a feature that uses a list of common spelling errors and typos to correct entries in your documents, is the tool making these corrections. For example, Word has already arranged to have the incorrect spelling of "t-e-h" to be replaced with "the." You can also add your own words to the AutoCorrect feature. For example, if you always spell aardvark as ardvark, you can set up AutoCorrect to correct this spelling error every time you type it.

You've already seen that the Spelling feature provides you with the option of placing misspelled words into the AutoCorrect library. You can also manually enter pairs of words (the incorrect and correct spellings) into the AutoCorrect dialog box.

To place words in the AutoCorrect list, follow these steps:

1. Click the **Tools** menu, and then click **AutoCorrect Options**. The AutoCorrect dialog box appears as shown in Figure 4.7.

2. In the **Replace** box, enter the word as you misspell it. In the **With** box, enter the correct spelling of the word.

3. Click **Add** to add the entry to the AutoCorrect list.

4. When you have completed adding entries, click **OK** to close the dialog box.

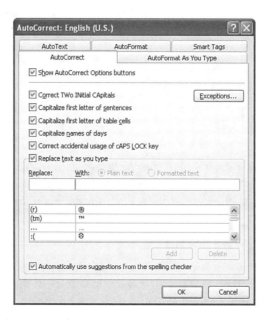

Figure 4.7 The AutoCorrect feature enables you to build a list of commonly misspelled words for automatic correction.

Now when you misspell the word, Word corrects it for you automatically. You can also use the AutoCorrect dialog box to delete AutoCorrect entries that you do not use (highlight the entry and click **Delete**) or that inadvertently correct items that you want to have in your document (clear the applicable check box).

This feature can also be used to help speed your typing along. For example, suppose that you are writing a technical paper that includes a long organizational name, such as the National Museum of American Art. If you tell the AutoCorrect feature to replace "nmaa" with "National Museum of American Art," it saves you a lot of typing.

TIP **Override the AutoCorrect Feature** If you type a text entry that is automatically changed by the AutoCorrect feature but you want it spelled your original way, immediately place your mouse on the corrected text. The AutoCorrect Smart Tag (it has a lightning bolt symbol on it) appears. When you click this Smart Tag's arrow, you can choose to return the word to its original text, among other options.

Changing How Text Looks

In this lesson, you learn basic ways to change the look of your text. You work with fonts and learn how to change font attributes. You also work with text alignment, such as centering and right justification.

Understanding Fonts

When you work in Word, you want to be able to control the look of the text in the documents that you create. The size and appearance of the text is controlled for the most part by the font or fonts you choose to use in the document. Each available font has a particular style or typeface. A variety of fonts exists, with names such as Arial, Courier, Times New Roman, CG Times, Bookman Old Style, and so on; the fonts you can choose depend on the fonts that have been installed on your computer (Windows offers a large number of default fonts; other font families are added when you install Office, and you can purchase software for special lettering and printing projects). Each font has a particular look and feel that makes it unique.

 TIP   **Keep Your Business Documents Standard**   The standard point size for most business documents is 12 points, which is 1/6 of an inch tall. So, when selecting a new font, it's generally a good idea to make sure that you use 12 points for documents such as business letters and memos.

You can change the font or fonts used in a document whenever you need to, and you can also manipulate the size of the characters and their attributes, including bold, underlining, and italic. You can select a new font before you begin typing your document, or you can select text and change its fonts and text attributes at any time.

Changing Font Attributes

The easiest way to change font attributes is through the use of the buttons provided on the Word Formatting toolbar. Figure 5.1 shows the Word Formatting toolbar with some of the most common font attribute buttons displayed.

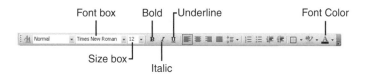

Font box   Bold   ┌Underline   Font Color

Size box┘
Italic

Figure 5.1 The Word Formatting toolbar gives you quick access to control the font attributes in your documents.

You can quickly change the font of selected text by clicking the **Font** box and selecting a new font from the list that appears. Other attributes, such as bold, italic, and underline, require that you select the text and then click the appropriate button once to add that attribute to the text. For example, you might want to apply special formatting to a heading so that it stands out from the rest of the text. You can do that by adding bold to the text.

To add bold to text in a document, follow these steps:

1. Select the word or other text to be bold.

2. Click the **Bold** button on the Formatting toolbar. The text appears in bold.

3. Click any other part of the document to deselect the text and view the results of your formatting.

You can use this same technique to underline and italicize text in your documents.

TIP   **I Don't Have Those Buttons on My Toolbar** Click the **Toolbar Options** drop-down arrow, point at **Add or Remove Buttons**, and then select the name of the toolbar you want to add the buttons to (such as the Formatting toolbar). From the drop-down list, select the buttons that you want to add to the Formatting toolbar. If you don't see the Formatting toolbar at all, right-click any of the toolbars and select **Formatting** on the menu that appears.

You can also use the various font buttons to select font attributes for the new text you type into a new document or insert into an existing document. Select the appropriate font attributes on the Formatting toolbar, and then type the text. To turn off a particular attribute, such as bold or italic, click the appropriate button a second time. To change to a new font or size, use the appropriate drop-down box.

When you are typing in a document, you might find that selecting font attributes from the toolbar actually slows you down because you must remove one hand from the keyboard to use the mouse to make your selection. You can also turn on or off a number of the formatting attributes using shortcut keys on the keyboard. Table 5.1 shows some of the common keyboard shortcuts for formatting attributes.

Table 5.1 Font Attribute Shortcut Keys

Attribute	Shortcut Keys
Bold	Ctrl+B
Italic	Ctrl+I
Underline	Ctrl+U
Double underline	Ctrl+Shift+D
Subscript	Ctrl+equal sign (=)
Superscript	Ctrl+Shift+plus sign (+)

To use any of the shortcut key combinations, press the keys shown simultaneously to turn the attribute on, and then repeat the key sequence to turn the attribute off. For example, to turn on bold while you are typing, press the **Ctrl** key and the **B** key at the same time. Press these keys again to turn the bold off.

Working in the Font Dialog Box

Although the Formatting toolbar certainly provides the quickest avenue for controlling various font attributes, such as the font and the font size, you can access several more font attributes in the Font dialog box. The Font dialog box gives you control over common attributes, such as font, font size, bold, and so on, and it also provides you with control over special font attributes, such as superscript, subscript, and strikethrough.

To open the Font dialog box, click the **Format** menu, and then select **Font**. The Font dialog box appears, as shown in Figure 5.2.

As you can see, the Font dialog box enables you to choose from several font attributes. You can control the font, the font style, and other character attributes such as strikethrough, superscript, and shadow.

- To change the font, click the **Font** drop-down box and select the new font by name.
- To change the font style to italic, bold, or bold italic, make the appropriate selection in the **Font Style** box.
- To change the size of the font, select the appropriate size in the **Size** scroll box.
- For underlining, click the **Underline Style** drop-down box and select an underlining style.
- To change the color of the font, click the **Font Color** drop-down box and select a new color.
- To select any special effects, such as strikethrough, superscript, or shadow, select the appropriate check box in the lower half of the dialog box.

Figure 5.2   The Font dialog box provides you with control over several font attributes not found on the Formatting toolbar.

As you make the various selections in the Font dialog box, a sample of what the text will look like appears in the Preview box at the bottom of the dialog box. After you have made all your selections in the Font dialog box, click **OK**.

TIP   **Change the Default Font**   To change the default font that you use for your documents (those created using the current or desired template), select the font attributes in the Font dialog box and then click the **Default** button at the lower left of the dialog box. Click **Yes** when Word asks for a confirmation of the change.

Aligning Text

Another important basic attribute of the text in your documents is how that text is oriented on the page. When you first start typing in a new document, all the text begins at the left margin and moves to the right as you type; this means the text is left-justified using the default align left feature. Left-justified text is characterized by text that is straight or unvarying on the left margin but has a ragged right-edged margin.

Text that serves a special function in a document, such as a heading, would probably stand out better in the document if it is placed differently than the rest of the text. Word makes it easy for you to change the alignment of any text paragraph. Several alignment possibilities are available:

• **Align Left**—The default margin placement for normal text, aligned on the left.

 • **Align Right**—Text is aligned at the right margin and text lines show a ragged left edge.

 • **Center**—The text is centered between the left and right margins of the page (with both margins having irregular edges).

 • **Justify**—The text is spaced irregularly across each line so that both the left and the right margins are straight edged and uniform (often used in printed publications such as the daily newspapers).

CAUTION

Remember How Word Sees a Paragraph   Any text followed by a paragraph mark—created when you press the **Enter** key—is considered a separate paragraph in Word. This means that when you use alignment features, such as those discussed in this section, only the paragraph that currently holds the insertion point will be affected by the alignment command that you select (such as Center). If you need to align multiple lines that are in separate paragraphs, select that text before selecting the alignment command.

Figure 5.3 shows examples of each of the alignment possibilities.

The easiest way to change the alignment of text in the document is to use the alignment buttons on the Formatting toolbar. Also, a button exists in the Paragraph dialog box for each of the alignment possibilities.

These justification buttons can be used to align new text or selected text. Again, if you are typing new text with a particular justification, your selected justification will still be in force even after you press Enter. You must change the justification as needed.

Aligning Text with Click and Type

Word offers a unique and quick way to insert and align text or to insert graphics, tables, and other items in a blank area of a document. Before entering text or another item, place the mouse pointer on a blank line on the page. As you move the mouse pointer from right to left on the blank line, the pointer (or I-beam, in this case) changes shape as you move it, denoting a particular line alignment. This makes it very easy to center or right-align the insertion point before you insert the text or other item.

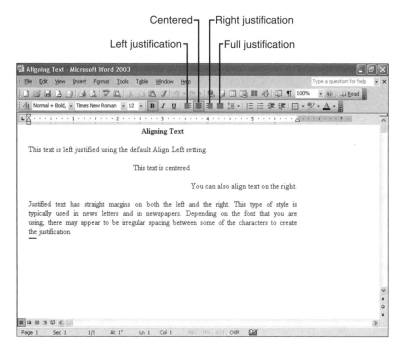

Figure 5.3 You can align the text in your document to suit your particular needs on a document page.

CAUTION

Click and Type Option Must Be On To use Click and Type, you must also make sure that the **Enable Click and Type** box is selected on the **Edit** tab of the Options dialog box (select **Tools**, **Options** to open this dialog box).

To use the Click and Type feature, you must be in the Print Layout or Web Layout view. The feature is not available in the Normal view. To switch to the Print Layout or Web Layout view, select **View**, and then select the appropriate view from the View menu.

Then, to use Click and Type to align your new text, follow these steps:

1. Move the mouse pointer toward the area of the page where you want to place the insertion point. The pointer icon changes to

• Center (the centering pointer appears)

• Right (the align-right pointer appears)

2. After the mouse pointer shows the centering or right-align icon, double-click in the document. The insertion point moves to the selected justification. In the case of the align-right pointer, the insertion point is placed at the mouse position and the text is right aligned from that position.

3. Type your new text.

After you've typed the centered or right-aligned text and you've pressed **Enter** to create a new line, you can return to left justification by placing the mouse on the left of the line (the align-left icon appears on the mouse pointer) and double-clicking.

Automatically Detecting Formatting Inconsistencies

Word can help you out as you work with formatting by marking formatting inconsistencies in your document. This allows you to make sure that the text in your document is formatted as you intended. The Detect Formatting feature keeps track of the formatting in your document and can also be configured to flag any formatting inconsistencies.

To configure the Detect Formatting feature to flag formatting inconsistencies, follow these steps:

1. Select **Tools**, and then select **Options**. The Options dialog box opens.

2. On the Options dialog box, select the **Edit** tab.

3. Under Editing options, select the **Keep Track of Formatting** check box, if it is not already selected. Also select the **Mark Formatting Inconsistencies** check box.

4. Click **OK** to close the Options dialog box.

Now, formatting inconsistencies will be marked with a wavy blue line as you type. When you find a word or paragraph that has been flagged with the wavy blue line, right-click the word or paragraph. A shortcut menu appears as shown in Figure 5.4.

Use the menu choices on the shortcut menu to either replace the direct formatting with an available style or ignore the direct formatting occurrence. To ignore this occurrence of the formatting, click **Ignore Once**. If you want all occurrences of the formatting that has been flagged by the Detect Formatting feature to be ignored in the document, click the **Ignore Rule** choice on the shortcut menu.

Be advised that the Detect Formatting feature doesn't always catch formatting errors. For example, if you have most of your text in a 12-point font, some font that you might have inadvertently formatted for 14 points won't necessarily be flagged. Word assumes you might be using the 14 points for a heading or other special text.

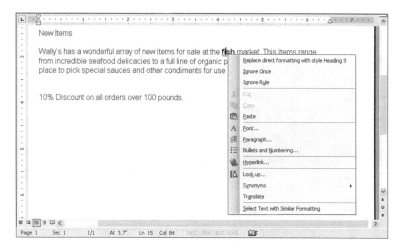

Figure 5.4 You can have formatting inconsistencies flagged in your documents.

The Detect Formatting feature is best at detecting direct formatting changes that you have made to text in a document (such as directly adding bold to text, as shown in Figure 5.4), where other text that has been bolded has been formatted using a "bold" style that you created (styles are covered in Lesson 10, "Working with Styles"). The inconsistency that Word picks up on is that you didn't use the style to bold the item as you had done in the rest of the document.

Reveal Formatting

Another useful feature in relation to text formatting is the Reveal Formatting feature. This feature allows you to quickly review the font and paragraph formatting (and section formatting, sections are discussed in Lesson 20, "Working with Larger Documents") used on your text.

To use Reveal Formatting, select the text for which you want to view the formatting information. Select the **Format** menu and then select **Reveal Formatting**. The Reveal Formatting task pane will open as shown in Figure 5.5. To view the formatting on a word, click on the word. To view the formatting on more than one word of text, select the text.

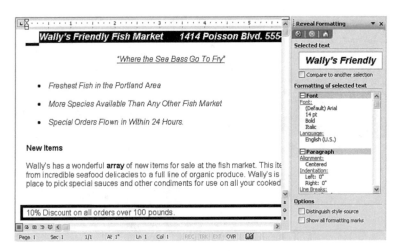

Figure 5.5 You can quickly view text formatting using the Reveal Formatting task pane.

Using Borders and Colors

In this lesson, you learn how to use borders and colors to emphasize text in your documents.

Adding Borders in Word

In Lesson 5, "Changing How Text Looks," you learned that you can use various font attributes, such as font size, bold, italic, and underline, to emphasize and otherwise denote certain text in your document. You also learned that alignment, such as centering, can be used to set off certain text lines on a page. Word provides you with the capability to add borders to your text and even place a shadow on the edge of a border for greater emphasis. You can add borders to text on a page or to an entire page.

Adding Borders to Text

A border can be placed around any text paragraph (any line followed by a paragraph mark). This means that one line of text or several lines of text can have a border placed around them.

 TIP ¶ **Remember How Word Views a Paragraph** Whenever you type a line or several lines of text and then press Enter, you are placing an end-of-paragraph mark at the end of the text. Word views any line or lines followed by a paragraph mark as a separate paragraph. If you need to view the paragraph marks in your document, click the **Show/Hide** button on the Word Standard toolbar.

To place a border around a text paragraph, follow these steps:

1. Place the insertion point in the paragraph that you want to place the border around. If you want to place a border around multiple paragraphs, select all the paragraphs.
2. Select the **Format** menu, and then **Borders and Shading**. The Borders and Shading dialog box appears, as shown in Figure 6.1.
3. Make sure the **Borders** tab is selected on the dialog box. You are provided with several settings for how the border should appear around the text.

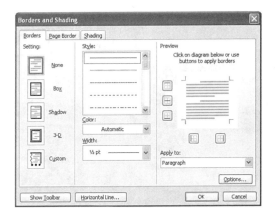

Figure 6.1   The Borders and Shading dialog box enables you to place a border around your text.

4. In the Setting area of the dialog box, select the type of box you want around your text; choose **Box**, **Shadow**, **3-D**, or **Custom** by clicking the appropriate setting sample. The Custom option enables you to create a border that uses different line styles for the various sides of the border.

TIP   **Removing a Border from a Paragraph**   If you want to remove the border from a paragraph, choose **None** in the Setting area of the Borders and Shading dialog box.

5. Several line styles are available for your border. Click the **Style** scroll box to scroll through the various line styles, and then click the style you want to use.

6. To change the color of the border lines, click the **Color** drop-down arrow and select a color from the color palette that appears.

7. As you select the various parameters for your border (in cases where you have selected Box, Shadow, or 3-D as the border setting), you can view a preview of the border in the Preview box. The Preview box also makes it easy for you to place an incomplete border around a paragraph in cases where you might only want a line above or below the text (refer to Figure 6.1).

8. When you have finished selecting the settings for the border, click the **OK** button. The border appears around the paragraph or paragraphs in the document, as shown in Figure 6.2.

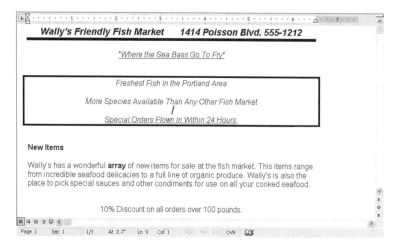

Figure 6.2 A border appears around the selected text after you set the border parameters in the Borders and Shading dialog box.

Borders Around More Than One Paragraph If you select several paragraphs that are using the same style and indents, Word places one border around all the paragraphs. If you want separate borders around the paragraphs, assign borders to them one at a time. For more discussion about indents, see Lesson 7, "Working with Tabs and Indents." You can find more information about styles in Lesson 10, "Working with Styles."

CAUTION

You also can quickly place a border around a paragraph or other selected text by using the Tables and Borders toolbar. Right-click anywhere on one of the currently shown toolbars and select **Tables and Borders** from the toolbar list. The Tables and Borders toolbar appears in the document window. Figure 6.3 shows the Tables and Borders toolbar.

The Borders button

Figure 6.3 You can add borders to selected text using the Tables and Borders toolbar.

To apply a border to a paragraph, make sure the insertion point is in the paragraph, and then click the drop-down arrow on the **Borders** button located on the Tables and Borders toolbar (this button also appears on the Formatting toolbar). From the border list provided, select the type of border you want to place around the text.

Placing a Border Around a Page

If you find that you would like to place a border around an entire page or pages in your document, you need to use the Page Border feature.

Follow these steps to place a border around the entire page:

1. Open the Borders and Shading dialog box (click the **Format** menu and select **Borders and Shading**) and click the **Page Border** tab (see Figure 6.4).

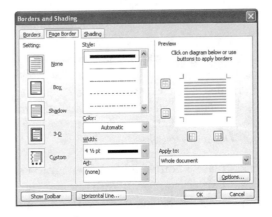

Figure 6.4 Borders can be placed around an entire page.

2. Select the **Border** setting and style as you would for a paragraph border.

3. Click the **Apply To** list drop-down arrow and select one of the following:

- **Whole Document**—Places a border around each page in the document.
- **This Section**—Places a border around each page in the current section of the document.
- **This Section-First Page Only**—Places a border around the first page of the current section.
- **This Section-All Except First Page**—Places a border around each page of the current section except the first page of the section.

To put a border around pages in a section, you must place sections in your document. Sections enable you to break a large document into smaller parts that can have radically different formatting attributes. For more about sections and how to create them, see Lesson 20, "Working with Larger Documents."

Section A portion of a document that has been defined as a discrete part. Each section can then have different formatting and even headers and footers defined for the section.

Adding Shading to the Paragraph

You can place a color or a grayscale pattern behind the text in a paragraph or paragraphs. This color or pattern is called *shading* and can be used with or without a border around the text.

To add shading to text, you must select the text for a particular paragraph—just make sure the insertion point is in the paragraph. After you've designated the text that you want to place the shading behind, follow these steps:

1. Select **Format, Borders and Shading**. The Borders and Shading dialog box appears.

2. Select the **Shading** tab, as shown in Figure 6.5.

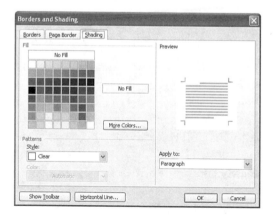

Figure 6.5 You can apply shading to a paragraph or selected text.

3. To select a fill color, click one of the colors on the color palette in the **Fill** area.

4. To select a pattern for the fill color, click the **Style** drop-down arrow and select a pattern from the list.

5. Use the **Apply To** drop-down arrow to designate whether the current paragraph or selected text should be shaded.

6. When you have completed your selections, click **OK**.

Your selected text or paragraph will now be shaded.

TIP **Take Advantage of More Colors** If the color you want to use is not shown on the Shading tab, click the **More Colors** button. This opens the Colors dialog box, which provides a huge number of colors on a color palette. You can even click the **Custom** tab on this dialog box and mix your own custom colors.

Changing Font Colors

When using the shading options, you might find that the current text color does not show up that well on the fill color or pattern that you selected. You can quickly change the font color for selected text anywhere in your document.

To change the color of text, follow these steps:

1. Select the text that you want to change to a different font color.

2. Select the **Format** menu and select **Font**. The Font dialog box appears.

3. In the Font dialog box, click the **Font Color** drop-down arrow and select the color you want to use (Word automatically defaults to black-colored fonts because this is typically what you use in business documents that you print).

4. When you have completed your selection, click **OK**.

You might find that you have to play around with the fill color and the font color to get an ideal combination on the page. You might even have to print out a sample page to see whether the colors work well on a printed page. Intensity of color typically varies between color printers. You might also find that by bolding the text that you've placed on top of a fill color, the text becomes more readable.

TIP **Quickly Change Font Color Using the Font Color Button** You can also change the font color of selected text using the Font Color button on the Formatting toolbar. Select the text and then click the Font Color drop-down arrow. Select the new font color from the color palette provided.

Working with Tabs and Indents

In this lesson, you learn how to set and use tabs and indents in your documents.

Aligning Text Using Tabs

Although the left and right alignment of text in your document is governed by the margins set in the document, there are times when you want to align the text to emphasize a list of items or otherwise offset text from the rest of the items on the page. In Chapter 5, "Changing How Text Looks," you worked with centering and justification as a way to change the alignment of text. Another way to align text in a document is to use tabs. Tabs are set every half inch by default in a new document. Every time you press the Tab key on the keyboard, you offset the text line from the left margin one tab stop.

You can customize tab stops to align text lines in columns. Word gives you complete control over where the tab stops are set in your document. Word also provides different tabs that enable you to align text in different ways:

- **Left Tab**—Aligns the beginning of the text line at the tab stop
- **Center Tab**—Centers the text line at the tab stop
- **Right Tab**—Right-aligns the text line at the tab stop
- **Decimal Tab**—Lines up numerical entries at their decimal point

Each of these tab types makes it easy for you to create lists that are offset from other text elements in the document. Your tab stops fall between the left and right margins on each page of the document. Each paragraph in the document can potentially have a different set of tab stops with different kinds of tabs set at the stops.

Setting Tabs in the Tabs Dialog Box

One way to set tabs in your document is using the Tabs dialog box. Select the **Format** menu, and then select **Tabs**. The Tabs dialog box requires that you specify a tab position in the Tab Stop Position box (the position you specify is the number of inches from the left margin); use the spinner box arrows to specify the position for the tab or type a position directly in the box.

After the tab stop position is set, click the appropriate Alignment option button to select the type of tab you want to create at the tab stop (see Figure 7.1). If you want to have a leader (a repeating element, such as a dash) fill the empty space to the left of the tab stop, select one of the leader option buttons in the Leader box. After you have specified a position and a tab type (and an optional leader), add the tab by clicking **Set**.

As you create the tabs, they will appear in the Tabs list on the left of the dialog box. If you want to remove a particular tab from the list, select it, and then click the **Clear** button. If you want to clear all the tabs listed (and start over), click the **Clear All** button.

Figure 7.1 You can set and remove tab stops in the Tabs dialog box.

After you have finished setting your tabs, click **OK**. Although you can certainly set all the tabs for a document or section in the Tabs dialog box, it is not necessarily the best place to quickly set the tabs for your documents. It does not provide you with a visual display of how the tabs will look in the document. However, if you are creating tabs that include leading characters (such as dot leaders often seen in a table of contents) and you want to precisely set the tab positions to previously determined settings, the Tabs dialog box gives you complete control over all the settings.

Setting Tabs on the Ruler

An excellent alternative to setting tabs in the Tabs dialog box is to use the Word Ruler and actually set the tabs on the Ruler itself. This enables you to visually check the position of the tab stops and makes it easy for you to change the type of tab at a particular tab stop and delete unwanted tabs.

To view the Ruler in the Word document window, select **View**, and then **Ruler**. The Ruler appears at the top of your document.

 TIP **Quickly View the Ruler** If the Ruler is not displayed in the Word window, place the mouse pointer at the top of your current document, below the toolbars. If you wait for just a moment, the Ruler drops down onto the document. This allows you to view current tab settings. When you remove the mouse, the Ruler folds up.

To set a tab on the Ruler, click the **Tab** button on the far left of the Ruler to select the tab type (Left, Center, Right, or Decimal). Each time you click the Tab button, you are cycled to the next tab type. If you go past the type of tab you want to set, keep clicking until the tab type appears on the Tab button.

After you have the appropriate tab type selected on the Tab button, place the mouse pointer on the ruler where you want to create the tab stop. Click the mouse and the tab is placed on the ruler. It's that simple.

Figure 7.2 shows the Ruler with each of the tab types set. The figure also shows how text aligns at each of the tab types.

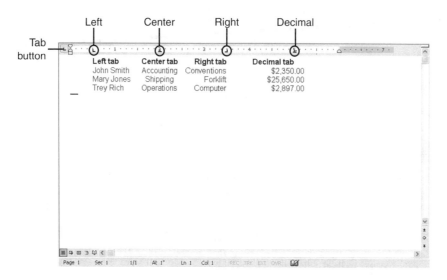

Figure 7.2 Setting tabs on the Ruler allows you to view their position and type.

TIP   **Moving or Removing Tabs**   If you want to delete a tab on the Ruler, use the mouse to drag the tab off the Ruler. If you need to reposition a particular tab, click and drag it to a new location on the Ruler.

CAUTION   **I Adjust the Tabs But It Works for Only One Line**   Remember that Word treats each line followed by a paragraph mark as a separate paragraph. When you adjust the tab positioning on the ruler, it affects only the paragraph containing the insertion point. To adjust the tabs for several paragraphs, select all the lines (or the entire document if you want) and then adjust the tabs on the Ruler.

Working with Indents

Although tabs enable you to align text at various tab stops on the Ruler, you might want to indent or offset lines and paragraphs from the left or right margins. Word provides different indent settings that indent the text at a particular setting on the Ruler.

TERM   **Indent**   The offset of a particular paragraph or line of text from the left or right margin.

The easiest way to indent a paragraph from the left margin is to use the **Increase Indent** button on the Formatting toolbar. Place the insertion point in the paragraph you want to indent, and then click the **Increase Indent** button on the toolbar. Remember that you can also use the Click and Type feature for left indents (see the previous chapter, "Using Borders and Colors").

Each time you click the button, you are increasing the indent one-half inch. You can also decrease the left indent on a particular paragraph. Click the **Decrease Indent** button on the Formatting toolbar.

Setting Indents on the Ruler

You can also indent a paragraph from both the left and right margins using the Ruler. The Ruler has a left and right indent marker on the far left and far right, respectively (see Figure 7.3).

To indent a paragraph from the left margin, use the mouse to drag the **Left Indent** marker to the appropriate position. Grab the marker at the very bottom, because the top of the marker is the First Line indent marker. These two markers separate if you don't grab both markers together at the bottom. You can also indent a paragraph from the right margin using the Right Indent marker. Slide the marker to the appropriate position on the ruler to create your indent.

Left Indent marker

First Line
indent marker

Right Indent marker

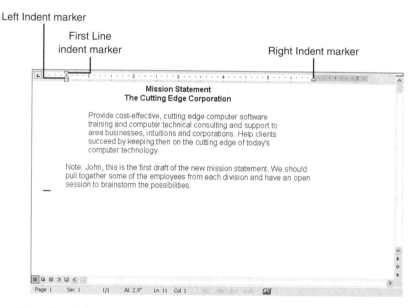

Figure 7.3   The Left Indent and Right Indent markers can be used to indent paragraphs from the left and right margins, respectively.

Creating Hanging Indents

The hanging indent is a special kind of indent. With this type of indent, the text (a single line or multiple lines) that wraps under the first line of the paragraph is indented more than the first line. Hanging indents are created by separating the First Line Indent marker from the Left Indent marker on the ruler.

To create a hanging indent, follow these steps:

1. Place the insertion point in the paragraph that you want to indent.

2. Drag the **Left Indent marker** (drag it by the square bottom of the marker) to the position where you want to indent the second and subsequent lines of the paragraph.

3. Drag the **First Line Indent marker** (drag it by the top of the marker) back to the position where you want the first line to begin.

Figure 7.4 shows a paragraph with a hanging indent. You can increase or decrease the offset between the first line and the rest of the paragraph by dragging either the First Line Marker or the Left Indent Marker. If you prefer to enter numerical information for your hanging indents, choose the **Indents and Spacing** tab (select **Format** menu and then **Paragraph**) and in the **Special** list under **Indentation**, select **Hanging**. Then, set the amount of space **By** box.

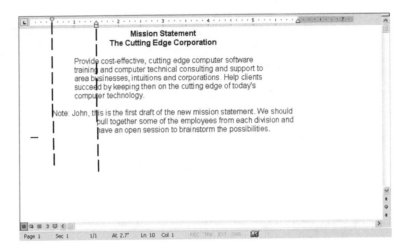

Figure 7.4   Hanging indents enable you to offset the indent on the first line of a paragraph and the remainder of the paragraph.

Examining Your Documents in Different Views

In this lesson, you learn how to examine your document using the different document displays offered in Word.

Changing the Document Display

Word provides you with several viewing possibilities as you work on your documents in the Word application window. Each of these display modes provides a different look at your document. For example, the Normal view provides you with a look at all the font and paragraph formatting in the document, but does not give you a view of the document as it would appear on the printed page. Instead, the Print Layout view supplies this viewpoint.

Using the different document views to your advantage can help you visualize and create great-looking documents in Word. Special views are even supplied for creating outlines and creating Web pages in Word. You take advantage of these different views using the View menu. Table 8.1 shows the various views available to you and describes, in general terms, for what they are best used.

Table 8.1   The Word Views

View	*Typical Use*
Normal	Use for general word processing tasks.
Web Layout	Use for designing HTML documents and viewing Web pages.
Print Layout	Use for document layout and documents containing graphics and embedded or linked objects.
Outline	Use to view document as an outline.
Reading Layout	Allows you to view the document in a side-by-side screen view. This is a view mode only, so you cannot edit the text when in this view.
Full Screen	Use when you want to use the entire screen to view the document and avoid seeing the toolbars and other marginal information.

The Normal View

The Normal view provides you with a view that is perfect for most word processing tasks. It is the default view for Word; to change to the Normal view (from any of the other views), select **View**, and then **Normal**.

 TIP   **Switch to Normal with a Click**   You can also change from view to view in Word using the View toolbar in the lower-left corner of the Word window. To go to the Normal view, click the **Normal** icon.

This view displays character and paragraph formatting that you place in the document (see Figure 8.1). Normal view, however, does not display the document headers and footers or show graphics in the document as they will print. Also, items created using the Drawing toolbar are not displayed in the Normal view.

View controls

Figure 8.1   The Normal view shows all the formatting in the document but does not show graphics, margins, and other special elements as they will appear on the printed page.

In the Normal view, you see the following:

- Page breaks appear as dashed lines.
- Headers and footers are displayed in the header/footer-editing area and you are temporarily switched to the print Layout (when **Header and Footer** is selected on the **View** menu). Only the header or footer can be edited at this point. When you close the Header and Footer toolbar you are returned to the Normal view.

- Footnotes and endnotes are displayed in a footnote or endnote editing area (when **Footnotes** is selected on the **View** menu). Only the footnote or endnote can be edited at this point.
- Margins and column borders are not displayed in this view.

Web Layout View

The Web Layout view is perfect for designing *HTML* documents that you want to use as Web pages. The Web Layout view displays your document as it would appear in your Web browser window. To switch to the Web Layout view, select **View**, and then **Web Layout**.

 TERM   **HTML**   Hypertext Markup Language—This document format is used for the creation of Web pages for the World Wide Web. The special document format is read using a Web browser or some other application (such as Word) that can display HTML documents.

In the Web Layout view, text is wrapped to fit in the window and graphics are placed as they will appear online. Any backgrounds present on the page are also seen in this view. Figure 8.2 shows a Web page in the Web Layout view.

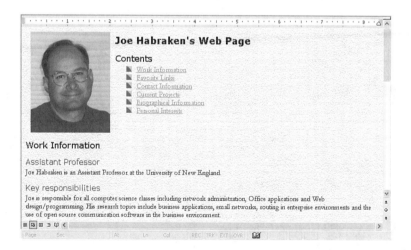

Figure 8.2   The Web Layout view allows you to look at and edit your HTML documents as they will appear in a Web browser.

 TIP   **Switch to Web Layout View Quickly**   To switch to the Web Layout view, click the **Web Layout** icon on the **View** toolbar.

The Web Layout view is the perfect view for designing your personal Web pages or for viewing Web pages using the Web Page Wizard (for more about Word and the Web, see Lesson 21, "Creating Web Pages in Word").

Print Layout View

The Print Layout view shows your document exactly as it will appear on the printed page. Working in this view allows you to fine-tune your document and work with graphic placement and text formatting as you prepare your document for printing.

To switch to the Print Layout view, select **View, Print Layout**. This view enables you to view headers, footers, footnotes, endnotes, and the margins in your document. Graphics are also positioned and sized as they will appear on the printed page. Figure 8.3 shows the same document that appeared earlier in Figure 8.1. Notice that in the Page Layout view, the margins of the document and (more importantly) a graphic in the document appear.

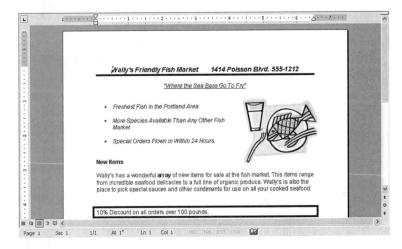

Figure 8.3   The Print Layout view enables you to fine-tune your document for printing.

  Switch to Print Layout View Quickly   To switch to the Print Layout view, click the **Print Layout** icon on the **View** toolbar.

Outline View

The Outline view allows you to create and edit your document in an outline format. Using the Word built-in heading styles is the key to creating the document in this view (for more about styles, see Lesson 10, "Working with Styles"). Each heading (Heading 1, 2, 3, and so on) is treated as a different level in the outline. For example, a heading assigned the Heading 1 style would be a Level 1 heading in the outline. You can promote and demote headings using the appropriate buttons on the Outline toolbar (a special toolbar that appears when you are in Outline view).

The Outline toolbar also provides an Outline Levels drop-down box that allows you to quickly change the level of the text where the insertion point currently resides. These levels coincide with different styles used by the outline feature. For example, Level 1 is equivalent to the Heading 1 style.

You can also collapse and expand the outline to better organize your document. Collapsing the document to all Level 1 Headings allows you to ignore the body text in the document and concentrate on the overall organization of the document.

 TIP   **Move a Heading and Associated Text**   You can drag a heading to a new position, and the subheading and body text associated with the heading move to the new position as well. This makes it very easy for you to reorganize the text in your document.

To change to the Outline view, select **View**, and then click **Outline**. You can easily select a heading and the text that is subordinate to it by clicking the hollow plus symbol (+) to the left of the text (see Figure 8.4). After you select the text, you can drag it to a new position.

When you have finished creating and editing a document in the Outline view, you can switch to any of the other views (such as the Print Layout view) to see your document in a more typical format.

 TIP   **Switch to Outline View Quickly**   To switch to the Outline view, click the **Outline** icon on the **View** toolbar.

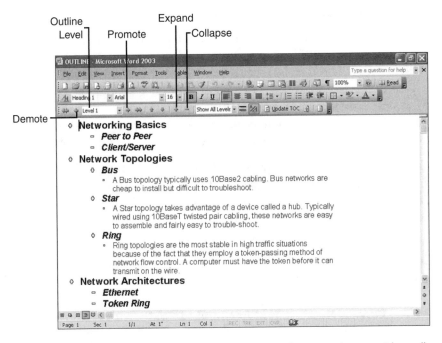

Figure 8.4 The Outline view makes it very easy to organize your document by collapsing and expanding different levels.

Reading Layout

A new view that has been added to Word is the Reading Layout view. This view splits the window into two side-by-side panes. Each pane shows one document screen (it does not show an entire page) as shown in Figure 8.5.

You can advance through the document screen by screen using the **Page Down** button on the vertical scrollbar. You can view thumbnails of each document screen by clicking the **Thumbnails** button provided on the Reading Layout toolbar. To quickly read one of the thumbnails provided, click the thumbnail and it and the preceding screen will appear in the Reading window.

Although you cannot edit the text in the Reading Layout view, it does allow you to read the text in a document and quickly advance from screen to screen. When you have completed reading the text in the document, click the **Stop Reading** button on the toolbar to return to the previously selected view (such as Normal or Print Layout).

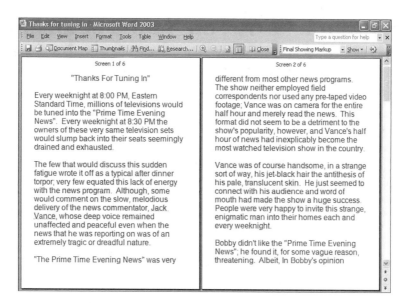

Figure 8.5 The Reading Layout view makes it easy to quickly read through the text in a document.

 TIP **Switch to Reading View Quickly** To switch to the Reading Layout view, click the **Start Reading** icon on the **View** toolbar.

Using the Full Screen View

In situations where you want to concentrate on the text and other items in your document, it is great to be able to clear all the visual clutter from the screen (toolbars, scrollbars, and other Word tools) and view only your document. For example, you might be proofreading a particular page and want to place as much of the page's text on the screen as you can. You can switch to a view where your document occupies all the space available on the screen. Select **View, Full Screen**.

You can still add or edit the text in your document when you are in the Full Screen view. You can also quickly return to the previous view you were using (such as Normal view or Print Layout view) before you switched to the Full Screen view. Click the **Close Full Screen** box that appears in the document window and you return to the previous view.

Zooming In and Out on Your Document

You can use the Zoom command to zoom in and out on your documents. This allows you to increase the magnification of items on the page, such as small fonts, or to step back (zoom out) from the document to view its general layout.

You can use Zoom in any of the Word views (except the Reading Layout view). In Normal, Print Layout, Web Layout, and Outline views, the effect of zooming in or out just changes the magnification of the onscreen elements. When you use Zoom on the Print Layout view, you get a very good look at how the document is laid out on the printed page.

To zoom in or out on your current document, select **View**, **Zoom**. The Zoom dialog box appears (see Figure 8.6).

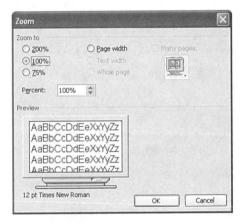

Figure 8.6   The Zoom dialog box can be used to change the current zoom level of your document.

A series of option buttons is used to change the zoom setting for the current document. When you click a particular option button (such as the **200%** option button), you see a preview of this magnification in the Preview box.

You can also set a custom zoom level in the **Percent** box. Use the click arrows in the box to increase or decrease the current zoom percentage. When you have selected the zoom level for the current document, click **OK**.

 TIP   **View Multiple Pages on Your Screen**   When you are in the Print Layout view, you can use the Zoom dialog box to view two or more pages at the same time. Click the **Many Pages** option button (when in Zoom option), and then click the **Computer** icon below the option button. Drag over the page boxes to select the number of pages you want to display, and then click **OK**.

100% ▼ You can also quickly change the zoom level in your current document using the Zoom drop-down box on the Word Standard toolbar. Click the drop-down arrow on the **Zoom** box and select the appropriate zoom level. If you want to set a custom zoom level, select the current zoom percentage on the Zoom box, and then type your own value.

Working with the Document Map

The Document Map view is somewhat similar to the Outline view in that it gives you a quick reference to the overall structure of your document. A special pane appears in the document window (on the left) that shows the headings in your document. You can use the Document Map to quickly move from one area of a document to another by clicking the appropriate heading.

To open the Document Map, select **View, Document Map**; the map pane appears in the document window (see Figure 8.7). You can change the width of the document map pane by placing the mouse on the border between the pane and your document. The mouse arrow changes to a sizing tool—a double-headed arrow. Drag the sizing tool to create a custom document map width.

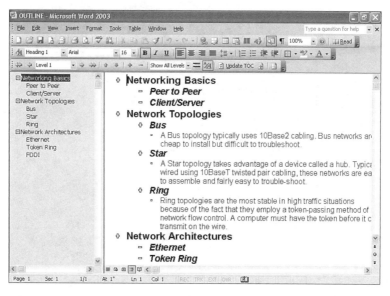

Figure 8.7   The Document Map view makes it easy to jump to a particular part of a document by clicking the appropriate heading.

The document map pane is available in any of the Word views. When you want to close the Document Map, select **View**, and then **Document Map** to deselect it.

Splitting the Document Window

Another useful way to view your documents is to split the current document window into two panes. This allows you to view the same document in both panes, which is particularly useful when you want to view two different parts of the same document.

You can use the two panes to drag and drop information from one part of a document into another. Remember that changes you make in either of the split panes will affect the document.

To split the document screen into two panes, select **Window, Split**. A horizontal split appears across the document window. Notice that as you move the mouse in the document window, the split bar moves with it. Place the mouse where you want to split the document window, and then click the left mouse button.

A set of vertical and horizontal scrollbars appears for each pane in the split window (see Figure 8.8). Use the scrollbars in each pane as needed.

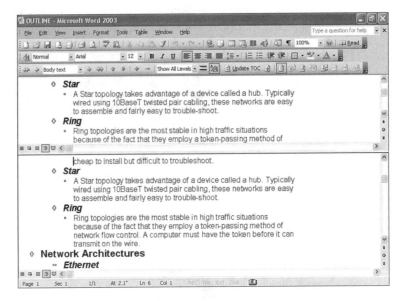

Figure 8.8   You can split the document screen to view different areas of a long document.

When you have finished working in the split document window, select **Window**, and then **Remove Split**. The splitter bar is removed from the document.

TIP   **Split a Window Using the Splitter Bar**   You can split a document window by manually dragging the splitter bar down into the document window. Place the mouse just above the Up arrow on the vertical scrollbar on the splitter bar. Your mouse becomes a splitter sizing tool. Drag to split the window as needed, and then click the mouse to set the bar.

Comparing Documents Side by Side

In cases where you would like to compare two documents or two versions of the same document (saved under different filenames) you can use the Compare Side by Side feature on the Windows menu. This is a new feature in this latest version of Word.

Open the documents in Word. Then use the Window menu or taskbar to go to the first of the two documents. To open the second document in a side-by-side window pane, select the **Window** menu, and then select **Compare Side by Side With**. The Compare Side By Side dialog box opens. Select the other document from the list provided in the dialog box. The two documents will appear side by side in the Word application window as shown in Figure 8.9.

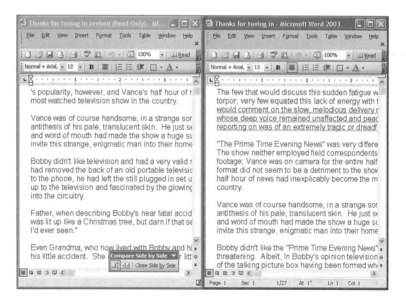

Figure 8.9   You can view documents side by side in the Word window.

By default, the two documents are synchronized when you scroll in either document. So you can advance through the documents at the same pace as you scroll up or down. If you want to turn off the synchronized scrolling and scroll through each document independently, click the **Synchronous Scrolling** button on the Compare Side by Side toolbar. When you have completed viewing the two documents in the side-by-side windows, click **Break Side by Side** on the Compare Side by Side toolbar and you will be returned to individual document windows.

Working with Margins, Pages, and Line Spacing

In this lesson, you learn how to set margins, insert page breaks into your documents, and control line spacing and line breaks in your documents.

Setting Margins

Margins control the amount of white space between your text and the edge of a printed page. Four margins—Left, Right, Top, and Bottom—can be set for your pages. The default margin settings for documents based on the Word Normal template are shown in Table 9.1.

Table 9.1   Default Margin Settings for the Normal Template

Margin	Setting (in Inches)
Left	1.25
Right	1.25
Top	1
Bottom	1

You can change any of the margin settings for your document or a portion of your document at any time. The Page Setup dialog box provides you with access to all these margin settings. You also have control over how your margins affect the layout of multiple pages in a document. For example, you can set up your pages to be laid out in book folio fashion (two pages arranged horizontally on each piece of paper) or two pages per sheet arranged vertically.

To change the margin settings for your document, follow these steps:

   1. Select **File**, **Page Setup**. The Page Setup dialog box appears as shown in Figure 9.1.

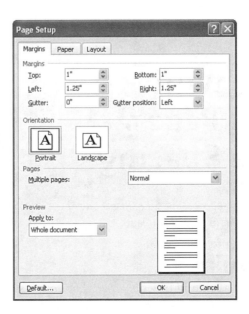

Figure 9.1 Use the Margins tab of the Page Setup dialog box to set your document margins and arrange them on multiple pages if necessary.

TIP **Margins Can Be Different for Different Parts of the Document** You can set different margin settings for different portions of your document. The easiest way to do this is to divide your document into sections. Each section can then have a different set of margins. For information on creating sections in your documents, see Lesson 20, "Working with Larger Documents."

2. Click the **Margins** tab if necessary. Use the click arrows in the **Top**, **Bottom**, **Left**, or **Right** margin boxes to increase or decrease the current setting. Or double-click in any of the boxes and type in a new value.

CAUTION **Maximum and Minimum Margins** Be advised that your printer defines the minimum margins for a page. For example, most inkjet printers limit you to a minimum top and bottom margins of .25" and .5", respectively, and left and right margins of .25". If you set margins less than the minimum, a dialog box appears when you close the Page Setup dialog box, letting you know that your margins are outside the printable area of the page. Click the **Fix** button on this dialog box to set the margins to the minimum for your printer. For maximum margins, Word notifies you by a dialog box if you select margins that overlap or negate any usable space on the page.

3. After you have selected the new margin settings, you can apply the margins to the entire document, to a section of the document (this option is available only if you have more than one section in the document), or to the document from the current page forward in the document. Using the last choice allows you to have different margin settings in the same document without requiring you to divide the document into sections (for more about sections, see Lesson 20). Click the **Apply To** drop-down box and select **Whole Document** (the default setting), **This Point Forward**, or **This Section** (if available).

4. After you have finished selecting your new margin settings and the amount of the document that they will affect, click **OK**.

TIP   **Set a Gutter for Bound Documents**   If your document will be bound (left or top) or placed into a three-ring notebook, set a value in the Gutter box to provide extra space for the binding or punch holes. Setting the **Mirror Margins** (under multiple pages) ensures that margins on facing pages are similar.

The new margins take effect in your document. The best way to view how these margins will look when you print the document is to switch to the Print Layout view (if you are not already in this view). Select **View**, **Print Layout**. The margins you've selected appear on the top, left, right, and bottom of your document in the Word document window.

When you are in the Print Layout view, you can also adjust the margins in your document using the Ruler. To view the Ruler, select **View**, **Ruler**. The vertical ruler is visible in the Print Layout View only.

In the Print Layout view, horizontal and vertical rulers appear in the document window. The margins appear as shaded areas on the edge of the respective ruler. For example, the left margin is a gray-shaded area on the left side of the horizontal ruler (see Figure 9.2).

TIP   **Open the Page Setup Dialog Box Using the Ruler**   Double-click any of the margins shown on the vertical or horizontal ruler. This opens the Page Setup dialog box.

To adjust a margin, place the mouse pointer between the gray margin and the white document area on the ruler. A margin-sizing arrow appears. Drag the gray margin to increase or decrease the respective margin. Figure 9.2 shows the margin-sizing arrow on the top margin on the vertical ruler.

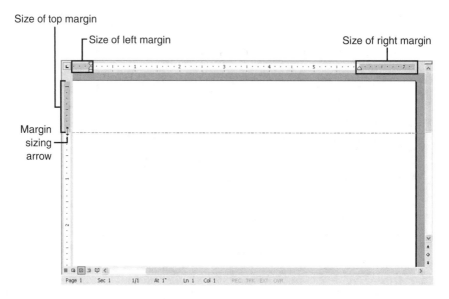

Figure 9.2 Drag the respective margin-sizing arrow to increase or decrease a margin.

Controlling Paper Types and Orientation

Other page attributes that you need to control in your documents are the paper size and the page orientation. Word's default settings assume that you will print to paper that is a standard 8.5 by 11 inches. The default page orientation is portrait, meaning that the maximum distance from the left edge to the right edge of the page is 8.5 inches.

You can select different paper sizes, which is particularly important if you want to print to envelopes or a different paper size, such as legal-size paper. You can also change the orientation of your text and images as they appear on a page from portrait to landscape, where the page contents are rotated so that the distance between the left and right edges on a standard sheet of paper would be 11 inches.

Paper size and page orientation are both set in the Page Setup dialog box. Follow these steps to edit the settings for these page attributes:

1. Select **File**, **Page Setup**. The Page Setup dialog box opens.
2. Click the **Paper** tab on the dialog box (see Figure 9.3).

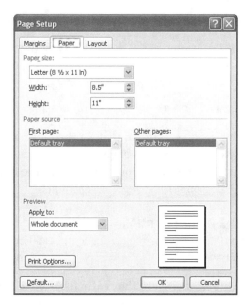

Figure 9.3 The Paper tab of the Page Setup dialog box enables you to set your paper size and source.

3. To select a new paper size, click the **Paper Size** drop-down box and select the paper type. For nonstandard paper sizes, select **Custom Size** in the **Page Size** box, and then type the paper's width into the **Width** box and its height into the **Height** box.

4. To change the orientation of the page to portrait or landscape, select the **Margins** tab and click the **Portrait** or the **Landscape** option button as needed (refer to Figure 9.1).

5. Finally, in the Apply To drop-down box, select **Whole Document** to apply the new settings to the new document or **This Point Forward** to apply the settings to the document from the current page forward.

6. When you complete editing the settings, click **OK**.

Inserting Page Breaks

As you create your document, Word automatically starts a new page when you fill the current page with text or other document items (such as graphics, tables, and so on). However, you can insert your own page breaks in the document as needed. These types of page breaks are often referred to as *hard*, or manual, page breaks.

To insert a page break into your document, follow these steps:

1. Place the insertion point in the document where you want to force a page break.

2. Select **Insert**, **Break**. The Break dialog box appears.

3. Make sure the Page Break option button is selected, and then click **OK**.

A page break is placed in your document. In the Normal view, the page break appears as a dashed line across the page, with "Page Break" denoted at the center of the line. In the Print Layout view, you can move to the new page by clicking the **Next Page** button on the bottom of the vertical scrollbar.

 TIP   **Use the Keyboard to Place a Page Break**   You can also place a page break in your document using the keyboard. Hold down the **Ctrl** key, and then press the **Enter** key.

To remove a page break, switch to the Normal view (select **View**, **Normal**). The page break appears as a dotted line in the document and is denoted as a "page break." Select the page break with a mouse and press **Delete** to remove it.

Changing Line Spacing

Another setting that greatly influences the amount of whitespace on the page is line spacing. When you consider whether you want your text single-spaced or double-spaced, those text attributes are controlled by changing the line spacing.

Line spacing can be set for each paragraph in the document or for selected text. Setting line spacing for a blank document allows you to set a default line spacing for all text paragraphs that will be placed in the document.

To set the line spacing for a new document, a paragraph, or selected text, follow these steps:

1. Select the **Line Spacing drop-down arrow** on the Formatting toolbar. A list of line spacing possibilities such as 1.0, 1.5, 2.0, and so on will appear. Select the line spacing you want to use.

2. **(optional)**   If you want to set a custom line spacing, select **More** from the Line Spacing button's drop-down list. The Paragraph dialog box appears (see Figure 9.4) with the Indents and Spacing tab selected.

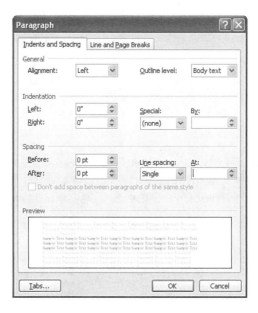

Figure 9.4   The Indents and Spacing tab allows you to fine-tune the line spacing for your text.

3. **(optional)**   To change the line spacing on the Indents and Spacing tab, click the **Line Spacing** drop-down box and select one of the following choices:

- **Single**—Spacing accommodates the largest font size found on the lines and adds a small amount of whitespace (depending on the font used) between lines.
- **1.5**—The line spacing is 1 and 1/2 times greater than single spacing.
- **Double**—Twice the size of single line spacing.
- **At Least**—(The default setting) line spacing adjusts to accommodate the largest font on the line and special items, such as graphics.
- **Exactly**—All lines are equally spaced, and special font sizes or items such as graphics are not accommodated. These items, if larger than the setting used here, appear cut off in the text. You can still accommodate these items by using the Multiple box (described next) to shift all the text lines to a higher spacing percentage that accommodates special items.
- **Multiple**—You specify the line spacing by a particular percentage. This feature is used in conjunction with the Exactly option to set a line spacing percentage that accommodates special font sizes or graphics found in the

document. For example, if you want to decrease the line spacing by 20%, you enter the number 0.8. To increase the line spacing by 50%, you enter 1.5.

4. The **Line Spacing** option selected in step 3 is influenced by the point size entered in the **At** box (this applies only when you have selected At Least, Exactly, or Multiple). Use the click arrows to increase or decrease the point size of the line spacing, if needed.

TIP **Set Spacing Before and After a Paragraph**—You can also set special spacing **Before** and **After** a particular paragraph. This is particularly useful for headings or other special text items.

5. When you complete setting the line spacing parameters, click **OK**.

If you find that you don't like the new line spacing settings for a particular paragraph, click the **Undo** button on the Standard toolbar to reverse the changes that you have made.

Working with Styles

10

In this lesson, you learn how to create character and paragraph styles. You also learn how to edit your styles and take advantage of the styles in the Style Gallery.

Understanding Styles and the Style Task Pane

Word styles provide an excellent way to manage the character and paragraph formatting in a document. A *style* is a grouping of formatting attributes identified by a style name. You can create styles for text that contain character-formatting attributes such as bold, italic, or a particular font size; these types of styles are called *character styles*. You can also create styles for paragraphs that include paragraph attributes, such as alignment information, indents, and line spacing; this type of style is called a *paragraph style*.

You view the style names in the Styles and Formatting task pane (see Figure 10.1). To open the Styles and Formatting task pane, select the **Format** command, and then click **Styles and Formatting**.

 TIP **Select Styles and Formatting at the Touch of a Button** The easiest way to access the Styles and Formatting task pane is to use the **Styles and Formatting** button on the Formatting toolbar.

Word includes several built-in styles, such as the headings, that you can take advantage of in your documents. Styles are particularly useful because if you use them to format text or paragraphs in the document, you can change the attributes saved in the style at any time. These changes immediately take effect on all the text that has been assigned that style.

Updating the look of text or the layout of paragraphs by editing a style allows you to quickly edit the look of text in your document. Using styles also provides you with a way to make certain categories of text, such as headings or figure captions, look uniform throughout the document without having to assign character or paragraph attributes to each of them individually.

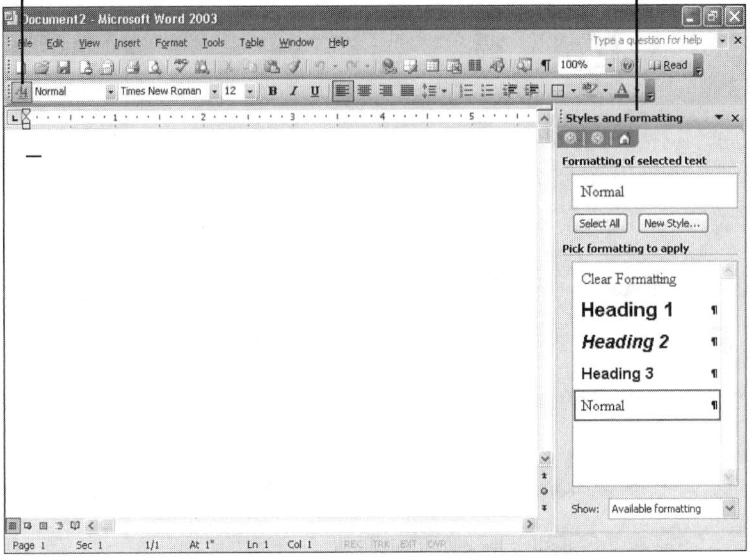

Click the Styles and
Formatting button...

...to open the Styles and Formatting task pane

Figure 10.1   The Styles and Formatting task pane is the starting place for creating, editing, and managing the styles and formatting in your documents.

CAUTION

Paragraph Styles Versus Character Styles   Paragraph styles (the more commonly used option) assign both character and paragraph attributes to the paragraph containing the insertion point. Character styles affect only the word or words you select before you apply the style.

Creating Character Styles

Creating character styles is extremely easy. Select the text you want to emphasize with special character formatting and assign it all the character attributes (font type, bold, underline, italic, and so on) that you want to include in the style. You may assign the attributes using either the Font dialog box (by selecting **Format**, **Font**) or the appropriate buttons on the Formatting toolbar. Fonts are covered in Lesson 5, "Changing How Text Looks."

Make sure that the desired text is selected, and then follow these steps to create the style:

1. Open the **Styles and Formatting** task pane and then **New Style**; the New Style dialog box appears as shown in Figure 10.2.

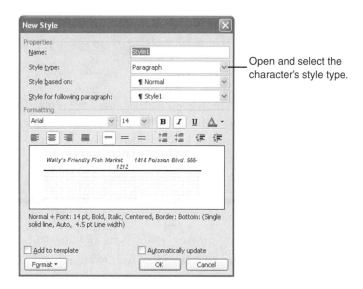

Open and select the character's style type.

Figure 10.2 The New Style dialog box allows you to create styles.

2. Click the **Style Type** drop-down box and select **Character** for the style type.

3. Look in the Formatting area of the New Style dialog box. It shows the text attributes that you have assigned to your selected text. Note that the new style is based on the current style (the default paragraph style or the normal style) plus your added attributes.

4. Type a name for your new style into the Name box.

5. Click **OK** to conclude the style creation process. You are returned to the Styles and Formatting task pane. Notice that your new style now appears in the Pick Formatting to Apply list in the task pane.

You can now assign the new character style to text in your document as needed. Simply select the text to which you want to assign this unique style, and then select the **Styles and Formatting** task pane. Select your unique style from the list provided. The style is applied to the selected text.

TIP **View All the Text Assigned a Style** To select all the text in a document that has been assigned a particular style, select the style in the Styles and Formatting task pane, and then click the Select All button.

When you create your styles, you also have the option of assigning shortcut keys to styles. This allows easy access to a style that you use a great deal in a document.

Styles can also be assigned to custom toolbar buttons making it easy to assign a style with one click of the mouse.

Creating Paragraph Styles

Creating paragraph styles is similar to creating character styles. Apply to a paragraph the formatting that you want to include in the style (you can use alignment settings, indents, and all the paragraph attributes that you are familiar with). Make sure that the insertion point is in the paragraph, and then follow these steps to create the style:

1. Open the **Styles and Formatting** task pane, and then click **New Style**; the New Style dialog box appears.

2. Click the **Style Type** drop-down box and select **Paragraph** for the style type.

3. Type a unique name into the **Name** box for the style.

4. Click **OK** to return to the Styles and Formatting task pane. The style is now available on the Style list. You can now apply the style to any paragraph in the document by placing the insertion point in the paragraph.

 TIP   **Have Word Automatically Update Your Styles**   When you create a paragraph or character style (or modify either type), you can have Word update the style automatically when you make formatting changes to text to which the style has been applied. Select the Automatically Update check box in the New Style or Modify Style dialog box.

Editing Styles

You can also edit or modify the attributes found in any of your styles or the default styles in the document. You edit styles using the Styles and Formatting task pane. Remember that when you edit a style, all the text to which the style was applied reflects the new text and paragraph attributes of your edited style.

To edit a style, follow these steps:

1. Open the **Styles and Formatting** task pane.

2. Under **Pick Formatting to Apply**, select the style you want to edit and place the mouse pointer on it until you see the box outline and down arrow appear. Then, click the down arrow and press **Modify**. The Modify Style dialog box appears as shown in Figure 10.3.

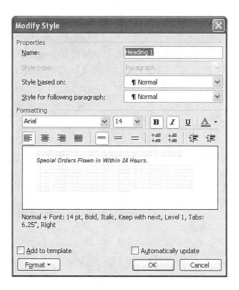

Figure 10.3   The Modify Style dialog box allows you to edit the name of a style and modify all the attributes found in the style.

3. To modify the style, select the **Format** button. A menu appears, allowing you to modify the following attributes in the style:

- Font
- Paragraph
- Tabs
- Borders
- Language
- Frame
- Numbering
- Shortcut key

4. Select one of the choices provided in the Format box. The appropriate dialog box appears, allowing you to edit the settings for the chosen attributes. For example, if you want to modify the font attributes for the style, click the **Format** arrow and select **Font** from the list provided. The Font dialog box appears.

5. When you have finished modifying the Font or other attributes for the style, click **OK**. You are returned to the **Modify Style** dialog box.

6. Modify other attributes of the style as needed by making the appropriate choices from the drop-down lists.

7. When you have completed your style modifications, click **OK** in the Modify Style dialog box and you return to the task pane with the changes made.

TIP **You Can Delete Unwanted Styles** You can delete styles that you've created that you no longer need. Open the **Styles and Formatting** task pane and place the mouse pointer on the style in the **Pick Formatting to Apply** list. Wait for the box outline and down arrow to appear, and then click the **Delete** button under the down arrow. The style is removed from the Style list.

Using the Style Organizer

Word also has the capability to copy styles from other documents and templates into your current document. This provides you with an easy way to add already existing styles to a document (rather than reinventing the wheel or style).

To copy styles from another document or template, follow these steps:

1. Select the **Tools** menu, and then choose **Templates and Add-Ins**.

2. In the Templates and Add-Ins dialog box, click the **Organizer** button. The Organizer dialog box appears as shown in Figure 10.4.

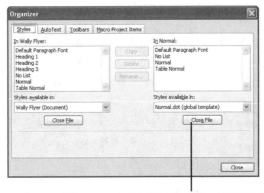

When you close a file, this button changes to Open File.

Figure 10.4 The Organizer dialog box makes it easy for you to copy a style or styles from one document to another.

3. The styles in the current document appear on the left side of the Organizer dialog box. Styles in the template that your current document was based on are shown on the right side of the Organizer dialog box (all documents are based on a template, even if it is just the Word Normal template). To close the template file on the right side of the dialog box, click the **Close File** button (in Figure 10.4, click **Close File** under the Normal.dot template on the right of the dialog box).

4. Now you can open a new template or document and copy the styles that it contains to the current document (shown on the left of the dialog box). Click **Open File** on the right side of the Organizer dialog box. Locate the document or template from which you want to copy the styles. Double-click the file in the Open dialog box to open the file.

5. You are returned to the Organizer dialog box, and the styles for the recently opened template or document are listed on the right side of the dialog box. To copy a style or styles, select the style and click the **Copy** button. The style is copied to the styles in your current document.

 TIP   **Copy More Than One Style at a Time**   To select several styles to copy to your document simultaneously, click the first style you want to copy and then hold down the **Shift** key and click the last style you want to copy. All the styles in between these two are also selected. To select styles that are not in a series, click the first style you want to copy, and then hold down the **Ctrl** key and click any other styles you want to select.

6. When you have finished copying styles (styles can be copied from either of the documents in the Organizer dialog box), click **Close** to close the Organizer dialog box.

As you can see, the Organizer makes it very easy for you to share the styles that you create between your documents. Remember, styles that you create reside only in the document where you create them. The only way to copy those styles to another document is to use the Style Organizer.

Using AutoFormatting to Change Text Attributes

In this lesson, you learn how to quickly change the look of your text with AutoFormat and apply text attributes automatically as you type.

Understanding AutoFormatting

AutoFormat is a great feature that helps you create professional-looking documents. AutoFormatting actually examines the text elements that you have placed in your document (such as headings, tables, lists, regular body text, and other items) and then automatically formats these elements using an appropriate Word style. Even though this formatting is automatic, you can accept or reject the changes AutoFormatting makes. You can also make additional changes to the document as you see fit by using other styles or font and paragraph formatting attributes (for more about styles, see Lesson 10, "Working with Styles").

You will also find that AutoFormat does more than just apply styles to your document elements. It can remove extra paragraph breaks between paragraphs and apply the hyperlink styles to e-mail addresses or Web addresses that you place in your documents.

You can use AutoFormat in two ways. You can turn on AutoFormatting so that items are formatted as you type, or you can create a new document and then use AutoFormat to format the entire document at once.

Formatting As You Type

You can have your document elements formatted as you type. However, this feature requires that you supply Word with certain cues so that the correct formatting is applied to the text. For example, if you turn on AutoFormat As You Type and want to create a bulleted list that is automatically formatted by the AutoFormat feature, you must begin the bulleted line with a dash, an asterisk, or a lowercase "o" so that Word knows to apply the bulleted list formatting.

Many AutoFormat As You Type features are enabled by default, although others are not. To customize the AutoFormat As You Type feature, follow these steps:

1. Select **Tools**, then **AutoCorrect Options**. The AutoCorrect dialog box appears.

2. Select the **AutoFormat As You Type** tab on the dialog box (see Figure 11.1).

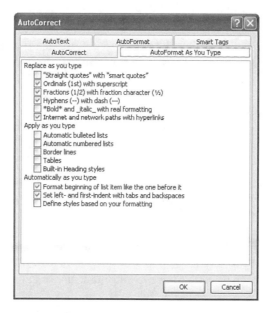

Figure 11.1　Use the AutoFormat As You Type tab to select the automatic formatting options.

3. A series of check boxes on the AutoFormat As You Type tab allows you to select which document elements will be formatted as you type. Again, you need to type certain characters for a particular element so that the AutoFormat feature recognizes and then formats the text. Some of the most often used AutoFormat possibilities are as follows:

   - **Automatic Bulleted Lists**—Select this check box to create bulleted lists automatically. Start each line in the list with an asterisk (*), a dash (-), or a lowercase "o."

   - **Automatic Numbered Lists**—Select this check box to create numbered lists. When you start a line with a letter or number, it is turned into a numbered list item. If the Format Beginning of List Item Like the One Before It check box is selected, paragraphs following the first numbered line are numbered sequentially.

- **Built-In Heading Styles**—Select this check box to have all headings that you apply to an outline or a legal document be automatically assigned the appropriate built-in heading style (using Headings 1–9).

- **Border Lines**—Select this check box to have borders automatically placed between paragraphs. You must type three dashes (-) for a thin border, three underscores (_) for a bold line, or three equal signs (=) for a double-line border.

- **Tables**—Select this check box to automatically create tables. You must type a series of plus symbols (+) and dashes (-) to signify the number of columns (+) and the distance between the columns (-).

Other AutoFormatting check boxes include features that format your quotation marks, ordinals (1st), and fractions (1/2). Select (or deselect) the various AutoFormat As You Type options and then click **OK** to close the dialog box.

 TIP **Create Styles As You Type** If you select the Define Styles Based on Your Formatting check box, Word automatically takes your character and paragraph formatting attributes and turns them into styles. You can then use the created styles to format other paragraphs.

Although formatting as you type might seem like a real timesaver, you must remember which special characters to use to automatically begin a particular formatting type.

Applying AutoFormat to a Document

The alternative to AutoFormatting as you type is to create the document and then format it after the fact with AutoFormat. Waiting to format a document until after its completion allows you to concentrate on the document content as you type. You then can concentrate on the look and feel of the document by selecting from the various AutoFormatting options. Heads, numbered or bulleted lists, and other items you have designated throughout the text are identified and formatted.

To AutoFormat a document, follow these steps:

1. Make sure that you are in the Print Layout view (select View, then Print Layout; this allows you to see the various formatting tags applied to the document when you review the autoformat changes; see Lesson 8, "Examining Your Documents in Different Views," for more information). Select **Format**, then **AutoFormat**. The AutoFormat dialog box appears (see Figure 11.2).

Figure 11.2 The AutoFormat dialog box allows you to immediately format the document or review each of the suggested formatting changes.

2. You can increase the accuracy of the formatting process by choosing a particular document type. Click the General Document Type drop-down arrow and select from the document types listed on the drop-down list (the default setting is **General Document**; you can also select **Letter** or **Email** as the document type from the list).

3. Now you can AutoFormat the document. If you want to AutoFormat the current document without reviewing the formatting changes, click the **AutoFormat Now** radio button and then click **OK**. The document is automatically formatted.

4. If you want to review the AutoFormatting process after the changes are made, click the **AutoFormat and Review Each Change** radio button. Then click **OK**.

5. The document is formatted, and then the AutoFormat/Review Changes dialog box appears. If you already know whether you are happy with the results, choose to **Accept All** or **Reject All** using the appropriate button in the dialog box. You can also click **Review Changes** to review the changes to your document so that you can decide whether you're happy with the results on a change-by-change basis. The Review AutoFormat Changes dialog box appears (see Figure 11.3).

Figure 11.3 This dialog box enables you to review each of the formatting changes made in the document.

6. Click the **Find** (forward) button (this button has a right-pointing arrow) to begin the review process. Notice that all the changes that AutoFormat has made to the document are tagged with a red line and a description box in the document.

7. When you are asked to review a particular change (the change appears in the Changes box), either select **Reject** to reject the change or click the **Find** button to skip to the next formatting change in the document. You can also choose to **Accept All** or **Reject All** using the appropriate button in the dialog box.

8. When you reach the bottom of the document, Word notifies you that it can start searching for changes at the top of the document. If you had the insertion point at the top of the document when you began the review process, click **Cancel**. Then, click **Cancel** to close the two subsequent dialog boxes as well.

To safeguard any automatic formatting changes that have been made, be sure to immediately save your document.

Changing AutoFormat Options

You can customize certain options related to the AutoFormat feature. The dialog box that has the options can be reached by selecting the **Tools** menu and then **AutoCorrect Options**. Make sure that the **AutoFormat** tab is selected.

The options that you have control over on the AutoFormat tab are similar to those found on the AutoFormat As You Type tab. You can choose check boxes that automatically format headings, lists, and so on (see Figure 11.4).

You can also choose to have Word retain the style that you have already placed in the document (prior to running AutoFormat). Select the **Styles** check box to do so.

 TIP **AutoFormat Text-Only E-Mail Automatically** If you use Word as your e-mail editor for Outlook (see Part III of this book for information on using Outlook), you can have any text-only e-mail messages that you receive automatically formatted so they look better when you read them. Select the **Plain Text Wordmail Document** check box at the bottom of the AutoFormat tab.

After you select the options you want to set for AutoFormat, select **OK**. You can now run AutoFormat, and your options will be in force as your document is formatted.

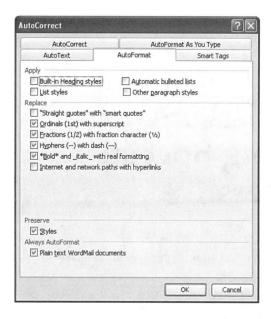

Figure 11.4   You can set the various options for automatic formatting on the AutoFormat tab of the AutoCorrect dialog box.

Adding Document Text with AutoText and Using Special Characters

In this lesson, you learn how to quickly add repeating text elements to your documents using the AutoText feature. You also learn how to add special characters to your document, such as the copyright symbol.

Understanding AutoText

AutoText provides you with a way to build a library of words and text phrases that you use often in your documents. AutoText makes it easy for you to quickly insert items from your AutoText list into any document. Creating AutoText entries is also very straightforward. An AutoText entry can consist of a company name, your name, or an entire paragraph that you commonly place in your documents.

Creating AutoText Entries

You can create an AutoText entry using text from an existing document, or you can type the text that you want to add to the AutoText list in a blank document. Then it's just a matter of copying the text to your AutoText list.

To create an AutoText entry, follow these steps:

1. Type the text you want to use for the AutoText entry or open the document containing the text that will serve as the AutoText entry.

2. Select the text.

3. Select the **Insert** menu, point at **AutoText**, and then select **New** from the cascading menu. The Create AutoText dialog box appears as shown in Figure 12.1.

TIP   **AutoText Isn't on My Insert Menu**   Remember that Word uses a personalized menu system that places your most recently used commands on the various menus. If you click a menu and don't see a particular command, rest your pointer in the menu for a moment; the menu will expand and provide a list of all the commands available on that particular menu.

Figure 12.1 Creating the Wally's AutoText saves you from typing Wally's Friendly Fish Market.

4. Type the name that you want to use to retrieve this AutoText entry in the text box provided (for one-word text entries, the selected text can also serve as the entry name).

5. After providing the name for the AutoText entry, click **OK**.

Your selected text is added to the AutoText list. You can repeat this procedure and add as many text items to the AutoText list as you want.

Inserting AutoText Entries

After you add an AutoText entry or entries to the list, you can insert them into any Word document. One method of inserting an AutoText entry into the current document is to pull the entry directly from the AutoText list.

To insert an AutoText entry into a document, follow these steps:

1. Place the insertion point in the document where you want to insert the AutoText entry.

2. Select the **Insert** menu, point at **AutoText**, and then select **AutoText**. The AutoCorrect dialog box appears as shown in Figure 12.2 (with the AutoText tab selected).

3. The AutoText tab of the AutoCorrect dialog box displays an alphabetical list (as well as various default entries that Word provides) of the AutoText entries that you have added to the AutoText list. Select the entry you want to insert and click **Insert**. Or double-click any entry on the list to insert it into the document.

An alternative to manually inserting AutoText into the document is using the AutoComplete feature to automatically insert an entry into your document. For example, if you have an entry in your AutoText list that reads "I am pleased to announce," you can automatically insert this entry into your document by beginning to type the entry. As you type the first few letters in the AutoText entry, an AutoComplete box appears, containing the complete AutoText entry, as shown in Figure 12.3.

Figure 12.2   Insert your AutoText entries from the AutoCorrect dialog box.

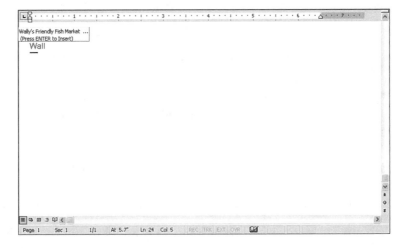

Figure 12.3   AutoComplete automatically places entries from your AutoText list into your documents.

To insert the entry into the document, press the **Enter** key. AutoComplete also helps you enter items that are not included on your AutoText list into your document. These items include the current date, days of the week, and names of months. For example, as you begin to type the name of a month, the AutoComplete box message appears, telling you to press **Enter** to insert the complete word.

 TIP   **Use the AutoText Toolbar to Quickly Insert AutoText Entries**   Right-click any toolbar, and then select **AutoText** from the menu. To add an entry into the current document, click the **All Entries** button on the AutoText toolbar and select your AutoText from the list.

Deleting AutoText Entries

You can easily delete items on the AutoText list when you no longer need them. This is done on the AutoText tab of the AutoCorrect dialog box.

To delete an AutoText entry, follow these steps:

1. Select the **Insert** menu, point at **AutoText**, and then select **AutoText** from the cascading menu. The AutoCorrect dialog box appears.
2. Select any of the entries in the AutoText list.
3. Click **Delete** to remove the entry from the list.

After you have completed your deletion of AutoText entries, click **OK** to close the AutoText dialog box.

Using Special Characters and Symbols

Special characters and symbols are characters that can't be found on your keyboard and that are not part of what is considered to be the standard character set. Characters such as the German "u" with an umlaut (ü) are special characters, and an item such as the trademark is an example of a symbol.

Many special characters and symbols exist. Table 12.1 lists some of the commonly used special characters and symbols.

Table 12.1   Common Special Characters and Symbols

Special Character or Symbol	Use
Copyright symbol ©	Used in a copyright notice in a document.
Trademark symbol ™	Placed to the right of official trademarks placed in a document.

Table 12.1 Continued

Special Character or Symbol	Use
Em dash —	Used to bracket asides or sudden changes in emphasis in a sentence—rather than using a comma. It appears as a long dash.
En dash –	Slightly shorter than an em dash, this dash is commonly used to separate numbers from capital letters, such as Figure B–1.
Wingdings	A group of special icons that can be used in your documents for emphasis or as bullets.
Foreign language font (á)	Characters that include special accents.

The basic special characters and symbols are held in three groups:

- **Symbol**—This group contains mathematical symbols, arrows, trademark and copyright symbols, and letters from the Greek alphabet.

- **Normal Text**—This group provides you with special characters containing accents and other special marks.

- **Wingdings**—Special icons and symbols for many purposes.

Additional special character sets might be available to you, depending on which fonts have been installed on your computer (you can purchase software with unique fonts and symbols, as well).

 TIP **Shortcut to Making an Em Dash** As you are typing along, you can quickly insert an em dash into the text by pressing **Ctrl+Alt+the minus sign** on the number pad. The em dash appears.

You can easily insert special characters and symbols into your documents using the Insert Symbol feature. To insert a special character or symbol, follow these steps:

1. Place the insertion point in your document where you want to insert the special character or symbol. Select **Insert**, **Symbol**. The Symbol dialog box appears as shown in Figure 12.4.

2. To insert a symbol, make sure the Symbol tab is selected on the Insert dialog box (if you want to insert a special character from the current symbol set, go to step 5). Use the Font drop-down box to select the symbol set from which you want to choose your symbol. The symbol set that you choose dictates which symbols are available, so select a symbol set that provides the symbol you want to insert. You will find that the normal text symbol set provides most of the commonly used symbols, such as copyright and trademark.

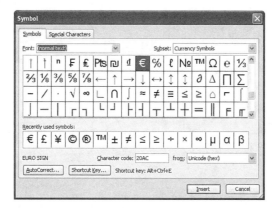

Figure 12.4 The Symbol dialog box gives you access to symbols and special characters that you can insert into your document.

3. After you select the symbol set (such as normal text, Symbol, Wingdings, or another font family), click to select the symbol you want to insert.

4. After selecting the symbol, click the **Insert** button.

5. If you want to insert a special character, such as the copyright symbol or an em dash, click the **Special Characters** tab on the Symbol dialog box.

6. Select the special character and then click **Insert**.

7. When you have finished inserting your symbol or special character, click the **Close** button on the Symbol dialog box.

CAUTION

My Key Combination Turns into a Symbol—The Word AutoCorrect feature is set up to replace several character combinations with special characters. You can override these changes made by the AutoCorrect feature by immediately pressing the **Backspace** key. For more on AutoCorrect, see Lesson 4, "Using Proofreading and Research Tools."

After you've inserted the symbol or special character into the document, you can continue typing or editing your text. Symbols and special characters give your document a finished, typeset look.

Adding Headers, Footers, and Page Numbers

In this lesson, you learn how to add headers, footers, and page numbers to your documents.

Understanding Headers and Footers

Another aspect of creating a document is using headers and footers to insert information that you want repeated on every page of the document or in the pages of a particular document section.

Header   The header resides inside the top margin on the page; it holds information such as the date or draft number that appears at the top of every page of the document. Every section of a document could potentially have a separate header.

Footer   The footer resides inside the bottom margin of the page; it holds information such as the page number or other information that appears at the bottom of every page of the document. Every section of a document could potentially have a separate footer.

Headers and footers provide you with a way to include a document title, the current date, or the current page number on the top or bottom of each page in the document. Headers can include text, graphics, or other items.

Adding Headers and Footers

You can add a header or footer to a document in any view. To add a header or footer, follow these steps:

1. Select **View**, **Header and Footer**. You are temporarily switched to the Print Layout mode and placed in the header area of the document (see Figure 13.1). The regular text area is dimmed and unavailable while you work in the header or footer box.

2. Type your text into the header area. If you want to create a footer, click the **Switch Between Header and Footer** button on the Header and Footer toolbar, which is also available in the document window.

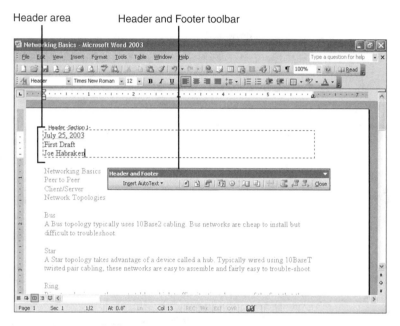

Figure 13.1 The header area of the page is where you type your header text. The Header and Footer toolbar provides you with tools to insert page numbers, the date, and to switch between your headers and footers.

3. You can add a page number, the current date, the current time, and other elements using the appropriate buttons on the Header and Footer toolbar (see Table 13.1).

4. When you need to align or format the text, use the appropriate buttons on the Word Formatting toolbar (while in the header/footer areas) as you would for text on the document page.

5. When you have finished entering your header and footer text, click the **Close** button on the Header and Footer toolbar.

You are returned to your document text. In the Normal view, you are not able to see your header or footer. In the Print Layout view, however, header and footer text appears dimmed.

You can edit your headers and footers by selecting **View**, **Header and Footer**. Move to the appropriate header or footer using the navigation buttons on the Header and

Footer toolbar shown in Table 13.1. To quickly enter a header or footer box, in the Print Layout view double-click the header or footer text.

Table 13.1   The Header and Footer Toolbar Buttons

Button	Purpose
	Inserts the page number
	Inserts the page count or number of total pages
	Edits the format of the page number
	Inserts the current date
	Inserts the current time
	Opens the Page Setup dialog box to the Layout tab, where you can change the header and footer settings
	Hides the document text while you work on your header and footer
	Sets up the next header the same as the current header (or footer)
	Switches between your header and footer
	Moves to the previous header or footer in the document
	Moves to the next header or footer in the document

Several toolbar choices, such as Same As Previous and Move to Previous or Next (header or footer) relate to documents that have several sections and so have different headers or footers within the same document. You can also have more than one header or footer in the document if you choose to have different headers or footers for odd- and even-numbered pages.

Using Odd- and Even-Numbered Page Headers and Footers

By default, the header and footer layout settings in Word assume that one header or footer appears on all the pages of a document (except in cases where the document is divided into more than one section; each section can have different headers and footers). You can change the header and footer settings so that different headers and/or footers appear on the odd- and even-numbered pages of your document (or the odd- and even-numbered pages of a document section).

To change the layout settings for Word Headers and Footers, follow these steps:

1. After activating the Header and Footer view (so that the Header and Footer toolbar appears), click the **Page Setup** button.

 TIP   **Changing Header and Footer Layout When You Aren't in the Header or Footer**   To get to the header and footer layout options when you don't have the header or footer displayed, select **File**, then **Page Setup**. The Page Setup dialog box appears. If it is not already selected, click the **Layout** tab.

2. In the Page Setup dialog box, click the **Different Odd and Even** check box to enable odd and even headers and/or footers in the current document (or document section).

3. If you want to have a header or footer (or none) on the first page of your document that is different from subsequent pages in the document, click the **Different First Page** check box (see Figure 13.2).

 TIP   **Headers and Footers Can Be Applied to Document Sections**   The only way to specify where a header or footer begins in a document (other than the first page of the document) is to break the document into sections. Creating sections is discussed in Lesson 20, "Working with Larger Documents."

4. Click **OK** to close the Page Setup dialog box. If you are returned to your document, select **View, Header and Footer** to add the odd- or even-numbered page headers to the document. If you were already in the Header and Footer view when you exited the Page Setup dialog box, you are returned to the current header and footer.

5. If you want to specify how close the header or footer is to the margin edge of the top or bottom of the document, respectively, use the Header or Footer spin boxes to set the distance.

6. When you have finished adding your odd- and even-numbered page headers and/or footers or your first page and subsequent page headers, click the **Close** button on the Header and Footer toolbar.

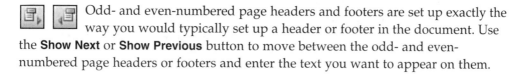 Odd- and even-numbered page headers and footers are set up exactly the way you would typically set up a header or footer in the document. Use the **Show Next** or **Show Previous** button to move between the odd- and even-numbered page headers or footers and enter the text you want to appear on them.

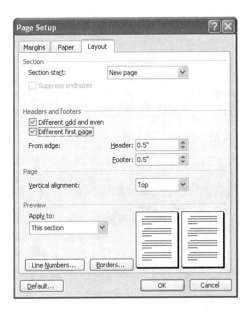

Figure 13.2 On the Layout tab of the Page Setup dialog box, you can select whether to have different odd- and even-numbered page headers/footers or a different header/footer on the first page of the document.

Adding Page Numbering to a Document

Headers and footers enable you to place repeating information in your documents, including the date, other important text, and most important—page numbers. When you want to place only page numbers on your document pages, you can skip the Header and Footer command and quickly add page numbers using the Insert menu.

To place page numbers in your document, follow these steps:

1. Select **Insert**, **Page Numbers**. The Page Numbers dialog box appears (see Figure 13.3).

2. To select the position for your page numbers, select the **Position** drop-down arrow and select **Top of Page (Header)** or **Bottom of Page (Footer)**.

3. You can select the alignment for the page numbers using the **Alignment** drop-down box. Select **Center**, **Left**, or **Right** to position the page numbers. When you are using mirror margins on a document that will be printed on both sides of the paper, select **Inside** or **Outside** (relative to a central binding, like that of a book) to position your page numbers.

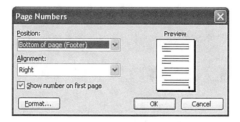

Figure 13.3   Use the Page Numbers dialog box to select the position and alignment of page numbers in your document.

4. To select the format for your page numbers, click the **Format** button. The Format dialog box appears.

5. Use the **Page Number Format** drop-down box (shown in Figure 13.4) to choose the format for your page numbers (Arabic numerals—1, 2, 3—is the default). When you have selected your number format, click **OK** to return to the Format dialog box.

6. To have the page numbering start on a specific page in the document, click the **Start At** option button and then use the spinner box to specify the page number.

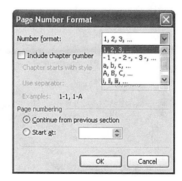

Figure 13.4   Use the Page Number Format drop-down box to choose the format for your page numbers.

7. Click **OK** to close the Page Number Format dialog box.

The page numbers are placed in the header or footer of your document according to your positioning and formatting choices. You can edit the page numbers and add text if you want by selecting **View**, **Header and Footer**.

Printing Documents

In this lesson, you learn how to preview your documents and then print them.

Sending Your Document to the Printer

When you have finished a particular document and are ready to generate a hard copy, Word makes it easy for you to get your document to the printer. In fact, you have three choices:

- You can send the document directly to the printer (no questions asked) by clicking the **Print** button on the Standard toolbar.

- You can open the Print dialog box (select **File**, **Print**) and set any print options that you want, such as printing a particular range of pages or printing multiple copies of the same document.

- You also have the option of previewing your hard copy before printing. This enables you to view your document exactly as it will appear on the printed page.

To preview your document before printing, click the **Print Preview** button on the Word Standard toolbar. The Print Preview window opens for the current document (see Figure 14.1).

You will find that the Print Preview window provides several viewing tools that you can use to examine your document before printing.

- **Zoom In or Out**—In the Print Preview window, the mouse pointer appears as a magnifying glass. Click once on your document to zoom in, and then click a second time to zoom out. To turn this feature off (or on again), click the **Magnifier** button.

- **Zoom by Percentage**—You can change to different zoom levels on the current document by using the **Zoom** drop-down arrow.

- **View Multiple Pages**—You can also zoom out and view several pages at once in the Preview window. Click **Multiple Pages**, and then drag to select the number of pages to be shown at once.

Figure 14.1 The Print Preview mode enables you to view your document the way it will print.

-  **Shrink to Fit**—If you have a two-page document and only a small amount of text appears on the second page, you can condense all the text to fit on the first page only; click the **Shrink to Fit** button.

When you have completed viewing your document in the Print Preview mode, you can click the **Print** button to print the document, or if you want to edit the document before printing, click the **Close** button on the toolbar.

Changing Print Settings

In some situations, you might want to print only the current page or a certain range of pages. These options are controlled in the Print dialog box. The Print dialog box supplies you with several options, including the printer to which you send the print job, the number of copies, and the page range to be printed.

To open the Print dialog box, select **File**, then **Print**. The Print dialog box is shown in Figure 14.2.

Depending on your home or office situation, you might have your computer connected to more than one printer (especially if you are on a network). The Print dialog box has a drop-down box that lists all the printers to which you have access. To select a printer other than the current printer, click the drop-down arrow in the **Name** box and choose your printer from the list.

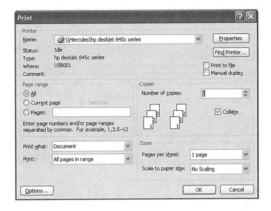

Figure 14.2   The Print dialog box gives you control over the options for your document.

The Print dialog box also enables you to select the range to be printed. This range can consist of a page, a group of specific pages in a sequence, or all the pages in the document.

- **All Pages**—To print all the pages in the document, make sure the **All** option button is selected.
- **Current Page**—To print a single page, click the **Current Page** option button (this prints the page that the insertion point is parked on).
- **Page Range**—To designate a range of pages, click the **Pages** option button and type the page numbers into the Pages box.

TIP   **Specifying Page Ranges**   To print a continuous range of pages, use the 1–5 format (where 1 is the start and 5 is the end of the range). For pages not in a continuous range, use the 5,9,13 format (where each distinct page number to be printed is separated by a comma). You can also mix the two formats. For example, you could specify 1–5,9,13.

- **Number of Copies**—In the Copies area of the Print dialog box, use the increment buttons in the Number of Copies box to select the number of copies you want to print. You can also double-click inside the Number of Copies box and type in a particular value for the number of copies you want.
- **Collate**—In addition to specifying the number of copies, you can select whether to collate your document by checking the Collate box in the copies area. *Collate* means that the document is printed in the proper order for stapling or binding.

For example, a 10-page document would be printed from page 1 through 10 and then the subsequent copies would also print in this "collated" arrangement. If you do not choose to collate, all the copies of page 1 will be printed, then page 2, and so on.

You can also choose to print all the pages in a chosen range or print only the odd or even pages. Click the **Print** drop-down box (near the bottom left of the dialog box) and select **All Pages in Range**, **Odd Pages**, or **Even Pages**, as required.

Another print option worth mentioning is the Zoom print option in the Print dialog box. This feature enables you to place several document pages on one sheet of paper. To use Zoom print, click the **Pages per Sheet** drop-down box in the **Zoom** area of the Print dialog box and select the number of document pages you want to place on a sheet of paper. To select a scale for the print job (the scale is the relative size of the mini-pages on the printout page, such as 8.5 by 11 inches or legal size), click the **Scale to Paper Size** drop-down box.

After you select these two options, proceed with your print job. Be advised, however, that the more pages you place on a single sheet, the smaller the text appears.

Finally, you can print special items that you have placed in your document, such as comments, styles, and AutoText entries. When you choose to print one of these items, you are supplied with a page or pages separate from the main document that lists the comments, styles, or other items you've selected.

Select the **Print What** drop-down arrow and select from the list of items as follows:

- **Document**—Prints the document.
- **Document Properties**—Prints a summary of the information found in the document properties dialog (click File, Properties).
- **Document Showing Markup**—Shows the document with markup from tracking changes by multiple authors.
- **List of Markup**—Prints a list of changes added to a document involving multiple authors.
- **Styles**—Lists the styles in the document.
- **AutoText Entries**—Provides a list of the AutoText entries in the document.
- **Key Assignments**—Shows the shortcut key assignments for the document.

If you want to print more than one of these optional items with the document printout, you must select them in the Print options dialog box.

Selecting Paper Trays, Draft Quality, and Other Options

Several additional print options are also available from the Print dialog box. Each printer, depending on the features it provides, will have its own set of unique options. To access these options, click the **Options** button on the bottom left of the Print dialog box (see Figure 14.3).

Figure 14.3 In the Print options dialog box, you can select or deselect certain options associated with your print job.

The Print options dialog box, using a series of check boxes, gives you control over the output of the print job as well as other options. You can also select the paper tray in your printer that you want to use for the print job (this is very useful in cases where you have a specific tray for letterhead, envelopes, and so on). Several of these options are described in Table 14.1.

Table 14.1   Print Options on the Print Dialog Box

Option	Purpose
Draft Output	Prints the document faster with less resolution
Reverse Print Order	Prints pages last to first, collating your document on printers that output documents face up
Background Printing	Prints the document quickly to a memory buffer so that you can work while the output is actually sent out to the printer
Document Properties	Prints the document properties

When you have finished selecting the various options for the printing of your document, click the **OK** button. You are returned to the Print dialog box. When you are ready to print the document, click **OK**.

Creating Numbered and Bulleted Lists

In this lesson, you learn how to create and edit numbered and bulleted lists.

Understanding Numbered and Bulleted Lists

You can add emphasis to a list of points or delineate a list of items in a document by adding numbers or bullets to the items in the list. Numbered lists are great for steps or points that should be read in order. Bulleted lists work best when you want to separate and highlight different items or points in a list, but the items do not have to appear in any particular order.

The style and look of the numbers or bullets that you apply to a list can easily be edited, and you can even change the starting number for a numbered list. The list then renumbers itself automatically. Also, as you add new lines to numbered or bulleted lists, the items are automatically set up with the same numbering style (with the proper number in the list sequence) or bullet style.

Creating a Numbered or a Bulleted List

You can create numbered or bulleted lists from scratch or add numbers or bullets to an existing list.

To create a new numbered list, follow these steps:

1. Place the insertion point where you want to begin the numbered list in your document.
2. Select **Format**, **Bullets and Numbering**. The Bullets and Numbering dialog box appears.
3. For a numbered list, select the **Numbered** tab (see Figure 15.1).

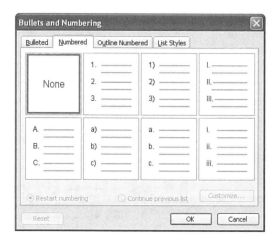

Figure 15.1 Use the Numbered tab on the Bullets and Numbering dialog box to select a number style for your numbered list.

TIP **Quickly Start a Numbered or Bulleted List Using the Formatting Toolbar** To start a numbered or bulleted list using the default number or bullet style, click the **Numbering** or **Bullets** button on the Formatting toolbar. To turn off the numbers or bullets, click the appropriate button on the toolbar.

4. On the **Numbered** tab, click the style box for the particular style that you want to use for the numbers in the list. If you want to customize any of the default styles offered, select the style box and then click the **Customize** button. The Customize Numbered List dialog box appears (see Figure 15.2).

5. Use this dialog box to change the number style, the format, the start number, the font for the numbers, or the number position. A preview of your changes appears at the bottom of the dialog box.

6. When you have selected your options for the number style for your list, click **OK**. You are returned to the Bullets and Numbering dialog box. Click **OK** to return to the document.

You can also easily create a bulleted list using the Bullets and Numbering dialog box; follow these steps:

1. To start a bulleted list, open the Bullets and Numbering dialog box, as previously discussed (select **Format, Bullets and Numbering**). Click the **Bulleted** tab.

Figure 15.2   The Customize Numbered List dialog box enables you to set the number style, format, and start number for the list.

2. Select the bullet style you want to use by clicking the appropriate box. If you need to customize your bullet style, click the **Customize** button. The Customize Bulleted List dialog box will open (see Figure 15.3).

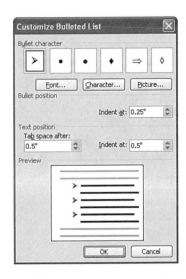

Figure 15.3   Use the Customize Bulleted List dialog box to select the bullet style or shape for your bulleted list.

3. The Customize Bulleted List dialog box enables you to select any symbol available in the various font symbol sets or create your button from a graphic available in the Office clip art library. Use the **Font** and **Character** buttons to select your bullet style from the various symbol sets (as discussed in Lesson 12, "Adding Document Text with AutoText and Using Special Characters"). If you want to use a graphic as the bullet, click the **Picture** button. Use the Picture Bullet dialog box that appears to select the bullet graphic you want to use, and then click **OK** (see Figure 15.4).

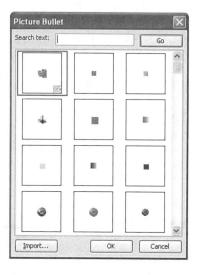

Figure 15.4 You can select from a number of bullet graphics using the Picture Bullet dialog box.

TIP **Import Pictures to the Organizer** If you have scans or digital photos on your computer that you want to use as bullet graphics, add them to the Organizer using the **Import** button.

4. Your new bullet style (selected either from a symbol set or from the Picture Bullet dialog box) will appear in the Customize Bulleted List dialog box. Click **OK** to return to the Bullets and Numbering dialog box.

5. When you are ready to begin the bulleted list, click **OK** to close the Bullets and Numbering dialog box. The first bullet for the list will appear in your document.

Adding Items to the List

After you've turned on numbering or bulleting, you will notice that a number or a bullet appears at the beginning of the line that holds the insertion point. Type the text for this numbered or bulleted item.

Press the **Enter** key to begin a new line. The numbering (sequentially) or bulleting continues with each subsequent line. Just add the needed text and press **Enter** whenever you are ready to move to the next new item in the list.

You can turn off the numbering or bulleting when you have finished creating your list. Click the **Numbering** button or the **Bullets** button, respectively, on the Formatting toolbar.

Creating a Numbered or a Bulleted List from Existing Text

You can also add numbers or bullets to existing text. Select the text list, as shown in Figure 15.5, and then select **Format, Bullets and Numbering**. Select the appropriate tab on the Bullets and Numbering dialog box and select the style of bullets or numbers you want to use.

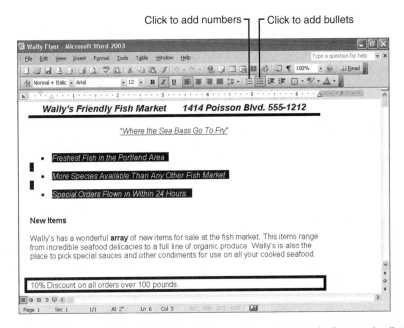

Figure 15.5 Select an existing text list and then add numbers or bullets to the list.

When you have completed making your selection, click **OK**. The numbers or bullets appear on the text list.

TIP **Add Numbers or Bullets with a Click** You can quickly add numbers or bullets to an existing list that is not yet formatted with bullets or numbers. Select the list of items and click the **Numbering** or **Bullets** buttons, respectively, on the Formatting toolbar.

Creating Multilevel Lists

You can also create multilevel lists by using the numbering and bullet feature. Multilevel lists contain two or more levels within a particular list. For example, a multilevel list might number primary items in the list, but secondary items (which fall under a particular primary item) in the list are denoted by sequential letters of the alphabet. Figure 15.6 shows a numbered, multilevel list.

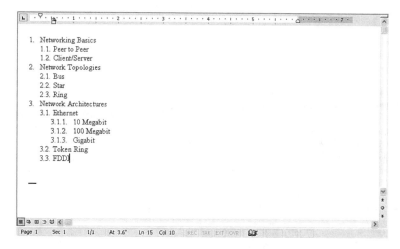

Figure 15.6 A multilevel numbered list uses several levels of numbering, as an outline does.

To create a multilevel list, follow these steps:

1. Place the insertion point where you want to begin the list, or select text in an already existing list.

2. Select **Format, Bullets and Numbering**. The Bullets and Numbering dialog box opens.

3. Click the **Outline Numbered** tab to view the multilevel options (see Figure 15.7).

Figure 15.7 Use the Outline Numbered tab to select the outline style for your multilevel list.

4. Select the style of multilevel list you want to use in your document.

5. After customizing the list options in the Customize Outline Numbered list, click **OK** to return to the Outline Numbered tab.

6. Click **OK** to close the Bullets and Numbering dialog box and return to the document.

7. To enter first-level items in the list, type the item (it will be automatically numbered as appropriate). Press **Enter** to move to the next line.

8. To demote the next line to the next sublevel (the next level of numbering), press the **Tab** key. Then, type your text. Press **Enter** to move to the next line.

9. If you decide to promote a line that you have demoted using the **Tab** key, make sure the insertion point is on the line, and then press **Shift+Tab**. When you have finished with the current line, press **Enter** to continue.

  TIP **Promote or Demote with the Toolbar** You can also promote or demote items using **Decrease Indent** and **Increase Indent** on the Formatting toolbar.

When you have completed your list, you can turn off the numbering by clicking the **Numbering** button on the Formatting toolbar (this deactivates numbering).

Using Word Tables

In this lesson, you learn how to create and format tables in your Word document. You also learn how to place math formulas in a table.

Understanding Tables and Cells

A Word table is made up of vertical columns and horizontal rows—a tabular format. A tabular format gives you flexibility to arrange text and graphics in an organized fashion using columns and rows. Tables enable you to enter and work with information in a self-contained grid. Information is entered into a table cell.

 Cell A table cell is the intersection of a column and row.

Word makes it easy for you to create a table of any size with any number of columns and rows in your document and then edit it. In addition to editing text or graphics in a table, you have access to several formatting options related to the table itself, such as row and column attributes and the capability to easily add or delete rows and columns from the table.

Creating Tables

Word offers you several approaches for actually placing the table into the document. You can insert the table into the document or draw the table using the Draw Table command.

Let's take a look at inserting a table, which allows you to quickly specify the number of rows and columns to be used. We can then look at drawing a table into a document.

Inserting a Table

One option for placing a table into your document is inserting the table. Inserting a table enables you to select the number of rows and columns in the table. The height and the width of the rows and columns are set to the default (one line space [based on the current font height] for the row height and 1.23 inches for the column width). Using the Insert command for a new table is the simplest way to select the number of rows and columns for the table. Also, to place the table, you need only place the insertion point at the position where the new table is to be inserted. The insertion point marks the top-left starting point of the table.

Inserted tables are static; you can move them to a new location in a document only by selecting the entire table and then using cut and paste. If you want to have better control over the placement of the table, you might want to draw a table (as described in the next section). This type of table can be dragged to any location in the document because it is created inside a portable frame.

To insert a table into your document, follow these steps:

1. Place the insertion point in the document where you want to place the table; select **Table**, and then point to **Insert**. Select **Table** from the cascading menu. The Insert Table dialog box appears (see Figure 16.1).

Figure 16.1   The Insert Table dialog box enables you to specify the number of columns and rows for your new table.

2. Use the spin arrows in the **Number of Columns** text box to set the number of columns. Use the click arrows in the **Number of Rows** text box to set the number of rows.

3. If you want to set the number of columns and rows as the default for subsequent tables, click the **Remember Dimensions for New Tables** check box.

4. To set the table so that it automatically adjusts the column widths to accommodate the text that you type in the column, select the **AutoFit to Contents** option button. If you are going to save the Word document containing the table as a

Web document (and use it on a Web site), select the **AutoFit to Window** option button. This allows the table to automatically adjust within a Web browser window so that it can be viewed when the browser window is sized.

5. When you have completed your settings for the table, click **OK**.

The table is inserted into your document.

 TIP   **Use the Toolbar to Insert a Table**   Click the **Insert Table** button on the Standard toolbar, and then drag down and to the right to select the number of rows and columns (a column and row counter shows you the number selected). Release the mouse to insert the table (or click Cancel if you change your mind).

Drawing a Table

An alternative to inserting a table into your document is to draw the table. This method creates a table that resides inside a table frame. The frame can then be dragged to any position in the document. You actually draw the table with a drawing tool and use the tool to add rows and columns to the table.

When you draw the table, you will find that it is created without any rows or columns. You then must manually insert the rows and columns using the Table Drawing tool. Although you can build a highly customized table using this method, it is not as fast as inserting a table with a prescribed number of rows and columns, as described in the previous section.

To draw a table in your document, follow these steps:

1. Select **Table, Draw Table**. The mouse pointer becomes a "pencil" drawing tool. The Tables and Borders toolbar also appears in the document window.

2. Click and drag to create the table's outside borders (its box shape). Release the mouse when you have the outside perimeter of the table completed.

3. To add rows and columns to the table, use the pencil to draw the row and column lines (hold down the left mouse button and drag the mouse; see Figure 16.2).

4. When you have completed your table, click the **Draw Table** button on the Tables and Borders toolbar to deactivate the Draw Table feature (this button is a toggle and can also turn the drawing tool back on when clicked).

Line being drawn will add a fourth column

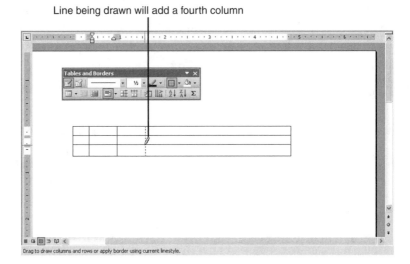

Figure 16.2 With the table drawing tool, you can draw a table in your document, and then draw in the row and column lines. The borders all snap to right-angled lines on an unseen grid so that your table will always have straight lines.

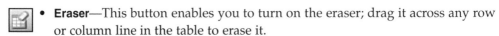

TIP **Right-Click Any Toolbar to Show the Tables and Borders Toolbar** Right-click on any toolbar in the Word application window, and then select **Tables and Borders** to open the Tables and Borders toolbar.

The Tables and Borders toolbar provides you with buttons that enable you to edit the attributes of the table. Several of the buttons on the Tables and Borders toolbar are useful for customizing your table:

- **Distribute Rows Evenly**—This button makes the row heights in the table all the same.

- **Distribute Columns Evenly**—This button makes all the column widths consistent.

- **Eraser**—This button enables you to turn on the eraser; drag it across any row or column line in the table to erase it.

- **Line Style**—This drop-down box enables you to change the weight and style of the row or column lines you create.

You can also move the table anywhere on the document page (it's not anchored in one place like tables that are placed on the page using the Insert Table command). Place the mouse on the upper-left edge of the table and a Move icon (a four-headed arrow) appears. Drag the icon to a new location on the page. When you release the mouse, the table is placed in the new location.

CAUTION

When I Insert or Draw a Table, My Screen View Changes For you to be able to see the table formatting as it occurs, Word automatically sets your document view to Print Layout. If you previously were in the Normal view, your screen will look different because it is now showing all layout instructions. To switch back, select your desired page view from the **View** menu.

Entering Text and Navigating in a Table

Entering text into the table is very straightforward. Click in the first cell of the table (the open box where the first column and first row of the table meet) and enter the appropriate text. To move to the next cell (horizontally, then vertically), press the **Tab** key. You can continue to move through the cells in the tables by pressing **Tab** and entering your text. If you want to back up a cell, press **Shift+Tab**. This moves you to the cell to the left of the current cell and selects any text entered in that cell.

Several other keyboard combinations are useful as you work in your table:

- **Alt+Home**—Takes you to the first cell in the current row
- **Alt+Page Up**—Takes you to the top cell in the current column
- **Alt+End**—Takes you to the last cell in the current row
- **Alt+Page Down**—Takes you to the last cell in the current column

Of course, you can use the mouse to click any cell of the table at any time.

Deleting text in the table is really no different from deleting text in your document. Select text in the table and press **Delete** to remove it. If you want to delete text in an entire row, but you want to keep the row in the table, place the mouse pointer at the left edge of the particular row. The mouse arrow pointer appears in the selection area. Click to select the entire row. When you press **Delete**, all the text in the cells in that particular row is deleted. You can also use a column pointer (a solid black arrow; place the mouse at the top of any column) to select an entire column and delete text using the Delete key.

Inserting and Deleting Rows and Columns

Even after creating your table, you still have complete control over the number of rows and columns in it. You can delete empty or filled rows and columns depending on your particular need.

To insert a row or column into the table, place the insertion point in a cell that is in the row or column next to where you want to place a new row or column. Select the **Table** menu and then point to **Insert** to see the available options. Options can be selected from a cascading menu:

- **Rows Above**—Insert a new row above the selected row.
- **Rows Below**—Insert a new row below the selected row.
- **Columns to the Left**—Insert a new column to the left of the selected column.
- **Columns to the Right**—Insert a new column to the right of the selected column.

You can also easily delete columns or rows from your table. Select the rows or columns, and then select the **Table** menu. Point at **Delete**, and then select **Columns** or **Rows** from the cascading menu, as appropriate. The columns or rows selected are removed from the table.

 TIP   **Quick Select Multiple Columns**   To select several cells, drag the mouse across them. You can also click the first cell in the series and then hold down the **Shift** key as you click the last cell you want to select.

Formatting a Table

Formatting a table can involve several things: You can change the width of a column or the height of a row, and you can also format the various table borders with different line weights or colors. Some of the table attributes can be modified directly on the table, but other attributes are best handled by modifying settings in the Table Properties dialog box or by using the AutoFormat dialog box.

Modifying Cell Size

An important aspect of working with your rows and columns is adjusting column widths and row heights to fit the needs of the information that you place inside the table cells. Both of these formatting tasks are mouse work. However, when you want to enter an actual value for all the column widths or row heights, you can use the Table Properties dialog box discussed in this section.

Place the mouse pointer on the border between any columns in your table. A sizing tool appears (see Figure 16.3). Drag the sizing tool to adjust the width of the column.

 TIP   **Use the Ruler As Your Guide**   You can also use the column border markers on the ruler to adjust the width of a column or columns in your table. This provides a method of sizing columns using the ruler as a measurement guide. Drag the marker on the ruler to the appropriate width. To view the ruler, select **View**, **Ruler**.

Sizing tool icon

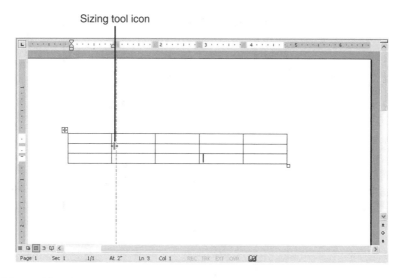

Figure 16.3 Use the column sizing tool to adjust the width of a column.

CAUTION

Be Careful When Sizing Columns If a Cell Is Selected If a cell is selected anywhere in a column and you attempt to drag the sizing tool to change the column width, only the width of the row holding the selected cell is changed. Make sure no cells are selected if you want to size the entire column.

You can also adjust the column widths and the row heights in the table using the Table Properties dialog box. If you want to adjust the row or column attributes for just one row or column, make sure the insertion point is in that row or column. If you want to adjust the values for the entire table, click anywhere in the table, choose the **Table** menu, point at **Select**, and then choose **Table**. This selects the entire table.

Follow these steps to open the dialog box and adjust the various properties associated with the current table:

1. Select **Table**, **Table Properties**. The Table Properties dialog box appears.

2. To adjust column widths using the dialog box, select the **Column** tab.

3. Make sure the **Specify Width** check box is selected, and then use the width click arrows to adjust the width (see Figure 16.4).

4. If you want to change the width of the next column, click the **Next Column** button. The **Previous Column** button enables you to adjust the width of the previous column.

5. When you have completed adjusting column widths, click the **OK** button.

Figure 16.4 Adjust your column widths using the Column tab of the Table Properties dialog box.

You can adjust row heights in a like manner. Use the **Row** tab of the Table Properties dialog box. You can use the **Specify Height** box to specify the row height and the **Previous Row** and **Next Row** buttons to specify the row for which you want to adjust the height.

TIP **Working with Drawn Tables** If you've created your table using the Draw Table command and then inserted your rows and columns with the Drawing tool, you might find it faster to align any irregularly sized elements (such as rows or columns) with the mouse (and the Tables and Borders toolbar) rather than using the Table Properties dialog box.

Formatting Table Borders

Formatting your table borders is a matter of selecting the cells (or the entire table) and then selecting the formatting parameters. After you've selected the appropriate cells, select the **Format** menu, and then select **Borders and Shading**.

TIP **Select the Entire Table** A fast way to select the entire table is to place the insertion point in the table and then select **Table**, point at **Select**, and then select **Table**.

The Borders and Shading dialog box appears as shown in Figure 16.5. Select the style of border that you want to place on the selected area of the table.

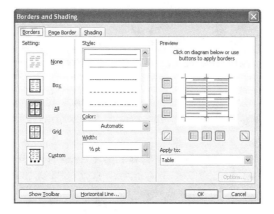

Figure 16.5 Use the Borders and Shading dialog box to select the border options for your table.

To select the border style, choose from one of the following:

- **Box**—This places a box around the outside of the table.
- **All**—This places a box around the table, gridlines inside the table, and also applies any shadow and color parameters that have been set in Word.
- **Grid**—This places a border around the table and places a border (grid) on the row and column lines.
- **Custom**—When you select **Custom**, you must then specify on the Preview table the border lines you want to format. To change the style, color, and width of your border lines, use the **Style**, **Color**, and **Width** drop-down boxes to select the options for your border lines. When you have completed your selections, click **OK** to return to the table.

The border options that you selected are used to format the cells that you selected in the table.

Automatically Formatting the Table

You can also format your table in a more automatic fashion using the Table AutoFormat feature. This feature enables you to select from a list of predetermined table formats that configure the borders and provide text and background colors in the cells; you can even select a particular font for the text contained in the cells.

To AutoFormat your table, click any cell of the table and then follow these steps:

1. Select **Table**, **Table AutoFormat**. The Table AutoFormat dialog box appears.

2. To preview the various formats provided, click a format in the **Formats** scroll box. A preview of the format is shown.

3. When you have found the format that you want to use (you can choose from about 50), select the format and then click **Apply**.

TIP **Select the Table Items You Want to Format with AutoFormat** The AutoFormat dialog box provides several check boxes (Borders, Shading, Font, Color, and so on) that can be deselected if you don't want your AutoFormat selection to format these particular items in your table (otherwise, the entire table will be formatted).

Placing a Formula in a Table

You can also place formulas in your tables that can do a variety of calculations. You can add cells to show a total, calculate an average, and do statistical calculations such as max and min, which return the maximum or minimum (respectively) from a list of numbers.

Before working with formulas, however, you should become familiar with how cell addresses are determined. Each column in the table is given a letter designation starting with A. So, the first column is A, the second is B and so on. The first row in the table is 1. The second row would be 2 and so on. The first cell in a table, which is in column A and row 1 would be cell A1. Each cell's address is the column letter followed by the row number.

To specify a group of cells to be acted on by a formula, you have to specify the first cell in the group and then the last cell in the group. So if you were adding cells B2, B3, B4, and B5, you would designate the cell group as B2:B5. This tells Word where the cells to act on begin and end.

Another thing you should know is that table formulas have to be created in a very specific way. Each formula must start with an equal sign (=) followed by the name of the formula (such as SUM for adding or AVERAGE for average). The cells to be acted on are then entered in parentheses following the name of the formula. A formula that provides you the average of cells B2:B5 would look like this:

=AVERAGE(B2:B5)

To place a formula in a table, follow these steps:

1. Click in the table cell where you will place the formula.

2. Select **Table**, **Formula**. The Formula dialog box appears as shown in Figure 16.6.

Figure 16.6   The Formula dialog box allows you to insert a formula into a Word table.

3. In many cases, the Formula dialog box will use cell position to interpret the best formula to insert into the table. For example, in Figure 16.6, Word "sees" that you have a column of numbers above the formula cell and so will probably want to add (SUM) cells above. If this is the appropriate formula, click **OK** and the formula (and its result) will be inserted into the table.

4. If you want to paste a different formula into the table cell, select and **Delete** the formula provided.

5. In the Formula box, type an equal sign (=) and then click the **Paste Function** drop-down list to insert a new formula.

6. To specify the cells to be acted on by the formula, place the starting and ending addresses of the cell grouping (separated by a colon).

7. Click OK to place the formula in the table.

TIP   **Understanding Word Formulas**   The formulas that Word provides for use in your tables are simplified versions of Excel functions. For more about how functions work and are used, see Lesson 5, "Performing Calculations with Functions," in the Excel section of this book.

Creating Columns in a Document

In this lesson, you learn how to create and edit column settings in your document.

Understanding Word Columns

Word makes it easy for you to insert and format columns for newsletters, brochures, and other special documents. It gives you complete control over the number of columns, column widths, and the space between the columns. You can insert columns for the entire page run of a document or place columns only in a particular document section.

The columns that you work with in Word are called newspaper columns or "snaking columns." This means that if you have two columns on a page and fill the first column, the text snakes over into the second column and continues there. This format is typical of your daily newspaper's columns.

TIP **For Side-by-Side Columns, Use a Table** If you want to create columns that allow you to place paragraphs of information side by side in a document, place the text in a table that is not formatted with a visible border. This gives you great control over the individual text blocks in the separate columns that you create (see Lesson 16, "Using Word Tables").

Creating Columns

You can format a new document for columns, or you can select text and then apply column settings to that specific text. When you apply column settings to any selected text, Word automatically places the text (now in the number of columns you selected) into its own document section with a section break above and below the text. This enables you to switch from text in regular paragraphs (which are basically one column that covers all the space between the left and right margins) to text placed in multiple columns. You can also turn off the columns and return to text in paragraphs with very little effort on your part. Figure 17.1 shows a document that contains a section of text in paragraphs followed by text in columns, followed by text in paragraphs (three sections in the same document). Sections are covered in Lesson 20, "Working with Larger Documents."

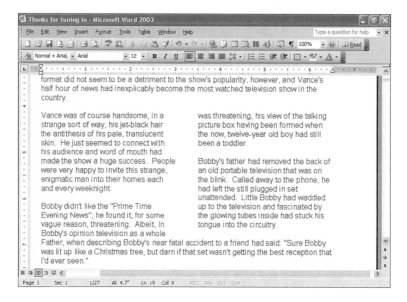

Figure 17.1 Documents can contain text in paragraphs and text in columns, as needed.

To place additional columns into a document, follow these steps:

1. Place the insertion point where you want the columns to begin or select the text that you want to format with the columns.

2. Select **Format**, **Columns**, and the Columns dialog box appears (see Figure 17.2).

3. To select the number of columns you want to place in the document, you can choose from several preset options or specify a number of custom columns. To use the Presets, select one of the following (all presets create columns separated by a half-inch space):

   - **One**—The default setting; this removes columns from the document and places all text in the normal one-column configuration.

   - **Two**—Creates two equal columns.

   - **Three**—Creates three equal columns.

   - **Left**—Creates two columns where the left column is half as wide as the right column.

   - **Right**—Creates two columns where the right column is half as wide as the left column.

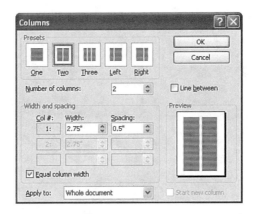

Figure 17.2 The Columns dialog box enables you to set the number of columns and column options for the columns that you place into your document.

4. If you want to select a custom number of columns (rather than using the Presets), use the **Number of Columns** spin box (or type a number in the box). Use the **Width and Spacing** box, located beneath the Number of Columns spinner box, to specify the width for each column and the distance between each of the columns.

5. If you want to place a vertical line between the columns, select the **Line Between** check box.

6. You can apply these new columns to the entire document (if you have selected text, the column settings apply only to that particular text) or click the **Apply To** drop-down box and select **Whole Document** or **This Point Forward**. If you choose This Point Forward, the columns are placed in the document from the insertion point to the end of the document (in their own section).

7. When you have finished selecting your column options, click **OK**.

 TIP **Create Columns with a Click of the Mouse** You can also create columns for currently selected text or insert columns into the text using the Columns button on the Standard toolbar. Click the **Columns** button and then select 1, 2, 3, or 4 columns from the drop-down box (you can choose **Cancel** if you change your mind by clicking outside the Columns button's pop-up menu). If you choose to create multiple columns using this method, columns of equal width are created.

Editing Column Settings

If you want to edit any of the column settings in your document, such as column number or column width, you can return to the Column dialog box to change any of the options.

1. Make sure that you click in the document section that contains the columns you want to modify.

2. Select **Format**, **Columns**. The Column dialog box appears.

3. Edit the various settings, described in the "Creating Columns" section, as needed. When you have completed your selections, click **OK**.

Inserting a Column Break

Because you are working with continuous, newspaper-type column settings, at times you might want to force a column break in a column. This enables you to balance the text between columns or end the text in a column at a particular point and force the rest of the text into the next column. To force a column break, follow these steps:

1. Place the insertion point in the column text where you want to force the break.

2. Select **Insert**, **Break**. The Break dialog box appears.

3. Select the **Column Break** option button.

4. Click **OK** to place the break in the column.

 TIP   **Use the Keyboard to Insert a Column Break**   You can also quickly place a column break in a column by pressing **Ctrl+Shift+Enter**.

The text at the break is moved into the next column in the document. Column breaks in the Print Layout view appear the way they will print, and you'll notice that all the column borders show in this view. In the Normal view, multiple columns are displayed as a single continuous column. The column break appears as a dotted horizontal line labeled Column Break.

Removing Column Breaks

Removing column breaks is very straightforward. Methods do vary, however, depending on the view that you are currently in.

In the Normal view, you can actually see the column break line; it appears as a dashed line and is designated as a Section Break. Select the break line with the mouse and then press **Delete**. Remember that in the Normal view you do not actually see the text in the multiple columns. To see the text as it will appear when you print the columns, use the Print Layout view.

In Print Layout mode, you can go from multiple columns back to a single column without actually removing the section break that specifies the beginning of the columns. Place the insertion point at the beginning of the text just after the break, click the **Columns** button on the Standard toolbar, and then drag to select one column. Again, this doesn't remove the section break that was inserted when you created the multiple column layout, but it does return the text to a single or default column setting.

Adding Graphics to Documents

In this lesson, you learn how to insert graphics, such as clip art, into your document and how to use the Word drawing tools to create your own graphics.

Inserting a Graphic

Adding a graphic to your document is really just a matter of identifying the place in the document where you want to place the picture and then selecting a specific graphic file. Word provides you with a large clip-art gallery of ready-made graphics (in the Windows metafile format, .wmf), and you can also place images into your document that you find on the World Wide Web, that you receive attached to e-mail messages, that are imported from a scanner or digital camera, and more.

Word also embraces several graphic file formats, including the following file types:

- CompuServe GIF (.gif)
- Encapsulated PostScript (.eps)
- Various paint programs (.pcx)
- Tagged Image File format (.tif)
- Windows bitmap (.bmp)
- JPEG file interchange format (.jpg)
- WordPerfect graphics (.wpg)

To add a graphic file to your document, you insert the image using the Insert menu.

Follow these steps to add a graphic to your document:

1. Place the insertion point where you want to place the graphic in the document.
2. Select **Insert**, **Picture**, and then select **From File** on the cascading menu. The Insert Picture dialog box appears.
3. Use the **Look In** box to locate the drive and folder that contains the picture file. After you locate the picture, click the file to view a preview (see Figure 18.1).

Figure 18.1 Picture files are inserted using the Insert Picture dialog box.

    4. After you select the picture you want to insert into the document, click **Insert** in the lower-right corner of the Insert Picture dialog box.

The picture is placed in your document, and the Picture toolbar appears in the document window. The Picture toolbar provides several tools you can use to modify and edit the graphics in your document. See the "Modifying Graphics" section in this lesson for more information on this toolbar.

Probably the first thing you will want to do to any graphic or picture that you insert into a document is to size the image so that it fits better on the page in relation to your text. Most inserted graphics, even those from the Office clip-art library, tend to be inserted into a document in a fairly large size.

To size a graphic, click it to select it. Sizing handles (small boxes) appear on the border of the graphic. Place the mouse on any of these sizing handles. The mouse pointer becomes a sizing tool with arrows pointing in the directions in which you can change the size; drag to size the graphic. To maintain the height/width ratio of the image (so you don't stretch or distort the image), use the sizing handles on the corners of the image and drag diagonally.

TIP **Add a Graphic with Copy and Paste** You can copy (Ctrl+C) a graphic to the Windows Clipboard from any Windows graphics program that you are running and then paste (Ctrl+V) it into your Word document.

Using the Word Clip Art

If you don't have a collection of your own pictures and graphics to place in your document, don't worry; Word provides a large collection of clip-art images you can use to liven up your documents. The clip-art library is organized by theme. For example, if you want to peruse the animal clip art that Word provides, you can select the **Animal** theme.

To insert Word clip art into your document, follow these steps:

1. Place the insertion point where you want to place the graphic in the document.
2. Select **Insert**, **Picture**, and then select **Clip Art** on the cascading menu. The Clip Art task pane appears (see Figure 18.2).

Figure 18.2   The Clip Art task pane gives you access to the Word clip art gallery.

3. Type the name of a clip-art theme, such as **Animals**, into the **Search For** box.
4. (Optional) By default, the search will be conducted on all your media collections, including the Office and Web Collections. If you want to exclude certain collections from the search (to speed up the search process), click the **Search In** drop-down arrow and clear the check mark from any of the locations listed.
5. (Optional) If you want to exclude certain file types from the search (to speed up the search process), select the **All Media File Types** drop-down box and deselect any of the file types (ClipArt, Photographs, and so on) as required.

TIP   **Sound and Action Imagery Available, Too**   You can insert sound or movie clips into your document from the Clip Art task pane. By default they are included in the results for any search you conduct.

6. Click the **Go** button, and various clip-art images that fit your search criteria appear.

7. When you have located the clip art you want to place in the document, click the image. An image drop-down box appears. Select **Insert** to place the image in your document (see Figure 18.3).

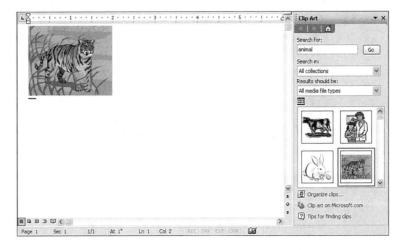

Figure 18.3   Click a particular clip-art category to view the clip-art images.

If used appropriately, pictures and clip art can definitely improve the look and feel of your documents, particularly special documents such as flyers, newsletters, and brochures. If you find that the clip-art library provided doesn't have what you need, click the **Clip Art on Microsoft.com** link near the bottom of the task pane. Your Web browser opens and takes you to Microsoft's online clip-art library, which offers additional clip-art images for your use.

Images and Copyright   Clip-art images, such as those that ship with Microsoft Word, are considered "free" images and can be used in any of your Word documents. Other images that you find on the World Wide Web might be copyrighted. You are responsible for determining whether you have the right to use an image before copying it. Sometimes you can pay a fee for one-time use or make another agreement.

CAUTION

Modifying Graphics

You can modify the images you place into your documents. An invaluable tool for modifying images is the Picture toolbar. It provides buttons that enable you to modify several picture parameters. You can also easily crop and resize your graphics.

When you click a picture (a picture file or Word clip art) in the document, the Picture toolbar automatically appears. You can use the toolbar to adjust the brightness or contrast of the image. You can also add a border to the graphic or adjust other picture properties. Word's Picture toolbar offers a large number of possibilities. Table 18.1 provides a list of the most commonly used buttons on the Picture toolbar.

Table 18.1   The Picture Toolbar Buttons and Their Purpose

Button	Click To
	Insert a new picture at the current picture position.
	Change the image to grayscale or black and white.
	Crop the image (after selecting, you must drag the image border to a new cropping position).
	Rotates the picture to the left 90 degrees.
	Select a line style for the image border (you must first use the Borders and Shading command to add a border to the image).
	Control how text wraps around the image (square, tight, behind image, and so on).
	Open the Format Picture dialog box.
	Reset the image to its original formatting values.

You can select from several formatting options for your picture when you select the **Format Picture** button; this opens the Format Picture dialog box (see Figure 18.4).

The Format Picture dialog box provides several tabs that can be used to control various formatting attributes related to the picture. These tabs are

- **Colors and Lines**—This tab enables you to change the fill color (or background color) for the picture. This tab also provides settings for line weight and color and the style of arrows used on lines. Line options are available only if you have created the image using the tools on the Drawing toolbar.

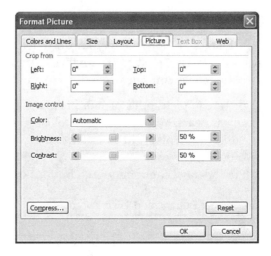

Figure 18.4   The Format Picture dialog box offers several ways to modify your picture.

- **Size**—This tab enables you to specify the height and width of the image in inches. It also enables you to specify the height and width scale (in percentages) for the image.
- **Layout**—This tab enables you to specify how text should wrap around the image (see Figure 18.5). Other options enable you to place the image behind or in front of the text.

Figure 18.5   The Layout tab of the Format Picture dialog box enables you to select how text near the image is wrapped.

- **Picture**—This tab enables you to crop the picture (refer to Figure 18.4). It also provides an Image control area that lets you control the brightness and contrast of the image. You can also change the color of the image from the default (Automatic) to Grayscale, Black and White, and Washout using the Color drop-down box.

- **Web**—This tab enables you to include message text for the image that will appear as the image is loaded on a Web page. You need to use this option only if the Word document containing the image is going to be saved as a Web page and used on a Web site.

CAUTION   **Why Is the Text Box Tab Unavailable?**   The Text Box tab is available only when you are using the Format Picture dialog box to change the format options on a text box that you have created. To create a Text Box, you must use the Text Box tool on the Drawing toolbar (shown later, in Figure 18.6).

After making formatting changes to the picture using the Format Picture dialog box, click **OK** to return to your document.

TIP   **Formatting Drawings You Create**   If you create your own image in a Word document using the tools on the Drawing toolbar, you can format the drawing using the Format Drawing Canvas dialog box, which contains the same tabs as those found on the Format Picture dialog box. To open the Format Drawing Canvas dialog box, select the drawing you have created, and select **Format**, **AutoShape**.

TIP   **Resize or Crop with the Mouse**   Select the picture, and then drag the resizing handles (the black boxes on the picture borders) to increase or decrease the size of your picture. If you want to crop the picture, hold down the **Shift** key as you drag any of the resizing handles.

You can delete a picture you no longer want in the document by clicking the picture and then pressing the **Delete** key on the keyboard. You can also move or copy the picture to another place in the current document—or to another document—using the **Cut**, **Copy**, and **Paste** commands(for general information about moving, copying, and pasting items in Word, see Lesson 3, "Editing Documents").

Using the Word Drawing Toolbar

You can also create your own graphics in your documents using the drawing tools provided on the Word Drawing toolbar. This toolbar provides several tools, including line, arrow, rectangle, oval, and text box tools. You can also use the appropriate tools to change the fill color on a box or circle, change the line color on your drawing object, or change the arrow style on arrows you have placed on the page.

To display the Drawing toolbar, select **View**, point at **Toolbar**, and then select **Drawing** from the toolbar list.

TIP **Quickly Access Toolbars** You can also right-click any toolbar in the Word window to access the toolbar list; then select **Drawing**.

The Drawing toolbar appears at the bottom of the document window just above the Word status bar. Figure 18.6 shows the Drawing toolbar and the tools available on it.

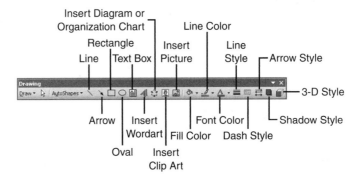

Figure 18.6 The Drawing toolbar makes it easy for you to create your own graphics in your documents.

Word provides you with an add-on program called WordArt that enables you to create special text effects in your document. You can create text that wraps around a circle, as well as a number of other special text "looks." In Word, click the **WordArt** button on the Drawing toolbar to start the WordArt program. WordArt can also be used in other Office programs, such as PowerPoint, to create visually exciting text items.

Another useful Drawing tool is the Insert Diagram or Organization Chart button. Click this button to add predesigned organizational charts and other special diagrams to a document.

Creating a New Object

To draw a particular object, click the appropriate button on the toolbar. Then, drag the mouse to create the object in your document. To draw a square or circle, click the **Rectangle** tool or the **Oval** tool and hold down the **Shift** key as you draw the object with the mouse. If you find that you aren't very good at actually drawing graphical objects, click the **AutoShapes** drop-down arrow (near the left side of the drawing toolbar) and select a particular object shape from the list provided.

Modifying Drawn Objects

You can also control the various attributes for a particular object that you've drawn. You must first select the object using the selection pointer (click the **Select Objects** tool, and then click the object). You can manipulate the object's line style, fill color, and line color. Just choose the appropriate tool on the toolbar, and make your selection from the list of possibilities.

You can also size and move objects that you draw. Select an object, and use the sizing handles to increase or decrease the size of the particular object. If you want to move the object to a new position, place the mouse pointer in the middle of the selected object and drag it to a new position.

If you draw several related objects, you can select all the objects at once and drag them together to a new location. Select the first object and then hold down the **Shift** key and select subsequent objects, as needed. When you drag any of the objects to a new location, all the selected objects move together.

At times you will want to delete a particular object from your document. Simply select the object and then press **Delete** to remove it.

You will find that the Drawing toolbar provides you with all the tools (except natural artistic ability) you need to create fairly sophisticated custom images. A little practice with the various tools goes a long way in helping you create objects that add interest to your documents.

Creating Personalized Mass Mailings

In this lesson, you learn how to create form letters, envelopes, and mailing labels for mass mailings using the Word merge feature.

Understanding the Mail Merge Feature

Word makes it easy for you to take a list of names and addresses and merge them with a form letter, an envelope template, or mailing labels. This enables you to quickly create items for mass mailings that appear to be customized for each person on the mailing list.

Although the Mail Merge Wizard walks you through the merge process, the entire procedure can be somewhat confusing. Two different documents are used during the merge process: a main document and a data source. The main document is your form letter or mailing label template, and the data source is a Word document that provides the list of names and addresses that are inserted into the main document during the merge. The data source can be created prior to the mail merge or during the process.

The information in the data source is inserted into the form letter or mailing label using placeholder codes called *merge fields*. Each merge field in the main document relates to a piece of information in the data source document, such as first name or street address, and the merge field gets its name from that particular field in the data source.

 Merge Fields   Codes serve as placeholders in your main document; for example, {FirstName} is an example of a merge field code that serves as a placeholder for the first-name information that is pulled from the data source.

 Data Source   The file of information, such as a list of names and addresses, to be merged into the main document (such as form letters, envelopes, or mailing labels). Data sources in Word typically take the form of a table, with each row in the table containing the name and address of a different individual.

The best way to understand how the various elements of the merge process—the main document, the data source, and field codes—relate is to actually perform a merge. Working through a merge that creates form letters for the entire list of people in a data source is a good place to start because creating other merge documents, such as labels and envelopes, is a similar process.

Because the merge process really consists of four different actions—creating the main document, creating the data source, inserting the merge fields into the main document (based on the data in the data source), and finally running the merge—this lesson breaks down each of these actions in their own section. We begin with starting the Mail Merge Wizard and creating the main document.

Specifying the Main Document

The first step in the merge process is to specify a main document for the merge. The main document can be the currently open document in the Word workspace, or you can open a pre-existing document during the merge process. To begin the merge process and designate a main document for the merge, follow these steps:

1. Open a new, blank document in the Word window; click the **New Blank Document** icon on the Standard toolbar.

2. Select **Tools**, point at the **Letters and Mailing** arrow, and then select **Mail Merge Wizard**. The Mail Merge task pane opens, as shown in Figure 19.1.

3. Under **Select Document Type** on the Mail Merge task pane, choose the type of main document you want to create using one of the following option buttons: Letters, E-Mail Messages, Envelopes, Labels, or a Directory. A directory, in this case, is a list of names and addresses that the wizard creates (like a phone book). It does not create a separate item for each person in the data source as the other options do.

4. After selecting the appropriate option button (for this example, **Letters** has been selected), click the **Next: Starting Document** link at the bottom of the task pane.

5. The next wizard step provided in the task pane provides three different option buttons; select one of the following:

   • **Use the Current Document**—This option enables you to build your main document using the new, blank document that was opened in step 1 (and this will be the approach that we use in the steps that follow in this section).

Figure 19.1 The Mail Merge task pane walks you through the steps of merging a main document with a data source.

- **Start from a Template**—When this option button is selected, a Select Template link appears in the Mail Merge task pane. Click **Select Template**, and the Select Template dialog box appears. This dialog box enables you to base your main document on any of Word's document templates. After selecting a particular template on one of the dialog box tabs, click **OK** to return to the Mail Merge task pane.

- **Start from Existing Document**—If you select this option button, a Start from Existing File box appears in the task pane. Click the **Open** button at the bottom of the box. The Open dialog box appears. Use it to select the existing Word document that will serve as the main merge document. Click **OK** to close the Open dialog box and return to the task pane.

6. After selecting one of the options (as discussed in step 5), click the **Next: Select Recipients** link at the bottom of the task pane. This allows you to either create or specify the document that contains the names and addresses (the data source) that you will use for the merge. We discuss the data source document in the next section.

A few things should be said about the options available in step 4. When you select one of these options, you are only setting the stage for how the main document will look when it is completed (meaning when the merge fields and any text that the document will include have been inserted).

If you use a blank document, you will have to add any special formatting or document layout features that you want to include in the document (as well as all the text that the document will contain). If you use an existing document, it can already contain the body text for the form letter and various formatting attributes. Using the document template option enables you to use one of Word's templates to determine the overall look of the document. Templates also often insert placeholder text in a document, allowing you to quickly replace it with text of your own. Of course, there's no guarantee that the style of templates Word provides by default will suit your needs.

No matter how you create the main document (using the options we discussed in this section), field or merge codes will need to be inserted. The actual field codes used will be determined by the data source document, which we discuss in the next section.

Creating or Obtaining the Data Source

The next step in the process is to open or create a data source document. This document not only provides the names and addresses that will be merged into your form letter, but it also dictates the merge fields that are placed in the main document (as placeholders for the actual data that will be placed in the form letters during the merge).

Creating a data source during the Mail Merge process is very straightforward because the Mail Merge Wizard provides you with a form that you use to enter people's names, addresses, and other information. When you enter the information for a particular person, you are creating a record. Each record pertains to one person.

However, you also can use existing data sources for the merge. For example, you can use Access database tables (see Part VI, "Access," for information on creating databases in Access), your Outlook Contacts list, or any Word data source document that you created for a previous merge.

To provide you with a complete, from-scratch look at the merge process, we will create a new data source document in this section of the lesson. The following steps pick up from the preceding section, where we specified the main document for the merge.

Record Information in the data source that contains information about a particular person (or place or thing).

Merge Field   A code that tells Word to automatically insert information into your main document during the merge. For example, the Last Name field inserts your letter recipient's last name.

Using Your Outlook Contacts As a Data Source   The Word Mail Merge Wizard also enables you to use information from your Outlook Contacts list as the data source for a mail merge. For more about the Outlook Contacts list, see Lesson 11, "Creating a Contacts List," in Part III of this book.

1. In the Mail Merge task pane (which currently shows Step 3 of 6, as shown in Figure 19.2), choose one of the following options to specify the data source for the merge:

Figure 19.2   You can use an existing document or your Outlook Contacts list as the data source, or you can create a new data source from scratch.

- **Use an Existing List**—This option is selected by default. If you have a Word document that contains a table or an Access table that contains the name and address information you want to use for the merge, select the **Browse** button in the task pane. This opens the Select Data Source dialog box. Locate your data source file, select it, and then click **Open** to return to the Word window and the Mail Merge task pane. The Mail Merge Recipients dialog box appears in the Word window, providing a data source list based on the source file (it will look the same as the Mail Merge Recipients dialog box shown later in Figure 19.4).

- **Select from Outlook Contacts**—This option enables you to select the names and addresses for the merge from your Outlook Contacts. When this option is selected, a Choose Contacts Folder link appears in the task pane. Click the link and specify the location of your Contacts folder in the Select Contact List Folder dialog box that opens (in almost all cases it finds your Contacts folder for you). Click **OK** to return to Word and the task pane. The Mail Merge Recipients dialog box appears containing a list of your contacts (it is the same as the dialog box shown later in Figure 19.4).

- **Type a New List**—This option enables you to create a new data source (you will use this option to explore how you create a new data source). After selecting this option, click the **Create** button in the task pane to open the New Address List dialog box (you explore this dialog box in step 2).

2. After selecting one of the options listed in step 1 and clicking the **Create** link, either the Mail Merge Recipients dialog box appears (when you select either the existing list or Outlook Contacts list options; we discuss the Mail Merge Recipients dialog box in step 5) or, in the case of the **Type a New List** option (which we select here as we explore this feature), the New Address List dialog box appears (see Figure 19.3).

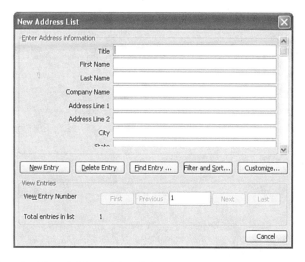

Figure 19.3   Use the New Address List dialog box to create the new data source for the merge.

3. Enter the name, address, and other information that you want to place in the record for the first recipient. When you have finished entering the data, click the **New Entry** button on the New Address List dialog box to enter the next record.

4. Enter additional records as needed. When you have finished entering your records, click the **Close** button on the New Address List dialog box. The Save Address List dialog box opens.

5. Enter a name for the file and specify a location (if necessary—by default, the address list is saved in a special My Data Sources folder that was created when you installed Office). Click **Save** to save the data source file.

6. The Mail Merge Recipients list appears (see Figure 19.4). If you used your Outlook Contacts list or an existing data source, this dialog box appears after you completed step 1 in this section.

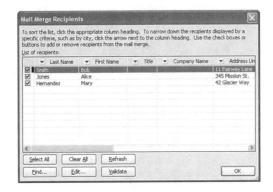

Figure 19.4   Use the Mail Merge Recipients dialog box to sort or select the recipients of the form letter.

7. If you want to deselect any of the recipients in the Mail Merge Recipients dialog box, clear the check box to the left of their records. If you want to sort the list by a particular field (such as last name), click that column's heading.

TIP   **Editing Recipient Information**   If you want to edit one of the records in the Mail Merge Recipients dialog box, select the record and click the **Edit** button. To add a new record, open an existing record using the **Edit** button and click **New Entry**.

8. After selecting recipients or sorting the recipient list, click **OK** to close the Mail Merge Recipients dialog box.

After creating your recipient list as discussed in this section, you are ready to complete the main document and enter the merge fields. These topics are discussed in the next section.

Completing the Main Document and Inserting the Merge Fields

Now that you have specified the recipients for the merge, you can add text, such as the body of the letter, to the main document. The merge fields that pull information from the data source can also be inserted.

Inserting merge fields is a very straightforward process. You can insert individual merge fields for information, such as first name and last name, or you can allow Word to automatically insert several fields into the letter. For example, you can click the Address Block icon that the Mail Merge task pane provides. This inserts the merge fields for the recipient's name and the appropriate address merge fields.

Follow these steps:

1. After specifying or creating a data source (as detailed in the last section), click the **Next: Write Your Letter** link at the bottom of the task pane.

2. The Write Your Letter (step 4 of 6) part of the merge process appears in the Mail Merge task pane (see Figure 19.5).

Figure 19.5   You can insert merge fields into the form letter using the icons in the task pane.

3. A good practice is to go ahead and click in the blank main document and type your letter text, such as the body of the letter. You can also add the closing of the letter or any other information.

4. You can insert the merge fields after typing the text for the letter. Place the insertion point in the main document where you want to place the first merge field. For example, to place recipients' addresses in a form letter, place the insertion point four lines above the greeting. Click the **Address Block** icon in the task pane. The Insert Address Block dialog box appears.

5. The Insert Address Block dialog box provides you with different formats for inserting the recipient's name and their address information. Choose one of the formats listed (see Figure 19.6).

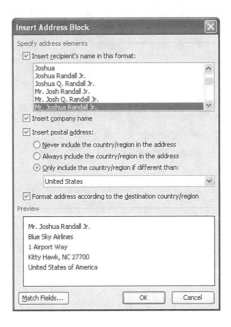

Figure 19.6 You can insert merge fields into the form letter using the icons in the task pane.

TIP   **Matching Fields**   Insertion commands such as Address Block or Greeting Line are configured to use the default field names that Word creates for its data source documents. If you created your data source in another application, such as Microsoft Access, you must specify the field names that you used for merge fields that specify information such as the recipient's name or address. Click the **Match Fields** button on the Address Block or Greeting Line dialog box and use the drop-down lists to select the field name that you used for fields such as Last Name, First Name, and Address. Then, click **OK** to return to the Address Block or Greeting Line dialog box.

6. Option buttons related to the inclusion of the country/region field in the address block are also included. Select the appropriate option button, and click **OK** to close the dialog box. Word inserts the Address Block code into the letter.

Now that you've inserted an Address field, move the insertion point to the position where you want to place the next set of merge fields—for example, the Greeting line.

To insert a Greeting line, click the **Greeting Line** icon on the task pane. The Greeting Line dialog box appears. Use the drop-down lists to select the format for your letter's greeting line, including the punctuation used at the end of the line, such as a comma or a colon, and to insert the appropriate merge fields, such as Last Name, that would be included on the greeting line. Then, click **OK**.

You can insert any other merge fields, as needed, into the document. If you want to insert individual merge fields into the letter, click the **More Items** icon on the task pane. The Insert Merge Field dialog box appears. Select a merge field, and then click **Insert**. When you have finished inserting any needed merge fields, click **Close**.

Finally, you might want to insert a date at the top of your form letter (the main document). Press **Ctrl+Home** to go to the top of the document, and then select **Insert**, **Date and Time**. Select your date format in the Date and Time dialog box, and then click **OK** to insert the date.

Figure 19.7 shows a main document that has been completed. Note that it contains merge fields for the address block and greeting line.

After you've finished your form letter (including the insertion of the appropriate merge fields), you are ready to complete the merge. The next section discusses the completion of the merge and the viewing of your finished form letters.

 TIP **Save the Main Document for Future Merges** To save the completed main document for use in future merges, click the **Save** button on the Standard toolbar. Provide a name and location for the document in the Save As dialog box, and click **Save** to save the document.

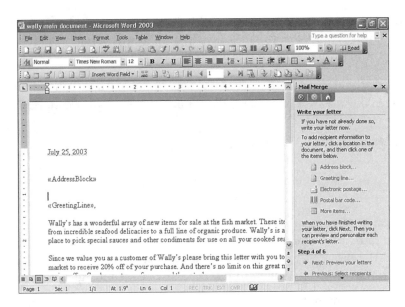

Figure 19.7   Your finished main document will include merge fields, a date, and the body text for the letter.

Merging the Documents

The next step in the merge process is to have Word create the merged documents so that you can preview the letters that are created. This enables you to be sure that the merge worked correctly (based on the merge fields you placed in the main document). It also enables you to edit any of the form letters created before you print them. Although the Mail Merge task pane allows you to preview each letter separately, the merge process actually creates a single document that places each form letter on a separate page.

Follow these steps:

1. Click the **Next: Preview Your Letters** link at the bottom of the task pane (refer to Figure 19.6; this is step 4 of 6 and picks up where the previous section left off).

2. The first form letter appears in the Word window (see Figure 19.8). Check to be sure that the merge fields have placed the appropriate information into the form letter. To view the next recipient's letter, click the **Next** button (>>) at the top of the task pane.

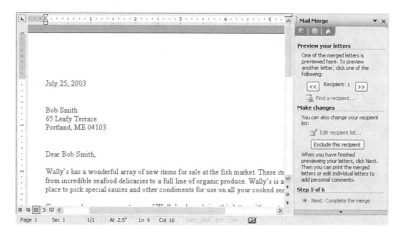

Figure 19.8 You can view each form letter created by the merge.

3. Continue to view the form letters that were created during the merge (using the **Next** button; if you want to go back to a previous letter, click the **Previous** button, <<). If you come across a letter to a recipient that you do not want to keep as part of the merge, click the **Exclude This Recipient** button. The form letter is deleted and the form letter for the next recipient appears in the Word window.

4. When you have finished viewing the form letters created by the merge and are ready to complete the merge process, click the **Next: Complete the Merge** link at the bottom of the task pane.

5. To send the form letters to your printer, click the **Print** icon on the task pane. Word sends the letters to your printer.

6. If you want to save the form letters so that you can print them in the future (or save them for later reference), click the **Save** button on the Standard toolbar. Provide a name and location for the document in the Save As dialog box. Then, click **Save** to save the document.

After you print the form letters or save the merged document, the merge process is complete. At this point, you can close the task pane, if you want to. Click its **Close** (**X**) button.

Creating Envelopes and Mailing Labels

The procedure for using the merge feature discussed in this lesson assumes that you are using a form letter as your main document and creating copies of the letter for each person listed in the data source. You can also use the merge feature to create other document types, such as envelopes and labels.

The procedure for creating envelopes, mailing labels, or letters is almost the same. In each case, you use the Mail Merge Wizard to specify the type of document that you are creating, and then the wizard walks you through the entire merge process. The steps that follow discuss how to create envelopes using the Mail Merge Wizard, but you can just as easily create mailing labels using this process.

To create envelopes using the Mail Merge Wizard, follow these steps:

1. Open a new blank document (click the **New Blank Document** icon on the Standard toolbar). Select **Tools**, point at **Letters and Mailing**, and then select **Mail Merge Wizard**. The Mail Merge task pane opens.

2. Under **Select Document Type**, select **Envelopes**.

3. Click **Next: Starting Document** at the bottom of the task pane.

4. On the next task pane screen, select the **Change Document Layout** option button (if necessary). To select the envelope type to use for the merge, click the **Envelope Options** icon. The Envelope Options dialog box will appear (see Figure 19.9).

5. Select the envelope type you want to use for the merge using the **Envelope Size** drop-down list. If you want to edit any of the fonts for the envelope, use the appropriate **Font** button on the dialog box. When you have finished setting your envelope options, click **OK**.

6. To proceed to the next step in the merge, click **Next: Select Recipients** at the bottom of the task pane.

7. You will need to open or create a data source document. After you open or create a new data source (as discussed earlier in this lesson), the Mail Merge Recipients dialog box appears. Click **OK** to close this dialog box.

8. To proceed to the next step in the merge process and place the merge fields on the envelope, click **Next: Arrange Your Envelope**.

9. Insert the merge fields on the envelope using the **Address Block** or **More Items** icons provided in the Mail Merge task pane. To center the recipient address on the envelope, press **Enter** as required and then click the **Center** icon on the Formatting toolbar.

Figure 19.9   Choose the type of envelope you need in the Envelope Options dialog box.

10. After placing the merge fields on the envelope, click **Next: Preview Your Envelopes**. Use the **Next (>>)** or **Previous (<<)** buttons as needed to view all the envelopes. Remove any envelopes that you do not want to create by clicking the **Exclude This Recipient** button on the task pane.

11. To complete the merge, click **Next: Complete the Merge** at the bottom of the task pane.

At this point, you can click the **Print** icon on the task pane to send the envelopes to your printer. You also can save the envelope document created (each recipient's envelope is placed on a separate page in the merged document) and then print individual pages as needed (click the **Save** button on the Standard toolbar).

Working with Larger Documents

In this lesson, you learn how to work with larger documents, including inserting section breaks and building a table of contents.

Adding Sections to Documents

When you work with larger documents, you might have several parts in the document, such as a cover page, a table of contents, and then the body of the document. In most cases, these different parts of the document require different formatting and layout attributes. To divide a document into different parts that have different layouts, you use sections. A *section* can contain its own set of formatting options. You can divide a document into as many sections as you need.

 Section A portion of a document (defined with section breaks that you insert) that can be formatted differently from the rest of the document or other distinct sections of the document.

When you first begin a new document, the document consists of one section with consistent page formatting throughout the document. If you look at the status bar in a new document, you find that it reads "Sec 1," which means that the insertion point is currently in Section 1 of the document (which would be the entire document, in this case).

Sections are defined in your document as section breaks (which mean a certain position in the document serves as the break between the existing section and the new section you insert). To place additional section breaks in a document, follow these steps:

1. Place the insertion point where you would like to insert the new section break.
2. Select **Insert**, **Break**. The Break dialog box appears. In the lower half of the Break dialog box, several section break types are available (see Figure 20.1).

Figure 20.1   Select your type of section break in the Break dialog box.

- **Next Page**—A page break is placed in the document, and the new section begins on this new page.
- **Continuous**—The new section starts at the insertion point and continues for the rest of the document (or until it comes to the next defined section).
- **Even Page**—The new section starts on the next even-numbered page.
- **Odd Page**—The new section starts on the next odd-numbered page.

3. Select the option button for the type of section break you want to place in the document.

4. Click **OK** to insert the new section into the document.

Your new section break appears in the document. In the Normal view, the section break appears as a double horizontal line marked with the text "Section Break" followed by the type of section you selected. If you are working in the Print Layout view, the only way to see which section you're in is to look at the number displayed on the status bar (see Figure 20.2).

After you have the new section in the document, you can apply page formatting to it as needed.

If you want to delete a section break, place the mouse pointer in the selection area and select the section break the same as you would any other line of text (this won't work in the Print Layout view). After the section break is selected, press the **Delete** key to remove it.

Section breaks are only visible in the Normal view

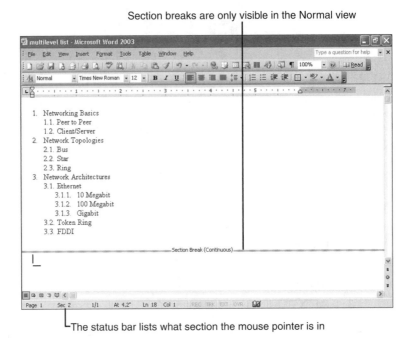

The status bar lists what section the mouse pointer is in

Figure 20.2 You can easily find out which section of a document you are in by reading the status bar or switching the document to Normal View.

Creating a Table of Contents

If you want to make it easy for the reader of a large document to find specific sections or parts of the document, you must include a table of contents. Creating a table of contents in Word relies heavily on using specific text styles to format and organize your document. As long as you do this, creating a table of contents is actually very straightforward.

For example, you can use either Word's built-in heading styles (Heading 1, Heading 2, Heading 3, and so forth) to format the different levels of headings in the document, or you can create your own styles to do so. Using these headings requires you to use some methodology to break down the contents of your document, such as using section levels or chapter levels. The important thing is that you use them consistently to format the various headings that you use in the document.

A good example is a document that is divided into parts and then further subdivided into chapters (each part contains several chapters). If you use Word's heading styles to format the different division levels in the document, you would use

Heading 1 for the parts (Part I, Part II, and so forth) and Heading 2 for the chapter titles. By assigning these built-in styles (or your own) to your different headings, you can generate a table of contents that shows two levels: parts and chapters. This process works because Word can pinpoint a particular heading level by the style that you've assigned to it (for more about working with and creating styles, see Lesson 10, "Working with Styles").

After you've placed your various headings for parts, chapters, or other divisions into your document and have assigned a particular style to each group of headings, you are ready to use the Word Table of Contents feature to generate the actual table of contents.

To create a table of contents using the Word heading styles—or unique styles that you have created—follow these steps:

1. Create a blank page at the beginning of your document for your table of contents (or create a new section in which to place your table of contents) and place your insertion point in it.

2. On the **Insert** menu, choose **Reference**, then **Index and Tables**.

3. When the Index and Tables dialog box appears, select the **Table of Contents** tab (see Figure 20.3).

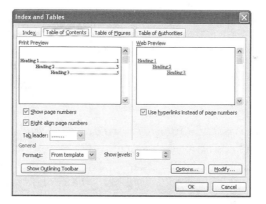

Figure 20.3   The Table of Contents tab on the Index and Tables dialog box is where you specify the options for your new table of contents. You see both a Print Preview and a Web Preview.

4. The Table of Contents tab provides you with a preview of the table of contents (TOC) hierarchy for Word's built-in heading styles. If you used the Word heading styles to format and specify the various division levels in your document,

you can skip down to step 7. If you made your own unique heading or section styles, click the **Options** button.

5. The Table of Contents Options dialog box appears. This is where you specify the styles you used to format the various TOC levels in your document. Scroll down through the **Available Styles** list. To specify a style as a TOC hierarchical level, type the level number (1, 2, 3, and so on) into the appropriate style's TOC level box.

6. When you have selected the styles that serve as your various TOC levels, click **OK** to return to the Table of Contents tab.

7. To select a style for the TOC, click the **Formats** drop-down list. You can choose from several styles, such as Classic, Distinctive, and Fancy. After you select a format, a preview is provided in the Print Preview and Web Preview areas of the dialog box.

TIP **Open the Outlining Toolbar for Quick Access to TOC Features** If you will be editing headings in the document that will affect the TOC after you generate it, you might want to click the **Show Outlining Toolbar** button on the Table of Contents tab. This opens the Outlining toolbar. After generating the TOC and doing any editing in the document, you can use the Update TOC button on the Outlining toolbar to quickly regenerate the TOC. The toolbar also provides a Go to TOC button that can be used to quickly move from anywhere in the document back to the TOC.

8. Use the various check boxes on the tab to select or deselect options for formatting the table of contents. After you've specified options such as right align, page numbers, and the tab leader style, you are ready to generate the table of contents; click **OK**.

Your new table of contents appears in the document (see Figure 20.4). You can add a title to the table of contents (such as Table of Contents) and format the text as needed. If you want to remove the table of contents from the document, place the mouse pointer in the selection area to the left of the table of contents. Click to select the TOC. Press the **Delete** key to remove it from the document.

TIP **Use the TOC to Quickly Move to a Particular Chapter** A slick feature associated with a table of contents in your document is that you can use it to quickly jump to a particular part of your document. For example, if you wanted to move to the beginning of Chapter 3 in the document, from the TOC, press **Ctrl+click** on the Chapter 3 notation in the table of contents. You are taken directly to the beginning of Chapter 3.

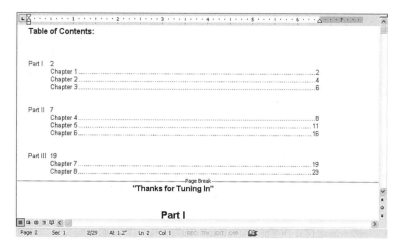

Figure 20.4   The table of contents is generated at the insertion point in your document. You can add your own title.

Creating Web Pages in Word

In this lesson, you learn how to work with Word's capability to build World Wide Web pages, and you learn how to add hyperlinks to your documents that quickly take you to a particular Web page.

Using Word to Create Web Pages

To have a presence on the World Wide Web, you need a Web page. You can create Web pages using a number of different tools; you will find, however, that Word makes it easy for you to create Web pages for the Web. You can create your own personal Web site or create Web pages for use on your corporate Web site.

Creating a Web page in Word is very straightforward. One way to create a Web page is to take any Word document that you have created and save it as a Web page.

However, you will probably agree from browsing the Web that Web pages typically have a particular look and feel. They are often divided into sections with distinct headings and use hyperlinks (discussed later in the lesson) to move around on a page or from page to page within a particular Web site.

Let's take a look at saving a Word document as a Web page and then look at some of the basics of creating a Web page from scratch using the blank Web Page template that is provided by Word.

Saving a Word Document as a Web Page

One way to create an HTML file from a Word document is to create the document in Word (as a typical document) and then save it in the HTML file format. For example, you can create your resume or a special report in Word using all of Word's familiar layout features. You can then save the document as a Web page so that it can be viewed online using a Web browser.

HTML Hypertext Markup Language is the coding system used to create Web pages for the World Wide Web. Basically, all documents must be translated into this universal language before being published to the WWW.

Even if you save the document in the HTML file format, you can still open it in Word and edit the document when needed. To save a Word document as an HTML file, follow these steps:

1. Create the document the same as you would any other Word document. You can include graphics, links to objects, and so on.

2. Select **File**, **Save As Web Page**. The Save As dialog box appears.

3. Using the **Save In** drop-down box, select the location where you would like to save the HTML file. Also type a name for your HTML document into the **File Name** box (the format of the HTML document has already been selected for you in the Save As Type box).

   If you are on a corporate network that has an Internet Web server (a computer that hosts the company's Web site), or if you are supplied with Web space on your Internet service provider's Web server, you can save your HTML document directly to the server itself. All you need to know is the FTP address of the server (something like `ftp.webserver.com`).

   In the **Save In** drop-down box, select **Add/Modify FTP Locations**. The Add/Modify FTP Locations dialog box appears. Type in the name of the FTP site and provide your username and password. When you click **OK**, the FTP site is added to the list of folders in the Save In drop-down box. Select the FTP site as the location to which you save the file. Then click **OK** to save the file.

 FTP   FTP, or File Transport Protocol, is an Internet service used to send and receive files. An FTP server is a computer on the Internet that enables you to save and retrieve files using the File Transport Protocol, which is supported by all the Office applications.

4. Click **Save** to save the HTML document to the specified location.

Even though your file is now in the HTML format, you can still open the document in Word and edit it as needed. Figure 21.1 shows a document in the HTML format open in the Word window.

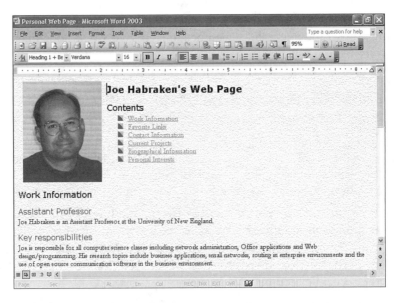

Figure 21.1 Use Word's various desktop publishing features to design a document, and then save it as a Web page for use on your Web site.

Creating a Web Page from Scratch

Because Web pages fulfill a particular purpose, you will probably create many of your pages from scratch, which means you have to add the various elements (pictures, hyperlinks, and so on) that make up the page. To create a Web page from scratch, follow these steps:

1. Select **File**, **New**. The New Document task pane will appear.

2. Click the **Web Page** link under the new heading. A new Web document opens in the Web Layout view.

3. Divide the page up into specific areas using headings. Remember that the longer the page, the more the reader will have to scroll using their Web browser. Keep pages short and use multiple pages in cases where you have to impart a large amount of information. The pages can then be linked together using hyperlinks (discussed later in the lesson).

4. Add the various elements (text and graphics) to your document as required, the same as you would a normal Word document. For headings on your Web page, use the heading styles provided in the **Style** drop-down box on the Word Formatting toolbar (or create your own styles or modify the available styles, if you want).

5. After adding the text and other elements to the new Web document, save the file. It is automatically saved in the Web document (HTML) format.

Selecting a Theme for Your Web Page

After you have edited your new Web page, you may want to add a theme. A *theme* provides design elements, background colors, and font colors that "dress" up your Web page (or any Word document).

1. To select a theme for the Web page, select **Format** and then select **Theme**. The Theme dialog box will appear (see Figure 21.2).

Figure 21.2   Select a theme for your Web page.

2. Select any of the themes in the Choose a Theme list to view a preview of the theme.

3. When you have found the theme that you want to use for the Web page, click OK.

The theme will be added to the Web page as shown in Figure 21.3. Remember to save your new Web page. Click the **Save** button on the Standard toolbar. Provide the filename and location for the Web page in the Save As dialog box. Then click **Save** to save the document.

Figure 21.3   The theme will be applied to your Web page.

Adding Hyperlinks to a Document

An important aspect of creating Web pages is being able to insert a *hyperlink* into a particular document. Hyperlinks provide the main navigational tool for the Web. If you've spent any time on the Web at all, you know that you move from site to site using hyperlinks.

You can also designate graphics that you create and pictures that you place on your Web pages as hyperlinks. Rather than clicking a text link, you click a picture, and it takes you to the referenced Web site.

 Hyperlink   A hyperlink references another Web page or site. Hyperlinks can appear as text or graphics on a Web page. When the hyperlink is clicked, you are taken to that page or site.

 Hyperlinks Can Reference Regular Documents and Files   Hyperlinks don't have to reference Web pages or Web sites. They can be used to link typical Word documents. For example, you can use a hyperlink to open another Word file on your hard drive.

When you create Web pages using the Web Page Wizard, hyperlinks are automatically created in your Web documents. They appear as underlined text elements. They also appear in a particular color. After you use a hyperlink, it appears in a different color when you return to the page containingThis lets you know that you've used that particular link before.

To place a hyperlink into a Word document, follow these steps:

1. Select the text or other items that will serve as the hyperlink.

2. Select **Insert**, **Hyperlink** or click the Insert Hyperlink button on the Standard toolbar. The Insert Hyperlink dialog box appears (see Figure 21.4).

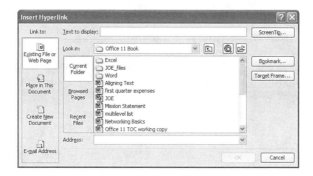

Figure 21.4   Enter the Web site address or the local filename for the new hyperlink into the Insert Hyperlink dialog box.

3. Enter the Web site address (URL—Uniform Resource Locator name—such as www.mcp.com) into the **Address** box.

4. To have text other than the actual hyperlink address appear as the hyperlink, type the text into the Text to Display box.

5. Click **OK**. You return to your document. The hyperlink is underscored and appears in a different color, denoting it as a hyperlink.

6. Repeat steps 2–4 as necessary to create all the hyperlinks for your document.

You can also create nontext hyperlinks. To make a picture, button, or other design element a hyperlink, right-click the object and select **Hyperlink** from the shortcut menu. Enter the address for the Web site into the **Web Page Name** box of the Insert Hyperlink dialog box. Click **OK**. Now when you click the picture hyperlink, you are taken to the referenced Web address.

Previewing Your Web Pages

You can preview your Web pages in the Internet Explorer Web browser as you work on them. This enables you to get a Web-based view of how your pages are turning out. In the Internet Explorer window, you can also check out any hyperlinks that you've placed on your Web page.

To preview your Web page in Internet Explorer, follow these steps:

1. Select **File**, **Web Page Preview**. Microsoft Internet Explorer opens with your Web page in its window.

2. Test your hyperlinks and other command elements as needed.

3. When you have finished viewing your Web page in Internet Explorer, click the **Close** (**X**) button on the upper-right corner of the window. You return to the Word window and your document.

Creating Web pages in Word can be quite easy (and very satisfying) because you are working in an environment that you use to create a variety of other, more "typical" documents.

Excel

Creating a New Workbook

In this lesson, you learn how to start and exit Excel and you become familiar with the Excel window. You also learn how to create new workbooks and open existing workbook files.

Starting Excel

Excel is a spreadsheet program that can help you create worksheets and invoices and do simple and sophisticated number crunching; it is designed to help you calculate the results of formulas and help you organize and analyze numerical data.

To start Excel from the Windows desktop, follow these steps:

1. Click the **Start** button, and the Start menu appears.

2. Point at **All Programs** (in Windows XP; in Windows 2000 select **Programs**), and the Programs menu appears.

3. Select the **Microsoft Office** program group and then **Microsoft Office Excel 2003** to start the program.

Understanding the Excel Window

When you click the Microsoft Excel icon, the Excel application window appears, displaying a blank workbook labeled Book1 (see Figure 1.1). On the right side of the Excel window is the Getting Started task pane. This task pane enables you to connect to Microsoft online. It also allows you to open existing Excel workbooks or create new workbooks (which is discussed later in the lesson).

TIP **Close the Task Pane** If you would like a little more room in the Excel window to work on the current workbook sheet, click the **Close** (**X**) button on the task pane.

When you work in Excel, you use workbook files to hold your numerical data, formulas, and other objects, such as Excel charts. Each Excel workbook can consist of several sheets; each sheet is called a worksheet.

Workbook   An Excel file is called a workbook. Each workbook consists of several worksheets made up of rows and columns of information.

You enter your numbers and formulas on one of the workbook's worksheets. Each worksheet consists of 256 columns. The columns begin with column A and proceed through the alphabet. The 27th column is AA, followed by AB, AC, and this convention for naming subsequent columns continues through the entire alphabet until you end up with the last column (column 256), which is designated IV.

Each worksheet also consists of 65,536 rows. The intersection of a column and a row on the worksheet is called a cell. Each cell has an address that consists of the column and row that intersect to make the cell. For example, the very first cell on a worksheet is in column A and row 1, so the cell's address is A1.

Worksheet   One sheet in an Excel workbook. Each worksheet consists of 256 columns and 65,536 rows (plenty of space to create even the most enormous spreadsheets).

Cell   Where a row and column intersect, each cell has an address that consists of the column letter and row number (A1, B3, C4, and so on). You enter data and formulas in the cells to create your worksheets.

Figure 1.1 shows cell A1 highlighted in worksheet 1 (designated as Sheet1 on its tab) of Workbook 1 (designated in the title bar as Book1; this will change to a particular filename after you name the workbook using the Save function).

The Excel window shown here includes many of the various elements available in other Office applications, such as Word or PowerPoint. These elements include a menu bar (from which you select commands), a status bar (which displays the status of the current activity), and toolbars (which contain buttons and drop-down lists that provide quick access to various commands and features).

In addition, the window contains several elements that are unique to Excel, as shown in Table 1.1.

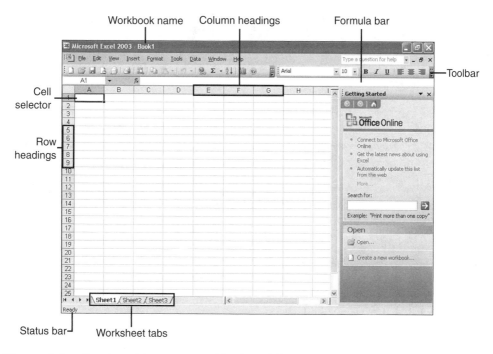

Figure 1.1   Excel provides a new workbook and the menus and toolbars necessary for doing some serious number crunching.

Table 1.1   Elements of the Excel Window

Element	Description
Formula bar	When you enter information into a cell, it appears in the Formula bar. You can use the Formula bar to edit the data later. The cell's location also appears in the Formula bar.
Column headings	The letters across the top of the worksheet, which identify the columns in the worksheet.
Row headings	The numbers down the side of the worksheet, which identify the rows in the worksheet.
Cell selector	The dark outline that indicates the active cell. (It highlights the cell you are currently working in.)
Worksheet tabs	These tabs help you move from worksheet to worksheet within the workbook.

Starting a New Workbook

As you've already seen, when you start Excel, it opens a new blank workbook. It is ready to accept data entry, which is discussed in Lesson 2, "Entering Data into the Worksheet."

The empty workbook that appears when you start Excel is pretty much a blank canvas, but Excel also enables you to create new workbooks based on a template. A *template* is a predesigned workbook that you can modify to suit your needs. Excel contains templates for creating invoices, expense reports, and other common business accounting forms.

To create a new workbook, follow these steps:

1. Open the **File** menu and select **New**. The New Workbook task pane appears on the right side of the Excel window (if you did not close it as outlined earlier, it should already be open).

2. The New Workbook task pane enables you to create new blank workbooks or create workbooks based on an existing workbook or a template (see Figure 1.2).

Figure 1.2   The New Workbook task pane provides quick access to commands for creating new Excel workbooks.

3. To create a blank workbook, click the **Blank Workbook** icon. A new blank workbook opens in the Excel window.

Blank templates are fine when you have a design in mind for the overall look of the workbook. However, for some help with workbook layout and formatting, you can base your new workbook on an Excel template. To use an Excel template, follow these steps:

1. Click the **On My Computer** link in the Templates pane of the New Workbook task pane. The Templates dialog box appears.

2. Click the **Spreadsheet Solutions** tab on the Templates dialog box. The various workbook template icons appear (see Figure 1.3).

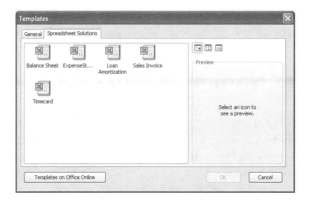

Figure 1.3   The Spreadsheet Solutions templates.

3. Select a template by clicking its icon, and then click **OK** or press **Enter**. A new workbook opens onscreen with a default name based on the template you chose. For example, if you chose the Timecard template, the new workbook is named Timecard1, as shown at the top of Figure 1.4.

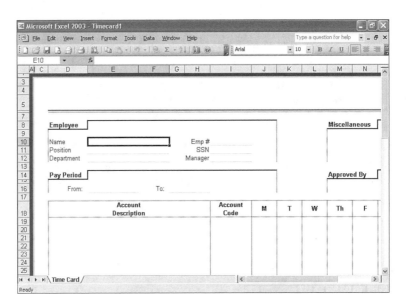

Figure 1.4 A new workbook based on a template provides a basic layout for a particular business form.

Saving and Naming a Workbook

Whether you build your workbook from a blank template or use one of the Excel templates, after you enter some data into the workbook, you should save the file (you learn about data entry in Lesson 2). Also, because changes that you make to the workbook are not automatically saved, you should occasionally save the edited version of your work.

The first time you save a workbook, you must name it and specify a location where it should be saved. Follow these steps to save your workbook:

1. Open the **File** menu and select **Save**, or click the **Save** button on the Standard toolbar. The Save As dialog box appears (see Figure 1.5).

2. Type the name you want to give the workbook in the **File Name** text box. You can use up to 218 characters, including any combination of letters, numbers, and spaces.

3. Normally, Excel saves your workbooks in the My Documents folder. To save the file to a different folder or drive (such as a network drive), select a new location using the **Save In** list.

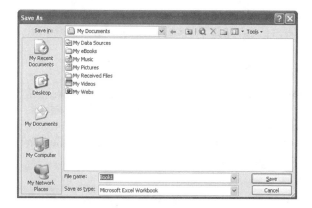

Figure 1.5 Specify the name and location for your new workbook in the Save As dialog box.

The Folder I Want to Save In Doesn't Exist! You can create a new folder from the Save As dialog box: click the **Create New Folder** button on the toolbar of the Save As dialog box, type a name for the new folder, and then press **Enter**.

CAUTION

4. Click **Save** to save your workbook and close the Save As dialog box.

To save changes that you make to a workbook that you have previously saved, just click the **Save** button on the Standard toolbar. You can also press the shortcut key combination of **Ctrl+S** to save changes to your workbook.

Saving a Workbook Under a New Name or Location

There might be an occasion when you want to save a copy of a particular workbook under a different name or in a different location. Excel makes it easy for you to make duplicates of a workbook. Follow these steps:

1. Select the **File** menu and select **Save As**. The Save As dialog box opens, just as if you were saving the workbook for the first time.

2. To save the workbook under a new name, type the new filename over the existing name in the **File Name** text box.

3. To save the new file on a different drive or in a different folder, select the drive letter or the folder from the **Save In** list.

4. To save the new file in a different format (such as WK4, which is a Lotus 1-2-3 format), click the **Save As Type** drop-down arrow and select the desired format.

5. Click the **Save** button or press **Enter**.

 TIP **Saving Excel Workbooks in Other File Formats** Occasionally, you might share Excel workbook data with coworkers or colleagues who don't use Excel. Being able to save Excel workbooks in other file formats, such as Lotus 1-2-3 (as discussed in step 4), enables you to provide another user a file that they can open in their spreadsheet program.

Opening an Existing Workbook

If you have a workbook you've previously saved that you would like to work on, you must open the file first, before you can make any changes. Follow these steps to open an existing workbook:

 1. Open the **File** menu and select **Open**, or click the **Open** button on the Standard toolbar. The Open dialog box shown in Figure 1.6 appears.

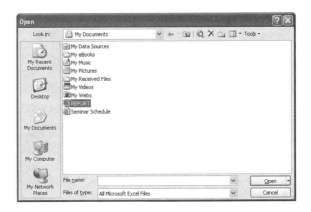

Figure 1.6 Use the Open dialog box to locate and open an existing Excel workbook.

2. If the file is not located in the current folder, open the **Look In** drop-down list box and select the correct drive and folder.

3. Select the file you want to open in the files and folders list.

4. To see a preview of the workbook before you open it, click the **Views** button and select **Preview**. Excel displays the contents of the workbook in a window to the right of the dialog box.

5. Click **Open** to open the currently selected workbook.

TIP   **Recently Used Workbooks**   If the workbook you want to open is one of your four most recently used workbooks, you'll find it listed at the bottom of the File menu. It will also be listed at the top of the New Workbook task pane (if the task pane is active).

Closing Workbooks

When you have finished with a particular workbook and want to continue working in Excel, you can easily close the current workbook. Click the **Close (X)** button in the upper-right corner of the workbook. (There are two Close buttons; the one on top closes Excel, and the one below it closes the current workbook window.) You can also close the current workbook by selecting **File, Close**. If you have changed the workbook since the last time you saved it, you will be prompted to save any changes.

TIP   **It's Closing Time!**   If you have more than one workbook open, you can close all of them at once by holding down the **Shift** key, selecting the **File** menu, and then selecting **Close All**.

Exiting Excel

When you have finished working with Excel, you need to exit the application. This closes all workbooks that are currently open. To exit Excel, select the **File** menu and select **Exit**. Or you can click the **Close (X)** button at the upper-right corner of the Excel window.

If you have changed any of the workbooks that you were working with, you are prompted to save changes to these workbook files before exiting Excel.

Entering Data into the Worksheet

In this lesson, you learn how to enter different types of data into an Excel worksheet.

Understanding Excel Data Types

When you work in Excel, you enter different types of information, such as text, numbers, dates, times, formulas, and functions (which is a special built-in formula provided by Excel). Excel data basically comes in two varieties: labels and values.

A label is a text entry; it is called a label because it typically provides descriptive information such as the name of a person, place, or thing. A label has no numerical significance in Excel; it's just there to describe accompanying values.

 Label   Any text entry made on an Excel worksheet.

A value is data that has numerical significance. This includes numbers, dates, and times that you enter on your worksheet. Values can be acted on by formulas and functions. Formulas are discussed in Lesson 3, "Performing Simple Calculations," and Excel functions in Lesson 5, "Performing Calculations with Functions."

 Values   Entries, such as numbers and dates, that have numerical significance and can be acted upon by formulas or functions.

Entering Text

Text is any combination of letters, numbers, and spaces. By default, text is automatically left-aligned in a cell, whereas numerical data is right-aligned.

 TIP   **Entering Numbers As Text**   To enter a number that you want treated as text (such as a ZIP code), precede the entry with a single quotation mark ('), as in '46220. The single quotation mark is an alignment prefix that tells Excel to treat the following characters as text and left-align them in the cell. You do not have to do this to "text" numerical entries, but it ensures that they will not be mistakenly acted upon by formulas or functions.

To enter text into a cell, follow these steps:

1. Use your mouse or the keyboard arrows to select the cell in which you want to enter text.

2. Type the text. As you type, your text appears in the cell and in the Formula bar, as shown in Figure 2.1.

Formula bar

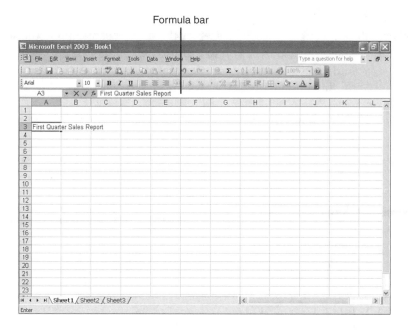

Figure 2.1   Data that you enter into a cell also appears in the Formula bar as you type it.

3. Press **Enter**. Your text appears in the cell, left-aligned. The cell selector moves down one cell. You can also press **Tab** or an arrow key to enter the text and move to the next cell to the right (or in the direction of the arrow).

CAUTION

But My Entry Doesn't Fit!   When text does not fit into a cell (because of the column width set for that column), Excel displays the information in one of two ways: If the next cell is empty, the text overflows into that cell, allowing you to see your entire entry. If the cell to the right of your entry is not empty, you will be able to see only the portion of your entry that fits within the confines of the cell. This can easily be remedied by changing the column width. You learn about changing column widths in Lesson 12, "Inserting and Removing Cells, Rows, and Columns."

Tips on Entering Column and Row Labels

Column and row labels identify your data. Column labels appear across the top of the worksheet beneath the worksheet title (if any). Row labels are entered on the left side of the worksheet.

Column labels describe what the numbers in a column represent. Typically, column labels specify time intervals such as years, months, days, quarters, and so on. Row labels describe what the numbers in each row represent. Typically, row labels specify data categories, such as product names, employee names, or income and expense items in a budget.

When entering your column labels, enter the first label and press the **Tab** key instead of pressing Enter. This moves you to the next cell on the right so that you can enter another column label. When entering row labels, use the down-arrow key or Enter instead of the Tab key. Figure 2.2 shows the various labels for a quarterly sales summary.

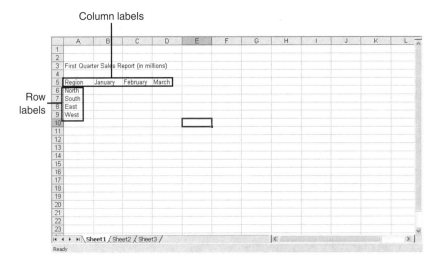

Figure 2.2   Column and row headings serve as labels for the data you enter on the worksheet.

If you need to enter similar data (such as a series of months or years) as column or row labels, you can enter them quickly as a series; this technique is discussed later in this lesson.

Adding Comments to Cells

You can add comments to particular cells, although the comments are not really considered cell content (such as labels and values). These comments allow you to associate information with a cell—information that does not appear (by default) with the worksheet when sent to the printer.

Comments are similar to placing a Post-it note on a cell, reminding you that an outstanding issue is related to that cell. For example, if you need to check the value that you've placed in a particular cell to make sure that it's accurate, you can place a comment in the cell (see Figure 2.3). Cells containing comments are marked with a red triangle in the upper-right corner of the cell. To view a comment, place the mouse pointer on the comment triangle.

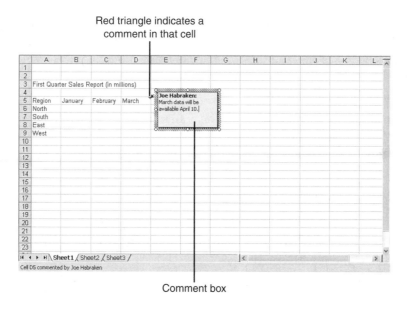

Red triangle indicates a
comment in that cell

Comment box

Figure 2.3   Comments can be added to cells as a kind of electronic Post-it note.

To insert a comment into a cell, follow these steps:

1. Click the cell in which you want to place the comment.
2. Select **Insert, Comment**. A comment box appears next to the cell.
3. Type your information into the comment box.
4. Click anywhere else in the worksheet to close the comment box.

You can also easily remove comments from cells. Select the cell, and then select **Edit** and point at **Clear**. On the cascading menu, select **Comments** to remove the comment.

TIP **Right-Click a Cell to Add Comment** You can add a comment to a cell by right-clicking on the cell and then selecting **Insert Comment** from the shortcut menu that appears.

Entering Numbers

Data that serves as the values in your workbooks can include the numeric characters 0–9. Because formulas are also considered values (you learn about simple calculations in Lesson 3), other valid value characters include symbols such as +, –, /, and *. You can also use characters such as a comma (,), a percent sign (%), or a dollar sign ($) in your values. You will find, however, that you can save yourself a few data-entry keystrokes and add these characters using different Excel formatting options (you learn about Excel formatting in Lesson 9, "Changing How Numbers and Text Look").

For example, you could enter the dollar amount $700.00 including the dollar sign and the decimal point. However, it's probably faster to enter the 700 into the cell and then format all the cells that contain dollar amounts after you have entered all the data.

To enter a value, follow these steps:

1. Click in the cell where you want to enter the value.
2. Type the value. To enter a negative number, precede it with a minus sign or surround it with parentheses.
3. Press **Enter** or the **Tab** key; the value appears in the cell right-aligned. Figure 2.4 shows various values entered into a simple worksheet.

TIP **What Are All Those Pound Signs?** If you enter a number and it appears in the cell as all pound signs (#######) or in scientific notation (such as 7.78E+06), the cell just isn't wide enough to display the entire number. To fix it, double-click the right border of the column's heading. The column expands to fit the largest entry in that column. See Lesson 12 for more information on working with column widths.

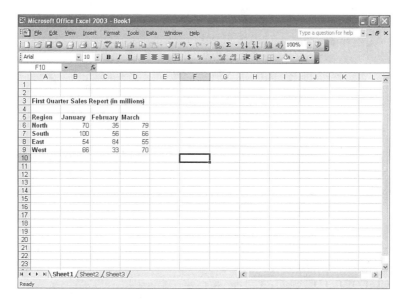

Figure 2.4   Values are right-aligned in a cell.

Entering Dates and Times

Dates that you enter into an Excel workbook have numerical significance. Excel converts the date into a number that reflects the number of days that have elapsed since January 1, 1900. Even though you won't see this number (Excel displays your entry as a normal date), the number is used whenever you use this date in a calculation. Times are also considered values. Excel sees them as the number of seconds that have passed since 12 a.m.

Follow these steps to enter a date or time:

1. Click in the cell where you want to enter a date or a time.
2. To enter a date, use the format MM/DD/YY or the format MM-DD-YY, as in 5/9/03 or 5-9-03.

   To enter a time, be sure to specify a.m. or p.m., as in 7:21 p or 8:22 a.

TIP   **A.M. or P.M.?**   Unless you type am or pm after your time entry, Excel assumes that you are using a 24-hour international clock. Therefore, 8:20 is assumed to be a.m., not p.m. (20:20 would be p.m.: 8 plus 12 hours). Therefore, if you mean p.m., type the entry as 8:20 pm (or 8:20 p). Note that you must type a space between the time and the am or pm notation.

3. Press **Enter**. As long as Excel recognizes the entry as a date or a time, it appears right-aligned in the cell. If Excel doesn't recognize it, it's treated as text and left-aligned.

After you enter your date or time, you can format the cells to display the date or time exactly as you want it to appear, such as September 16, 2003, or 16:50 (international time). If you're entering a column of dates or times, you can format the entire column in one easy step. To format a column, click the column header to select the column. Then open the **Format** menu and select **Cells**. On the **Numbers** tab, select the date or time format you want to use (you learn more about formatting text and numbers in Lesson 9).

Copying Data to Other Cells

Another way to enter labels or values onto a sheet is to use the Fill feature. You can copy (fill) an entry into surrounding cells. For example, suppose you have a list of salespeople on a worksheet, and they will each get a $100 bonus. You can enter the 100 once and then use the Fill feature to insert multiple copies of 100 into nearby cells. To use the Fill feature for copying, follow these steps:

1. Click the fill handle of the cell (the small block in the lower-right corner of the cell) that holds the data that you want to copy (see Figure 2.5).

2. Drag the fill handle down or to the right to copy the data to adjacent cells. A data tag appears to let you know exactly what data is being copied into the cells.

3. Release the mouse button. The data is "filled" into the selected cells.

When you release the mouse, a shortcut box for Fill options appears at the end of the cells that you filled. Copy Cells is the default option for the Fill feature, so you can ignore the shortcut box for the moment. It does come into play when you enter a series in the next section.

Watch That Fill!   The data you're copying replaces any existing data in the adjacent cells that you fill.

CAUTION

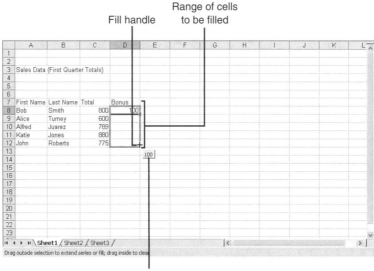

Figure 2.5 Drag the fill handle to copy the contents of a cell into neighboring cells.

Entering a Series of Numbers, Dates, and Other Data

Entering a value *series* (such as January, February, and March or 1, 2, 3, 4, and so on) is accomplished using the Fill feature discussed in the preceding section. When you use the Fill feature, Excel looks at the cell holding the data and tries to determine whether you want to just copy that information into the adjacent cells or use it as the starting point for a particular series of data. For example, with Monday entered in the first cell of the series, Excel automatically inserts Tuesday, Wednesday, and so on into the adjacent cells when you use the Fill feature.

Sometimes Excel isn't quite sure whether you want to copy the data when you use Fill or create a series. This is where the Fill options shortcut box comes in. It enables you to select how the Fill feature should treat the data that you have "filled" into the adjacent cells. Figure 2.6 shows the creation of a data series using Fill.

When you create a series using Fill, the series progresses by one increment. For example, a series starting with 1 would proceed to 2, 3, 4, and so on. If you want to create a series that uses some increment other than 1, you must create a custom series.

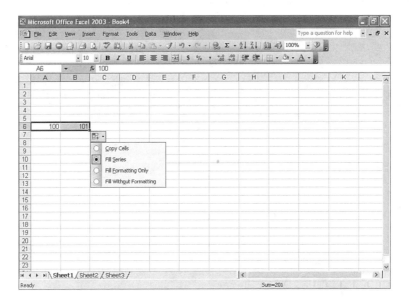

Figure 2.6   Fill can also be used to create a series of data in adjacent cells.

Entering a Custom Series

If you want to create a series such as 10, 20, 30, where the series uses a custom increment between the values, you need to create a custom series. Excel provides two
ways to create a custom series. To create a custom series using Fill, follow these
steps:

1. Enter the first value in the series into a cell.

2. Enter the second value in the series into the next cell. For example, you might
   enter **10** into the first cell and then **20** into the second cell. This lets Excel know
   that the increment for the series is 10.

3. Select both cells by clicking the first cell and dragging over the second cell.

4. Drag the fill handle of the second cell to the other cells that will be part of the
   series. Excel analyzes the two cells, sees the incremental pattern, and re-creates
   it in subsequent cells.

You can also create a custom series using the Series dialog box. This enables you to
specify the increment or step value for the series and even specify a stop value for
the series.

1. Enter the first value in the series into a cell.

2. Select the cells that you want included in the series.

3. Select the **Edit** menu, point at **Fill**, and then select **Series**. The Series dialog box opens (see Figure 2.7).

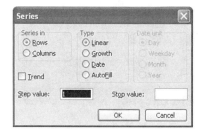

Figure 2.7   The Series dialog box enables you to create a custom series.

4. Enter the Step Value for the series. You can also enter a Stop Value for the series if you did not select the cells used for the series in step 2. For example, if you want to add a series to a column of cells and have clicked in the first cell that will receive a value, using a Stop Value (such as 100 for a series that will go from 1 to 100) will "stop" entering values in the cells when it reaches 100—the Stop Value.

5. Click **OK** to create the series.

TIP   **Different Series Types**   Not only can you create a linear series using the Series dialog box (as discussed in the steps in this section), but you can also create growth and date series. In a growth series, the data you're copying replaces any existing data in the adjacent cells that you fill.

Taking Advantage of AutoComplete

Another useful feature that Excel provides to help take some of the drudgery out of entering information into a workbook is the AutoComplete feature. Excel keeps a list of all the labels that you enter on a worksheet by column. For example, suppose you have a worksheet tracking sales in Europe and you are entering country names, such as Germany, Italy, and so on, multiple times into a particular column in the worksheet. After you enter Germany the first time, it becomes part of the AutoComplete list for that column. The next time you enter the letter G into a cell in that column, Excel completes the entry as "Germany."

You can also select an entry from the AutoComplete list. This allows you to see the entire list of available entries. Follow these steps:

1. Enter your text and value data as needed onto the worksheet.

2. If you want to select a text entry from the AutoComplete list, to fill an empty cell, right-click that cell. A shortcut menu appears.

3. Select **Pick from List** from the shortcut menu. A list of text entries (in alphabetical order) appears below the current cell.

4. Click a word in the list to insert it into the current, empty cell.

TIP **Adding Data to Excel Using Voice Recognition** The Office Speech Recognition feature can also be used to enter data into an Excel worksheet and to perform voice commands. If you have a computer that is set up with a sound card and microphone, you can use this feature. See Lesson 4, "Using the Office Speech Feature," in Part 1 of this book to learn how to get the voice feature up and running and to use it to enter information into Office applications such as Excel.

Performing Simple Calculations

In this lesson, you learn how to use formulas to calculate results in your worksheets.

Understanding Excel Formulas

One way to add calculations to an Excel workbook is to create your own formulas. Formulas are typically used to perform calculations such as addition, subtraction, multiplication, and division. More complex calculations are better left to Excel functions, which is a built-in set of formulas that provide financial, mathematical, and statistical calculations. You learn more about functions in Lesson 5, "Performing Calculations with Functions."

Formulas that you create typically include cell addresses that reference cells on which you want to perform a calculation. Formulas also consist of mathematical operators, such as + (addition) or * (multiplication). For example, if you wanted to multiply two cells, such as C3 and D3, and then divide the product by 3, you would design a formula that looks like this:

`=(C3*D3)/3`

Notice that the formula begins with the equal sign (=). This lets Excel know that the information that you are placing in the cell is meant to do a calculation. The parentheses are used to let Excel know that you want C3 multiplied by D3 before the result is divided by 3. Creating appropriate formulas requires an understanding of the order of mathematical operations, or what is often called the rules of precedence. The natural order of math operations is covered in the next section.

Formula Operators

As previously mentioned, you can create formulas that add, subtract, and multiply cells in the worksheet. Table 3.1 lists some of the operators that you can use and how you would use them in a simple formula.

Table 3.1   Excel's Mathematical Operators

Operator	Performs	Sample Formula	Result
^	Exponentiation	=A1^3	Enters the result of raising the value in cell A1 to the third power
+	Addition	=A1+A2	Enters the total of the values in cells A1 and A2
–	Subtraction	=A1–A2	Subtracts the value in cell A2 from the value in cell A1
*	Multiplication	=A2*A3	Multiplies the value in cell A2 by cell A3
/	Division	=A1/B1	Divides the value in cell A1 by the value in cell B1

Figure 3.1 shows some formulas that have been created for an Excel worksheet. So that you can see how I wrote the formulas, I've configured Excel so that it shows the formula that has been placed in a cell rather than the results of the formula (which is what you would normally see).

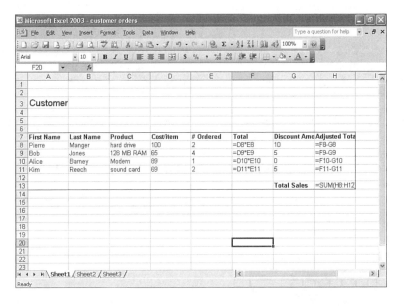

Figure 3.1   You can create formulas to do simple calculations in your worksheets.

Order of Operations

The order of operations, or *operator precedence*, simply means that some operations take precedence over other operations in a formula. For example, in the formula =C2+D2*E2, the multiplication of D2 times E2 takes precedence, so D2 is multiplied by E2 and then the value in cell C2 is added to the result.

You can force the precedence of an operation by using parentheses. For example, if you want C2 and D2 added before they are multiplied by E2, the formula would have to be written =(C2+D2)*E2.

The natural order of math operators follows:

1. Exponent (^) and calculations within parentheses
2. Multiplication (*) and division (/)
3. Addition (+) and subtraction (–)

In the case of operations such as multiplication and division, which operate at the same level in the natural order, a formula containing the multiplication operator followed by the division operator will execute these operators in the order they appear in the formula from left to right. If you don't take this order into consideration, you could run into problems when entering your formulas. For example, if you want to determine the average of the values in cells A1, B1, and C1, and you enter =A1+B1+C1/3, you'll get the wrong answer. The value in C1 will be divided by 3, and that result will be added to A1+B1. To determine the total of A1 through C1 first, you must enclose that group of values in parentheses: =(A1+B1+C1)/3.

Entering Formulas

You can enter formulas in one of two ways: by typing the entire formula, including the cell addresses, or by typing the formula operators and selecting the cell references. Take a look at both ways.

To type a formula, perform the following steps:

1. Select the cell where you will place the formula.
2. Type an equal sign (=) into the cell to begin the formula.
3. Enter the appropriate cell references and operators for the formula. Figure 3.2 shows a simple multiplication formula. The formula also appears in the Formula bar as you type it. The cells that you specify in the formula are highlighted with a colored border.
4. Press **Enter** when you have finished the formula, and Excel calculates the result.

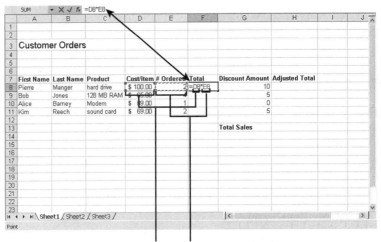

Cell border and cell text reference have matching color

Figure 3.2   The formula appears in the cell and in the Formula bar as you type it.

TIP   **Unwanted Formula**   If you start to enter a formula and then decide you don't want to use it, you can skip entering the formula by pressing **Esc**.

To enter a formula by selecting cell addresses, follow these steps:

1. Click in the cell where you will place the formula.
2. Type the equal sign (=) to begin the formula.
3. Click the cell whose address you want to appear first in the formula. You can also click a cell in a different worksheet or workbook. The cell address appears in the cell and in the Formula bar.
4. Type a mathematical operator after the value to indicate the next operation you want to perform. The operator appears in the cell and in the Formula bar.
5. Continue clicking cells and typing operators until the formula is complete.
6. Press **Enter** to accept the formula and have Excel place its results into the cell.

Error!   If ERR appears in a cell, you probably made a mistake somewhere in the formula. Be sure you did not commit one of these common errors: dividing by zero, using a blank cell as a divisor, referring to a blank cell, deleting a cell used in a for-

CAUTION   mula, or including a reference to the same cell in which the formula appears.

TIP   **Natural Language Formulas**   Excel also enables you to create what are called Natural Language formulas. You can refer to a cell by its column heading name and the corresponding row label. For example, if you had a column labeled Total and a column labeled Discount for each customer, you can write a formula such as =Smith Total–Smith Discount. You are referring to cells by the labels that you have placed in the worksheet rather than the actual cell addresses.

Using the Status Bar AutoCalculate Feature

Using a feature that Excel calls , you can view the sum of a column of cells simply by selecting the cells and looking at the status bar. The values in the selected cells are added. You can also right-click the AutoCalculate area of the status bar and choose different formulas, such as average, minimum, maximum, and count.

This feature is useful if you want to quickly check the total for a group of cells or compute the average. It also allows you to "try out" an Excel function (discussed in Lesson 5) before actually entering it into a cell. You can also view the average, minimum, maximum, and count of a range of cells. To display something other than the sum, highlight the group of cells you want the operation performed on, right-click the status bar, and select the option you want from the shortcut menu that appears (see Figure 3.3).

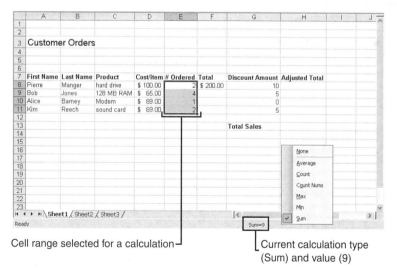

Cell range selected for a calculation ⎤   Current calculation type (Sum) and value (9)

Figure 3.3   You can view the results of different built-in formulas in the status bar.

Displaying Formulas

Normally, Excel does not display the formula in a cell. Instead, it displays the result of the calculation. You can view the formula by selecting the cell and looking in the Formula bar. However, if you're trying to review all the formulas in a large worksheet, it would be easier if you could see them all at once (and even print them). If you want to view formulas in a worksheet, follow these steps:

1. Open the **Tools** menu and choose **Options**.
2. Click the **View** tab.
3. In the Window options area of the View tab (near the bottom of the tab), click to select the **Formulas** check box.
4. Click **OK**.

Editing Formulas

Editing a formula is the same as editing any entry in Excel. The following steps show how you do it:

1. Select the cell that contains the formula you want to edit.
2. Click in the Formula bar to place the insertion point in the formula, or press **F2** to enter Edit mode (the insertion point is placed at the end of the entry in that cell).

3. Press the left-arrow key or the right-arrow key to move the insertion point within the formula. Then, use the **Backspace** key to delete characters to the left, or use the **Delete** key to delete characters to the right. Type any additional characters.
4. When you finish editing the data, click the **Enter** button on the Formula bar or press **Enter** to accept your changes.

Manipulating Formulas and Understanding Cell References

In this lesson, you learn how to copy formulas, use relative and absolute cell references, and change calculation settings.

Copying Formulas

Copying labels and values in Excel is no big deal. You can use the Copy and Paste commands (discussed in Lesson 8, "Editing Worksheets") or you can use some of the Fill features discussed in Lesson 2, "Entering Data into the Worksheet." Copying or moving formulas, however, is a little trickier.

Suppose that you create the formula =D8*E8 and place it into cell F8, as shown in Figure 4.1. You have designed the formula to reference cells D8 and E8. However, Excel looks at these cell references a little differently. Excel sees cell D8 as the entry that is located two cells to the left of F8 (where the formula has been placed, in this example). It sees cell E8 as being the location that is one cell to the left of F8.

Excel's method of referencing cells is called *relative referencing.* The great thing about this method of referencing cells is that when you copy a formula to a new location, it adjusts to the relative cell references around it and provides you with the correct calculation.

For example, you could copy the formula in cell F8 to cell F9, and Excel would use relative referencing to change the cell addresses in the formula. The original formula =D8*E8 would appear as D9*E9 when copied to cell F9.

Relative referencing is very useful in most situations where you copy a formula to several cells in the same column. However, it can get you into trouble when you cut and paste a formula to a new location or copy the formula to a location where it can no longer reference the appropriate cells to provide you with the correct calculation.

In these situations, you must use absolute referencing so that the formula references only specified cells and does not change the cell references in the formula when pasted to the new location. Absolute referencing is discussed in the next section.

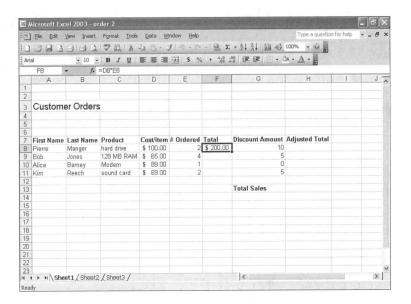

Figure 4.1   Formulas you place in Excel use relative referencing for calculations.

You can copy formulas using the Copy and Paste commands (see Lesson 8); however, when you need to copy a formula to multiple locations, you can also use the Fill feature discussed in Lesson 2.

Because Excel uses relative referencing by default, the formula adjusts to each of its new locations. An alternative way to "copy" a formula to multiple adjacent cells is to select all cells that will contain the formula before you actually write the formula in the first cell. Follow these steps:

1. Select all the cells that will contain the formula (dragging so that the cell that you will write the formula in is the first of the selected group of cells).

2. Enter the formula into the first cell.

3. Press **Ctrl+Enter** and the formula is placed in all the selected cells.

TIP   **Get an Error?**   If you get an error message in a cell after copying a formula, verify the cell references in the copied formula. For more information on sorting out cell referencing, see the next section in this lesson.

Using Relative and Absolute Cell Addresses

As mentioned at the beginning of this lesson, when you copy a formula from one place in the worksheet to another, Excel adjusts the cell references in the formulas relative to their new positions in the worksheet. There might be occasions when you don't want Excel to change the reference related to a particular cell that appears in a formula (or in an Excel function, which is discussed in Lesson 5, "Performing Calculations with Functions").

Absolute Versus Relative An *absolute reference* is a cell reference in a formula that does not change when copied to a new location; you designate it as absolute. A *relative reference* is a cell reference in a formula that is adjusted when the formula is copied.

For example, suppose you have a worksheet that computes the commission made on sales by each of your salespeople. Sales have been so good that you've decided to give each person on the sales team a $200 bonus. Figure 4.2 shows the worksheet that you've created.

$ character makes cell reference absolute

	A	B	C	D	E	F	G
SUM ▾ ✕ ✓ ƒ =E6+$E$15							
1							
2	Employee Commissions						
3							
4							
5		First Name	Last Name	Sales	Commission	Total Compensation	
6		Bob	Smith	6000	=D6*0.1	=E6+$E$15	
7		Alice	Turney	4500			
8		Alfred	Juarez	5000			
9		Katie	Jones	7200			
10		John	Roberts	6350			
11							
12							
13							
14							
15				June Bonus	200	the bonus amount is located in cell E15	
16							
17							
18							
19							
20							
21							
22							
23							

Sheet1 / Sheet2 / Sheet3 /

Cell E15 commented by Joe Habraken

Figure 4.2 Some formulas require absolute references.

Notice that the bonus amount is contained in only one cell on the worksheet (cell E15). Therefore, when you create the formula used in F6 and then copied to cells F7 through F11, you need to make sure that the bonus amount in cell E15 is always referenced by the formula. This is a case where you must "absolutely" reference the bonus amount in cell E15.

To make a cell reference in a formula absolute, add a $ (dollar sign) before the column letter and before the row number that make up the cell address. For example, in Figure 4.2, the formula in F6 must read as follows:

=E6+$E$15

The address, $E$15, refers to cell E15, meaning that cell E15 is absolutely referenced by the formula. This cell reference remains "locked" even when you copy the formula to the other cells in the E column.

To create an absolute reference in a formula (or a function, which is discussed in Lesson 5), create your formula as you normally would (as detailed in Lesson 3, "Performing Simple Calculations"). After typing or pointing out a cell address in a formula that needs to be an absolute reference, press **F4**. A dollar sign ($) is placed before the cell and row designation for that cell. Once data is labeled as absolute, you will find that if you move the data to a different cell (or cells), the formula will update itself to reference the new location.

Some formulas might contain cell addresses where you will make the column designation absolute, but not the row (or vice versa). For example, you could have a formula $A6/2. You are telling Excel that the values will always be contained in column A (it is absolute), but the row reference (6) can change when the formula is copied. Having a cell address in a formula that contains an absolute designation and a relative reference is called a *mixed reference*.

Mixed References   A reference that is only partially absolute, such as A$2 or $A2. When a formula that uses a mixed reference is copied to another cell, only part of the cell reference (the relative part) is adjusted.

Absolute referencing and mixed references are also required by some of Excel's built-in functions. You work with functions in the next lesson.

Recalculating the Worksheet

Excel automatically recalculates the results in your worksheet every time you enter a new value or edit a value or formula. This is fine for most workbooks. However, if you have a computer with limited memory and processing power, you might find that having Excel recalculate all the results in a very large worksheet every time you make a change means that you are sitting and waiting for Excel to complete the recalculation.

You can turn off the automatic recalculation. However, this won't be necessary except in situations where you are working with huge workbooks that contain a very large number of formulas, functions, and data. Turning off the automatic calculation feature also means that you must remember to manually recalculate the values in the worksheet before you print. To change the recalculation setting, take the following steps:

1. Open the **Tools** menu and choose **Options**.
2. Click the **Calculation** tab to display the options shown in Figure 4.3.

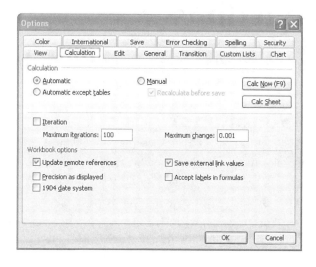

Figure 4.3 You can turn off the automatic recalculation feature.

3. Select one of the following Calculation options:

   • **Automatic**—This is the default setting. It recalculates the entire workbook each time you edit or enter a formula.

   • **Automatic Except Tables**—This automatically recalculates everything except formulas in a data table (data tables are used to provide a range of data for one formula and function and are used for an advanced Excel feature called "What If Analysis").

   • **Manual**—This option tells Excel to recalculate only when you say so. To recalculate manually, press the **F9** key. When this option is selected, you can turn the Recalculate Before Save option off or on.

4. Click **OK**.

Performing Calculations with Functions

In this lesson, you learn how to perform calculations with functions and how to use the Insert Function feature to quickly insert functions into your worksheets.

What Are Functions?

You already learned in Lesson 3, "Performing Simple Calculations," how to create your own formulas in Excel. When you work with more complex calculations, you are better off using Excel's built-in formulas—functions.

Functions are ready-made formulas that perform a series of operations on a specified range of values. For example, to determine the sum of a series of numbers in cells A1 through H1, you can enter the function =SUM(A1:H1). Excel functions can do all kinds of calculations for all kinds of purposes, including financial and statistical calculations.

Every function consists of the following three elements:

- The = sign, which indicates that what follows is a function (formula).
- The function name, such as SUM, that indicates which operation will be performed.
- A list of cell addresses, such as (A1:H1), which are to be acted upon by the function. Some functions can include more than one set of cell addresses, which are separated by commas (such as A1,B1,H1).

 TIP **How Ranges Are Designated** When a range of cells (a contiguous group of cells) is referenced in Excel, the format A1:H1 is used. This tells you that the range of cells starts at A1 and includes all the cells from A1 to (:) and including cell H1. We look at cell ranges in more detail in Lesson 11, "Working with Ranges."

You can enter functions into the worksheet by typing the function and cell references (as you did with your own formulas), or you can use the Insert Function feature, which walks you through the process of creating a function in a worksheet (you will work with the Insert Function feature in a moment). Table 5.1 lists some of the Excel functions that you will probably use most often in your worksheets.

Table 5.1 Commonly Used Excel Functions

Function	Example	Description
AVERAGE	=AVERAGE(B4:B9)	Calculates the mean or average of a group of cell values.
COUNT	=COUNT(A3:A7)	Counts the number of cells that hold values in the selected range or group of cells. This can also be used to tell you how many cells are in a particular column, which tells you how many rows are in your spreadsheet.
IF	=IF(A3>=1000,"BONUS","NO BONUS")	Allows you to place a conditional function in a cell. In this example, if A3 is greater than or equal to 1000, the true value, BONUS, is used. If A3 is less than 1000, the false value, NO BONUS, is placed in the cell.
MAX	=MAX(B4:B10)	Returns the maximum value in a range of cells.
MIN	=MIN(B4:B10)	Returns the minimum value in a range of cells.
PMT	=PMT(.0825/12,360,180000)	Calculates the monthly payment on a 30-year loan (360 monthly payments) at 8.25% a year (.0825/12 a month) for $180,000.
SUM	=SUM(A1:A10)	Calculates the total in a range of cells.

 TIP **Specify Text with Quotation Marks** When you are entering text into a function, the text must be enclosed within quotation marks. For example, in the function =IF(A5>2000,"BONUS","NO BONUS"), if the condition is met (the cell value is greater than 2000), the word BONUS will be returned by the function. If the condition is not met, the phrase NO BONUS will be returned in the cell by the function.

Excel provides a large number of functions listed by category. There are Financial functions, Date and Time functions, Statistical functions, and Logical functions (such as the IF function described in Table 5.1). The group of functions that you use most often depends on the type of worksheets you typically build. For example, if you do a lot of accounting work, you will find that the Financial functions offer functions for computing monthly payments, figuring out the growth on an investment, and even computing the depreciation on capital equipment.

Although some commonly used functions have been defined in Table 5.1, as you become more adept at using Excel you might want to explore some of the other functions available. Select **Help**, **Microsoft Excel Help**. On the Contents tab of the Help window, open the **Function Reference** topic. Several subtopics related to Excel functions and their uses are provided.

Using AutoSum

Adding a group of cells is probably one of the most often-used calculations in an Excel worksheet. Because of this fact, Excel makes it very easy for you to place the SUM function into a cell. Excel provides the AutoSum button on the Standard toolbar. AutoSum looks at a column or row of cell values and tries to select the cells that should be included in the SUM function.

To use AutoSum, follow these steps:

1. Select the cell where you want to place the SUM function. Typically, you will choose a cell that is at the bottom of a column of values or at the end of a row of data. This makes it easy for AutoSum to figure out the range of cells that it should include in the SUM function.

 2. Click the **AutoSum** button on the Standard toolbar. AutoSum inserts =SUM and the cell addresses that it thinks should be included in the function (see Figure 5.1).

3. If the range of cell addresses that AutoSum selected is incorrect, use the mouse to drag and select the appropriate group of cells.

4. Press the **Enter** key. AutoSum calculates the total for the selected range of cells.

 TIP **Quick AutoSum** To bypass the step where Excel displays the SUM formula and its arguments in the cell, select the cell in which you want the sum inserted and double-click the **AutoSum** button on the Standard toolbar.

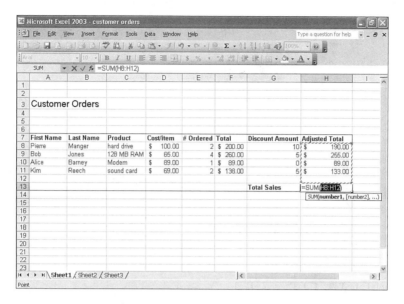

Figure 5.1 AutoSum inserts the SUM function and selects the cells that will be totaled by the function.

Using the Insert Function Feature

After you become familiar with a function or a group of functions, you place a particular function in an Excel worksheet by typing the function name and the cells to be referenced by the function (the same as you have done for formulas that you create as outlined in Lesson 3). However, when you are first starting out with functions, you will find it much easier to create them using the Insert Function feature. The Insert Function feature leads you through the process of inserting a function and specifying the appropriate cell addresses in the function.

For example, suppose you want to compute the average, maximum, and minimum of a group of cells that contain the weekly commissions for your sales force. Figure 5.2 shows how these three functions would look on a worksheet (the display has been changed in Excel to show you the functions rather than their results). You could use the Insert Function feature to create any or all of these functions.

To use the Insert Function feature, follow these steps:

1. Click in the cell where you want to place the function.

2. Click the arrow button next to the **AutoSum** button and select **More Functions**. The Insert Function dialog box appears (see Figure 5.3).

AutoSum button

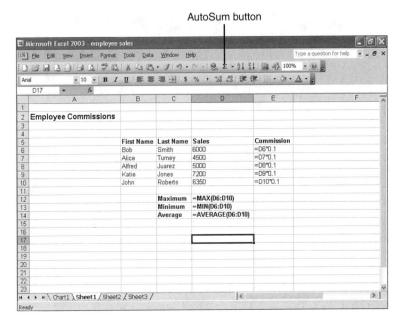

Figure 5.2 Functions such as Average, MIN, and MAX can be placed into a worksheet using the Insert Function feature.

Figure 5.3 The Insert Function dialog box helps you select the function you want to use.

3. To search for a particular function, type a brief description of what you want to do in the Search for a Function box (for example, you could type `monthly payment` and Excel would show you financial functions that help you calculate monthly payments), and then click **Go** to conduct the search. You also can select a function category, such as Financial or Statistical, using the Select a

Category drop-down box. In either case, a list of functions is provided in the
Select a Function dialog box.

Recently Used Functions The Insert Function dialog box by default lists the
functions that you have used most recently.

4. From the Functions list, select the function you want to insert. Then click **OK**.
The Function Arguments dialog box appears. This dialog box allows you to
specify the range of cells (some functions require multiple ranges of cells) that
the function acts upon (see Figure 5.4).

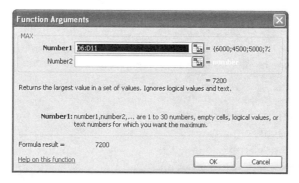

Figure 5.4 The Function Arguments dialog box is where you specify the cells that will be
acted upon by the function.

5. Next, you must enter the range of cells that will be acted upon by the function.
Click the **Collapse** button on the far right of the Number1 text box in the
Function Arguments dialog box. This returns you to the worksheet.

6. Use the mouse to select the cells that you want to place in the function (see
Figure 5.5). Then click the **Expand** button on the right of the Function
Arguments dialog box.

7. Click **OK**. Excel inserts the function and cell addresses for the function into the
selected cell and displays the result.

If you find that you would like to edit the list of cells acted upon by a particular
function, select the cell that holds the function and click the **Insert Function** button
on the Formula bar. The Function Arguments dialog box for the function appears.
Select a new range of cells for the function, as discussed in steps 4 and 5.

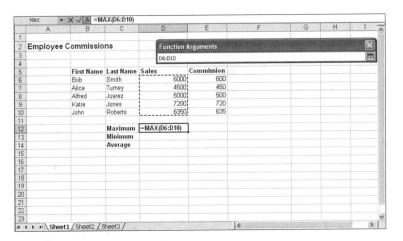

Figure 5.5   The Function Arguments dialog box collapses and allows you to select the cells that will be acted upon by the function.

Excel 2003 also makes it easy for you to bypass the Insert Function dialog box and insert commonly used functions such as Average, Count, Max, and Min. Click the arrow to the right of the AutoSum button on the Excel Standard toolbar and select a function from the list provided. To complete the function select the range of cells that you want the function to act on, and then press the **Enter** key.

What's This Function?   If you'd like to know more about a particular function, click the **Help on This Function** link at the bottom of the Function Arguments dialog box. The Help window will open with help on this specific function.

Getting Around in Excel

In this lesson, you learn the basics of moving around in a worksheet and within a workbook.

Moving from Worksheet to Worksheet

Now that you've taken a look at how to enter labels, values, formulas, and functions, you should take a look at how to navigate the space provided by Excel workbooks and worksheets. By default, each workbook starts off with three worksheets. You can add or delete worksheets from the workbook as needed. Because each workbook consists of one or more worksheets, you need a way of moving easily from worksheet to worksheet. Use one of the following methods:

- Click the tab of the worksheet you want to go to (see Figure 6.1). If the tab is not shown, use the tab scroll buttons to bring the tab into view, and then click the tab.
- Press **Ctrl+PgDn** to move to the next worksheet or **Ctrl+PgUp** to move to the previous one.

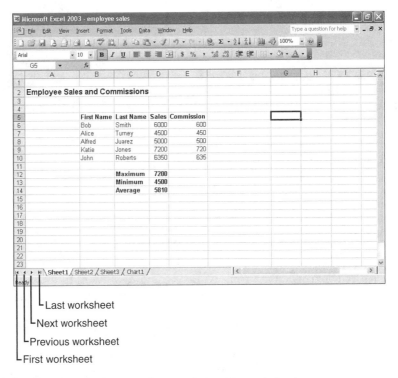

First worksheet
Previous worksheet
Next worksheet
Last worksheet

Figure 6.1   Use the tabs to move from worksheet to worksheet.

Switching Between Workbooks

Switching between the different workbooks that you have opened on the Windows desktop is very straightforward. By default, each workbook has its own button on the Windows taskbar and opens in its own Excel application window. To switch between workbooks, click the button for the workbook you want.

If you don't want to have a separate taskbar entry for each open Excel workbook, you can turn this feature off using the Windows in Taskbar option on the View tab of the Options dialog box (click **Tools**, **Options**). Keep in mind, however, that disabling this feature means that you will have to use the Window menu to switch between Excel workbooks. To do so, select the Window menu, and then select the name of the workbook you want to make the current workbook in the Excel application window.

Moving Within a Worksheet

To enter your worksheet data, you need some way of moving to the various cells within the worksheet. Keep in mind that the part of the worksheet displayed onscreen is only a small piece of the actual worksheet.

Using the Keyboard

To move around the worksheet with your keyboard, use the key combinations listed in Table 6.1.

Table 6.1   Moving Around a Worksheet with the Keyboard

To Move	Press This
Up one cell	Up-arrow key
Down one cell	Down-arrow key
Right one cell	Right-arrow key
Left one cell	Left-arrow key
Up one screen	Page Up
Down one screen	Page Down
Leftmost cell in a row (column A)	Home
Lower-right corner of the data area	Ctrl+End
Cell A1	Ctrl+Home
Last occupied cell to the right of a row	End+right-arrow key

You can also quickly go to a specific cell address in a worksheet using the Go To feature. Press **Ctrl+G** (or select **Edit**, **Go To**). Type the cell address you want to go to into the Reference box, and then click the **OK** button (see Figure 6.2).

Figure 6.2   The Go To feature can be used to move to a specific cell address on the worksheet.

The Go To feature keeps a list of cells that you have recently moved to using the Go To feature. To quickly move to a particular cell in the Go To list, double-click that cell address.

TIP **Even Faster Than Go To** To move quickly to a specific cell on a worksheet, type the cell's address (the column letter and row number; for example, **C25**) into the Name box at the left end of the Formula bar and press **Enter**.

Using a Mouse

To scroll through a worksheet with a mouse, follow the techniques listed in Table 6.2.

Table 6.2 Moving Around a Worksheet with the Mouse

To Move	Click This
Move the selector to a particular cell	Any cell
View one more row, up or down	Up or down arrows on the vertical scrollbar
View one more column, left or right	Left or right arrows on the horizontal scrollbar
Move through a worksheet quickly	The vertical or horizontal scrollbar; drag it up or down or right and left, respectively (as you drag, a ScreenTip displays the current row/column number)

TIP **Watch the Scroll Box** The size of the scroll box changes to represent the amount of the total worksheet that is currently visible. If the scroll box is large, you know you're seeing almost all of the current worksheet in the window. If the scroll box is small, most of the worksheet is currently hidden from view.

Using a Wheel-Enabled Mouse

If you use a wheel-enabled mouse (like the Microsoft IntelliMouse), you can move through a worksheet even faster than you can by using the scrollbars and a conventional mouse. Table 6.3 shows how.

Table 6.3 Moving Around a Worksheet with a Wheel-Enabled Mouse

To:	Do This:
Scroll a few rows (scroll up and down)	Rotate the wheel in the middle of the mouse forward or backward.
Scroll faster (pan)	Click and hold the wheel button, and then drag the mouse in the direction in which you want to pan. The farther away from the origin mark (the four-headed arrow) you drag the mouse, the faster the panning action. To slow the pan, drag the mouse back toward the origin mark.
Pan without holding the wheel	Click the wheel once, and then move the mouse in the direction in which you want to pan. (You'll continue to pan when you move the mouse until you turn panning off by clicking the wheel again.)
Zoom in and out	Press the **Ctrl** key as you rotate the middle wheel. If you zoom out, you can click any cell you want to jump to. You can then zoom back in so you can see your data.

Different Ways to View Your Worksheet

In this lesson, you learn about the various ways in which you can view your worksheets.

Changing the Worksheet View

Excel provides many ways to change how your worksheet appears within the Excel window. Changing the view has no effect on how your worksheets look when printed (unless you choose to hide data onscreen, a topic covered later in this lesson). However, changing the view and getting a different perspective helps you to see the overall layout of the worksheet and allows you to view worksheet cells that might not appear in the default screen view. For example, you can enlarge or reduce the size of the worksheet so that you can view more or less of it at one time.

To enlarge or reduce your view of the current worksheet, use the Zoom feature. Simply click the **Zoom** button on the Standard toolbar and select the zoom percentage you want to use from the following: 25%, 50%, 75%, 100%, or 200%. If you want to zoom by a number that's not listed, just type the number into the Zoom box and press **Enter**.

You can also have Excel zoom in on a particular portion of a worksheet. This is particularly useful when you have created very large worksheets. Select the area of the worksheet you want to zoom in on, and then click the **Zoom** button list and click **Selection**. You can then select different zoom values on the Zoom list to zoom in or out on that particular portion of the worksheet. Keep in mind that Excel zooms in on the entire worksheet, not just the selected cells. (It just makes sure that you can see the selected cells when you change the zoom values.)

 TIP **Fast Zoom with a Wheel Mouse** If you use the Microsoft IntelliMouse or another compatible wheel mouse, you can zoom in and out quickly by holding down the **Ctrl** key as you move the wheel forward or back.

You also can display your worksheet so that it takes up the full screen. This eliminates all the other items in the Excel window, such as the toolbars, the Formula bar, the status bar, and so on. Figure 7.1 shows a worksheet in the Full Screen view. To use this view, select the **View** menu and select **Full Screen**. To return to Normal view, click **Close Full Screen**.

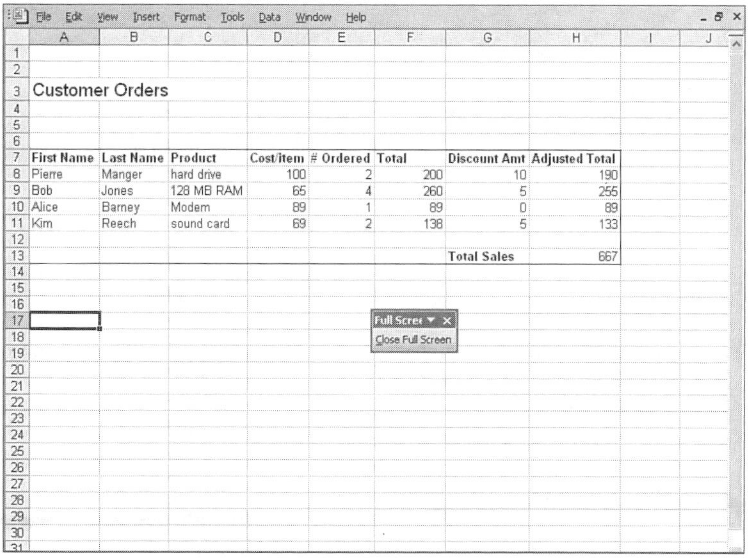

Figure 7.1 View your worksheet on the entire screen.

Freezing Column and Row Labels

When you work with very large worksheets, it can be very annoying as you scroll to the right or down through the worksheet when you can no longer see your row headings or column headings, respectively. For example, you might be entering customer data where the customer's name is in the first column of the worksheet, and when you scroll to the extreme right to enter data, you can no longer see the customer names.

You can freeze your column and row labels so that you can view them no matter how far you scroll down or to the right in your worksheet. For example, Figure 7.2 shows frozen column labels (columns A and B, which include the first names and last names) that allow you to see the customer names no matter how far you move to the right of the worksheet.

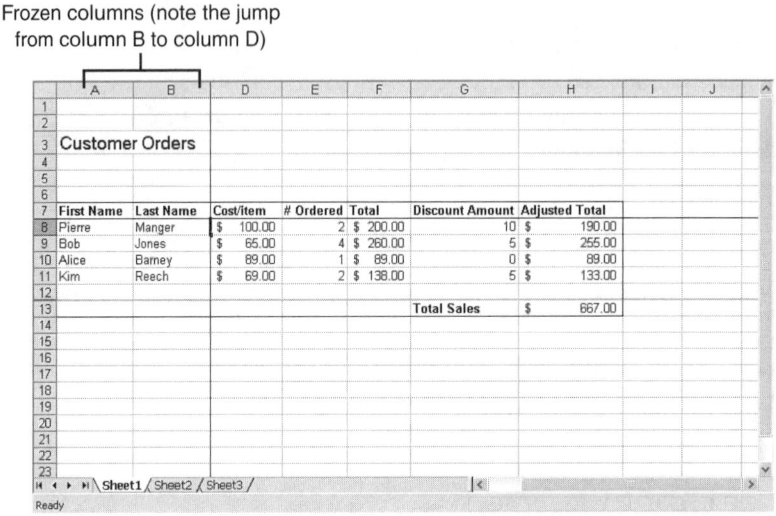

Frozen columns (note the jump
from column B to column D)

Figure 7.2   You can freeze row and column headings so that they remain onscreen as you scroll.

To freeze row or column headings (or both), follow these steps:

1. Click the cell to the right of the row labels and/or below any column labels you want to freeze. This highlights the cell.

2. Select the **Window** menu, and then select **Freeze Panes**.

You might want to experiment on a large worksheet. Freeze the column and row headings, and then use the keyboard or the mouse to move around in the worksheet. As you do, the row and/or column headings remain locked in their positions. This enables you to view data in other parts of the worksheet without losing track of what that data represents.

When you have finished working with the frozen column and row headings, you can easily unfreeze them. Select the **Window** menu again and select **Unfreeze Panes**.

Splitting Worksheets

When you work with very large worksheets, you might actually want to split the worksheet into multiple windows. This enables you to view the same worksheet in different windows. You can then scroll through the multiple copies of the same worksheet and compare data in cells that are normally far apart in the worksheet.

Figure 7.3 shows a worksheet that has been split into multiple panes. Each "copy" of the worksheet will have its own set of vertical and horizontal scrollbars.

	A	B	C	D	E	F	G	H	I	J
1										
2										
3	Employee List									
4										
5										
6										
7	FirstName	LastName	Extension	Department	Start Date					
8	Nancy	Davy	123	Living Room	1/23/2003					
9	Janet	Leverling	448	Porches and Decks	3/10/1997					
10	Steven	Buchanan	223	Architects	5/12/1997					
7	FirstName	LastName	Extension	Department	Start Date					
8	Nancy	Davy	123	Living Room	1/23/2003					
9	Janet	Leverling	448	Porches and Decks	3/10/1997					
10	Steven	Buchanan	223	Architects	5/12/1997					
11	Snidley	Backlash	110	Porches and Decks	1/28/1998					
12	Henry	Cotton	623	Kitchen	7/7/1996					
13	Alice	Smith	332	Bathroom	5/4/1997					
14	Bob	Palooka	234	Living Room	9/8/2002					
15	Cleo	Katrina	543	Architects	4/9/1999					
16	Robert	Buchanan	227	Bathroom	8/15/2003					
17	Richard	Jones	333	Porches and Decks	3/10/1999					
18	Carmella	Jones	434	Architects	2/1/2001					
19	Amy	Buchanan	654	Living Room	3/10/2001					

Employees

Ready

Figure 7.3 You can split a worksheet into two windows, making it easy to compare data in the worksheet.

To split a worksheet, follow these steps:

1. Click in the cell where you want to create the split. A split appears to the left of the selected cell and above the selected cell.

2. You can adjust the vertical or horizontal split bars using the mouse. Place the mouse on the split bar and drag it to a new location.

3. You can use the scrollbars in the different split panes to view data in the worksheet (different data can be viewed in each pane).

To remove the split, select the **Window** menu and select **Remove Split**.

 TIP **Create Splits with the Split Boxes** You can also create a vertical or horizontal split in a worksheet by using the split boxes. A horizontal split box rests just above the vertical scrollbar, and a vertical split box rests on the far right of the horizontal scrollbar. Place your mouse on either of these split boxes and drag them onto the worksheet to create a split bar.

Hiding Workbooks, Worksheets, Columns, and Rows

For those times when you're working on top-secret information (or at least information that is somewhat proprietary, such as employee salaries), you can hide workbooks, worksheets, columns, or rows from prying eyes. For example, if you have confidential data stored in one particular worksheet, you can hide that worksheet, yet still be able to view the other worksheets in that workbook. You can also hide particular columns or rows within a worksheet.

Use these methods to hide data:

- To hide a row or a column in a worksheet, click a row or column heading to select it (you can select adjacent columns or rows by dragging across them). Then, right-click within the row or column and select **Hide** from the shortcut menu that appears. The row or column will be hidden (see Figure 7.4). To unhide the row or column, right-click the border between the hidden item and rows or columns that are visible, and then select **Unhide** from the shortcut menu.

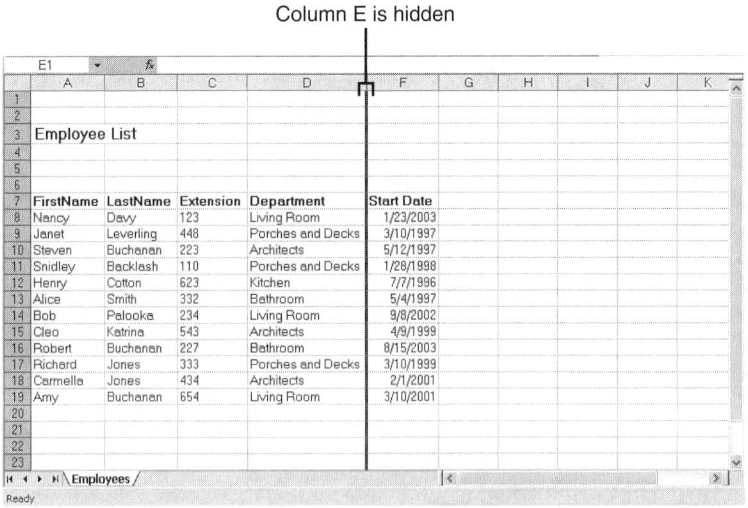

Figure 7.4   Column E, which contains employee salaries, has been hidden on a worksheet.

- To hide a worksheet, click its tab to select it. Then, open the **Format** menu and select **Sheet**, **Hide**. To unhide the worksheet, select **Format**, **Sheet**, and then **Unhide**. Select the worksheet to unhide in the Unhide dialog box that appears, and then click **OK**.

- To hide an entire workbook, open the **Window** menu and select **Hide**. This removes the workbook from the Excel window, even though the workbook is open. To unhide the workbook, select **Window**, **Unhide**.

Locking Cells in a Worksheet

In some situations, you might create a worksheet or worksheets and someone else will enter the data. In these situations, you might want to lock cells that contain formulas and functions so that the person doing the data entry does not accidentally overwrite or delete the worksheet formulas or functions. Locking cells in a worksheet is a two-step process. You must first select and lock the cells. Then, you must turn on protection on the entire worksheet for the "lock" to go into effect.

Follow these steps to lock cells on a worksheet:

1. Select the cells in the worksheet that you want to lock. These are typically the cells that contain formulas or functions.

2. Select **Format** and then **Cells**. The Format Cells dialog box appears. Click the **Protection** tab on the dialog box (see Figure 7.5).

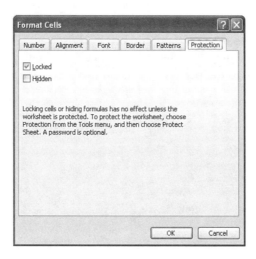

Figure 7.5   Cells can be locked using the Protection tab of the Format Cells dialog box.

3. Be sure the Locked check box is selected on the Protection tab. Then click **OK**.

4. Now you must protect the entire worksheet to have the lock feature protect the cells that you selected. Select the **Tools** menu, point at **Protections**, and then select **Protect Sheet**. The Protect Sheet dialog box appears (see Figure 7.6).

Figure 7.6   The worksheet must be protected if you want to lock cells containing formulas or functions.

5. Enter a password if you want to require a password for "unprotecting" the worksheet. Then click **OK**.

The cells that you locked in steps 1, 2, and 3 will no longer accept data entry. Every time someone tries to enter data into one of those cells, Excel displays a message stating that data will not be accepted. The cells are now protected, and you can pass the workbook on to the person who handles the data entry.

Editing Worksheets

In this lesson, you learn how to change data and how to undo those changes if necessary. You also learn how to search for data and replace it with other data, how to spell check your work, and how to copy, move, and delete data.

Correcting Data

You've taken a look at entering text, values, formulas, and functions. There will definitely be occasions when you need to edit information in a cell. One way to change an entry in a cell is to replace it by selecting the cell and then entering new data. Just press **Enter** after entering the information. If you just want to modify the existing cell content, you can also edit data within a cell.

To edit information in a cell, follow these steps:

1. Select the cell in which you want to edit data.
2. To begin editing, click in the Formula bar to place the insertion point into the cell entry. To edit within the cell itself, press **F2** or double-click the cell. This puts you in Edit mode; the word Edit appears in the status bar.
3. Press the right- or left-arrow key to move the insertion point within the entry. Press the **Backspace** key to delete characters to the left of the insertion point; press the **Delete** key to delete characters to the right. Then, type any characters you want to add.
4. Press the **Enter** key when you have finished making your changes.

   If you change your mind and you no longer want to edit your entry, click the **Cancel** button on the Formula bar or press **Esc**.

 TIP **Moving to the Beginning or End of a Cell Entry**   In Edit mode, you can quickly move to the beginning or end of a cell's contents. Press **Home** to move to the beginning of the entry; press **End** to move to the end of the entry.

Undoing an Action

Although editing a worksheet is supposed to improve it, you might find that you've done something to a cell or range of cells that you had not intended. This is where the Undo feature comes in.

 You can undo just about any action while working in Excel, including any changes you make to a cell's data. To undo a change, click the **Undo** button on the Standard toolbar (or select **Edit, Undo**).

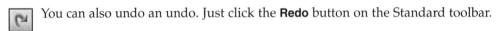 You can also undo an undo. Just click the **Redo** button on the Standard toolbar.

> **TIP** **Undoing/Redoing More Than One Thing** The Undo button undoes only the most recent action. To undo several previous actions, click the **Undo** button multiple times or click the drop-down arrow on the Undo button and select the number of actions you want undone.

Using the Replace Feature

Suppose you've entered a particular label or value into the worksheet and find that you have consistently entered it incorrectly. A great way to change multiple occurrences of a label or value is using Excel's Replace feature; you can locate data in the worksheet and replace it with new data. To find and replace data, follow these steps:

1. Select the **Edit** menu, and then select **Replace**. The Find and Replace dialog box appears, as shown in Figure 8.1.

Figure 8.1 Find and replace data with the Find and Replace dialog box.

2. Type the text or value that you want to find into the **Find What** text box.

3. Click in the **Replace With** text box and type the text you want to use as replacement text.

4. To expand the options available to you in the dialog box, click the **Options** button (Figure 8.1 shows the dialog box in its expanded form).

5. If you want to match the exact case of your entry so that Excel factors in capitalization, click the **Match Case** check box. If you want to locate cells that contain exactly what you entered into the Find What text box (and no additional data), click the **Match Entire Cell Contents** check box.

6. To search for entries with particular formatting, click the **Format** button on the right of the Find What box. The Find Format dialog box appears (see Figure 8.2). You can search for entries that have been assigned number, alignment, font, border, patterns, or protection using the appropriate tab on the Find Format dialog box. After making your selection, click the **OK** button.

Figure 8.2   The Find Format dialog box enables you to search for entries that have been assigned a particular formatting.

7. You can also replace your entries with a particular formatting. Click the **Format** button on the right of the Replace With box. The Replace Format dialog box appears. It is the same as the Find Format dialog box. Simply select any formats you want to assign to your replacement, and then click **OK**.

8. Click **Find Next** to find the first occurrence of your specified entry.

9. When an occurrence is found, it is highlighted. Click **Replace** to replace only this occurrence and then click **Find Next** to find the next occurrence.

10. If you want to find all the occurrences, click **Find All**; you can also replace all the occurrences of the entry with **Replace All**.

11. When you have finished working with the Find and Replace dialog boxclick **Close**.

Search an Entire Workbook If you want to search an entire workbook for a particular entry, click the **Within** drop-down list in the Find and Replace dialog box and select **Workbook**.

If you don't need to replace an entry but would like to find it in the worksheet, you can use the Find feature. Select **Edit**, **Find**, and then type the data you want to locate into the Find What text box and click **Find Next**.

Checking Your Spelling

Because worksheets also include text entries, you might want to make sure that you check for any misspellings in a worksheet before printing the data. Excel offers a spell-checking feature that finds and corrects misspellings in a worksheet.

To run the Spelling Checker, follow these steps:

1. Click the **Spelling** button on the Standard toolbar (or select **Tools**, **Spelling**). The Spelling dialog box appears. Excel finds the first misspelled word and displays it at the top of the Spelling dialog box. A suggested correction appears in the Suggestions box (see Figure 8.3).

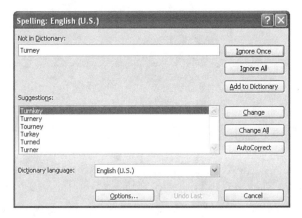

Figure 8.3 Correct spelling mistakes with the options in the Spelling dialog box.

2. To accept the suggestion in the Suggestions box, click **Change**, or click **Change All** to change all occurrences of the misspelled word.

3. If the suggestion in the Suggestions box is not correct, you can do any of the following:

- Select a different suggestion from the Suggestions box, and then click **Change** or **Change All**.
- Type your own correction into the Change To box, and then click **Change** or **Change All**.
- Click **Ignore Once** to leave the word unchanged.
- Click **Ignore All** to leave all occurrences of the word unchanged.
- Click **Add to Dictionary** to add the word to the dictionary so that Excel won't flag it as misspelled again.
- Click **AutoCorrect** to add a correctly spelled word to the AutoCorrect list so that Excel can correct it automatically as you type.
- If you make a mistake related to a particular entry, click the **Undo Last** button to undo the last change that you made.

4. You might see a message asking whether you want to continue checking spelling at the beginning of the sheet. If so, click **Yes** to continue. When the Spelling Checker can't find any more misspelled words, it displays a prompt telling you that the spelling check is complete. Click **OK** to confirm that the spelling check is finished.

 TIP   **Setting Spelling Options**   If you want to set options related to the Spelling feature, such as ignoring words in uppercase and words with numbers, click the **Options** button in the Spelling dialog box. This takes you to the Options dialog box for the Spelling Checker. Set options as needed and then click **OK** to return to the Spelling dialog box.

Copying and Moving Data

In Lesson 2, you learned how to use the Fill feature to copy a particular entry to multiple cells. In this section, you take a closer look at the Copy feature. When you copy or cut data in a cell, that data is held in a temporary storage area (a part of the computer's memory) called the Clipboard.

Excel 2003 (and all the Office 2003 applications) makes it easy for you to work with the Clipboard because it can be viewed in the Office Clipboard task pane (you look at the Clipboard later in this lesson). This enables you to keep track of items that you have copied or cut to the Clipboard. The Clipboard not only enables you to copy or move data with Excel, but it enables you to place Excel data directly into another application (see Lesson 7, "Sharing Office Application Data," in Part I of this book).

 Clipboard The Clipboard is an area of memory that is accessible to all Windows programs. The Clipboard is used to copy or move data from place to place within a program or between programs.

When you copy data, you create a duplicate of data in a cell or range of cells. Follow these steps to copy data:

1. Select the cell(s) that you want to copy. You can select any range or several ranges if you want. (See Lesson 11, "Working with Ranges," for more information).

 2. Click the **Copy** button on the Standard toolbar. The contents of the selected cell(s) are copied to the Clipboard.

3. Select the first cell in the area where you would like to place the copy. (To copy the data to another worksheet or workbook, change to that worksheet or workbook first.)

 4. Click the **Paste** button. Excel inserts the contents of the Clipboard at the location of the insertion point.

 Watch Out! When copying or moving data, be careful not to paste the data over existing data (unless, of course, you intend to).

CAUTION

You can copy the same data to several places by repeating the **Paste** command. Items remain on the Clipboard until you remove them.

Using Drag and Drop

The fastest way to copy something is to drag and drop it. Select the cells you want to copy, hold down the **Ctrl** key, and drag the border of the range you selected (see Figure 8.4). When you release the mouse button, the contents are copied to the new location. To insert the data between existing cells, press **Ctrl+Shift** as you drag.

To drag a copy to a different sheet, press **Ctrl+Alt** as you drag the selection to the sheet's tab. Excel switches you to that sheet, where you can drop your selection into the appropriate location.

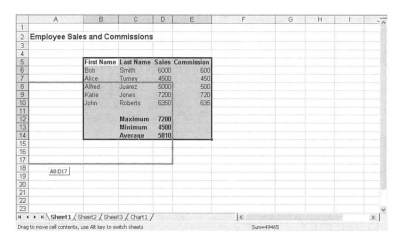

Figure 8.4   Dragging is the fastest way to copy data.

Moving Data

Moving data is similar to copying except that the data is removed from its original place and placed into the new location.

To move data, follow these steps:

1. Select the cells you want to move.

 2. Click the **Cut** button.

3. Select the first cell in the area where you want to place the data. To move the data to another worksheet, change to that worksheet.

4. Click **Paste**.

Using Drag and Drop to Move Data

You can also move data using drag and drop. Select the data to be moved, and then drag the border of the selected cells to its new location. To insert the data between existing cells, press **Shift** while you drag. To move the data to a different worksheet, press the **Alt** key and drag the selection to the worksheet's tab. You're switched to that sheet, where you can drop your selection at the appropriate point.

Using the Office Clipboard

You can use the Office Clipboard to store multiple items that you cut or copy from an Excel worksheet (or workbook). You can then paste or move these items within Excel or to other Office applications. The Office Clipboard can hold up to 24 items.

What a Drag! You can't use the drag-and-drop feature to copy or move data to the Office Clipboard.

CAUTION

The Office Clipboard is viewed in the Clipboard task pane. Follow these steps to open the Office Clipboard:

1. Select the **Edit** menu, and then select **Office Clipboard**. The Clipboard task pane appears. Any items that you have cut or copied appear on the Clipboard (see Figure 8.5).

Figure 8.5   The Clipboard provides a list of items that you have cut or copied.

2. To paste an item that appears on the Clipboard, click in a cell on the worksheet, and then click the item on the Clipboard. It is then pasted into the selected cell.

You can remove any of the items from the Clipboard. Place the mouse pointer on an item listed on the Clipboard and click the drop-down arrow that appears. Click **Delete** on the shortcut menu that appears.

You can also clear all the items from the Clipboard. Click the **Clear All** button at the top of the Clipboard task pane.

 TIP **Open the Clipboard from the System Tray** You can quickly open the Office Clipboard in any Office application by double-clicking the Clipboard icon in the Windows System Tray (at the far right of the Windows taskbar).

Deleting Data

To delete the data in a cell or range of cells, select them and press **Delete**. Excel also offers some additional options for deleting cells and their contents:

- With the **Edit**, **Clear** command, you can delete only the formatting of a cell (or an attached comment) without deleting its contents. The formatting of a cell includes the cell's color, border style, numeric format, font size, and so on. You'll learn more about this option in a moment.

- With the **Edit**, **Delete** command, you can remove cells and then shift surrounding cells over to take their place (this option is described in more detail in Lesson 12, "Inserting and Removing Cells, Rows, and Columns").

To use the Clear command to remove the formatting of a cell or a note, follow these steps:

1. Select the cells you want to clear.

2. Open the **Edit** menu and point at **Clear**. The Clear submenu appears.

3. Select the desired Clear option: **All** (which clears the cells of all contents, formatting, and notes), **Formats**, **Contents**, or **Comments**.

Changing How Numbers and Text Look

In this lesson, you learn how to customize the appearance of numbers in your worksheet and how to customize your text formatting to achieve the look you want.

Formatting Text and Numbers

When you work in Excel, you work with two types of formatting: value formatting and font formatting. In value formatting, you assign a particular number style to a cell (or cells) that holds numeric data. You can assign a currency style, a percent style, or one of several other numeric styles to values.

Another formatting option available to you in Excel relates to different font attributes. For example, you can add bold or italic to the contents of a cell or cells. You can also change the font used for a range of cells or increase the font size.

Next, you take a look at numeric formatting, and then you look at how different font attributes are controlled in Excel.

Using the Style Buttons to Format Numbers

The Formatting toolbar (just below the Standard toolbar) contains several buttons for applying a format to your numbers, including the following:

Button	Name	Example/Description
$	Currency Style	$1,200.90
%	Percent Style	20.90%
,	Comma Style	1,200.90
+.0 .00	Increase Decimal	Adds one decimal place
.00 +.0	Decrease Decimal	Deletes one decimal place

To use one of these buttons, select the cell or cells you want to format, and then click the desired button. If you would like more formatting options for numeric values, read on; they are covered in the next section.

Numeric Formatting Options

The numeric values that you place in your Excel cells are more than just numbers; they often represent dollar amounts, a date, or a percentage. If the various numeric style buttons on the Formatting toolbar (discussed in the previous section) do not offer the exact format you want for your numbers, don't worry. Excel's Format Cells dialog box offers a wide range of number formats and even allows you to create custom formats.

To use the Format Cells dialog box to assign numeric formatting to cells in a worksheet, follow these steps:

1. Select the cell or range that contains the values you want to format.

2. Select the **Format** menu and select **Cells**. The Format Cells dialog box appears.

3. Click the **Number** tab. The different categories of numeric formats are displayed in a Category list (see Figure 9.1).

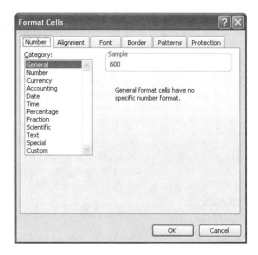

Figure 9.1 Apply a numeric format in the Number tab of the Format Cells dialog box.

4. In the Category list, select the numeric format category you want to use. The sample box displays the default format for that category.

5. Click **OK** to assign the numeric format to the selected cells.

As you can see from the Number tab on the Format Cells dialog box, Excel offers several numeric formatting styles. Table 9.1 provides a list of these different number formats.

Table 9.1   Excel's Number Formats

Number Format	Examples	Description
General	10.6 $456,908.00	Excel displays your value as you enter it. In other words, this format displays currency or percent signs only if you enter them yourself.
Number	3400.50 €120.39	The default Number format has two decimal places. Negative numbers are preceded by a minus sign, but they can also appear in red and/or parentheses.
Currency	$3,400.50 €$3,400.50	The default Currency format has two decimal places and a dollar sign. Negative numbers appear with a minus sign, but they can also appear in red and/or parentheses.
Accounting	$3,400.00 $978.21	Use this format to align dollar signs and decimal points in a column. The default Accounting format has two decimal places and a dollar sign.
Date	11/7	The default Date format is the month and day separated by a slash; however, you can select from numerous other formats.
Time	10:00	The default Time format is the hour and minutes separated by a colon; however, you can opt to display seconds, a.m., or p.m.
Percentage	99.50%	The default Percentage format has two decimal places. Excel multiplies the value in a cell by 100 and displays the result with a percent sign.
Fraction	1/2	The default Fraction format is up to one digit on each side of the slash. Use this format to display the number of digits you want on each side of the slash and the fraction type (such as halves, quarters, eighths, and so on).
Scientific	3.40E+03	The default Scientific format has two decimal places. Use this format to display numbers in scientific notation.
Text	135RV90	Use Text format to display both text and numbers in a cell as text. Excel displays the entry exactly as you type it.
Special	02110	This format is specifically designed to display ZIP codes, phone numbers, and Social Security numbers correctly so that you don't have to enter any special characters, such as hyphens.

Table 9.1 Continued

Number Format	Examples	Description
Custom	00.0%	Use Custom format to create your own number format. You can use any of the format codes in the Type list and then make changes to those codes. The # symbol represents a number placeholder, and 0 represents a zero placeholder.

You can also open the Format Cell dialog box using a shortcut menu. Select the cell or cells that you want to assign a numeric format to, and then right-click those cells. On the shortcut menu that appears, select **Format Cells**. Then, select the **Number** tab to select your numeric format.

CAUTION

That's Not the Date I Entered! If you enter a date into a cell that is already formatted with the Number format, the date appears as a value that represents the number of days between January 1, 1900, and that date. Change the cell's formatting from a Number format to a Date format and select a date type. The entry in the cell then appears as an actual date.

TIP

How Do I Get Rid of a Numeric Format? To remove a number format from a cell (and return it to General format), select the cell whose formatting you want to remove, open the **Edit** menu, select **Clear**, and select **Formats**.

How You Can Make Text Look Different

When you type text into a cell, Excel automatically formats it in the Arial font with a text size of 10 points. The 12-point font size is considered typical for business documents (the higher the point size, the bigger the text is; there are approximately 72 points in an inch). You can select from several fonts (such as Baskerville, Modern, or Rockwell) and change the size of any font characters in a cell. You can also apply special font attributes, such as bold, italic, and underline.

TERM

Font A font is a set of characters that have the same typeface, which means they are of a single design (such as Times New Roman).

Before you take a look at applying different font attributes to the cells in a worksheet, take a look at how you change the default font for all your Excel workbooks. This enables you to select a different font and font size for your worksheets.

To change the default font, follow these steps:

1. Select **Tools** and then click **Options** to open the Options dialog box.

2. Click the **General** tab (see Figure 9.2).

3. In the Standard Font area, use the drop-down list to select a new font. Use the Size drop-down list to select a new default font size.

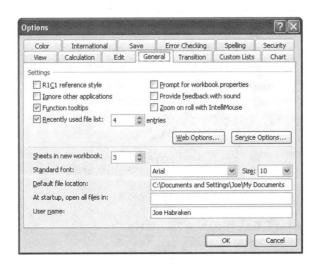

Figure 9.2 You can set a new default font and font size for your Excel workbooks.

4. When you click the **OK** button, Excel makes your preference the default font and size.

Changing Text Attributes with Toolbar Buttons

When you are working on your various Excel worksheets, you will probably apply a variety of formatting options to the different cells in a particular worksheet. A fast way to assign text attributes, such as bold and italic, is to use the various font attribute buttons on the Excel Formatting toolbar.

To use the Formatting toolbar to change text attributes, follow these steps:

1. Select the cell or range that contains the text whose look you want to change.

2. To change the font, click the **Font** drop-down list, and select a new font name. To change the font size, click the **Font Size** drop-down list and select the size you want to use. You can also type the point size into the Font Size box and then press **Enter**.

3. To add an attribute such as bold, italic, or underlining to the selected cells, click the appropriate button: **Bold**, **Italic**, or **Underline**, respectively.

> **TIP**   **Font Keyboard Shortcuts**   You can apply certain attributes quickly by using keyboard shortcuts. First select the cell(s), and then press **Ctrl+B** for bold, **Ctrl+I** for italic, **Ctrl+U** for single underline, or **Ctrl+5** for strikethrough.

You can also change the color of the font in a cell or cells. Select the cell or cells and click the **Font Color** drop-down arrow on the Formatting toolbar. Select a font color from the Color palette that appears.

Accessing Different Font Attributes

If you would like to access a greater number of font format options for a cell or range of cells, you can use the Font tab of the Format Cells dialog box. It provides access to different fonts, font styles, font sizes, font colors, and other text attributes, such as strikethrough and superscript/subscript. To format cells using the Font tab of the Format Cells dialog box, follow these steps:

1. Select the cell or range that contains the text you want to format.

2. Select the **Format** menu and select **Cells**, or press **Ctrl+1**. (You can also right-click the selected cells and choose **Format Cells** from the shortcut menu.)

3. Click the **Font** tab. The Font tab provides drop-down lists and check boxes for selecting the various font attributes (see Figure 9.3).

4. Select the options you want.

5. Click **OK** to close the dialog box and return to your worksheet.

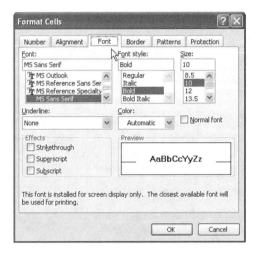

Figure 9.3 The Font tab provides access to all the font attributes.

Aligning Text in Cells

When you enter data into a cell, that data is aligned automatically. Text is aligned on the left, and numbers are aligned on the right (values resulting from a formula or function are also right-aligned). Both text and numbers are initially set at the bottom of the cells. However, you can change both the vertical and the horizontal alignment of data in your cells.

Follow these steps to change the alignment:

1. Select the cell or range you want to align.

2. Select the **Format** menu and then select **Cells**. The Format Cells dialog box appears.

3. Click the **Alignment** tab (see Figure 9.4).

4. Choose from the following options to set the alignment:

   - **Horizontal**—Lets you specify a left/right alignment in the cells. (The **Center Across** selection centers a title or other text within a range of cells, which is discussed in a moment.)

   - **Vertical**—Lets you specify how you want the text aligned in relation to the top and bottom of the cells.

   - **Orientation**—Lets you flip the text sideways or print it from top to bottom instead of left to right.

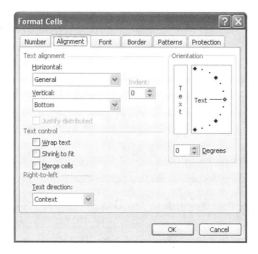

Figure 9.4   Select from the Alignment options on the Alignment tab of the Format Cells dialog box.

- **Wrap Text**—Tells Excel to wrap long lines of text within a cell without changing the width of the cell. (Normally, Excel displays all text in a cell on one line.)

- **Shrink to Fit**—Shrinks the text to fit within the cell's current width. If the cell's width is adjusted, the text increases or decreases in size accordingly.

- **Merge Cells**—Combines several cells into a single cell. All data is overlaid, except for the cell in the upper-left corner of the selected cells.

5. Click **OK** when you have finished making your selections.

TIP   **Changing Text Orientation**   The Alignment tab also provides an Orientation box that enables you to rotate text within a cell or a group of merged cells. Drag the degree dial on the Alignment tab or use the Degree box to specify the amount of rotation for the text.

Aligning Text from the Toolbar

As with the font attributes such as bold and italic, you can also select certain alignment options directly from the Formatting toolbar. Table 9.2 lists the buttons that enable you to align the text.

Table 9.2 Alignment Buttons

Button	Name	Description
	Align Left	Places data at left edge of cell
	Align Right	Places data at right edge of cell
	Center	Centers data in cell
	Merge and Center	Centers data in selected cell range

Excel also enables you to indent your text within a cell. If you're typing a paragraph's worth of information into a single cell, for example, you can indent that paragraph by selecting **Left Alignment** from the Horizontal list box in the Format Cells dialog box (as explained earlier). After selecting Left Alignment, set the amount of indent you want with the Indent spin box in the Format Cells dialog box.

In addition, you can add an indent quickly by clicking the buttons on the Formatting toolbar, as listed in Table 9.3.

Table 9.3 Indent Buttons

Button	Name	Description
	Decrease Indent	Removes an indent or creates a negative indent
	Increase Indent	Adds an indent

Combining Cells and Wrapping Text

As shown in Table 9.2 in the last section, you can center text across a range of cells or merge several cells to hold a sheet title or other text information. If you want to center a title or other text over a range of cells, select the entire range of blank cells in which you want the text centered. This should include the cell that contains the text you want to center (which should be in the cell on the far left of the cell range). Then, click the **Merge and Center** button on the Formatting toolbar.

Combining a group of cells also allows you to place a special heading or other text into the cells (this works well in cases where you use a large font size for the text). Select the cells that you want to combine. Then, select **Format**, **Cells** and select the **Alignment** tab of the Format Cells dialog box.

Click the **Merge Cells** check box and then click **OK**. The cells are then merged.

If you have a cell or a group of merged cells that holds a large amount of text (such as an explanation), you might want to wrap the text within the cell or merged cells. Click the cell that holds the text entry, and then select **Format**, **Cells**. Select the **Alignment** tab of the Format Cells dialog box.

Click the **Wrap Text** checkbox. Then click **OK**.

Copying Formats with Format Painter

After applying a numeric format or various font attributes to a cell or cell range, you can easily copy those formatting options to other cells. This works whether you're copying numeric or text formatting or shading or borders, as you'll learn in upcoming lessons. To copy a format from one cell to another, follow these steps:

1. Select the cells that contain the formatting you want to copy.

 2. Click the **Format Painter** button on the Standard toolbar. Excel copies the formatting. The mouse pointer changes into a paintbrush with a plus sign next to it.

3. Click one cell or drag over several cells to which you want to apply the copied formatting.

4. Release the mouse button, and Excel copies the formatting and applies it to the selected cells.

 TIP   **Painting Several Cells**   To paint several areas with the same formatting at one time, double-click the **Format Painter** button to toggle it on. When you're through, press **Esc** or click the **Format Painter** button again to return to a normal mouse pointer.

Adding Cell Borders and Shading

In this lesson, you learn how to add borders and shading to your worksheets.

Adding Borders to Cells

As you work with your worksheet onscreen, you'll notice that each cell is identified by gridlines that surround the cell. By default, these gridlines do not print; even if you choose to print them, they don't look very good on the printed page. To create well-defined lines on the printout (and onscreen, for that matter), you can add borders to selected cells or entire cell ranges. A border can appear on all four sides of a cell or only on selected sides; it's up to you.

> **TIP** **Printing the Gridlines** It's true that gridlines do not print by default. But if you want to try printing your worksheet with gridlines, just to see what it looks like, open the **File** menu, select **Page Setup**, click the **Sheet** tab, check the **Gridlines** box, and click **OK**.

To add borders to a cell or range, perform the following steps:

1. Select the cell(s) around which you want a border to appear.
2. Open the **Format** menu and choose **Cells**. The Format Cells dialog box appears.
3. Click the **Border** tab to see the Border options shown in Figure 10.1.
4. Select the desired position, style (thickness), and color for the border. The position of the border is selected using the buttons along the left of the Border box. You can also click inside the **Border** box itself to place the border.
5. Click **OK** or press **Enter**.

When you're adding borders to a worksheet, hiding the gridlines onscreen gives you a preview of how the borders will look when printed. To hide gridlines, select the **Tools** menu, select **Options** (this opens the Options dialog box), and then select the **View** tab. Remove the check mark from the Gridlines check box, and then click **OK** to return to the worksheet. Selecting this option has no effect on whether the gridlines actually print, only on whether they are displayed onscreen.

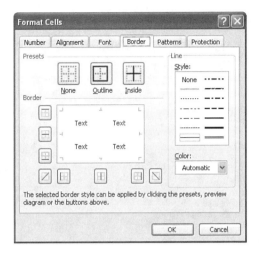

Figure 10.1   Choose Border options from the Format Cells dialog box.

 TIP   **Add Borders from the Toolbar**   You can use the Borders button on the Formatting toolbar to add a border to cells or cell ranges. Select the cells, and then click the **Borders** drop-down arrow on the Formatting toolbar to select a border type.

Adding Shading to Cells

Another way to offset certain cells in a worksheet is to add shading to those cells. With shading, you can add a color or gray shading to the background of a cell. You can add shading that consists of a solid color, or you can select a pattern as part of the shading options, such as a repeating diagonal line.

Follow these steps to add shading to a cell or range. As you make your selections, keep in mind that if you plan to print your worksheet with a black-and-white printer, the colors you select might not provide enough contrast on the printout to provide any differentiation between ranges of cells. You can always use the Print Preview command (as explained in Lesson 14, "Printing Your Workbook") to view your results in black and white before you print.

1. Select the cell(s) you want to shade.
2. Open the **Format** menu and choose **Cells**.
3. Click the **Patterns** tab. Excel displays the shading options (see Figure 10.2).
4. Click the **Pattern** drop-down arrow to see a grid that contains colors and patterns.

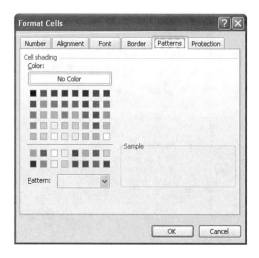

Figure 10.2 Choose colors and patterns from the Patterns tab of the Format Cells dialog box.

5. Select the shading color and pattern you want to use. The Color options let you choose a color for the overall shading. The Pattern options let you select a black or colored pattern that is placed on top of the cell-shading color you selected. A preview of the results appears in the Sample box.

6. When you have finished making your selections, click **OK**.

TIP **Add Cell Shading with the Toolbar** Select the cells you want to shade. Click the **Fill Color** drop-down arrow on the Formatting toolbar and then select the fill color from the Color palette that appears.

Using AutoFormat

If you don't want to take the time to test different border types and shading styles, you can let Excel help you with the task of adding some emphasis and interest to the cells of your worksheet. You can take advantage of AutoFormat, which provides various predesigned table formats that you can apply to a worksheet.

To use predesigned formats, perform the following steps:

1. Select the cell(s) that contain the data you want to format. This could be the entire worksheet.

2. Select the **Format** menu, and then select **AutoFormat**. The AutoFormat dialog box appears (see Figure 10.3).

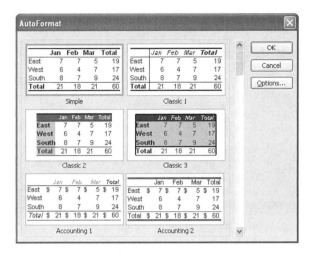

Figure 10.3 Select a format from the AutoFormat dialog box.

3. Scroll through the list to view the various AutoFormat styles provided. When you find a format that you want to use, click it to select it.

4. To prevent AutoFormat from overwriting certain existing formatting (such as numbers, alignment, or fonts), click the **Options** button and deselect the appropriate check boxes.

5. Click **OK** and your worksheet is formatted.

 TIP **Yuck! I Chose That?** If you don't like what AutoFormat did to your worksheet, click the **Undo** button (or press **Ctrl+Z**).

Applying Conditional Formatting

Another useful formatting feature that Excel provides is conditional formatting. Conditional formatting allows you to specify that certain results in the worksheet be formatted so that they stand out from the other entries in the worksheet. For example, if you wanted to track all the monthly sales figures that are below a certain amount, you can use conditional formatting to format them in red. Conditional formatting formats only cells that meet a certain condition.

To apply conditional formatting, follow these steps:

1. Select the cells to which you want to apply the conditional formatting.

2. Select the **Format** menu and select **Conditional Formatting**. The Conditional Formatting dialog box appears, as shown in Figure 10.4.

527

Figure 10.4 Apply formats conditionally to highlight certain values.

3. Be sure that **Cell Value Is** is selected in the Condition 1 drop-down box on the left of the dialog box.

4. In the next drop-down box to the right, you select the condition. The default is Between. Other conditions include Equal To, Greater Than, Less Than, and other possibilities. Use the drop-down box to select the appropriate condition.

5. After selecting the condition, you must specify a cell or cells in the worksheet that Excel can use as a reference for the conditional formatting. For example, if you select Less Than as the condition, you must specify a cell in the worksheet that contains a value that can be used for comparison with the cells that you are applying the conditional formatting to. Click the **Shrink** button on the Conditional Formatting dialog box. You are returned to the worksheet. Select the reference cell for the condition.

6. Click the **Expand** button on the Conditional Formatting dialog box to expand the dialog box.

7. Now you can set the formatting that will be applied to cells that meet your condition. Click the **Format** button in the Conditional Formatting dialog box and select the formatting options for your condition in the Format Cells dialog box. Then click **OK**. Figure 10.5 shows a conditional format that applies bold and italic to values that are greater than the value contained in cell F8.

Figure 10.5 Set the various options for your conditional formatting.

8. After setting the conditions to be met for conditional formatting (you can click **Add** to set more than one condition), click **OK**.

You are returned to the worksheet. Cells that meet the condition you set up for conditional formatting will be formatted with the options you specified. Figure 10.6 shows cells that the settings used in Figure 10.5 conditionally formatted.

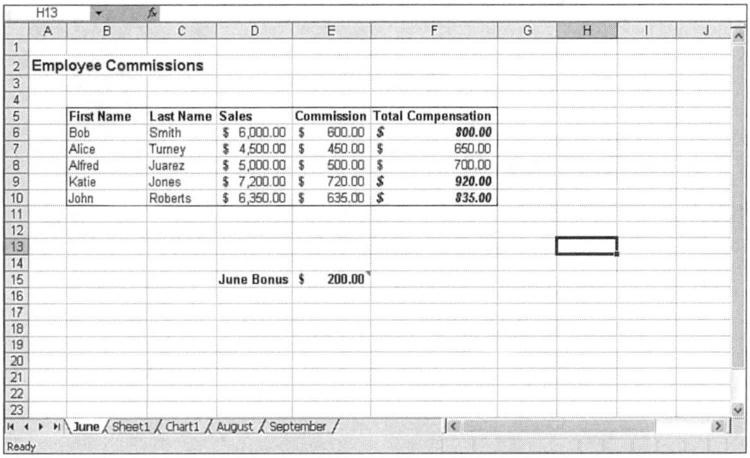

	A	B	C	D	E	F	G	H	I	J
1										
2	Employee Commissions									
3										
4										
5		First Name	Last Name	Sales		Commission	Total Compensation			
6		Bob	Smith	$ 6,000.00	$	600.00	*800.00*			
7		Alice	Turney	$ 4,500.00	$	450.00	650.00			
8		Alfred	Juarez	$ 5,000.00	$	500.00	700.00			
9		Katie	Jones	$ 7,200.00	$	720.00	*920.00*			
10		John	Roberts	$ 6,350.00	$	635.00	*835.00*			
11										
12										
13										
14										
15				June Bonus	$	200.00				
16										
17										
18										
19										
20										
21										
22										
23										

Figure 10.6 Conditional formatting formats only the cells that meet your conditions.

> **TIP** **Conditional Formatting Applied to Formulas** You can also set up conditional formatting to highlight cells that contain a particular formula or function. Select **Formula Is** for Condition 1 in the Conditional Formatting dialog box and then type the formula or function in the box to the right.

Working with Ranges

In this lesson, you learn how to select and name ranges.

What Is a Range?

When you select a group of cells (which you have done numerous times in the various Excel lessons), you are in fact selecting a range. A cell range can consist of one cell or any group of contiguous cells.

Ranges are referred to by their anchor points (the upper-left corner and the lower-right corner). For example, a range that begins with cell C10 and ends with I14 is referred to as C10:I14.

TERM   **Range**   A group of contiguous cells in an Excel worksheet.

Selecting ranges is certainly not rocket science, but you can do a number of things with a selected range of cells. For example, you can select a range of cells and print them (rather than printing the entire worksheet). You can also name ranges, which makes it much easier to include the cell range in a formula or function (you learn about range names and using range names in formulas later in this lesson). A few tricks for selecting cell ranges are discussed in the next section.

Selecting a Range

To select a range using the mouse, follow these steps:

1. Move the mouse pointer to the upper-left corner of a range.

2. Click and hold the left mouse button.

3. Drag the mouse to the lower-right corner of the range and release the mouse button. The cells are highlighted on the worksheet (see Figure 11.1).

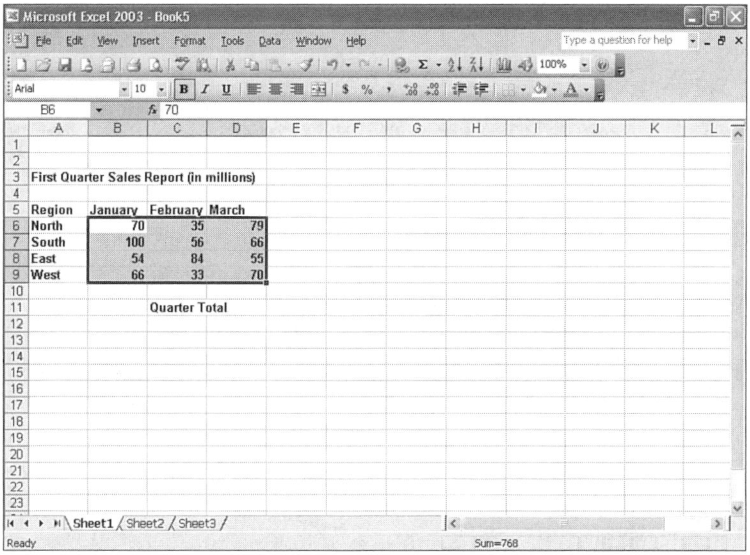

Figure 11.1 A range is any combination of cells that forms a rectangle or a square.

Techniques that you can use to quickly select a row, a column, an entire worksheet, or several ranges are shown in Table 11.1.

Table 11.1 Selection Techniques

To Select This	Do This
Several ranges	Select the first range, hold down the **Ctrl** key, and select the next range. Continue holding down the **Ctrl** key while you select additional ranges.
Row	Click the row heading number at the left edge of the worksheet. You also can press **Shift+Spacebar**. To select several adjacent rows, drag over their headers. To select nonadjacent rows, press **Ctrl** as you click each row's header.
Column	Click the column heading letter at the top edge of the worksheet. You also can press **Ctrl+Spacebar**.
Entire worksheet	Click the **Select All** button (the blank rectangle in the upper-left corner of the worksheet, above row 1 and left of column A). You also can press **Ctrl+A**.
The same range on several sheets	Press and hold **Ctrl** as you click the worksheets you want to use, and then select the range in the usual way.
Range that is out of view	Press **Ctrl+G** (**Go To**) or click in the **Name** box on the Formula bar and type the address of the range you want to select. For example, to select the range R100 to T250, type **R100:T250** and press **Enter**.

TIP   **Deselecting a Range**   To deselect a range, click any cell in the worksheet.

Selected cells are highlighted in a slightly grayed tone, so you can still read your data.

Naming Ranges

Up to this point, when you have created formulas or functions or formatted cells in a worksheet, you have specified cells and cell ranges using the cell addresses. You can also name a cell or range of cells. You could select a range of values and assign that range a name. For example, you could select a range of cells that includes your expenses and name that range EXPENSES. You can then name a range of cells that includes your income and name that range INCOME. It would be very simple to then create a formula that subtracts your expenses from your income using the range names that you created. The formula would be written as follows:

`=SUM(INCOME)-SUM(EXPENSES)`

You are telling Excel to add the INCOME range and add the EXPENSES range. The formula then subtracts the total EXPENSES from the total INCOME. Note that the SUM function is used along with simple subtraction in this formula to provide the desired results.

Using range names in formulas and functions can definitely make your life easier. Range names are very useful when you create formulas or functions that pull information from more than one worksheet in a workbook or different workbooks. You can even use a range name to create a chart (you learn about charts in Lesson 15, "Creating Charts").

Follow these steps to name a range:

1. Select the range you want to name (the cells must be located on the same worksheet). If you want to name a single cell, simply select that cell.

2. Select the **Insert** menu, point at **Name**, and then select **Define**. The Define Name dialog box appears (see Figure 11.2).

3. Type the name for the range in the box at the top of the dialog box. You can use up to 255 characters, and valid range names can include letters, numbers, periods, and underlines, but no spaces.

4. Click the **Add** button to name the range. The name is added to the list of range names.

5. Click **OK**.

Figure 11.2 Use the Define Name dialog box to name a cell range.

TIP **Selecting a Different Range** You can change the selected range from the Define Name dialog box. Click the **Shrink** button at the bottom of the dialog box, and then select the range on the worksheet. To return to the dialog box, click the **Expand** button on the Define Name dialog box.

You can also use the Define Name dialog box to delete any unwanted range names. Select **Insert**, point at **Name**, and then select **Define**. Select an unwanted range name from the list and click the **Delete** button. To close the dialog box, click **OK**.

TIP **Quickly Create a Range Name** You can also create a range name by typing it into the Name box on the Formula bar (this box normally shows the location of the selected range or cell). Select the cell range, click in the Name box, and type the name for the range. Then press **Enter**.

Creating Range Names from Worksheet Labels

You can also create range names using the column and row labels that you have created for your worksheet. The row labels are used to create a range name for each row of cells, and the column labels are used to create a range name for each column of cells. Follow these steps:

1. Select the worksheet, including the column and row labels.
2. Select the **Insert** menu, point at **Name**, and then select **Create**. The Create Names dialog box appears (see Figure 11.3).
3. Click in the check boxes that define the position of the row and column labels in the worksheet.
4. After specifying the location of the row and column labels, click **OK**.

Figure 11.3   Use the Create Names dialog box to create range names for the cells in the worksheet.

You can check the range names (and their range of cells) that were created using the Create Name feature in the Define Name dialog box. Select **Insert**, point at **Name**, and then select **Define**. All the range names that you created appear in the Names in Workbook list.

Inserting a Range Name into a Formula or Function

As previously discussed in this lesson, range names make it easy for you to specify a range of cells in a formula or function. To insert a range name into a formula or function, follow these steps:

1. Click in the cell where you want to place the formula or function.

2. Type the formula or function (begin the formula or function with the equal sign).

3. When you are ready to insert the range name into the formula or function, select the **Insert** menu, point at **Name**, and then select **Paste**. The Paste Name dialog box appears (see Figure 11.4).

Figure 11.4   Use the Paste Name dialog box to insert a range name into a formula or function.

4. Select the range name you want to place in the formula or function, and then click **OK**.

5. Finish typing the formula or function (including the appropriate operators).

6. Press **Enter** to place the formula or function into the cell and return the calculated value.

TIP   **Type the Name of a Range**   When you are creating a formula or function using a range name and you remember what that range name is, you can type it into the formula or function. You don't have to use the Paste Name dialog box.

Inserting and Removing Cells, Rows, and Columns

In this lesson, you learn how to rearrange the data in your worksheet by adding and removing cells, rows, and columns. You also learn how to adjust the width of your columns and the height of your rows to make the best use of the worksheet space.

Inserting Rows and Columns

As you edit and enhance your worksheets, you might need to add rows or columns within the worksheet. Inserting entire rows and columns into your worksheet is very straightforward. Follow these steps:

1. To insert a single row or column, select a cell to the right of where you want to insert a column or below where you want to insert a row.

To insert multiple columns or rows, select the number of columns or rows you want to insert. To insert columns, drag over the column letters at the top of the worksheet. To insert rows, drag over the row numbers. For example, select three column letters or row numbers to insert three rows or columns.

2. Select the **Insert** menu, and then select **Rows** or **Columns**. Excel inserts rows above your selection and columns to the left of your selection. The inserted rows or columns contain the same formatting as the cells (or rows and columns) you selected in step 1. Figure 12.1 shows a worksheet to which additional columns have been added.

As you can see, when you insert rows or columns, the Insert Options shortcut icon appears to the right of the inserted columns or below inserted rows. Use the Insert Options menu to specify the column or row from which the new column or row should copy its formatting. For example, in the case of inserted columns, you can choose to copy the formatting from the column to the right or left of the inserted column or columns, or you can choose to clear the formatting in the inserted columns.

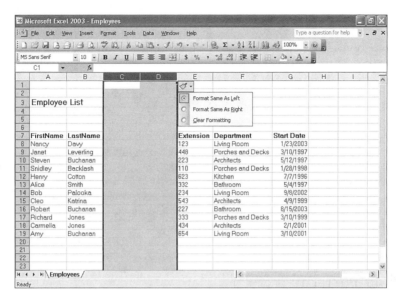

Figure 12.1   Columns can easily be inserted into an Excel worksheet.

  TIP   **Fast Insert**   To quickly insert rows or columns, select one or more rows or columns, right-click one of them, and choose **Insert** from the shortcut menu.

Removing Rows and Columns

When you delete a row in your worksheet, the rows below the deleted row move up to fill the space. When you delete a column, the columns to the right shift left.

Follow these steps to delete a row or column:

1. Click the row number or column letter of the row or column you want to delete. You can select more than one row or column by dragging over the row numbers or column letters.

2. Select the **Edit** menu and then select **Delete**. Excel deletes the rows or columns and renumbers the remaining rows and columns sequentially. All cell references in formulas and functions are updated appropriately.

Inserting Cells

Although inserting rows and columns makes it easy to dramatically change the layout of a worksheet, on occasion you might need to insert only a cell or cells into a worksheet. Inserting cells causes the data in existing cells to shift down a row or over a column to create a space for the new cells.

Watch Your Formulas and Functions   Inserting cells into a worksheet can throw off the cell references in formulas and functions. Double-check your formulas and functions after inserting cells to make sure that the calculations are acting upon the appropriate cell addresses.

CAUTION

To insert a single cell or a group of cells, follow these steps:

1. Select the area where you want the new cells inserted. Excel inserts the same number of cells as you select.

2. Select the **Insert** menu and then select **Cells**. The Insert dialog box appears (see Figure 12.2).

Figure 12.2   You can insert cells into a worksheet using the Insert dialog box.

3. Select **Shift Cells Right** or **Shift Cells Down** (or you can choose to have an entire row or column inserted).

4. Click **OK**. Excel inserts the cells and shifts the adjacent cells in the direction you specify.

You will find that inserting cells is useful if you have entered rows of information and have mismatched data, such as a customer's name with someone else's order information. Inserting a couple of cells enables you to quickly edit the data without having to delete data or insert a new row.

TIP   **Drag Insert Cells**   A quick way to insert cells is to select the number of cells you want, hold down the **Shift** key, and then drag the fill handle up, down, left, or right to set the position of the new cells.

Removing Cells

You already learned about deleting the data in cells back in Lesson 8, "Editing Worksheets," and you learned that you could also delete cells from a worksheet. Eliminating cells from the worksheet rather than just clearing their contents means that the cells surrounding the deleted cells in the worksheet are moved to fill the gap that is created. Remove cells only if you want the other cells in the worksheet to shift to new positions. Otherwise, just delete the data in the cells or type new data into the cells.

If you want to remove cells from a worksheet, use the following steps:

1. Select the cell or range of cells you want to remove.

2. Open the **Edit** menu and choose **Delete**. The Delete dialog box appears (see Figure 12.3).

Figure 12.3   Use the Delete dialog box to specify how the gap left by the deleted cells should be filled.

3. Select **Shift Cells Left** or **Shift Cells Up** to specify how the remaining cells in the worksheet should move to fill the gap left by the deleted cells.

4. Click **OK**. Surrounding cells are shifted to fill the gap left by the deleted cells.

As with inserting cells, you should check the cell references in your formulas and functions after removing cells from the worksheet. Be sure that your calculations are referencing the appropriate cells on the worksheet.

Adjusting Column Width and Row Height with a Mouse

It doesn't take very long when you are working in Excel to realize that the default column width of 8.43 characters doesn't accommodate long text entries or values that have been formatted as currency or other numeric formats. You can adjust the width of a column quickly using the mouse.

You can also adjust row heights, if you want, using the mouse. However, your row heights will adjust to any font size changes that you make to data held in a particular row. Row heights also adjust if you wrap text entries within them (see Lesson 9, "Changing How Numbers and Text Look," for more about wrapping text). You will probably find that you need to adjust column widths in your worksheets far more often than row heights.

CAUTION

What Is ########? When you format a value in a cell with numeric formatting and Excel cannot display the result in the cell because of the column width, Excel displays ######## in the cell. This lets you know that you need to adjust the column width so that it can accommodate the entry and its formatting.

To adjust a column width with the mouse, place the mouse pointer on the right border of the column. A sizing tool appears, as shown in Figure 12.4. Drag the column border to the desired width. You can also adjust the column width to automatically accommodate the widest entry within a column; just double-click the sizing tool. This is called AutoFit, and the column adjusts according to the widest entry.

Sizing tool

	A	B	C	D	E	F	G	H	I	J
1										
2	Employee Commissions									
3										
4										
5		First Name	Last Name	Sales	Commission	Total Compensation				
6		Bob	Smith	#####	$ 600.00	$ 800.00				
7		Alice	Turney	#####	$ 450.00	$ 650.00				
8		Alfred	Juarez	#####	$ 500.00	$ 700.00				
9		Katie	Jones	#####	$ 720.00	$ 920.00				
10		John	Roberts	#####	$ 635.00	$ 835.00				
11										
12										
13										
14										
15				June Bo	$ 200.00					
16										
17										
18										
19										
20										
21										
22										
23										

G16 — Width: 8.86 (67 pixels)

June / Sheet1 / Chart1 / August / September /

Ready

Figure 12.4 Use the column width sizing tool to adjust the width of a column.

If you want to adjust several columns at once, select the columns. Place the mouse on any of the column borders and drag to increase or decrease the width. Each selected column is adjusted to the width you select.

Changing row heights is similar to adjusting column widths. Place the mouse on the lower border of a row and drag the sizing tool to increase or decrease the row height. To change the height of multiple rows, select the rows and then drag the border of any of the selected rows to the desired height.

Using the Format Menu for Precise Control

If you want to precisely specify the width of a column or columns or the height of a row or rows, you can enter specific sizes using a dialog box. This provides you with a little more control than just dragging a row height or column width.

To specify a column width, follow these steps:

1. Select the columns you want to change.

2. Select the **Format** menu, point at **Column**, and then select **Width**. The Column Width dialog box appears (see Figure 12.5).

Figure 12.5   Column widths can also be specified in the Column Width dialog box.

3. Type the column width into the dialog box (the width is measured in number of characters).

4. Click **OK**. Your column(s) width is adjusted accordingly.

Adjusting row heights is similar to adjusting column widths. Select the row or rows, and then select the **Format** menu, point at **Rows**, and select **Height**. In the Row Height dialog box that appears, type in the row height and then click **OK**.

Managing Your Worksheets

In this lesson, you learn how to add and delete worksheets within workbooks. You also learn how to copy, move, and rename worksheets.

Selecting Worksheets

By default, each workbook consists of three worksheets whose names appear on tabs at the bottom of the Excel window. You can add or delete worksheets as desired. One advantage of having multiple worksheets within a workbook is that it enables you to organize your data into logical chunks. Another advantage of having separate worksheets for your data is that you can easily reorganize the worksheets (and the associated data) in a workbook.

Before you learn about the details of inserting, deleting, and copying worksheets, you should know how to select one or more worksheets. Selecting a single worksheet is a method of moving from worksheet to worksheet in a workbook.

Selecting multiple worksheets in a workbook, however, is another story. Selecting multiple workbooks enables you to apply the same AutoFormatting or cell formatting to more than one worksheet at a time. This is particularly useful in cases where you might have several worksheets in a workbook that will end up looking very much the same. For example, you might have a workbook that contains four worksheets—each of the worksheets serving as a quarterly summary. Because the design of these worksheets is similar, applying formatting to more than one sheet at a time enables you to keep the sheets consistent in appearance.

To select a worksheet or worksheets, perform one of the following actions:

- To select a single worksheet, click its tab. The tab becomes highlighted to show that the worksheet is selected.
- To select several neighboring or adjacent worksheets, click the tab of the first worksheet in the group and then hold down the **Shift** key and click the tab of the last worksheet in the group. Each worksheet tab will be highlighted (but only the first sheet selected will be visible).

- To select several nonadjacent worksheets, hold down the **Ctrl** key and click each worksheet's tab.

If you select two or more worksheets, they remain selected as a group until you ungroup them. To ungroup worksheets, do one of the following:

- Right-click one of the selected worksheets and choose **Ungroup Sheets**.
- Hold down the **Shift** key and click the tab of the active worksheet.
- Click any worksheet tab to deselect all the other worksheets.

Inserting Worksheets

When you create a new workbook, it contains three worksheets. You can easily add additional worksheets to a workbook.

 TIP **Start with More Sheets**   You can change the default number of worksheets Excel places in a new workbook by opening the **Tools** menu, selecting **Options**, clicking the **General** tab, and then changing the number in the **Sheets in New Workbook** option. Click **OK** to save your changes. The maximum value for the number of worksheets in a workbook is determined by the amount of memory on your computer. If you use more than 20 worksheets in a workbook and the worksheets are full of data, you might find that Excel's overall performance starts to slow down.

Follow these steps to add a worksheet to a workbook:

1. Select the worksheet that you want to be to the right of the inserted worksheet. For example, if you select the August sheet shown in Figure 13.1, the new sheet will be inserted to the left of August.

2. Select the **Insert** menu.

3. Select **Worksheet**. Excel inserts the new worksheet to the right of the previously selected worksheet.

 TIP **Use the Shortcut Menu**   A faster way to work with worksheets is to right-click the worksheet's tab. This brings up a shortcut menu that enables you to insert, delete, rename, move, copy, or select all worksheets.

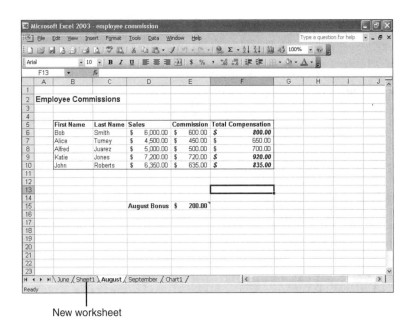

New worksheet

Figure 13.1 Excel inserts the new worksheet to the left of the active worksheet.

Deleting Worksheets

If you find that you have a worksheet you no longer need, or if you plan to use only one worksheet of the three that Excel puts into each workbook by default, you can remove the unwanted worksheets. Here's how you remove a worksheet:

1. Select the worksheet(s) you want to delete.

2. Select the **Edit** menu and then select **Delete Sheet**.

3. If the sheet contains data, a dialog box appears, asking you to confirm the deletion. Click **Delete** to delete the sheet. You will lose any data that the sheet contained.

You can delete multiple sheets if you want. Use the techniques discussed earlier in this lesson to select multiple sheets, and then use steps 2 and 3 in this section to delete the sheets.

Moving and Copying Worksheets

You can move or copy worksheets within a workbook or from one workbook to another. Copying a worksheet enables you to copy the formatting of the sheet and other items, such as the column labels and the row labels. Follow these steps:

1. Select the worksheet or worksheets you want to move or copy. If you want to move or copy worksheets from one workbook to another, be sure the target workbook is open.

2. Select the **Edit** menu and choose **Move or Copy Sheet**. The Move or Copy dialog box appears, as shown in Figure 13.2.

Figure 13.2 The Move or Copy dialog box asks where you want to copy or move a worksheet.

3. To move the worksheets to a different workbook, be sure that workbook is open, and then select that workbook's name from the To Book drop-down list. If you want to move or copy the worksheets to a new workbook, select **(New Book)** in the To Book drop-down list. Excel creates a new workbook and then copies or moves the worksheets to it.

4. In the Before Sheet list box, choose the worksheet you want to follow the selected worksheets.

5. To move the selected worksheet, skip to step 6. To copy the selected worksheets instead of moving them, select the **Create a Copy** option.

6. Select **OK**. The selected worksheets are copied or moved as specified.

Moving a Worksheet Within a Workbook with Drag and Drop

A fast way to copy or move worksheets within a workbook is to use drag and drop. First, select the tab of the worksheet(s) you want to copy or move.

Move the mouse pointer over one of the selected tabs, click and hold the mouse button, and drag the tab where you want it moved. To copy the worksheet, hold down the **Ctrl** key while dragging. When you release the mouse button, the worksheet is copied or moved.

Moving or Copying a Worksheet Between Workbooks with Drag and Drop

You can also use the drag-and-drop feature to quickly copy or move worksheets between workbooks.

1. Open the workbooks you want to use for the copy or move.

2. Select **Window** and select **Arrange**. The Arrange dialog box opens.

3. You can arrange the different workbook windows horizontally, vertically, tiled, or cascaded in the Excel application window. For more than two open workbooks, your best selection is probably the **Tiled** option.

4. After making your selection, click **OK** to arrange the workbook windows within the Excel application window. Figure 13.3 shows three open workbooks that have been tiled.

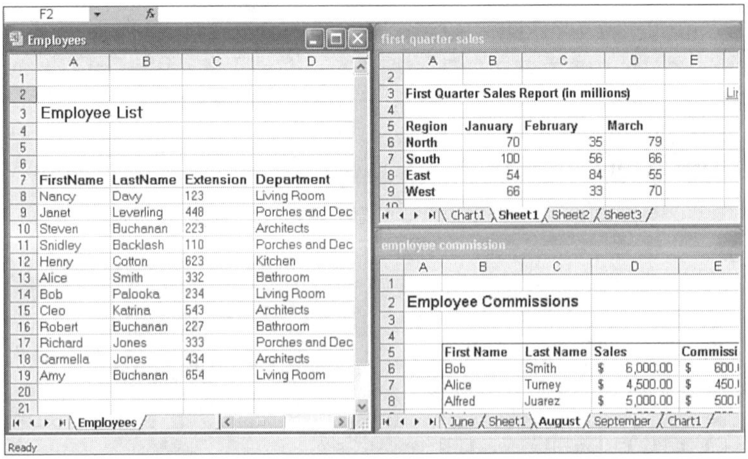

Figure 13.3   You can arrange multiple workbooks in the Excel window and then move or copy worksheets.

5. Select the tab of the worksheet(s) you want to copy or move.

6. Move the mouse pointer over one of the selected tabs, click and hold the mouse button, and drag the tab where you want it moved. To copy the worksheet, hold down the **Ctrl** key while dragging.

7. When you release the mouse button, the worksheet is copied or moved.

 TIP   **Compare Workbooks Side-by-Side**   You can display two workbooks side-by-side for a quick comparison of the data. With the workbooks open in Excel, select **Window** and then **Compare Side by Side**. If only one other workbook is open, the workbook name will appear as part of the Compare Side by Side command on the menu. When you're working with multiple open workbooks, a Compare Side by Side dialog box will open listing the other open workbooks. Select the workbook for comparison and then click **OK**.

Changing Worksheet Tab Names

By default, all worksheets are named SheetX, where X is a number starting with the number 1. So that you'll have a better idea of the information each sheet contains, you should change the names that appear on the tabs. Here's how to do it:

1. Double-click the tab of the worksheet you want to rename. The current name is highlighted.

2. Type a new name for the worksheet and press **Enter**. Excel replaces the default name with the name you type.

Printing Your Workbook

In this lesson, you learn how to preview your print jobs, repeat
row and column headings on pages, and add headers and footers
to your worksheets. You also learn how to print an entire workbook and large worksheets.

Previewing a Print Job

After you've finished a particular worksheet and want to send it to the printer, you
might want to take a quick look at how the worksheet will look on the printed page.
You will find that worksheets don't always print the way that they look on the
screen.

To preview a print job, select the **File** menu and then select **Print Preview**, or
click the **Print Preview** button on the Standard toolbar. Your workbook appears
in the same format that it will be in when sent to the printer (see Figure 14.1).

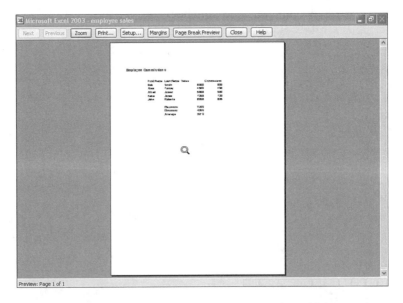

Figure 14.1　By previewing the worksheet, you can determine which page layout attributes need adjusting.

From this view you can zoom in on any area of the preview by clicking it with the mouse pointer (which looks like a magnifying glass). Or use the **Zoom** button on the Print Preview toolbar.

 TIP   **Access Print Preview from Other Dialog Boxes**   The Page Setup and Print dialog boxes explained later in this lesson also include a Preview button, so you can check any last-minute changes you made in either dialog box without having to close the box first.

When you have finished previewing your worksheet, you can print the worksheet by clicking the **Print** button, or you can return to the worksheet by clicking **Close**.

Changing the Page Setup

After you preview your worksheet, you might want to adjust page attributes or change the way the page is set up for printing. For example, you might want to print the column and row labels on every page of the printout. This is particularly useful for large worksheets that span several pages; then you don't have to keep looking back to the first page of the printout to determine what the column headings are.

Printing column and row labels and other worksheet page attributes, such as scaling a worksheet to print out on a single page or adding headers or footers to a worksheet printout, are handled in the Page Setup dialog box. To access this dialog box, select the **File** menu and then select **Page Setup** (see Figure 14.2).

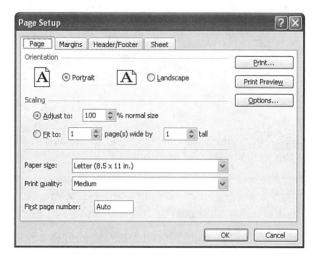

Figure 14.2   Access the Page Setup dialog box to make sure your worksheet page is set to print correctly.

The following sections provide information on some of the most common page setup attributes that you will work with before printing your Excel worksheets.

Printing Column and Row Labels on Every Page

Excel provides a way for you to select labels and titles that are located on the top edge and left side of a large worksheet and to print them on every page of the printout. This option is useful when a worksheet is too wide to print on a single page. If you don't use this option, the extra columns or rows are printed on subsequent pages without any descriptive labels.

Follow these steps to print column or row labels on every page:

1. Select the **File** menu and then select **Page Setup**. The Page Setup dialog box appears.

2. Click the **Sheet** tab to display the Sheet options (see Figure 14.3).

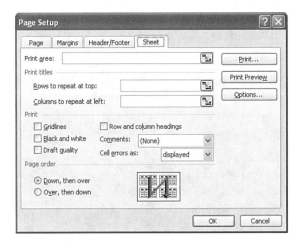

Figure 14.3   Use the Sheet tab to specify headings you want to repeat in the printout.

3. To repeat column labels and a worksheet title, click the **Shrink** button to the right of the Rows to Repeat at Top text box.

4. Drag over the rows that you want to print on every page. A dashed line border surrounds the selected area, and absolute cell references with dollar signs ($) appear in the Rows to Repeat at Top text box.

5. Click the **Expand** button on the collapsed dialog box to expand the Page Setup dialog box.

6. To repeat row labels that appear on the left of the worksheet, click the **Shrink** button to the right of the Columns to Repeat at Left text box. Excel reduces the Page Setup dialog box.

7. Select the columns that contain the row labels you want to repeat.

8. Click the **Expand** button to return again to the Page Setup dialog box.

9. To print your worksheet, click **Print** to display the Print dialog box. Then click **OK**.

 TIP   **Select Your Print Area Carefully**   If you select rows or columns to repeat, and those rows or columns are part of your print area, the selected rows or columns might print twice. To fix this, select your print area again, leaving out the rows or columns you're repeating.

Scaling a Worksheet to Fit on a Page

If your worksheet is too large to print on one page even after you change the orientation and margins, consider using the **Fit To** option. This option shrinks the worksheet to make it fit on the specified number of pages. You can specify the document's width and height.

Follow these steps to scale a worksheet to fit on a page:

1. Select the **File** menu and then select **Page Setup**. The Page Setup dialog box appears.

2. Click the **Page** tab to display the Page options.

3. In the Fit to XX Page(s) Wide by XX Tall text boxes, enter the number of pages into which you want Excel to fit your data (don't try to cram too much information on a page; this will make the font very small and the data difficult to read).

4. Click **OK** to close the Page Setup dialog box and return to your worksheet, or click the **Print** button in the Page Setup dialog box to display the Print dialog box, and then click **OK** to print your worksheet.

 TIP   **Change the Page Orientation**   The Page tab of the Page Setup dialog box also enables you to change the orientation of the worksheet from Portrait to Landscape. Landscape orientation is useful if you have a worksheet with a large number of columns.

Adding Headers and Footers

Excel enables you to add headers and footers to your worksheets that will appear at the top and bottom of every page of the printout (respectively). The information can include any text, as well as page numbers, the current date and time, the workbook filename, and the worksheet tab name.

You can choose the headers and footers that Excel suggests, or you can include any text plus special commands to control the appearance of the header or footer. For example, you can apply bold, italic, or underline to the header or footer text. You can also left-align, center, or right-align your text in a header or footer (see Lesson 9, "Changing How Numbers and Text Look," for more information).

To add headers and footers, follow these steps:

1. Select the **File** menu and then select **Page Setup**. The Page Setup dialog box appears. Click the **Header/Footer** tab on the dialog box (see Figure 14.4).

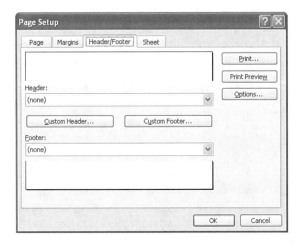

Figure 14.4   Add headers and footers with Header/Footer options.

2. To select a header, click the **Header** drop-down arrow. Excel displays a list of suggested header information. Scroll through the list and click a header you want. The sample header appears at the top of the Header/Footer tab.

 TIP   **Don't See One You Like?**   If none of the suggested headers or footers suit you, click the **Custom Header** or **Custom Footer** button and enter your own information.

3. To select a footer, click the **Footer** drop-down arrow. Excel displays a list of suggested footer information. Scroll through the list and click a footer you want. The sample footer appears at the bottom of the Header/Footer tab.

4. Click **OK** to close the Page Setup dialog box and return to your worksheet, or click the **Print** button to display the Print dialog box and click **OK** to print your worksheet.

TIP **Don't Want Headers or Footers Any More?** To remove the header and/or footer, choose **(None)** in the **Header** and/or **Footer** lists.

Setting Sheet Settings

The Sheet tab of the Page Setup dialog box allows you to specify a number of print settings such as the area of the worksheet to be printed and whether or not gridlines should be included on the printout. Figure 14.5 shows the Sheet tab.

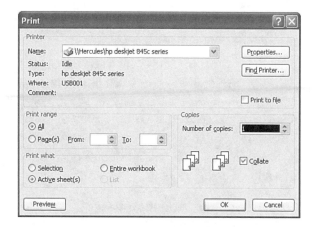

Figure 14.5 The Sheet tab gives you control over a number of print-related parameters.

Settings related to printing that are controlled on the Sheet tab are as follows:

• **Print area**—You can specify what part of a worksheet is printed. Click the Shrink button to the right of the Print area box and then select the area to print. Press Enter to return to the dialog box.

• **Print titles**—You can specify columns or rows to be printed on each page of the printout. This is used to repeat column headings or row headings on each page of a large worksheet. Use the appropriate shrink button to specify the range of the rows or columns to repeat.

- **Print settings**—The Print area of the Sheets tab allows you to specify what should be placed on the printed pages. This includes check boxes for gridlines, black and white, or draft printout and row and column headings (the number and letter designations of the row and columns).

- **Page order**—This allows you to specify how subsequent pages are created as a worksheet that will not fit on a single page is printed. The default **Down, and then over** moves down the worksheet, printing additional pages; when it reaches the bottom of the sheet it moves over to continue printing the data. The **Over, and then down** option moves across the worksheet from left to right printing pages and then moves down as it continues printing the worksheet.

After you have set the options of the Sheet tab, you can close the Page Setup dialog box. Click **OK** to close it.

Printing Your Workbook

After adjusting the page settings for the worksheet and previewing your data, it is time to print. You can print selected data, selected sheets, or the entire workbook.

To print your workbook, follow these steps:

1. If you want to print a portion of the worksheet, select the range of cells you want to print. To print only a chart, click it (you learn about creating charts in Lesson 15, "Creating Charts"). If you want to print one or more worksheets within the workbook, select the worksheet tabs (see Lesson 13, "Managing Your Worksheets"). To print the entire workbook, skip this step.

2. Select the **File** menu and then select **Print** (or press **Ctrl+P**). The Print dialog box appears, as shown in Figure 14.6.

 TIP **Print Using the Default Settings**   If you click the **Print** button (instead of using the **File** menu and clicking **Print**), Excel prints your current worksheet without letting you make any selections.

3. Select the options you would like to use:
   - **Print Range**—Enables you to print one or more pages. For example, if the selected print area contains 15 pages and you want to print only pages 5–10, select **Page(s)** and then type the numbers of the first and last page you want to print into the **From** and **To** boxes.
   - **Print What**—Enables you to print the currently selected cells, the selected worksheets, or the entire workbook.

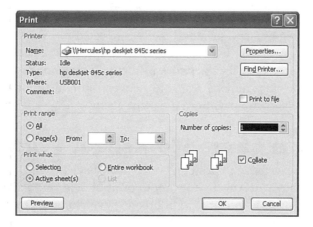

Figure 14.6   In the Print dialog box, select your printer and a page range to print.

- **Copies**—Enables you to print more than one copy of the selection, worksheet, or workbook.

- **Collate**—Enables you to print a complete copy of the selection, worksheet, or workbook before the first page of the next copy is printed. This option is available when you print multiple copies.

4. Click **OK** to print your selection, worksheet, or workbook.

While your job is printing, you can continue working in Excel. If the printer is working on another job that you (or someone else, in the case of a network printer) sent, Windows holds your current job until the printer is ready for it.

Sometimes you might want to delete a job while it is printing or before it prints. For example, suppose you think of other numbers to add to the worksheet or realize that you forgot to format some text; you'll want to fix these things before you print the file. To display the print queue and delete a print job, follow these steps:

1. Double-click the **Printer** icon in the Windows system tray (at the far right of the taskbar), and the print queue appears.

2. Click the job you want to delete.

3. Select the **Document** menu and then select **Cancel Printing**, or just press **Delete**.

To delete all the files from the print queue, open the **Printer** menu and select **Purge Print Documents**. This cancels the print jobs but doesn't delete the files from your computer.

The amount of control you have over printing documents depends on whether or not you are printing to a printer directly connected to your computer or a networked printer. In the case of a directly connected computer, you have the ability to cancel any and all print jobs. On a network printer you may not have the appropriate rights to purge or delete print jobs. See your network administrator if you cannot delete your own print documents from the print queue.

Selecting a Large Worksheet Print Area

You don't always have to print an entire worksheet; instead, you can easily tell Excel what part of the worksheet you want to print by selecting the print area yourself. If the area you select is too large to fit on one page, no problem; Excel breaks it into multiple pages. When you do not select a print area yourself, Excel prints either the entire worksheet or the entire workbook, depending on the options set in the Print dialog box.

To select a print area, follow these steps:

1. Click the upper-left cell of the range you want to print.

2. Drag downward and to the right until the range you want is selected.

3. Select the **File** menu, point at **Print Area**, and then select **Set Print Area**.

To remove the print area so you can print the entire worksheet again, select the **File** menu, select **Print Area**, and select **Clear Print Area**.

Adjusting Page Breaks

When you print a workbook, Excel determines the page breaks based on the paper size, the margins, and the selected print area. To make the pages look better and to break information in logical places, you might want to override the automatic page breaks with your own breaks. However, before you add page breaks, try these options:

- Adjust the widths of individual columns to make the best use of space.
- Consider printing the workbook using the Landscape orientation.
- Change the left, right, top, and bottom margins to smaller values.

After trying these options, if you still want to insert page breaks, Excel offers you an option of previewing exactly where the page breaks appear and then adjusting them. Follow these steps:

1. Select the **View** menu and select **Page Break Preview**.

2. If a message appears telling you how to adjust page breaks, click **OK**. Your worksheet is displayed with page breaks, as shown in Figure 14.7.

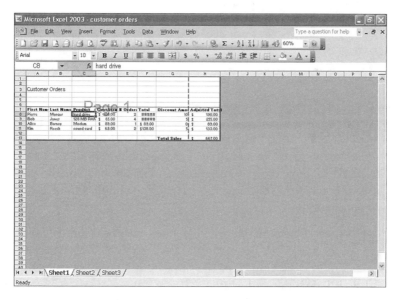

Figure 14.7   Check your page breaks before printing your worksheet.

3. To move a page break, drag the blue line to the desired location.

   To delete a page break, drag it off the screen.

   To insert a page break, move to the first cell in the column to the right of where you want the page break inserted, or move to the row below where you want the break inserted. For example, to insert a page break between columns G and H, move to cell H1. To insert a page break between rows 24 and 25, move to cell A25. Then, open the **Insert** menu and select **Page Break**. A dashed line appears to the left of the selected column or above the selected row.

4. To exit Page Break Preview and return to your normal worksheet view, open the **View** menu and select **Normal**.

Once you have modified the page breaks, you may want to take a look at the pages in Print Preview (click the **Print Preview** button on the Standard toolbar). This allows you to see how well balanced the pages are in terms of the amount of printed data and white space on the page.

Creating Charts

In this lesson, you learn how to create graphical representations (charts) of workbook data.

Understanding Charting Terminology

Charts enable you to create a graphical representation of data in a worksheet. You can use charts to make data more understandable to people who view your printed worksheets. Before you start creating charts, you should familiarize yourself with the following terminology:

- **Data Series**—The bars, pie wedges, lines, or other elements that represent plotted values in a chart. For example, a chart might show a set of similar bars that reflects a series of values for the same item. The bars in the same data series would all have the same pattern. If you have more than one pattern of bars, each pattern would represent a separate data series. For example, charting the sales for Territory 1 versus Territory 2 would require two data series—one for each territory. Often, data series correspond to rows of data in your worksheet (although they can correspond to columns of data if that is how you have arranged the information in your worksheet).

- **Categories**—Categories reflect the number of elements in a series. You might have two data series that compare the sales of two territories and four categories that compare these sales over four quarters. Some charts have only one category, and others have several. Categories normally correspond to the columns in your worksheet, with the category labels coming from the column headings.

- **Axis**—One side of a chart. A two-dimensional chart has an x-axis (horizontal) and a y-axis (vertical). The x-axis contains the data series and categories in the chart. If you have more than one category, the x-axis often contains labels that define what each category represents. The y-axis reflects the values of the bars, lines, or plot points. In a three-dimensional chart, the z-axis represents the vertical plane, and the x-axis (distance) and y-axis (width) represent the two sides on the floor of the chart.

- **Legend**—Defines the separate series of a chart. For example, the legend for a pie chart shows what each piece of the pie represents.

- **Gridlines**—Typically, gridlines appear along the y-axis of the chart. The y-axis is where your values are displayed, although they can emanate from the x-axis as well (the x-axis is where label information normally appears on the chart). Gridlines help you determine a point's exact value.

Working with Different Chart Types

With Excel, you can create many types of charts. Some common chart types are shown in Figure 15.1. The chart type you choose depends on the kind of data you're trying to chart and on how you want to present that data. The following are the major chart types and their purposes:

- **Pie**—Use this chart type to show the relationship among parts of a whole.

- **Bar**—Use this chart type to compare values at a given point in time.

- **Column**—Similar to the bar chart; use this chart type to emphasize the difference between items.

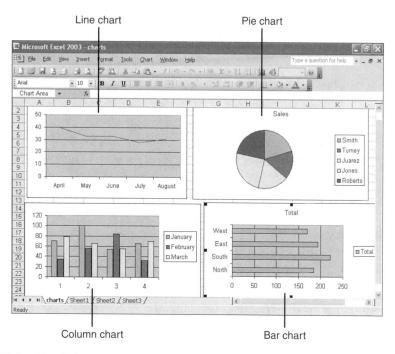

Figure 15.1   Excel chart types enable you to analyze and present your data.

- **Line**—Use this chart type to emphasize trends and the change of values over time.

- **Scatter**—Similar to a line chart; use this chart type to emphasize the difference between two sets of values.

- **Area**—Similar to the line chart; use this chart type to emphasize the amount of change in values over time.

Most of these basic chart types also come in three-dimensional varieties. In addition to looking more professional than the standard flat charts, 3D charts can often help your audience distinguish between different sets of data.

Creating and Saving a Chart

You can place your new chart on the same worksheet that contains the chart data (an embedded chart) or on a separate worksheet (a chart sheet). If you create an embedded chart, it is typically printed side by side with your worksheet data. Embedded charts are useful for showing the actual data and its graphical representation side by side. If you create a chart on a separate worksheet, however, you can print it independently. Both types of charts are linked to the worksheet data that they represent, so when you change the data, the chart is automatically updated.

The **Chart Wizard** button on the Standard toolbar enables you to quickly create a chart. To use the Chart Wizard, follow these steps:

1. Select the data you want to chart. If you typed column or row labels (such as Qtr 1, Qtr 2, and so on) that you want included in the chart, be sure you select those, too.

2. Click the **Chart Wizard** button on the Standard toolbar.

3. The **Chart Wizard - Step 1 of 4** dialog box appears (see Figure 15.2). Select a **Chart Type** and a **Chart Sub-Type** (a variation on the selected chart type). Click **Next**.

4. Next, Excel asks whether the selected range is correct. You can correct the range by typing a new range or by clicking the **Shrink** button (located at the right end of the **Data Range** text box) and selecting the range you want to use.

5. By default, Excel assumes that your different data series are stored in rows. You can change this to columns if necessary by clicking the **Series in Columns** option. When you're ready for the next step, click **Next**.

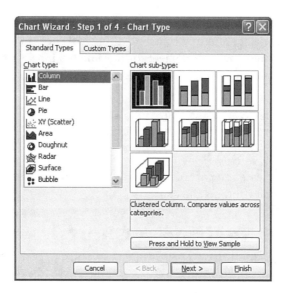

Figure 15.2 Choose the chart type using the Chart Wizard.

6. Click the various tabs to change options for your chart (see Figure 15.3). For example, you can delete the legend by clicking the **Legend** tab and deselecting **Show Legend**. You can add a chart title on the **Titles** tab. Add data labels (labels that display the actual value being represented by each bar, line, and so on) by clicking the **Data Labels** tab. When you finish making changes, click **Next**.

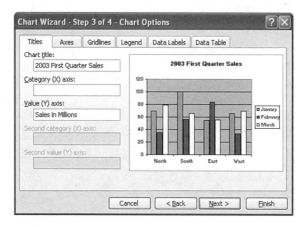

Figure 15.3 Select from various chart appearance options.

7. Finally, Excel asks whether you want to embed the chart (as an object) in the current worksheet (or any other existing worksheet in the workbook) or if you want to create a new worksheet for it. Make your selection and click the **Finish** button. Your completed chart appears.

 TIP **Create a Chart Fast!** To create a chart quickly, select the data you want to use and press **F11**. Excel creates a column chart (the default chart type) on its own sheet. You can then customize the chart as needed.

The charts you create are part of the current workbook. To save a chart, simply save the workbook that contains the chart.

Moving and Resizing a Chart

To move an embedded chart, click anywhere in the chart area and drag it to the new location. To change the size of a chart, select the chart and then drag one of its handles (the black squares that border the chart). Drag a corner handle to change the height and width, or drag a side handle to change only one dimension. (Note that you can't really resize a chart that is on a sheet by itself.)

Printing a Chart

If a chart is an embedded chart, it will print when you print the worksheet that contains the chart. If you want to print just the embedded chart, click it to select it, and then open the **File** menu and select **Print**. Be sure the **Selected Chart** option is turned on. Then, click **OK** to print the chart.

If you created a chart on a separate worksheet, you can print the chart separately by printing only that worksheet. For more information about printing, refer to Lesson 14, "Printing Your Workbook."

Access

Working in Access

In this lesson, you learn how to start Microsoft Access and become familiar with the Access application window. You will also learn what a database is and how to plan one.

Starting Access

Microsoft Access 2003 is a powerful, relational database application that allows you to create simple and complex databases. We will discuss what a database is and what Access database objects are in a moment, but first let us take a look at the Access application window. You can start Access in several ways, depending on how you've installed it. One way is to use the Start menu button. Follow these steps:

1. Click the **Start** button. A menu appears.

2. Point to **All Programs**. A menu of software applications installed on your computer appears. Select the Microsoft Office icon.

3. On the submenu that appears, click **Microsoft Office Access 2003**; Access starts.

 TIP   **Moving Programs Around on the Start Menu**   If you prefer to have Access in a different program group, open the **Start** menu and drag the Access item to another location of your choice.

You can also start Access using either of the following:

- Create a shortcut icon for Access that sits on your desktop; you can then start Access by double-clicking the icon. To create the shortcut icon, right-click on the Access icon on the Start menu and then click **Create Shortcut** on the shortcut menu that appears. A second Access icon appears on the Start menu. Drag it from the Start menu to the desktop.

- When you're browsing files in Windows Explorer, you can double-click any Access data file to start Access and open that data file.

Parts of the Access Window

Access is much like any other Office application: It contains menus, toolbars, a status bar, the Ask a Question box, and so on. Figure 1.1 provides a look at these different areas of the Access window. This view assumes that you have either created a new database or opened an existing database in the Access workspace. Creating a new database and opening an existing database are discussed in Lesson 2, "Creating a New Database."

Notice that in Figure 1.1 the Database window provides a list of icons on the left side for items such as Tables, Queries, Forms, and so on. It is these different items, called *Access objects*, that will make up your database. We will describe how each of these objects fits into the overall database later in the lesson.

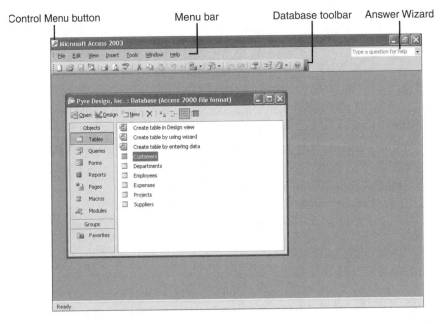

Figure 1.1   Access provides the typical tools provided by the members of the Microsoft Office suite of applications.

 Access Object   Access objects are the different items that make up a database such as tables, forms, queries, and reports.

You probably have noticed that most of the buttons on the toolbar are unavailable if you have opened Access and have not created or opened a database. That's because you haven't created any database objects, such as tables or forms, for the new database. The toolbar currently displayed in the Access window is the Database toolbar. Access differs from the other Office applications in that it has a different toolbar for each database object. In some cases, multiple toolbars exist for an object, depending on whether you are entering data into the object or changing the design parameters of the object.

For example, Access tables have two toolbars. The Table Datasheet toolbar provides you with tools that help you enter and manipulate the data in the table when you work with it in the Datasheet view. If you switch to the Design view of the table, a Table Design toolbar helps you manipulate the design settings for the table.

Because you will be working with each Access object type, you will also become familiar with each object toolbar. As you work with the various buttons on the toolbars, remember that you can place the mouse pointer on any toolbar button to see a ToolTip. The ToolTip shows the name of the button, which usually indicates what the particular tool is used for.

One other thing that should be mentioned related to the Access window is that only one database at a time can be open in the Access window. It doesn't enable you to work on multiple databases at the same time, as you could work with multiple documents in Word, or multiple workbooks in Excel.

 TIP **Choose Your Toolbars** As you work in Access on the various objects, right-click any toolbar to view a shortcut menu that provides a list of available toolbars. Typically, you are limited to the toolbar specific to the object that you are working on.

Exiting Access

Even though you have only barely gotten your feet wet with Access, take a look at how you exit the application. You can exit Access in several ways:

- Select **File**, and then select **Exit**.
- Click the Access window's **Close** (**X**) button on the upper right of the Access window.
- Press **Alt+F4**.

Now that you are familiar with the Access window, it is important for you to understand what makes up an Access database and how information or data is actually arranged and viewed in a database. We will begin the discussion by defining what a database is and how different objects in Access make up a database.

Understanding Access Databases and Objects

Strictly speaking, a *database* is any collection of information. Your local telephone book, for example, is a database, as is your Contacts folder in Outlook. Microsoft Access makes creating databases very straightforward and relatively simple. The electronic container that Access provides for holding your data is called a *table* (see Figure 1.2).

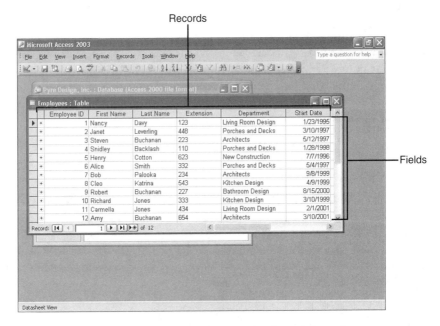

Figure 1.2 A table serves as the container for your database information.

A table consists of rows and columns. Access stores each database entry (for example, each employee or each inventory item) in its own row; this is a *record*. Each record contains specific information related to one person, place, or thing.

Table A container for your database information consisting of columns and rows.

Each record is broken up into discrete pieces of information, called fields. Each *field* consists of a separate column in the table. Each field contains a different piece of information and all the fields in one row make up a particular record. For example,

Last Name is a field. All the last names in the entire table (all in the same column) are the data that is held in the Last Name field of each record.

Record   A row in a table that contains information about a particular person, place, or thing.

Field   A discrete piece of information that is part of a record. Each column in the Access table is a different field.

Access is a special kind of database called a *relational database*. A relational database divides information into discrete subsets. Each subset groups information by a particular theme, such as customer information, sales orders, or product information. In Access, these subsets of data reside in individual tables like the one described previously.

Access enables you to build relationships between tables. These relationships are based on a field that is common to two tables. Each table must have a field called the primary key (you learn how to specify a field as the primary key in Lessons 3 and 4). The primary key must uniquely identify each record in the table. So, the primary key field is typically a field that assigns a unique number (no duplicates within that table) to each record.

For example, a Customers table might contain a Customer Identification field (shown as Customer ID in Figure 1.3) that identifies each customer by a unique number (such as your Social Security number). You might also have a table that holds all your customer orders. To link the Orders table to the Customers table, you include the Customer Identification field in the Order table. This identifies each order by customer and links the Order table data to the Customers table data.

Relational Database   A collection of individual tables holding discrete subsets of information that are linked by common data fields.

You will find that even a simple database consists of several tables that are related. Figure 1.3 shows a database and the different table relationships. Lesson 9, "Creating Relationships Between Tables," provides information on creating table relationships.

Indicates a link between tables

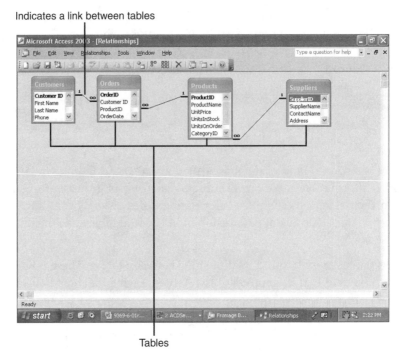

Tables

Figure 1.3 A relational database contains related tables.

The table is just one type of object found in Access. There are several more with which you can work, including forms, queries, and reports.

- A *form* is used to enter, edit, and view data in a table, one record at a time.
- A *query* enables you to ask your database questions. The answer to the query can be used to manipulate data in a table, such as deleting records or viewing the data in a table that meets only certain criteria.
- A *report* enables you to summarize database information in a format that is suitable for printing.

In essence, each of these different database objects gives you a different way of viewing and manipulating the data found in your tables. Each of these objects (including the table) should also be considered as you plan a new database.

Planning a Database

When you do create a new database, you want to make sure that the database is designed not only to meet your data entry needs, but also to meet your needs for viewing and reporting the data that is held in the various tables that make up the database. Taking a little time to plan your database before you create it can save you from headaches down the road. The sections that follow provide some tips on planning a database.

Determining Your Tables

Technically, you need only one table to make a database. However, because Access is a relational database program, it's meant to handle many tables and create relationships among them. For example, in a database that keeps track of customer orders, you might have the following tables:

- Customers
- Orders
- Products
- Salespeople
- Shipping Methods

Using many tables that hold subsets of the database information can help you avoid making redundant data entries. For example, suppose you want to keep contact information on your customers along with a record of each transaction they make. If you kept it all in one table, you would have to repeat the customer's full name, address, and phone number each time you entered a new transaction. It would also be a nightmare if the customer's address changed; you would have to change the address in every transaction record for that customer.

A better way is to assign each customer an ID number. Include that ID number in a table that contains names and addresses, and then use the same ID number as a link to a separate transactions table. Basically, then, each table in your database should have a particular theme—for example, Employee Contact Information or Customer Transactions. Don't try to have more than one theme per table.

A table design requirement is to be sure that every table you create uses the first field (the first column of the table) as a way to uniquely identify each record in the table. This field can then serve as the table's primary key. For example, customers can be assigned a customer number, or sales transactions can be assigned a transaction number. The primary key is the only way that you can then link the table to another table in the database.

It's a good idea to do some work on paper and jot down a list of tables that will be contained in the database and the fields that they will contain. Restructuring tables because of poor planning isn't impossible, but it isn't much fun, either. Tables are discussed in more detail in Lessons 3, 4, and 5.

Determining Your Forms

As already mentioned, forms are used for data entry. They allow you to enter data one record at a time (see Figure 1.4). Complex forms can also be constructed that actually allow you to enter data into more than one table at a time (this is because fields can be pulled from several tables in the same database into one form).

Figure 1.4 A form allows you to enter data one record at a time.

Planning the forms that you use for data entry is not as crucial as planning the tables that make up the database. Forms should be designed to make data entry easier. They are great in that they allow you to concentrate on the entry or editing of data one record at a time. You might want to have a form for each table in the database, or you might want to create composite forms that allow you to enter data into the form that is actually deposited into more than one table.

The great thing about forms is that they don't have to contain all the fields that are in a particular table. For example, if you have someone else enter the data that you keep in an employee database, but you don't want that data entry person to see the employee salaries, you can design a form that does not contain the salary field. Forms are discussed in more detail in Lessons 10, 11, and 12.

Determining Your Queries

Queries enable you to manipulate the data in your database tables. For example, a query can contain criteria that allow you to delete old customer records, or it can provide you with a list of employees who have worked at the company for more than 10 years.

Deciding the queries that you will use before all the data is entered can be difficult. However, if you are running a store—a cheese shop, for example—and know that it is important for you to keep close tabs on your cheese inventory, you will probably want to build some queries to track sales and inventory.

Queries are an excellent way for you to determine the status of your particular endeavor. For example, you could create a query to give you total sales for a particular month. Queries are, in effect, questions. Use queries to get the answers that you need from your database information. For more about Access queries, see Lessons 15 and 16.

Determining Your Reports

A report is used to publish the data in the database. It places the data on the page (or pages) in a highly readable format. Reports are meant to be printed (unlike tables and forms, which are usually used onscreen). For example, if you were running a club, you might want a report of all people who haven't paid their membership dues or who owe more than $1,000 on their account.

A report is usually for the benefit of other people who aren't sitting with you at your computer. For example, you might print a report to hand out to your board of directors to encourage them to keep you on as CEO. A report can pull data from many tables at once, perform calculations on the data (such as summing or averaging), and present you with neatly formatted results. Figure 1.5 shows a database report.

You can create new reports at any time; you don't have to plan them before you create your database. However, if you know you will want a certain report, you might design your tables in the format that will be most effective for that report's use. For more information on creating Access reports, see Lessons 17 and 18.

Designing good databases is an acquired skill. The more databases that you work with, the better each will be. Now that you've gotten your feet wet with database planning, take a look at how to start Access.

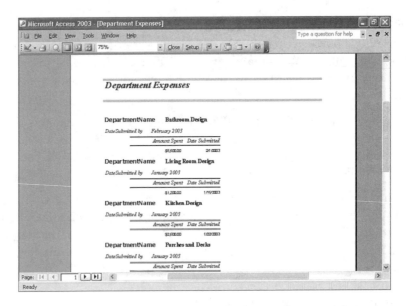

Figure 1.5 Reports allow you to organize and summarize database information.

Creating a New Database

In this lesson, you learn how to create a blank database and how to create a new database using a database template and the Database Wizard. You also learn how to close your database, open it, and how to find a misplaced database file.

Choosing How to Create Your Database

Before you can create your database tables and actually enter data, you must create a database file. The database is really just a container file that holds all the database objects, such as the tables, forms, and reports that I introduced in Lesson 1. You have three options for creating a new database: You can create a blank database from scratch, create a new database based on a database template, or you can create a new database based on the structure of an existing database file. This option actually creates a copy of the existing database file including the database's structure and the objects contained in the database (minus the data it contains). The third alternative would be great in situations where you want to share the structure for a database with a colleague and also show them how your data is organized in the database.

 TIP **What Are Projects?** Another option when you use the New File Task Pane is a project. Projects are Access front-ends or conduits to powerful SQL databases maintained on a server running Microsoft SQL Server. Access allows you to access this remote data just as you would a database that you created that you have saved on your computer.

Creating a new database based on a template (a template other than the Blank Database template) means that you take advantage of a Database Wizard, which not only creates your new database file but also helps you quickly create tables, forms, and other objects for the database.

 TIP **Database Wizard** Access provides several templates for creating new database files, and the Database Wizard walks you through the process of creating objects, such as tables, for the new database.

Whether you create your new database from scratch or use one of the database templates depends on how closely one of the Access templates meets your database needs. If one of the templates provides you with the type of tables and other objects necessary for your database, it makes sense to use a template. For example, if you want to create a database that helps you manage your company's inventory, you can take advantage of the Inventory Control template that Access provides. This template provides you with the basic tables and other objects to start the process of getting a handle on your inventory database.

In some cases, the templates might not meet your needs. For example, if you want to create a complex database that allows you to track sales, customers, and employee performance, it might be easier to create a blank database and then create each table for the database as needed. Let's start the overview of database creation with creating a blank database.

Selecting a Database File Type

One thing to discuss before you look at creating a new database is the database file format. By default, new databases created in Access are created in the Access 2000 file format. This makes your database files compatible with earlier versions of Access, such as Access 2000 and Access 97.

Saving the database in the Access 2000 file format does not prevent you from using any of the tools or features available in Access 2003. If you use your database files only in Access 2002 or 2003, you can set the default file format for new databases to Access 2002-2003. You must have a database (blank or otherwise) open to access the Options dialog box. Select the **Tools** menu, and then select **Options**. The Options dialog box opens.

Select the **Advanced** tab on the Options dialog box. Click the **Default File Format** drop-down box and select **Access 2002-2003**. Now let's take a look at creating new databases.

Creating a Blank Database

Creating a blank database is very straightforward. As mentioned previously, you are just creating the container file that holds all the objects that actually make up the database. To create a blank database, follow these steps:

1. In the Access window select the **New** button on the Database toolbar or select **File**, then **New**. The New File Task Pane will appear.

2. Select **Blank Database** in the task pane. The File New Database dialog box appears (see Figure 2.1).

Figure 2.1   Provide a location and a name for the new database file.

3. Use the Save In drop-down box to locate the folder in which you want to save the new database. Type a name for the new file into the File Name text box.

4. When you are ready to create the database file, click **Create**. The new database window appears in the Access workspace (see Figure 2.2).

Figure 2.2   A new database window opens in Access.

The database window provides you with a set of icons that enable you to select a particular object type. For example, the Tables icon is selected by default after you create the new database (which makes sense, because you need to create at least one table before you can create any of the other object types, such as a form or a report).

Shortcuts for different methods of creating tables are provided at the top of the Object pane. After you create a new table for the database, it is listed in this pane. In Lesson 3, "Creating a Table with the Table Wizard," and Lesson 4, "Creating a Table from Scratch," you will take a look at creating tables.

The database window enables you to view the different objects that you've created for a particular database (or those that were created when you used the Database Wizard). When you want to switch the database window's focus to a different Access object, all you have to do is click the appropriate icon in the Objects list.

 TIP **Different Ways to View the Database Windows** The toolbar on the database window provides buttons for opening or creating a particular database object, such as a table or a form. The toolbar also provides buttons that can be used to change the view in the Object pane: **Large Icons**, **Small Icons**, **List** (the default view) and **Details** (which provides information such as when the object was last modified). To collapse the icons shown on the left side of the Database window to categories such as Objects, click the **Groups** button.

Creating a Database from a Template

Another option for creating a new database is using one of the Access database templates. Templates are available for asset tracking, contact management, inventory control, and other database types. Another perk of using an Access template to create a new database is that a Database Wizard creates tables and other objects, such as forms and reports, for the new database. The wizard also sets up the relationships between the various tables (making your database relational).

Your interaction with the Database Wizard is somewhat limited; the wizard allows you to select the fields that will be used in the tables that it creates for the database. However, you don't have a say about which tables are initially created (tables can always be deleted later if you don't need them). You are, however, given the opportunity to select the format for screen displays (for forms and reports) and select the format for printed reports.

To create a database from a template, follow these steps:

1. In the Access window, open the New File task pane: Select **File**, **New**. In the Templates area of the New File task pane, click the **On My Computer** link.

2. The Templates dialog box appears. If necessary, click the Databases tab on the dialog box to view the database templates (see Figure 2.3).

3. Click the database template you want to use (for example, the Contact Management template) and then click **OK**. The File New Database dialog box appears (refer to Figure 2.1).

Figure 2.3 Access provides several database templates.

4. Specify a location for the database using the Save In drop-down list, type a name for the database, and then click **Create** to continue. A new database file is created, and then the Database Wizard associated with the template starts. For example, if you chose the Contact Management template, the wizard appears and explains the type of information that the database holds.

5. To move past the wizard's opening screen, click **Next**. On the next screen, a list of the tables that will be created appears (see Figure 2.4). The tables in the database are listed on the left of the screen and the selected table's fields appear on the right.

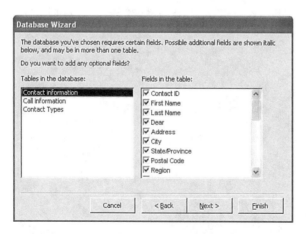

Figure 2.4 You can examine and deselect (or select) the fields that will be contained in each table.

6. Select a table to examine its fields. If you do not want to include a field in the table, clear the check box next to the field name. Optional fields are also listed for each field and are shown in italics. To include an optional field, click it to place a check mark next to it. When you have finished viewing the tables and their fields, click **Next** to continue.

CAUTION

Be Careful Deselecting Fields!   Because you are stuck with the tables that the Database Wizard creates, you must be very careful removing fields from the tables. This is especially true of fields that uniquely identify the records in a table, such as Contact ID. These fields are often used to relate the tables in the database. You might want to leave all the fields alone initially when you use the wizard.

7. The next screen asks you to select the screen display style you want to use. This affects how forms appear on the screen. Click a display style in the list to preview the style; after selecting the style you want to use, click **Next**.

8. On the next screen, the wizard asks you to choose a visual style for your printed reports. Click a report style and examine the preview of it. When you decide on a style, click it, and then click **Next**.

TIP

Report Background   The colored backgrounds used for some report styles look nice onscreen, but they don't print well on a black-and-white printer. Unless you have access to a color printer, stick to plain backgrounds for the best report printouts.

9. On the next wizard screen, you are asked to provide a title for the database. This title appears on reports and can be different from the filename. Enter a title as shown in Figure 2.5.

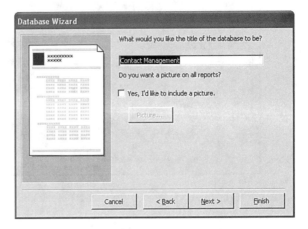

Figure 2.5   Enter a title for the database, and as an option, choose a graphic to use for a logo.

10. (Optional) To include a picture on your forms and reports (for example, your company's logo), click the **Yes, I'd Like to Include a Picture** check box. Then click the **Picture** button, choose a picture file from your hard drive (or other source), and click **OK** to return to the wizard.

11. Click **Next** to continue. You are taken to the last wizard screen. On this screen there is a checkbox that says "Yes, start the database." Make sure that this is selected so that the database will open when you complete the process. Click **Finish** to open the new database. The wizard goes to work creating your database and its database objects.

When the wizard has finished creating the database, the database's Main Switchboard window appears (see Figure 2.6). The Main Switchboard opens automatically whenever you open the database.

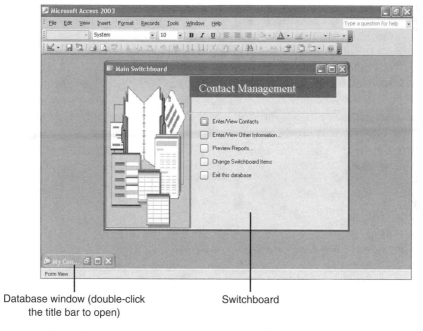

Database window (double-click   Switchboard
the title bar to open)

Figure 2.6 The Switchboard window is a database navigation tool provided by the Database Wizard.

All the databases created using one of the Access templates (other than the Blank Database template) include a Main Switchboard. The Switchboard is actually a form with some programming built into it. It enables you to perform common tasks related to database management by clicking a button. It is very useful when a person is unfamiliar with how to manipulate the various objects in a database.

For example, to enter or view contacts in the database shown in Figure 2.6, you would click **Enter/View Contacts**. This action opens a form (which is used to view and edit data into a database table) that allows you to view and enter contact information. If you click the Preview Reports button, a second Switchboard opens and you are provided with a list of ready-made reports that are available for you to view. Again, these reports were created by virtue of the fact that you used a template to create your new database.

Using the Main Switchboard for a database is a quick and straightforward way of quickly getting data into a database and taking advantage of a number of ready-made objects that were created for you. You will find, however, that as you become more familiar with Access, you will probably want to work with your database objects directly (such as tables, forms, and reports) and will no longer use the Main Switchboard. To close the Switchboard, click its **Close** (**X**) button.

TIP   **I Hate That Switchboard!**   To prevent the Switchboard from opening when you open the database, choose **Tools**, **Startup**. In the Startup dialog box, select the **Display Form/Page** drop-down list and select **[None]**. Click **OK**.

After you close the Switchboard window, you will find that the database window has been minimized in the Access workspace. Just double-click its title bar (at the bottom-left corner of the screen) to open it. To see the tables that the wizard created, click the **Tables** object type. Click the other object types (such as forms) to see the other objects that were created by the wizard.

The tables that the wizard creates are, of course, empty. After you fill them with data (either inputting the data directly into the table or using a form), you will be able to run queries and create reports.

Opening a Database

You have already taken a look at how to close a database; next, you walk through the process of opening a database file. The next time you start Access or after you finish working with another database, you need to know how to open your other database files.

One of the easiest ways to open a database you've recently used is to select it from the File menu. Follow these steps:

1. Open the **File** menu. You'll see up to four databases that you've recently used listed at the bottom of the menu.

2. If the database you need is listed there, click it.

TIP   **Want to See More Files?**   To increase the number of files displayed in this list, open the **Tools** menu and select **Options**. Then, from the **General** tab of the Options dialog box, select a number from 1 to 9 (the default is 4) in the **Recently Used Files** drop-down list.

A list of recently used databases also appears on the tip of the Access task pane. You can open any of the files by clicking the filename (to open the task pane, select **View, Toolbars, Task Pane**).

If a file you want to open is not listed either on the File menu or the task pane, you can open it using the Open command. Follow these steps:

1. Select **File, Open**, or click the toolbar's **Open** button. The Open dialog box appears.

2. If the file isn't in the currently displayed folder, use the Look In drop-down list to access the correct drive, and then double-click folders displayed in the dialog box to locate the file.

3. When you have located the database file, double-click the file to open it.

Closing a Database

When you finish working with a database, you might want to close it so that you can concentrate on creating a new database (as you do in the next section). However, because Access allows you to have only one database open at a time, as soon as you begin creating a new database the currently open database closes. Opening an existing database also closes the current database (which is something you do later in this lesson).

If you want to close a database, there are a couple of possibilities: you can click the **Close** (**x**) button on the database window, or you can select **File, Close**. In either case, the database window closes, clearing the Access workspace.

Creating a Table with the Table Wizard

In this lesson, you learn how to create a table by using the Table Wizard.

Tables Are Essential

As discussed in Lesson 1, your tables really provide the essential framework for your database. Tables not only hold the data that you enter into the database, but they are designed so that relationships can be established between the various tables in the database. Tables can be created from scratch, as discussed in the next lesson, or they can be created using the Table Wizard.

Working with the Table Wizard

The Table Wizard can save you a lot of time by supplying you with all the needed fields and field formats for entering your database information. Access provides a large number of different kinds of tables that you can create with the wizard. The wizard is also fairly flexible, allowing you to select the fields the table will contain and the way in which they will be arranged. You can also change the name of a field during the process. If the wizard doesn't provide a particular field, you can always add it to the table later, as discussed in Lesson 5, "Editing a Table's Structure."

To create a table using the Table Wizard, make sure you've opened a database as described in Lesson 2 and then follow these steps:

1. In the database window, click the **Tables** object icon, and then double-click the **Create Table by Using Wizard** icon. The Table Wizard opens.

   TIP **Alternative Routes** You can also start the Table Wizard by clicking the **New** button in the database window or choosing **Insert**, **Table**. In both cases, the New Table dialog box opens. Then, choose **Table Wizard** and click **OK**.

2. On the first Table Wizard screen, you can select from two categories of table types: **Business** or **Personal**. Your choice determines the list of sample tables that appears (see Figure 3.1).

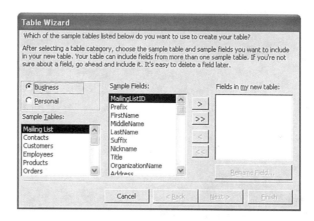

Figure 3.1 Select either the Business or Personal category to view a list of tables.

3. Select a table in the Sample Tables list; its fields appear in the Sample Fields list.

4. To include a field from the Sample Fields list in the table, select the field and click the **Add (>)** button to move it to the **Fields in My New Table** list. You can include all the fields in the Sample Fields list by clicking the **Add All (>>)** button.

5. If you want to rename a field that you have added, click the **Rename Field** button, type a new name into the Rename Field box, and then click **OK**.

> **TIP** **Remove Unwanted Fields** If you add a field that you don't want in the table, select the field in the **Fields in My New Table** list and click the **Remove (<)** button. To remove all the fields and start over, click **Remove All (<<)**.

6. Repeat steps 3 and 4 as needed to select more fields for the table. You can select fields from more than one of the sample tables for the table that you are creating (remember that you want fields in the table related only to a particular theme, such as customer information). When you're finished adding fields, click **Next** to continue.

7. The next screen asks you to provide a name for the table (see Figure 3.2). Type a more descriptive name if necessary to replace the default name.

8. This dialog box also asks whether you want the wizard to create a primary key for the table or allow you to select the primary key yourself. For example, CustomerID is an excellent primary key because each customer is assigned a different ID number. In this case, click **Yes, Set a Primary Key for Me** to have the wizard choose your primary key field. You can learn to set your own primary keys in Lesson 4, "Creating a Table from Scratch."

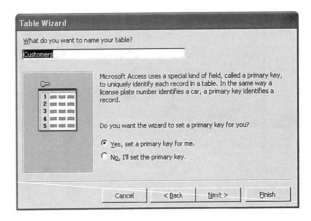

Figure 3.2   Provide a name for the table and allow the wizard to select a primary key for the table.

 Primary Key   The field that uniquely identifies each record in the table. Every table must have a primary key. This is usually an ID number because most other fields could conceivably hold the same data for more than one record (for example, you might have several people with the last name of Smith).

9. Click **Next** to continue. Because you're allowing the wizard to select the primary key, you are taken to the last wizard screen. On the last wizard screen, you have the options of modifying the table's design, entering data directly into the new table, or having the wizard create a data entry form for you. To see the table the wizard created, go with the default: Enter Data Directly into the Table (see Figure 3.3).

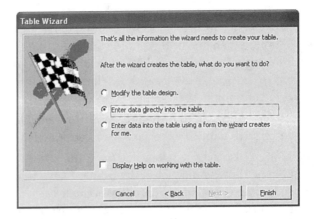

Figure 3.3   After completing the table, you can have the wizard open it so that you can enter data.

10. Click **Finish**.

The new table appears in the Access workspace (see Figure 3.4). From here you can enter data into the table, the specifics of which are discussed in Lesson 6, "Entering Data into a Table." When you close the table, it appears in the Object pane of the database window (you must also select the Tables object icon).

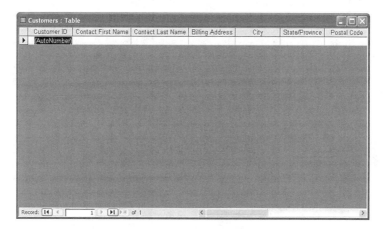

Figure 3.4   Your new table appears in the Access workspace when you close the Table Wizard.

Creating a Table from Scratch

In this lesson, you learn how to create a table in Table Design view.

Creating Tables Without the Wizard

Although the Table Wizard provides an easy method for quickly creating tables, it does not provide you with complete control over all the aspects of creating the table's structure. It does allow you to select the fields used in the table from a set list, but it restricts you to only those predefined fields (there are also several types of fields, each used for a different data type).

When you work with tables you work in two different views: the Datasheet view and the Design view. The Datasheet view is used to enter, view and edit data. The Design view is available to create and edit a table's structure. Creating tables from scratch in the Design view allows you to build the table from the bottom up and gives you complete control over all aspects of the table's design.

Design View   This view allows you to enter field names, select the data type that a field will hold, and customize each field's properties. A Design view is available for all the Access objects, including tables, forms, queries, and reports.

The Design view isn't the only way to create a table from scratch in Access. You can also create a table in the Datasheet view by labeling your field columns directly on the table's datasheet; this method is similar to creating a worksheet in Excel. We will take a look at both methods for creating a new table.

Datasheet View   This view places each record in a separate row and each field in a separate column (column headings are provided by the field names). This view is used to enter data directly into the table. You will use the Datasheet view whenever you want to view the records in the table or add or edit records.

Creating a Table in Table Design View

When you create a table in the Design view, you are creating the structure for the table; you create a list of the fields that will be in the table. You also select the data type for each field. (Fields can hold text, numbers, even graphics—you learn the types of fields that can be created later in this lesson.) You also have the option of entering a description for each field. Field descriptions are useful in that they provide a quick summary of the type of data that goes into the field.

Another issue that relates to creating a table in the Design view (or editing a table's structure in the Design view) is that any changes you make must be saved before closing the table. If you have worked in other applications, such as Word or Excel, you might think that saving your work is just common sense. However, when you actually start working on entering data into a table or a form, Access automatically saves your records as you enter them. Therefore, in Access, you need to remember to save only the changes that you make to the structure of a table, form, query, or report. You learn more about this in Lesson 5, "Editing a Table's Structure."

 TIP **Field Naming Rules** Field names in Access can be up to 64 characters long and can contain spaces and both alphanumeric and numeric characters. You can't use periods or exclamation points in your field names. Also, avoid special characters (such as $, %, or #) in field names because some of these characters have special meanings in Access code. Access lets you know if you've used an invalid character and allows you to make the necessary corrections.

To create a table in Table Design view, follow these steps:

1. In the database window (of any database) click the **Tables** icon if necessary, and then double-click **Create Table in Design View**. The Table Design view opens (see Figure 4.1).

2. Be sure that the insertion point is in the first row of the Field Name column. Type the field name for the first field in your table. Then, press **Tab** or **Enter** to move to the Data Type column.

3. When you move to the Data Type column, an arrow appears for a drop-down list. The default data type setting is Text; several other data types are available, such as AutoNumber, which automatically numbers each of your records (incrementally). This field type is excellent for customer number fields or employee ID fields. Click the **Data Type** drop-down list and select a field type that suits your needs. The different data types are discussed later in this lesson, in the section "Understanding Data Types and Formats."

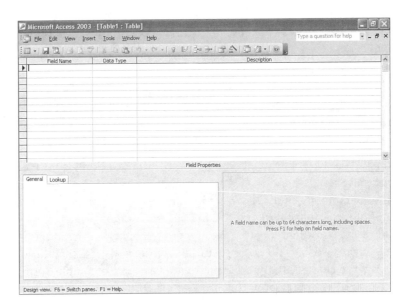

Figure 4.1   The Table Design view allows you to create the structure for your table.

4. After selecting the data type, press **Enter** to move to the Description column; type a description for the field. (This is optional—the table will work fine without it—however, describing the fields reminds any user of the database what type of information should go into that particular field.)

 TIP   **Deleting a Field**   If you enter a field and decide that you don't want it in the table's structure, select the field (its entire row) and press the **Delete** key.

5. Enter other fields and their field types (descriptions are optional) as needed. Figure 4.2 shows the structure for a table that will be used to enter product information.

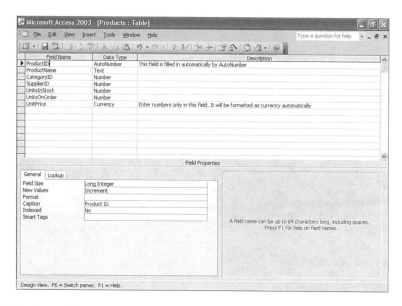

Figure 4.2 A table's structure consists of several fields; fields may differ by field type.

Setting the Primary Key

An important aspect of table structure design is that each table must have a field that is used to uniquely identify the records in the table. This field is called the *primary key*. Setting an appropriate key is trickier than it seems because no two records can have the same key value. In a table of customers, for example, you might think the Last Name field would be a good key, but this theory falls flat as soon as you have more than one customer with the same last name. A more appropriate primary key for your customers is a Social Security number (although people don't like to give these out) because it uniquely identifies each customer.

A good general rule is to create an identification field, such as a customer number, that allows you to assign a sequential number to each customer as you add them to your database table. Access can even help you out with the assigning of numbers to the customers because you can make the field type for the Customer Number field AutoNumber. An AutoNumber field type assigns a number to each record starting with the number 1.

TIP **Creating the Primary Key** Typically, the first field in the table serves as the primary key.

To set a primary key, follow these steps:

1. In Table Design view, select the field that you want for the primary key.

2. Select **Edit**, **Primary Key**, or click the **Primary Key** button on the toolbar. A key symbol appears to the left of the field name, as shown in Figure 4.3.

Primary Key

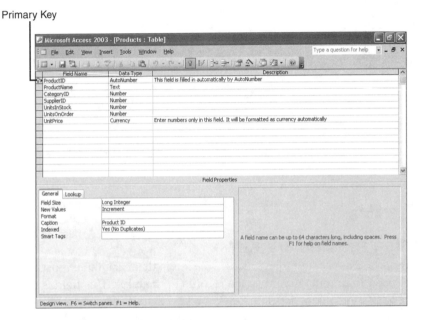

Figure 4.3   The primary key field is marked by a key symbol.

3. After you select the primary key and have finished entering your table fields, you should save the table. Click the **Save** button on the Table Design toolbar to open the Save As dialog box.

4. Enter a name for the table, and then click **OK**.

5. After saving the table, you can either switch to the Datasheet view (to enter data) by clicking the **View** button on the toolbar, or you can choose to close the table by clicking the table's **Close** (**X**) button.

TIP   **No Primary Key!**   If you attempt to close your new table in the Design view without specifying a primary key (even if you have saved the table), a message appears, letting you know that no primary key has been assigned. Click **Yes** on the message box to have Access assign a primary key to the table. If you have set up your table to contain an AutoNumber field, Access will make this field the primary key. Otherwise, Access creates a new AutoNumber field in the table and specifies it as the primary key. You can change the name of this new field as needed.

Understanding Data Types and Formats

To assign appropriate data types to the fields you create in a table, it is necessary for you to know what differentiates the different data types available for use with your table fields. When you create a field, you want to assign it a data type so that Access knows how to handle its contents. The following are the different data types you can choose:

- **Text**—Text and numbers up to 255 characters (numbers that are not going to be used in calculations).
- **Memo**—Lengthy text.
- **Number**—Numbers used in mathematical calculations.
- **Date/Time**—Date and time values.
- **Currency**—Numbers formatted for currency.
- **AutoNumber**—Sequentially numbers each new record. Only one AutoNumber field can be placed in a table. This field type is typically used for the primary key field.
- **Yes/No**—Lets you set up fields with a true/false data type.
- **OLE (Object Linking and Embedding)**—A picture, spreadsheet, or other item from another software program.
- **Hyperlink**—A link to another file or a location on a Web page. This field type lets you jump from the current field to information in another file.
- **Lookup Wizard**—This field type chooses its values from another table.

In addition to a field type, each field has other formatting options you can set. They appear in the bottom half of the dialog box, in the Field Properties area. The formatting options change depending on the field type; there are too many to list here, but Table 4.1 shows some of the most important ones you'll encounter.

Table 4.1 Formatting Options for Data Types

Formatting Option	Description
Field Size	The maximum number of characters a user can input in that field (applies only to text fields).
Format	A drop-down list of the available formats for that field type. You can also create custom formats.
Decimal Places	For number fields, you can set the default number of decimal places that a number shows.

Table 4.1   Continued

Formatting Option	Description
Default Value	If a field is usually going to contain a certain value (for example, a certain ZIP code for almost everyone), you can set that as the Default Value option. It always appears in a new record, but you can type over it in the rare instances when it doesn't apply.
Required	Choose **Yes** if a particular field is required to be filled in each record.

The best general rule for setting the data type for the field is to take a moment to consider what kind of data will go into that field. For example, if you are working with the monetary value of a product, you will probably want to use currency.

The different formatting options provided for a field in the Field Properties box are often used to help make sure that data is entered correctly. For example, the Field Size option can be used to limit a Number data type field to only a single or double digit. In the case of the default value, you can actually save data entry time because you use this option when a particular field almost always has a certain value or text entry.

Creating a Table in the Datasheet View

After you feel comfortable creating new tables in the Design view, you might want to dive right in and create tables in the Datasheet view. Creating tables this way immediately creates a table with 20 field columns and 30 record rows. This method still requires, however, that you enter the Table Design view to specify the key field, the field data types, field descriptions, and any field property changes.

Creating tables in the Datasheet view is really useful only if you feel the need to quickly enter some data into the table before setting up the table's properties. To create a table in the Datasheet view, follow these steps:

1. In the database window (with the Table icon selected), double-click **Create Table by Entering Data**. A new table in Datasheet view appears in the Access workspace (see Figure 4.4).

2. To enter the field names, double-click any field column heading (Field1, Field2, and so on). Then, type in the field name.

3. After you have placed the field names, you can begin entering data.

Creating a table in the Datasheet view might be fine for quickly entering data, but you will still probably need to switch to the Table Design view at some point and set up the various field data types and properties.

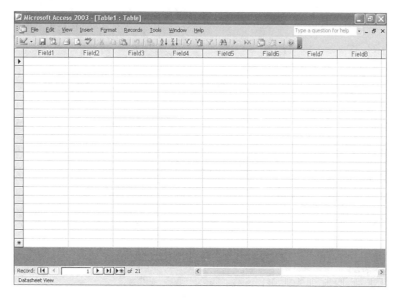

Figure 4.4   Tables can be created in the Datasheet view.

 You can switch to the Design view from the Datasheet view by clicking the **View** icon on the Table Datasheet toolbar. Remember to save any changes to the table's design that you make in the Design view.

TIP   **Use Copy and Paste to Build Tables**   You can copy fields from a table in the Design view and paste these fields into another table that you have open in the Design view. This is an easy way to "borrow" fields from a table and quickly create the structure for a new table. Copy and paste can also be used to copy records and field data from one open table to another (when in the Datasheet view).

Editing a Table's Structure

In this lesson, you learn how to change your table structure by adding and removing fields and using the Input Mask Wizard.

Editing Fields and Their Properties

After you've created a table with the Table Wizard or from scratch, you might find that you want to fine-tune the table's structure. This requires that you edit your fields and their properties.

You can delete fields, add new fields, or change the order of fields in the table. You also can change a field's data type. Because the table's structure is discussed here and not the data, you need to work in the Table Design view.

Get the Table's Structure Down Before Entering Data You should try to finalize the table's field structure and properties before you enter data. Changing data types or other field properties can actually delete data that you've already CAUTION entered into the table.

You can open an existing table in the Table Design view in several ways:

- In the database window, click the **Table** object icon, select the table you want to work with in the right pane of the database window, and then click the **Design** button on the database window's toolbar.
- Right-click the table in the database window and select **Design View** from the shortcut menu that appears.
- If you are in the table's Datasheet view, click the **View** button on the Table Datasheet view toolbar.

Changing Field Names and Data Types

When you are in the Design view (see Figure 5.1), you can enhance or rework your table's structure. For example, you can change a field's name. Just double-click the field's current name and type in a new one.

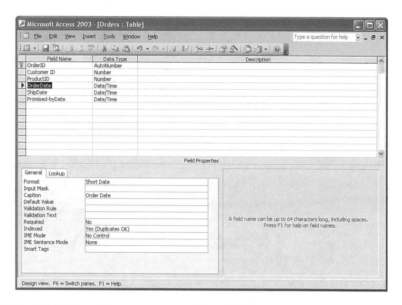

Figure 5.1 A table's existing structure can be edited in the Design view.

You can also change the data type for an existing field. Click the field's Data Type box and select a new data type from the drop-down list. Remember that when you change a field name or a field's data type, you must save the changes that you've made to the table's structure.

Setting Field Properties

Field properties can also be edited for each field using the various Properties boxes found in the Field Properties pane on the lower half of the table's window in Design view. Lesson 4, "Creating a Table from Scratch," provides a quick overview of some of the properties that are available.

Another very useful field property, particularly for fields that use text entries (remember that text entries can include numbers) is an *input mask*. An input mask is used to format data as you enter it into a field. For example, you might want to enter a date in a particular format, such as the format xx/xx/xxxx. The input mask can be used so that when you enter the data into the date field, all you need to enter is the two-digit input for the month and day, and four digits for the year. Access automatically places the slashes in the field for you.

Input Mask A field property that limits the number of characters that can be entered in a field.

Input masks are also very useful for entering ZIP codes. The input mask limits the number of characters that can be entered (such as those in a ZIP code), and if you use the 5-4 ZIP code format, the input mask can place the dash into the ZIP code for you.

To create an input mask for a field (such as a date field), follow these steps:

1. Click in the **Field Name box** to select the field for which you want to create the input mask.

2. In the Field Properties pane, click in the **Input Mask box**. The Input Mask Wizard button appears in the box.

3. Click the **Input Mask Wizard** button to open the dialog box shown in Figure 5.2.

Figure 5.2 The Input Mask Wizard helps you create an input mask for a field.

4. The Input Mask Wizard offers a list of possible masks for the field based on the field's data type. For example, Figure 5.2 shows the Input Mask Wizard used for a field with the Date data type. Select one of the mask formats listed, and then click **Next**.

5. The next wizard screen shows you the input mask you have chosen and gives you the opportunity to change the format. You can also test the input mask format by typing some data into the Try It box. Edit the input mask format if necessary and then click **Next** to continue.

6. You are taken to the last wizard screen. Click **Finish** to create the input mask. The input mask appears in the Input Mask box in the Field Properties pane (see Figure 5.3).

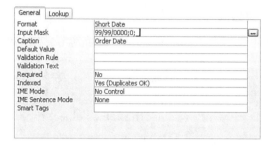

Figure 5.3   The input mask appears in the Input Mask box.

7. Click the **Save** button to save changes that you have made to the table structure.

Adding, Deleting, and Moving Fields

You can also add additional fields to your table's structure. All you have to do is add a new row to the field list and then enter the new field name and data type. Follow these steps:

1. Click the field selector (the gray square to the left of the field name) to select the field that will follow the new field that you create (in the field list).

2. Select **Insert**, **Row** (or click the **Insert Rows** button on the toolbar). A blank row appears in the Field Name list.

3. Enter a name, a data type, a description, and so on for the new field.

You can also delete any unwanted fields. Click the record selector for the field and then press the **Delete** key on the keyboard. A message box appears that requires you to confirm the field's deletion. Click **Yes** to delete the field.

CAUTION

Don't Remove Important Fields!   Be very careful about deleting fields after you start entering records into your table. When you delete a field, all the information stored for each record in that field is gone, too. The best time to experiment with deleting fields is before you enter any data into the table.

You can also rearrange the fields in the table. Click the record selector for the field to select the field. Then, use the mouse to drag the field to a new position in the field list. Remember to save any changes that you have made to the table's structure.

Deleting a Table

No matter how hard you work on a table's design, you might find as you design the other tables for your database that you just don't need a particular table. It's easy to delete a table (although it might not be easy to forget the time that you spent creating the table); simply follow these steps:

1. In the database window, click the **Tables** object type.

2. In the right pane of the database window, select the table you want to delete.

3. Select **Edit**, **Delete**, or press the **Delete** key on your keyboard.

4. A message appears asking whether you're sure you want to do this. Click **Yes**.

Entering Data into a Table

6

In this lesson, you learn how to add records to a table, print the table, and close it.

Entering a Record

After you've created the table and fine-tuned its structure, you are ready to enter data into the table. This means that you should have access to all the data that you need to enter. Then, all you have to do is open the table and input the data records.

> **TIP** **Using Forms to Enter Data** Access doesn't limit you to entering data directly into the table. You can also enter data using a form. Form creation and data entry using a form are covered in Lesson 11, "Modifying a Form."

First, from the database window, double-click the table in which you want to enter the records. The table opens in the Datasheet view (see Figure 6.1). If this is the first time you have entered data into the table, only one empty record appears in the table. As you complete each record, a new blank record (a new row) appears.

To enter records into the table, follow these steps:

1. Click in the first field of the first blank record (if necessary). If the first field is an identification field, such as Customer ID, and you selected the AutoNumber data type for the field, press **Tab** to advance to the next field (the AutoNumber field is automatically filled in for you).

2. Type the value for that field.

3. Press **Tab** to move to the next field and enter that field's data.

4. Continue pressing **Tab** and entering data until you complete the last field in the record. When you press **Tab** in the last field, a new record (a new row) appears, and the insertion point moves to the first field in the new record.

5. Continue entering field information in the records as required.

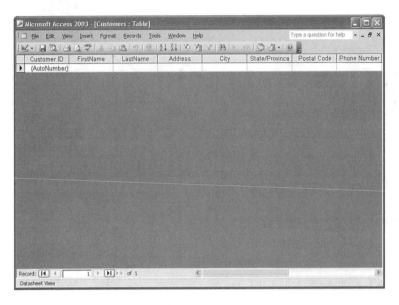

Figure 6.1   Enter data in the table's Datasheet view.

 TIP   **Data Entry Tricks**   Access offers some hotkey combinations for entering dates and data found in the same field in a previous record. To insert the current date, press **Ctrl+;** (semicolon). To insert the current time, press **Ctrl+:** (colon). To repeat the value from the same field in the previous record, press **Ctrl+'** (apostrophe).

You should be aware that, as you enter each field's data and move on to the next field, Access automatically saves your table data. This is very different from other Office applications, such as Word or Excel, where you must save your data after entering it.

 TIP   **Voice Data Entry**   Access and the other Office applications can accept data that is entered by voice. See Lesson 4, "Using the Office Speech Feature," in the "Office Introduction and Shared Features" section of this book.

Moving Around in a Table

So far, you've used the Tab key only to move from field to field in the table. You might have also used the mouse to move the insertion point from a field in one record to another field in that record, or to a field in a different record. Because you do your data entry from the keyboard, Access provides several keystrokes that can be used to navigate the various fields in the table. For example, you can back up one field in a record by pressing **Shift+Tab**. Table 6.1 summarizes the various keyboard shortcuts for moving around in a table.

Table 6.1   Table Movement Keys

To Move To	Press
Next field	Tab
Previous field	Shift+Tab
Last field in the record	End
First field in the record	Home
Same field in the next record	Down-arrow key
Same field in the previous record	Up-arrow key
Same field in the last record	Ctrl+down-arrow key
Same field in the first record	Ctrl+up-arrow key
Last field in the last record	Ctrl+End
First field in the first record	Ctrl+Home

Hiding a Field

When you are entering data into the table, you might find that you have not actually collected the data that you need to enter into a particular field. This means that you must skip this field in all the records as you enter your data (until you come up with the data).

You can hide a field or fields in the table datasheet. This doesn't delete the field column or disrupt any of the field properties that you set for that particular field. It just hides the field from your view as you enter your data. To hide a field, follow these steps:

1. In the Datasheet view, select the field or fields that you want to hide (click a field's column heading, as shown in Figure 6.2). To select multiple contiguous fields, click the first field, and then hold down the **Shift** key and click the last field.

2. Select **Format** and then **Hide Columns,** or right-click the column and select **Hide Columns**. The column or columns disappear.

3. Enter your data records into your table; the hidden column is skipped as you move from column to column.

4. When you have finished entering data into the other fields in the table, you can unhide the column. Select **Format, Unhide Columns**. The Unhide Columns dialog box appears (see Figure 6.3). Fields with a check mark next to them are unhidden; fields without a check mark are hidden.

		Customer ID	First Name	Last Name	Phone	Street	City	State	
▶	+	1	Pierre	Manger	(216) 555-1234	111 Eiffel Blvd	Paris	PA	5533(
	+	3	Bob	Jones	(216) 555-5436	1340 America Dr.	Crystal	PA	3501:
	+	4	Alice	Barney	(216) 555-7777	1420 Mineshaft Street	Big City	PA	6543:
	+	5	Kim	Reech	(512) 555-3843	55 Platinum St.	Los Angeles	OH	4424(
	+	6	Larry	Curly-Moe	(216) 555-8444	3 Stooges Lane	Hollywood	OH	4424(
	+	7	Edward	Reech	(345) 555-7778	456 Rural Lane	Friendly Heights	VA	6454
✳		(AutoNumber)							

Figure 6.2 You can select a column and then hide it.

Figure 6.3 The Unhide Columns dialog box shows you which columns are currently hidden.

5. Click the **check box** of any hidden field to "unhide" the field.

6. Click **Close**. The hidden column (or columns) reappears in the table.

Freezing a Column

Another useful manipulation of the field columns in an Access table that can make data entry easier is freezing a column. For example, if a table has a large number of fields, as you move to the right in the table during data entry, fields in the beginning of the table scroll off the screen. This can be very annoying if you lose your place, because you might not remember which customer you were entering data for.

You can freeze columns so that they remain on the screen even when you scroll to the far right of a table record. Follow these steps:

1. Click the column heading of the field column you want to freeze. This selects the entire column of data.

2. Click the **Format** menu; then click **Freeze Columns**.

3. The frozen field column moves over to the first field position in the table. Click anywhere in the table to deselect the field column.

4. When you move through the fields in a record toward the far right of the table, the frozen field column remains on the screen. This allows you to see important data such as the customer's name as you attempt to enter other data into a particular record.

You can freeze multiple columns if you want, such as the Last Name field and the First Name field. When you want to unfreeze the column or columns in the table, select the **Format** menu, and then select **Unfreeze All Columns**.

Using the Spelling Feature

To ensure your data entry accuracy, you can quickly check the spelling of the data that you have input into your table. This should help you clear up any typos that you might have made while you were entering the table records.

The Spelling feature, obviously, won't be able to check the numerical information that you input or help you enter proper names, but it can help you avoid embarrassing misspellings. To check the spelling in a table, follow these steps:

1. Click the **Spelling** button on the Table Datasheet toolbar, or you can select **Tools**, **Spelling** to open the Spelling dialog box (see Figure 6.4).

Figure 6.4   The Spelling feature enables you to quickly check for typos and misspellings in your Access table.

2. Words flagged as misspelled appear in the dialog box. A list of suggestions also appears from which you can choose a correct spelling. You can either correct the misspellings manually or click one of the suggestions. When you're ready, click **Change** to correct the spelling. The Speller then moves to the next misspelled word.

3. If you want to add the flagged word to the dictionary, click the **Add** button. If a flagged word is correctly spelled, click the **Ignore** button to ignore the word and continue with the spell check.

4. If the field containing the flagged word is a field that typically holds proper names or other values that the Spelling feature will always flag as misspelled, click the **Ignore "Field Name"** button.

Closing a Table

After you have finished entering data into a particular table and checking the spelling, you should close that table. Because the table is just like any other window, click the table's **Close (X)** button to close the table. You are returned to the database window.

Editing Data in a Table

In this lesson, you learn how to edit information in a field, select records, and insert and delete records.

Changing a Field's Content

After you enter the records in a table, you will probably find that you need to make some changes; sometimes data is entered incorrectly or the data for a particular record might actually change. Editing a field's content is easy. You can replace the old field content entirely or edit it.

Replacing a Field's Content

If the data in a field must be updated or has been entered incorrectly, the easiest way to replace this data is to enter the new data from scratch. To replace the old content in a field, follow these steps:

1. You can use the **Tab** key to move to the field you want to edit (the contents of the field will be selected), or select the contents of a field with the mouse. To use your mouse, place the mouse pointer on the upper left or right edge of the field. The mouse pointer becomes a plus sign (+) as shown in Figure 7.1. Click the field to select its content.

2. Type the new data, which replaces the old data.

3. You can then use the **Tab** key or the mouse to move to the next field you need to edit.

Field Selector

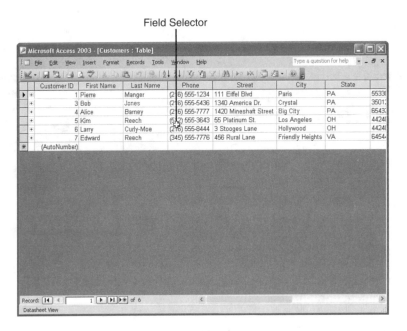

Figure 7.1   To select a field's entire content, make sure that the mouse pointer is a plus sign when you click.

Editing a Field's Content with a Mouse

Replacing the entire contents of a field is kind of a heavy-handed way to edit a field if you need to correct the entry of only one or two characters. You can also fine-tune your entries by editing a portion of the data in the field. Follow these steps:

1. Place the mouse pointer over the position in the field where you want to correct data. The mouse pointer should become an I-beam.

2. Click once to place the insertion point at that position in the field (see Figure 7.2). Now you can edit the content of the field.

	Customer ID	First Name	Last Name	Phone	Street	City	State	
+	1	Pierre	Manger	(216) 555-1234	111 Eiffel Blvd	Paris	PA	5533(
+	3	Bob	Jones	(216) 555-5436	1340 America Dr.	Crystal	PA	3501:
+	4	Alice	Barney	(216) 555-7777	1420 Mineshaft Street	Big City	PA	6543:
+	5	Kim	Reech	(512) 555-3643	55 Platinum St.	Los Angeles	OH	4424(
+	6	Larry	Curly-Moe	(216) 555-8444	3 Stooges Lane	Hollywood	OH	4424(
+	7	Edward	Reech	(345) 555-7776	456 Rural Lane	Friendly Heights	VA	6454-
*	(AutoNumber)							

Insertion point

Figure 7.2   Place the insertion point into a field to edit its content.

3. Press **Backspace** to remove the character to the left of the insertion point or **Delete** to remove the character to the right of the insertion point.

4. Enter new text into the field as needed. New entries in the field are inserted, meaning they displace the current entry but do not overwrite it.

Moving Around a Field with the Keyboard

Although the mouse provides a quick way to place the insertion point into a field, you might want to be able to navigate inside a field using the keyboard, especially when you are editing a fairly long field entry. Access provides several keyboard possibilities for moving inside a cell. Table 7.1 lists these keyboard-movement keys.

Table 7.1 Moving Within a Field

To Move	Press
One character to the right	Right-arrow key
One character to the left	Left-arrow key
One word to the right	Ctrl+right-arrow key
One word to the left	Ctrl+left-arrow key
To the end of the line	End
To the beginning of the line	Home

Moving and Copying Data

As in any Office application, you can use the Cut, Copy, and Paste commands to copy and move data in your table fields. This is particularly useful if you want to quickly copy a ZIP code that is the same for more than one customer, or you want to cut data that you put in the wrong field, so that you can paste it into the appropriate field. To use copy, cut, and paste, follow these steps:

1. Select the entire field or the portion of a field's content that you want to cut or copy.

2. Select **Edit**, and then **Cut** (to move) or **Copy** (to copy). Or press **Ctrl+X** to cut or **Ctrl+C** to copy.

3. Position the insertion point where you want to insert the cut or copied material.

4. Select **Edit**, **Paste**, or press **Ctrl+V** to paste.

 TIP   **Toolbar Shortcuts** You can also use the Cut, Copy, and Paste buttons on the Table Datasheet toolbar to manipulate text in the table fields.

Inserting and Deleting Fields

You can also insert and delete fields in the Table Datasheet view. This allows you to quickly enter the data into a new field or delete an unneeded field. It is preferable, however, to insert new fields into the table in the Design view and then enter data. This is because you will eventually have to switch to Table Design view to specify the data type or other properties of the new field (Lesson 5, "Editing a Table's Structure," covered inserting and deleting fields in the Design view).

To insert a field, follow these steps:

1. Select the existing field column in which you want to insert the new field. The new field column is inserted to the left of the currently selected field column.

2. Select **Insert, Column**. The new column appears in the table (see Figure 7.3).

Newly inserted field

Customer ID	First Name	Last Name	Field1	Phone	Street	City	
1	Pierre	Manger		(216) 555-1234	111 Eiffel Blvd	Paris	PA
3	Bob	Jones		(216) 555-5436	1340 America Dr.	Crystal	PA
4	Alice	Barney		(216) 555-7777	1420 Mineshaft Street	Big City	PA
5	Kim	Reech		(512) 555-3643	55 Platinum St.	Los Angeles	OH
6	Larry	Curly-Moe		(216) 555-8444	3 Stooges Lane	Hollywood	OH
7	Edward	Reech		(345) 555-7776	456 Rural Lane	Friendly Heights	VA
(AutoNumber)							

Figure 7.3   New field columns can be added to the table in the Datasheet view.

3. To name the new field, double-click the field heading (such as Field1) and type the new name for the field.

4. Enter data into the new field as needed.

Deleting a field or fields is also very straightforward. Remember, however, that deleting a field also deletes any data that you have entered into that field. Select the field that you want to delete and then select **Edit, Delete Column**. You are asked to verify the deletion of the field. If you're sure, click **Yes**.

Inserting New Records

As your customer base increases or other new data becomes available for your database, you will definitely be adding records to the various tables in the database. New records are inserted automatically. As soon as you begin to enter data into a record, a new blank record appears at the bottom of the table.

TIP   **Quickly Go to the Bottom of the Table Using the New Record Button**
As you enter records a new, blank record is automatically created at the bottom of
the table for you. However, you can use the New Record Button on the toolbar to
move from anywhere in the table (such as in an existing record) to the bottom of the
table and a blank new record.

This process is re-created every time you complete a record and then start a new
record. Inserting information into the first field of the new record inserts another
new record below the one you are working on.

You can't insert new records between existing ones or at the top of the table. New
records are always entered at the bottom of the table, below the last completed
record.

TIP   **What If I Want the Records in a Different Order?**   Although you can enter
new records only at the bottom of the table, you can rearrange the order of your
records if you want. This can be done using the sorting feature discussed in Lesson
15, "Creating a Simple Query."

Deleting Records

You will probably find that certain records in the table become outdated or no longer
pertinent to the database (such as an employee who has left your company but still
has a record in the Employee table). You can delete a record or several records at
a time.

To delete a record or records, follow these steps:

1. To select the record that you want to delete, click the **record selector** button (the
small gray box to the left of the record, as shown in Figure 7.4). If you want to
select multiple records, click and drag the record selector buttons of the contiguous records.

	First Name	Last Name	Phone	Street	City	State	Zip
+	Pierre	Manger	(216) 555-1234	111 Eiffel Blvd	Paris	PA	55330-4433
+	Bob	Jones	(216) 555-5436	1340 America Dr.	Crystal	PA	35012-6894
+	Alice	Barney	(216) 555-7777	1420 Mineshaft Street	Big City	PA	65437-8765
+	Kim	Reech	(512) 555-3643	55 Platinum St.	Los Angeles	OH	44240-9354
▶ +	Larry	Curly-Moe	(216) 555-8444	3 Stooges Lane	Hollywood	OH	44240-3210
+	Edward	Reech	(345) 555-7776	456 Rural Lane	Friendly Heights	VA	64544-3343
*							

Selected record

Figure 7.4   Select the record or records you want to delete.

2. To delete the record or records, perform any of the following:

- Click the **Delete Record** button on the toolbar.
- Press the **Delete** key on the keyboard.
- Select **Edit, Delete Record**.

3. A dialog box appears, letting you know that you are deleting a record and will not be able to undo this action. To delete the record or records, click **Yes**.

CAUTION

Deleting Records Affects the AutoNumber Sequence   When you delete records in the table that were assigned an identification number using the AutoNumber data type, that number (or numbers) will be lost from the sequence. For example, if you delete a customer with the AutoNumber customer ID of 3, the number 3 is removed from the sequence. When listing your customers, the customer numbers would then appear as 1, 2, 4, 5, and so on.

Formatting Access Tables

In this lesson, you learn how to improve the look of a table by adjusting the row and column sizes, changing the font, and choosing text alignment options.

Changing the Look of Your Table

Most people don't spend a lot of time formatting Access tables because they don't always use the table for data entry; instead, they use a form. Most people also don't typically print their tables. They use data-entry forms to see the records onscreen and reports to print their records. The tables are merely holding tanks for the raw data.

However, creating forms and reports might be more work than you want to tackle right now. And formatting a table so that data entry is a little less tedious (and less hard on the eyes) or so that you can quickly print a copy of a table (covered in Lesson 20, "Printing Access Objects") is certainly no crime. Making a table more readable onscreen is certainly nice for the person using the table to enter data.

Changing Column Width and Row Height

One common problem with a table is that you can't see the complete contents of the fields. Fields often hold more data than will fit across a column's width. This causes the data in your table to appear to be cut off.

You can fix this problem in two ways: make the column wider so that it can display more data, or make the row taller so that it can display more than one line of data.

Changing Column Width

Access offers many ways to adjust column width in a table; you can choose the method you like best. One of the easiest ways to adjust the column width is to drag the column headings. Follow these steps:

1. Position the mouse pointer between two field names (column headings) so that the pointer turns into a vertical line with left- and right-pointing arrows; this is the sizing tool (see Figure 8.1). You'll be adjusting the column on the left; the column on the right will move to accommodate it.

Column width sizing tool icon

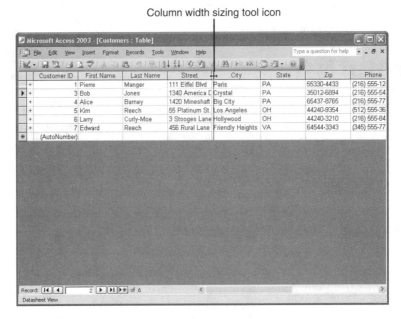

Figure 8.1   Position the mouse pointer between two column headings.

2. Click and hold the mouse button and drag the edge of the column to the right or left to increase or decrease the width.

3. Release the mouse button when the column is the desired width.

Alternatively, you can double-click the column's vertical border when the sizing tool is showing, which automatically adjusts the width of the column on the left so that it accommodates the largest amount of data entered in that particular field.

Another, more precise, way to adjust column width is to use the Column Width dialog box. Follow these steps:

1. Select the column(s) for which you want to adjust the width.

2. From the **Format** menu, choose **Column Width**, or right-click and choose **Column Width** from the shortcut menu. The Column Width dialog box appears (see Figure 8.2).

3. Do one of the following to set the column width:

- Adjust the column to exactly the width needed for the longest entry in it by clicking **Best Fit**.

- Set the width to a precise number of field characters by typing a value in the **Column Width** text box.

Figure 8.2   Adjust the column width precisely in the Column Width dialog box.

- Reset the column width to its default value by selecting the **Standard Width** check box.

4. Click **OK** to apply the changes.

Because changing the width of a field column in the table is actually changing the field's length (which you designated in the Design view when you created the table), you do need to save these changes. Click the **Save** button on the Table Datasheet toolbar.

Changing Row Height

You can also change the height of the rows or records in the table. This allows you to see more text in a field that contains a large amount of data, such as a memo field.

CAUTION

Adjusting One Row Height Adjusts Them All   If you change the height of one row, it changes the height of all the rows or records in the table. Edit the row height only in cases where it allows you to see more data in a particular field for each record.

One way to make rows taller (or shorter) is to drag a particular row's border, enlarging the record's row. Position the mouse pointer between two rows in the row selection area, and then drag up or down. Remember that this changes the height of all the rows in the table (meaning all the records).

Another way is to use the Row Height dialog box. It works the same as the Column Width dialog box, except that no Best Fit option is available. Select the **Format** menu and then choose **Row Height**. The Row Height dialog box appears.

Enter the height for the table's rows into the dialog box (or click **Standard Height** to return the rows to the default height) and click **OK**.

Changing the Font and Font Size

Unlike other Access views (such as Report and Form), the Datasheet view doesn't allow you to format individual fields or portions of the data that are entered in a particular view. You can format the font style only for the entire table. Font changes are automatically applied to all data in the table, including the field column headings.

Font changes that you make in Datasheet view won't affect the way your data looks in other Access objects, such as your reports, queries, or forms. They affect only the table itself.

There are some good reasons for changing the font style in a table. For example, you might want to increase the font size so that the field contents are easier to read. Or you might bold the data in the table so that you get a nice, crisp printout when you print the table.

Changing the Default Font Style

If the default style used in Access for tables has been bugging you from the beginning, you can change the default font used in Datasheet view for all the tables you create in Access.

Select **Tools**, and then **Options**. Select the **Datasheet** tab of the Options dialog box (see Figure 8.3).

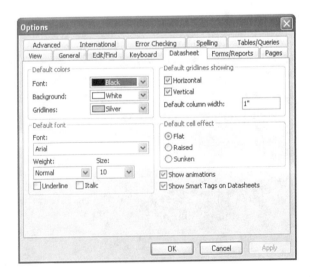

Figure 8.3   You can change the default Datasheet font properties in the Options dialog box.

Use the different drop-down menus in the Default Font box of the Datasheet tab to select the font name, font weight, or font size. When you have finished making your changes, click **OK**.

Changing the Font Style for a Table

Font changes that you make to a specific table override the default font settings. To choose a different font for a currently open table datasheet, follow these steps:

1. From the **Format** menu, choose **Font**. The Font dialog box appears (see Figure 8.4).

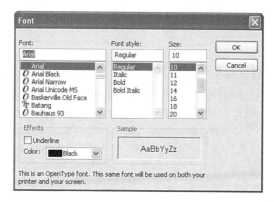

Figure 8.4   Select the different font options in the Font dialog box.

2. Select a font from the **Font** list box.

3. Select a style from the **Font Style** list box.

4. Select a size from the **Size** list box.

5. Select a color from the **Color** drop-down list.

6. (Optional) Click the **Underline** check box if you want underlined text.

7. You can see a sample of your changes in the Sample area. When you're happy with the look of the sample text, click **OK**.

Another way you can change the look of your table is with the Datasheet Formatting dialog box (choose **Format, Datasheet**). You can change the cell special effects, background color, the color of the grid lines between each row and column, and whether the lines show.

Creating Relationships Between Tables

In this lesson, you learn how to link two or more tables using a common field and create a relational database.

Understanding Table Relationships

You've already learned in Lesson 1, "Working in Access," that the best way to design a database is to create tables that hold discrete types of information. For example, one table can contain customer information, and another table can hold order information. By creating relationships between tables, you make it possible to combine information from the tables into forms, queries, and reports to produce meaningful results.

Suppose that you have two tables in your database. One table, Customers, contains names and addresses; the other, Orders, contains orders the customers have placed. The two tables both contain a common field: Customer ID. All records in the Orders table correspond to a record in the Customers table. (This is called a one-to-many relationship because one customer could have many orders.)

The secret to creating relationships revolves around the primary keys for your tables. For example, in a Customers table, the primary key is the Customer ID. It uniquely identifies each customer record. Then, when you design an Orders table, you make sure that you include the Customer ID field. In the Orders table, the Customer ID is not the primary key (it is actually called the foreign key); a field such as Order Number would be the primary key field. You include the Customer ID field in the Orders table so that order information can be linked to customer information in the Customers table.

 Foreign Key   A primary key field in a table that is duplicated in a second table (where it is not the primary key) and used to link the tables together.

Creating a Relationship Between Tables

To create a relationship between tables, open the Relationships window. Before you can create relationships between tables, you must first add the tables to the Relationships window. Follow these steps:

1. In the database, select **Tools**, **Relationships**, or click the **Relationships** button on the toolbar to open the Relationships window.

2. If you haven't selected any tables yet, the Show Table dialog box appears automatically (see Figure 9.1). If it doesn't appear, choose **Relationships**, **Show Table**.

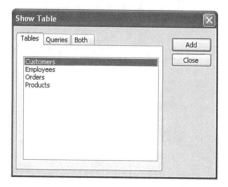

Figure 9.1   Add tables to your Relationships window with the Show Table dialog box.

3. Click a table that you want to include in the Relationships window, and then click the **Add** button.

> **TIP**   **Well-Designed Databases and Relationships**   In a well-designed database, every table in the database is related to at least one other table in the database. So, you might want to add all your tables to the Relationships window.

4. Repeat step 3 to select all the tables you require in the Relationships window, and then click **Close**. Each table appears in its own box in the Relationships window, as shown in Figure 9.2. Each table box lists all the fields in that table.

> **TIP**   **Enlarge the Table Box**   If you can't see all the fields in a table's box, drag the table border to make it large enough to see all the fields.

Fields in table

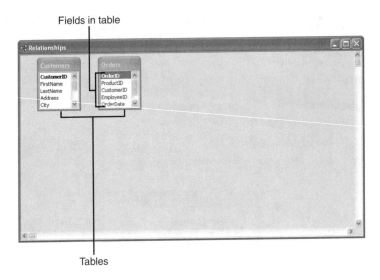

Tables

Figure 9.2 Tables in the Relationships window.

5. After you have the tables available in the Relationships window, you can create the relationships you want to exist between them. Remember that you must link the tables using a common field. For example, you can link the Customers table to the Orders table using the Customer ID field, as shown in Figure 9.2. Select the common field in the table where it is the primary key (in this case, the Customer table). Drag the field and drop it on its counterpart (the same field name) in the other table (in this case, Orders). The Edit Relationships window opens (see Figure 9.3).

Field Type Matters The fields to be linked must be of the same data type (date, number, text, and so on). The only exception is that you can link a field with an AutoNumber format to another field with a number format.

CAUTION

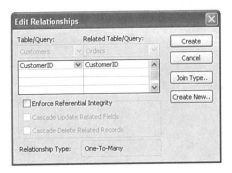

Figure 9.3 The Edit Relationships dialog box asks you to define the relationship you're creating.

6. The Edit Relationships dialog box shows the fields that will be related. It also allows you to enforce referential integrity, which you learn about in the next section. For now, click **Create**. A relationship is created, and you'll see a join line between the two fields in the Relationships window (see Figure 9.4).

Line shows relationship between tables

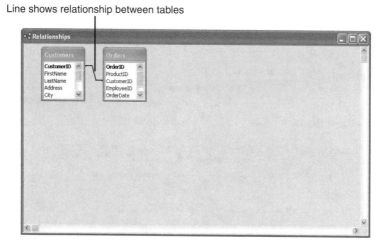

Figure 9.4   The join line represents a relationship between the two tables.

 When you create relationships between tables, it's important that you save them. Click the Save button on the Relationships toolbar to save the current relationships (and the list of tables available in the Relationships window).

Enforcing Referential Integrity

In the Edit Relationships box is a check box called Enforce Referential Integrity. What does this mean? *Referential integrity* means that data entered in a field that is used to link two tables must match from one table to another. Actually, the data entered in the table where the field does not serve as the primary key must match the entries that are in the table where the field serves as the primary key. This means that the table containing the primary key dictates what data can go into the foreign key field in the other table. If you don't have the data in the primary key field, it can't be entered in the foreign key field because it can't be referenced (and its integrity is in doubt).

TERM   **Referential Integrity**   When you enter data into the foreign key field used in the table relationship it must match data that is already contained in the primary key field in the other table. If the data differs, Access returns an error message.

For example, you could link a Customers table that has a Customer ID field as its primary key to an Orders table that also holds the Customer ID field, where it does not serve as the primary key (the Customer ID is providing the link for the relationship). If you enforce referential integrity, values entered into the Order table's Customer ID field must match values already entered into the Customers table's Customer ID field. Enforcing referential integrity is a way to make sure that data is entered correctly into the secondary table.

When referential integrity is breached during data entry, (meaning a value is entered into the secondary table in the relationship that was not in the linking field of the primary table), an error message appears (see Figure 9.5). This error message lets you know that the field value you have entered in the linking field is not contained in a record in the other table in the relationship (where the field is the primary key).

Figure 9.5 Enforcing referential integrity means that values entered in the linking field must be contained in the field in the table where it serves as the primary key.

Two other options are possible when data entered into a field violates referential integrity. Figure 9.6 shows the Edit Relationships dialog box with the Enforce Referential Integrity box selected. The two additional options provided are

- **Cascade Update Related Fields**—If this check box is selected, any data changes that you make to the linking field in the primary table (Customers, in this example) are updated to the secondary table. For example, if you had a customer in the Customers table listed with Customer ID 5 and you changed that to Customer ID 6, any references to Customer ID 5 would be updated to Customer ID 6 in the Orders table.

- **Cascade Delete Related Fields**—If this check box is marked and you change the linking field's data in the primary table so that it no longer matches in the secondary table, the field information is deleted from the secondary table. Therefore, if you changed a Customer ID number in the Customers table, the field data in the Customer ID field in the Orders table would be deleted.

You should probably set up your relationships and enforce referential integrity before you do any data entry in the related tables. You should also typically enter the data first into the table where the linking field is the primary key. For example, you should fill in as much of your Customers table information as possible before you try to fill the data fields in the related Orders table.

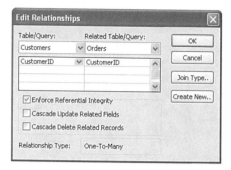

Figure 9.6   The Edit Relationships dialog box is used to change the options related to a particular relationship.

Be advised, however, that you do not have to enforce referential integrity for the tables to function correctly. The only risk that you run is that you can enter incorrect data into the foreign key field in the secondary table that does not match data in the primary key field in the primary table. This makes a mess out of forms, queries, and reports that you run taking advantage of the relationship between the tables (meaning Access won't be sure what to do with the incorrect data).

Editing a Relationship

You can edit any of the relationships that you create between your tables. Just double-click the relationship line, and the Edit Relationships dialog box appears (refer to Figure 9.6). For example, you might want to enforce referential integrity on an existing relationship or change other options related to the relationship as discussed in the previous section.

When you have finished editing the relationship, click OK to close the Edit Relationships dialog box. This returns you to the Relationships window.

Removing a Relationship

To delete a relationship, just click it in the Relationships window (the line between the tables turns bold to indicate that it is selected), and then press Delete. Access asks for confirmation; click Yes, and the relationship disappears.

If you delete relationships between tables, you are affecting how information in the tables can be combined in a query, form, or report. It is a good practice to design your tables so that they can be related. Remember that each table is supposed to hold a subset of the database information. If each table is set up correctly, it should have at least one other table in the database that it can be related to.

Creating a Simple Form

In this lesson, you learn how to create a form using the AutoForm, the Form Wizard, and from scratch.

Creating Forms

As discussed in Lesson 6, "Entering Data into a Table," entering data directly into a table has its downside. It can become difficult to concentrate on one record at a time, especially when you are working with a large number of fields and records, because information is constantly scrolling on and off the screen.

An alternative to entering data directly into the table is to use a form. With a form, you can allot as much space as you need for each field, you get to concentrate on one record at a time, and you can create forms that simultaneously enter data into more than one table. You can create a form in three ways:

- AutoForms provide very quick, generic forms that contain all the fields in a single table.
- The Form Wizard helps you create a form by providing a series of screens in which you can choose the fields and style for the form.
- Creating a form from scratch means that you work in the Form Design view and select the fields from the appropriate table or tables. This is the most difficult way to create a new form (at first), but it also provides the most control.

Creating a Form with AutoForm

The easiest way to create a form is with AutoForm. AutoForm takes the fields from a specified table and creates a form; it's not very flexible, but it is very convenient. To use the AutoForm feature, follow these steps:

1. From the database window, click the **Forms** object type.
2. Click the **New** button on the database window toolbar. The New Form dialog box appears (see Figure 10.1).

New Form button

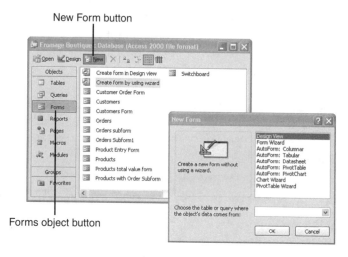

Forms object button

Figure 10.1   Choose how you want to create your form.

3. Select a type of form to create. Because we're going to use AutoForm, you can click several types of forms, including

- **AutoForm:Columnar**—A columnar form (the most popular kind). This creates a form that contains your fields in a single column, from top to bottom.

- **AutoForm:Tabular**—A form that resembles a table.

- **AutoForm:Datasheet**—A form that resembles a datasheet.

4. Open the drop-down list at the bottom of the dialog box and choose the table or query you want to use as the source of the form's fields.

5. Click **OK**. The form appears, ready for data entry (see Figure 10.2).

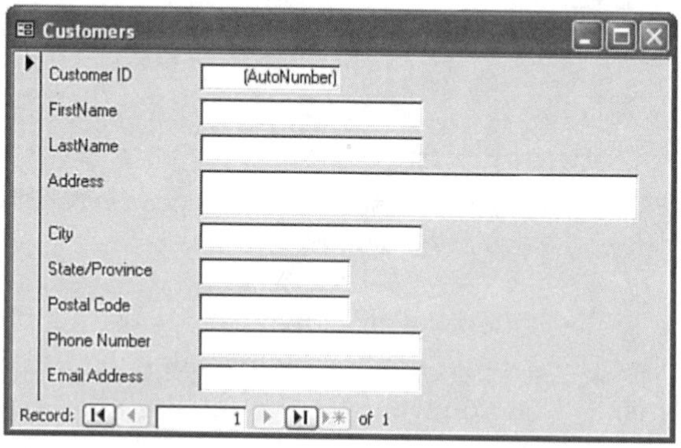

Figure 10.2   AutoForm creates a form based on a single table.

Forms created with AutoForm can be edited using the Form Design view, which is discussed later in this lesson. When you attempt to close the AutoForm, you are asked whether you want to save it. If you do, click Yes. Then, enter a name for the form into the Save As box and click OK.

TIP   **Create an AutoForm in the Table Datasheet View**   You can also create an AutoForm while you are working on a table in the Datasheet view. Click the AutoForm button on the Table Datasheet toolbar. A new form appears, based on the table's fields.

Creating a Form with the Form Wizard

The Form Wizard offers a good compromise between the automation of AutoForm and the control of creating a form from scratch. The wizard enables you to select the fields, layout, and look for the form. Follow these steps to use the Form Wizard:

1. From the database window, click the **Forms** object type.

2. Double-click the **Create Form by Using Wizard** option located in the database window to open the Form Wizard (see Figure 10.3).

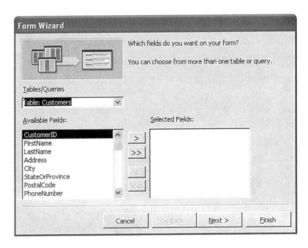

Figure 10.3   The Form Wizard enables you to choose which fields you want to include from as many different tables in the database as you like.

3. From the Tables/Queries drop-down list, choose a table or query from which to select fields. (By default, the first table in alphabetical order is selected, which probably isn't what you want.)

4. Click a field in the Available Fields list that you want to include on the form, and then click the **Add** (>) button to move it to the Selected Fields list.

5. Repeat step 4 until you've selected all the fields you want to include from that table. If you want to include fields from another table or query, go back to step 3 and choose another table.

 TIP   **Selecting All Fields**   You can quickly move all the fields from the Available Fields list to the Selected Fields list by clicking the Add All (>>) button. If you make a mistake, you can remove a field from the Selected Fields list by clicking it and then clicking either the **Remove** (<) button or the **Remove All** (<<) button.

6. Click **Next** to continue. You're asked to choose a layout: **Columnar**, **Tabular**, **Datasheet**, or **Justified**. Click each button to see a preview of that type (Columnar is the most common). Select the layout you want to use, and then click **Next**.

7. The next screen asks you to select a style for your form (see Figure 10.4). Click each style listed to see a preview of it; click **Next** when you've selected a style.

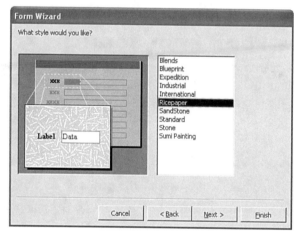

Figure 10.4   You can select from several form styles.

8. On the last screen, enter a title for the form into the text box at the top of the dialog box (if you want a title other than the default).

9. Click the **Finish** button. The form appears, ready for data entry (see Figure 10.5).

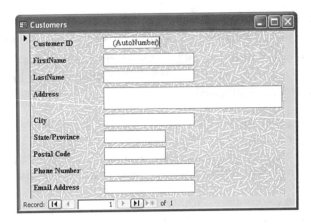

Figure 10.5 The Form Wizard creates a usable form using the fields, format, and style that you selected.

If your form's field labels are cut off or need some additional layout work, you can fix them in the Form Design view. You learn about modifying a form in Lesson 11, "Modifying a Form."

Creating a Form from Scratch

You can also create a form from scratch in the Form Design view. This method might seem difficult at first, but Access provides tools, such as the Field list and the Toolbox, to help you create your form. The most powerful and difficult way to create a form is with Form Design view. In this view, you decide exactly where to place each field and how to format it.

To open the Form Design view and create a new form, follow these steps:

1. From the database window, click the **Forms** object type.
2. Click the **New** button. The New Form dialog box appears (refer to Figure 10.1).
3. Click **Design View**.
4. Select a table or query from the drop-down list at the bottom of the dialog box. The table or query that you select provides a Field list that you can use to place fields on the form.
5. Click **OK**. A Form Design window appears (see Figure 10.6). You're ready to create your form.

Field list

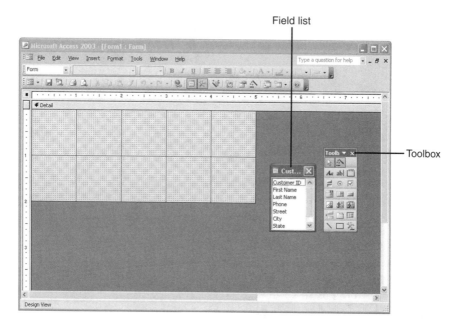

Toolbox

Figure 10.6   Form Design view presents a blank canvas for your new form.

Notice that a Field list and Toolbox appear in the Form Design view. You work with creating form controls (the equivalent of a field in a table) using these tools in the next section.

You can also start the process of building a form in the Design view by double-clicking the Create Form in Design View link in the database window. Because you are not specifying a table for the Field list to use (as you did in the steps outlined in this section), however, that Field list won't be available. Instead, you must specify a table for the Field list.

 To do this, click the Properties button on the Form Design toolbar. The form's properties dialog box appears (see Figure 10.7).

In the properties dialog box, be sure that the All tab is selected. Click in the Record Source box, and then use the drop-down arrow that appears to specify the table that will serve as the field source for the form. The Field list appears in the Design View window. Close the properties dialog box.

TIP   **Don't See the Toolbox or Field List?**   You need to use the Form Design toolbox and the Field list to help in the design of your form. If they're not visible, click the Toolbox button or the Field List button in the toolbar.

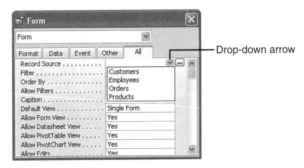

Drop-down arrow

Figure 10.7 The properties dialog box enables you to set a number of properties for the form including the source table.

Adding Controls to a Form

The basic idea of the Form Design window is simple: It's similar to a light table or a paste-up board where you place the elements of your form. The fields you add to a form appear in the form's Detail area. The Detail area is the only area visible at first; you'll learn how to add other areas in the next lesson.

TIP **Controls and Fields** When you are working with a table, you work directly with fields of data. On forms and reports, you work with controls, which are elements that display data from a field, hold informative text (such as titles and labels), display the results of a formula or calculation, or are purely decorative (such as lines and rectangles).

To add a control displaying a field to the form, follow these steps:

1. Display the Field list if it's not showing. Choose the **Field List** from the **View** menu to do so.

2. Drag a field from the Field list onto the Detail area of the form. The mouse pointer changes to show that a field is being placed.

3. Repeat step 2 to add as many fields as you like to the form (see Figure 10.8).

When you drag a field to a form from the Field list, it becomes a control that displays data from that table field on the form. It is basically a link between the table field and the control on the form. You can drag more than one field to the form at once using the steps described earlier. However, in step 2, rather than clicking and dragging a single field, do one of the following before dragging:

- To select a block of adjacent fields, click the first one you want and hold down the Shift key while you click the last one.

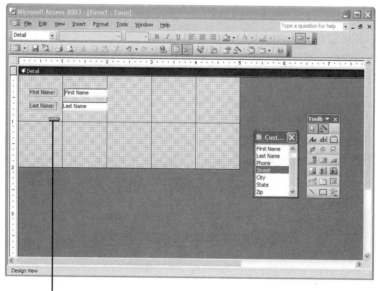

Field placement mouse icon

Figure 10.8   Drag fields from the Field list to the form grid.

- To select nonadjacent fields, hold down the Ctrl key as you click each one you want.

- To select all the fields on the list, double-click the Field List title bar.

You can move objects around on a form after you initially place them; you'll learn how to do this in the next lesson. Don't worry if your form doesn't look very professional at this point; in the next several lessons, you see how to modify and improve your form.

 TIP   **Using Snap to Grid**   If you find it hard to align the fields neatly, choose Snap to Grid from the Format menu to place a check mark next to that command. This forces the borders of the fields included on your form to "snap" to the grid that appears in the Design view. If you want to align the fields on your own, select Snap to Grid again to turn it off.

After you have placed all the controls on the form that relate to the fields in a particular table or tables, you are ready to do some data entry. First, however, you must save the form's structure. Click the Save button on the Form Design toolbar. Type a name for the form into the Save As dialog box. Then click OK.

Entering Data into a Form

The point of creating a form is so that you can enter data into your tables more easily. The form acts as an attractive mask that shields you from the stark reality of the table's Datasheet view. To enter data into a form, follow these steps:

1. Open the form. In the database window, click the **Forms** object, and then double-click the form's name.

2. Click in the field you want to begin with and type your data.

3. Press **Tab** to move to the next field. If you need to go back, you can press **Shift+Tab** to move to the previous field. When you reach the last field, pressing **Tab** moves you to the first field in a new, blank record (you can also use the mouse to move from field to field).

   To move to the next record before you reach the bottom field or to move back to previous records, click the right- and left-arrow buttons on the left end of the navigation bar at the bottom of the window.

4. Repeat steps 2 and 3 to enter all the records you like. They're saved automatically as you enter them.

Modifying a Form

In this lesson, you learn how to modify a form's design.

Working with Field Controls

After you've created a form, you might find that it doesn't quite look as good as you like. Controls might need realignment, or you might want to resize the label for a particular control or controls. You also might want to expand the form grid areas so that you can rearrange the form controls or add additional controls to the form.

You can accomplish all these actions in the Form Design view. Using this view, you can edit the structure of any form that you create, regardless of whether you created the form using AutoForm, the Form Wizard, or the Design view.

Moving Field Controls

The most common change to a form is to reposition a control. For example, you might want to move several controls down so you can insert a new control, or you might want to rearrange how the controls appear on the grid.

If you placed controls on the form to begin with (rather than using AutoForm or the Form Wizard), you have probably noticed that the control consists of two parts: a text label and the actual control. You can manipulate various aspects of the label and the control independently (such as their sizes or the distance between them). You work with label and control sizing later in this lesson.

 TIP **More Space** If you want to create extra space at the bottom of the controls so that you have more room to move them around, drag the bottom of the form down so that more of the Detail area is visible. You can also drag the right side of the grid to make the form wider. If you need more space at the top of the form, highlight all the controls and move them down as a group.

To move a control, follow these steps:

1. ![Design] From the database window, select a form in the Form list, and then click the **Design** button on the database window toolbar. The form is opened in Design view.

2. Click a control's label to select it. Selection handles appear around the label (a displacement handle, which looks like a hand with a pointing figure, also appears on the control, but don't touch it because it will move the label and control apart; we discuss it later in the lesson). You can select several controls by holding down **Shift** as you click each control's label.

3. Position the mouse pointer on the edge of the control's label so that the pointer becomes a hand (see Figure 11.1). If you're moving more than one selected control, you can position the mouse pointer on any selected control's label.

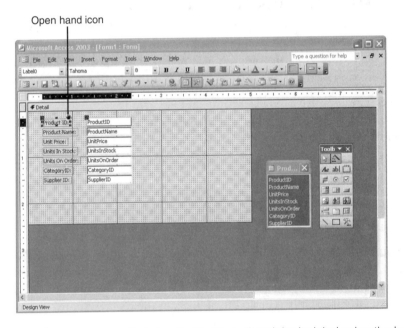

Figure 11.1 To move a control, first select it. Then, drag it by its label using the hand pointer.

4. Drag the control's label and the control to a new location.

5. Release the mouse button when the control is at the desired new location.

CAUTION

The Label Moved Without the Control Attached! When you position the mouse pointer over the control to be moved, be sure the pointer changes to an open hand, as shown in Figure 11.1. If you see a pointing finger, you are on the control's displacement box. The pointing finger is used to move controls and labels independently, as you'll learn in the next section.

Moving Controls and Field Labels Independently

Depending on how you are laying out the controls in your form, you might want to separate the control label from the control. For example, you might want to arrange the form in a tabular format where the control names are positioned over the controls. Separating controls and labels also allows you to move the control so that the field label isn't cut off. Then you can resize the label.

 TIP **Field Controls: The Most Commonly Used Controls** Controls related to fields in a table and their attached labels are discussed in this lesson, but the same methods can be used with other controls that have attached labels, such as combo boxes and list boxes (which are discussed in Lesson 12, "Adding Special Controls to Forms").

To move a control or its attached label by itself, follow these steps:

1. Click the control that you want to separate from its label.

2. Position the mouse pointer over the displacement handle at the top left of the label or the control (the large box handle on the top left of the label or the control). The mouse pointer becomes a pointing finger (see Figure 11.2).

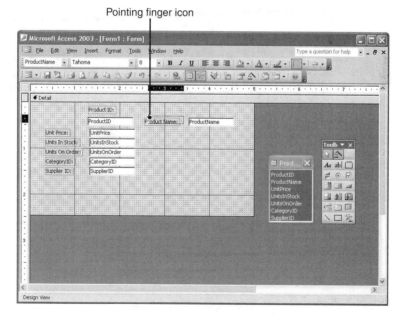

Figure 11.2 Drag the displacement handle to move the control or label independently.

3. Drag the label or the control to a new position.

TIP **Deleting Labels** If a certain control is self-explanatory (such as a picture), you might want to delete its attached label. To do so, select the label and press Delete.

Separating the label from a control allows you to arrange your controls in all kinds of tabular and columnar arrangements on the form grid. Just make sure that you keep the correct label in close proximity to the appropriate control.

Changing Label and Control Sizes

You can also change the width or height of a label or control. Separating a label from its control, as discussed in the previous section, provides you with the room to resize the label or the control independently. To change a label's or control's width (length):

1. Click the label or the control to select it. If you are going to resize the control itself, be sure you click the control. Selection handles (small boxes) appear around it.

2. Position the mouse pointer on either the right or left of the label or control until the mouse pointer becomes a sizing tool (a horizontal double-headed arrow, as shown in Figure 11.3).

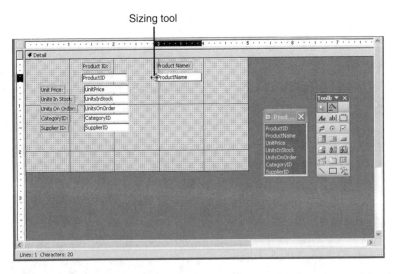

Figure 11.3 You can change the size of a label or control by dragging a sizing box.

3. Drag the label's or control's sizing handle to increase or decrease the length as needed. Then release the mouse button.

Viewing Headers and Footers

So far, you have been working in the main part of the form grid called the Detail area. The Detail area is where you place the various field controls for the form (and additional controls, such as those discussed in the next lesson).

Forms have other areas as well. For example, a form header can be used to include a title for the form (header information appears at the top of the form). The form areas are

- **Form Header**—An area at the top of the form that can be used for repeating information, such as a form title.

- **Form Footer**—An area at the bottom of the form that can be used for repeating information, such as the current date or explanatory information related to the form.

- **Page Header**—Forms that are built to add data to multiple tables can consist of multiple pages. You can also include a Page Header area on a form that enables you to include information that you want to repeat on each page of the form when it is printed out, such as your name or company information.

- **Page Footer**—This area enables you to place information, such as page numbering, that appears on every page when the form is printed.

These different areas of the form grid aren't displayed by default; to display these areas, such as the Form Header/Footer, use the View menu. To show the Form Header/Footer, for example, select View, Form Header/Footer.

When you create a form with the Form Wizard, the Form Header and Form Footer areas appear in Design view, but nothing is in them. To make some room to work in the Form Header, click the Detail Header bar to select it, position the mouse pointer between the bars, and drag downward (see Figure 11.4).

The Detail section contains controls whose data changes with every record. As already mentioned, the Form Header contains text you want repeated on each onscreen form. This makes the Form Header a great place to add a label that contains a title for the form.

Sizing tool

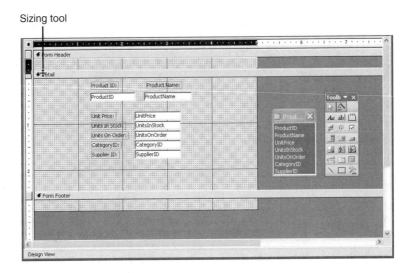

Figure 11.4 Drag the Detail border bar down to create space to add text in the Form header.

Adding Labels

You can add a label to any of the areas in the form. Adding labels to the form enables you to place titles, subtitles, or explanatory text on the form. Because you will want these types of labels to repeat at the top or bottom of the form, the best place to add them is to the form's header or footer. To add titles and other general information to a header or a footer or to add information specific to particular controls to the Detail area, follow these steps:

1. If the toolbox isn't displayed, choose **Toolbox** from the **View** menu, or click the **Toolbox** button on the toolbar.

2. Click the **Label** tool in the Toolbox. The mouse pointer changes to a capital A with a plus sign next to it.

3. Place the Label pointer on an area of the form grid, such as the Form Header area. Drag to create a box or rectangle for text entry (see Figure 11.5).

4. When you release the mouse button, a new label box appears with an insertion point inside it. Type the text you want the label box to contain.

Label tool pointer icon

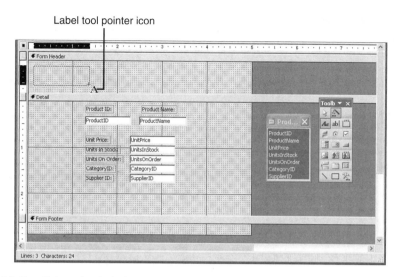

Figure 11.5 Select the Label tool in the toolbox.

TIP **You Must Type the Text Now** If you don't type anything before you go on to step 5, the box disappears as soon as you click any other area of the form.

5. Click anywhere outside the control's area to finish, or press **Enter**.

Don't worry about positioning the label as you create it; you can move a label control in the same way that you move other controls. Just click it, position the mouse pointer so that the hand appears, and then drag it to where you want it to go.

Formatting Text on a Form

After you place all your information on the form (that is, the controls you want to include and labels to display any titles or explanatory text), the next step is to make the form look more appealing.

All the formatting tools you need are on the Formatting toolbar (the top toolbar in the Form Design view). Table 11.1 describes several of the formatting tools. To format a control or label, select it, and then click the appropriate formatting tool to apply the format to the control or label.

Table 11.1   Tools on the Formatting Toolbar

Tool	Purpose
B	Toggles bold on/off
I	Toggles italic on/off
U	Toggles underline on/off
≡	Left-aligns text
≡	Centers text
≡	Right-aligns text
	Fills the selected box with the selected color
A	Colors the text in the selected box
	Colors the outline of the selected box
	Controls the border width on the selected box
	Adds a special effect to the selected box

Some tools, such as the Font and Size tools, are drop-down lists. You click the down arrow next to the tool and then select from the list. Other tools are simple buttons for turning bold and italic on or off. Still other tools, such as the Color and Border tools, combine a button and a drop-down list. If you click the button, it applies the current value. You can click the down arrow next to the button to change the value.

You can change the color of the form background, too. Just click the header for the section you want to change (for example, Detail) to select the entire section. Then right-click and choose Fill/Back color to change the color.

TIP   **AutoFormat**   You can use a shortcut for formatting your form. Choose Format, AutoFormat. You can choose from among several premade color and formatting schemes. If you don't like the formatting after you apply it, press Ctrl+Z to undo.

Changing Tab Order

When you enter data on a form, press Tab to move from control to control in the order they're shown in the form. The progression from control to control on the form is the tab order. When you first create a form, the tab order runs from top to bottom.

When you move and rearrange controls, the tab order doesn't change automatically. For example, suppose you had 10 controls arranged in a column and you rearranged them so that the tenth one was at the beginning. It would still require 10 presses of the Tab key to move the insertion point to that control, even though it's now at the top of the form. This makes it more difficult to fill in the form, so you'll want to adjust the tab order to reflect the new structure of the form.

TIP **Tab Order Improvements** To make data entry easier, you might want to change the tab order to be different from the obvious top-to-bottom structure. For example, if 90% of the records you enter skip several controls, you might want to put those controls last in the tab order so that you can skip over them easily.

Follow these steps to adjust the tab order:

1. Choose **View, Tab Order**. The Tab Order dialog box appears (see Figure 11.6).

Figure 11.6 Use the Tab Order dialog box to decide what tab order to use on your form.

2. Choose the section for which you want to set the tab order. The default is Detail.

3. The controls appear in their tab order. To change the order, click a control and then drag it up or down in the list.

4. To quickly set the tab order based on the controls' current positions in the form (top to bottom), click the **Auto Order** button.

5. Click **OK**.

When you have finished making different enhancements to your form, you must save the changes. Click the Save button on the Form Design toolbar.

Adding Special Controls to Forms

In this lesson, you learn about some special controls you can include on your forms.

Using Special Form Controls

So far, you've taken a look at adding controls to a form that directly relate to fields that exist in an associated table or tables. This means that unless the control is linked to a table's field that uses the AutoNumber data type, you are going to have to type all the data that you enter into the form (exactly as you would in the table).

Fortunately, Access offers some special form controls that can be used to help you enter data. For example, a list box contains a list of entries for a control from which you must choose when entering data. All you have to do is select the appropriate entry from the list. Other special controls also exist that can make it easier to get your data into the form. These controls are:

- **List Box**—Presents a list from which you choose an item.
- **Combo Group**—Like a list box, but you can type in other entries in addition to those on the list.
- **Option Group**—Provides you with different types of input buttons (you can select only one type of button when you create an Option group). You can use option buttons, toggle buttons, or check boxes.
- **Command Button**—Performs some function when you click it, such as starting another program, printing a report, saving the record, or anything else you specify.

Figure 12.1 shows some special controls in the Form view. In this lesson, you create each of these control types.

All these special controls can be created using the buttons on the Toolbox. Wizards are also available that walk you through the steps of creating each of these special control types. To use the wizard for a particular special control, make sure that the Control Wizards button is activated on the Toolbox. Figure 12.2 shows the Toolbox and the buttons that you are working with in this lesson.

Command button   List box

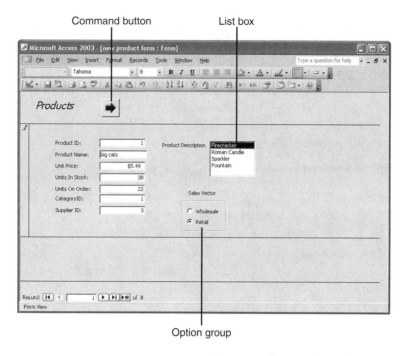

Option group

Figure 12.1   Special controls can make data entry easier.

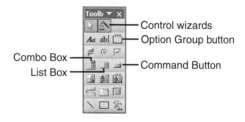

Control wizards
Option Group button
Combo Box
Command Button
List Box

Figure 12.2   To use wizards, make sure that the Control Wizards button is selected.

Creating a List Box or a Combo Box

A *list box* or a *combo box* can come in handy if you find yourself repeatedly typing certain values into a field. For example, if you have to enter the name of one of your 12 branch offices each time you use a form, you might find it easier to create a list box containing the branch office names, and then you can click to select a particular name from the list. With a list box, the person doing the data entry is limited to the choices that display on the list.

A combo box is useful when a list box is appropriate, but it's possible that a different entry might occasionally be needed. For example, if most of your customers come from one of six states, but occasionally you get a new customer from another state, you might use a combo box. During data entry, you could choose the state from the list when appropriate and type a new state when it's not. The combo box only allows data to be entered that is not on the list if you select the **I Will Type In the Values That I Want** option when you are creating the combo box (this is discussed in the set of steps that follow).

Follow these steps to create a list box or combo box from Form Design view:

1. Make sure that the **Control Wizards** button on the Toolbox is selected.

2. Click the **List Box** or **Combo Box** button in the Toolbox. The mouse pointer changes to show the type of box you selected.

3. Drag your mouse to draw a box on the grid where you want the new element to be placed. When you release the mouse button, the list or combo box wizard starts.

4. On the wizard's first screen (see Figure 12.3), click the option button **I Will Type In the Values That I Want**. Then click **Next**.

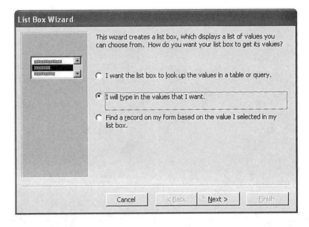

Figure 12.3   The wizard walks you through the steps of creating a list box or a combo box.

TIP   **Another Way to Enter Values**   List boxes and combo boxes can also be set up so that they pull their list of values from an existing table in the database (or a query that you've created). Select I Want the List Box to Look Up the Values in a Table or Query on the first wizard screen, and then specify the table or query that should supply the values for the list. A third option for setting up your list box or combo box is to allow the box to pull its list of values from a control field in the form. For example, product names could be pulled from a Product Name field in the form. Use the **Find a Record on My Form Based on the Value I Selected in My List Box** option on the Wizard screen to have the list pulled from a form field.

5. On the next screen, a column of boxes (only one box shows before you enter your values) is provided that you use to enter the values that you want to appear in the list. Type them in (as shown in Figure 12.4), pressing the **Tab** key after each one. Then click **Next**.

TIP   **Adding Columns to the List or Combo Box**   You can add additional columns to the list box that allow you to include additional data or information related to the names or data that is included in the first column of the list or combo box. For example the first column might include product names; a second column could include the price of each of the products. In most cases, however, you will find that you only work with a List or Combo box that contains one column.

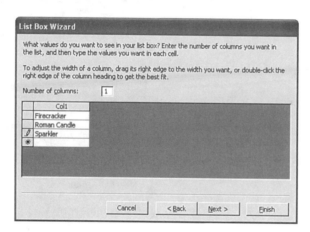

Figure 12.4   Type the values for the list or combo box.

6. On the next screen, you choose the option of Access either remembering the values in the list for later use (such as in a calculation) or entering a value selected from the list in a particular field. Because you are using this box for data entry, select **Store That Value in This Field**, and then choose a field from the drop-down list that is supplied. For example, if you want this list to provide data from your Product Description field, select it in the drop-down list. Click **Next** to continue.

TIP **Tying a List or Combo Box to a Field** The best way to approach list and combo boxes is to create a form that includes all the fields from a particular table. Then, you can delete the controls for fields in the Form Design view that you want to "re-create" as list or combo boxes. You then store the values from the list or combo box in one of the fields that you removed from the form.

7. On the next screen, type the label text for the new list or combo box control.

8. Click **Finish**. Your new list or combo box appears on your form. This box will show a list, so expand the control box as shown in Figure 12.5.

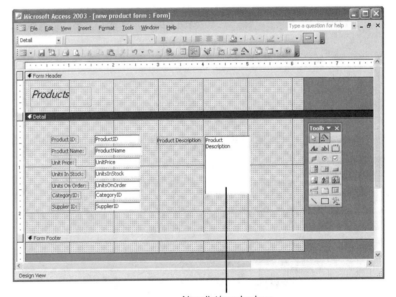

New list/combo box

Figure 12.5 Your list or combo box appears on the form grid.

 Where Are My Values? Don't be alarmed that the values you entered for the control don't appear in the box in the Design view. The values will be available when you switch to the Form view and do data entry on the form.

CAUTION

 TIP **I Picked the Wrong Box Type!** You can easily switch between a list box and a combo box, even after you create it. In Form Design view, right-click the control, click Change To from the shortcut menu that appears, and select a new control type.

Creating an Option Group

Another useful special control is the *option group*. An option group provides different types of buttons or input boxes that can be used to quickly input information into a form. An option group can use one of the following types of buttons:

- **Option buttons**—A separate option button is provided for each choice you supply on the form. To make a particular choice, click the appropriate option button.

- **Check boxes**—A separate check box is provided for each item you place in the option group. To select a particular item, click the appropriate check box.

- **Toggle buttons**—A button is provided for the response required, which can be toggled on and off by clicking the button.

Option groups work best when a fairly limited number of choices are available, and when you create your option group, you should select the type of button or box that best suits your need. If you have several responses where only one response is valid, use option buttons. If you have a situation in which more than one response is possible, use check boxes. Toggle buttons are used when only one response is possible, and a toggle button responds to a "yes or no" type question. The option button is then turned on or off with a click of the mouse.

 TIP **Other Options** You can create a series of option buttons or check boxes using the Option Group button, or you can opt to directly create option buttons or check boxes by clicking the required button (the Option button or the Check Box button, respectively) on the Toolbox.

To create an Option Group control (you will create a control that uses option buttons), follow these steps:

1. Make sure that the **Control Wizards** button in the Toolbox is selected.

 2. Click the **Option Group** button on the Toolbox. Your mouse pointer changes to show the Option Group icon.

3. Drag your mouse pointer on your form to draw a box where you want the option group to appear. When you release the mouse button, the wizard starts.

4. The wizard prompts you to enter the labels you want for each button (or check box or toggle button), as shown in Figure 12.6. You will need a label for each button that will appear in the group. These labels should be the same as the type of data you would normally insert into the field you are building the option group for (which you will specify in step 7). Enter the labels needed, pressing **Tab** after each one; then click **Next**.

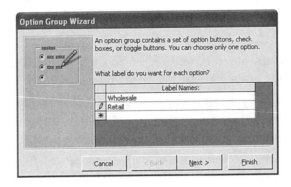

Figure 12.6 Enter the labels you want for each option here.

5. On the next screen, you can select one of the labels that you input in step 4 as the default choice for the option group. Specify the label, and then click **Yes, the Default Choice Is**. Or click **No, I Don't Want a Default As the Other Possibility**. Then click **Next**.

6. On the next screen, the wizard asks what value you want to assign to each option (such as 1, 2, and so on). These values provide a numerical equivalent for each label you listed in step 4 and are used by Access to store the response provided by a particular option button or check box. You should use the default values that Access provides. Click **Next** to continue.

7. On the next screen, you decide whether the value that you assigned to each of your option labels is stored in a particular field or saved by Access for later use. Because you are using the option group to input data into a particular field, be sure the **Store the Value in This Field** option button is selected. This stores the data that the option group provides in a particular field. Select the field from the drop-down list provided. Then, click **Next** to continue.

8. On the next screen, select the type of control (option button, check box, or toggle button—see Figure 12.7) you want to use and a style for the controls; then click **Next**.

9. On the last screen, type a label for the new control. Then click **Finish**.

Your new option control appears on the grid area of the form. All the different option values that you entered appear in the control. When you switch to the Form view to enter data, you can use the various option buttons or check boxes to select an actual value for that particular field.

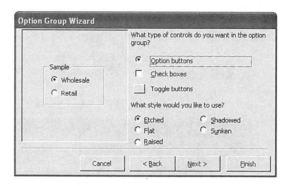

Figure 12.7   You can choose different input controls for your Option group.

Adding Command Buttons

Another special control type that you can add to your form is a command button. Command buttons are used to perform a particular action. For example, you could put a command button on a form that enables you to move to the next record or to print the form. Access offers different command button types that you can place on your forms:

- **Record Navigation**—You can add command buttons that allow you to move to the next, previous, first, or last record.

- **Record Operations**—You can make buttons that delete, duplicate, print, save, or undo a record.

- **Form Operations**—Command buttons can print a form, open a page (on a multiple page form), or close the form.

- **Application**—Command buttons can exit Access or run some other application.

- **Miscellaneous**—Command buttons can print a table, run a macro, run a query, or use the AutoDialer to dial a phone number specified on a form.

 TIP   **Placing Command Buttons**   Form headers or footers make a great place to put any command buttons that you create. Placing them in the header makes it easy for you to go to the top of the form and click a particular command button.

To place a command button on a form, follow these steps:

1. Be sure that the **Control Wizards** button in the Toolbox is selected.

 2. Click the **Command Button** in the Toolbox. Your mouse pointer changes to show the Command Button icon.

3. Click your form where you want the command button to appear (such as the header of the form). The Command Button Wizard opens.

4. On the first wizard screen, select an action category in the Categories list, and then in the Actions box (see Figure 12.8), select the action that the button should perform. Then click **Next**.

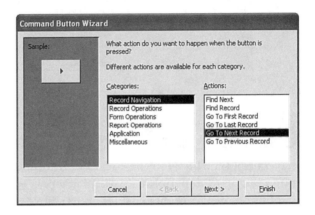

Figure 12.8   Choose what action you want the command button to execute.

5. On the next screen, you can select to have either text or a picture appear on the command button. For text, choose **Text** and then enter the text into the appropriate box. To place a picture on the button, select **Picture** and then select a picture from the list provided (you can use your own bitmap pictures on the buttons if they are available; use the **Browse** button to locate them). Then click **Next**.

6. On the next screen, type a name for your new button. Then click **Finish**. The button appears on your form. You can move it around like any other control.

Searching for Information in Your Database

In this lesson, you learn how to search for data in a database using the Find feature and how to find and replace data using the Replace feature.

Using the Find Feature

Whether you are viewing the records in the table using the Datasheet view or a form, the Find feature is useful for locating a particular record in a table. For example, if you keep a database of customers, you might want to find a particular customer's record quickly by searching using the customer's last name. You can search the table using a specific field, or you can search the entire table (all the fields) for a certain text string.

Although the Find feature is designed to find information in a table, you can use the Find feature in both the Table Datasheet view and the Form view. The results of a particular search display only the first match of the parameters, but you can repeat the search to find additional records (one at a time).

 TIP **Finding More Than One Record** If you need to find several records at once, Find is not the best tool because it locates only one record at a time. A better tool for locating multiple records is a filter, discussed in the next lesson.

To find a particular record, follow these steps:

1. Open your table in the Datasheet view or open a form that is used to enter data in the table that you want to search.
2. Click in the field that contains the data you want to search for.
3. Select **Edit, Find**, or press **Ctrl+F**. The Find and Replace dialog box appears (see Figure 13.1) with the Find tab on top.

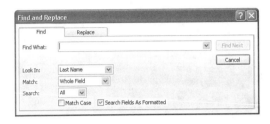

Figure 13.1 Use the Find and Replace dialog box to find data in a record.

4. Type the data string that you want to find into the **Find What** text box.

5. The default value for Look In is the field you selected in step 2. If you want to search the entire table, click the **Look In** list drop-down box and select the table's name.

6. From the **Match** drop-down list, select one of the following:

   - **Whole Field**—Select this to find fields where the specified text is the only thing in that field. For example, "Smith" would not find "Smithsonian."

   - **Start of Field**—Select this to find fields that begin with the specified text. For example, "Smith" would find "Smith" and "Smithsonian," but not "Joe Smith."

   - **Any Part of Field**—Select this to find fields that contain the specified text in any way. "Smith" would find "Smith," "Smithsonian," and "Joe Smith."

7. To limit the match to entries that are the same case (uppercase or lowercase) as the search string, select the **Match Case** check box.

8. To find only fields with the same formatting as the text you type, select **Search Fields As Formatted** (this option can slow down the search on a large table, so don't use it unless you think it will affect the search results).

9. When you are ready to run the search, click **Find Next**.

10. If needed, move the Find and Replace dialog box out of the way by dragging its title bar so that you can see the record it found. If Access finds a field matching your search, it highlights the field entry containing the found text (see Figure 13.2).

11. To find the next occurrence, click **Find Next**. If Access can't find any more occurrences, it tells you the search item was not found. Click **OK** to clear that message.

12. When you finish finding your data, click the Find and Replace dialog box **Close** (**x**) button.

Text found and highlighted during search

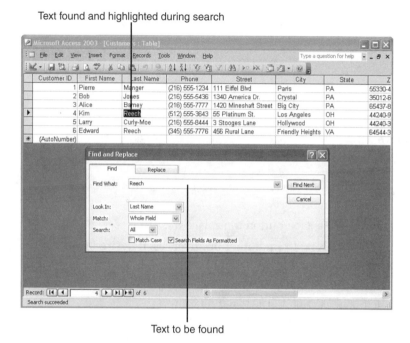

Text to be found

Figure 13.2   Access finds records, one record at a time, that contain the search text.

Using the Replace Feature

The Replace feature is similar to the Find feature, except that you can stipulate that a value, which you specify, replace the data found during the search. For example, if you found that you misspelled a brand name or other value in a table, you could replace the word with the correct spelling. This is useful for correcting proper names because the Spelling Checker doesn't help correct those types of spelling errors.

To find and replace data, follow these steps:

1. Select **Edit**, **Replace**, or press **Ctrl+H**. The Find and Replace dialog box appears with the Replace tab displayed (see Figure 13.3).

2. Type the text you want to find into the **Find What** text box.

3. Type the text you want to replace it with into the **Replace With** text box.

4. Select any options you want using the Match drop-down list or the check boxes on the Search tab. They work the same as the options discussed on the Find tab (in the previous section).

Figure 13.3 You can find specific text in a table and then replace it using the Replace feature.

5. To start the search, click **Find Next**. Access finds the first occurrence of the search string.

6. Click the **Replace** button to replace the text.

7. Click **Find Next** to find other occurrences, if desired, and replace them by clicking the **Replace** button.

8. If you decide that you would like to replace all occurrences of the search string in the table, click the **Replace All** button.

9. When you have found the last occurrence of the search string (Access lets you know that the string can no longer be located, which means you are at the end of the table), click the **Close (X)** button on the Find and Replace dialog box.

The Find and Replace feature works well when you want to work with data in a particular field, but it is limited because you can work with only one record at a time. Other, more sophisticated ways exist to locate records that contain a particular parameter. For example, you can filter records (discussed in the next lesson) using a particular field's content as the filter criteria. This provides you with a subset of the current table, showing you only the records that include the filter criteria.

Queries also provide you with a method for creating a subset of records found in a database table. Queries are discussed in Lesson 15, "Creating a Simple Query," and Lesson 16, "Creating Queries from Scratch."

Sorting, Filtering, and Indexing Data

In this lesson, you learn how to sort and filter data and you also learn how to speed up searches with indexing.

Sorting Data

Although you probably entered your records into the table in some kind of logical order, perhaps by employee number or employee start date, being able to change the order of the records in the table based on a particular field parameter can be extremely useful. This is where the Sort feature comes in.

Using Sort, you can rearrange the records in the table based on any field in the table (more complex sorts can also be created that allow you to sort by more than one field, such as Last Name and then First Name). You can sort in either ascending (A to Z, 1 to 10) or descending (Z to A, 10 to 1) order.

 TIP **Which View?** You can sort either in Form view or Datasheet view, but the Datasheet view is better because it shows you all the records in the table in their new sort order.

The fastest way to sort is to use either the **Sort Ascending** or **Sort Descending** button on the Table toolbar. However, this easy road to sorting limits you to sorting by one field or adjacent fields.

Follow these steps to sort records:

1. Place the insertion point in the field by which you want to sort the table (if you want to sort by more than one adjacent field, select the field columns by clicking and dragging the Field Column names). Figure 14.1 shows a Customers table where the insertion point has been placed in the Country field.

2. To sort the records in the table by that field in ascending order (alphabetically from A to Z), click the **Sort Ascending** button. Figure 14.2 shows the results of an ascending sort by Country field on the table that was shown in Figure 14.1.

Insertion point

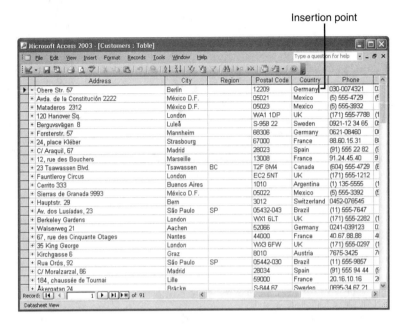

Figure 14.1 Place the insertion point in the field you want to sort that table by.

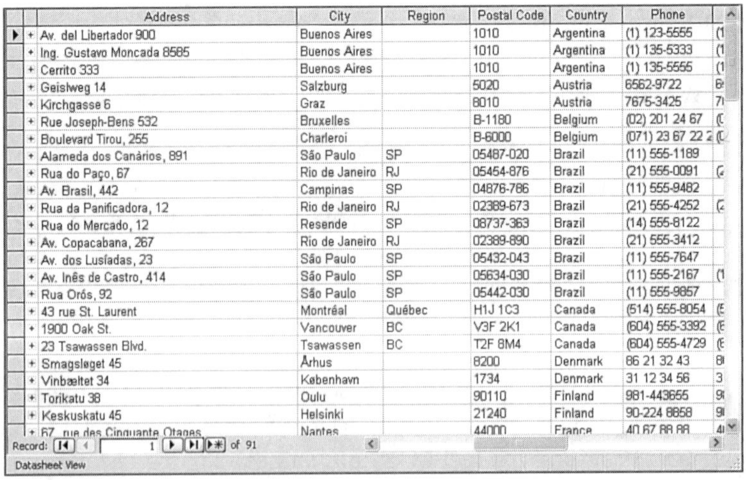

Figure 14.2 The table records are sorted based on the field that you selected.

3. To sort the records in descending order, click the **Sort Descending** button.

4. To place the records back in their presorted order, select the **Records** menu, and then select **Remove Filter/Sort**.

As already mentioned, you can sort a table by adjacent fields using the sort buttons. All you have to do is select the field headings for those particular field columns, and then click the correct sort button. For example, if you wanted to sort a customer table by last name and then first name, the last name would have to be in the column that is directly to the left of the First Name field.

Filtering Data

Although sorting rearranges the records in the table, you might need to see a subset of the records in a table based on a particular criterion. Filtering is used for this purpose. The Filter feature temporarily hides records from the table that do not meet the filter criteria.

For example, you might want to view only the records in an employee table for the employees who have exceeded their sales goal for the year. Or in an order table, you might want to find orders that were placed on a particular date. Filters can help you temporarily narrow down the records shown in the table based on your criteria.

You can apply a filter in three ways: Filter by Selection (or Filter Excluding Selection), Filter by Form, and Advanced Filter/Sort. The first two methods are very easy ways to quickly filter the records in a table.

The Advanced Filter/Sort feature uses a Design view that is almost the same as the Query Design view (covered in Lesson 16). If you learn how to create queries (which are really nothing more than advanced filters/sorts), you will be able to work with the Advanced Filter/Sort feature.

This section covers Filter by Selection and Filter by Form. Next, take a look at how you filter by selection.

Filter by Selection

Filtering by selection is the easiest method of filtering, but before you can use it, you must locate a field that contains the value that you want to use to filter the table.

To filter by selection, follow these steps:

1. Locate a field in a record that contains the value you want to use to filter the table. For example, if you want to see all the customers in Germany, you would find a field in the Country field column that contains the text, "Germany."

2. Click in the field that contains the value you will use as the filter.

 3. Click the **Filter by Selection** button on the toolbar, or select **Records**, point at **Filter**, and then choose **Filter by Selection**. The records that match the criteria you selected appear, as shown in Figure 14.3.

TIP **Fine-Tuning Filter by Selection** You can also filter the table by selecting only a portion of an entry in a field. For example, if you want to filter the records by last names beginning with the letter S, select the S in a last name that appears in the Last Name field in a record.

Selected data

Address	City	Region	Postal Code	Country	Phone	
+ Adenauerallee 900	Stuttgart		70563	Germany	0711-020361	0711
+ Luisenstr. 48	Münster		44087	Germany	0251-031259	0251
+ Taucherstraße 10	Cunewalde		01307	Germany	0372-035188	
+ Mehrheimerstr. 369	Köln		50739	Germany	0221-0644327	0221
+ Heerstr. 22	Leipzig		04179	Germany	0342-023176	
+ Magazinweg 7	Frankfurt a. M.		60528	Germany	069-0245984	069-
+ Maubelstr. 90	Brandenburg		14776	Germany	0555-09876	
+ Berliner Platz 43	München		80805	Germany	089-0877310	089-
+ Walserweg 21	Aachen		52066	Germany	0241-039123	0241
+ Forsterstr. 57	Mannheim		68306	Germany	0621-08460	0621
+ Obere Str. 57	Berlin		12209	Germany	030-0074321	030-

Figure 14.3 The table will be filtered by the field data you selected.

With Filter by Selection, you can filter by only one criterion at a time. However, you can apply successive filters after the first one to further narrow the list of matching records.

You can also filter for records that don't contain the selected value. Follow the same steps as outlined in this section, but choose Records, point at Filter, and choose Filter Excluding Selection in step 3.

After you have finished viewing the records that match your filter criteria, you will want to bring all the table records back on screen. Select Records, Remove Filter/Sort.

Filter by Form

Filtering by form is a more powerful filtering method than filtering by selection. With Filter by Form, you can filter by more than one criterion at a time. To filter by form, follow these steps:

1. With the table open in the Datasheet view, click the **Filter by Form** button on the toolbar, or select **Records**, point at **Filter**, and then select **Filter by Form**. A blank form appears, resembling an empty datasheet with a single record line.

2. Click in the field for which you want to set a criterion. A down arrow appears for a drop-down list. Click the arrow and select the value you want from the list (see Figure 14.4). You also can type the value directly into the field if you prefer.

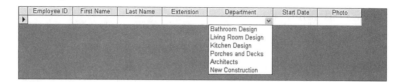

Figure 14.4 Set the criteria for the filter using the drop-down list in each field.

3. Enter additional criteria for the filter as needed using the drop-down lists provided by the other fields in the table.

4. After you enter your criteria, click the **Apply Filter** button on the toolbar. Your filtered data appears in the Table window.

As in Filter by Selection, you can remove a filter by clicking the Remove Filter button (same icon as for Apply Filter) or by selecting Records, Remove Filter/Sort.

Saving Your Filter As a Query

If you design a filter that you would like to keep, it resides on the Query list in the database window. You will work with queries in Lessons 15 and 16.

To save a filter as a query, follow these steps:

1. Display the filter in Filter by Form view.

2. Select **File, Save As Query**. Access asks for the name of the new query.

3. Type a name and click **OK**. Access saves the filter as a query.

Indexing Data

Although not a method of manipulating data like a sort or a filter, indexes provide a method for speeding up searches, sorts, and filters by cataloging the contents of a particular field. The primary key field in a table is automatically indexed. If you have a large database table and frequently search, sort, or filter by a field other than the primary key field, you might want to create an index for that field.

Can't Be Indexed You can't index a field whose data type is Memo, Hyperlink, or OLE Object. There is no way for Access to verify the content of fields containing these types of entries, making it impossible to create an index.

CAUTION

To index a field, follow these steps:

1. Open the table in Design view.
2. Select the field that you want to index.
3. In the Field Properties pane on the General tab, click in the **Indexed** box.
4. From the Indexed field's drop-down list, select either **Yes (Duplicates OK)** or **Yes (No Duplicates)**, depending on whether that field's content should be unique for each record (see Figure 14.5). For example, in the case of indexing a last name field, you would want to allow duplicates (Duplicates OK), but in the case of a Social Security number field where you know each entry is unique, you would not want to allow duplicates (No Duplicates).

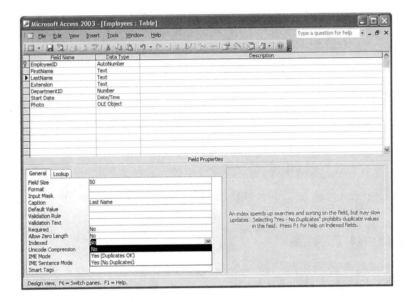

Figure 14.5   To index a field, set its Indexed value to one of the Yes choices.

5. Save your changes to the table's structure by clicking the **Save** button on the Design toolbar.
6. Close the Design view of the table.

Indexes aren't glamorous. They work behind the scenes to speed up your searches and filters. They don't really have any independent functions of their own.

Creating a Simple Query

In this lesson, you create a simple query.

Understanding Queries

As you learned in the previous lesson, Access offers many ways to help you narrow down the information you're looking at, including sorting and filtering. The most flexible way to sort and filter data, however, is using a query.

A *query* is a question that you pose to a database table or tables. For example, you might want to know which of your customers live in a specific state or how many of your salespeople have reached a particular sales goal. The great thing about queries is that you can save queries and use them to create tables, delete records, or copy records to another table.

Queries enable you to specify

- The table fields that appear in the query
- The order of the fields in the query
- Filter and sort criteria for each field in the query

Query   A query enables you to "question" your database using different criteria to sort, filter, and summarize table data.

Queries are a powerful tool for analyzing and summarizing database information. In this lesson, you take a look at the queries you can create using a wizard. Creating queries in the Design view is covered in Lesson 16, "Creating Queries from Scratch."

Using the Simple Query Wizard

The easiest way to create a query is with the Simple Query Wizard, which enables you to select the table fields you want to include in the query. A simple query is useful when you want to weed out extraneous fields but still want to see every record in the database table. The Simple Query Wizard helps you create a *select query*.

TERM   **Select Query**   The select query is used to select certain data from a table or tables. It not only filters the data, but it can also sort the data. It can even perform simple calculations on the results (such as counting and averaging).

To create a select query with the Simple Query Wizard, follow these steps:

1. In the Access window, open the database you want to work with and select the **Queries** icon in the database window.

2. Double-click the **Create Query by Using Wizard** option found in the database window. The first dialog box of the Simple Query Wizard appears (see Figure 15.1).

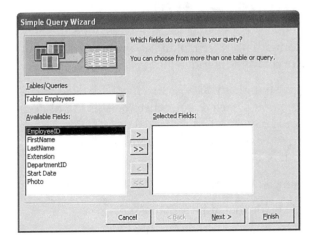

Figure 15.1   The Simple Query Wizard first asks what fields you want to include in the query.

3. Choose the table from which you want to select fields from the Tables/Queries drop-down list.

4. Click a field name in the Available Fields list; then click the **Add >** button to move the field name to the Selected Fields list. Add fields as needed, or move them all at once with the **Add All >>** button.

5. (Optional) Select another table or query from the Tables/Queries list and add some of its fields to the Selected Fields list (this enables you to pull data from more than one table into the query). When you have finished adding fields, click **Next**.

CAUTION

Relationships Required   If you're going to use two or more tables in your query, they must be joined by a relationship. See Lesson 9, "Creating Relationships Between Tables," for more information.

6. The next screen asks if you want to create a detail or summary query. A detail query lists all the fields that you selected in step 4 and 5. A summary query allows you to summarize data in numerical fields using the formulas sum (total), avg (average), max (maximum), and min (minimum).

7. (Optional) To summarize field data using a formula, click the **Summary** option button. Then click **Summary Options**. Any fields containing numerical data will be listed on the Summary Options screen. In our example, you could summarize the data by the AmountSpent field (as shown in Figure 15.2). Use the formula check boxes (such as sum or avg) to select the calculation that will be used to summarize the field data in the query. Then click **OK**. Click **Next** to continue.

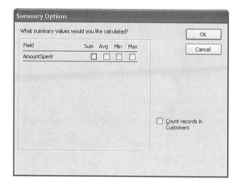

Figure 15.2   You can summarize data in the query such as totaling the values (using the SUM formula) in a particular field.

8. On the next screen, enter a title for the query. Then, click **Finish** to view the query results. Figure 15.3 shows the results of a simple query.

The problem with queries created using the Simple Query Wizard is that you do not have the option of setting sort parameters for the records or the capability to filter them by particular criteria. Simple queries just allow you to select the fields. For this query to provide a little more manipulation of the table data, you would have to edit this in Query Design view, which is discussed in the next lesson. Building queries from scratch provides you with a lot more control over how the data is filtered, sorted, and summarized.

First Name	Last Name	DepartmentName	Amount Spent	Date Submitted
Nancy	Davy	Living Room Design	$1,200.00	1/15/2003
Janet	Leverling	Porches and Decks	$300.00	1/18/2003
Richard	Jones	Kitchen Design	$2,600.00	1/22/2003
Steven	Buchanan	Architects	$1,800.00	1/23/2003
Henry	Cotton	New Construction	$920.00	1/24/2003
Snidley	Backlash	Porches and Decks	$1,560.00	2/3/2003
Alice	Smith	Porches and Decks	$2,200.00	2/5/2003
Robert	Buchanan	Bathroom Design	$5,500.00	2/7/2003
Bob	Palooka	Architects	$1,400.00	2/8/2003

Figure 15.3 Queries such as this detail query can be created using the Simple Query Wizard.

Saving a Query

When you create a query, Access saves it automatically. You don't need to do anything special to save it. When you are finished viewing the results of the query, click its **Close** (**x**) button. The new query is then listed in the Query list that the database window provides.

Rerunning a Query

At any time, you can rerun your query. If the data has changed in the table fields that you included in a query, rerunning the query provides you with an updated set of results.

To rerun a query, follow these steps:

1. Open the database containing the query.

2. Select the **Queries** icon in the database window.

3. In the Query list, double-click the query you want to run, or click it once and then click the **Open** button.

TIP **Query Results Look Like Tables** Query results can be manipulated in the Datasheet view just like a table. You can use the Sort and Filter features on the results, or you can delete records from them. You cannot add data to a query, however, as you can to a table (unless you use the Create Table Query and make a new table from the query results).

Using Other Query Wizards

Access's different query features are quite powerful; they can do amazingly complicated calculations and comparisons on data from several tables. Queries also can do calculations to summarize data or arrange the query data in a special format called a crosstab. Creating more advanced queries means that your database tables must be joined by the appropriate relationships; otherwise, the query cannot pull the data from multiple tables.

You can create very complex queries from the Query Design view, which you learn about in the next lesson. However, Access also provides some wizards that can be used to create some of the more complex query types. These wizards include the following:

- **Crosstab Query Wizard**—This wizard displays summarized values, such as sums, counts, and averages, from a field. One field is used on the left side of the Query datasheet to cross-reference other field columns in the Query datasheet. For example, Figure 15.4 shows a Crosstab table that shows the different products that each customer has ordered, sorted on the customer's last name (and then sorted by promised by date). Note that some customers have multiple orders.

First Name	Last Name	Promised-by Date	Total Of Quantity	Brie	Cheddar	Gouda	Swiss
Alice	Barney	1/17/2003	3				3
Larry	Curly-Moe	2/10/2003	2			2	
Larry	Curly-Moe	4/30/2003	1	1			
Bob	Jones	4/30/2003	2	2			
Pierre	Manger	4/30/2003	1	1			
Pierre	Manger	5/9/2003	2			2	
Kim	Reech	3/29/2003	4		4		
Edward	Reech	5/12/2003	9	2		3	4

Figure 15.4   Crosstab queries allow you to cross-tabulate information between table fields. This query is sorted on the Last Name field.

- **Find Duplicates Query Wizard**—This query is used to compare two tables and find duplicate records.
- **Find Unmatched Query Wizard**—This wizard compares two tables and finds all records that don't appear in both tables (based on comparing certain fields).

You can access any of these query wizards from the database window. With the Queries icon selected, click the New button on the database window toolbar. The New Query dialog box appears, as shown in Figure 15.5.

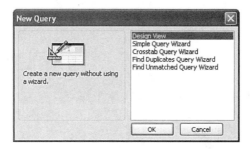

Figure 15.5   The other query wizards can be accessed from the New Query dialog box.

Select the wizard that you want to use for your query and click OK. Work with the wizard as it walks you through the steps for creating your new query.

Understanding Access Query Types

Before this lesson ends, you should spend a little time learning about the different types of queries that Access offers. In this lesson, you created a simple select query that "selects" data from a table or tables based on your query criteria. You can also build other types of queries in Access and most are based on the select query. For example, a select query pulls certain data from a table or tables. If you wanted to make a table from the data that the query pulls together for you, all you would have to do is create the select query and then change it to a Make Table query. The query type is changed in the Query Design view using the Query menu. We will work in the Query Design view in the next lesson.

The different query types are

- **Make Table Query**—This type of query is similar to a select query, but it takes the data pulled together by the criteria and creates a new table for the database.

- **Update Query**—This query updates field information in a record. For example, you might have placed a certain credit limit for customers and want to update it in all the records. You would use an Update query.

- **Append Query**—This type of query is used to copy records from one table and place them (append them) into another table. For example, you might want to append employee records from an Active Employee table to a Former Employee table.

- **Delete Query**—This type of query is used to delete records from a table. For example, you might want to delete old records from a table based on particular criteria. Again, you could create a select query using the Wizard (the select query pulls the information together) and then change the query to a delete query in the Design view. The delete query would select the same data designated in the query, but it would delete it from the specified table or tables.

Now, you might be thinking that all these query types are a little too much to handle. However, you create different query types just as you would a select query. As a matter of fact, you actually design each of these different query types as a select table (using a wizard, Query Design view, or a combination of both), and then you change the query type in the Query Design view. It's just a matter of selecting the query type from the Query menu.

For example, Figure 15.6 shows a select query that was created with the wizard and then opened in the Query Design view. The Query was then changed to a delete query using the Query menu (as shown in the figure). The purpose of this delete query was to remove customers from the Customers table that resided in Minnesota (MN). Note that under the State field in the query grid, the parameter "MN" was added to the criteria line (because MN is the information that will be used to delete certain records).

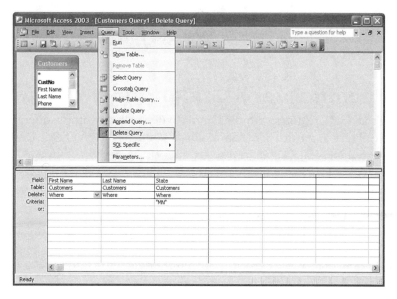

Figure 15.6   Special query types such as delete queries can be quickly created from select queries.

When you run this query (by selecting **Query**, then **Run),** any customer in the Customers table who is from Minnesota will be removed from the table. We will be working with the Query grid and the Query Design view commands in the next lesson. So, keep in mind that the special queries that we have discussed in this section are really just modified select queries.

Creating Queries from Scratch

In this lesson, you learn how to open a query in Design view, how to select fields to include in it, and how to specify criteria for filtering the records.

Introducing Query Design View

In Lesson 15, "Creating a Simple Query," you created a simple query using the Simple Query Wizard. This wizard allows you to select the fields from a particular table and then create a standard select query. Although the Simple Query Wizard makes it easy to create a query based on one table, you will find that building more sophisticated queries is best done in the Query Design view.

The Query Design view provides two distinct areas as you work. A Table pane shows you the tables currently being used for the query. The bottom pane, the Query Design grid (see Figure 16.1), enables you to list the fields in the query and select how these fields will be sorted or the information in them filtered when you run the query.

Opening a Query in Query Design View

One thing that you can do in the Query Design view is edit existing queries, such as the simple query that you created in the previous lesson. You can change the fields used in the query and change the action that takes place on that field (or fields) when you run the query. To open an existing query in Query Design view, follow these steps:

1. In the database window, click the **Queries** icon.
2. In the Query list, select the query you want to edit.
3. Click the **Design** button on the database window toolbar.

The query opens in the Query Design window.

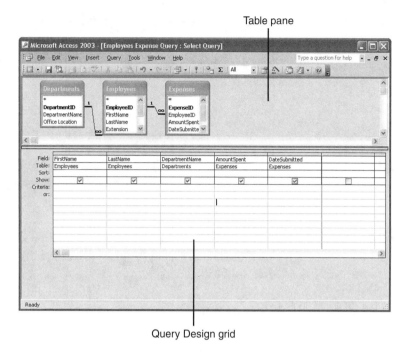

Table pane

Figure 16.1   The Query Design view is divided into a Table pane and a Query Design grid.

Starting a New Query in Query Design View

Creating a new query from scratch in the Query Design view allows you to select both the tables and the fields that you use to build the query. To begin a new query in Query Design view, follow these steps:

1. Click the **Queries** icon in the database window.

2. In the Query list, double-click **Create Query in Design View**. The Show Table dialog box appears, listing all the tables in the database (see Figure 16.2).

3. Click a table that contains fields you want to use in the query, and then click the **Add** button (you can also build queries from existing queries or a combination of tables, queries, or queries and tables). Repeat for each table you want to add.

4. Click **Close** when you finish adding tables. The Query Design view window opens.

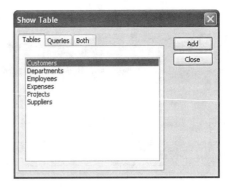

Figure 16.2   Choose which tables you want to include in the query.

The tables chosen for the query appear in the top pane of the Query Design view. Field names do not appear in the Query Design grid until you add them. Adding fields to the query is covered in the next section.

 TIP   **Create Table Relationships**   When you create queries from multiple tables, these tables must be related. See Lesson 9, "Creating Relationships Between Tables," for more information.

Adding Fields to a Query

Whether you create your query from scratch or modify an existing query, the Query Design view provides the capability to add the table fields that will be contained in the query. Be sure that the tables that contain the fields for the query are present in the design window.

 TIP   **Adding More Tables**   You can add tables to your query at any time. Click the Show Table button on the toolbar, or select Query, Show Table. Then, select the tables you want and click Add. Click Close to return to your query design.

To add a field to the query, follow these steps:

1. In the first field column of the query grid, click in the **Field** box. A drop-down arrow list appears.

2. Click the drop-down list and select a field (see Figure 16.3). Because all the fields available in the tables you selected for the query are listed, you might have to scroll down through the list to find the field you want to use.

3. Click in the next field column and repeat the procedure. Add the other fields that you want to include in the query as needed.

Drop-down list of fields

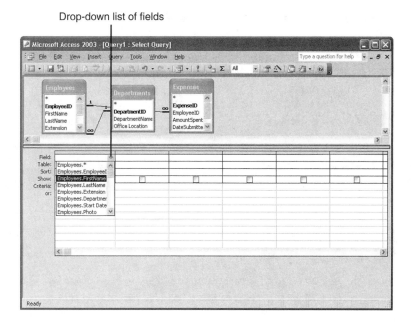

Figure 16.3   Scroll through the Field list to locate the field you want to place in the query.

As you add the fields to the query from left to right, be advised that this will be the order in which the fields appear in the query when you run it. If you need to change the field that you've placed in a particular field column, use the Field drop-down list in the column to select a different field.

TIP   **Quickly Add Fields to the Query**   You can also add fields to the query directly from the tables that appear in the Table pane of the Query Design view. In one of the tables, locate the field that you want to place in the first field column and double-click the field name (in the table itself). The field appears in the Field box in the first field column of the query grid. To add the next field, locate it in a table, and then double-click it. This method enables you to select the fields from specific tables rather than scrolling through a long, continuous list of field names.

Deleting a Field

If you place a field that you don't want into a field column, you can replace it using the drop-down list in the Field box (of that column) to select a different field. If you don't want a field in that field column at all, you can delete the field from the query. Deleting the field deletes the entire field column from the query. You can use two methods for deleting a field column from the query:

- Click anywhere in the column and select Edit, Delete Columns.
- Position the mouse pointer directly above the column so that the pointer turns into a downward-pointing black arrow. Then click to select the entire column. To delete the selected field column, press Delete.

After you have selected the fields that you will use in the table, you are ready to set the criteria for the query.

Adding Criteria

The criteria that you set for your query determine how the field information found in the selected fields appears in the completed query. You set criteria in the query to filter the field data. The criteria that you set in a query are similar to the criteria that you worked with when you used the filtering features in Lesson 14, "Sorting, Filtering, and Indexing Data."

For example, suppose you have a query where you have selected fields from an Employee table and a Department table (which are related tables in your company database). The query lists the employees and their departments. You would also like to list only employees that were hired before March 2003. This means that you would set a criteria for your Start Date field of <03/01/2003. Using the less-than sign (<) simply tells Access that you want the query to filter out employee records where the start date is before (less than) March 1, 2003.

To set criteria for a field in your query, follow these steps:

1. In Query Design view, click the **Criteria** row in the desired field's column.
2. Type the criteria you want to use (see Figure 16.4).

Field:	DepartmentName	LastName	FirstName	Start Date		
Table:	Departments	Employees	Employees	Employees		
Sort:						
Show:	☑	☑	☑	☑	☐	☐
Criteria:				<03/01/2003		
or:						

Figure 16.4 Enter your criteria into the Criteria row of the appropriate field's column.

3. Queries can contain multiple criteria. Repeat steps 1 and 2 as needed to add additional criteria to field columns in the query.

Query criteria can act both on alphanumeric field data (text) and numeric data (dates are seen by Access as numerical information). For example, suppose you have a Customer table that lists customers in two states: Ohio (OH) and Pennsylvania (PA). The criterion used to filter the customer data in a query so that only customers in PA is shown in the query results would be PA. It's that simple.

When you work with criteria, symbols are used (such as the less-than sign that appears in the criteria in Figure 16.4) to specify how the query should evaluate the data string that you place in the Criteria box. Table 16.1 provides a list of some of these symbols and what you use them for.

Table 16.1 Sample Criteria for Queries

Symbol	Used For
< (less than)	Matching values must be less than (or before in the case of dates) the specified numerical string.
> (greater than)	Matching values must be greater than (or after in the case of dates) the specified numerical string.
<= (less than or equal to)	Matching values must be equal to or less than the value used in the criteria.
>= (greater than or equal to)	Matching values must be equal to or greater than the value used in the criteria.
= (equal to)	Matching values must be equal to the criteria string. This symbol can be used both with text and numeric entries.
Not	Values matching the criteria string will not be included in the results. For example, Not PA filters out all the records in which PA is in the state field.

Using the Total Row in a Query

You can also do calculations in a query, such as totaling numeric information in a particular field or taking the average of numeric information found in a particular field in the query. To add calculations to a query, you must add the Total row to the Query Design grid.

After the Total row is available in the query grid, different calculations can be chosen from a drop-down list in any of the fields that you have chosen for the query. For example, you can sum (total) the numeric information in a field, calculate the average, and even do more intense statistical analysis with formulas such as minimum, maximum, and standard deviation.

To add a calculation to a field in the query grid, follow these steps:

1. In Query Design view, click the **Totals** button on the Query Design toolbar. The Total row is added to the Query Design grid (just below the Table row).

2. Click in the Total row for a field in the Query Design grid that contains numerical information. A drop-down arrow appears.

3. Click the drop-down arrow (see Figure 16.5) to select the formula you want to place in the field's Total box. The following are some of the more commonly used formula expressions:

   - **Sum**—Totals the values found in the field.
   - **Avg**—Calculates the average for the values found in the field.
   - **Min**—Displays the lowest value (the minimum) found in the field.
   - **Max**—Displays the highest value (the maximum) found in the field.
   - **Count**—Calculates the number of entries in the field; it actually "counts" the entries.
   - **StDev**—Calculates the standard deviation for the values in the field. The standard deviation calculates how widely values in the field differ from the field's average value.

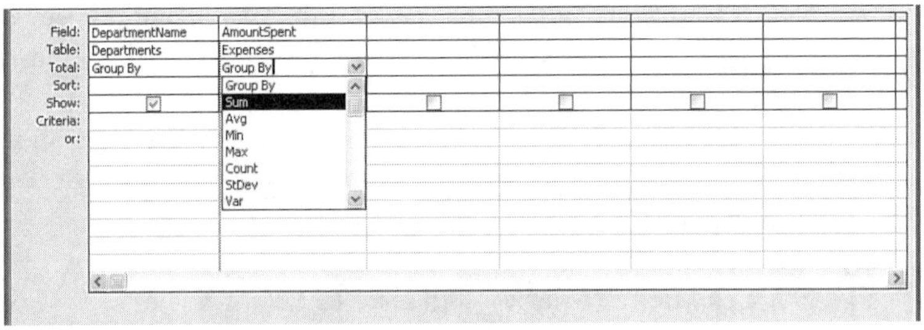

Figure 16.5   Calculations added to the Total row are chosen from a drop-down list.

4. Repeat steps 2 and 3 to place formulas into other field columns.

When you use the Total row, you can summarize the information in a particular field mathematically when you run the query. For example, you might want to total the number of orders for a particular product, so you would use the sum formula provided by the Total drop-down list.

Viewing Query Results

After you have selected the fields for the query and have set your field criteria, you are ready to run the query. As with tables created in the Design view and forms created in the Design view, you should save the query after you have finished designing it.

Just click the Save button on the Query Design toolbar. Supply a name for the query and then click Yes.

Now, you are ready to run the query. Click the Run button on the Query Design toolbar, or choose Query, Run. The query results appear in a datasheet that looks like an Access table (see Figure 16.6).

	First Name	Last Name	DepartmentName	Amount Spent	Date Submitted
▶	Nancy	Davy	Living Room Design	$1,200.00	1/15/2003
	Janet	Leverling	Porches and Decks	$300.00	1/18/2003
	Richard	Jones	Kitchen Design	$2,600.00	1/22/2003
	Steven	Buchanan	Architects	$1,800.00	1/23/2003
	Henry	Cotton	New Construction	$920.00	1/24/2003
	Snidley	Backlash	Porches and Decks	$1,560.00	2/3/2003
	Alice	Smith	Porches and Decks	$2,200.00	2/5/2003
	Robert	Buchanan	Bathroom Design	$5,500.00	2/7/2003
	Bob	Palooka	Architects	$1,400.00	2/8/2003
*					

Figure 16.6   The results of the query appear as a table datasheet.

After you have reviewed the results of your query, you can quickly return to the Query Design view to edit the query fields or criteria. Just click the Design View button on the toolbar.

Creating a Simple Report

17

In this lesson, you learn how to create reports in Access by using the AutoReport feature and the Report Wizard.

Understanding Reports

So far, the discussion of Access objects has centered on objects that are used either to input data or manipulate data that has already been entered into a table. Tables and forms provide different ways of entering records into the database, and queries enable you to sort and filter the data in the database.

Now you are going to turn your attention to a database object that is designed to summarize data and provide a printout of your database information—an Access report. Reports are designed specifically to be printed and shared with other people.

You can create a report in several ways, ranging from easy to difficult. An AutoReport, the simplest possibility, takes all the records in a table and provides a summary that is ready to print. The Report Wizard, an intermediate possibility, is still simple to use but requires more decisions on your part to select the fields and the structure of the report. Finally, the most difficult method of creating a report is building a report from scratch in the Report Design view. You learn about the Report Design view in the next lesson.

Using AutoReport to Create a Report

The fastest way to take data in a table and get it into a format that is appropriate for printing is AutoReport. The AutoReport feature can create a report in a tabular or columnar format. A tabular report resembles a datasheet in that it arranges the data from left to right on the page. A columnar report resembles a form in that it displays each record in the table from top to bottom. The downside of AutoReport is that it can create a report from only one table or query.

To use the AutoReport feature to create a simple report, follow these steps:

1. Open the database containing the table or query that you will use to create the report.

2. Click the **Reports** icon in the left pane of the database window.

3. Click the **New** button on the database window's toolbar. The New Report dialog box appears (see Figure 17.1).

Figure 17.1   Choose one of the AutoReport formats in the New Report dialog box.

4. Select one of the two available AutoReport options: **AutoReport:Columnar** or **AutoReport:Tabular**.

5. In the drop-down list at the bottom of the dialog box, select the table or query on which you want to base the report.

6. Click **OK**. The report appears in Print Preview. The Print Preview mode allows you to examine your report before printing. You learn more about Print Preview later in this lesson.

> **Create an AutoReport from an Open Table**   You can also create an AutoReport directly from an open table. With the table open in the Access window, click the New Object drop-down list on the Table Datasheet toolbar and select AutoReport. This creates a simple columnar report.

AutoReport produces fairly simple-looking reports. To have more control over the report format and layout, you can create a report using the Report Wizard.

Creating a Report with the Report Wizard

The Report Wizard offers a good compromise between ease-of-use and control over the report that is created. With the Report Wizard, you can build a report that uses multiple tables or queries. You can also choose a layout and format for the report. Follow these steps to create a report with Report Wizard:

1. Open the database containing the table or query on which you want to report.

2. Click the **Reports** icon in the database window.

3. In the Reports pane of the database window, double-click **Create Report by Using Wizard** to start the Report Wizard (see Figure 17.2). The first wizard screen enables you to choose the fields to include in the report.

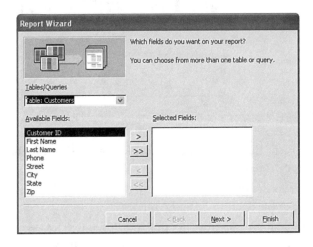

Figure 17.2   The first Report Wizard screen enables you to select the fields for the report.

4. From the Tables/Queries drop-down list, select a table or query from which you want to include fields.

5. Click a field in the Available Fields list, and then click the **Add >** button to move it to the Selected Fields list. Repeat this step to select all the fields you want, or click **Add All >>** to move all the fields over at once.

6. For a report using fields from multiple tables, select another table or query from the Tables/Queries list and repeat step 5. To build the report from more than one table, you must create a relationship between the tables. When you finish selecting fields, click **Next** to continue.

7. On the next wizard screen, Access gives you the option of viewing the data by a particular category of information. The wizard provides this option only when you build a report from multiple tables. For example, if you have a report that includes fields from a Customer table, a Products table, and an Orders table, the information in the report can be organized either by customer, product, or order information (see Figure 17.3). For example, if you organize the report by customer, each section of the report will be by customer. If you want the report to be viewed from the perspective of your product line, you will organize it by product. Select the viewpoint for the data from the list on the left of the wizard screen; then select **Next** to continue.

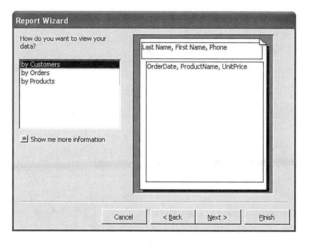

Figure 17.3 Data in the report can be arranged from a particular viewpoint based on the tables used to create the report.

8. On the next wizard screen, you can further group records in the report by a particular field. To group by a field, click the field and then click the **>** button. You can select several grouping levels in the order you want them. Then click **Next** to move on.

TIP   **Grouping?**   By default, the field data in the report are not grouped. By selecting different group levels, you can group information by department, product, or any field that you select. Grouping the data enables you to create a report that has been divided into logical subsections.

9. The wizard asks whether you would like to sort the records in the report (see Figure 17.4). If you want to sort the records by a particular field or fields (you can sort by more than one field, such as by last name and then first name), open the top drop-down list and select a field by which to sort. From the drop-down lists, select up to four fields to sort by, and then click **Next**.

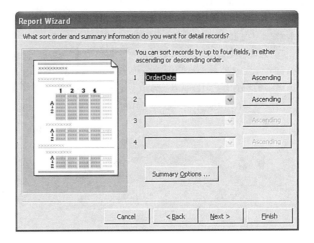

Figure 17.4 Set the sort order for your records.

10. On the next wizard screen, choose a layout option from the Layout section. When you click an option button for a particular layout, the sample in the box changes to show your selection.

TIP **Where Are All the Layouts?** If you don't choose any groupings in your report, you are limited to three layout choices: Columnar, Tabular, and Justified. More layouts are available when you have set grouping options for the report.

11. In the next wizard dialog box, choose a report style. Several are listed; click one to see a sample of it, and then click **Next** when you're satisfied with your choice.

12. On the last wizard screen, you're asked for a report title. Enter one into the Report text box, and click **Finish** to see your report in Print Preview.

Viewing and Printing Reports in Print Preview

When you create a report with either AutoReport or the Report Wizard, the report appears in Print Preview (as shown in Figure 17.5). From there, you can print the report if you're happy with it or go to Report Design view to make changes. (You'll learn more about the Report Design view in Lesson 18, "Customizing a Report.")

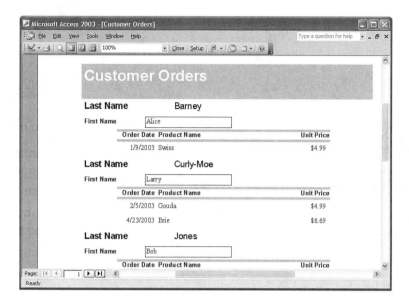

Figure 17.5 Either AutoReports or reports created with the wizard automatically open in Print Preview.

In the Print Preview mode, you can zoom in and out on the report using the Zoom tool (click once to zoom in and click again to zoom out). Using the appropriate button on the Print Preview toolbar, you can also display the report as one page, two pages, or multiple pages.

If you want to print the report and specify any print options (such as the number of copies), choose File, Print. If you want a quick hard copy, click the toolbar's Print button.

If you click the Close (X) button on the Print Preview toolbar, you are taken directly to the Report Design view. You learn about the Report Design view in the next lesson.

Customizing a Report

18

In this lesson, you learn how to use Report Design view to make your reports more attractive.

Working in the Report Design View

You've already seen that you can create reports using AutoReport and the Report Wizard. After you've created a report using either of these methods, you can edit or enhance the report in the Report Design view. You can also create reports from scratch in the Report Design view.

The Report Design view is similar to the Form Design view that you worked with in Lesson 11, "Modifying a Form," and Lesson 12, "Adding Special Controls to Forms." Like forms, reports are made up of controls that are bound to fields in a table or tables in the database.

To edit an existing report in the Design view, follow these steps:

1. Click the **Reports** icon in the database window.
2. In the list of reports provided, select the report you want to modify.
3. Click the **Design** button on the database toolbar. The report appears in Design view, as shown in Figure 18.1.

As you can see in Figure 18.1, the report's underlying structure contains several areas. The Detail area contains the actual controls that relate to the table fields included in the report. Above the Detail area is the Page Header, which contains the labels that are associated with the controls in the Detail area. At the very top of the report is the Report Header. It contains a text box that displays the name of the report.

At the bottom of the report are two footers. The Page Footer contains formulas that display the current date and print the page number of the report. At the very bottom of the report is the Report Footer. The Report Footer is blank in Figure 18.1. It can be used, however, to insert a summary formula or other calculation that works with the data that appears in the Detail area (you will add a calculation to a report later in the lesson).

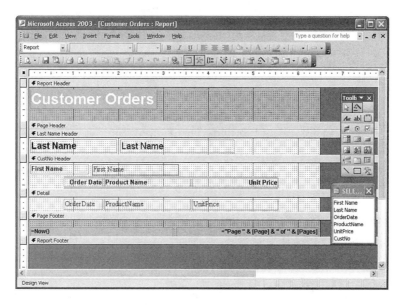

Figure 18.1 The report is divided into several areas in the Design view.

As already mentioned, the Report Design view is similar to Form Design view. The Report Design view also supplies the Toolbox, which is used to add text boxes and special controls to the report. The Field list allows you to add field controls to the report.

CAUTION

Using Special Controls on a Report Access enables you to place any type of control on a report, even command buttons or combo boxes. These won't do you much good on a report, however. It's better to stick to text boxes, labels, and graphics on reports—items that enhance the overall look of the report when it is printed.

Working with Controls on Your Report

Working with report controls in Report Design view is the same as working with controls in Form Design view. You might want to turn back to Lesson 11 to review how you manipulate controls and their labels. The following is a brief review:

- **Selecting Controls**—Click the control to select it. Selection handles appear around the control.
- **Moving Objects**—To move a control, first select it. Next, position the mouse pointer over a border so that the pointer turns into an open hand. Then, click and drag the control to a new location.

TIP **Moving Between Report Areas** You can't drag a control from one section of the report to another, but if you do need to move it, you can use cut and paste. Select the control (or label) and press Ctrl+X to cut it. Then, click the title of the section where you want to move it and press Ctrl+V to paste it into the newly selected section.

- **Resizing Objects**—First, select the object. Then, position the mouse pointer over a selection handle and drag it to resize the object.

- **B** **I** **U** **Formatting Text Objects**—Use the Font and Font Size drop down lists on the toolbar to choose fonts; then use the Bold, Italic, and Underline toolbar buttons to set special attributes.

You can add any controls to the report that the Toolbox provides. For example, you might want to add a graphic to the report, such as a company logo. The next section discusses adding an image to a report.

Adding an Image to a Report

You can add graphics, clip art, or even images from a digital camera to your Access reports. For example, if you want to add a company logo to a report, all you need is access to the logo image file on your computer (or a company's network). If you want to include an image, such as a company logo, on the very first page of the report, you will want to add it to the Report Header. Any information or graphics placed in the Report Header will appear at the very top of the report. Images that you want to use to illustrate information in the report should go in the Details area.

To add an image to a report, follow these steps:

1. Expand the area of the report (such as the Report Header) in which you want to place the image. For example, to expand the Report Header, drag the Page Header's title bar downward using the mouse (the mouse becomes a sizing tool when you place it on an area's border).

2. Click the **Image** button on the Toolbox. The mouse pointer becomes an image drawing tool.

3. Drag to create a box or rectangle that will contain the image in the appropriate area of the report. When you release the mouse, the Insert Picture dialog box appears (see Figure 18.2).

4. Use the Look In drop-down list to locate the drive that contains the image file, and then open the appropriate folder by double-clicking.

5. When you locate your image, click the filename to select it, and then click **OK**. The image is inserted into the report.

Figure 18.2 Use the Insert Picture dialog box to locate and insert your picture into the report.

You might find that the image file is larger than the image control that you have created. To make the image fit into the control, right-click the Image control and select Properties from the shortcut menu that appears. In the Properties dialog box, select the Format tab. Then, click in the Size Mode box and select Zoom from the drop-down list. This automatically sizes the graphic to fit into the control (which means that it typically shrinks the image to fit into the control). You can then close the Properties box. Figure 18.3 shows a picture that has been added to the header of a report. Note that in Print Preview the graphic appears at the top of the report.

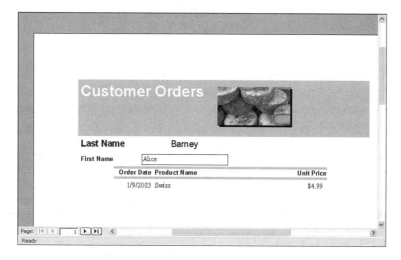

Figure 18.3 Images can be placed on reports.

TIP **Check Your Report Design in Print Preview**   As you work on the structure of your report in the Design view, you can check to see how things will look by switching to the Print Preview mode. Click the Print Preview button on the Report Design toolbar.

Arranging and Removing Controls

As already mentioned, you can move or resize the controls on the report. This also goes for any new controls that you add from the Toolbox or by using the Field list. You can also remove unwanted controls from the report.

To delete a control, select it by clicking it, and then press Delete. Deleting a control from the report doesn't delete the field from the associated table.

Adding Text Labels

You can also add descriptive labels to your report. For example, you might want to add a text box containing descriptive text to the Report Header.

 Click the Label button on the Toolbox. The mouse pointer becomes a label drawing tool. Drag with the mouse to create a text box in any of the areas on the report. When you release the mouse, you can begin typing the text that will be contained in the text label.

Placing a Calculation in the Report

Controls (also called text boxes in a report) most commonly display data from fields, as you've seen in the reports that you have created. However, text boxes can also hold calculations based on values in different fields.

TIP   **Calculations Can Be Added with the Wizard**   When you create a report with the Report Wizard, you are provided with options for placing summary calculations in the report. You can also add calculations to a report "after the fact" as discussed in this section.

Creating a text box holding a calculation is a bit complicated: First, you must create an unbound control/text box (that is, one that's not associated with any particular field), and then you must type the calculation into the text box. Follow these steps:

 1. Click the **Text Box** tool in the Toolbox, and then click and drag on the report to create a text box.

2. Change the label to reflect what's going in the text box. For example, if it's sales tax or the total of your orders multiplied by the price of your various products, change the label accordingly. Position the label where you want it.

3. Click in the text box and type the formula that you want calculated. (See the following list for guidance.)

4. Click anywhere outside the text box when you finish.

Figure 18.4 shows a control that provides the total value of the orders for each item. This control multiplies the Quantity control (which is tied to a field that supplies the number of orders for each item) by the UnitPrice control (which provides the price of each item).

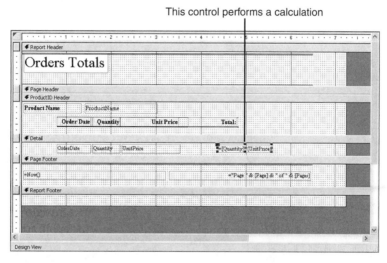

This control performs a calculation

Figure 18.4 You can add controls to the report that do calculations.

The formulas you enter into your calculated text box use standard mathematical symbols:

+	Add
-	Subtract
*	Multiply
/	Divide

All formulas begin with an equal sign (=), and all field names are in parentheses. The following are some examples:

- To calculate a total price where a control called Quantity contains the number of items and a control called Price holds the price of each item, you would multiply these data in these two controls. The formula would look like this: **=[Quantity]*[UnitPrice]**.

- To calculate a 25% discount off the value in the field, such as a field called Cost, you would type the formula **=[Cost]*.075**.
- To add the total of the values in three fields, enter **[Field1]+[Field2]+[Field3]** (where Field# is the name of the field).

 TIP   **More Room**   If you run out of room in the text box when typing your formula, press Shift+F2 to open a Zoom box, which gives you more room within the control.

Taking Advantage of Database Relationships

In this lesson, you learn how to view related table data and use related tables in forms and reports.

Reviewing Table Relationships

When we first discussed creating a database in the Access section of this book, we made a case for creating tables that held discrete subsets of the data that would make up the database. We then discussed the importance of creating relationships between these tables in Lesson 9, "Creating Relationships Between Tables." In this lesson, you take a look at how you can take advantage of related tables when creating other Access objects, such as forms, queries, and reports.

As previously discussed in Lessons 1 and 9, tables are related by a field that is common to each table. The common field serves as the primary key in one of the tables and as the foreign key in the other table. (The foreign key is the same field, but it is held in a table where it does not serve as the primary key.)

For example, in Figure 19.1, an Employees table is linked to two other tables: Expenses and Departments. The Employees table and the Expenses table are related because of the EmployeeID field. The Employees table and the Departments table are related by the DepartmentID field.

The more complex your database, the more tables and table relationships the database contains. For example, Figure 19.2 shows a complex company database that contains several related tables.

More important to the discussion in this lesson is how you take advantage of related tables to create complex forms and reports. First, take a look at how related table data can be viewed in the Table Datasheet view.

Denotes foreign key⌐   ⌐Denotes primary key

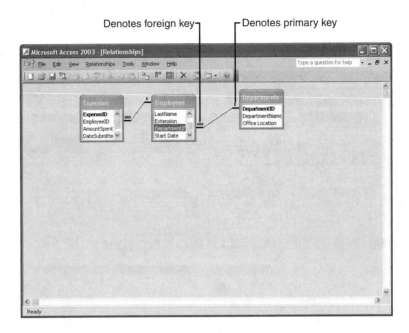

Figure 19.1   Related tables share a common field.

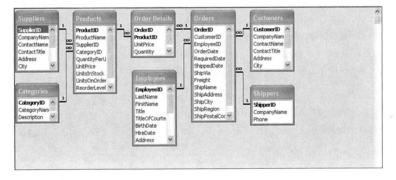

Figure 19.2   Complex databases contain many related tables.

Viewing Related Records in the Datasheet View

When working with a table in the Datasheet view, you can view data held in a related table. The information that can be viewed is contained in any table that is subordinate to the table you currently have open in the Datasheet view. Tables subordinate to a particular table hold the foreign key (which is the primary key in the top-level table in the relationship).

For example, suppose you are viewing the Departments table that was included in the table relationships shown in Figure 19.1. A plus sign appears to the left of each record in the table (see Figure 19.3). To view related data for each record, click the plus sign (which then changes to a minus sign). A table appears that contains the related data for that record. In this example, the Employees table provides the related data (which, if you look back at Figure 19.1, was related subordinately to the Departments table).

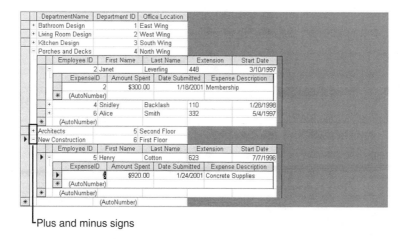

Plus and minus signs

Figure 19.3 Display related records in the linked table by clicking a plus sign next to a record. Contract them again by clicking the minus sign.

When related records are displayed, the plus sign turns into a minus sign. Click that minus sign to hide the related records again.

As you can see in Figure 19.3, even the related records can have linked information. For example, clicking any of the plus signs next to the records containing employee information shows data pulled from the Expenses table (which, again referring to Figure 19.1, is related to the Employees table).

Creating Multi-Table Queries

The real power of relational databases is to use the related tables to create other Access objects, such as queries. Multi-table queries enable you to pull information from several related tables. You can then use this query to create a report or a form.

The easiest way to create a multi-table query is in the Query Design view. Follow these steps:

1. From the database window (with the Queries icon selected), double-click **Create Query in Design View**. The Show Table dialog box appears.

2. In the Show Table dialog box (see Figure 19.4), select the related tables that you want to include in the query. For example, using the tables shown in Figure 19.4, you could create a query using the Employees, Departments, and Expenses tables that would show you each employee, the department, and any expenses that the employee has incurred.

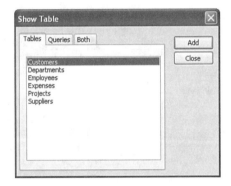

Figure 19.4 Select the tables that will be used to create the multi-table query.

3. After you have selected the tables for the query, click **Close** to close the Show Table dialog box. The tables and their relationships appear at the top of the Query Design window.

4. Add the fields to the Query grid that make up the query. The fields can come from any of the tables that you have included in the query. Figure 19.5 shows a multi-table query that includes fields from the Employees, Departments, and Expenses tables.

5. When you have finished designing the multi-table query, you can run it. Click the **Run** button on the toolbar.

The query results appear in the Datasheet view. Combining data from related tables into one query allows you to create other objects from that query, reports.

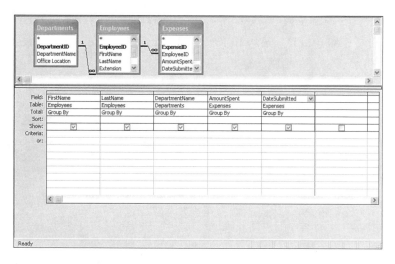

Figure 19.5 Multi-table queries enable you to pull data from fields on more than one table.

Creating Multi-Table Forms

Forms can be created from more than one table using the Form Wizard or the Form Design view. Creating a form from fields that reside in more than one table allows you to enter data into more than one table using just the single form.

A very simple way to create a multi-table form is to add a *subform* to an existing form. For example, you might have a form that is based on a Customers table. If you would also like to be able to view and enter order information when you work with the Customers form, you can add an Orders subform to it. It is important that the tables used to create the two forms (the main form and the subform) are related tables.

 Subform A form control that actually consists of an entire form based on another table or tables.

The easiest way to create a subform is to actually drag an existing form onto another form in the Design view. The following steps describe how you do it:

1. Use the AutoForm feature, the Form Wizard, or the Form Design view to create two forms: the form that serves as the main form and the form that serves as the subform. These forms should be based on tables that are related (see Lessons 10 and 11 for more about creating forms).

2. In the Form Design view, open the form that will serve as the main form.

3. Size the Form Design window so that you can also see the database window in the Access workspace (see Figure 19.6).

Click and drag

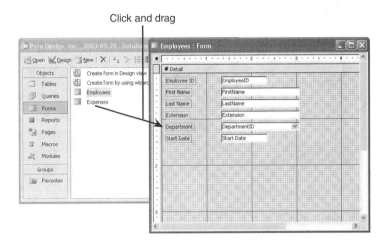

Figure 19.6 The subform is dragged from the database window onto the Design view of the main form.

4. In the database window, be sure that the Forms list is showing. Then, drag the form that will serve as the subform onto the main form that is open in the Design view. When the mouse pointer enters the Design view, it becomes a control pointer. Release the mouse button when you are in the general area where you want to place the subform. The subform control appears on the main form.

5. Maximize the Form Design window. Reposition or size the subform in the Design view until you are happy with its location (see Figure 19.7).

6. Save the changes that you have made to the main form (specifically, the addition of the subform).

7. To change to the Form view to view or add data to the composite form, click the **View** button on the Form Design toolbar.

Figure 19.8 shows the main form and the subform in the Form view. The form can be used to view or enter data into two tables at once.

Main form

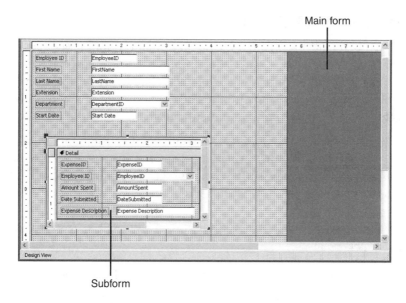

Subform

Figure 19.7   The subform becomes another control on the main form.

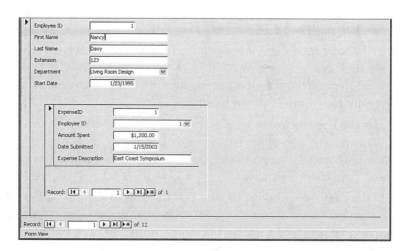

Figure 19.8   The composite form can be used to view and enter data into more than one table.

Creating Multi-Table Reports

You can also create reports that include information from more than one table or query. The process is the same as the procedure that you used in Lesson 17, "Creating a Simple Report," when you used the Report Wizard to create a report. All you have to do is select fields from related tables during the report creation process. This allows the report to pull information from the related tables.

An alternative to creating reports that contain fields from more than one table is to create a report that contains a *subreport*. The procedure is similar to the procedure discussed in the previous section, when you created a main form that held a subform.

 TERM **Subreport**   A report control that consists of an entire report based on another table or tables.

To create a report that contains a subreport, follow these steps:

1. Use the AutoReport feature, the Report Wizard, or the Report Design view to create two reports: the report that serves as the main report and the report that serves as the subreport. These reports should be based on tables that are related (see Lessons 17 and 18 for more about Access reports).

2. In the Report Design view, open the report that will serve as the main report. Size the area in which you will place the subreport. For example, you might want to place the subreport in the Report Header area so that it can be viewed on any page of the printed report.

3. Size the Report Design window so that you can also see the database window in the Access workspace (working with reports and subreports is similar to working with forms and subforms; see Figure 19.6 when arranging the report and database windows).

4. In the database window, be sure that the Reports list is showing. Then, drag the report that will serve as the subreport onto the main report in the Design view window. Don't release the mouse until you have positioned the mouse pointer in the area (such as the Report Header) where you want to place the subreport.

5. Size or move the subreport control as needed and then save any changes that you have made to the main report.

When you view the composite report in the Print Preview mode, the subreport appears as part of the main report. Figure 19.9 shows the composite report in the Print Preview mode. Placing subreports on a main report enables you to include summary data that can be referenced while data on the main report is viewed either on the screen or on the printed page.

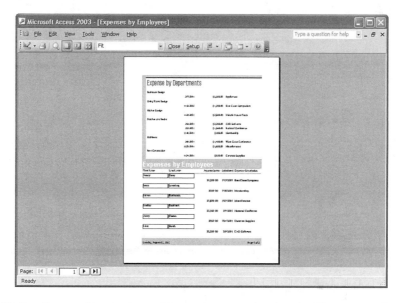

Figure 19.9   Composite reports enable you to report the data in different ways on the same report.

Printing Access Objects

In this lesson, you learn how to print Access tables, forms, queries, and reports.

Access Objects and the Printed Page

You have probably gotten a feel for the fact that tables, forms, and queries are used mainly to view and manipulate database information on your computer's screen, whereas the report is designed to be printed. This doesn't mean that you can't print a table or a form; it's just that the report provides the greatest amount of control in placing information on the printed page.

First, this lesson discusses printing Access objects with the report. Then, you look at printing some of the other Access objects, such as a table or form.

Printing Reports

As you learned earlier in this section of the book, the Access report is the ideal format for presenting database information on the printed page. Using reports, you can add page numbering controls and other header or footer information that repeat on each page of the report.

Whether you create a report using AutoReport or the Report Wizard, the completed report appears in the Print Preview mode, as shown in Figure 20.1.

 You can immediately send the report to the default printer by clicking the Print button on the Print Preview toolbar. If you find that you would like to change the margins on the report or change how the report is oriented on the page, click the Setup button on the Print Preview toolbar. The Page Setup dialog box appears (see Figure 20.2).

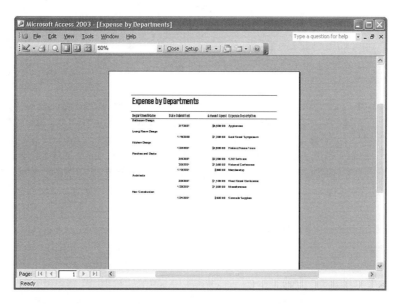

Figure 20.1 Reports created using AutoReport or the Report Wizard open in the Print Preview mode.

Figure 20.2 The Page Setup dialog box page orientation of the printed report.

Three tabs are on the Page Setup dialog box:

- **Margins**—This tab enables you to set the top, bottom, left, and right margins. To change one of the default settings (1 inch), type the new setting in the appropriate margin box.

- **Page**—This tab enables you to change the orientation of the report on the printed page. Portrait, which is the default setting, orients the report text from top to bottom on a regular 8 1/2-inch by 11-inch page. Landscape turns the page 180 degrees, making it an 11-inch by 8 1/2-inch page. Landscape orientation works well for reports that contain a large number of fields placed from left to right on the report. This tab also enables you to select the type of paper that you are going to use for the printout (such as letter, legal, and so on).

- **Columns**—This tab enables you to change the number of columns in the report and the distance between the columns. Because the columns for the report are determined when you create the report using AutoReport or the Report Wizard, you probably won't want to tamper with the column settings. It's easier to change the distance between field controls in the Report Design view.

 TIP **Use the Report Design View to Make Design Changes**   If you find that the report needs some major structural changes, click the View button to go to the Design view.

After you have finished making your choices in the Page Setup dialog box, click OK to close the dialog box. You can now print the report.

Printing Other Database Objects

The fastest way to print a database object, such as a table, form, or query, is to select the object in the database window. Just select the appropriate object icon in the database window and select an object in the object list, such as a table.

 After the object is selected, click the Print button on the database toolbar. Your database object is sent to the printer.

If you would like to preview the printout of a table, form, or query, either select the particular object in the database window or open the particular object and then click the Print Preview button. The object is then displayed in the Print Preview mode, such as the table shown in Figure 20.3.

When you print tables, forms, or queries, the name of the object and the current date are placed at the top of the printout. Page numbering is automatically placed at the bottom of the printout. You can control the margins and the page layout (portrait or landscape) for the table printout (or other object) using the Page Setup dialog box (discussed earlier in this lesson).

Figure 20.3 Any database object, such as a table, can be viewed in Print Preview.

Using the Print Dialog Box

So far, this discussion of printing in Access has assumed that you want to print to your default printer. You can also print a report or other database object to a different printer and control the range of pages that are printed or the actual records that are printed. These settings are controlled in the Print dialog box.

From the Print Preview mode or with a particular object open in the Access window, select File, Print. The Print dialog box appears (see Figure 20.4).

To select a different printer (one other than the default), click the Name drop-down list and select a printer by name. If you want to select a range of pages to print (such as a range of pages in a report), click the Pages option button and then type the page range into the page boxes.

In the case of tables and queries, you can also print selected records. Before you open the Print dialog box, select the records in the table or query. Then, when you open the Print dialog box, click the Selected Record(s) option button.

When you have finished changing the default printer or specifying a page range or the printing of select records, you are ready to print the object. Click the OK button. This closes the Print dialog box and sends the object to the printer.

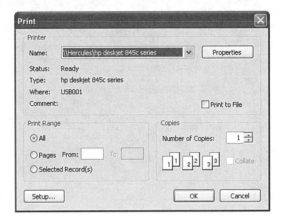

Figure 20.4   The Print dialog box enables you to select a different printer or specify a print range.

PowerPoint

Working in PowerPoint

In this lesson, you learn how to start and exit PowerPoint. You also learn about the PowerPoint presentation window.

Starting PowerPoint

PowerPoint is a powerful application that enables you to create presentations that can be viewed on a computer. Using PowerPoint, you can print handouts or create film slides for a presentation. PowerPoint also enables you to add animation and sound to your presentations, which makes it the perfect tool for business presentations or classroom lectures.

To start PowerPoint, follow these steps:

1. Click the **Start** button.

2. Move your mouse pointer to **Programs** (**All Programs** on Windows XP). A menu of programs appears. Point at the **Microsoft Office** icon.

3. Move your mouse pointer to the **Microsoft Office PowerPoint** icon and click it. The PowerPoint application window opens, as shown in Figure 1.1.

The first thing you see when you open PowerPoint is that the application window is divided into different areas. The default view for PowerPoint is the Normal view (you learn about the different PowerPoint views in Lesson 3, "Working with Slides in Different Views"). On the left of the screen is a pane that can be used to switch between an Outline and Slides view of the current presentation. In the center of the PowerPoint application window is the Slide pane; this is where you work individually on each slide in the presentation.

Below the Slide pane is the Notes pane, which enables you to add notes to the presentation for each slide. On the far right of the application window is the New Presentation task pane. The task pane provides different commands and features depending on what you are currently doing in PowerPoint.

Slide pane   Outline and Slides pane   Task pane

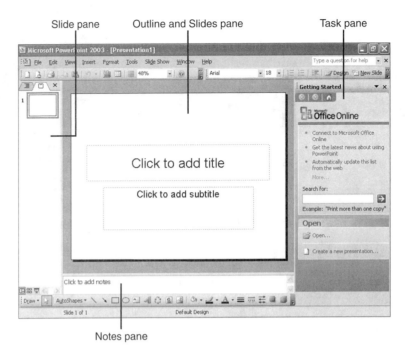

Notes pane

Figure 1.1   The PowerPoint window is divided into several panes.

Getting Comfortable with the PowerPoint Window

Although PowerPoint looks a little different from the other Office applications, such as Word and Excel, all the standard Office application components, such as the menu bar and various toolbars, are available to you as you design your presentations. The basic element of a presentation is a slide, to which you add text and other objects, such as images, using the Slide pane (which is discussed in the next lesson). PowerPoint provides several slide layouts; each layout provides the necessary text boxes or clip-art boxes for creating a particular type of slide.

Adding text to a slide is very straightforward. Each slide that you add to a presentation (Lesson 5, "Inserting, Deleting, and Copying Slides," discusses inserting slides into a presentation) contains placeholder text that tells you what to type into a particular text box on the slide. For example, Figure 1.2 shows a title slide. Note that the top text box on the slide says Click to Add Title.

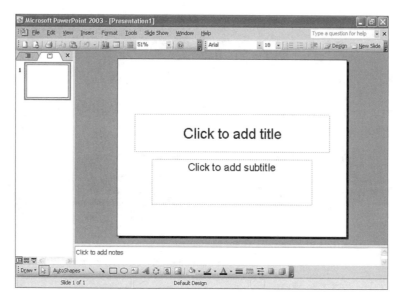

Figure 1.2   Click the placeholder text to input text into a slide.

To replace the placeholder text with your own text, just click the placeholder text. Then, you can type your entry into that text box.

Because a presentation consists of several slides, PowerPoint provides a thumbnail view of each slide in the presentation to the left of the Slides pane. Figure 1.3 shows an example of a complete presentation with a series of these thumbnail slides. This view can be used to keep track of your slides as you add them to the presentation and can even be used to rearrange slides in the presentation.

Because presentations require a certain logical arrangement of information, you can view the slides in the presentation as an outline. This enables you to make sure that you have the facts presented by each slide in the proper order for the presentation. The Outline pane also enables you to move topics within the presentation and even move information from slide to slide. Figure 1.4 shows the Outline pane for a presentation that contains several slides.

You learn about using the Slides and Outline pane in Lesson 3, "Working with Slides in Different Views."

Lesson 3 shows you how you can edit the presentation's text in either the Outline or the Slide pane. Changes in one pane are reflected in the other pane. When you want to place a nontext object on a slide (such as a graphic), you do so in the Slide pane.

Thumbnail slide images

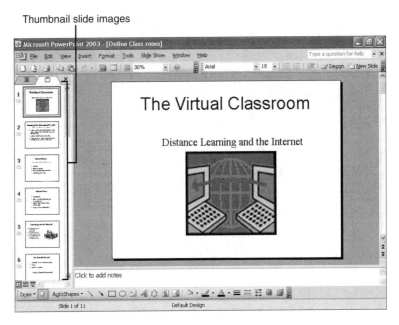

Figure 1.3   The Slides pane enables you to view thumbnails of the slides in the presentation.

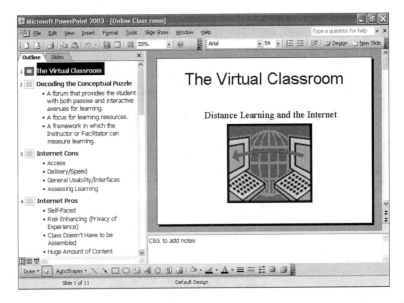

Figure 1.4   The Outline pane enables you to view the topic of each slide and each piece of text information included in a slide.

Exiting PowerPoint

When you finish using PowerPoint, you can exit the application. This closes any open presentations (PowerPoint might prompt you to save changes to those presentations).

To exit PowerPoint, perform one of the following:

- Click the PowerPoint window's **Close (X)** button.
- Double-click the **Control Menu** icon in the left corner of the title bar, or click it once to open the Control menu and then select Close.
- Open the **File** menu and select **Exit**.
- Press **Alt+F4**.

Creating a New Presentation

2

In this lesson, you learn several ways to create a presentation. You also learn how to save, close, and open an existing presentation.

Starting a New Presentation

PowerPoint offers several ways to create a new presentation. Before you begin, decide which method is right for you:

- The AutoContent Wizard offers the highest degree of help. It walks you through each step of creating the new presentation. When you're finished, you have a standardized group of slides, all with a similar look and feel, for a particular situation. Each slide created includes dummy text that you can replace with your own text.

- A design template provides a professionally designed color, background, and font scheme that applies to the slides you create yourself. It does not provide sample slides.

- You can also start a new presentation based on an existing presentation. This "copies" all the slides in the existing presentation and allows you to save the new presentation under a new filename.

- You can start from scratch and create a totally blank presentation. That means that you build the presentation from the ground up and create each slide in the presentation. (Beginners might want to use the wizard or templates until they get a feel for the overall design approach used to create a cohesive slide presentation.)

Design Template   A design template is a preformatted presentation file (without any slides in it). When you select a template, PowerPoint applies the color scheme and general layout of the template to each slide you create for the presentation.

Creating a New Presentation with the AutoContent Wizard

With the AutoContent Wizard, you select the type of presentation you want to create (such as corporate, sales, or various projects), and PowerPoint creates an outline for the presentation.

The following steps describe how you use the AutoContent Wizard:

1. Select the **File** menu and select **New**. The New Presentation task pane appears on the right of the PowerPoint window, as shown in Figure 2.1 (if the Presentation task pane was already open in the window, you can skip to step 2).

Figure 2.1   Start the AutoContent Wizard from the task pane.

2. Click the **From AutoContent Wizard** link on the task pane.
3. The AutoContent Wizard starts. The opening wizard screen summarizes the process you should follow to create a new presentation. Click **Next** to continue.
4. The wizard provides you with category buttons for different categories of presentations: General, Corporate, Projects, and Sales/Marketing. Select a category by selecting the appropriate button (see Figure 2.2). A list of specific presentations will appear to the right of the category buttons. To see all the AutoContent presentations available, click the **All** button.

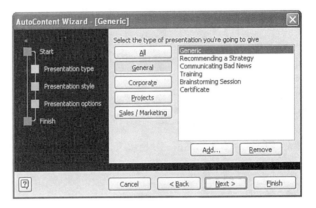

Figure 2.2 Select a category button to view a list of presentation types.

5. After selecting a particular category of presentations, select a presentation type in the list provided. You can choose to create a generic presentation, or presentations recommending a strategy, communicating bad news, or for a brainstorming session (among others). After selecting the type of presentation (I selected generic), click **Next** to continue.

6. On the next screen, you select how you will give the presentation. Select one of the following options:

   - **Onscreen Presentation**—Choose this if you plan to use a computer and your PowerPoint file to present the show.
   - **Web Presentation**—Choose this if you are planning to distribute the presentation as a self-running or user-interactive show.
   - **Black-and-White Overheads**—Choose this if you plan to make black-and-white transparencies for your show.
   - **Color Overheads**—Choose this if you plan to make color transparencies for your show.
   - **35mm Slides**—Choose this if you plan to send your PowerPoint presentation to a service bureau to have 35mm slides made. (You probably don't have such expensive and specialized equipment in your own company.)

7. After selecting how you will give the presentation, click **Next** to continue.

8. On the next screen, type the presentation title into the text box provided (see Figure 2.3). If you want to add a footer (such as your name or other) that will appear at the bottom of each slide of the presentation, click in the Footer box and type the appropriate text. If you do not want a date and/or slide number on each slide, deselect the **Date Last Updated** and/or **Slide Number** check boxes.

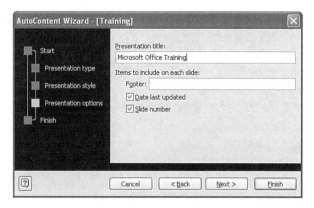

Figure 2.3   Provide a title for the presentation.

9. After supplying the presentation title and any optional information, click **Next** to continue.

10. PowerPoint takes you to the last wizard screen, where you should simply click **Finish**.

The title slide of your new presentation appears in the Slide pane. The entire presentation, including the dummy text placed on each slide, appears in the Outline pane on the left of the PowerPoint window (see Figure 2.4).

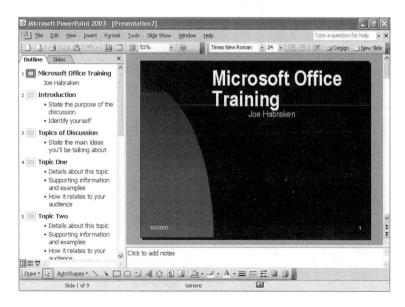

Figure 2.4   Your new presentation appears in the PowerPoint window.

You can start working on your presentation right away by replacing the dummy text on the slides with your own text. Just select the existing text in a text box and type right over it. You learn about editing text in slide text boxes in Lesson 7, "Adding and Modifying Slide Text."

Creating a New Presentation with a Design Template

A template is the middle ground between maximum hand-holding (the AutoContent Wizard) and no help at all (Blank Presentation). Two kinds of templates are available: presentation templates and design templates.

When you use the AutoContent Wizard, you use a presentation template. It contains not only formatting, but also sample slides that contain placeholder text. The other kind of template is a design template. It contains the overall formatting for the slides of the presentation but does not actually create any slides. If you want to use a presentation template that includes placeholder text, use the AutoContent Wizard, as explained in the preceding section.

To start a new presentation using a design template, follow these steps:

1. Select the **File** menu and select **New**. The New Presentation task pane appears on the right of the PowerPoint window.

TIP   **Select Your Task Pane**   If the task pane is already open for another PowerPoint feature, click the drop-down arrow on its title bar and select **New Presentation** from the list that appears.

2. On the New Presentation task pane, click the **From Design Template** link. PowerPoint switches to the Slide Design side pane, which displays a list of design templates, as shown in Figure 2.5. A blank title slide for the presentation appears in the Slide pane.

3. Click a template from the Available For Use section of the task pane. PowerPoint then formats the title slide in the Slide pane using the selected template.

You can select different templates to determine the best look for your presentation. When you have found the design template that you want to use, you can immediately start working on the slides for the presentation.

TIP   **The Next Step?**   Add more slides by clicking the **New Slide** button on the toolbar. Inserting slides into a presentation is covered in Lesson 5, "Inserting, Deleting, and Copying Slides."

Figure 2.5   Design templates are listed in the task pane.

Creating a New Presentation from an Existing Presentation

Another alternative for creating a new presentation is to use an existing presentation. This creates a copy of the existing presentation (and all its slides) and allows you to quickly save the presentation under a new filename.

1. Select the **File** menu and select **New**. The New Presentation task pane appears on the right of the PowerPoint window.

2. Select **From Existing Presentation** in the New Presentation task pane. The New from Existing Presentation dialog box opens (see Figure 2.6).

3. Use the Look in drop-down list to locate the drive and the folder that holds the existing presentation. When you locate the existing presentation, select it and then click **Create New**.

4. A "copy" of the existing presentation will open in the PowerPoint window.

When you have the copy of the existing presentation open, you can edit it as needed. You can then save the presentation under a new filename as discussed later in this lesson.

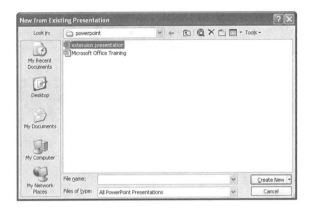

Figure 2.6 Open the existing presentation that the new presentation will be based on.

 TIP   **What Is the Photo Album?**   An additional choice, Photo Album, appears on the New Presentation task pane. This new presentation option provides you with a quick way to create a presentation that contains pictures and other images. We discuss the Photo Album in Lesson 9, "Adding Graphics to a Slide."

Creating a Blank Presentation

Your fourth option for creating a new presentation is to create a blank presentation. This means that you have to create all the slides from scratch. A design for the slides can then be selected using the Slide Design task pane. You open this task pane by selecting **Format**, **Slide Design**. In the Slide Design task pane, be sure that the Design Templates icon is selected.

Creating a new, blank presentation takes only a click: Click the **New** button on the Standard toolbar or click the **Blank Presentation** link on the New Presentation task pane. The new presentation appears in the PowerPoint window. A blank title slide is ready for you to edit.

Saving a Presentation

After you create a new presentation, it makes sense to save it. To save a presentation for the first time, follow these steps:

 1. Select **File**, **Save**, or just click the **Save** button on the Standard toolbar. The Save As dialog box appears (see Figure 2.7).

2. In the **File Name** text box, type the name you want to assign to the presentation. Your filenames can be as long as 255 characters and can include spaces.

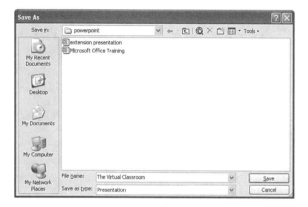

Figure 2.7   Type a name for your presentation into the Save As dialog box.

3. The Save In box shows in which folder the file will be saved. The default is My Documents. To select a different drive location for the file, click the **Save In** drop-down arrow and select one from the list that appears. To save to a specific folder in the drive location you've selected, double-click the folder in which you want to store the file.

4. Click **Save**.

Now that you have named the file and saved it to a disk, you can save any changes you make simply by pressing **Ctrl+S** or clicking the **Save** button on the Standard toolbar. Your data is saved under the filename you assigned to the presentation in the Save As dialog box.

To create a copy of a presentation under a different filename or location, select **File**, **Save As**. The Save As dialog box reappears; follow steps 2 to 4 as discussed in this section to give the file a new name or location.

Closing a Presentation

You can close a presentation at any time. Note that although this closes the presentation window, it does not exit PowerPoint as do the methods discussed in Lesson 1. To close a presentation, follow these steps:

1. If more than one presentation is open, click a presentation's button on the Windows taskbar to make it the active presentation, or you can select the **Window** menu and select the presentation from the list provided.

2. Select **File**, **Close,** or click the presentation's **Close** (**x**) button. (It's the lower of the two Close buttons; the upper one is for the PowerPoint window.) If you

haven't saved the presentation or if you haven't saved since you last made changes, a dialog box appears, asking whether you want to save.

3. To save your changes, click **Yes**. If this is a new presentation that has never been saved, refer to the steps in the preceding section for saving a presentation. If you have saved the file previously, the presentation window closes.

Opening a Presentation

A presentation, like Rome, is not built in a day, so you will probably fine-tune a presentation over time. To open a saved presentation file that you want to work on, follow these steps:

1. Select **File**, **Open**, or click the **Open** button on the Standard toolbar. The Open dialog box appears (see Figure 2.8).

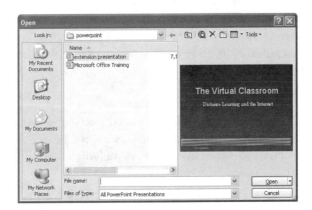

Figure 2.8 Select the presentation you want to open.

2. If the file isn't in the currently displayed folder, select the **Look In** drop-down arrow to choose from a list of other drives and/or folders.

3. Browse to the location containing the file and double-click it to open it in PowerPoint.

Finding a Presentation File

If you're having trouble locating your file, PowerPoint can help you look. Follow these steps to find a file:

1. Select **File**, **Open** (if the Open dialog box is not already open).

2. Click the **Tools** drop-down button in the Open dialog box and select **Search**. The File Search dialog box appears (see Figure 2.9).

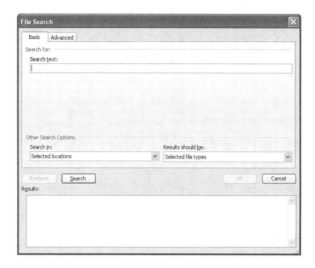

Figure 2.9   Use the File Search dialog box to find a presentation on your computer.

3. In the **Search Text** box, type text that is contained in the presentation's filename. Use the Search In box to specify where you want the search to be conducted. In the Results Should Be box, specify the file types you want to be included in the search.

4. When you are ready to conduct the search, click the **Search** button.

5. Files that meet the search criteria are listed in the Results box (if you see your file in the Results box and the search is continuing, click the **Stop** button).

6. To open a file in the Results box, double-click the filename.

7. You are returned to the Open dialog box with the file listed in the File Name box. Click **OK** to open the file. A PowerPoint presentation then opens in the PowerPoint window.

Working with Slides in Different Views

In this lesson, you learn how to display a presentation in different views and how to edit slides in the Outline and Slide views.

Understanding PowerPoint's Different Views

PowerPoint can display your presentation in different views. Each of these views is designed for you to perform certain tasks as you create and edit a presentation. For example, Normal view has the Outline/Slides, Slide, and Notes panes; it provides an ideal environment for creating your presentation slides and for quickly viewing the organization of the slides or the information in the presentation (using the Outline or the Slides tabs). Another view, the Slide Sorter view, enables you to quickly rearrange the slides in the presentation (and is similar to the Slides view that shares the pane with the Outline tab when you are in the Normal view).

To change views, open the **View** menu and choose the desired view: **Normal**, **Slide Sorter**, **Slide Show**, or **Notes Page**.

- **Normal**—The default, three-pane view (which is discussed in Lesson 1, "Working in PowerPoint").
- **Slide Sorter**—This view shows all the slides as thumbnails so that you can easily rearrange them by dragging slides to new positions in the presentation (Figure 3.1 shows the Slide Sorter).
- **Slide Show**—A specialized view that enables you to preview and present your show onscreen. It enables you to test the presentation as you add slides, and it is used later when your presentation is complete.
- **Notes Page**—This view provides a large pane for creating notes for your speech. You can also type these notes in Normal view, but Notes Page view gives you more room and allows you to concentrate on your note text.

An even faster way to switch to certain views is to use the view buttons that are provided along the lower-left corner of the PowerPoint window. These buttons, from left to right, are Normal View, Slide Sorter View, and Slide Show (from current slide) button. A button not provided for the Notes view.

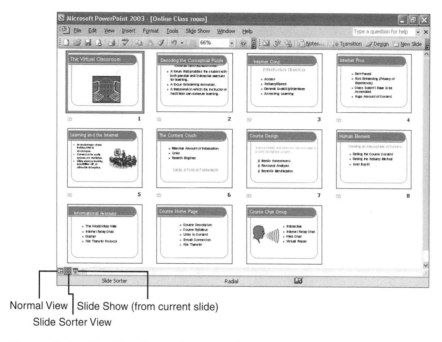

Normal View | Slide Show (from current slide)
Slide Sorter View

Figure 3.1 The Slide Sorter view is used to rearrange the slides in a presentation.

Moving from Slide to Slide

PowerPoint provides several ways to move from slide to slide in the presentation. The particular view you are in somewhat controls the procedure for moving to a specific slide.

In the Normal view, you can move from slide to slide using these techniques:

- Click the **Outline** tab on the far left of the window. To go to a particular slide in the outline, click the slide icon next to the slide number (see Figure 3.2). The slide opens in the Slide pane.

- Press the **Page Up** or **Page Down** keys to move to the previous or next slide, respectively.

- Click the **Previous Slide** or **Next Slide** button just below the vertical scrollbar (refer to Figure 3.2), or drag the scroll box inside the vertical scrollbar until the desired slide number is displayed.

- Click the **Slides** tab on the far left of the PowerPoint window. This enables you to move from slide to slide in the Normal view by selecting a particular slide's thumbnail. When you click the thumbnail, the slide appears in the Slide pane.

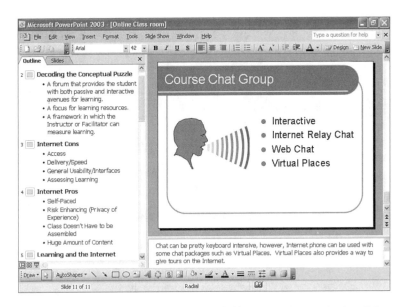

Figure 3.2　The Outline view can be used to quickly move to a particular slide.

You can also move from slide to slide in other views, such as the Slide Sorter view or the Slide Show view. In the Slide Sorter view (refer to Figure 3.1), just click a slide's thumbnail to move to that slide. You then can use any of the tools that PowerPoint provides to format the selected slide (or delete it). If you want to actually open a slide when you are working in the Slide Sorter view, so that you can edit the text it contains, double-click the slide. You are returned to the Normal view.

When you are actually showing a presentation in the Slide Show view, you can use the **Page Up** or **Page Down** keys to move from slide to slide (unless you have set up timers to change slides). You can also click a slide with the mouse to move to the next slide. You learn more about the Slide Show view in Lesson 12, "Presenting an Onscreen Slideshow."

Introduction to Inserting Slide Text

If you created a presentation in Lesson 2 using the AutoContent Wizard, you already have a presentation that contains several slides, but they won't contain the text you want to use. Slides created by the wizard contain placeholder text that you must replace. If you created a blank presentation or based a new presentation on a design template, you have only a title slide in that presentation, which, of course, needs to be personalized for your particular presentation. This means that additional slides will need to be added to the presentation. Lesson 5, "Inserting, Deleting, and Copying Slides," covers the creation of new slides for a presentation.

The sections that follow in this lesson look at the basics of inserting text into the text boxes provided on slides. You will look at adding new text boxes and formatting text in text boxes in Lesson 7, "Adding and Modifying Slide Text." Upcoming lessons also discuss how to add pictures and other objects to your PowerPoint slides.

 Object   An object is any item on a slide, including text, graphics, and charts.

Editing Text in the Slide Pane

The text on your slides resides within boxes (all objects appear on a slide in their own boxes for easy manipulation). As shown in Figure 3.3, to edit text on a slide, click the text box to select it and then click where you want the insertion point moved, or select the text you want to replace.

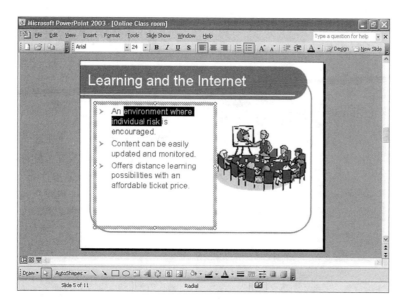

Figure 3.3   You can edit your text directly on the slide in the Slide pane.

When you work with the Slide pane, you might want to close the Outline/Slides pane. Just click the pane's **Close** button (X) to provide the Slide pane with the entire PowerPoint window (refer to Figure 3.3). In Lesson 7, "Adding and Modifying Slide

Text," you'll learn more about adding text to a slide, including creating your own text boxes on a slide.

TIP **Opening the Outline Pane** If you close the Outline pane to concentrate on the Slide pane, click **View**, **Normal (Restore Panes)** to restore it to the application window.

Editing Text in the Outline Pane

The Outline pane provides another way to edit text in a slide. To switch to the Outline view on the Outline/Slides pane, click the **Outline** tab. You simply click to move the insertion point where you want it (or select the range of text you want to replace) in the outline, and then type your text (see Figure 3.4). If you've placed the insertion point in the slide text (without selecting a range), press the **Delete** key to delete characters to the right of the insertion point or press the **Backspace** key to delete characters to the left. If you've selected a range of text, either of these keys deletes the text. If you want to move the highlighted text, simply drag it to where you want it moved.

TIP **Larger Outline** You might want to enlarge the Outline pane by dragging its divider to the right in the Normal view.

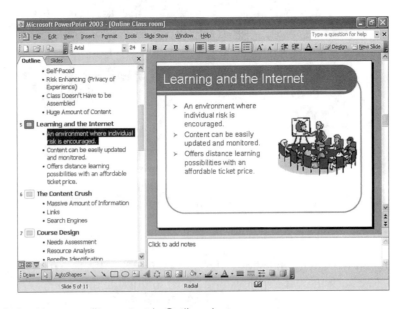

Figure 3.4 You can edit your text in Outline view.

> **TIP** **Auto Word Select** When you select text, PowerPoint selects whole words. If you want to select individual characters, open the **Tools** menu, select **Options**, click the **Edit** tab, and click the **When Selecting, Automatically Select Entire Word** check box to turn it off. Click **OK**.

Moving Text in the Outline Pane

As you work in the Normal view, you can also view your presentation slides as an outline using the Outline pane. This provides you with a quick way to move text items around on a slide or move them from slide to slide. Just select the text and drag it to a new position.

As already mentioned, you can also drag text from one slide to another. All you have to do is select a line of text in the Outline pane and drag it to another slide. You can also move a slide in the Outline pane. Drag the slide's icon in the Outline pane to a new position (under the heading for another slide).

If you aren't that confident with your dragging skills, PowerPoint provides you with help in the form of the Outlining toolbar. It provides buttons that make it easy to move text up or down on a slide (with respect to other text on the slide) or to move a slide up or down in the presentation.

To turn on the Outlining toolbar, right-click one of the PowerPoint toolbars and select **Outlining**. Figure 3.5 shows the Outlining toolbar on the left side of the Outline pane (the Outline pane has also been expanded to take up more of the PowerPoint window).

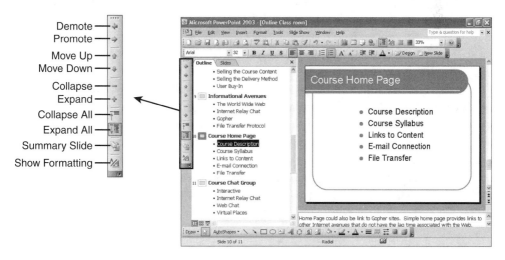

Figure 3.5 You can use the Outlining toolbar to move text and slides in the presentation.

- To move a paragraph or text line up in a slide, select it and click the **Move Up** button.

- To move a paragraph or text down in a slide, select it and click the **Move Down** button.

You can also use the **Move Up** and **Move Down** buttons to move entire slides up or down in the presentation. Click the slide's icon and then use the appropriate button (it might take several clicks to move a slide up or down with respect to another slide).

If you want to see how the text is actually formatted on the slides that you are viewing in the Outline pane, click the **Show Formatting** button on the Outlining toolbar. Viewing the text as it is formatted can help you determine where the text should appear on a slide as you move the text (or whether you will have to reformat the text later).

Rearranging Text in the Outline Pane

As you can see from Figure 3.5, your presentation is organized in a multilevel outline format. The slides are at the top level of the outline, and each slide's contents are subordinate under that slide. Some slides have multiple levels of subordination (for example, a bulleted list within a bulleted list).

You can easily change an object's level in Outline view with the Tab key or the Outlining toolbar:

- To demote a paragraph in the outline, click the text, and then press the **Tab** key or click the **Demote** button on the Outlining toolbar.

- To promote a paragraph in the outline, click the text, and then press **Shift+Tab** or click the **Promote** button on the Outlining toolbar.

In most cases, subordinate items on a slide appear as items in a bulleted list. In Lesson 8, "Creating Columns and Lists," you learn how to change the appearance of the bullet and the size and formatting of text for each entry, as well as how much the text is indented for each level.

 TIP **Create Summary Slides in the Outline Pane** If you would like to create a summary slide for your presentation that contains the headings from several slides, select those slides in the Outline pane (click the first slide, and then hold down the **Shift** key and click the last slide you want to select). Then, click the **Summary Slide** button on the Outlining toolbar. A new slide appears at the beginning of the selected slides containing the headings from the selected slides. You then can position the Summary slide anywhere in the presentation as you would any other slide.

Changing a Presentation's Look

In this lesson, you learn various ways to give your presentation a professional and consistent look.

Giving Your Slides a Professional Look

PowerPoint comes with dozens of professionally created designs and color schemes that you can apply to your presentations. These designs include background patterns, color choices, font choices, and more. When you apply a design template to your presentation, it applies its formatting to a special slide called the Slide Master.

The Slide Master is not really a slide, but it looks like one. It is a master design grid that you make changes to; these changes affect every slide in the presentation. When you apply a template, you are actually applying the template to the Slide Master, which in turn applies it to each slide in the presentation.

 Master Slide   A slide that contains the master layout and color scheme for the slides in a presentation.

You don't have to work with the Slide Master itself when you apply template or color scheme changes to your presentations. Just be aware that you can open the Slide Master (select **View**, point at **Master**, and then select **Slide Master**) and change the style and fonts used by the text boxes in a presentation (see Figure 4.1). You can also select a custom background color for the slides in the presentation. Any changes that you make to the Slide Master affect all the slides in the presentation.

You will probably find that PowerPoint provides enough template and color scheme options that you won't need to format the Slide Master itself very often. Edit its properties only if you have a very strict formatting need for the presentation that isn't covered in the templates and color schemes provided. For example, one good reason to edit the Slide Master would be a situation in which you want a graphic to appear on every slide (such as a company logo); you can place the image on the Slide Master instead of pasting it onto each slide individually.

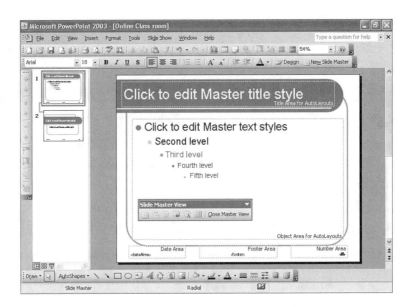

Figure 4.1 The Slide Master holds the default design and color options for the entire presentation.

 TIP **Close the Slide Master** If you open the Slide Master, you can close it by clicking **Close Master View** on the Master View toolbar.

Applying a Different Design Template

You can apply a different template to your presentation at any time, no matter how you originally created the presentation. To change the design template, follow these steps:

1. Select **Format**, **Slide Design** to open the Slide Design task pane. Then, if necessary, click the **Design Templates** icon at the top of the task pane. This provides a listing of PowerPoint's many design templates (see Figure 4.2).

2. Click the template that you want to use in the list. The template is immediately applied to the slide in the Slide pane.

 3. When you have decided on a particular template (you can click on any number of templates to see how they affect your slides), save the presentation (click the **Save** button on the toolbar).

Figure 4.2   Choose a different template from the Design Templates task pane.

The Design Template Changes Custom Formatting   If you spent time bolding text items on a slide or changing font colors, these changes are affected (lost) when you select a new design template. For example, if you have customized **CAUTION**   bold items in black in your original design template and switch to another template that uses white text, you lose your customizations. You should choose your design template early in the process of creating your presentation. Then, you can do any customized formatting at the end of the process so that it is not affected by a design template change.

When you work with design templates, you can apply them to all the slides in the presentation (as discussed in the steps provided in this section), or you can apply the template to selected slides in the presentation. Follow these steps to apply a template to a selected group of slides in a presentation:

1. Switch to the Slide Sorter view (select **View**, **Slide Sorter**).

2. Open the Slide Design task pane as outlined in the previous steps.

3. Now you must select the slide (or slides) to which you want to apply the template. Click the first slide you want to select, and then hold down the **Ctrl** key as you click other slides you want to select. To select a series of slides, click the first one and then Shift+click on the last slide to select them all.

4. Point at the design template you want to use in the Slide Design task pane; a drop-down arrow appears.

5. Click the template's drop-down arrow and select **Apply to Selected Slides** (see Figure 4.3).

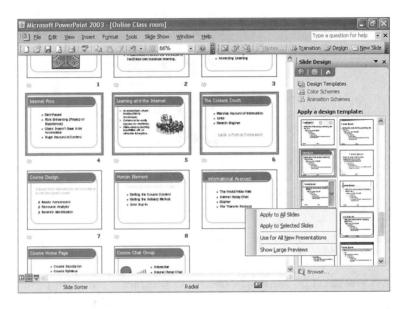

Figure 4.3 Design templates can be assigned to selected slides in a presentation.

The template's design is then applied to the selected slides.

 TIP **View a Larger Design Sample** To expand the view of the design templates, click the drop-down arrow on the template and select **Show Large Previews**.

Using Color Schemes

Design templates enable you to change the overall design and color scheme applied to the slides in the presentation (or selected slides in the presentation, as discussed in the previous section). If you like the overall design of the slides in the presentation but would like to explore some other color options, you can select a different color scheme for the particular template that you are using.

The number of color schemes available for a particular design template depends on the template itself. Some templates provide only three or four color schemes, whereas other templates provide more. As with design templates, you can assign a new color scheme to all the slides in the presentation or to selected slides.

To change the color scheme for the presentation or selected slides, follow these steps:

1. In the Normal or Slide Sorter view (use the Slide Sorter view if you want to change the color scheme for selected slides), open the task pane by selecting **View**, **Task Pane** (if the task pane is already open, skip to the next step).

2. Select the task pane's drop-down arrow and then select **Slide Design-Color Schemes**. This switches to the Color Schemes section of the Slide Design task pane. The color schemes available for the design template that you are using appear in the Apply a Color Scheme section (see Figure 4.4).

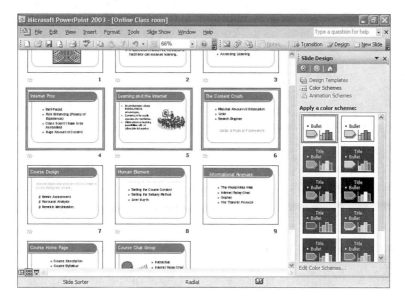

Figure 4.4   You can choose from a list of color schemes for the presentation or selected slides.

3. (Optional) If you are in the Slide Sorter view and want to assign a new color scheme only to selected slides, select those slides (click the first slide and then hold down **Ctrl** and click additional slides).

4. To assign the new color scheme to all the slides in the presentation, click a scheme in the Slide Design task pane. If you are assigning the color scheme only to selected slides, point at the color scheme and click its drop-down arrow. Select **Apply to Selected Slides**.

The new color scheme is applied to the slides in the presentation (or selected slides in the presentation). If you decide you don't like the color scheme, select another scheme from the task pane.

Changing the Background Fill

You can also fine-tune the color scheme that you add to a slide or slides by changing the background fill. This works best in cases where the design template and color scheme that you selected don't provide a background color for the slide or slides. You must be careful, however, because you don't want to pick a background color that obscures the text and graphics that you place on the slide or slides.

To change the background fill on a slide or slides, follow these steps:

1. Switch to the Slide Sorter view (select **View**, **Slide Sorter**).

2. (Optional) If you are going to change the background fill for selected slides, select those slides in the Slide Sorter window.

3. Select the **Format** menu and then select **Background**. The Background dialog box appears (see Figure 4.5).

Figure 4.5   Use the Background dialog box to add a fill color to a slide or slides.

4. Click the drop-down arrow at the bottom of the dialog box and choose a fill color from the color palette that appears.

5. To assign the fill color to all the slides in the presentation, click **Apply to All**. To assign the fill color to selected slides (if you selected slides in step 2), click **Apply**.

Inserting, Deleting, and Copying Slides

In this lesson, you learn how to insert new slides, delete slides, and copy slides in a presentation.

Inserting Slides into a Presentation

You can insert slides into your presentation. You can insert blank slides or you can insert slides from other presentations.

Let's look at inserting blank slides. Then we can look at inserting existing slides from another presentation.

Inserting a New, Blank Slide

You can insert a slide into a presentation at any time and at any position in the presentation. To insert a new slide, follow these steps:

1. On the Outline or Slides pane, select the slide that appears just before the place where you want to insert the new slide (you can also insert a new slide in the Slide Sorter view, if you want).

2.  Choose the **Insert** menu and then **New Slide**, or click the **New Slide** button on the PowerPoint toolbar. A new blank slide appears in the PowerPoint window, along with the Slide Layout task pane (see Figure 5.1).

3. In the Slide Layout task pane, select the slide layout that you want to use for the new slide. Several text slide layouts and layouts for slides that contain graphics are provided.

4. Follow the directions indicated on the slide in the Slide pane to add text or other objects. For text boxes, you click an area to select it and then type in your text. For other object placeholders, you double-click the placeholder.

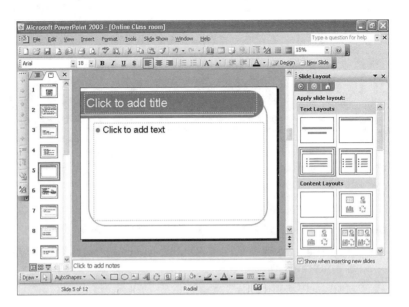

Figure 5.1   Your new slide appears in the PowerPoint window.

 TIP   **Cloning a Slide**   To create an exact replica of an existing slide (in any view), select the slide you want to duplicate. Click **Insert** and then select **Duplicate Slide**. The new slide is inserted after the original slide. You can then choose a different layout for the slide if you want.

Inserting Slides from Another Presentation

If you want to insert some or all of the slides from another presentation into the current presentation, perform these steps:

1. Open the presentation into which you want to insert the slides.

2. Select the slide located before the position where you want to insert the slides.

3. Select the **Insert** menu and select **Slides from Files**. The Slide Finder dialog box appears (see Figure 5.2).

4. Click the **Browse** button to display the Browse dialog box. In the Browse dialog box, locate the presentation that contains the slides that you want to insert into the current presentation (use the **Look In** drop-down arrow to switch drives, if necessary).

5. When you locate the presentation, double-click it.

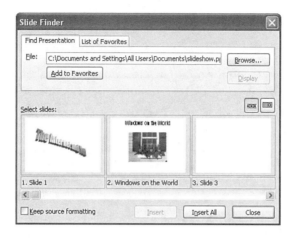

Figure 5.2   Use the Slide Finder dialog box to insert slides from another presentation.

6. The slides in the presentation appear in the Slide Finder's Select Slides box. To select the slides that you want to insert into the current presentation, click the first slide and then hold down **Ctrl** and click any subsequent slides.

7. When you have selected all the slides you want to insert, click **Insert** (if you want to insert all the slides, click **Insert All**).

8. PowerPoint inserts the slides into the presentation at the point you originally selected. Click **OK** to close the Slide Finder dialog box.

Creating Slides from a Document Outline

If you have created a document in Word that includes outline-style headings and numbered or bulleted lists (see Lesson 8, "Examining Your Documents in Different Views," in the Word section of this book for more information), PowerPoint can pull the headings and the text from the document and create slides. To create slides from a document outline, follow these steps:

1. Choose the **Insert** menu, and then choose **Slides from Outline**. The Insert Outline dialog box appears (it is similar to the Open dialog box used to open a presentation or other file).

2. Use the **Insert Outline** dialog box to locate the document file you want to use.

3. Double-click the name of the document file.

PowerPoint then uses all the first-level headings to create slides for your presentation. Any text in the document below a first-level outline heading is added to the slide in an additional text box.

Deleting Slides

You can delete a slide from any view. To delete a slide, perform the following steps:

1. Select the slide you want to delete. You can delete multiple slides by selecting more than one slide (on the Outline or Slides pane or in the Slide Sorter view).

2. Choose the **Edit** menu, and then choose **Delete Slide**. The slide is removed from the presentation.

 TIP **Use the Delete Key** You can quickly delete slides by selecting the slide or slides and then pressing the **Delete** key on the keyboard.

 Oops! If you deleted a slide by mistake, you can get it back. Select **Edit, Undo**, or press **Ctrl+Z**. This works only if you do it immediately. You cannot undo the change if you exit PowerPoint and restart the application.

CAUTION

Cutting, Copying, and Pasting Slides

In Lesson 6, "Rearranging Slides in a Presentation," you learn how to rearrange slides using the Slide Sorter and the Outline/Slides pane. Although dragging slides to new positions in the Slide Sorter is probably the easiest way to move slides, you can use the **Cut, Copy,** and **Paste** commands to move or copy slides in the presentation. Follow these steps:

1. Change to Slide Sorter view, or display Normal view and work with the Outline or Slides panes.

2. Select the slide(s) you want to copy or cut.

3. Open the **Edit** menu and select **Cut** or **Copy** to either move or copy the slide(s), respectively, or you can use the **Cut** or **Copy** toolbar buttons.

 TIP **Quick Cut or Copy** From the keyboard, press **Ctrl+C** to copy or **Ctrl+X** to cut.

4. In Slide Sorter view, select the slide after which you want to place the cut or copied slide(s), or on the Outline pane, move the insertion point to the end of the text in the slide after which you want to insert the cut or copied slide(s).

5. Select the **Edit** menu and choose **Paste**, or click the **Paste** toolbar button. PowerPoint inserts the cut or copied slides.

 TIP **Keyboard Shortcut** You can also press **Ctrl+V** to paste an item that you cut or copied.

Rearranging Slides in a Presentation

*In this lesson, you learn how to rearrange your slides using the
Slide Sorter view and the Outline/Slides pane.*

Rearranging Slides in Slide Sorter View

Slide Sorter view shows thumbnails of the slides in your presentation. This enables
you to view many if not all slides in the presentation at one time. Slide Sorter view
provides the ideal environment for arranging slides in the appropriate order for your
presentation. To rearrange slides in Slide Sorter view, perform the following steps:

1. If necessary, switch to Slide Sorter view by selecting **View** and then choosing
   Slide Sorter.
2. Place the mouse pointer on the slide you want to move.
3. Hold down the left mouse button and drag the slide to a new position in the
   presentation. The mouse pointer becomes a small slide box.
4. To position the slide, place the mouse before or after another slide in the presentation. A vertical line appears before or after the slide (see Figure 6.1).

Destination Not in View?   If you have more than just a few slides in your presentation, you might not be able to see the slide's final destination in the Slide Sorter.
Don't worry; just drag the slide in the direction of the destination, and the Slide Sorter
pane scrolls in that direction.

CAUTION

5. Release the mouse button. PowerPoint places the slide into its new position and
   shifts the surrounding slides to make room for the inserted slide.

You can also copy a slide in Slide Sorter view as easily as you can move a slide.
Simply hold down the **Ctrl** key while you drag the slide. When you release the
mouse, PowerPoint inserts a copy of the selected slide into the presentation.

Although the Slides pane on the left side of the Normal view window does not provide as much workspace as the Slide Sorter, you can use the techniques discussed in
this section to move or copy a slide. The Slides pane probably works best when you

have only a few slides in the presentation. When you have a large number of slides, you might want to switch from the Normal view to the Slide Sorter view.

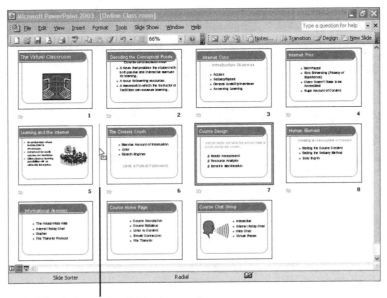

Vertical line indicates the slide's placement

Figure 6.1   Drag a slide in the presentation to a new position.

Rearranging Slides in the Outline Pane

In the Outline pane of the Normal view, you see the presentation as an outline that numbers each slide and shows its title and slide text. This provides you with a pretty good picture of the content and overall organization of your presentation. To rearrange the slides in your presentation using the Outline pane, follow these steps:

1. Switch to the Normal view by selecting **View**, **Normal**, or by clicking the **Normal** button on the bottom left of the PowerPoint window.

2. Click the slide number you want to move. This highlights the contents of the entire slide.

3. Place the mouse on the slide icon for that particular slide and drag the slide up or down within the presentation; then release the mouse.

TIP   **Use the Up or Down Buttons**   You can also move a slide in the outline by selecting the slide and then using the **Move Up** or **Move Down** buttons on the Outlining toolbar.

Hiding Slides

Before you give a presentation, you should try to anticipate any questions that your audience might have and be prepared to answer those questions. You might even want to create slides to support your answers to these questions and then keep the slides hidden until you need them. To hide one or more slides, perform the following steps:

1. In the Slide Sorter view or the Slides pane of the Normal view, select the slides you want to hide.

2. Select the **Slide Show** menu and then select **Hide Slide**. In the Slide Sorter view and in the Slides pane, the hidden slide's number appears in a box with a line through it (see Figure 6.2).

Hidden slides

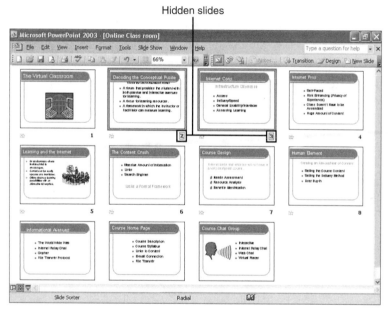

Figure 6.2   Hidden slides are denoted by a line through the slide number (slides 2 and 3 in this figure).

3. To unhide the slides, display or select the hidden slides, choose the **Slide Show** menu, and then select **Hide Slide** (the Hide Slide command toggles the slides from hidden to unhidden).

Remember that the slides are only hidden when you actually show the presentation. You can still edit or otherwise manipulate the slides in PowerPoint (in the other views, such as Normal view) even if you have marked them as "hidden."

 TIP   **Right-Click Shortcut**   To quickly hide a slide, you can right-click it and select **Hide Slide** from the shortcut menu that appears. To unhide the slide, right-click it again and select **Hide Slide** again.

Adding and Modifying Slide Text

In this lesson, you learn how to add text boxes to a slide and change the text alignment and line spacing.

Creating a Text Box

As you learned in Lesson 3, "Working with Slides in Different Views," the text on slides resides in various text boxes. To edit the text in a text box, click in the box to place the insertion point, and then enter or edit the text within the box. If you want to add additional text to a slide that will not be contained in one of the text boxes already on the slide, you must create a new text box.

 Text Box A text box acts as a receptacle for the text. Text boxes often contain bulleted lists, notes, and labels (used to point to important parts of illustrations).

To create a text box, perform the following steps:

1. If necessary, switch to the Normal view (select **View**, **Normal**). Use the Slides or Outline tab on the left of the workspace to select the slide that you want to work on. The slide appears in the Slide pane.

 2. Click the **Text Box** button on the Drawing toolbar (if the Drawing toolbar isn't visible, right-click any toolbar and select **Drawing**).

3. Click the slide where you want the text box to appear. A small text box appears (see Figure 7.1). (It will expand as you type in it.)

4. Type the text that you want to appear in the text box. Press **Enter** to start a new paragraph. Don't worry if the text box becomes too wide; you can resize it after you are done typing.

5. When you are finished, click anywhere outside the text box to see how the text appears on the finished slide.

If the text does not align correctly in the text box, see the section "Changing the Text Alignment and Line Spacing" later in this lesson to learn how to change it.

Inserted text box

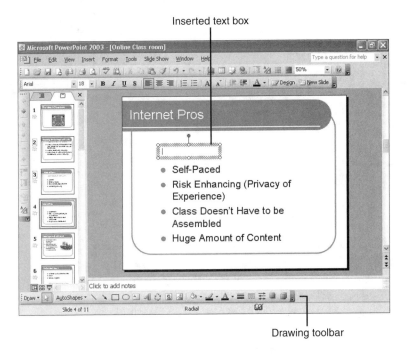

Drawing toolbar

Figure 7.1   Text boxes can be inserted from the Drawing toolbar.

You can also add a text box via the Insert menu. Select **Insert**, then **Textbox**. Then use the mouse to "draw" the text box on the slide. Using this command set to create a textbox actually allows you to create the width of the text box before you enter the text.

Sizing and Moving Text Boxes

You can size any of the text boxes on a slide. You can also move them on the slide. To size a text box follow these steps:

1. Select the text box.

2. Place the mouse on any of the sizing handles that appear on the box (they will be small round circles).

3. When you place the mouse on the sizing handle a sizing tool appears. Click and drag the sizing handle to change the size of the box. To retain the height-width ratio of the text box, use a sizing handle on any of the text box corners and drag on the diagonal. To move a text box, place the mouse pointer on any of the box borders. The mouse pointer becomes a move tool. Drag the box to any location on the slide.

TIP   **Rotate a Text Box**   You can rotate a text box using the green rotation handle that appears at the top center of a selected text box. Place the mouse pointer on the handle, and the rotation icon appears. Use the mouse to drag the rotation handle to the desired position to rotate the box.

Deleting a Text Box

You can delete text boxes from your slides. Select the text box (so that handles appear around it and no insertion point appears inside it), and then press the **Delete** key.

If you want to delete multiple text boxes, select the first text box and then select other text boxes with the mouse while holding down the **Ctrl** key. This will select each additional text box. Press the **Delete** key to delete the text boxes.

Changing Font Attributes

You can enhance your text by using the Font dialog box or by using various tools on the Formatting toolbar. Use the Font dialog box if you want to add several enhancements to your text at one time. Use the Formatting toolbar to add one font enhancement at a time.

Fonts, Styles, and Effects   In PowerPoint, a font is a family of text that has the same design or typeface (for example, Arial or Courier). A style is a standard enhancement, such as bold or italic. An effect is a special enhancement, such as shadow or underline.

Using the Font Dialog Box

The font dialog box offers you control over all the attributes you can apply to text. Attributes such as strikethrough, superscript, subscript, and shadow are available as check boxes in this dialog box.

You can change the font of existing text or of text you are about to type by performing the following steps:

1. To change the font of existing text, select text by clicking and dragging the I-beam pointer over the text in a particular text box. If you want to change font attributes for all the text in a text box, select the text box (do not place the insertion point within the text box).

2. Choose the **Format** menu and then choose **Font**. The Font dialog box appears, as shown in Figure 7.2.

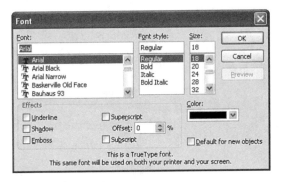

Figure 7.2   The Font dialog box enables you to change all the text attributes for selected text.

TIP   **Right-Click Shortcut**   You can right-click the text and select **Font** from the shortcut menu to open the Font dialog box.

3. From the **Font** list, select the font you want to use.

4. From the Font Style list, select any style you want to apply to the text, such as **Bold** or **Italic**. (To remove styles from text, select **Regular**.)

5. From the Size list, select any size in the list, or type a size directly into the box. (With TrueType fonts—the fonts marked with the TT logo—you can type any point size, even sizes that do not appear on the list.)

6. In the Effects box, select any special effects you want to add to the text, such as **Underline**, **Shadow**, or **Emboss**. You can also choose **Superscript** or **Subscript**, although these are less common.

7. To change the color of your text, click the arrow button to the right of the Color list and click the desired color. (For more colors, click the **More Colors** option at the bottom of the Color drop-down list; to select a color, use the dialog box that appears.)

8. Click **OK** to apply the new look to your selected text.

TIP   **Title and Object Area Text**   If you change a font on an individual slide, the font change applies only to that slide. To change the font for all the slides in the presentation, you need to change the font on the Slide Master. Select **View**, point at **Master**, and then select **Slide Master**. Select a text area and perform the preceding steps to change the look of the text on all slides. Be careful, however, because these changes override any font styles that are supplied by the design template assigned to the presentation.

Formatting Text with the Formatting Toolbar

The Formatting toolbar provides several buttons that enable you to change font attributes for the text on your slides. It makes it easy for you to quickly bold selected text or to change the color of text in a text box.

To use the different Formatting toolbar font tools, follow these steps:

1. To change the look of existing text, select the text, or select a particular text box to change the look of all the text within that box.

2. To change fonts, open the **Font** drop-down list and click the desired font.

3. To change font size, open the **Font Size** drop-down list, click the desired size or type a size directly into the box, and then press **Enter**.

 TIP  **Incrementing the Type Size**   To increase or decrease the text size to the next size up or down, click the Increase Font Size or Decrease Font Size buttons on the Formatting toolbar.

4. To add a style or effect to the text (bold, italic, underline, and/or shadow), click the appropriate button(s):

Bold   **B**

Italic   *I*

Underline   U

Shadow   S

As you have already seen, you can change the font color through the Font dialog box. You can also change it with the Font Color button on the Formatting toolbar. Just do the following:

1. Select the text for which you want to change the color.

 2. Click the down-pointing arrow next to the **Font Color** button on the Formatting toolbar. A color palette appears (see Figure 7.3).

Figure 7.3   When you click the arrow next to the Font Colors button, a color palette appears.

3. Do one of the following:

- Click a color on the palette to change the color of the selected text or the text box (the colors available are based on the design template and color scheme you have selected for the presentation).

- Click the **More Font Colors** option to display a Colors dialog box. Click a color on the Standard tab or use the Custom tab to create your own color. Then click **OK**. The color is applied to the text.

Copying Text Formats

If your presentation contains text with a format you want to use, you can copy that text's format and apply it to other text on the slide (or other slides). To copy text formats, perform the following steps:

1. Highlight the text with the format you want to use.

 2. Click the **Format Painter** button on the toolbar. PowerPoint copies the format.

3. Drag the mouse pointer (which now looks like the Format Painter icon) across the text to which you want to apply the format.

If you want to apply a format to different text lines or even different text boxes on a slide or slides, double-click the Format Painter button. Use the mouse to apply styles to as many text items as you want. Then, click the Format Painter button again to turn off the feature.

Changing the Text Alignment and Line Spacing

When you first type text, PowerPoint automatically places it against the left edge of the text box. To change the paragraph alignment, perform the following steps:

1. Click anywhere inside the paragraph you want to realign (a paragraph is any text line or wrapped text lines followed by a line break—created when you press the **Enter** key).

2. Select the **Format** menu and then select **Alignment**. The Alignment submenu appears (see Figure 7.4).

3. Select **Align Left**, **Center**, **Align Right**, or **Justify** to align the paragraph as required.

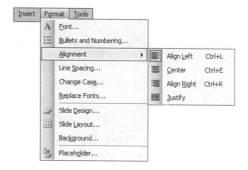

Figure 7.4 You can align each text line or paragraph in a text box.

 TIP   **Some Alignment Shortcuts** To quickly set left alignment, press **Ctrl+L** or click the **Align Left** button on the Formatting toolbar. For centered alignment, press **Ctrl+C** or click the **Center** button. For right alignment, press **Ctrl+R** or click the **Align Right** button.

If you want to align all the text in a text box in the same way (rather than aligning the text line by line), select the entire text box (click the box border) and then use the Alignment menu selection or the alignment buttons on the Formatting toolbar.

You can also change the spacing between text lines (remember, PowerPoint considers these to be paragraphs) in a text box. The default setting for line spacing is single space. To change the line spacing in a paragraph, perform these steps:

1. Click inside the paragraph you want to change, or select all the paragraphs you want to change by selecting the entire text box.

2. Select **Format**, **Line Spacing**. The Line Spacing dialog box appears, as shown in Figure 7.5.

3. Click the arrow buttons to the right of any of the following text boxes to change the spacing for the following:

Figure 7.5 Select Format, Line Spacing to open the Line Spacing dialog box.

- **Line Spacing**—This setting controls the space between the lines in a paragraph.
- **Before Paragraph**—This setting controls the space between this paragraph and the paragraph that comes before it.
- **After Paragraph**—This setting controls the space between this paragraph and the paragraph that comes after it.

4. After you make your selections, click **OK**.

 TIP   **Lines or Points?**   The drop-down list box that appears to the right of each setting enables you to set the line spacing in lines or points. A line is the current line height (based on the current text size). A point is a unit commonly used to measure text. One point is 1/72 of an inch.

Adding a WordArt Object

PowerPoint comes with an add-on program called WordArt (which is also available in other Office applications, such as Word and Excel) that can help you create graphical text effects. You can create text wrapped in a circle and text that has 3D effects and other special alignment options. To insert a WordArt object onto a slide, perform the following steps:

1. In the Slide view, display the slide on which you want to place the WordArt object.

 2. Click the **Insert** menu, point at **Picture**, and then select **WordArt** (or select the WordArt button on the Drawing toolbar). The WordArt Gallery dialog box appears, showing many samples of WordArt types.

3. Click the sample that best represents the WordArt type you want and click **OK**. The Edit WordArt Text dialog box appears (see Figure 7.6).

Figure 7.6   Enter the text, size, and font to be used into the Edit WordArt Text dialog box.

   4. Choose a font and size from the respective drop-down lists.

   5. Type the text you want to use into the Text box.

   6. Click **OK**. PowerPoint creates the WordArt text on your slide, as shown in Figure 7.7.

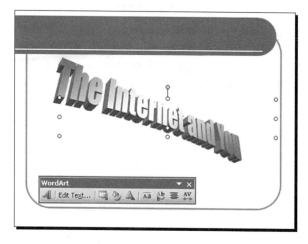

Figure 7.7   The WordArt toolbar is available when your WordArt object is selected.

After you have created WordArt, you have access to the WordArt toolbar, shown in Figure 7.7. You can use it to modify your WordArt. Table 7.1 summarizes the toolbar's buttons.

Table 7.1   Buttons on the WordArt Toolbar

To Do This	Click This
Insert a new WordArt object	
Edit the text, size, and font of the selected WordArt object	Edit Text...
Change the style of the current WordArt object in the WordArt Gallery	
Open a Format WordArt dialog box	
Change the shape of the WordArt	
Make all the letters the same height	Aa
Toggle between vertical and horizontal text orientation	Ab b
Change the text alignment	
Change the spacing between letters	AV

You can rotate a WordArt object by dragging the rotation handle on the WordArt box. To edit the WordArt object, double-click it to display the WordArt toolbar and text entry box. Enter your changes and then click outside the WordArt object. You can move the object by dragging its border or resize it by dragging a handle.

Creating Columns, Tables, and Lists

In this lesson, you learn how to use tabs to create columns of text, bulleted lists, numbered lists, and other types of lists.

Working in Multiple Columns

Depending on the type of slide that you are creating, you might need to arrange text on a slide in multiple columns. PowerPoint provides three options for placing text into columns on a slide:

- You can use the Title and 2 Column slide layout to create a slide with side-by-side text columns.
- You can place tab stops in a single text box and press **Tab** to create columns for your text.
- You can use a table to create a two- or multiple-column text grid.

In this lesson, you learn about all these methods.

Creating Columns with a Slide Layout

The easiest way to create columns of text is to change a slide's layout so that it provides side-by-side text boxes. Because the default layout for slides is a slide with a title box and a single text box, you will probably need to use the Slide Layout task pane to change its format to include two text columns. Follow these steps:

1. Create a new slide or select a slide that you want to format with the two-column layout (using the Outline or Slides pane).
2. Open the task pane (select **View**, **Task Pane**).
3. Select the task pane drop-down arrow and select **Slide Layout**.
4. Click the **Title and 2 Column** slide layout from the Text Layouts section of the Slide Layout task pane to format the slide (see Figure 8.1).

You can then type the text that you want to appear in the two text boxes provided on the slide.

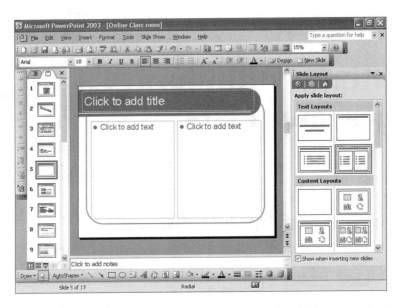

Figure 8.1 A two-column slide layout provides two panes in which to enter text.

TIP **Position the Cursor on a Slide Layout to See Its Description** If you position the cursor on any of the slide layouts in the Slide Layout task pane, a tip appears, describing the layout.

Using Tabs to Create Columns

You can also create multiple columns in a text box using tab stops. To set the tabs for a multicolumn list, perform the following steps:

1. Open the presentation and select the slide you want to work with in Slide view.

2. Make sure that the ruler is showing in the PowerPoint window (select **View**, then **Ruler** if necessary).

3. Select **Insert**, then **Textbox**. Drag the mouse to create a textbox that is as wide as the area on the ruler that you will use to set the tabs. The ruler area will display the usable area on the slide (white) and the margins on the slide (dark gray). If you do not see the ruler, select the **View** menu and then select **Ruler** to display the ruler.

Text Box from the Drawing Toolbar   You cannot easily place tabs in a textbox created using the Drawing toolbar. Use the Insert menu as outlined in the steps to place a textbox that will contain tabs.

CAUTION

4. Click anywhere inside the text box. After the insertion point is in the text box, you can set the tabs.

5. If you already typed text inside the text box, select the text.

6. Click the **Tab** button at the left end of the ruler until it represents the type of tab you want to set (see Table 8.1 for more information on the type of tabs available).

7. Click in various positions on the ruler to place a tab stop using the type of tab you currently have selected. Figure 8.2 shows several tab stops that have been placed in a text box.

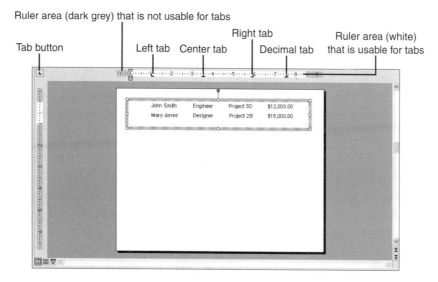

Figure 8.2   The ruler enables you to create tab stops for a text box.

8. Repeat steps 6 and 7 if you want to set different types of tab stops at different positions.

9. To change the position of an existing tab stop setting, drag it on the ruler to the desired position. To delete an existing tab stop setting, drag it off the ruler.

10. (Optional) To hide the ruler, select the **View** menu and then select **Ruler**.

Table 8.1 Tab Button Stop Types

Button Appearance	Tab Stop Type
	Aligns the left end of the line against the tab stop.
	Centers the text on the tab stop.
	Aligns the right end of the line against the tab stop.
	Aligns the tab stop on a period. This is called a decimal tab and is useful for aligning a column of numbers that uses decimal points.

Creating a Table

Tables can also be used to place text in side-by-side columns. You can create tables that provide two columns, three columns, or any number of columns that you require. Tables are also very useful when you want to display numerical information in a grid layout or information that you want to arrange in rows. A table is a collection of intersecting columns and rows. The block created when a column and a row intersects is often referred to as a *cell*. The easiest way to create a table on a slide is to use the Table layout. Follow these steps:

1. Create a new slide or select a slide that you want to format with the Table layout (using the Outline or Slides pane).

2. Open the task pane (select **View**, **Task Pane**).

3. Select the task pane drop-down arrow and select **Slide Layout**.

4. Scroll down through layouts in the task pane, and then click the **Title and Table** layout. This assigns the Title and Table layout to the current slide (see Figure 8.3).

5. After you assign the Title and Table layout to the slide, you can set the number of columns and rows for the table. Double-click the Table icon on the slide. The Insert dialog box appears.

6. Specify the number of columns and rows that you want in the table and then click **OK**. The table is placed on the slide.

You can also insert a table onto an existing slide. This allows you to include a table on a slide where you don't want to change the slide's layout as discussed in the preceding steps. Follow these steps:

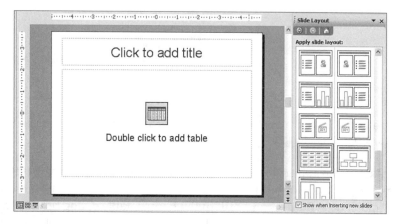

Figure 8.3   The Table layout enables you to place a table on a slide.

1. Display the slide on which you want to place the table.

2. Select the **Insert** menu and then choose **Table**. The Insert Table dialog box appears.

3. Enter the number of columns and rows that you want to have in the table.

4. Click **OK**. The table appears on the slide.

When the table appears on the slide, the Tables and Borders toolbar also appears in the PowerPoint window (we will use this toolbar in a moment). After you have a table on a slide, you can work with it like this:

- Click inside a table cell and enter your text. You can move from cell to cell by pressing **Tab** to go forward or **Shift+Tab** to go back. Enter text as needed.

- If you need to resize the table, drag a selection handle, the same as you would any object.

- To adjust the row height or column width, position the mouse pointer on a line between two rows or columns and drag. The mouse pointer becomes a sizing tool when you place it on any column or row border.

- If you want to change the style of the borders around certain cells on the table (or the entire table), select the cells (drag the mouse across the cells to select them). You can then use the buttons on the Tables and Borders toolbar to change the border attributes (see Figure 8.4). Use the Border Style button and the Border Width button to change the border style and border line weight, respectively. If you want to change the border color, use the Border Color button. Use the buttons on the Tables and Borders toolbar to adjust the thickness and style of the table gridlines.

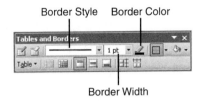

Border Style   Border Color

Border Width

Figure 8.4   Border attributes for the table can be changed using the buttons on the Tables and Borders toolbar.

To make a table appear to be multiple columns of text without the table borders, turn off all the gridlines in the table. To do so, select all the cells in the table; then right-click and choose **Borders and Fill**. In the Format Table dialog box that appears (see Figure 8.5), click each of the border buttons provided on the table diagram to turn the border off for each side of each cell in the table. Click **OK** to return to the table.

Figure 8.5   The Format Table dialog box can be used to control border lines and other table attributes.

Making a Bulleted List

When you enter new slides into a presentation, the default layout provides a title box and a text box that is set up as a simple bulleted list. Therefore, just creating a new slide creates a bulleted list.

You can turn off the bullets in front of any paragraphs by selecting the paragraphs and clicking the **Bullets** button on the Formatting toolbar to toggle the bullets off. If you want to remove the bullets from all the paragraphs (remember a text line followed by the Enter key is a paragraph), select the entire text box and click the **Bullets** button.

When you insert your own text boxes using the Text Box button on the Drawing toolbar, the text does not have bullets by default. You can add your own bullets by following these steps:

1. Click the text line (paragraph) that you want to format for bullets. If you want to add bullets to all the text lines in a text box, select the text box.

2. Select the **Format** menu, and then select **Bullets and Numbering**. The Bullets and Numbering dialog box appears (see Figure 8.6).

Figure 8.6   The Bullets and Numbering dialog box enables you to select the bullets for your bulleted items.

 TIP   **Quick Bullets**   To bypass the dialog box, click the **Bullets** button on the Formatting toolbar to insert a bullet, or right-click and select **Bullet** from the shortcut menu. You can click the **Bullets** button again to remove the bullet.

3. Select the bullet style you want to use from the list PowerPoint provides.

4. Click **OK**. PowerPoint formats the selected text into a bulleted list. (If you press **Enter** at the end of a bulleted paragraph, the next paragraph starts with a bullet.)

 TIP   **Create Your Own Bullets**   You can select from a number of pictures and symbols for the bullets that you apply to text in PowerPoint. In the Bullets and Numbering dialog box, select **Picture** to choose from several bullet pictures. Select **Customize** to select from several bullet symbols.

Working with Numbered Lists

Numbered lists are like bulleted lists, except they have sequential numbers instead of symbols. You can convert any paragraphs to a numbered list by selecting them and clicking the **Numbering** button on the Formatting toolbar. Select the paragraphs again and click the **Numbering** button again to toggle the numbering off.

You can also create numbered lists with the Bullets and Numbering dialog box, the same as you did with bullets. Follow these steps:

1. Select the paragraphs that you want to convert to a numbered list.

2. Choose **Format**, and then select **Bullets and Numbering**.

3. Click the **Numbered** tab on the dialog box. The numbered list styles appear (see Figure 8.7).

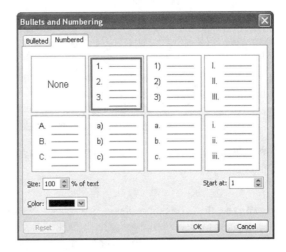

Figure 8.7 Choose the numbering style you want or turn numbering off by choosing None.

4. Click the number style you want for your list.

5. (Optional) Change the Size and/or Color of the numbers.

6. (Optional) If you want the list to start at a number other than 1, enter it into the **Start At** text box.

7. Click **OK**.

Adding Graphics to a Slide

In this lesson, you learn how to add PowerPoint clip art to your presentations and how to add images from other sources.

Using the Clip Art Task Pane

The Clip Art task pane provides you access to all the clip art provided with Microsoft Office. It also includes a search engine that you can use to search for clip art, photographs, movies, and sounds that are stored on your computer. You can also search for clip art and other items using Microsoft's online clip library. (You must be connected to the Internet when using PowerPoint to access the Microsoft online library.)

Figure 9.1 shows the Clip Art task pane. You can use this task pane to search for and insert images onto your slides, or you can take advantage of slides that use a layout that contains a placeholder for images and clip art.

You learn about using the Clip Art task pane and slide layouts that provide image placeholders in this lesson. In Lesson 10, "Adding Sounds and Movies to a Slide," you take a look at using the Clip Art task pane to add movies and slides to your PowerPoint slides.

 Clip Art   A collection of previously created images or pictures that you can place on a slide. Microsoft Office provides clip art and other media types, such as movies and sounds.

You can open the Clip Art task pane in any of these ways:

- Click the **Insert Clip Art** button on the Drawing toolbar.
- Select the **Insert** menu, point at **Picture**, and then choose **Clip Art**.
- Open the task pane, click the task pane drop-down arrow, and then select **Insert Clip Art** to switch to the Clip Art task pane.

Figure 9.1 The Clip Art task pane manages pictures, motion clips, and sounds—all in one convenient place.

When you use the Clip Art task pane, you search for images by keywords. In the following sections, you take a look at inserting clip art from the task pane and learn how you can insert clip art using some of the slide layouts (that provide a clip art placeholder on the slide).

TIP **Clip Organizer Scan** The first time you open the Clip Art task pane, PowerPoint prompts you to allow the Clip Organizer (which is discussed later in the lesson) to search your hard drive. Clip Organizer then creates category folders and image indexes from the clip art and images that it finds there. Click **Yes** to allow this process to take place.

Inserting an Image from the Task Pane

As previously mentioned, the Clip Art task pane allows you to search for clip art files using keywords. If you wanted to search for clip art of cats, you would search for the word "cats." To insert a piece of the clip art using the task pane, follow these steps:

1. Select the slide on which you want to place the image so that it appears in the Slide pane.

2. Select **Insert**, point at **Picture**, and then select **Clip Art**. The Clip Art task pane appears.

3. Type keywords into the Search Text box in the task pane that will be used to find your clip art images.

4. Click the **Search** button. Images that match your search criteria appear in the task pane as thumbnails.

5. In the Results list, locate the image that you want to place on the slide. Then click the image, and the clip art is placed on the slide (see Figure 9.2).

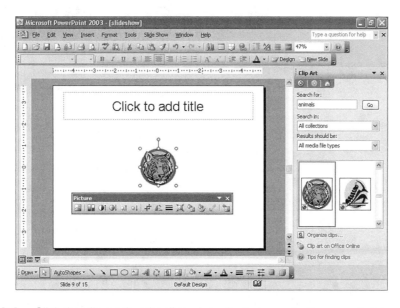

Figure 9.2   Click the clip art thumbnail to place the image onto the current slide.

You can use the sizing handles on the image to size the clip art box. Or you can drag the clip art box to a new location on the slide.

Inserting an Image from an Image Box

Another way that you can add clip art images to a slide in your presentation is to create the slide using a slide format that supplies a clip art placeholder box on the slide. These slide layout types are called content layouts because they make it easy to insert objects such as clip art, charts, and other items onto a slide. You can then use the object placeholder on the slide to access the clip art library and insert a particular image onto the slide.

Follow these steps:

1. Create a new slide or select the slide you want to assign a layout to that contains a clip art placeholder box.

2. Open the task pane (**View**, **Task Pane**) and then click the task pane drop-down menu and select **Slide Layout** (the Slide Layout task pane automatically opens if you've just created a new slide).

3. Scroll down through the layouts provided until you locate either the Content layout or the Text and Content layout. Both of these layout categories provide slide layouts that contain object placeholders or object placeholders and text boxes, respectively.

4. Select the layout that best suits the purpose of your slide (see Figure 9.3).

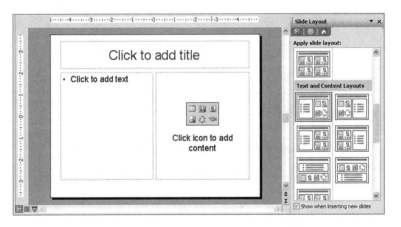

Figure 9.3   Select a slide layout that contains an object placeholder.

5. The slide layout you choose provides you with a placeholder box that contains icons for tables, charts, clip art, and other objects. Click the **Insert Clip Art** icon in the placeholder box. The Select Picture dialog box appears (see Figure 9.4).

6. Scroll down through the list of clip art and other images to find a particular image (the list will be lengthy because it includes all the Office Clip Art and any other images that were located on your computer when the Clip Organizer cataloged the images on your computer).

7. If you want, you can search for particular images by keyword. Type the search criteria into the Search Text box and then click **Search**. Images that match the search criteria appear in the Select Picture dialog box.

8. Click the picture thumbnail that you want to place on the slide. Then click **OK**.

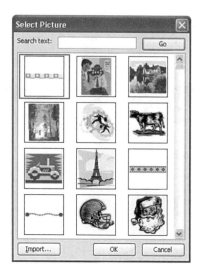

Figure 9.4 The Select Picture dialog box enables you to scroll through or search through the entire clip art and image library on your computer.

PowerPoint places the image on the slide in the object placeholder box. You can size the box or move it on the slide.

Inserting a Clip from a File

If you have an image stored on your computer that you would like to place on a slide, you can insert the picture directly from the file. This means that you don't have to use the Clip Art task pane to search for and then insert the image.

To place a graphical image on a slide directly from a file, follow these steps:

1. Select the slide on which the image will be placed.

2. Select the **Insert** menu, point at **Picture**, and then select **From File**. The Insert Picture dialog box appears (see Figure 9.5).

3. Select the picture you want to use. You can view all the picture files in a particular location as thumbnails. Select the **Views** button, and then select **Thumbnails** on the menu that appears.

4. Click **Insert** to place the image on the slide.

If the picture is too big or too small, you can drag the selection handles (the small squares) around the edge of the image to resize it. Hold down the **Shift** key to proportionally resize the image (this maintains the height/width ratio of the image so that you cannot stretch or distort it). See Lesson 11, "Working with PowerPoint Objects," for more details about resizing and cropping images and other objects on a slide.

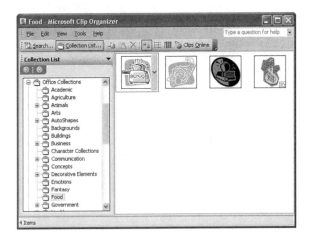

Figure 9.5   Use the Insert Picture dialog box to place images on a slide.

 TIP   **Link It Up**   You can link a graphic to the presentation so that whenever the original changes, the version in the presentation changes, too. Just open the drop-down list on the Insert button in the Insert Picture dialog box (refer to Figure 9.5) and choose **Link to File**.

Managing Images in the Clip Organizer

Occasionally, you might want to add or delete clip art images from folders on your computer. Managing images is accomplished using the Clip Organizer. When you install Microsoft Office 2003 (using the default installation), a fairly large library of clip art is placed on your hard drive in different category folders. You can manage these clip art images and other images on your computer, such as scanned images or pictures from a digital camera. To open the Clip Organizer, follow these steps:

1. With the Clip Art task pane open in the PowerPoint window, click the **Clip Organizer** link near the bottom of the task pane to open the Clip Organizer.

2. (optional) The first time you open the Organizer, you will be given the opportunity to catalog all the media files (clip art, photos, videos) on your computer. Click the **Now** button to catalog all media.

3. To view the clip art categories Microsoft Office has provided, click the plus sign (+) to the left of the Office Collections folder in the Collection list (this folder is located on the left side of the Clip Organizer window). Category folders such as Academic, Agriculture, and so on will appear in the Collection list.

4. Click one of the category folders to view the clip art that it holds (for example, click **Food**). The clip art in that category folder appears in the Clip Organizer window (see Figure 9.6).

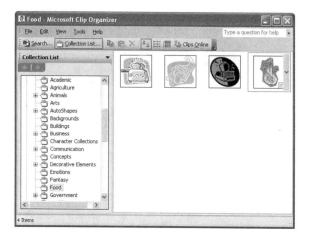

Figure 9.6   Use the Clip Organizer to manage your clip art and image files.

Not only does the Clip Organizer allow you to browse the various clip art and other images on your computer, it allows you to copy, delete, or move images. For example, if you find an image you no longer want to store on your computer, select the image in the Clip Organizer window and press **Delete**. A dialog box appears, letting you know that this image will be removed from all collections on the computer. Click **OK** to delete the image.

You can also use the Clip Organizer to copy or move clip art images from a location on your hard drive to one of the clip art collections. Locate the images you want to move or copy to a particular collection and then select them.

To move the images to a collection, select the **Edit** menu, and then **Move to Collection**. The Move to Collection dialog box appears (see Figure 9.7). Select a location in the dialog box and click **OK** to move the selected image or images.

Figure 9.7   You can move images from one location to another using the Clip Organizer.

You can also copy images to a new location using the Copy to Collection command. Select the images in a particular folder on your computer using the Clip Organizer window. Select the **Edit** menu and then **Copy to Collection**. Select a location in the Copy to Collection dialog box where you would like to place copies of the images, and then click **OK**.

Adding Sounds and Movies to a Slide

In this lesson, you learn how to add sound and video clips to a PowerPoint presentation.

Working with Sounds and Movies

A great way to add some interest to your PowerPoint presentations is to add sounds and movies to your slides. Sounds enable you to emphasize certain slides, and movie animations can add humor and style to your presentations. Next, you take a look at adding sounds and then adding movie animations to your slides.

Too Much Media Can Be Distracting   Too many sounds, movies, and even images can be distracting to your audience and clutter your slides. Use sounds, movies, and images to add interest, not confusion.

CAUTION

Including Sounds in a Presentation

Sounds can be used to add emphasis to information on slides or to add some auditory interest to your presentation. You can place sound files on your slides in two different ways:

- You can insert a sound clip as an icon on a slide. When you click the icon, the sound plays.
- You can assign a sound to another object on a slide so that when you click the object, the sound plays. For example, you could assign a sound to an image. When you click the image, the sound plays (sounds added to PowerPoint animations play when the animation plays).

Inserting a Sound onto a Slide

To insert a sound clip as an object onto a slide, you can either use the Clip Art task pane or insert the sound as a file. The Clip Art task pane can provide you only with sound files that have been included in the Office clip art library or sound files that you have added to your collection using the Clip Organizer (which is discussed in the previous lesson). Any sound file that you have recorded or otherwise acquired can be inserted as a file.

To insert a sound clip from the Clip Art task pane, follow these steps:

1. Select the slide on which you will place the sound, so that it appears in the Slide pane.

2. Select **Insert**, point at **Movies and Sounds**, and then select **Sound from Clip Organizer**. The Clip Art task pane appears with a list of sound files. You can use the Search For box to search for a particular type of sound file by keyword.

3. To preview a particular sound file, point at the file and click the menu arrow that appears. Select **Preview/Properties** from the menu. The Preview/Properties dialog box for that sound file appears (see Figure 10.1).

Figure 10.1   Preview a sound clip before placing it onto a slide.

4. The sound will play automatically when the Preview/Properties dialog box opens. You can click the **Stop, Pause,** or **Play** buttons in the dialog box to perform that particular function. When you have finished previewing a sound file, click **Close** to close the Preview/Properties dialog box.

5. When you are ready to insert a sound file onto the slide, click the sound file on the task pane.

6. A dialog box opens, asking you whether you want the sound to play automatically when you run the slide show. Click **Yes** to have the sound played

automatically. Click **No** to set up the sound so that you will have to click it during the slide show to play the sound.

Regardless of whether you choose to have PowerPoint play the sound automatically, it appears as a sound icon on the slide.

If you have recorded a sound file or have acquired a sound file that you want to use on a slide without using the Clip Art task pane, you can insert it as a file. To insert a sound clip from a file, follow these steps:

1. Choose the **Insert** menu, point at **Movies and Sounds**, and then choose **Sound from File**.

2. In the Insert Sound dialog box, navigate to the drive and folder containing the sound you want to use (see Figure 10.2).

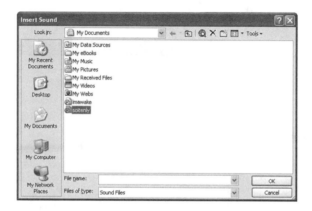

Figure 10.2 Choose the sound clip you want to include on your slide.

3. Select the sound clip and then click **OK**.

4. A dialog box opens, asking you whether you want the sound to play automatically when you run the slide show or play when you click on the sound icon on the slide. Click **Automatically** to have the sound played automatically or **When Clicked** to set up the sound so that you will have to click it during the slide show to play the sound.

The sound file appears on the slide as a sound icon. If you want to play the sound file on the slide, right-click the sound icon and select **Play Sound** from the shortcut menu.

Associating a Sound with Another Object on the Slide

If you want to avoid having a sound icon on your slide, you can associate the sound with some other object already on the slide, such as a graphic. To do so, follow these steps:

1. Right-click the object (such as a clip art image) to which you want to assign the sound.

2. Choose **Action Settings** from the shortcut menu. The Actions Settings dialog box appears.

3. If you want the sound to play when the object is pointed at, click the **Mouse Over** tab. Otherwise, click the **Mouse Click** tab. The Mouse Click option requires that the sound icon be clicked on for the sound to play.

4. Click the **Play Sound** check box. A drop-down list of sounds becomes available (see Figure 10.3).

Figure 10.3   Choose a sound to be associated with the object.

5. Open the **Play Sound** drop-down list and choose the sound you want.

   If the sound you want is not on the list, choose **Other Sound** and locate the sound using the Add Sound dialog box that appears. Select the sound from there and click **OK**.

6. When you have chosen the sound you want, click **OK** to close the Action Settings dialog box.

Now, when you are giving the presentation, you can play the sound by either click-ing or pointing at the object (depending on how you configured the sound to play). To test this, jump to the Slide Show view (select the **View** menu and then click **Slide Show**) and try it out. Press **Esc** to return to the Normal view when you are finished testing the sound file.

Placing a Movie onto a Slide

The procedure for placing a movie onto a slide is very much the same as that for a sound. You can place a movie using the Clip Art task pane or from a file. You will find that the task pane Clip Organizer provides several movies that can be used to add interest to your slides. To insert a movie onto a slide, follow these steps:

1. Choose the **Insert** menu, point at **Movies and Sounds**, and then select **Movies from Clip Organizer**. Use the Search box if you want to locate movies using a keyword search.

2. Scroll through the movies listed on the Clip Art task pane.

3. Point at a movie clip you want to preview. Click the menu arrow that appears and select **Preview/Properties**. The Preview Properties dialog box for the movie appears.

4. PowerPoint previews the movie on the left side of the dialog box (see Figure 10.4). If you want to place a caption onto the movie clip, click in the **Caption** box below the Preview pane and type a caption.

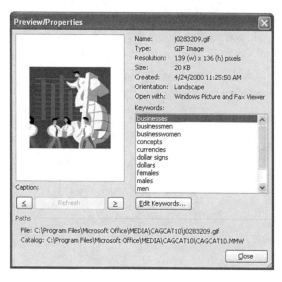

Figure 10.4   Preview a movie in the Preview/Properties dialog box.

5. Click **Close** to close the Preview/Properties dialog box. To insert the movie into your slide, click the movie in the task pane.

6. A dialog box will open allowing you to choose how the movie will be started during the slide show. Click **Automatically** to start the movie automatically when the slide is shown during the slide show or **When Clicked**, which will require that you click the movie to play it during the slide show.

After the movie icon is in place on your slide, you can size the movie box using the usual sizing handles or move it to another position on the slide. If you want to test view the movie on the slide, jump to the Slide Show view (select the **View** menu and then click **Slide Show**) and try it out. Press **Esc** to return to the Normal view when you are finished testing the movie.

 TIP **Clip Organizer Movies Really Aren't Movies** The Clip Organizer movies provided by Microsoft Office are really just animations. They are designed to play automatically when the slide containing the image is opened during a slide show.

You can also place actual videos on a slide as a file. This enables you to place video captures that you have created or video files from other sources.

Follow these steps:

1. Choose the **Insert** menu, point at **Movies and Sounds**, and then choose **Movie from File**.

2. In the Insert Sound dialog box that appears, navigate to the drive and folder containing the movie file you want to use.

3. Select the file and click **OK** to place it on the slide.

4. A dialog box appears that enables you to have the movie play when the slide appears in the slide show. Click **Automatically**. To require that you click the movie's icon to make it play during the slide show, click **When Clicked**.

After you make your selection in step 4, PowerPoint places the movie onto the slide. To preview the video file on the slide, right-click the video icon and then select **Play Movie**.

Working with PowerPoint Objects

In this lesson, you learn how to manipulate objects on your slides, such as clip art and other items, to create impressive presentations.

Selecting Objects

In the previous two lessons, you learned about inserting clip art, image files, sound files, and movie files onto the slides of your PowerPoint presentation. Any type of special content that you place on a slide is called an object. In addition to the object types just listed, objects could also be items from other Office applications. For example, you could create an object on a slide that is actually an Excel worksheet or chart (for more about sharing information between Office applications, see Lesson 7, "Sharing Office Application Data," in Part 1, "Office Introduction and Shared Features," of this book.

After you select an object, you can do all kinds of things to it, such as copying, moving, deleting, or resizing it. The following is a review of ways you can select objects on a PowerPoint slide:

- To select a single object, click it. (If you click text, a frame appears around the text. Click the frame to select the text object.)
- To select more than one object, hold down the **Ctrl** or **Shift** key while clicking each object. Handles appear around the selected objects, as shown in Figure 11.1 (this temporarily groups the objects so that you can move them all simultaneously on the slide).
- To deselect selected objects, click anywhere outside the selected object or objects.

 TIP   **Select Objects Tool**   Use the Select Objects tool on the Drawing toolbar to drag a selection box around several objects you want to select. When you release the mouse button, PowerPoint selects all the objects inside the box.

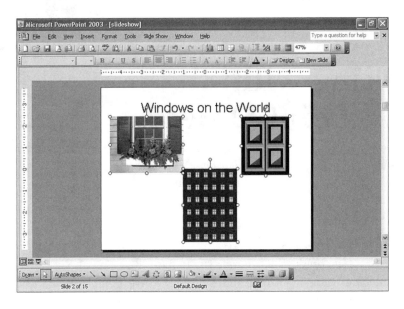

Figure 11.1 You can select multiple objects on a slide.

Working with Layers of Objects

As you place objects onscreen, they might start to overlap, creating layers of objects where the lower layers are often difficult or impossible to select. To move objects in layers, perform the following steps:

1. Click the object you want to move up or down in the stack. If the Drawing toolbar is not available in the PowerPoint window, right-click on any toolbar and select **Drawing** from the menu that appears.

2. Click the **Draw** button on the Drawing toolbar to open the Draw menu, and select **Order**, as shown in Figure 11.2.

3. Select one of the following options:

- **Bring to Front**—Brings the object to the top of the stack.
- **Send to Back**—Sends the object to the bottom of the stack.
- **Bring Forward**—Brings the object up one layer.
- **Send Backward**—Sends the object back one layer.

Using the different layering settings allows you to superimpose images on top of other images. For example, you could place an image of a bird on top of a picture of the sky. You can also use these settings to superimpose text on a graphic.

Figure 11.2 Use the Draw menu on the Drawing toolbar to change the layer on which a graphic appears on your slide.

Grouping and Ungrouping Objects

Each object on a slide, including text boxes, is an individual object. However, sometimes you want two or more objects to act as a group. For example, you might want to make the lines of several objects the same thickness or group several objects so that they can easily be moved together on the slide. If you want to treat two or more objects as a group, perform the following steps:

1. Select the objects you want to group. Remember, to select more than one object, hold down the **Shift** or **Ctrl** key as you click each one.

2. Click the **Draw** button on the Drawing toolbar to open the Draw menu, and then select **Group**.

3. To ungroup the objects, select any object in the group and select **Draw**, and then choose **Ungroup**.

Cutting, Copying, and Pasting Objects

You can cut, copy, and paste objects onto a slide (or onto another slide) the same as you would normal text. When you cut an object, PowerPoint removes the object from the slide and places it in a temporary holding area called the Office Clipboard. When you copy or cut an object, a copy of the object, or the object itself when you use Cut, is placed on the Office Clipboard. You can place multiple objects onto the Clipboard and paste them as needed onto a slide or slides in your presentation.

To view the Office Clipboard, select **View**, **Task Pane**. Then, on the task pane drop-down menu, select **Clipboard**. Figure 11.3 shows the Clipboard task pane.

Figure 11.3 Use the Clipboard to keep track of objects that you have cut or copied.

To cut or copy an object, perform the following steps:

1. Select the object(s) you want to cut, copy, or move.

2.  Select the **Edit** menu and then choose **Cut** or **Copy**. Or you can use the **Cut**, **Copy**, and **Paste** buttons on the Formatting toolbar.

> TIP **Right-Click Shortcut** Right-click a selection to choose Cut or Copy from the shortcut menu.

3. Display the slide on which you want to paste the cut or copied objects.

4. Select **Edit** and then choose **Paste**. PowerPoint pastes the objects onto the slide.

> TIP **Keyboard Shortcuts** Instead of using the toolbar buttons or the menu, you can press Ctrl+X to cut, Ctrl+C to copy, and Ctrl+V to paste.

To remove an object without placing it on the Clipboard, select the object and press the **Delete** key.

Rotating an Object

When you select an object on a slide, a handle with a green end on it appears at the top center of the object. This is the rotation handle, and it can be used to rotate any object on a slide. The rotation handle enables you to revolve an object around a center point.

To rotate an object, do the following:

1. Click the object you want to rotate.

2. Place the mouse pointer on the object's **Rotation** handle (the green dot) until the Rotation icon appears.

3. Hold down the mouse button and drag the **Rotation** handle until the object is in the position you want.

4. Release the mouse button.

The Draw menu (on the Drawing toolbar) also enables you to rotate or flip an object. You can flip an object horizontally left or right or flip the object vertically from top to bottom. To flip an object, click the **Draw** button on the Drawing toolbar and then point at **Rotate and Flip**. Select either **Flip Horizontal** or **Flip Vertical** from the menu that appears.

 TIP **Can't Find the Drawing Toolbar?** If the Drawing toolbar does not appear at the bottom of the PowerPoint application window, right-click any visible toolbar and select **Drawing**.

Resizing Objects

You will find that objects such as pictures and clip art are not always inserted onto a slide in the correct size. You can resize the object by performing these steps:

1. Select the object to resize. Selection handles appear.

2. Drag one of the following handles (the squares that surround the object) until the object is the desired size:

   • Drag a corner handle to change both the height and width of an object. PowerPoint retains the object's height-to-width ratio.

   • Drag a side, top, or bottom handle to change the height or width alone.

   • To keep the original center of the object stationary while sizing, hold down the **Ctrl** key while dragging a sizing handle.

3. Release the mouse button when you have completed resizing the object.

Cropping a Picture

In addition to resizing a picture, you can crop it; that is, you can trim a side or a corner off the picture to remove an element from the picture or cut off some whitespace. This enables you to clean up the picture within the object box.

To crop a picture, perform the following steps:

1. Click the picture you want to crop.
2. To crop the picture, you need the Picture toolbar. Right-click any toolbar currently showing in the PowerPoint window and select **Picture**. The Picture toolbar appears.

 3. Click the **Crop** button on the Picture toolbar. Cropping handles appear around the picture (see Figure 11.4).

Figure 11.4 Use the cropping handles on the figure to crop portions of the picture.

4. Move the mouse pointer over one of the cropping handles. The mouse pointer becomes the same shape as the cropping handle. (Use a corner handle to crop two sides at once. Use a side, top, or bottom handle to crop only one side.)
5. Hold down the mouse button and drag the pointer until the crop lines are where you want them.
6. Release the mouse button. PowerPoint crops the image.
7. After cropping that image, move or resize the picture as needed.

Stop That Crop! To undo the cropping of a picture immediately after you crop it, select **Edit** and then choose **Undo Crop Picture**.

CAUTION

Presenting an Onscreen Slide Show

In this lesson, you learn how to view a slide show onscreen, how to make basic movements within a presentation, and how to set show options. You also learn how to create a self-running show with timings and how to work with slide transitions.

Viewing an Onscreen Slide Show

Before you show your presentation to an audience, you should run through it several times on your own computer, checking that all the slides are in the right order and that the timings and transitions between the slides work correctly. This also enables you to fine-tune any monologue you might have to give as you show the slides so that what you are saying at any point in the presentation is synchronized with the slide that is being shown at that moment.

You can preview a slide show at any time; follow these steps:

1. Open the presentation you want to view.

2. Choose the **Slide Show** menu and choose **View Show**. The first slide in the presentation appears full screen (see Figure 12.1). A series of icons appear at the bottom left of the presentation screen. There is a previous slide arrow, a pen icon, a menu icon, and a next slide arrow. We will discuss the pen and menu icons later in the lesson.

3. To display the next or the previous slide, do one of the following:

   - To display the next slide, click the left mouse button, press the **Page Down** key, or press the right-arrow or down-arrow key. You can also click the right-pointing arrow that appears at the bottom left of the slide.

   - To display the previous slide, click the right mouse button, press the **Page Up** key, or press the left-arrow or up-arrow key. You can also click the left-pointing arrow that appears at the bottom left of the slide.

4. When you have finished running the slide show, press the **Esc** key.

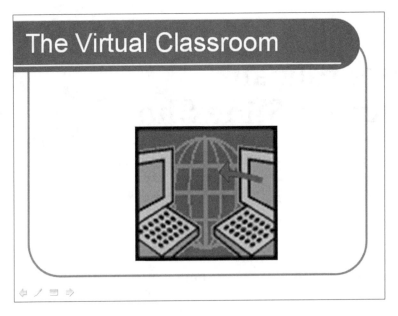

Figure 12.1 When you run your slide show, the entire screen is used to display the sides.

 TIP **Start the Show!** You can also start a slide show by clicking the **Slide Show** button in the bottom-left corner of the presentation window or by pressing **F5**.

Setting Slide Animation Schemes

After running the slide show a few times, you might find that the presentation doesn't really provide the visual impact that you had hoped. Even though you have designed your slides well and created slides that include images and movies, you are still looking for something with a more "artsy" feel. A great way to add visual impact to the presentation is to assign an animation scheme to a slide or slides in the presentation.

An animation scheme controls how the text in the text boxes on the slide appear or materialize on the slide during the presentation. For example, you can select a slide animation scheme called Bounce, where the text on the slide "bounces" onto the slide when it appears onscreen during the slide show.

 TERM **Animation Scheme** A scheme that controls how objects materialize onto the slide during the slide show.

PowerPoint provides three categories of animation schemes that you can assign to a slide: Subtle, Moderate, and Exciting. Each of these categories provides a number of animation schemes. The great thing about the animation schemes is that you can assign them to a slide or slides and then try them out in the Normal view. If you don't like the animation scheme, you can select another.

To assign an animation scheme to a slide in the presentation, follow these steps:

1. Select the slide to which you will assign the animation scheme so that it appears in the Slide pane in the Normal view.

2. Select the **Slide Show** menu and select **Animation Schemes**. The Animation Schemes list appears in the Slide Design task pane on the right side of the PowerPoint window (see Figure 12.2).

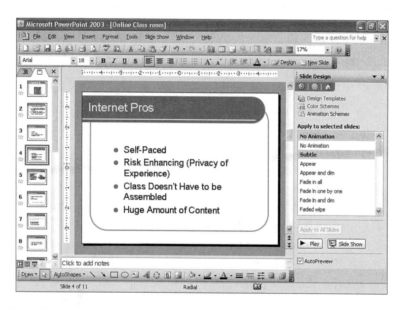

Figure 12.2   The task pane houses the animation schemes that you can assign to the slides in your presentation.

3. Scroll through the list of animation schemes. When you find a scheme that you want to try, select the scheme in the list box.

4. To try the scheme, click the **Play** button in the task pane.

5. If you don't like the scheme, select another.

6. If you find a scheme that you would like to apply to all the slides in the presentation, click the **Apply to All Slides** button.

TIP   **Assign Animation Schemes to Selected Slides**   You can select several slides in the Slide Sorter view and then use the Slide Design task pane to assign the same animation scheme to all the selected slides.

Setting Up a Self-Running Show

In a self-running show, the slide show runs itself. Each slide advances after a specified period of time. This allows you to concentrate on the narrative aspects of the presentation as you use the slide show for a speech or classroom presentation. For a self-running show, you must set timings. You can set the same timing for all slides (for example, a 20-second delay between each slide), or you can set a separate timing for each slide individually.

When you set up a self-running show, you can also select different slide transitions. A slide transition is a special effect that is executed when the slide appears during the slide show. For example, you can have a slide dissolve onto the screen, or you can have the slide appear on the screen using a checkerboard effect.

To configure the show to use timings and transitions, follow these steps:

1. Open the presentation you want to view.

2. Select the slide to which you would like to apply a timing or transition so that it appears in the Slides pane in the Normal view.

3. Select **Slide Show** and click **Slide Transition**. The Slide Transition task pane opens containing controls for the type of transition you want to use, the speed with which that transition executes, and the length of time the slide should remain onscreen (see Figure 12.3).

4. To select a transition for the slide, select one of the transitions supplied in the Apply to Selected Slides box.

5. To test the transition, click the **Play** button.

6. If you want to change the speed of the transition, click the Speed drop-down list and select **Slow**, **Medium**, or **Fast** (Fast is the default).

7. (Optional) If you want to select a sound to accompany the slide transition (such as Applause, Drum Roll, or Laser), click the Sound drop-down list and select one of the supplied sounds.

8. To set the timing for the slide in the Advance Slide section of the task pane, click the **Automatically After** check box. Use the click box below the check box to enter the number of seconds for the slide's automatic timing.

9. If you want to apply the selected transition and the timing to all the slides in the presentation, click the **Apply to All Slides** button.

Figure 12.3 The Slide Transition task pane houses the controls necessary for tailoring the way a slide transitions onto the screen during a presentation.

My Slides Don't Advance Using the Timings If you find when you run the slide show that the slides don't advance using the timings that you have set, select Slide Show, Set Up Show. In the Set Up Show dialog box, be sure that the Using Timings, If Present option button is selected. Then click OK.

CAUTION

When you run the slide show, the slides advance according to the timings that you have set. The slides also use any transitions that you have selected for them. Take the time to run the slide show several times so that you can gauge whether the transitions and timings work well. Remember that the slide must be onscreen long enough for your audience to read and understand the text on the slide.

TIP **Assign Transitions and Timings to Selected Slides** You can select several slides in the Slide Sorter view and then use the Slide Transition task pane to assign the same transition and/or timing to the selected slides.

Don't Get Too Fancy! If you are going to use slide transitions and animation schemes on each and every slide, you might find that your slide show is becoming "too exciting," like a film with too many explosions, car chases, and other special effects. Viewers of the slide show will probably have trouble concentrating on the text on the slides if too many things are going on at once. Remember, everything in moderation.

CAUTION

Using the Slide Show Menu Tools

PowerPoint also provides some other features that you will find very useful when you are running your slide show. For example, you can turn the mouse pointer into a pen (such as a ballpoint pen or a highlighter) that enables you to draw on a particular slide, enabling you to quickly emphasize a particular point visually. Other features include the ability to add speaking notes on the fly as you view the presentation. You can also blank out the current slide to a black or white screen, allowing you to pause for a moment and answer audience questions or comments.

These tools are accessed by clicking on the icons that appear on the bottom left of your presentation slides as you show the presentation. There is an icon for the pen feature and a second icon that brings up a menu that allows you to access screen settings and a Go To feature that allows you to quickly go to a particular slide in the presentation. We discuss the use of the pen, speaker notes, and the Go to feature in the sections that follow.

TIP   **Access the Slide Show Icons**   If you move the mouse over a slide being shown in the Slide Show window, a series of buttons appear on the bottom left side of the slide pane.

Drawing with a Pen

An extremely useful tool is the pen, which enables you to draw on a particular slide. This is great for highlighting information on a slide to emphasize a particular point.

To use the pen during the slide show, follow these steps:

1. With the slide show running, click on the Pen icon that appears on the bottom left of the current slide.

2. On the menu that appears, select one of the pen types such as the **Ball Point Pen**. The mouse pointer becomes a ball point pen. (You can also choose to use a felt tip pen or a highlighter.)

3. Click the left mouse button and draw on the slide as needed (see Figure 12.4).

4. After you've finished working with the pen, you can return to the arrow pointer. Click the **Pen** icon. Select **Arrow** on the menu that appears. You can now use the mouse to advance to the next slide.

You can also choose the pen color that you use to draw on the slides. After clicking on the **Pen** icon, point at **Ink Color**, and then select the pen color you want to use from the color palette that appears.

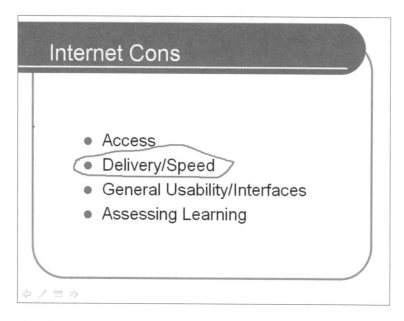

Figure 12.4 The pen provides you with an easy way to highlight a particular item on a slide.

Taking Speaker Notes

Another useful tool that you can take advantage of while showing your slide presentation is the Speaker Notes feature. It enables you to quickly take notes related to the discussion or to audience comments made during your presentation.

To use the Speaker Notes feature, follow these steps:

1. With the slide show running, point at the **Menu** icon on the bottom left of the current slide (it is the third icon from the left).

2. On the menu that appears, point at **Screen** and then select **Speaker Notes**. The Speaker Notes dialog box opens (see Figure 12.5.)

3. Type your notes into the Speaker Notes dialog box.

4. When you have finished adding notes, click the **Close** button to close the dialog box.

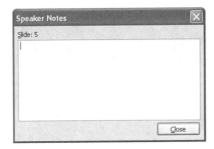

Figure 12.5 The Speaker Notes box allows you to record notes related to the current slide.

Finding a Particular Slide During the Show

As you reach the end of a presentation, you might be asked to reshow a particular slide or subset of slides that you included in your slide show. The easiest way to go to a particular slide when you are in the Slide Show view is to use the Go to Slide command on the Slide Show menu.

To go to a particular slide in the presentation, follow these steps:

1. With the slide show running, click the Menu button on the bottom left of the current slide.

2. On the menu that appears, point at **Go to Slide**. A submenu will appear showing all the slides (titles) in the presentation (see Figure 12.6).

3. To move to a particular slide, click the slide's title on the submenu. PowerPoint takes you to the selected slide.

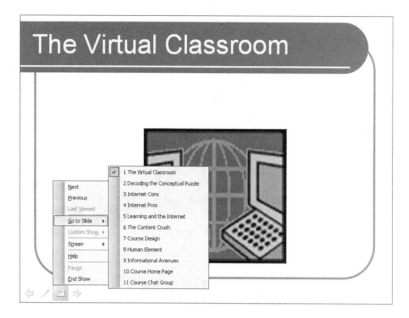

Figure 12.6 You can quickly go to any slide in the presentation.

Adding Action Buttons to User-Interactive Shows

You can create slide show presentations that will be played on a computer where your audience actually interacts with the slide show (for example, a computer at a trade show that tells potential customers about your company). This means that you need to give the audience some means of controlling the show. You can simply provide access to a keyboard and/or mouse and let the user control the show in the same way you learned earlier in this lesson, or you can provide action buttons onscreen that make it easy to jump to specific slides.

Action buttons are like controls on an audio CD player; they enable you to jump to any slide quickly, to go backward, to go forward, or even to stop the presentation.

TIP   **The Same Controls on All Slides?**   If you want to add the same action buttons to all slides in the presentation, add the action buttons to the Slide Master. To display the Slide Master, select **View**, point at **Master**, and then choose **Slide Master**.

To add an action button to a slide, follow these steps:

1. Display the slide in Normal view.

2. Select **Slide Show**, point at **Action Buttons**, and pick a button from the palette that appears. For example, if you want to create a button that advances to the next slide, you might choose the button with the arrow pointing to the right.

TIP   **Which Button Should I Choose?**   Consider the action that you want the button to perform, and then pick a button picture that matches it well. To change the button picture, you must delete the button and create a new one.

3. Your mouse pointer turns into a crosshair. Drag to draw a box on the slide where you want the button to appear. (You can resize it later if you want.) PowerPoint draws the button on the slide and opens the Action Settings dialog box (see Figure 12.7).

Figure 12.7   Set the action for your button in the Action Settings dialog box.

4. Select either the **Mouse Click** tab or **Mouse Over** tab to set the action for the button (Mouse Click options require a click; Mouse Over requires only that the mouse pointer be placed on the button).

5. Choose the type of action you want to happen when the user clicks the button. Click the **Hyperlink To** drop-down list and select an action such as **Next Slide**.

6. (Optional) If you want a sound to play when the user clicks the button, select the **Play Sound** check box and choose a sound from the drop-down list.

7. Click **OK**. Your button appears on the slide.

8. View the presentation (as you learned at the beginning of this lesson) to try out the button.

If you do use buttons on your slides so that users can run the slide show, be sure you use the same style of button on each of your slides for a particular action. This kind of consistency gives the viewer of the presentation a feeling of comfort and control.

> **TIP**   **Buttons Can Do Many Things**   You can also create action buttons that run a program or run a macro that has been created using the Visual Basic for Applications programming language. Although these are very advanced features not covered in this book, keep in mind as you learn more about PowerPoint that many possibilities exist for making very creative and complex slide show presentations.

Setting Slide Show Options

Depending on the type of show you're presenting, you might find it useful to make some adjustments to the way the show runs, such as making it run in a window (the default is full screen) or showing only certain slides. You'll find these controls and more in the Set Up Show dialog box, which you can open by clicking the **Slide Show** menu and selecting **Set Up Show** (see Figure 12.8).

Figure 12.8   Use the Set Up Show dialog box to give PowerPoint some basic instructions about how to present your slide show.

In this dialog box, you can choose from several options, including the following:

- Choose the medium for showing the presentation. Your choices are **Presented by a Speaker (Full Screen)**, **Browsed by an Individual (Window)**, and **Browsed at a Kiosk (Full Screen)**.

- Choose whether to loop the slide show continuously or to show it only once. You might want to loop it continuously so that it operates unaided at a kiosk at a trade show, for example.

- Show all the slides or a range of them (enter the range into the **From** and **To** boxes).

- Choose whether to advance slides manually or to use timings you set up.

- Choose a pen color. Use the Pen Color drop-down box to select a color.

Using the Set Up Show dialog box to set the various options for the show allows you to put the finishing touches on the presentation before you actually present it to your audience. For example, it negates the need to select a pen color on the fly, allowing you to concentrate on the slide content rather than trying to change the pen color with the audience watching.

This dialog box also allows you to set the viewing parameters for the environment that the presentation will be shown in. For example, if you are running the slideshow on a PC that will be used by individuals at a tradeshow booth, it makes sense to format the presentation to be viewed by an individual in a window. That way the individual can leave the presentation for a moment and take a look at any sample software or other items you have on the PC that support the presentation.

Printing Presentations, Notes, and Handouts

In this lesson, you learn how to select a size and orientation for the slides in your presentation and how to print the slides, notes, and handouts you create.

Using PowerPoint Notes and Handouts

Although PowerPoint presentations are designed to be shown on a computer screen, you might want to print some items related to the presentation. For example, as you design your presentation, you can enter notes related to each slide that you create in the Notes pane. These notes can then be printed out and used during the presentation.

Using speaker notes helps you keep on track during the presentation and provides you with the information that you want to present related to each slide in the presentation. When you print your notes, each slide is printed on a separate page with the notes printed below the slide.

If you want to make it easier for your audience to follow the presentation and perhaps take notes of their own, you can print out handouts. Handouts provide a hard copy of each slide. The number of slides printed on each page of the handout can range from 1 to 9 slides. If you choose to print three slides per page (this is set up in the Print dialog box, which is discussed later in this lesson), PowerPoint automatically places note lines on the printout pages to the right of each slide (which makes it even easier for your audience to take notes related to the slides in the presentation).

This lesson covers the options related to printing hard copies of your slides, notes, and handouts. Let's start with a look at printing out presentation slides.

Quick Printing with No Options

You can quickly print all the slides in the presentation. You don't get to make any decisions about your output, but you do get your printout without delay.

To print a quick copy of each slide in the presentation, choose one of these methods:

- Click the **Print** button on the Standard toolbar.
- Choose the **File** menu, choose **Print**, and click **OK**.
- Press **Ctrl+P** and click **OK**.

The downside of printing the presentation in this way is that you will get a printout of only one slide per page in the landscape orientation. It doesn't matter what view you are in—you just get the slides. This uses up a lot of printer ink or toner, and if you want to print the presentation as an outline or print the presentation so that you can see the presentation notes that you've made, you need to access printing options that provide more control over the printout.

One way to fine-tune some of the settings that control how pages will be printed is using the Page Setup dialog box.

Changing the Page Setup

The Page Setup dialog box enables you to select how slides, notes, and handouts should be oriented on the page (Portrait or Landscape) and the type of page that the slides should be formatted for, such as On-Screen Show, overhead sheets, or regular 8 1/2-inch by 11-inch paper.

To customize the Page Setup settings, follow these steps:

1. Select the **File** menu and select **Page Setup**. The Page Setup dialog box appears as shown in Figure 13.1.

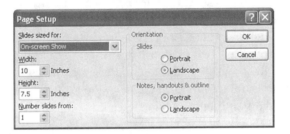

Figure 13.1 The Page Setup dialog box enables you to set the paper type and the orientation of slides and notes on the page.

2. Perform one of the following procedures to set the slide size:

   - To use a standard size, select a size from the **Slides Sized For** drop-down list. For example, you can have slides sized for regular 8 1/2-inch by 11-inch paper, overheads, or 35mm slides (if you have a special printer that can create slides).

   - To create a custom size, enter the dimensions into the **Width** and **Height** text boxes.

TIP   **Spin Boxes**   The arrows to the right of the Width and Height text boxes enable you to adjust the settings in those boxes. Click the up arrow to increase the setting by .1 inch or the down arrow to decrease it by .1 inch.

3. In the **Number Slides From** text box, type the number with which you want to start numbering slides. (This is usually **1**, but you might want to start with a different number if the presentation is a continuation of another.)

4. Under the Slides heading, choose **Portrait** or **Landscape** orientation for your slides.

5. In the Notes, Handouts & Outline section, choose **Portrait** or **Landscape** for those items.

6. Click **OK**. If you changed the orientation of your slides, you might have to wait a moment while PowerPoint repositions the slides.

Choosing What and How to Print

To really control your printouts related to a particular presentation, use the various options supplied in the Print dialog box. The Print dialog box enables you to specify what to print, such as handouts or the presentation as an outline; it also enables you to specify the printer to use for the printout. For example, you might want to use a color printer for overhead transparencies and a black-and-white printer for your handouts. To set your print options, follow these steps:

1. Select the **File** menu and select **Print**. The Print dialog box appears with the name of the currently selected printer in the Name box (see Figure 13.2).

2. If you want to use a different printer, open the Name drop-down list and select the printer you want.

TIP   **Printer Properties**   The Properties button enables you to adjust graphics quality, select paper size, and choose which paper tray to use, among other things.

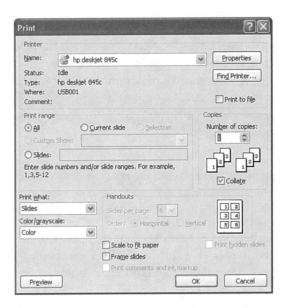

Figure 13.2   The Print dialog box enables you to control the printer and the printouts.

3. Choose what to print in the Print Range section:

- Choose **All** to print all the slides in the presentation.
- Choose **Current Slide** to print only the currently displayed slide.
- Enter a range of slide numbers into the **Slides** text box; for example, enter 2–4 to print slides 2, 3, and 4.

4. Open the **Print What** drop-down list and choose what you want to print. You can print slides, handouts, notes, or outlines.

5. If you want more than one copy, enter the number of copies you want into the **Number of Copies** box.

6. Use the Color/Grayscale drop-down box to specify whether the printout should be in color, grayscale, or black and white.

7. If you are printing handouts, use the Handouts box to specify the number of slides that should be printed per page and the orientation used for the printed page (Portrait or Landscape).

8. Select or deselect any of these check boxes in the dialog box, as required:

- **Print to File**—Select this option to send the output to a file rather than to your printer.

- **Collate**—If you are printing more than one copy, select this check box to collate (1, 2, 3, 1, 2, 3) each printed copy instead of printing all the copies of each page at once (1, 1, 2, 2, 3, 3).

- **Scale to Fit Paper**—If the slide (or whatever you're printing) is too large to fit on the page, select this check box to decrease the size of the slide to make it fit on the page. Now you won't have to paste two pieces of paper together to see the whole slide.

- **Frame Slides**—Select this check box if you want to print a border around each slide.

- **Print Hidden Slides**—If you have any hidden slides, you can choose whether to print them. If you don't have any hidden slides, this check box will be unavailable.

- **Print Comments and Ink Markup**—Prints all the comments on the slides of the presentation on a separate comments page. This option also prints any ink markups that you have made using the pen feature when viewing the presentation.

 TIP   **Preview Your Printout Selection**   After specifying the various options in the Print dialog box, you might want to preview the printout before you send it to the printer. Click the **Preview** button. You are taken to the Print Preview screen. If things look good on the Print Preview screen, click **Print** to send the printout to the printer.

9. Click **OK** to print.

Publisher

Getting Started with Publisher

*In this lesson, you learn how to start Publisher, and you become
familiar with the Publisher workspace. You also learn about the
process of planning a new publication and preview the options for creating a publication.*

Starting Publisher

Publisher makes it easy for you to create a variety of publication types. These publications can range from business cards to trifold brochures to World Wide Web pages. However, before you can take advantage of Publisher's sophisticated but easy-to-use tools for creating great-looking publications, you need to open the Publisher application window.

To start the Publisher program, follow these steps:

1. From the Windows XP Desktop, click **Start**, and point at **All Programs**. The Programs menu appears (in Windows 2000 select **Start**, then **Programs**).

2. Point at **Microsoft Office**, and then select **Microsoft Office Publisher 2003**. The Publisher program window appears on the desktop (see Figure 1.1).

The initial Publisher window supplies you with the launch point for new and existing publications. The New Publication task pane enables you to begin the process of starting a new publication (see Figure 1.1). It also enables you to open existing publications. When you begin a new publication (or open an existing publication), you will find that the Publisher workspace is similar to the workspaces in the other Office applications; it provides menus and toolbars with many of the tools that you are already familiar with if you use Word, Excel, or PowerPoint.

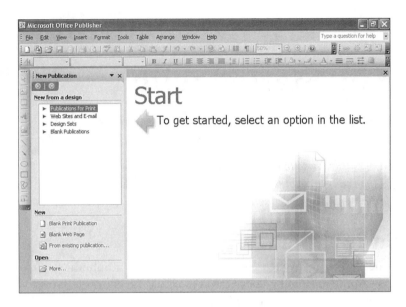

Figure 1.1 The New Publication task pane allows you to create a new publication or open existing publications.

Deciding How to Create a New Publication

A number of possible methods are available in the New Publication task pane to start a new publication. These possibilities are as follows:

- **Publications for Print**—If you want to create a specific type of publication for print such as a banner, brochure, or business card and would like to have a design template provided, you can view publications by category by clicking the **Publications for Print** heading in the New Publication task pane. Publication categories include Advertisements, Awards, Business Cards, and Gift Certificates, just to name a few. A Quick Publications category provides a number of template layouts for single-page publications that can be used as flyers and one-page posters. Creating a publication for print using one of the publication categories is discussed in Lesson 2, "Creating a New Publication."

- **Web Sites and E-Mail**—Publisher also provides a series of templates that can be used to quickly create Web sites and special e-mails such as newsletters and featured product sheets. Web sites and e-mail templates are accessed by clicking the Web Sites and E-Mail heading in the New Publication task pane. When you select a template such as a Web site, Publisher will use the Easy Web Site Builder to accumulate information needed for the site (see Figure 1.2) and walk you through the steps of completing the Web site's pages.

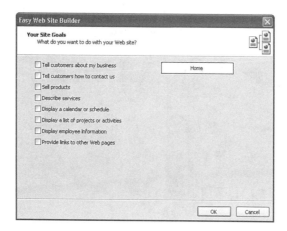

Figure 1.2   The Easy Web Site Builder will help you determine the purpose for your site and build your pages.

- **Design Sets**—Design sets enable you to create a family of publications that have the same look. Each master design set uses a particular set of design elements and colors that are consistent across all the publications in the set. For instance, you might want to create letterhead, business cards, and invoices that all have the same design look for your small business. You can create these publications by choosing a particular design set in the Design Sets pane and then selecting the particular publication (such as the business cards) in the Master Sets window. Specific families of publications such as personal stationery sets and fund-raising sets make it easy for you to create a group of publications with the same design and look for specific purposes.

- **Blank Publications**—Another possibility for creating your new publication is to create it from scratch. However, you will find that Publisher doesn't totally abandon you when you take this approach. To start a blank publication, select the **Blank Publications** heading in the New Publication task pane. You can then select the type of blank document you want to create such as a business card or flyer. Figure 1.3 shows a new blank publication. Notice that the Publication Designs task pane enables you to select color schemes and font schemes for the new blank publication.

 TIP   **Create a Publication from an Existing Publication**   You can also create a publication based on an existing publication. This allows you to use the design elements in an existing publication and modify it for a new purpose.

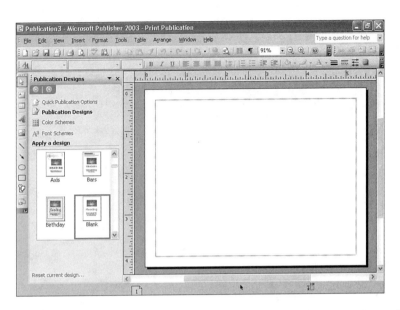

Figure 1.3 Publisher also provides help with design elements when you create a blank publication.

As far as selecting a route for creating your new publication, that will depend on your experience with Publisher and the particular design requirements of your publication. The various document templates and the design sets provide you with a lot of help as you initially design your publication. They also create placeholder objects in your new publication that you can replace with your own pictures or design elements.

For the new user, using a template for a print publication or Web site, or using the design sets offers a quick and easy way to create your new publications. Creating publications from scratch might be something that you hold off on until you have a good understanding of all the Publisher tools and some basic design principles.

Using the Publisher Workspace

After you've begun a publication using either a specific template, the design sets, or by starting your new publication from scratch, you work with the various commands and features that enable you to edit and enhance the publication. Publisher provides you with several ways to access the commands and features you use as you work on your publications. You can access these commands using the menus on the menu bar and the buttons on the toolbars that Publisher supplies.

You can also access a number of Publisher commands using shortcut menus. These menus are accessed by right-clicking a particular document element. The shortcut menu appears with a list of commands related to the item you are currently working on, such as a word or paragraph.

The Publisher Menu Bar

The Publisher menu bar gives you access to all the commands and features that Publisher provides. As in all Windows applications, Publisher's menus are found below the title bar and are activated by clicking a particular menu choice. The menu then opens, providing you with a set of command choices.

To access a particular menu, follow these steps:

1. Select the menu by clicking its title (such as **Insert**). The most recently used commands appear; wait just a moment for all the commands on a particular menu to appear.

2. Select the command on the menu that invokes a particular feature (such as **Object**).

TIP   Full Menus at Once   If you want to view all the commands available for the menu system, click the **Tools** menu, click **Customize**, and then click the **Options** tab on the Customize dialog box. To show all the commands on the menus, click the **Always Show Full Menus** check box. The figures in this book show the menus in Publisher with this option selected.

You will find that a number of the commands found on the menu are followed by an ellipsis (…). When one of these commands is selected, either a dialog box or a task pane will open. In both cases, you have to provide Publisher with additional information to create a particular command or task.

TIP   Activating Menus with the Keyboard   You can also activate a particular menu by holding down the **Alt** key and then pressing the keyboard key that matches the underscored letter in the menu's name. This underscored letter is called the hotkey. For instance, to activate the File menu in Publisher, you would press **Alt+F**.

Shortcut Menus

A fast way to access commands that are related to a particular document element is to hover the mouse pointer over a particular publication object, and then right-click. This opens a shortcut menu that contains commands related to the particular object you are working with.

Publisher Object   Any element found in a publication, such as text, a graphic, a hyperlink, or other inserted item.

If you select an object such as clip art, for instance, or a drawn object such as a circle, right-clicking the selected object opens a shortcut menu with commands such as Cut, Copy, Paste, and other commands related to that particular object.

Publisher Toolbars

The Publisher toolbars provide you with a very quick and straightforward way of accessing commands and features. When you start a new publication, Publisher displays the Standard, Formatting, and Publisher toolbars (most of the buttons on the toolbars will not become active until you start a new publication). The Standard and Formatting toolbars reside under the Publisher menu bar. These toolbars provide you with easy access to commands such as Save and Open, or to formatting features such as bold, underline, and centering.

To access a particular command using a Standard or Formatting toolbar button, click the button. Depending on the command, you see an immediate result in your publication (such as the bolding or centering of a selected text object) or a dialog box appears, requesting additional information from you.

Finding a Toolbar Button's Purpose   You can place the mouse pointer on any toolbar button to view a description of that tool's function.

The Objects toolbar is a special toolbar that allows you to add objects to a publication, such as text boxes and tables, and design elements, such as ovals and lines (see Figure 1.4). The Objects toolbar resides as a vertical toolbar on the left side of the Publication workspace.

The Objects toolbar

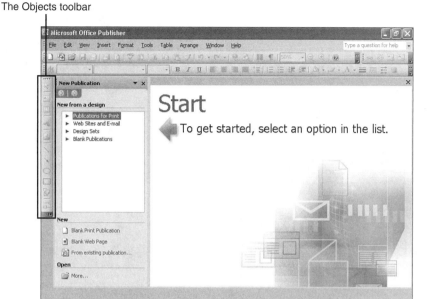

Figure 1.4   The Objects toolbar allows you to quickly insert objects such as tables into a publication.

Exiting Publisher

After you have completed your initial survey of the Publisher application window, or whenever you have completed a particular publication, you will want to exit the software. More than one way exists to close the Publisher window, which is the same as exiting the program.

You can exit Publisher by selecting the **File** menu, then **Exit**. Or you can close Publisher with one click of the mouse by clicking the **Close** (X) button in the upper-right corner of the application window.

When you do close Publisher, you might be prompted to save any work that you have done in the application window. If you were just experimenting as you read through this lesson, you can click **No**. The current document will not be saved and the Publisher application window closes. All the ins and outs of actually saving your publications are covered in Lesson 2.

Creating a New Publication

In this lesson, you learn how to create a new publication using the publication categories accessed from the print publication designs.

Using a Publication Category

A straightforward method of creating a new publication in which you are provided with design, layout, and page orientation help is using a design template provided in one of the publication categories. These categories are accessed using the Publications for Print Heading that is provided in the New Presentation task pane.

When you first start Publisher, the New Presentation task pane automatically opens. You can open the New Presentation task pane at any time by selecting **File**, then **New**.

With the New Presentation task pane open, follow these steps to create a new print publication:

1. In the New Publication task pane, select the **Publications for Print** option. A list of publication categories will appear (see Figure 2.1).

2. Scroll down through the list to view the publication categories. When you find the category you want to use, select it (for example, Business Cards).

3. A number of different designs supplied by the category will appear in the Preview window (see Figure 2.2). Select the design template you want to use for your publication by clicking the sample in the Preview window.

The new publication will be created and placed in the Publisher workspace. The New Publication task pane will be replaced by an option task pane with specific options available related to the type of publication you are creating.

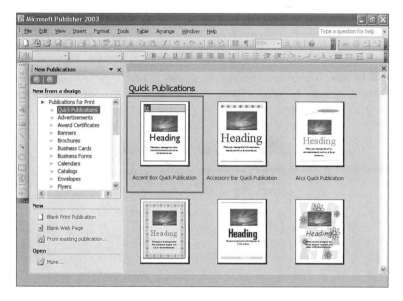

Figure 2.1 Publication categories provide design templates for different types of print publications.

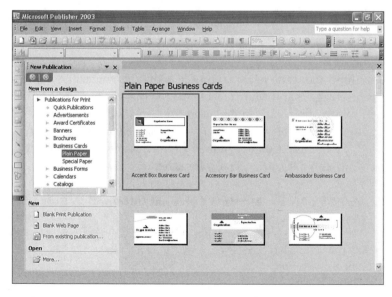

Figure 2.2 Select a publication category to view the designs supplied, and then select a specific design.

Creating a Personal Information Profile

Depending on the type of publication you are creating, the Personal Information dialog box may open asking you to create a personal profile. This profile contains information such as your name, company name, phone number, and other information. For business forms, business cards, and letterhead, you are prompted to create a new profile as shown in Figure 2.3.

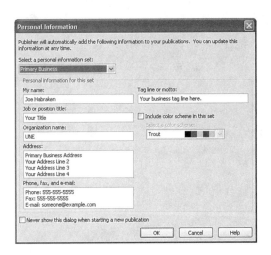

Figure 2.3   Personal information is requested to be used in the publication.

The best thing about the personal profile is that you enter the information once and it can be used again and again as you create your various publications. To edit the Personal Information, click in the appropriate text box and supply the appropriate information. You can also select to have a color scheme stored with the information set. Select the **Include Color Scheme in This Set** check box and then use the color scheme drop-down list to select a color scheme.

TIP   **You Can Create Multiple Personal Information Sets**   You can create more than one personal information set (up to four information sets can be created). Click the Select a Personal Information Set drop-down box at the top of the Personal Information dialog box. Select any of the four information set types provided. You can create a Primary Business, Secondary Business, Other Organization, and Home/Family information set.

After supplying the information, click **OK**. The information that you provided in the information set is placed in the current publication.

TIP   **Updating Personal Information**   You can update your personal information as needed. Select **Edit**, then **Personal Information** to open the Personal Information dialog box. When you have edited the information, click the **Update** button to close the dialog box.

Selecting a New Publication Design

After you have supplied the personal information if required (it is not required for all publication types), you are ready to begin working on your publication in the Publisher workspace. Depending on the type of publication you are working on, you are provided with options for the current publication in an Options task pane. For example, a business card created using a design from the print publication categories will have the Business Card Options task pane associated with it.

One option related to your publication is that you can change the overall publication design if you do not like the initial design that you chose. To select a new design for the publication, click the **Publication Designs** option in the task pane (see Figure 2.4).

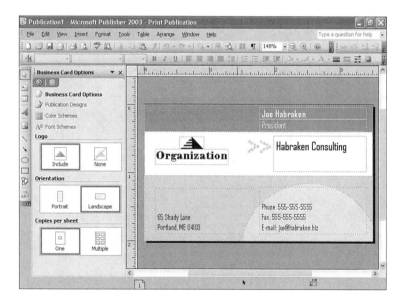

Figure 2.4   You can select a new design for your publication.

An Apply a Design scroll box will appear that allows you to view other available designs for the publication type. To select a new design, scroll through the design possibilities and then click on a new design.

Selecting a Publication Color Scheme

Another option that you control is the color scheme for the publication. When you select a particular design template for a publication, it supplies you with a default color scheme. You can modify the color scheme using the Color Schemes option in the Options task pane for your publication type.

Follow these steps:

1. Click the Color Schemes option in the task pane. An Apply a Color Scheme scroll box will appear on the task pane (see Figure 2.5).

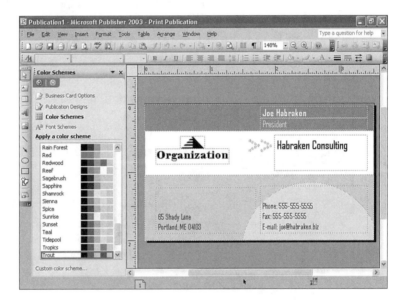

Figure 2.5   You can select a new color scheme for your publication.

2. Scroll through the list of color schemes provided.
3. When you have decided on a new color scheme, click the color scheme in the Apply a Color Scheme scroll box. The color scheme will be applied to your presentation.

Selecting a Font Scheme

Another aspect of the overall publication design that you control is the font scheme that is used in the publication. A font scheme is really a font family, meaning that you select a particular font such as Arial or Courier New and then the font is applied in the appropriate sizes to the different text areas of the publication. Other font attributes such as bold and italic are also applied to the font family depending on the requirements of the design template you selected.

To change the font scheme for a publication, follow these steps:

1. Click the Font Schemes option in the task pane. An Apply a Font Scheme scroll box will appear on the task pane (see Figure 2.6).

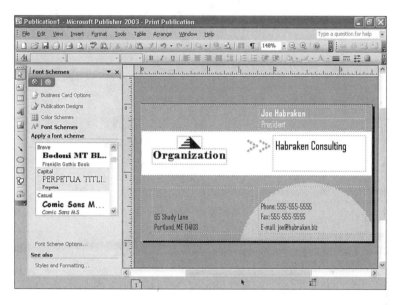

Figure 2.6   You can select a new font scheme for your publication.

2. Scroll through the list of font schemes provided.

3. When you have decided on a new font scheme, click the color scheme in the Apply a Font scheme scroll box. The font scheme will be applied to your presentation.

Selecting Page Orientation

Depending on the type of publication you are creating, you may also have the option of changing the page orientation in the publication's option task pane. For example, the business card in Figure 2.7 can be created in either a portrait or a landscape orientation.

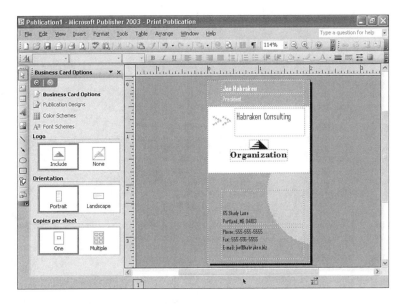

Figure 2.7   You can change the page orientation for the publication.

 TIP   **Portrait or Landscape**   If you are dealing with a regular 8 1/2 by 11-inch sheet of paper, Portrait orientation means that the height is 11 inches and the width is 8 1/2 inches. If you use Landscape orientation, the paper is turned on its side, so the height is 8 1/2 inches and the width is 11 inches.

In cases where you cannot change the publication page orientation in the Options task pane, you can change the page orientation using the Layout tab of the Page Setup dialog box.

Follow these steps:

1. Select the **File** menu, then **Page Setup**.
2. In the Page Setup dialog box, select the **Layout** tab.
3. On the Layout tab select either **Portrait** or **Landscape** as necessary.
4. Click **OK** to close the dialog box.

Understanding Placeholders

Depending on the type of publication you are creating, a number of placeholders are placed on the publication. These placeholders can be for company logos, pictures, or other graphical elements. For instance, in the case of business cards, you can have placeholders for company logos and the various text elements that make up the card.

Working with placeholders is very straightforward. For example, to edit a text box, click in the text placeholder to place the insertion point (see Figure 2.8). This selects the text box and you can now insert the appropriate text.

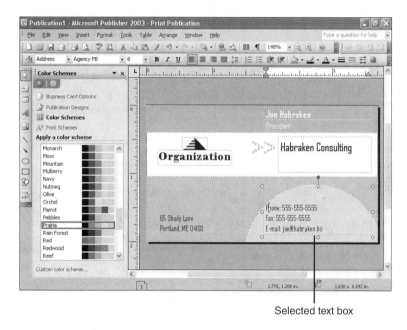

Selected text box

Figure 2.8   You can change the text in the placeholders provided on your publication.

Placeholder images may also be present in publications that you create using the various design templates available. Working with graphics is discussed in Lesson 8, "Working with Graphics."

 TIP   **Edit Text As You Would in Any Office Application**   You can edit text in a placeholder as you would in any Office application; you can use the mouse to select text and delete text with either the **Delete** key or the **Backspace** key.

Saving Your Publication

After you complete the various steps in selecting the design, colors, and fonts for the publication, you should save your publication. This protects all your hard work from unforeseen accidents such as power outages or computer malfunctions. It also enables you to take a breather before you begin the editing or enhancement process.

To save your new publication, follow these steps:

1. Select the **File** menu, and then select **Save**. The Save As dialog box appears.

2. Type a filename in the **File Name** box.

3. Click the **Save In** drop-down box and select the drive in which you want to save the publication.

4. When you have provided a filename and a location for your new publication, click the **Save** button. The publication is saved to your computer.

Using Design Sets

In this lesson, you learn how to create new publications as part of a design set. You also learn how to create a publication from scratch.

Understanding the Publication Design Sets

Publisher provides you with a way to create sets of publications that share the same color and design attributes. This makes it easy for you to create publications such as business cards, envelopes, brochures, and letterheads that share the same look.

Publisher provides a number of different design sets. Master sets provide a wide variety of different designs (there are 45 Master sets). Special design sets such as the Special Events set and the Restaurant set enable you to quickly create a family of publications for a specific purpose. There are eight different special design sets.

Selecting the Design Set

You select the design set for your new publication from the New Publication task pane, which appears when you start Publisher, or when you start a new publication from the File menu (**File**, **New**). To select a design set for a family of publications (and create a new publication from the family), follow these steps:

1. Start Publisher using the **Start** menu, or if you are already in the Publisher window, click the **File** menu, and then click **New**.

2. In the New Publication task pane, click the **Design Sets** option. A list of design sets will appear in the task pane (see Figure 3.1).

3. Select the set that you want to use for your current new publication. For example, you can select Master sets or one of the more specific sets such as the Personal Stationery set.

4. When you select a particular design set (such as the Master set), a subset of specific designs will appear in the Preview window. For example, in the Master set, you can select from designs such as Arcs, Blends, and Brocade. Select a particular design to see how the different publications (such as business cards or calendars) will appear if you use the design.

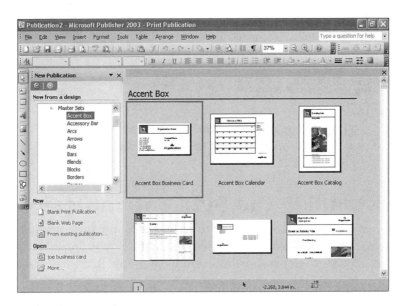

Figure 3.1 Design sets can be selected from the New Publication task pane.

5. When you have selected the design you want to use (one of the designs from a set), select the design from the list.

TIP **Use the Scrollbar to Peruse the Design List** To view all the design sets in the Design Sets list, click the down scroll arrow on the list's scrollbar.

Completing the Publication

After you've selected a particular design set, and a specific design, you can select a particular publication from the Preview window and create that publication. Repeating the steps discussed in the preceding section allows you to create an entire family of publications that use the same design set (you create the publications one at a time).

For example, to create an envelope using a master design, follow these steps:

1. After selecting a design set and then a specific design, click the **envelope** template shown in the Preview window. The new envelope and the Envelope Options task pane appear (see Figure 3.2).

2. (optional) Use the **Color Schemes** option on the Envelope to select a different color scheme for the envelope (remember that this will change the default colors, which you might not want to do if you are using the design set to create a family of "like" publications).

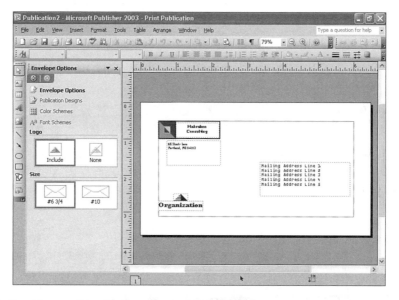

Figure 3.2 The new envelope can be modified using the Envelope Options task pane.

3. (optional) Use the Font Schemes option to change the font family used for the publication (again, you might not want to change the default if you are creating several publications that need to look the same).

4. If you do not want to include a log on the envelope, click the **None** option under Logo on the task pane.

5. Use the envelope size options under Size on the taskbar to size the envelope.

As with any other publication that you create from a design template, you can now replace any existing text or other items in a placeholder with the appropriate information. When you have completed editing the envelope, make sure that you save the presentation. After you complete the first publication in your set, you can use the New Publication task pane to select the appropriate design set and create other publications as needed.

Creating a Publication from Scratch

We have already discussed how you can create a publication from a design template (in Lesson 2, "Creating a New Publication") and how you create a publication family using design sets (as discussed in this lesson). You also have the option of creating a publication from scratch. However, you will find that even when you use this option, Publisher provides you with help in determining the overall layout of the publication.

To create a publication from scratch, follow these steps:

1. Open the New Presentation task pane (select **File**, then **New** to open the task pane), and select the **Blank Publications** option.

2. Scroll down through the list of blank publication types in the Preview window. Then select the publication type you want to create (such as banner).

The new blank publication appears in the Publisher workspace (see Figure 3.3). You can now add text boxes, picture frames, and other objects to complete your presentation. Color schemes and font schemes for the publication can be selected from the New Publication task pane as discussed in the preceding section of this lesson (and in Lesson 2).

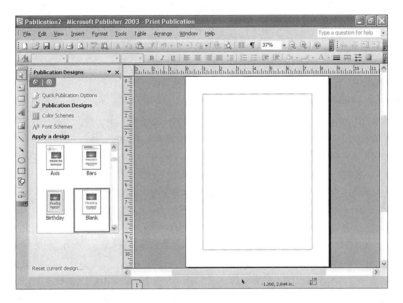

Figure 3.3   A number of blank publication types are available from the New Presentation task pane.

Adding text boxes and picture frames to a publication is discussed in Lesson 6, "Working with Publication Objects." For more about formatting text in a publication, see Lesson 7, "Changing How Text Looks."

Viewing Your Publications

4

In this lesson, you learn the different options for viewing your publication, including the Zoom feature. You also learn how to work with positioning tools such as the ruler and guides.

Changing the Publication Display

When you create publications in the Publisher window, the default view is the Whole Page view. This enables you to see the entire current page from a bird's-eye view, which is excellent for determining the overall layout of the page and the positioning of the various text boxes, picture frames, and other objects.

As you work with your publications, you will find that it's convenient to be able to change the view from a single page to a two-page spread and to zoom in and out on a particular page. The following sections describe the three basic views that are available to you.

Whole Page

The default view is Whole Page. It shows the entire current page and shows the margins for the page. Figure 4.1 shows a publication (a flyer) in the Whole Page view.

If you are in any other view and want to return to the Whole Page view, select the **View** menu, and then point at **Zoom**. Select **Whole Page** from the cascading menu.

 TIP **Go to Whole Page View Using the Keyboard** You can quickly go to the Whole Page view by pressing **Ctrl+Shift+L** on the keyboard.

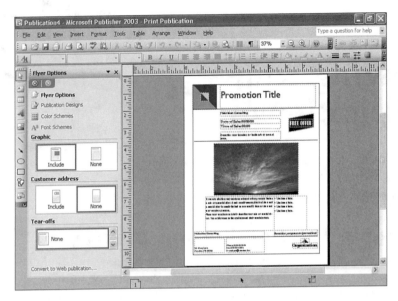

Figure 4.1　The Whole Page view enables you to view the spatial relations of all the items that you've placed on a particular page.

Page Width

Another useful view is the Page Width view. This enables you to zoom in on the publication page but still see the left and right margins. The Page Width view provides a view that is slightly larger than zooming to 50% (58%). Because this view maintains the total width of the page and enables you to see the left and right margins, you can easily scroll up and down on the page using the vertical scrollbar to see any hidden parts of your publication. Figure 4.2 shows the page depicted in Figure 4.1 (the Whole Page view) in the Page Width view.

To place the current publication page in the Page Width view, select the **View** menu, and then point at **Zoom**. Select **Page Width** from the cascading menu.

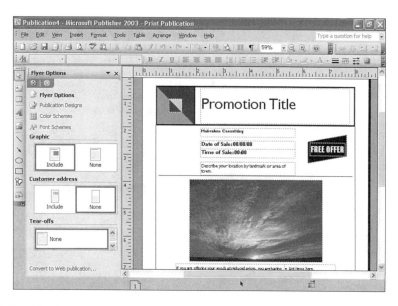

Figure 4.2 The Page Width view enables you to zoom in on your publication page, but it still shows the left and right margins for reference.

Two-Page Spread

Another useful view is the Two-Page Spread. This enables you to examine facing pages in a publication. This view is particularly useful when you want to make sure that the frames and objects on these two pages are balanced and arranged appropriately. Any publication that opens (for example, a greeting card or brochure) has facing pages inside it.

Figure 4.3 shows a three-page publication with the facing pages (pages 2 and 3) in the Two-Page Spread view. To view a publication in the Two-Page Spread view, select the **View** menu, and then select **Two-Page Spread**. A check mark appears next to the Two-Page Spread selection on the View menu.

 TIP **Move From Page to Page in a Multipage Publication** You can quickly move from page to page in a multipage publication by clicking the page icons on the Publisher taskbar.

When you want to return to the single-page view, select the **View** menu and click **Two-Page Spread** to remove the check mark.

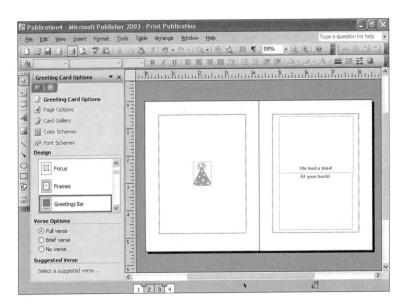

Figure 4.3 The Two-Page Spread view enables you to look at facing pages in your publication.

TIP **First Pages Don't Have Facing Pages** The very first page of your publication is considered a cover page. If you think about greeting cards and other booklet-type publications, the first page is visible when the publication is closed. The first inside page is page 2 (on the left of the open card), with page 3 as its right-facing page.

Using the Zoom Feature

Because your publication pages consist of various frames containing text and other items such as pictures, you will often need to edit or otherwise fine-tune these items. When you are trying to concentrate on a particular item on the page, you want to be able to zoom in on that item. Publisher provides you with the capability to zoom in and out on your publication pages using a range from 10% to 400% (the larger the percentage, the more you've zoomed in on your publication).

To zoom in or out on the current page, follow these steps:

1. Select the **View** menu, and then point at **Zoom**.

2. Select your Zoom percentage from the cascading menu (such as **66%**). Figure 4.4 shows a page zoomed at 66%.

Figure 4.4 Use the Zoom feature to zoom in and out on your publication pages.

 TIP **Zoom In and Out Quickly Using the Toolbar** You can also zoom in and out on your publication pages using the **Zoom** drop-down box on the Standard toolbar. Click it and select the zoom percentage.

Working with Rulers and Guide Lines

Another visual aspect of working on your publications is the use of the rulers and guides. A vertical ruler and a horizontal ruler are supplied in the Publication window to help you place items on the page. *Guides* are really extensions of the ruler and appear as guide lines (both vertical and horizontal) that you can drag onto the document page (from either ruler) to help you appropriately place text and pictures on the page.

 TERM **Guide** A layout guide is a nonprinting vertical or horizontal line that you place on the publication page to help you align the various elements that the publication contains. Guides appear on the document page in green.

 TIP **Where Are My Rulers?** If you don't see the rulers in the Publication window, select the **View** menu, and then select **Rulers**.

Using the Ruler

When you move the mouse on the page, you will notice that the vertical and horizontal positions of the mouse pointer are tracked by a tick mark (a line) on each of the rulers. The actual position (horizontal and vertical) of the mouse pointer is also displayed on the Publisher taskbar (see Figure 4.5).

Tick marks ⌐   ⌐Current position of pointer

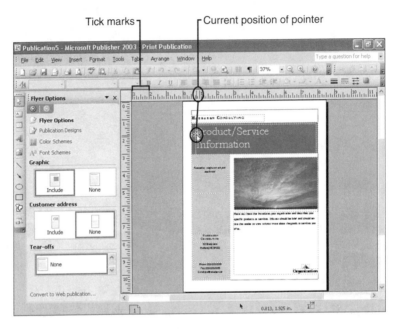

Figure 4.5   The rulers show you the position of the mouse pointer on the page.

Being able to see the position of the mouse pointer on the rulers and in the taskbar enables you to position object frames on the page with precision. For instance, to place a picture frame two inches down from the top of a page, you drag the object by its top (because you want the top at the two-inch mark) and watch until the vertical ruler tick mark reaches the two-inch mark. Then you release the object.

Using Layout Guides

Another tool that you can use to precisely position picture frames and text boxes on your Publisher page is the layout guide. These guides, as already mentioned, are nonprinting vertical and horizontal lines that you place on a publication page. The great thing about using layout guides is that they help you maintain the overall layout design on publications that run a number of pages (you set up the same layout guides on each page).

Placing guides on the page enables you to actually place a frame on the guide. This is called *snap to guide*. When you move the object near the guide, it snaps onto the guide, precisely positioning the item.

 TIP   **Turning On Snap to Guides**   If you are going to use guides in your publications to help you place items on the page, you should turn on the Snap to Guides feature. Select the **Tools** menu, and then select **Snap to Guides**.

Guides are created and positioned on your pages using the mouse. Follow these steps to create guides on a publication page:

1. To create a vertical layout guide, place the mouse pointer on the vertical ruler.

2. Drag the mouse onto the page. A vertical guideline appears (see Figure 4.6).

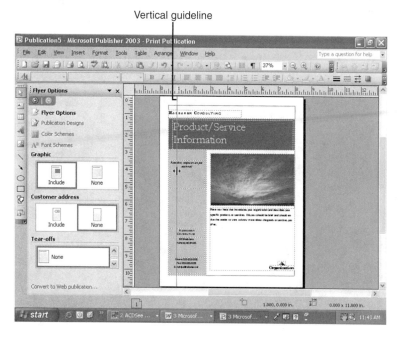

Figure 4.6   Position guides on your pages to help you align text boxes and picture frames.

3. Position the guideline at the appropriate position on the page and release the mouse button.

4. To create a horizontal layout guide, repeat steps 1–3, but drag a guide down from the horizontal ruler.

TIP **Where Are My Guides?** If you attempt to create guides and they don't appear in the Publication window, select the **View** menu, and then select **Boundaries and Guides**.

You can place as many guides as you need on your pages. If you find that you like using guides but don't like creating and positioning them with the mouse, you can also choose to have a series of horizontal and vertical guides created for you automatically. This forms a grid pattern on the publication, providing you with a sort of topography that you can use to appropriately align your publication items.

To create a grid system for a page, follow these steps:

1. Select the **Arrange** menu, and then select **Layout Guides**. The Layout Guides dialog box appears.

2. To set guides, click the Grid Guides tab and use the **Columns** and **Rows** click boxes to set the number of vertical (column) and horizontal (row) guides you want to place on the page.

3. After you have specified the number of columns and rows you want for the guides, click **OK**. The new guides appear on your publication page.

Working with Existing Publications

In this lesson, you learn how to open, close, and save an existing publication, add pages to the publication, and save the publication under a new filename. You also learn how to complete publications containing picture frames and placeholders.

Opening an Existing Publication

You will probably find that you end up with a library of saved publications that you use on a fairly regular basis. Items such as certificates, invitation cards, and various business forms can be created and saved to your computer and then used when needed.

 TIP **Saving Is Not Just for Finished Publications** If you've worked on a publication and don't really have its design or colors the way you want, you can, of course, save the file and then work on it again at your convenience.

The great thing about recycling publications in this way is that you take the time to design them well once, and then you can open them and edit them to fit your particular need. To open an existing publication, follow these steps:

1. In the Publisher window, select the **File** menu, and then select **Open**. The Open Publication dialog box appears (see Figure 5.1).

 TIP **Use the Open Button** To quickly open a publication, click the **Open** button on the Publisher Standard toolbar.

2. In the Open Publication dialog box, click the **Look In** drop-down box to select the drive on which your file is located.

3. After you select a drive, double-click the appropriate folder in the folder list that appears.

4. Select the file you want to open, and then click **Open**. The publication opens in the Publisher window.

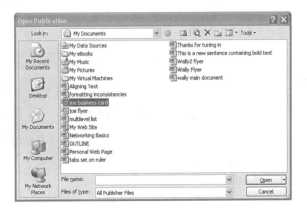

Figure 5.1   Select a location on your computer to open a specific file.

Completing a Design Template Publication

When you create publications using a design template, some information is added from your personal information profile, but this doesn't necessarily complete the publication for you. A number of text boxes and picture frames will probably be present in the publication; for example, a publication such as a certificate or an invitation requires that you fill in the recipient's name or the time and place of the event. So, much of the process related to completing a publication relates to replacing placeholder text and images with the appropriate content.

Editing Text in a Publication

When you work with text in Publisher, the text is held inside a frame called a *text box*. You learn more about creating and working with text boxes in Lesson 7, "Changing How Text Looks."

To modify or complete text entries in a publication, follow these steps:

1. To modify the contents of a text box, click the text box to select it (click anywhere on the box frame that is around the text).

 TIP   **Zoom In When Working on Text**   When you need to edit text in a text frame, you might want to zoom in on the publication for a closer look. Select the **View** menu, point at **Zoom**, and then select the zoom percentage from the cascading menu.

2. Double-click the text in the text frame to select all the text (see Figure 5.2). To select a portion of the text, use click-and-drag.

3. Type the appropriate text into the text frame. The selected placeholder text is deleted and replaced by the new text.

Selected text

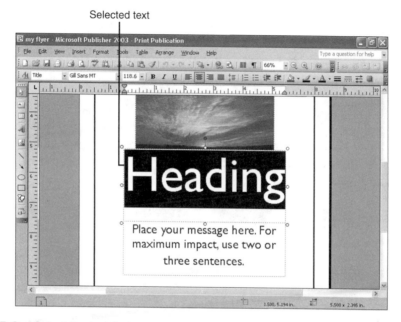

Figure 5.2 Select the text that you want to modify.

TIP **Select All the Text in a Story** Publisher refers to the text in text boxes as a *story*. In cases where you can't see all the text that is in a text box (because the text box isn't big enough to display all the text), you can press Ctrl+A to select all the text that actually resides in the text box.

Filling a Picture Frame

Not all the additions that you need to make to a design template–based publication are text, however. In some cases you need to fill other placeholders (such as for a company logo or a picture of the chairperson of the board) with the appropriate graphic. These graphics are held in a frame referred to as *picture frames*. See Lesson 8, "Working with Graphics," for more information on working with picture frames.

To fill a picture placeholder with a new picture, follow these steps:

1. Click the placeholder picture frame in the publication to select it.

2. Select the **Insert** menu, then point at **Picture**. From the cascading menu, select one of the following:

Clip Art—You can search for and select Office clip art from the Clip Art task pane.

From File—You can select a picture that you have stored on your computer.

Empty Picture Frame—You can place an empty picture frame on the page. You can then insert a picture into the frame at a later time.

From Scanner or Camera—If you have either of these devices connected to your computer, you can create a new image and place it immediately into Publisher.

Depending on your choice, you work with either the Clip Art task pane, the Insert File dialog box, or your scanner or camera. Figure 5.3 shows the Clip Art task pane after a search has been conducted for flag clip art. For more information on working with and manipulating pictures, see Lesson 8.

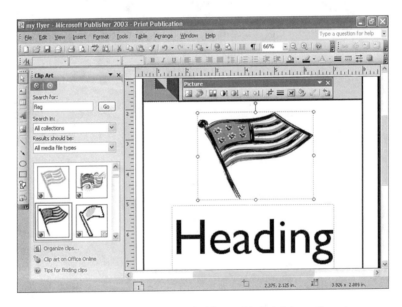

Figure 5.3   You can replace picture placeholders with Publisher clip art.

After you replace a placeholder item with a picture or graphic of your own, you can continue to edit the text and graphic items in the publication. The number of text frames and placeholder items that you need to edit to complete a particular publication depends on the publication itself. Typically, the more complex the publication, the more items you have to personalize.

Adding Pages to a Publication

You might find that as you complete a particular publication, you need to add additional pages to it. This can be a common need when you build publications from scratch.

To add pages to the current publication, follow these steps:

1. Select the **Insert** menu, and then select **Page**. The Insert Page dialog box appears (see Figure 5.4).

Figure 5.4   You can insert new pages into a publication before or after the current page.

2. Type the number of new pages you want to insert in the **Number of New Pages** box.

3. Click either the **Before Current Page** or **After Current Page** button to select the appropriate option.

4. In the Options area, select the appropriate option for your blank pages:

   Insert Blank Pages—The pages are inserted into the publication with no frames.

   Create One Text Box on Each Page—A text box is placed on each of the new pages.

   Duplicate All Objects on Page—Copies the objects on the designated page (type the number in the page box) and places them on the new page or pages inserted.

After you make your selections, click **OK**; the new page or pages are inserted into your document.

Saving a Revised Publication Under a New Name

When you work with publications that you use again and again, such as award certificates or invitations, you might want to keep your original publication incomplete (with award recipient names not filled in or other items left blank until the publication is made ready for printing) under a particular filename. For instance, you might create an award certificate and leave the recipient name blank. Then, when you are ready to create an award for a particular person, you open the award publication and edit the text frame that contains the recipient name.

You might also want to save the completed publication (the one with the recipient name or other information) under a different filename. This can be done using the Save As command.

To save a publication under a different filename, follow these steps:

1. Select the **File** menu, and then select **Save As**. The Save As dialog box appears.
2. Type a new name for the publication in the **File Name** box.
3. Use the **Save In** drop-down box to designate the drive to which you will save the file. Also, make sure to select a folder on that drive by double-clicking the folder.
4. Click **Save** to save the file.

You have now saved any changes that you made to your original publication under a new filename. This means that the original file under the original filename still exists, and it can be used whenever you need it to create personalized publications that can then be saved under a different filename.

Closing a Publication

After you have saved a particular publication and are finished working with it, you will want to close the publication. To close the current publication, select the **File** menu, and then select **Close**. The publication closes and Publisher opens a new blank publication in the Publisher window.

Working with Publication Objects

In this lesson, you learn the basics of working with objects: how to insert, copy, delete, and manipulate objects on your publication pages.

Inserting an Object

When you place an item such as text, a picture, or another item on a publication page, you are actually inserting an object that is surrounded by a frame. Being able to insert, delete, or move these object frames and manage their border and color attributes means that you can give your publication pages a customized look as you control the overall layout of individual pages.

Object A text box, picture, or other item inserted onto a publication page.

You can work with a number of different object types in a publication and format and size their frame borders. The most straightforward way to insert an object (and its frame) into a publication is to use the Objects toolbar (which appears on the left side of the Publisher window).

To insert an object, follow these steps:

1. Click an object tool on the Objects toolbar (such as the Text Box tool).

2. Place the mouse pointer on the page where you want to place the new object. The mouse pointer becomes a crosshair (see Figure 6.1).

3. Click and drag to create the object (you determine the height and width of the frame around the object).

The new object appears on your page. Your next action depends on the type of object you created. If you used the Text Box tool to create the object frame, you now type the text you want to place in the text box. If you used the Picture Frame tool, the Insert Clip Art dialog box appears, enabling you to insert your choice of pictures.

Object toolbar   Crosshair pointer

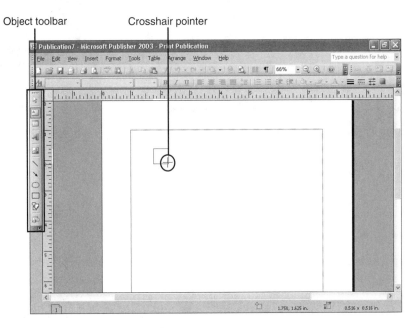

Figure 6.1   Use the crosshair mouse tool to place a new object on your publication page.

After you have the object on the page, a number of options are available to you. You can size the frame around the object, move the object, delete the object, or group the object with other objects on the page. These object manipulations are covered in the balance of this lesson.

Removing an object from a publication page is very straightforward. Select the object that you want to delete and then press the **Delete** key. This removes the object from the publication.

 TIP   **Text in Overflow Icon**   If you see an icon below a text box that contains an A followed by an ellipse, this is the Text in Overflow icon. This means that there is more text associated with the text box but that it cannot be shown in the box until you increase the size of the text box.

Sizing an Object Frame

You can change the width and height (or both) of an object's frame on a publication page. Changing the size of the object frame is accomplished using the sizing handles that appear on the selected object.

Select the object by clicking on it. The frame around the object will appear and sizing handles appear on the border of the frame. To change the frame size, select one of the options discussed in the following list:

- **Change the Width**—To change the width of the object frame, place the mouse pointer on one of the sizing handles on either the left or right vertical border of the frame. The mouse pointer changes to a Resize pointer. Drag to change the width of the object.

- **Change the Height**—To change the height of the object frame, place the mouse pointer on one of the sizing handles on either the top or bottom horizontal border of the frame. Drag to change the height of the object using the **Resize** pointer.

- **Change the Width and Height**—To change the width and height of the object frame simultaneously and maintain the current width and height ratio, place the mouse pointer on any of the diagonal sizing handles (handles positioned where the vertical and horizontal border meet in a corner) and drag to change the overall size of the object (see Figure 6.2).

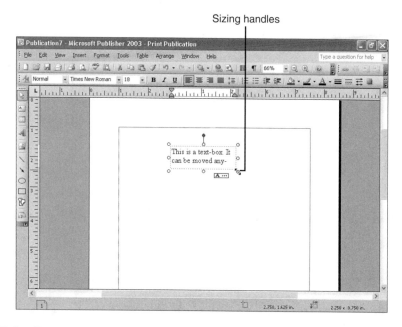

Figure 6.2   Drag any of the sizing handles to change the size of the frame.

TIP   **Zoom Out When Sizing an Object**   If you have zoomed in on a object to place text or some other item in it, you might want to zoom out to the Whole Page view when you size your frame. Select **View**, point at **Zoom**, and then select **Whole Page** to switch to the Whole Page view. Now you can size the object's frame in relation to other objects on the page.

If you require more exacting measurements for the height and width of a particular frame than you can attain with the mouse, you can also specify these measurements in the Size and Position dialog box. Follow these steps to specify an exact set of measurements for an object frame:

1. Right-click on an object such as a text box.

2. On the shortcut menu, select **Format Text Box** (if you are working with a picture frame, select **Format Picture**).

3. Select the **Size** tab on the dialog box (see Figure 6.3).

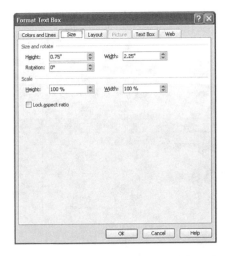

Figure 6.3   Use controls on the Size tab to change the size of your selected object.

4. Use the click arrows in the Size and Rotate area of the tab or type a new width in the **Width** box.

5. Use the click arrows or enter a new height in the **Height** box.

6. If you want to change the scale of the object width and height, use the Height and Width percentage spinner boxes in the Scale area.

7. When you have completed entering your settings, click **OK** to close the dialog box.

Your object is resized using the width and height values you entered.

Moving an Object

Publisher also enables you to move your objects on your publication pages. Any selected frame can be moved using the mouse.

Follow these steps to move an object:

1. Click anywhere on an object to select it.

2. Place the mouse pointer on any of the border edges surrounding the object (do not place the mouse pointer on the sizing handles). A Move pointer appears.

3. Drag the object to a new position on the page.

 TIP   **Snapping Objects to Grid and Ruler Guides**   Another way you can position objects with more accuracy is to turn on the Snap to Guides feature (select **Arrange**, point at **Snap,** and then select **To Guides**). Objects then snap to the nearest grid line guides. For more about guides, see Lesson 5, "Working with Existing Publications."

You might find that you want to fine-tune the position of an object in reference to other objects on a page. This can be done using the Nudge feature.

1. Click anywhere on an object to select it.

2. Select the **Arrange** menu, and then point at **Nudge**.

3. The Nudge menu appears. Select Up, Down, Left, or Right to "nudge" the object in that direction.

Copying an Object

You can also copy objects and place multiple occurrences of the same object on a page or copy an object to another page in your publication. This enables you to easily place repeating design elements on a page or within an entire publication.

To copy an object, follow these steps:

1. Click an object to select it.

2. Select the **Edit** menu, and then select **Copy** (or press Ctrl+C).

3. Select the page from the status bar on which you want to place the copy of the object, or remain on the current page.

4. Select the **Edit** menu, and then select **Paste** (or press Ctrl+V).

If you want to move the object from the current page to another page in the publication, select the **Edit** menu and select **Cut**, and then proceed with steps 3 and 4.

Grouping Objects

After you have objects placed on a page, you might want to adjust the overall positioning of all the objects in relation to the top or bottom of the page or some other special element on the page (such as a large banner heading). Moving each of the frames individually can be time-consuming and frustrating, especially if you have the objects currently positioned exactly where you would like them to be in relation to each other.

The solution to this problem is to group the objects and then move them together as one unit. This enables you to fine-tune the layout of the page without moving each object individually.

To group objects, follow these steps:

1. Select the first object that will be in the group by clicking it.
2. Hold down the **Ctrl** or **Shift** key and select additional objects. A Group Objects icon appears at the bottom of the selected group (see Figure 6.4).

You can now move the entire group of objects by placing the mouse on the group frame and dragging it to a new position. You could also delete all the selected objects at once, or copy the objects and then paste them on another page in your publication.

When you have finished manipulating the grouped objects, click anywhere outside the group to deselect it.

If you want to group the objects on a more permanent basis (to keep them together as a group), select the objects to be part of the group and select **Arrange**, then **Group Objects**. A group frame will appear around the objects. Even when you click outside of these grouped objects to deselect them, the group remains intact. Click any object in the group and all the objects are selected. Selecting the **Ungroup Objects** command on the **Arrange** menu ungroups the objects in a selected group.

Group objects icon

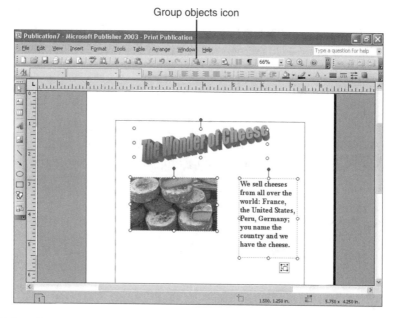

Figure 6.4 Group several objects and then move them together to a new position on the page.

Arranging Objects in Layers

You might find occasion to layer several objects on top of each other in a stack. For instance, you might decide to place a text object on top of a picture to produce an eye-catching heading for a publication. You can layer a number of objects using the layering commands on the Arrange menu.

To layer frames, follow these steps:

1. Drag an object onto another object to form a layer. For instance, drag a text box onto a picture frame.

2. The text in the text box seems to disappear. With the Text box still selected, click the **Arrange** menu, point at **Order**, and then click **Bring to Front**. The text box is placed on top of the Picture frame.

With some practice, you can layer several objects into complex arrangements on your publication pages. Understanding the layering commands on the Order menu (a submenu of the Arrange menu) will help you work with the objects that you have layered.

- **Bring to Front**—This moves the currently selected object to the top of the stack of objects you have layered.

- **Send to Back**—This moves the currently selected object to the bottom of the stack.

- **Bring Forward**—This moves the currently selected object up one position in the stack. For instance, if the object is the second object in the layer of the stacks, this moves the object to the first position, or the top of the stack.

- **Send Backward**—This moves the currently selected object down one position in the stack. For instance, an object in the second layer of the stack would be moved to the third layer.

 TIP   **Make Your Frame Stack One Group**   After you have layered several object and have them positioned and stacked appropriately, make the object a permanent group (select **Arrange**, then **Group Objects**). This prevents you from inadvertently disturbing the stack when you are working on the other elements on the publication page.

Adding Border and Colors to Object Frames

When you place an object on a publication page, the border around the object is transparent (you can't see the frame) and does not have a border. You can only see the border when you actually select the object. You can add borders to your objects and also place shading and background colors on any object you've created.

To add borders and background color to an object, follow these steps:

1. Right-click on the object you want to place the border around.

2. On the shortcut menu, select **Format Object** (where "object" is the name of the object, such as Picture or Text Box).

3. On the Format dialog box that appears, select the **Colors and Lines** tab (see Figure 6.5).

4. Use the Line **Color**, **Style**, and **Weight** drop-down lists to select the color, style, and thickness of the line for the border respectively.

5. To add a background color to the object (most useful on text boxes), click the Fill **Color** drop-down list and select the color for the object's fill color.

6. When you have made your selections, click **OK**.

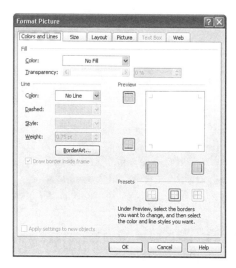

Figure 6.5 Use the Colors and Lines tab to add a border or background color to an object.

You can also set custom borders for an object on the Colors and Lines tab. Use the preset buttons under the Preview box. This allows you to place a border line under an object or to the right or left, without placing a border all around the object's frame.

Changing How Text Looks

In this lesson, you learn how to add text to your publications and change formatting options related to text, such as font selection, text alignment, and text color. You also learn how to add tables to your pages.

Adding Text to Your Publications

You can add text to your publication in text boxes by using the Text Box tool on the Objects toolbar. You will find that Publisher provides you with complete control over the look and formatting of text in the box, including the font style, font size, font attributes (such as bold and italic), and the color of your font. Any or all of these font parameters can be edited on a particular text box.

To add a text box to a publication page, follow these steps:

1. Click the **Text Box** tool on the Objects toolbar.

2. Place the mouse pointer on the page and drag to create the text box.

3. The insertion point appears in the text box. Type the text that you want to place in the box (see Figure 7.1).

 TIP **Zoom In to Concentrate on Your Text**   If you are in the Whole Page view when you place your text box on your page, you might want to zoom in on the text before you type the text or attempt to edit it. Click the **Zoom** drop-down box on the Standard toolbar and select a zoom percentage that zooms you in on your page.

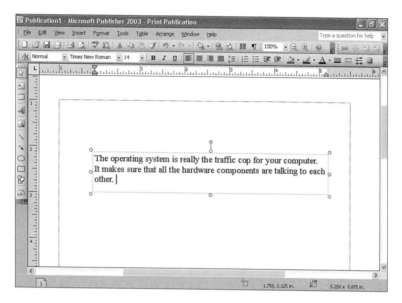

Figure 7.1   Add your text to the text box.

Inserting Text

You can also easily add additional text to a text box. To add text to a box that already contains text, follow these steps:

1. Place the mouse pointer on the text in the text box. The pointer becomes an I-beam.

2. Click the I-beam on the text where you want to place the insertion point.

3. Type the text you want to insert into the text box.

Selecting and Deleting Text

You can also easily delete text in a text box. Select the text you want to delete and press the **Delete** key. You will find that the mouse provides the easiest method for selecting text in the text box. Table 7.1 provides a list of ways to use the mouse to select text.

Table 7.1   Techniques for Using the Mouse to Quickly Select Text in a Box

Text Selection	Mouse Action
Selects the word	Double-click a word.
Selects a text block	Click and drag, or click at the beginning of text and then hold down the Shift key and click at the end of text block.
Selects all the text	Triple-click in the text box.

You will find that these selection techniques are also useful when you want to change the format (or color) of text in a text frame (as discussed in subsequent sections of this lesson).

TIP **Copy, Cut, and Paste Text**   You can also copy or cut selected text in a text box and then paste it into another text frame or in another position in the current text box. Use the **Copy** button, the **Cut** button, and the **Paste** button on the Standard toolbar, respectively.

Working with Fonts

The text that you type in a new text box is created in Publisher's default font, which is Times New Roman, 10 point. Each available font has a particular style or typeface.

A variety of font types exist, such as Arial, Courier, Times New Roman, CG Times, Bookman Old Style, and so on. You can select the font style for a particular publication using the Publications Design task pane or a specific task pane such as the Business Card Options task pane, depending on the type of document you are creating.

The size of the font is measured in points. A point is 1/72 of an inch, and the standard point size for business letters and other documents is 12 points. The higher the number of points (such as 18), the larger the font size.

You can change the font for existing text in a text box by following these steps:

1. Select the text in the text box (using the mouse) that you want to change to a different font type.

2. Click the **Font** drop-down box on the Formatting toolbar and select a new font from the list.

If you have finished working with a particular text box, click outside the box to deselect it. If you create a new text box, you can change the font that you use for the text that you place in the frame before you actually type any text. This, in effect, changes the default font for that particular text frame. To change to a different font, click the **Font** drop-down box and select a new font.

You can change the font size of text in a text box in much the same way. Select the text in the text box to which you would like to assign a new font size. Then click the **Font Size** drop-down box on the Formatting toolbar and select a new font size.

Changing Font Attributes

You also have control over other font attributes associated with the text in your text boxes. You can quickly change the style of the font to bold, italic, or underline. These font styles are readily available on the Formatting toolbar.

To change the font attributes for text in a text frame, follow these steps:

1. Select the text in the text box for which you want to change the font attributes (for example, changing the text style to bold).

2. Click the appropriate button on the Formatting toolbar.

You can also change font attributes for selected text in a frame by using the Font dialog box. Select the **Format** menu, and then select **Font**.

The Font dialog box enables you to change the font, the font style, the font size, and a number of other font attributes (such as superscript, subscript, small caps, and so on), as shown in Figure 7.2.

To select any of the font attributes in the Effects area of the dialog box, click the appropriate check box. A preview of the particular effect (and other attribute changes that you have made) appears in the Sample box. When you have completed making your font changes, click the **OK** button to return to your publication.

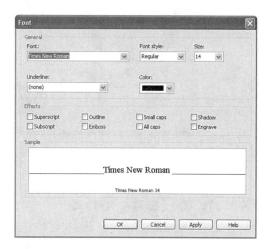

Figure 7.2 The Font dialog box gives you control over a number of font attributes.

Changing Font Colors

You can also change the color of the text in a text box. Changing font color enables you to emphasize certain text and can add interest to your publication pages.

To change the font color for text in a text box, follow these steps:

1. Select the text in the text box that you want to change to a different font color.

 2. Click the **Font Color** button on the Formatting toolbar.

3. Select a new color from the color box that appears (if you don't see a color you like, continue with step 4).

4. If you want to select from additional colors, click the **More Colors** selection in the color box. The Colors dialog box appears (see Figure 7.3).

5. Click anywhere in the color palette to select a new color range for the text.

6. After you've selected your new color, click **OK** to return to your publication.

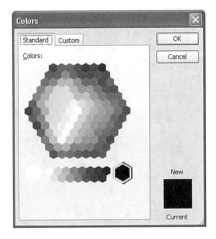

Figure 7.3   The Colors dialog box offers you all the colors of the spectrum for your text.

Aligning Text in a Text Box

You also have control over the alignment of the text in the box. You can center the text (in relation to the box border), right-align the text, left-align the text, or use different alignments on different text lines or paragraphs in a text box. For lines or paragraphs to be treated separately, place a line break (press **Enter**) between the line and the next line in the text box.

The alignments align the text to the left and right borders of the frame. Table 7.2 shows the alignment buttons available on the Formatting toolbar.

Table 7.2 Alignment Buttons for Changing Selected Text Alignment in a Frame

Formatting Toolbar Button	Alignment
	Left
	Center
	Right
	Justify (straight margins on the left and right)

To align text in a box, follow these steps:

1. Place the insertion point in the paragraph (any line or lines of text followed by a line break) that you want to align.

2. Click the appropriate button on the Formatting toolbar (as detailed in Table 7.2).

Your text is aligned according to the button you selected on the Formatting toolbar.

Adding Tables to a Publication

Another way to present text information in a publication is to use a table. A table enables you to place information into rows and columns, making it easy to arrange information in a highly accessible format. The intersection of a row and a column is called a cell; the cells are where you place your data. Publisher gives you complete control over the number of rows and columns in your table and their size.

Tables are added to a publication page in much the same way as any object (such as a text box or a picture frame). You use the Insert Table tool on the Objects toolbar.

To insert a table onto a page, follow these steps:

1. Click the **Insert Table** tool on the Objects toolbar.

2. Click and drag to create the table on the page.

3. In the Create Table dialog box, type the number of rows and columns for the table (see Figure 7.4).

4. Click **OK**. The table appears on the publication page.

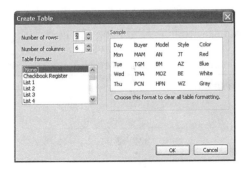

Figure 7.4 The Create Table dialog box enables you to select the number of rows and columns for the table.

When you want to place information side-by-side on the page, you will find that tables make it a simple task. Tables provide you with much more control over the placement of information as compared to trying to align items with indents or tabs.

Working with Graphics

In this lesson, you learn how to add pictures and clip art to your publications. You also learn how to crop pictures and clip art.

Inserting a Picture

Publisher provides you with a lot of flexibility as to the types of picture objects that you can add to your publication pages. You can add a picture file to a page, or you can choose to add a clip art image from the extensive clip art library that comes with Microsoft Office.

Pictures can come in a variety of file types, and pictures can consist of files you have on disk, items you copy from the World Wide Web, or pictures that you create using a scanner or a digital camera.

Publisher supports a wide variety of picture file formats that you can insert into a publication. Table 8.1 lists some of the most common picture file types.

Table 8.1   Picture File Formats Publisher Can Use

File Type	Extension
Windows Bitmap (Windows Paint)	.bmp
CorelDRAW!	.cdr
Encapsulated PostScript (QuarkXPress)	.eps
Graphics Interchange Format (CompuServe format)	.gif
Joint Photographics Expert Group (commonly used on the World Wide Web)	.jpeg or .jpg
Kodak PhotoCD and Pro PhotoCD	.pcd
PC Paintbrush	.pcx
Tagged Image File Format (TIFF) (PhotoDraw)	.tif
Windows Metafile (Microsoft Word Clip Art)	.wmf
WordPerfect Graphics	.wpg

Depending on the source of your image (clip art, or a picture file, or an image insert-ed from a scanner or camera), the procedure for inserting the picture varies slightly; the common avenue for inserting the image is the Picture Frame tool on the Objects toolbar, and then the steps required to complete the process will vary. For example, in the case of clip art insertions, you will find that the Clip Art task pane opens, allowing you to select the clip art that you will place on the page. In the case of a scanner or camera, you will actually be able to "pull" the image directly from either device.

Let's take a look at inserting a picture from a file on your computer; follow these steps:

1. Click the **Picture Frame** tool on the Objects toolbar. A list of picture tools appears: Clip Art, Picture from File, Empty Picture Frame, and From Scanner and or Camera.

2. Select Picture from File.

3. Place the mouse pointer on the page and drag to create the picture frame. The Insert Picture dialog box appears (see Figure 8.1).

4. Use the **Look In** drop-down arrow to select the drive on which the picture resides.

5. Double-click the folder that holds the file.

Figure 8.1 Use the Insert Picture dialog box to locate the picture file that you will place in your picture frame.

6. When you have selected the picture file, click the **Insert** button. The picture is placed in the picture frame on the publication page.

Using Clip Art

As already mentioned in this lesson, another way to add pictures to your publication pages is to use clip art. Clip art is a library of ready-made images that you can easily search using the Clip Art task pane.

To insert clip art onto a publication page, follow these steps:

1. Click the **Picture Frame** tool on the Objects toolbar. Select the **Clip Art** tool on the submenu.

2. The Clip Art task pane appears in the Publisher workspace (see Figure 8.2).

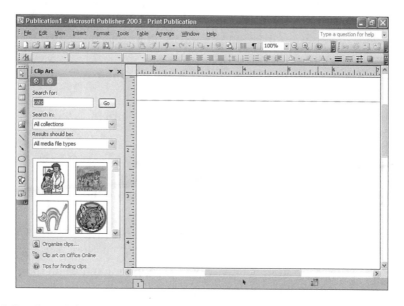

Figure 8.2 Search for your clip art by keyword.

3. Type a keyword or keywords that you want to use for your search parameters in the Search For box.

4. Click the Go button to initiate the search. Clip art matching your search criteria will appear in the task pane.

5. Click the **clip art** image that you want to insert and the image is inserted into your publication.

6. When you have finished working with the Clip Art task pane, close it.

Clip art reacts to changes in the frame size the same way other pictures do. Increase the size of the frame and the clip art inside the frame is enlarged.

To increase or decrease the size of an image, drag the image frame (drag the sizing handles provided). When scaling your pictures, however, you usually want to maintain the height/width ratio of the picture. Otherwise, images appear elongated or squashed if you only change their scale in one direction (such as just dragging one of the vertical borders to change the width). The easiest way to maintain the height/width ratio of an image is to drag diagonally to size a picture using one of the corner sizing handles.

Cropping Pictures

You might run across a situation where you want to trim the edges off a particular image. For instance, you have a clip art image that contains a picture surrounded by a border, and you want to crop the border and just keep the picture itself in the frame. Or you might have an image that contains several items, such as a picture of several people, and you want to crop the image so that only one person appears in the frame.

You can easily crop an image using the Publisher cropping tool. To crop a picture or clip art image, follow these steps:

1. Select the picture frame that holds the image you want to crop. When you select the image, the Picture toolbar should appear in the Publisher workspace (if you don't see the toolbar, right-click on any toolbar in the Publisher window and select **Picture**).

2. On the Picture toolbar, select the **Crop** tool. Cropping handles appear on the image and the mouse pointer becomes a cropping tool (see Figure 8.3).

3. Place the cropping tool on any of the cropping handles on the picture's frame and drag to crop the picture.

4. When you have completed cropping the picture, click the **Crop** button on the toolbar to turn off the cropping feature.

 TIP **Crop in More Than One Direction** After you invoke the cropping tool, you can crop the image in more than one direction (such as cropping it on the right and then cropping it on the top) in the same cropping session. The cropping tool disappears only when you click outside the picture frame and deselect it.

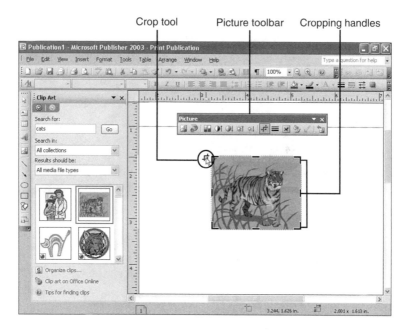

Figure 8.3 Use the cropping tool to crop an image in a picture frame.

Drawing Objects

Publisher provides you with several drawing tools, which are found on the Objects toolbar. You can draw a rectangle, oval, line, or arrow by clicking on the appropriate tool. The Objects toolbar also provides you with the AutoShapes tool, which allows you to quickly choose from a number of different object shapes such as connectors, block arrows, and flow chart items.

Drawing a Line

Publisher makeseasy for you to create a vertical, horizontal, or otherwise-oriented line. Lines that you create using the Line tool on the Publisher toolbar can also include arrowheads and be designed with different line weights and colors.

1. Click the **Line** tool on the Objects toolbar and place the mouse pointer on the page.

2. Drag on the publication page to create the line (dragging either vertically or horizontally to create the appropriate orientation).

3. Release the left mouse button and the line appears on the page.

TIP **Drawing a Straight Line** To draw a perfectly straight horizontal or vertical line, hold down the **Shift** key as you drag to create the line.

Drawing rectangles and ovals (circles) is similar to drawing a line. You select the appropriate tool on the Objects toolbar and then drag the mouse to draw the object on the page.

Drawing a Custom Shape

Publisher also provides you with the capability to draw a number of custom shapes using the AutoShapes tool. To draw a custom shape, follow these steps:

1. Click the **AutoShapes** tool on the Objects toolbar.

2. Point at a custom shape type listed on the submenu that appears.

3. For example, point at Block Arrows and a shape palette appears with different arrow shapes as shown in Figure 8.4. Select a shape from the palette.

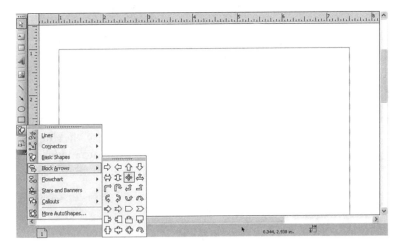

Figure 8.4 Select from a number of custom shapes.

4. Drag on the publication page to create the drawn object.

5. Release the left mouse button, and your new drawn object appears on the page.

TIP **The Design Gallery Provides Page Banners, Sidebars, and Other Custom Elements** To add graphical elements such as page banners, sidebars, logos, and calendars to a publication page, select the Design Gallery tool on the Objects toolbar. The Publisher Design Gallery opens, which provides many items that you can add to your Publisher pages.

Formatting Drawing Objects

You can change the outside border color and the interior fill color of any drawn object. Both of these color attributes can easily be changed on a selected object by using the Line Color and Fill Color buttons on the Formatting toolbar.

To change the border color of a drawn object, follow these steps:

1. Click the drawn object for which you want to change the line color.

2. Click the **Line Color** button on the Formatting toolbar.

3. Select a color on the color palette that appears.

Changing the fill color is a similar operation. Follow these steps:

1. Select the object for which you want to select a fill color.

2. Click the arrow on the right of the **Fill Color** button on the Formatting toolbar.

3. Click a fill color on the color palette that appears. If you want to choose from more colors than provided by the Fill Color menu, click **More Fill Colors** on the color palette. The Colors dialog box appears. Click color to select a new color for your fill color. Then click **OK** to close the dialog box. You are returned to the publication page.

Formatting Publication Pages

In this lesson, you learn how to change the margins on your publication pages. You also learn how to add a border to a page, add page numbers to pages, and work with publication master pages.

Changing Page Margins

When you start a new publication (particularly one that you create from scratch), you might want to change the margins for the publication pages. Publisher enables you to shift the margin guides (the blue and pink lines that surround the page) in the Layout Guides dialog box. You can adjust the top, bottom, left, and right margins.

To change the margins for the current page, follow these steps:

1. Select the **Arrange** menu, and then select **Layout Guides**. The Layout Guides dialog box appears (see Figure 9.1). Make sure the **Margin Guides** tab is selected.

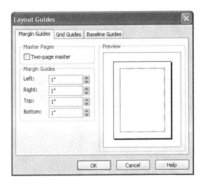

Figure 9.1   You can adjust your page margins using the Layout Guides dialog box.

2. Use the appropriate click arrows to increase (or decrease) the left, right, top, or bottom margins, as needed.

3. Click **OK**; the new margins appear on your page.

You can also manually drag the margins on a page to a new location with the mouse. However, you work in the master page view of the publication to manipulate the margins. The Master Page is used to provide the overall formatting for the pages in a publication such as margins, page numbers, and headers and footers.

Select **View**, then **Master Page**. You can now manipulate the margin guides. Hold down the **Shift** key and drag any margin to a new location. Working in the Master Page view is discussed later in this lesson.

Adding Page Borders

You can place borders around the edges of your pages. This gives you a design element that helps emphasize the objects that are placed within these borders.

When you create a new publication using a design template or a design set, the page border for the publication might be part of the design that you select for that particular publication. However, if you want to place a border around pages in a publication you created from a blank publication template (or by inserting a new page), you can use the Publications Design task pane.

To place a border around a publication page, follow these steps:

1. If the task pane is not open in the Publisher application window, click **View**, then **Task Pane**.

2. At the top of the current task pane, click the drop-down arrow and select **Publication Designs**.

3. In the Publications Design task pane, make sure the **Publications Design** option is selected. A number of publication designs including design elements and borders appear at the bottom of the task pane (see Figure 9.2).

4. Select the design (with border) that you want to apply to the publication.

 TIP **Open the Publication Designs Task Pane from the Format Menu** You can also open the Publication Designs task pane by selecting Format, Publication Designs.

You can try out as many of the border designs as you want. When you find the border you want to use, select it. Save the publication. You can then close the task pane, if you want.

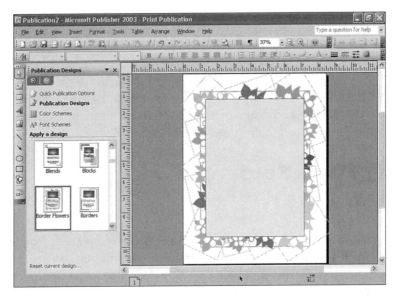

Figure 9.2 Different border types can be found in the different publication designs provided.

Working with Master Pages

When you place the various objects on a publication page, you are providing the design elements and information for that page only. If you want to add repeating elements to the pages of a publication such as a company logo, page numbers, or other repeating information, you use the master page for the publication.

To view the master **page** for a publication (there can actually be more than one master page for a publication, if you have very different groups of page types in a single publication), select **View** and then **Master Page**. The Master Page task pane appears and the master page assigned to the current publication page appears in the Publisher workspace (see Figure 9.3).

To insert a repeating element such as a company logo, you would insert the picture file as you would on any other publication page (use the Picture Frame tool on the Objects toolbar). However, any object placed on the master page will appear on all pages in the publication.

One use you may have for the master page is page numbering. When you create publications that contain multiple pages, you might want to number the pages.

The page number code would be placed on the master page in a text box. The great thing about using the page number feature is that even if you insert or delete pages in the publication, the appropriate page number always appears on your pages.

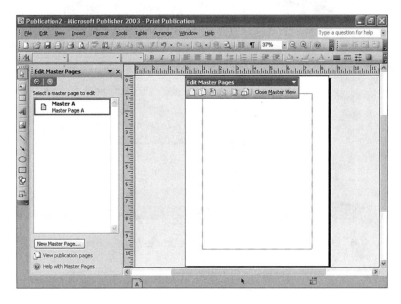

Figure 9.3 The master page is where you place repeating elements for the publication pages.

To create a page number frame on the master page, follow these steps:

1. On the master page, click the **Text box** tool on the Objects toolbar.

2. Drag the mouse to create the text box that will hold the page number code.

3. Select the **Insert** menu, then **Page Numbers**. A page number code is placed in the text frame (see Figure 9.4).

If you want to have page numbers that read Page 1 and so on, you can click the mouse just in front of the Page Number code (#) and add the appropriate text. You can also insert a date code into a text box on the master page to place the current date on all the publication pages. Remember that any element that you add to the master page will appear on all the pages in the presentation.

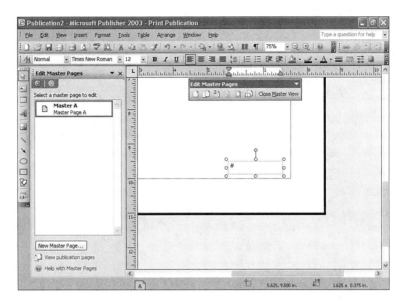

Figure 9.4   Place the page number code on the master page to number the pages in the publication.

Fine-Tuning Publisher Publications

In this lesson, you learn how to use the Spelling feature, control hyphenation in a text box, check your publication design with the Design Checker, and set up the AutoCorrect feature.

Using the Spell Checker

After you spend a lot of time designing a publication, you will want to print a hard copy of the final product. But first you should make sure that all the errors in the publication have been found and that you have checked the overall design of the publication. Publisher offers several tools that enable you to fine-tune your publication.

The Spelling feature checks your documents for misspellings and typos, and it displays each suspect word in the Spelling dialog box. You can choose to replace the word with a suggested correct spelling, ignore the word, or correct the misspelling yourself.

To use the Spelling feature, follow these steps:

1. Select a text box that you want to spell check.

2. Select **Tools**, and then select **Spelling** (or click the **Spelling** button on the Standard toolbar).

3. The Check Spelling dialog box appears (see Figure 10.1). The first suspect word (a word considered misspelled) appears in the Not in Dictionary box. To correct the word, choose one of the following:

   - Select the correct spelling in the **Suggestions** box and then click **Change**.

   - To change all occurrences of the word to the new spelling, click **Change All**.

   - To ignore the word (in cases where the word is correctly spelled), click **Ignore** (click **Ignore All** to ignore all occurrences of the word).

   - If you want to add the word to the dictionary file so that it will not be flagged as misspelled in the future, click **Add**.

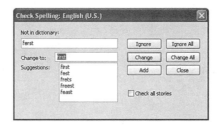

Figure 10.1   The Check Spelling dialog box offers you several options for a flagged word.

4. After you make your selection, the next flagged word is shown in the Not in Dictionary box. Correct other suspected misspellings as needed. When the current text box is completed, the Speller lets you know that the current "story" has been checked, and a dialog box appears asking if you want to continue checking the publication. Click **Yes** to correct the rest of the publication or **No** to stop spell checking with the currently selected text box.

TIP   **Check All the Text Boxes at Once**   If you want to automatically check all the text in the publication (all text boxes), click the **Check All Stories** check box in the Check Spelling dialog box.

You probably already noticed that Publisher actually flags suspected misspellings as you type (as do all the Office applications). A wavy red line appears under the flagged word. You can choose to correct a flagged misspelling without running the Spell Checker. Right-click the word and select a correct spelling from the list provided on the shortcut menu that appears.

Controlling Hyphenation in Text Boxes

Another element of fine-tuning a publication is determining where words are hyphenated in your text boxes. You can have Publisher automatically hyphenate the text in your text frames (which means it determines where to break words with a hyphen and continue the remaining portion of the word on the next line).

When you choose to use the automatic hyphenation feature, hyphens are only placed as needed. The great thing about the feature is that if you edit the text, unnecessary hyphens are removed (automatically) and new hyphens are placed as needed.

To hyphenate the text in a text frame automatically, follow these steps:

1. Click the text box that you want to automatically hyphenate.

2. Select the **Tools** menu, point at **Language**, and then select **Hyphenation**. The Hyphenation dialog box appears (see Figure 10.2).

Figure 10.2   You can automatically hyphenate text in a text frame.

3. Click the **Automatically Hyphenate This Story** check box in the Hyphenation dialog box.

4. Click **OK** to exit the dialog box and hyphenate the text.

You can also choose to hyphenate the text manually. To do this, click the **Manual** button in the Hyphenation dialog box. A Hyphenate dialog box appears, displaying the first word in the text frame that needs to be hyphenated.

To use the hyphenation shown in the Hyphenate box, click **Yes**. If you don't want to hyphenate the word, click **No**. The next word to be hyphenated is displayed, and you are given the same choices as already described. Continue through the text until all the words have either been hyphenated or rejected (by you) and not hyphenated.

Using the Design Checker

The Design Checker is another great tool for helping you fine-tune your publication. The Design Checker actually looks at the design elements and objects in your publication and helps you find empty frames, improperly proportioned pictures, font problems (such as too many fonts), and other design problems. The Design Checker also offers you help when it identifies a potential design problem.

To use the Design Checker, follow these steps:

1. Select the **Tools** menu, and then select **Design Checker**. The Design Checker task appears.

2. In the Design Checker task pane, the design flaws found in the publication will be listed (see Figure 10.3).

3. To go to the item that is listed as an error, click the item in the Design Checker list. The picture frame, text box, or other object will be selected on the appropriate publication page.

4. When you fix the error, it will disappear from the Design Checker list.

5. Repeat steps 3 and 4 until all the errors in the publication have been remedied.

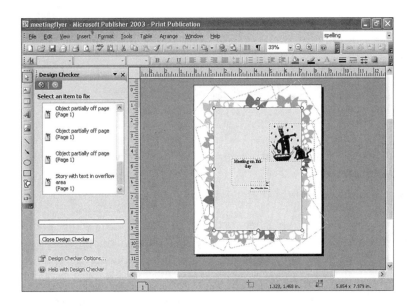

Figure 10.3   Use the Design Checker to check your publication for design flaws.

Setting Up AutoCorrect

When you add text to your publications, it's nice to have misspellings and typos corrected automatically. The Publisher AutoCorrect feature does this for you. You can set the various AutoCorrect options and add your own common misspellings and typos to the AutoCorrect list.

To set up AutoCorrect, follow these steps:

1. Select the **Tools** menu, and then select **AutoCorrect Options**. The AutoCorrect dialog box appears (see Figure 10.4).

2. To add a common misspelling or typo, type the misspelling in the **Replace** box and the correct spelling in the **With** box.

3. Click **Add** to add the items to the AutoCorrect list.

4. To remove an item from the AutoCorrect list, click the item and then click the **Delete** button.

5. Click **OK** when you have finished working in the AutoCorrect dialog box.

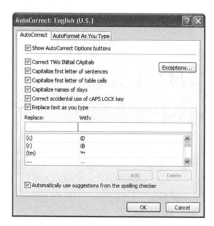

Figure 10.4   You can set the options for AutoCorrect in the AutoCorrect dialog box.

Printing Publisher Publications

In this lesson, you learn how to print your publications and also configure advanced print settings. You also learn how to compress a publication using Pack and Go.

Previewing the Publication

When you are working in Publisher, you are, in effect, always seeing each page as it will print. This means that objects, pictures, and text boxes on the Publisher pages are displayed as they will appear on printed pages.

The best strategy for previewing your publication is to go from the general to the specific. Zoom in and make sure that individual objects are correctly set up and that text boxes do not contain typos. When you zoom out on the publication, you can check placement of objects, the overall design of the publication, and the use of color.

Before you print, you will still probably want to preview the completed publication in the Print Preview window. Click **Print Preview** on the Standard toolbar.

The publication will appear in the Print Preview window as shown in Figure 11.1. You can zoom in and out on the publication and view multiple pages in the preview window. When you have completed viewing the publication, click the Close button to return to the Publisher workspace.

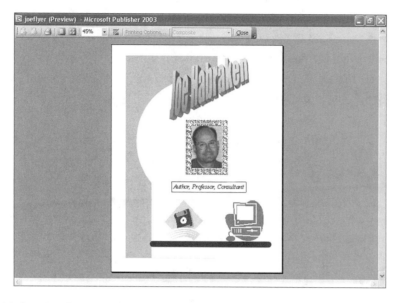

Figure 11.1 Use Print Preview to get an overall view of the publication as it will appear on the printed page.

Printing the Publication

No matter how hard you work on the color and design parameters of your publication, the final judge of your skills will be the actual printout of the publication. To print your publication, follow these steps:

1. Select the **File** menu, and then select **Print**. The Print dialog box appears (see Figure 11.2).

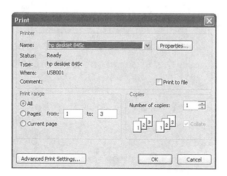

Figure 11.2 Select your print settings in the Print dialog box.

2. If necessary, click the **Name** drop-down box and select the printer to which you want to send the print job.

3. Set the page range of the printout, if necessary.

4. Use the **Number of Copies** click box to specify the number of copies.

5. Click **OK** to send the print job to the selected printer.

TIP **Print Quickly with the Print Button** You can send your publication directly to the printer and bypass the Print dialog box. Click the **Print** button on the toolbar.

Your publication is printed. In cases where you send your publication to an outside printing service, you will also have to work with the various advanced print options (discussed in the next section) to prepare the publication for printing.

Working with Print Options

When you print your publications yourself, you typically will not have to set advanced print options related to the color scheme settings and settings for graphics and fonts. If you use an outside print service, you may have to also set a number of print options before sending the publication files to the printer service. These options range from settings such as the color system used, whether printer's marks should be included, and how graphics are printed. Each of these options is accessed using the Advanced Print Settings dialog box.

To open the Advanced Print Settings dialog box, open the Print dialog box (**File**, then **Print**). On the Print dialog box click the **Advanced Print Settings** button (which opens the Advanced Print Settings dialog box).

Selecting Output Separation Settings

The color system that you use for your printout will depend on whether you are going to print the publication yourself or use an outside printing service. You can select the color system on the **Separations** tab of the Advanced Print Settings dialog box (see Figure 11.3).

By default the color scheme in the Output drop-down box is set to **Composite RGB** (Red, Green, Blue). This is the color scheme that is used by most color printers you will use at home or in the office. If you are going to print the publication yourself, you can leave the color scheme setting as Composite RGB.

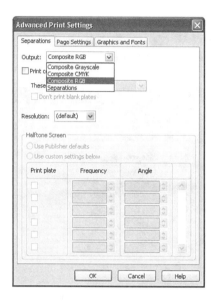

Figure 11.3   Select the color system for your printout.

If you are going to print the presentation on a non-color printer, you can change the color scheme to **Composite Grayscale**. This allows your black-and-white printer to substitute different shades of gray for the colors used in the publication.

If you are preparing the publication for printing by an outside service, the color scheme you use will be dictated by the print service. They should supply you with this information. Most commercial printers use process colors selected using the **Composite CMYK** setting. This color scheme works very well with color photos.

In some instances the print service may supply you with information on the number of separations and color settings that will be used to print the publication. In this case, you would select **Separations** from the Output drop-down menu and then select the **Use Custom Settings** option button. You must then supply the Frequency and Angle for each color that will be used in the separations as dictated by your print service. Again, this information will be supplied by the print service; you do not have to change these settings for a simple print job to your color printer.

Advanced Page Print Settings

Another of the tabs on the Advanced Print Settings dialog box is the Page Settings tab (see Figure 11.4). This tab allows you to set whether or not printer's marks, such as crop marks and job specifications, show on the printout. When complex publications such as books are published, print runs of the publication do provide the crop marks and the job information. Both of these settings (Crop Marks and Job Information) are selected by default on the Page Settings tab. You will only need to change these settings if directed by your print service.

Figure 11.4   Set options related to printer's marks and job specifications on the Page Settings tab.

The Page Settings tab also allows you to control bleeds. *Bleeds* are graphics that extend beyond the trim edge of the page. This is so that there is no border between the edge of the page and the border of the element that is allowed to bleed. Bleeds are allowed by default on the Page Settings tab. You will find that most color printers, particularly inkjet printers, don't allow you to bleed an element off the page. Again, this is a setting that you may work with if your publication is printed by a printing service.

Linked Graphics Print Settings

When you place your pictures and clip art on a publication page, you are making that image part of the page. When you have a publication printed by a commercial service, you typically have to provide the pictures and clip art images as separate files that are linked to the publication rather than placed in it.

The Graphic Manager task pane, which you open from the Tools menu, enables you to convert your publication images to linked objects. How these linked graphic images are then printed by your print service is controlled on the Graphics and Fonts tab of the Advanced Print Settings dialog box (see Figure 11.5).

Figure 11.5   Settings related to linked graphics and fonts are handled on the Graphics and Fonts tab.

By default linked graphics are printed in full resolution. You have the options of printing the graphics in low resolution or not printing the graphics at all (only empty frames will appear in the printed publication).

You can also choose whether to allow the substitution of fonts found in the publication. By default, the **Use Only Publication Fonts** option is selected. This means that the printer may have to render some of the fonts as graphics, which means their resolution may not be as crisp. There is an option to allow the printer to substitute fonts, but if you are using a particular font family for the publication, this can lead to an inconsistent look throughout the publication pages.

Using Pack and Go

You will find that a publication jam-packed with pictures, text boxes, and various design elements constitutes a file that is pretty large. In many cases, the publication may be too large to fit on a floppy disk, and it will be very large if sent as an e-mail attachment. However, you can compress your publications using Pack and Go. This makes it easy for you to take your publication to another computer or take it to a commercial printer.

To pack a presentation, follow these steps:

1. Select the **File** menu, point at **Pack and Go**, and then click **Take to Another Computer**. The Pack and Go Wizard appears.

2. Click **Next** to start the Pack and Go Wizard.

3. To pack the publication to a floppy disk, click **Next** (or specify another drive on your computer and then click **Next**).

4. To embed the fonts and pictures in the publication in the Pack and Go file, click the appropriate check boxes (see Figure 11.6), and then click **Next**.

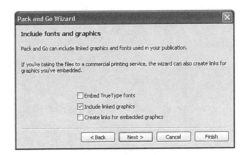

Figure 11.6   Select the items that should be included in the Pack and Go file.

5. Click **Finish** to pack the publication onto a disk.

If the packed publication will not fit on one floppy disk, the Pack and Go Wizard prompts you to place additional floppy disks in your floppy disk drive.

A copy of Unpack.exe is also placed on the floppy disk (or floppy disks) that hold your packed presentation. You can use this program to unpack your publication onto another computer.

To unpack a packed file, place the floppy disk in the other computer and then click **Start**, then **Run**. In the Run box, type **a:\unpack.exe**. You are prompted for a destination folder for the unpacking of your publication; specify the folder and then click **OK**.

Index

How can we make this index more useful? Email us at indexes@quepublishing.com

How can we make this index more useful? Email us at indexes@quepublishing.com

How can we make this index more useful? Email us at indexes@quepublishing.com

How can we make this index more useful? Email us at indexes@quepublishing.com

How can we make this index more useful? Email us at indexes@quepublishing.com

How can we make this index more useful? Email us at indexes@quepublishing.com

How can we make this index more useful? Email us at indexes@quepublishing.com

How can we make this index more useful? Email us at indexes@quepublishing.com

How can we make this index more useful? Email us at indexes@quepublishing.com

How can we make this index more useful? Email us at indexes@quepublishing.com

How can we make this index more useful? Email us at indexes@quepublishing.com

How can we make this index more useful? Email us at indexes@quepublishing.com

How can we make this index more useful? Email us at indexes@quepublishing.com

How can we make this index more useful? Email us at indexes@quepublishing.com

How can we make this index more useful? Email us at indexes@quepublishing.com

How can we make this index more useful? Email us at indexes@quepublishing.com

905

I

How can we make this index more useful? Email us at indexes@quepublishing.com

How can we make this index more useful? Email us at indexes@quepublishing.com

909

How can we make this index more useful? Email us at indexes@quepublishing.com

How can we make this index more useful? Email us at indexes@quepublishing.com

How can we make this index more useful? Email us at indexes@quepublishing.com

How can we make this index more useful? Email us at indexes@quepublishing.com

917

How can we make this index more useful? Email us at indexes@quepublishing.com

How can we make this index more useful? Email us at indexes@quepublishing.com

921

How can we make this index more useful? Email us at indexes@quepublishing.com

How can we make this index more useful? Email us at indexes@quepublishing.com

925

How can we make this index more useful? Email us at indexes@quepublishing.com

927

How can we make this index more useful? Email us at indexes@quepublishing.com

How can we make this index more useful? Email us at indexes@quepublishing.com

How can we make this index more useful? Email us at indexes@quepublishing.com

How can we make this index more useful? Email us at indexes@quepublishing.com

How can we make this index more useful? Email us at indexes@quepublishing.com

How can we make this index more useful? Email us at indexes@quepublishing.com

How can we make this index more useful? Email us at indexes@quepublishing.com

How can we make this index more useful? Email us at indexes@quepublishing.com

How can we make this index more useful? Email us at indexes@quepublishing.com

How can we make this index more useful? Email us at indexes@quepublishing.com

How can we make this index more useful? Email us at indexes@quepublishing.com

spell checking, 508-509
splitting, 500-501
status bar, 480
switching between, 493
ungrouping, 543
values, 464
views, 498-499
window elements,
455-457
wrapping text, 521-523

.wpg files, 849. *See also*
graphics

writing. *See* **composing**

X – Y – Z

**XML (Extensible Markup
Language), 13, 78**

**Yahoo! e-mail account
setup, 109**

**Yes/No data type (Access
tables), 593**

Zoom button
Access Print Preview
toolbar, 681
Excel Standard toolbar,
498, 549

**Zoom command (View
menu)**
Publisher, 822
Word, 350

**Zoom dialog box (Word),
350**

**Zoom, Page Width com-
mand (Publisher View
menu), 820**

**Zoom, Whole Page com-
mand (Publisher View
menu), 819**

zooming
Excel worksheets, 498
publications, 822-823
Word, 350-351, 388

How can we make this index more useful? Email us at indexes@quepublishing.com